Demography and Degeneration

Richard A. Soloway

Demography and Degeneration

Eugenics and the Declining Birthrate

in Twentieth-Century Britain

The University of North Carolina Press

Chapel Hill and London

© 1990 The University of North Carolina Press
All rights reserved
Manufactured in the United States of America

The paper used in this book meets the guidelines for permanence and
durability of the Committee on Production Guidelines for Book
Longevity of the Council on Library Resources.

94 93 92 91 90   5 4 3 2 1

Library of Congress Cataloging-in-Publication Data
Soloway, Richard A.
    Demography and degeneration : eugenics and the declining birthrate
in twentieth-century Britain / by Richard A. Soloway.
        p.   cm.
    Bibliography: p.
    Includes index.
    ISBN 0-8078-1865-8
    1. Eugenics—Great Britain—History—20th century.   2. Family
size—Great Britain—History—20th century.   I. Title.
HQ755.5.G7S65   1990
303.6'34'0941—dc20   89-33500
                                                            CIP

Contents

Acknowledgments

I am deeply grateful for the support and assistance this project has received from numerous individuals and institutions. Professors John Cell of Duke University and Bernard Semmel of the State University of New York at Stony Brook read the entire manuscript, and I believe they know how much I appreciate their thoughtful criticism and helpful suggestions for improvement. My colleagues Donald Mathews and Gillian Cell proved to be patient sounding boards for many of the ideas worked out in the book and have helped me on several occasions to clarify my sometimes muddled thoughts. Dr. Leslie Banner of Duke University lent her impressive editorial skills to the final draft of the manuscript in what I hope has been a successful effort to unravel my dense prose and make the book more readable as well as informative.

Special thanks are also due to Lesley Hall and the excellent staff of the Contemporary Medical Archives Center at the Wellcome Institute for the History of Medicine as well as to S. E. Walters, general secretary of the Eugenics Society, for her patient assistance and kindness while I was working for many months in the society's library. I am also indebted to the British Library, University College and Senate House Libraries of the University of London, the British Library of Political and Economic Science, the Department of Population Studies in the London School of Economics, the Public Record Office, the National Maritime Museum in Greenwich and the staff of the David Owen Centre for Population Growth Studies at University College, Cardiff.

My research in this country benefited particularly from access to materials in the Library of Congress; Widener Library, Harvard University; the Stirling Library, Yale University; the Perkins Library, Duke University; and the libraries of my own institution, the University of North Carolina. The project was generously assisted by fellowships from the National Endowment for the Humanities and the National Humanities Center as well as grants-in-aid from the American Council of Learned Societies and the Research Council of the University of North Carolina. Most of the book was completed during a wonderful year at the National Humanities Center; I am especially grateful for the support of the trustees, staff, and former colleagues at that institution and for the opportunity to write in such a stimulating environment.

Introduction

Demography and Degeneration represents the merging of several of my research interests associated with the great changes that have occurred during the past hundred years in European fertility in general and British fertility in particular. It is also the result of a wider historical preoccupation with how various influential and, for the most part, educated groups in society perceive, interpret, and respond to profound social change.

I first explored this topic in *Prelates and People* (1969), a study of ecclesiastical social thought in England in the first half of the nineteenth century. There I was concerned with how the leadership of a privileged, traditional, conservative institution, the Church of England, responded to the unprecedented economic, social, and demographic changes associated with the industrial revolution. In turning several years ago to the post-Malthusian population question of the late nineteenth and early twentieth centuries, I continued to be intrigued by contemporary analyses of important social developments—especially how, after a century of rapid demographic expansion tied to very high levels of marital fertility, the British responded to the ensuing decades of declining fertility and to the start of the modern birth control revolution. One result of that inquiry was *Birth Control and the Population Question in England, 1877–1930* (1982); another is the present volume.

In the course of my research for *Birth Control*, I was struck by two important characteristics of British demographic thought that justified separate study: the pervasiveness of qualitative, biological evaluations that fell under the broad mantle of eugenics; and the persistence of deep, intermittent cultural and social pessimism, accompanied by the sense of impending decadence and decline. The theme of pessimism and degeneration in literature and art since the fin de siècle is familiar enough, and a number of scholars have described the concerns people felt in the late Victorian and Edwardian years about national and even biological deterioration. But the intense relationship of these often emotional ideas to the dry, dull population statistics of the twentieth century, which preoccupied a significant segment of the educated British public for decades, has received little attention from historians and virtually none from demographers.

Demography and Degeneration considers an important aspect of that relationship in examining how differing scientific (and pseudoscientific) eugenicist theories of biological inheritance became popularized and enmeshed in the
prolonged, often contentious national debate stirred up by the relentless fall in
fertility from the 1870s to World War II. During that period the crude birthrate,
which had hovered around 34 births per 1,000 of the population for most of the
nineteenth century, dropped to under 15, while the number of children per
marriage fell from the prolonged high Victorian average of five or six to the
modern ratio of slightly more than two. By the 1930s more sophisticated
analyses convinced a great many people that it was only a matter of time before
the dwindling of the British family, which had fallen substantially below
replacement, would bring an end to population growth entirely, followed by a
relentless and potentially disastrous decline.

The overall decline of marital fertility in European countries, including
Great Britain, has been exhaustively examined over the past two decades in an
important series of books and articles by historical demographers associated
with the European Fertility Project in the Office of Population Research at
Princeton University.[1] Their macrolevel studies of national and provincial
fertility based upon aggregate census data and vital statistics have demonstrated that with few exceptions (such as France, where the decline started
much earlier) birthrates began to drop rapidly and relentlessly virtually everywhere in Europe between 1880 and 1930.[2] Indeed, by the end of World War I,
nearly 60 percent of all European provinces (excluding France) had experienced at least a 10 percent decline in marital fertility beyond which the fall
became irreversible. The decline came somewhat later in Ireland and in several countries in eastern and southern Europe, but by World War II their
birthrates were also on the same downward path. The length of time it took to
record a fall of 10 percent once the decline set in varied widely: in England,
where the change was most rapid, it took only 16 years; in Germany, 33 years;
and in Italy nearly 60 years. Less than 100 years separated the first provincial
decline in marital fertility rates from the last, and in most places the loss was at
least 50 percent. In England the birthrate was halved by 1917.

The timing and pace of the fertility decline not only differed from country to
country and among provinces within those countries, but it occurred under a
wide variety of social, economic, and demographic conditions which do not
conform very closely to the classical theory of demographic transition. According to its hypothesis, formulated as a model of modernization in the
1950s, the ideal of the small family emerged in urban, industrial societies
where the family was losing many of its functions in production, consumption,
recreation, and education.[3]

In contrast to the first stage of the transition, which was characterized by high fertility and mortality and slow population growth, the second stage was marked by a substantial decline in infant mortality while fertility remained relatively high. People, however, began to recognize they could conceive fewer children to achieve a certain family size; beyond that number the costs of rearing and educating an excessively large brood became an increasingly heavy burden. Consequently, the pressures for high fertility gradually weakened in the course of the nineteenth century, and the motivation and desire for limitation strengthened. In addition, the theory of demographic transition runs, women were finding a new independence from household obligations and new economic roles less compatible with childbearing.

All of these socioeconomic factors contributed to a strong predisposition to curtail marital fertility which was acted upon as the knowledge of birth control became widely dispersed throughout Europe in the decades after 1870. Once completed, as it is in most modern, industrialized societies, the demographic transition is characterized by low and approximately equal levels of mortality and fertility resulting in little or no population growth. Periodic "baby booms," such as occurred after World War II, and "baby busts," which many developed countries are experiencing today, do not in the long run appreciably alter the balance.

Some of the broad correlations of diminished fertility with socioeconomic development and modernization contained in the theory of demographic transition still appear to have general validity. But participants in the European Fertility Project have raised serious questions about a number of the theory's basic tenets and have pointed up numerous difficulties in trying to explain the rapid decline in the birthrate from macrolevel quantitative data. While they confirm a rough coincidence of socioeconomic modernization and the demographic transition in the nineteenth century, they also cite many exceptions in different countries and regions. For example, the birthrate began to fall suddenly and unambiguously in England and Hungary about the same time, although England by every socioeconomic measurement was at a much higher stage of development. Similarly, the decline had started decades earlier in France, well before that country had advanced very far along the path of modernization.

Moreover, although in general, relatively urban and industrialized provinces with lower levels of illiteracy and infant mortality were, as the model postulated, the leaders in the transition, this was not always the case. Even when it was, the difference in the lag time before fertility fell at least 10 percent in both urban and rural areas was usually small. Furthermore, according to the transitionary model, a decline in infant mortality should have preceded the decline in the birthrate; it did not, however, do so in half of the European countries and provinces, including England, where the fall in marital fertility not only came first but at least a decade before infant deaths began to diminish significantly. Indeed, as two of the investigators in the European Fertility Project, John Knodel and Etienne van de Walle, cautioned, "at this stage no definite conclusion can be reached on the role of declining mortality in the fertility transition in the West." In fact, they added, "an examination of the social, economic and mortality conditions at the times of the onset of the fertility decline in various European countries reveals no consistency in the level of development." The remarkable diversity of conditions revealed in their studies and those of their colleagues made it "safe to conclude that no obvious threshold of social and economic development was required for the fertility transition to begin."[4]

Once the fertility decline started, as Susan Watkins pointed out in her summary of the project's findings, contraception was the one unifying factor in reducing the birthrate and restricting childbearing to the early years of a woman's married life. It was the determination on the part of spouses to limit and, later in the transition, to space their children, once they knew how, rather than any significant change in the incidence of marriage or in contraceptive technology that accounts for the rapid fall in fertility.[5] While the impressive quantitative studies, buttressed by charts, graphs, tables, and multiple regression equations testing numerous variables, date and trace the decline and detail socioeconomic factors that might or might not have caused it at various points in time, they do not, as some of their authors acknowledge, really explain why people chose to limit their families. The answers to that question, Michael Teitelbaum admits in his indispensable examination of the *British Fertility Decline*, lie as much in the realm of qualitative cultural history as they do in the socioeconomic and technological. It is, he argues in his concluding chapter, fruitless to try to disentangle the subtle and complex interaction existing among the three contributing factors.[6] Although Teitelbaum, like other contributors to the European Fertility Project, concentrates upon a macrolevel analysis of aggregated statistical tabulations, he recognizes, as do Knodel and van de Walle, that qualitative studies of the population question, though closer to social history than demography, can help place quantitative results in their social, psychological, and cultural context.[7]

That is precisely what this book tries to accomplish. It is an unabashedly qualitative study in the history of ideas that examines how successive generations of mostly middle- and upper-class educated men and women in twentieth-century Britain, who were culturally inclined to think in socially conscious, value-laden, hereditarian terms, comprehended and responded to compelling quantitative changes brought about by the sudden and precipitous decline in the fertility of their countrymen. Birthrate statistics and net reproduction ratios provoked decades of controversy that engaged prominent as well as peripheral figures in government, politics, law, religion, education, science, medicine, the military, journalism, literature, and even the theater. Their explanations, arguments, concerns, and prognoses fixed not only upon the size of the population, but, more importantly, on the relative proportion of people within it from different socioeconomic groups or classes. To contemporaries, a reading of the demographic map of society often led to the discovery that the poorest and least educated, healthy, intelligent, and skilled portion of the population were continuing to reproduce themselves in large numbers, while more and more people in the wealthiest, best-educated, and highly skilled classes were rapidly reducing the size of their families.

Inverse correlations between fertility and social status focused public attention upon the highly subjective and emotional question of "race quality" and provoked alarming predictions that Britain not only faced substantial depopulation at some point in the future, but would also be swamped by the socially, and, if eugenicists were correct, genetically "unfit." This scary prospect of "race suicide," as the gloomier prophets described it, was revived time and again before World War I and, though often with more subtlety and with greater sophistication, in the interwar years as well. It was a myth not laid to rest until the baby boom following World War II. Current discussions about the consequences of the "birth dearth" brought on by a return since the 1970s to lower fertility and reproduction rates that have fallen well below replacement in many western countries, including Britain, suggest that the myth's slumber, like the postwar surge in the birthrate, might have been short lived.[8]

The post-Malthusian population question is still before us though the eugenic considerations that were once so pervasive in the answers, and with which this book is primarily concerned, have been discredited. Recent controversies, particularly in the United States, over the validity of sociobiology and the ethical, legal, and potential biological consequences of genetic engineering may or may not portend, as critics claim, a revival of some sort of new eugenics. Whatever the outcome, there are plenty of reasons to suggest that the old arguments about the relative role of nature and nurture, which were at the heart of eugenic evaluations of classes, ethnic and cultural groups, and societies and races, may not be as moribund as they once were. Although some historians of science continue to examine their subjects in isolation from the historical environment, much as some historians tend to examine great ideas as if they were expounded in a historical vacuum, students of both subjects are today much more inclined to recognize the extent to which scientists and their scientific inquiries are, like intellectuals and the ideas they espouse, deeply influenced by the values, beliefs, and assumptions of the culture and times in which they live.

Eugenics, this work contends, was the product of profound social, political, and cultural changes feeding upon a deeply entrenched belief in the primacy of heredity as an explanation for the human condition. It is not clear to what extent the unsavory association of eugenics with Nazism, racism, and anti-socialist, procapitalistic class prejudices made it an unattractive subject after the war for scholarly inquiry by historians of science as well as of the social and intellectual history of modern Britain. Perhaps the failure of eugenics to achieve credibility either as a science or, as its founder, Francis Galton, and his followers hoped, a new positivistic religion and powerful agent for social reform, made it seem inconsequential, a fate often reserved for failed movements of the past. It is not too surprising that some of the first scholarly studies of eugenics appearing in the 1960s concentrated upon the United States, where the movement, for reasons peculiar to this country, had more practical success as well as a substantial intellectual following.[9] The series of books and articles in the past two decades on eugenics in Britain, the land of its origins, was in many ways launched by an Australian, Lyndsay Farrall, whose 1969 doctoral dissertation at Indiana University, "The Origins and Growth of the English Eugenics Movement 1865–1925," though widely read and quoted in its unpublished form, has only recently appeared in print.[10]

Farrall's pioneering work has been followed by a wide range of studies exploring the relationship of eugenics to politics, imperialism, racism, the New Liberalism, the Left, the Right, the social hygiene movement, the emergence of middle-class consciousness, and the rise of the professions, as well as more explicitly scientific inquiries into the eugenical foundations of modern statistics and genetics.[11] In addition, Galton has been the subject of at least one recent scholarly biography, an insightful dissertation on his hereditarian ideas, and many articles on aspects of his eclectic scientific work.[12] These studies, along with a great many others, have provided a foundation of secondary sources for the most recent and, by far, the most impressive investigation of the subject, Daniel J. Kevles's comparative examination of eugenics in Britain and America, *In the Name of Eugenics: Genetics and the Uses of Human Heredity.*[13]

My own book obviously owes a great debt to the authors of this body of literature even when I do not entirely share some of their interpretations. I attempt to examine and explain the rise (and fall) of eugenics in twentieth-century Britain in a very different historical context shaped in large part by the rapid decline in the birthrate and the assessments of this new phenomenon by contemporaries trying to understand what was happening to their society. While concerns about the decline in fertility, particularly in its socially differential aspects, have been noted by analysts of the eugenics movement, none of them has explicitly examined the importance of demographic change and post-Malthusian ideas of population control. These developments, I would argue, were of central importance to the transformation of eugenics from an unfocused, comparatively unknown set of late Victorian ideas about heredity into an organized movement and, increasingly, an important facet of biological thinking prominent in educated middle- and upper-class circles. Though his own approach to the subject precluded his taking it up, Kevles observed in his survey of the literature that "an important history remains to be written of the general relationship among eugenics, demography, and population control."[14]

In exploring the relationship of eugenics to the precipitous decline of fertility in twentieth-century Britain, the following chapters do not pretend to be a study in historical demography, as defined by the quantitative investigators of the Princeton European Fertility Project, nor do they constitute a scientific history of eugenics. On the contrary, in them I examine eugenics as an evolving species of historically shaped, culturally fashioned social thought based upon biological assumptions about individual ability and social class, and as a reform movement created by both the real and the imagined consequences of long-term changes in reproductive behavior.

One of the major problems confronting scholars attempting to evaluate the importance of eugenics in Britain during this period was the chronic inability of its often prestigious and influential advocates to translate their hereditarian beliefs into concrete results. Eugenicists were more adept at influencing other groups and individuals and at reinforcing "eugenic tendencies" where they found them than they were in establishing a clear, dominant role for themselves and their movement. Another difficulty in assessing the role of eugenics stems from assumptions that the personnel and intellectual boundaries of eugenics were coterminus with the small, elite, slightly esoteric Eugenics Society founded in 1907 to promote the cause. While that organization attracted a number of prominent and respected physicians, scientists, academicians, businessmen, and public figures, its middle- and upper middle-class membership, drawn almost equally from both sexes, was never very large, and its journal, *The Eugenics Review*, started in 1909, though economically self-sustaining, never achieved a large readership.

I would argue, however, that the importance of eugenics greatly transcended the limited institutional boundaries of a formal organization. Rooted deeply in a tradition of hereditarian determinism and qualitative ideas of class, eugenics permeated the thinking of generations of English men and women worried about the biological capacity of their countrymen to cope with the myriad changes they saw confronting their old nation in a new century. More than anything else, eugenics was a biological way of thinking about social, economic, political, and cultural change. It was rooted not only in a supposed understanding of the laws of heredity but, perhaps more important, in what many people believed to be a common sense recognition that "like tends to beget like." The sophisticated arguments among scientists, social scientists, and mathematicians about heredity and population were undoubtedly beyond the comprehension of many contemporaries who grasped not the structure and logic of learned dialogue but the practical implications for their society. In a great many cases, however, as eugenics was absorbed and popularized, it gave scientific credibility, and, consequently, respectability to attitudes, values, beliefs, prejudices, anxieties, and fears that were prevalent primarily, but not exclusively, among the middle and upper middle classes.

Eugenics was therefore always more a product of the culture of the times than it was a viable science or social science. As the times changed so did eugenics. But ultimately its fundamental tenets were made irrelevant and obnoxious by a more sophisticated scientific understanding of the complexities of human heredity and by profound changes in the social and political culture that had nurtured the movement in the first place.

Though many critics in the past, as now, believed eugenics was nothing more than a right-wing ideology embraced by Conservative, middle-class reactionaries, it in fact attracted people across the political spectrum. Because eugenics lacked ideological rigor and its adherents were never entirely certain whether they were promoting a science, a social science, or even a new religion, it was open to a wide range of interpretations. People of differing persuasions and interests were able to find in it what they wanted while rejecting that which they found offensive or unpersuasive. Eugenics in effect tried to create an objective reality outside of culture and history to explain conditions that were cultural and historical. In doing so, it appealed to people on a number of different levels and for a number of different reasons. This eclecticism made for strange bedfellows at times; they ranged from unreconstructed Tory reactionaries to Liberal social reformers, a wide variety of socialists and even the occasional Communist. If for some people eugenics provided a scientific rationalization for opposing the growing demands of collectivist social reformers who would defy the laws of natural selection and encourage the proliferation of the unfit, for others it was a progressive, even a radical program for scientifically planning and guiding the course of needed social reform. While many advocates were certain true eugenic policies could only succeed in a totally laissez-faire, competitive, capitalistic environment, their opponents were equally convinced eugenics was only possible in a planned, cooperative socialist society where environmental inequities were neutralized.

As a facet of a society and culture in rapid transition, eugenics is not only of historical interest but in its wider context also has a special relevance to contemporary society as the progenitor of more recent ideas of sociobiological engineering. Indeed the rise of modern sociobiology, or "scientific racism" as some critics describe it, has paralleled the remarkable discoveries made in human genetics since World War II and has provoked a heated controversy in this country that continues off and on to the present day.[15] But its origins, and many of the disputes it has aroused about the innate abilities of particular racial and ethnic groups, can be found in the history of eugenics and in some of the anxieties, particularly about the size and social composition of the population, that for a time gave that movement considerable popular credence and scientific credibility.

One

The Turn of the Century

T he waning years of the Victorian era and the approach of a new age aroused a great deal of commentary on the recent past and anxious speculation about the future. Whatever their oracular proclivities, most contemporary observers were proud that within their lifetimes, as well as those of their parents and grandparents, their small island nation had been transformed into an extraordinarily wealthy, powerful, and populous empire. If, increasingly, some critics questioned the social, physical, and moral costs of Great Britain's dynamic achievements, most admired them and the inventive, energetic, and vital people who had brought them about. To the religious, there was no want of evidence of divine favor. For those of a more secular, Darwinist turn of mind, the truth of natural selection was everywhere manifest in the unprecedented progress of their "race," as the British people were loosely described.

Whether that favor would remain and progress continue in the new century was a source of considerable anxiety even before the old had passed away. Challenges to Britain's economic preeminence from industrializing, commercially expansive countries such as Germany and the United States raised serious questions in the 1880s and 1890s about the ability of the country to expand or even preserve its markets around the globe. The agricultural and industrial depression of those decades, coupled with the intensification of imperial rivalries in Africa and elsewhere, caused many people to doubt the durability of their nation's accomplishments and its predominant position in a rapidly changing world. The rise of the "Condition of England" question and the growth of socialism prompted lasting skepticism about long-held, fundamental social and economic assumptions. Darwinism had a similar effect upon traditional religious explanations of the human condition and stimulated a great deal of apprehension about the fitness of the mature, highly evolved British race to adapt to the new, complex challenges that unquestionably lay ahead.

The sudden death in January 1901 of Queen Victoria, whose sixty-four-year reign symbolized what many of her subjects believed to be a golden age of prosperity, power, and imperial grandeur, unleashed an orgy of nostalgia about the past and conjecture about the future. Her last prime minister, Lord Salisbury, eulogized her ameliorative role during Britain's remarkably peaceful transition from an old to a new society, but his nephew and political successor, Arthur James Balfour, was more to the point in his conclusion that the nation's grief was all the greater because "we feel that the end of a great epoch has come upon us."[1] Having said farewell to the "poor wicked nineteenth century" three weeks earlier, Wilfred Scawen Blunt, upon hearing of the queen's death, wrote in his diary, "the great Victorian age is at an end. . . . This is notable news. It will mean great changes in the world."[2] The *Times*, whose columns had entertained a dispute about whether the twentieth century began on 1 January 1900 or 1901, knew with Victoria's passing that it was resolved. The nineteenth century was irrevocably over and we feel "less secure of our position . . . and somewhat less abreast of the problems of the age than we ought to be."[3]

A number of commentators were more outspoken in their concern, questioning whether England would survive the new century. The *Westminster Review*, pondering "What should England do to be Saved?" complained that the country "has grown old, her national vitality is exhausted. She has arrived at the stage of senile decay, while the United States is just entering upon that of vigorous puberty." The popular *Daily Mail*, a paper of a very different stripe, also recognized that "in some inscrutable manner the old fire of energy seems to be waning within us. We are entering stormy seas, and the time may be near when we shall have to fight in very truth for our life."[4]

While the war in South Africa was not the sort of epic confrontation the *Daily Mail* had in mind, the British army's inauspicious performance in that costly, protracted, often humiliating conflict did little to assuage misgivings about the nation's capacity to measure up to the anticipated demands of the new age. Recalling Queen Victoria's stately funeral procession, the novelist Elinor Glyn sensed the passing of a great epoch "in which England had been supreme, and had attained to the height of her material wealth and power." There were many people, she wrote, "who wondered, doubted perhaps, whether that greatness could continue; who read in the failures of the early part of the Boer War a sign of decadence." Admittedly influenced, perhaps unduly, by Gibbon's *Decline and Fall* and by her French upbringing, Glyn felt she "was witnessing the funeral procession of England's greatness and glory."[5] Although Britain finally prevailed over the Boers in 1902, confidence in the nation's strength, vitality, and efficiency had been severely shaken. It was difficult not to wonder if a country forced to spend three years and £250 million to defeat a handful of unorganized farmers had the right to call itself the greatest power on earth.[6]

This unease about the future was perhaps more obvious because it was in such contrast to the confidence and optimism that had obtained for most of the nineteenth century. Until the closing years of the queen's reign, the Victorians had worshiped change, which they associated with human improvement and social and economic progress. Their Edwardian successors, confronting the consequences of the industrial-imperial society built in the preceding century, were certain changes would continue, perhaps even accelerate, but they were much less sanguine about their correlation with progress. As the Liberal reformer C. F. G. Masterman concluded in his popular 1909 study, *The Condition of England*, "We are uncertain whether civilization is about to blossom into flower, or wither in a tangle of dead leaves and faded gold." Optimism could still be found in competition with pessimism. But thirty years earlier it had been pessimism which had competed with optimism.[7]

The Diminishing Birthrate

An increasingly important factor in the shifting balance between pessimism and optimism was a growing awareness at the turn of the century that dramatic changes were under way in the rate at which the British were reproducing themselves. Despite the dire warnings of Thomas Robert Malthus and other early nineteenth-century political economists, generations of Victorians associated high fertility and large families with the vitality and progress of their country. Predictions of unchecked population growth inevitably outstripping basic subsistence seemed increasingly remote to a society whose economic productivity and expansionary appetites had brought it enviable prosperity and influence.[8] As Arthur Lyttelton, the master of Selwyn College, Cambridge, noted in 1891, there was no evidence that population had encroached upon wealth or was inimical to economic progress. Indeed, he argued, capital, property values, and trade had all increased far more than population, while declining prices and expanded opportunities had greatly improved the availability of subsistence.[9]

Decennial censuses starting in 1801 charted a more than threefold increase in population, from approximately 11 million to 37 million people 100 years later. At no time in that period did the rate of increase fall below 11 percent a decade, and, in the first half of the century, it was often substantially above the decennial average of 13.8 percent.[10] These increases were in large part sustained by a high level of fertility apparently beginning in the second half of the eighteenth century and continuing until the closing years of the nineteenth.[11] The civil registration of births and deaths after 1837 in England and Wales

revealed a slowly rising annual crude birthrate of approximately 30 births per
1,000 of the population to a recorded high of 36.3 in 1876.[12] It seems likely,
however, that this increase had less to do with rising fertility than with improved registration, so that the average rate even in the 1840s was already
probably closer to 35 per 1,000.[13]

Although the crude rates were distorted by changes in age structure and sex
composition and revealed nothing about patterns of nuptiality and marital
fertility, they demonstrated general trends and illustrated the rate at which the
population was being augmented by births. Moreover, these were the figures
most observers of population trends cited. Mortality figures, by contrast,
tended to be more sophisticated since sanitary reformers, public health officials, and government statisticians were more preoccupied with death rates in
various parts of the country. Until the late nineteenth and early twentieth
centuries, at least, high birthrates were taken for granted, and even then it was
not until the 1930s that significant steps were taken to improve systematically
the gathering and analysis of fertility statistics.[14]

By the time of Queen Victoria's death in 1901 it was, however, becoming
apparent that her subjects were reproducing themselves at markedly lower
rates than in earlier generations. The high figures of 35 and 36 per 1,000
persisting throughout much of her long reign had begun to diminish steadily in
the 1880s, and by the opening of the new century had fallen to 28.5, a decline
of more than 21 percent. This new trend had first been noticed nearly twenty
years earlier in the quarterly and annual reports of the registrar-general. The
Malthusian, the journal of the first birth control organization in the country,
the Malthusian League, founded in the aftermath of the sensational obscenity
trial of Charles Bradlaugh and Annie Besant in 1877, commented in 1883 on a
drop of 10 to 15 per 1,000 in the birthrate of such London districts as
Willesden, Kensington, and Hampstead compared to a decade earlier.[15] Furthermore, the *Malthusian* was encouraged to observe, the number of children
born in London in 1883 was already 400 less than the previous ten-year
average, despite a much larger population in the metropolis.[16]

Occasional comments and notices in the 1880s gave way to fuller discussion
in the 1890s as the relentless decline in fertility continued. Lyttelton, a critic of
the new, or neo-Malthusians, as well as the old, called attention to the downward trend in 1892, which he attributed to the changing economic conditions
and a tendency toward later marriage. Like most of his contemporaries, however, he was not yet particularly alarmed by the diminishing rates.[17] A decade
later the mood had changed considerably. The *Daily Mail* in 1903 assured its
many readers that among the problems the nation's leaders would have to

confront in the new century none was more important than stopping the decline in the birthrate that had "set in with ominous steadiness, and which is now beginning to menace the predominance of the race."[18] Not to be outdone, the *Daily Telegraph* remarked upon the anxiety caused by the recent course of national fertility and described "man power [as] the rock on which the whole edifice of the State is built." In calling for the creation of a "sound and patriotic public opinion" on the issue, the newspaper warned that no land could truly prosper when its fertility declined.[19]

The neo-Malthusians, invoking the teachings of their patron saint, insisted that just the opposite was the case, and until the increase of population was substantially curtailed poverty would remain endemic and economic growth would be constrained. J. A. Spender, the editor of the *Westminster Gazette*, recalling the fluctuations in popular demographic thought since Malthus's time, found it ironic that having finally achieved their goal, those who had long advocated a check on population now saw public opinion swinging to the opposite pole again. What was once regarded by Victorian political economists as "the special aim of statesmanship," he wrote, "is now regarded as a sign of decay." Despite the population having nearly quadrupled in the past 100 years, "in these days we find most of the newspapers and all the preachers in a state of despair about the slightest check in the percentage of increase."[20]

If not all of the press shared the medical journal *Lancet*'s gloomy assessment of the falling birthrate as "a national calamity seriously threatening the future welfare of our race," the quarterly and annual reports of the registrar-general were nevertheless important news items in the Edwardian years.[21] They inspired a periodic flood of editorials and articles ranging from the coolly analytical to the hysterically apocalyptical. The latter were usually punctuated by ominous cries of "race suicide." There was no end of comparisons with ancient and more recent civilizations and empires whose flagging reproductive energies explained their decline.

Only slightly less common were comparisons with contemporary nations, usually Germany and the United States, but sometimes China and Japan, whose higher fertility and larger populations implicitly constituted an immediate or eventual threat to Britain's extensive empire. The Liberal M.P., Leo Chiozza Money, was by 1912 reciting familiar statistics when he reminded readers of the *Nineteenth Century* that not only was the German rate of increase in the previous decade (15.2 percent) the largest in Europe and nearly 50 percent more than in Great Britain (10.9 percent), but since 1880 the demographic gap between the two countries had risen from 10 million to 20 million people. In an era of intense economic, political, and military rivalry, it was particularly alarming to realize that the country's most formidable challenger was increasing by 900,000 people a year, compared to only 111,500 in the United Kingdom.[22]

Equally worrisome were the parallels drawn with the French, whose comparatively low birthrate symbolized for many Englishmen the weakness and decadence of that unfortunate race, and in part explained its quick defeat by the virile Germans in 1870. Gallic fertility, the lowest in Europe, averaged nearly 10 fewer births per 1,000 than England throughout the nineteenth century, but by 1901 there was fear that the gap was narrowing. After analyzing vital statistics since 1878, J. Holt Schooling warned in the *Fortnightly Review* that the recent decline in the English birthrate was greater than in any other European country. Whatever the reason, only a similar fall in the death rate prevented "our approaching France's condition of a number of births insufficient to maintain the native population."[23]

Schooling, like many of his contemporaries, was initially uncertain whether the decline was accidental and temporary or the more permanent result of "an aggregate of individual intention to restrain the birth of children." What was evident, however, was that since 1878 there had been "an immense decline in the actual number of children that are born of . . . modern marriages." To demonstrate his argument, he drew up five-year fertility-of-marriage tables starting in 1846. They showed that the number of births per 100 marriages had risen steadily from 371 in 1846–50 to 441 in 1876–80 before falling to 346 at the end of the century. Schooling calculated that this decline resulted in some 2,000 fewer births a week than twenty years earlier.[24] One of the results, Sidney Webb noted in 1906, was a decline of 5,000 in the number of preschool children ages three to five in London since 1891, although the population had grown by more than 300,000 in the past ten years alone. Similar trends were evident throughout the country, he wrote the *Times*, and he informed its readers that the Fabian Society was studying the problem.[25]

The general pattern described by Schooling and some of the consequences observed by others were repeatedly confirmed in the early years of the new century by more sophisticated and authoritative analyses. Aware of the mounting interest in the vital statistics issued by his department, the registrar-general in his 1903 report placed special emphasis upon the use of corrected fertility rates as a more precise form of measurement. These figures, which enumerated the number of children born annually to married women ages fifteen to forty-five, had been available since mid-century but now took on new significance. Until the 1870s when it reached a recorded peak of 304, the corrected rate had averaged 288 births per 1,000 married women in their childbearing years. Since then the figure had fallen to 234, and showed every sign of continuing on its downward path.[26] Indeed, by 1914 it stood at 191.6 per 1,000, a decline of 37 percent since the prolific 1870s. The drop in corrected or marital fertility even exceeded the 33 percent slide to 24 per 1,000 in the crude birthrate.

Each new report from the registrar-general was followed by a spate of calculations estimating how many thousands of children would have been born if the corrected or crude birthrates had remained at the level of the 1870s. What it added up to, the medical officers Arthur Newsholme and T. H. C. Stevenson told the Royal Statistical Society in 1905, was that women of childbearing age were having fewer children with every passing year, irrespective of their marital status. Even illegitimacy had plummeted 40 percent in the last quarter of the century, indicating that some effective check to reproduction was clearly at work.[27]

Despite popular assumptions to the contrary, Newsholme wrote elsewhere, that check was not a peculiarity of the accelerated urbanization and geographic redistribution of population that resulted in more than three-quarters of the population living in large towns by 1901. Warnings about the sterilizing effects of crowded city life were nothing new by the early twentieth century, but extensive rural migration to the great towns since the 1870s had raised worrisome questions about the future replenishment of the population from healthy country stock. The revivifying flow from that presumably purer stream was threatened not only by the effects of the agricultural depression on village life but, as Newsholme demonstrated, by a 20 percent decline in the corrected rural birthrate that was actually 5 percent greater than in the cities.[28]

Both Sidney Webb, in his 1907 Fabian Society study, *The Decline in the Birth-Rate*, and Ethel Elderton, in her more extensive, statistically sophisticated 1914 Eugenics Laboratory memoir, *Report on the English Birth Rate*, though comparing different areas of the country, essentially confirmed Newsholme's findings.[29] Their work was part of the mushrooming volume of popular and scientific literature analyzing the plummeting birthrate in the decade before the Great War. Even the *Malthusian*, while delighted by the downward trend, complained about the impossibility of keeping up with press comment on the subject.[30] Much of that comment was in the form of a eulogy for the large Victorian family with its five or six children. Writers conjured up melancholy images of empty cradles and silent nurseries as they looked for explanations and contemplated consequences.

J. M. Robertson, the Radical-Liberal journalist and M.P. for Tyneside, criticized many of his professional and political colleagues for spouting "hollow . . . lugubrious humbug" about the extinction of the race or the "eclipse of the Anglo Saxon by more prolific stocks," when in fact the decline in the birthrate was by no means restricted to Great Britain.[31] That it was, as the optimistic Havelock Ellis argued, a characteristic of the "highly civilised" European and American races, brought little comfort to those of his contemporaries who mourned the dwindling family.[32] Evidence showing births exceeding deaths by more than 40 percent and the population still increasing by over 1 percent a year seemed to have no effect on the Edwardian prophets of race suicide. Not even the addition of another 4 million people during Edward VII's nine-year reign brightened the cheerless, constricted future they read in the remains of the statistical brew.

One of the major impediments to resolving the differing analyses and interpretations of the declining birthrate was the absence of reliable data about marital fertility. Comparisons of the size of past and present families as well as projections into the future had to be extrapolated from crude and corrected marriage and birth rates. Schooling, for example, in drawing up his quinquennial tables of marital fertility, assumed that most children would be born in the first five years of marriage. Starting with 1851–55 he therefore divided the number of children born in a five-year period by the number of marriages in the preceding five years to get an estimate of the number of births per marriage.[33]

Karl Pearson, Goldsmid Professor of Applied Mathematics and Mechanics at University College, London, a few years earlier, in the mid-1890s, had applied his much more formidable statistical talents to the problem. On the basis of the marital and fertility figures in the registrar-general's reports, he plotted a number of frequency curves that distinctly showed a decline in the number of families of five and six children and a corresponding increase in those with two, three, and four. Although the trend toward smaller families had not yet become an issue of national concern, Pearson correctly suspected that it soon would.[34]

The proliferation of unofficial investigations by individuals and organizations in the new century indicated how quickly demographic considerations were becoming a focus of wider apprehensions about the changes already occurring in British society and the problems and challenges that lay ahead. The most important of these inquiries was undertaken in 1913 by the National Birth-Rate Commission under the auspices of the eminently respectable National Council of Public Morals (NCPM), itself a descendant of an earlier social purity crusade. Buttressed by an impressive roster of peers, politicians, bishops, Anglican clergymen, Nonconformists, educators, physicians, editors, and even Beatrice Webb and James Ramsay MacDonald, the council condemned "the low and degrading views of the racial instinct" threatening, among other things, "our very life as a nation." [35]

The "regeneration of the race," the NCPM's director, the Presbyterian minister James Marchant, explained and the organization's motto proclaimed, was dependent upon a "strong, simple and pure" family life.[36] In emphasizing sexual purity, moral education, and traditional domestic values, the council, as Samuel Hynes has written, "sought to marshal the vague moral pieties of a past life against the social anxieties of a fearful present"—and, it should be added, an ominous future.[37] The falling birthrate became an important focus of those anxieties, and the goals of the National Birth-Rate Commission were to explore the extent and character of the decline, to determine its causes, to measure its effects upon marriage and the family, and to determine its likely impact upon the economy and the nation.[38]

The commission, under the cochairmanship of William Boyd Carpenter, the bishop of Ripon, and William Ralph Inge, the outspoken dean of St. Paul's, was created only when it became evident that the Liberal government was no more inclined than its Conservative predecessor to appoint a royal commission to resolve the often contentious arguments surrounding the fall in the birthrate. Like Balfour before him, Prime Minister Henry Asquith acknowledged the growing importance and emotionalism of the issue but went no further than promising to follow the birthrate commission's deliberations with interest.[39] More importantly, however, in part to ward off mounting demands for an official investigation, he had sanctioned the taking of an unprecedented *Fertility of Marriage Census* in conjunction with the decennial census of 1911.

Although the war delayed publication of the *Fertility of Marriage Census*, its author, T. H. C. Stevenson, who had become superintendent of statistics in the General Register Office, provided many of his findings to the National Birth-Rate Commission in 1913–14. By tabulating the fertility experience of millions of married women in all classes of society recorded in the special census returns, Stevenson expected to demonstrate precisely the social, regional, and generational characteristics of the decline in the birthrate since the middle of the nineteenth century. He also assumed the data would clarify the reasons for the rapid diminution in family size generating so much discussion among his contemporaries.

The returns certainly confirmed that the average number of children born to successive marriage cohorts had fallen by nearly half since the 1860s, when it stood at about six. By the end of the century it had dropped to four, and although the families of recent marriages were still not complete, there was little reason to believe they would average many more than three children. Furthermore, since the 1870s the percentage of large families with nine or ten offspring had fallen from nearly 14 to 4 percent, while those with only one or two children had risen from 12.5 percent to nearly one-third. Summarizing the evidence of the many tables reproduced in the census report, Stevenson noted "the universality of the decline for all classes and all ages at marriage. There is scarcely an exception to the rule that the fertility of the marriages of any period is less than that of the preceding period."[40] Later studies refined and corroborated this trend which continued, with slight fluctuations, until World War II. By then married couples were, with 2.04 children, barely reproducing themselves and predictions of an imminent decline in the population bordered on the hysterical.[41]

Differential Fertility

More alarming to the pre–World War I generation than the general decline in the birthrate was the realization that it was much more pronounced among the better-educated, economically successful middle and upper classes than among the poorer or lower classes of society. Indeed, the inverse correlation between fertility and socioeconomic status troubled even those who were otherwise unconcerned about the diminishing rate of increase in a country they believed to be already overcrowded. The extensive concern about differential fertility was evident in many of the unofficial investigations undertaken in the Edwardian years as well as in the *Fertility of Marriage Census*.

Stevenson and his colleagues in the General Register Office constructed an elaborate scale of social classification in which nearly 300 occupations were compressed into eight classes. They ranged from people in the professional, wealthy middle, and upper middle ranks in classes I and II through the skilled, semiskilled, and unskilled workers in classes III–V. Textile operatives, whose fertility proved to be contrastingly low, and miners and agricultural laborers, whose rate of reproduction was disconcertingly high, were placed in special classes VI–VIII.[42]

The architects of the census were well aware of the imprecision and confusion embedded in their complex, socially stratified categories, but, as Stevenson told the National Birth-Rate Commission in 1914, even the preliminary compilations showed that while the fall in the birthrate since the 1870s was evident among all classes, it was much more pronounced among people in classes I–III. A comparative analysis of older and more recent marriages proved conclusively that women in the poorer ranks not only began bearing children earlier than their social betters in the same age cohorts but continued to do so long after their more affluent counterparts stopped.[43] Contrary to popular belief, it was this rather than the class disparities in the age and frequency of marriage that accounted for the differential fertility patterns described in the census. While it was true that working-class women married earlier than those in classes I and II, the rise in the marriage age since 1850, from 22.5 to 25.3, noted by many demographic analysts, affected all ranks of society. In the new century the average age at which women in the highest classes were wed was, at 26, only 2 years older than those in the most fertile working-class categories.[44]

Women in the more elevated stations were, as the later Victorians and the Edwardians often complained, less likely to marry, but the frequency with which they eventually went to the altar was not statistically all that different. Many of these complaints reflected the presence of a large number of single women of childbearing age in all classes of British society. Between 1851 and 1931, for example, on average 43 percent of females ages 25–29 were unmarried, and the proportion actually increased slightly until 1911.[45]

The odds of women marrying were further reduced by the lower survival rates of male children to adulthood. By the later nineteenth century this differential had created a "surplus" of nearly a million females. Moreover, as Stevenson pointed out, late marriage was as prevalent among workers in several skilled and unskilled occupations as it was among men in the higher ranks, while the celibacy of agricultural laborers was close to that of men in the professional classes. The evidence, he argued, supported the conclusion "that frequency of marriage differs comparatively little in the various classes, much less so than fertility when married."[46] It was this fertility differential, he later recalled, that had changed dramatically since mid-century when the number of births had not varied much among social classes, but that now raised "new and formidable" questions "which must be left for the consideration of authorities on eugenics."[47]

Those questions, with their eugenic implications, arose from census data demonstrating that the birthrate among middle- and upper-class couples who had married in the 1870s and 1880s had declined anywhere from a third to as much as two-thirds more than fertility in working class marriages celebrated in the same decades. By 1911 this meant that the doctors, teachers, clergymen, scientists, bankers, barristers, chemists, accountants, military officers, businessmen, and prosperous landowners in classes I and II, whose families were complete, had sired an average of 3.4 children. This was nearly half the 6.1 reported for the more numerous coal miners, boilermakers, general laborers, shipyard workers, dockers, riveters, pig iron workers, coal heavers, and scavengers at the other end of the socioeconomic spectrum.

Despite the general decline in fertility since the 1870s, the class differential had actually widened so that in more recent marriages in which conception was still possible, the comparative figures when standardized were 1.8 and 3.7.[48]

Since it was clear that the wives of prosperous, successful, professional men in classes I and II, where small families were now the rule, stopped having children much sooner than those in the most progenitive classes, IV, V, VII, and VIII, there was every reason to believe the "inverse relation between brain work and fertility" that had characterized the nation's recent demographic experience would continue to grow.[49]

The *Fertility of Marriage Census* confirmed what most observers of the demographic scene already knew and, in many cases, feared. Social analysts such as Charles Booth and B. Seebohm Rowntree, in their important studies of London and York in the 1890s, had forcefully demonstrated the close relationship of poverty to high fertility. Booth, in particular, compared the swollen birthrate which averaged 37 per 1,000 in the poorest, most overcrowded areas of East London with the low figure of 24 per 1,000 recorded for a like number of the most fashionable and prosperous boroughs. Not even the substantially higher infant mortality suffered by the poor was enough to offset a net rate of population growth nearly one-third larger than that experienced by those at the top of the social ladder.[50]

Karl Pearson made the same point when, in 1897, after measuring existing disparities in family size, he calculated that 40 percent of the married population produced nearly 70 percent of the children. More striking was his much-quoted prediction that half of the next generation would be bred by no more than 20 to 25 percent of the present generation of married couples. His analysis of median fertility indicated that this unrestrained minority continued to have at least six or seven offspring while the majority was increasingly inclined to have no more than two to four. When the number of unmarried men and women was factored into the calculus, Pearson added, half of the next generation would be produced by as few as one-sixth of adults living today. "Any correlation between inheritable (physical or social) characteristics and fertility," he cautioned, "must thus sensibly influence the next generation."[51]

A Darwinist and fervent social imperialist who believed the competitive laws of natural selection were in the modern world more applicable to the struggle between nations than between individuals, Pearson was also a recent convert to Francis Galton's eugenically inspired, quantitative theories of human heredity. They suggested, among other things, the deleterious effects an excessively fertile minority could have on a comparatively infertile population. The two merged in Pearson's growing doubts about whether Britain was breeding any longer sufficient numbers of the sort of people needed to compete efficiently and successfully in the international arena.[52]

Although he believed natural selection through high infant mortality was still acting as something of a check on the excessive fertility of the unfit, Pearson thought it was no longer sufficient to moderate the widening reproductive disparities in English society. In fact, there was reason to believe that "survival of the most fertile, rather than the survival of the fittest, is very possibly now the keynote to evolution in civilised man." His Fabian socialist sympathies in the 1890s possibly restrained him from making the invidious class comparisons that frequently accompanied discussions of differential fertility, but as an accomplished professional statistician he also knew existing studies were unable to support reliable comparisons of marriage or birth rates among classes and occupational groups. Nevertheless, he predicted that statesmen rather than statisticians would soon have to become concerned with the "relative degrees of fertility in the various classes of a community, and the correlation of various social or anti-social characteristics with fertility."[53]

The absence of reliable data did not, however, prevent Pearson early in the new century from complaining about a dangerous decline in intelligence and talent. "The mentally better stock in the nation is not reproducing itself at the same rate as it did of old; the less able," he warned, "and the less energetic, are more fertile than the better stocks." Like many proponents of national efficiency, Pearson worried about Britain's ability to match qualitatively the formidable Germans and Americans, or, for a time, the lowly Boers.[54] It was therefore with considerable trepidation that he confronted "the commencement of an epoch which will be marked by a great dearth of ability." The cause of that privation was implied in his appeal for a census to determine accurately the "effective size of families among the intellectual classes" and compare it with the fertility of skilled and unskilled workers. There was no doubt in Pearson's mind the returns would conclusively demonstrate that "grave changes have taken place in relative fertility during the last forty years."[55]

Pearson's reproductive calculus was frequently cited during the debate over the falling birthrate in the decade before World War I. It was offered as confirming evidence in the *Fertility of Marriage Census* and figured prominently in the deliberations of the National Birth-Rate Commission in 1914. By then he had refined the data sufficiently to suggest that half the next generation might actually be supplied by no more than 12 percent of the population.[56] This dwindling minority of excessively fertile people were located, by a variety of demographic investigators, in the poorest districts of the great towns, especially London.

Some of these investigators, like David Heron, G. Udny Yule and Ethel Elderton, were Pearson's former students. On the basis of a detailed, comparative analysis of the fertility of married women in twenty-seven London districts, Heron, a fellow in the newly established Eugenics Laboratory in University College, London, was able to claim in 1906 that every statistical correlation proved that "the wives in the districts of least prosperity and culture have the largest families, and the morally and socially lowest classes in the community are those which are reproducing themselves with the greatest rapidity."[57] Moreover, like Yule, who had made a less thorough study of corrected birthrates in several London boroughs from 1871 to 1901, Heron found an ever-growing differential relationship between reproduction and undesirable social conditions. In admitting the contrast might not be as great in other parts of the country, Yule nevertheless warned the Royal Statistical Society of the impossibility of denying any longer that the "matter is one of the gravest social importance."[58]

Sidney Webb cited Heron's recent work in his own Fabian Society tract, *The Decline in the Birth-Rate*, but complained that the contrast of rich with poor districts and the concentration on London with its large population of Catholic Irish and immigrant Jews distorted the realities of differential fertility in the country. A review of the maternity claims made by the skilled artisans, mechanics, and responsible small shopkeepers who contributed to the two largest friendly benefit societies, the Hearts of Oak and the Royal Standard, showed a dramatic decline of more than 50 percent since 1880. Webb estimated that had the number of recipients of lying-in benefits been proportionally the same in 1904 as in 1880, their wives would have given birth to 67,000 more children than they did. The evidence satisfied Webb that the birthrate was not only falling conspicuously among the wealthy and middle classes, "but among the sections of every class in which there is most prudence, foresight and self-control."

Although his own inquiry concentrated upon the most successful and prosperous sector of the working and lower middle classes, Webb argued that the lack of similar evidence for the semiskilled and unskilled did not necessarily mean they were recklessly breeding in the great towns, as many people claimed. Moreover, he reminded his readers, the decline in the birthrate was, as Newsholme and Stevenson had recently proven, as great, if not greater, in rural counties with their large numbers of badly paid agricultural laborers. The danger of "race suicide" was not then a consequence of differential fertility, Webb concluded, but of the loss of some 200,000 potential children a year to all classes.[59]

If Heron's *On the Relation of Fertility in Man to Social Status* was the most comprehensive study before the 1911 census, Webb's tract was probably more widely read by the public and reviewed by the press. Even Pearson, who

criticized Webb's methodology, statistical techniques, and questionable conclusions, acknowledged that *The Decline in the Birth-Rate* helped focus on the
issue of differential reproduction. Nevertheless his own incomplete examination of poorer working-class marriages found little to sustain Webb's suppositions about a generalized distribution of diminishing fertility. On the contrary,
his sample of 1,205 families averaged 6.4 to 6.6 children, a figure well above
that estimated by Webb for skilled workers and middle-class couples.[60]

Elderton's 1914 *Report on the English Birth Rate* north of the Humber river,
was an attempt to shift the emphasis on differential fertility studies away from
London. But it too focused upon the fertility of the working classes since the
data gathered in the 1911 census for the middle and upper classes was not yet
available. Unlike previous studies, however, Elderton supplemented census
materials with questionnaires, interviews, and the health reports of medical
officers in sample districts.[61] Her findings, elaborately embellished with
graphs and correlative tables for the industrial and rural areas in the nine
counties surveyed, corroborated those made by Heron, Pearson, Newsholme,
Stevenson, and others in previous years. These included a preliminary measurement of "The Correlation of Fertility with Social Value" in the manufacturing towns of Blackburn, Preston, and Salford where she and her colleagues
in the Galton Eugenics Laboratory established that "in almost every case a bad
social condition is associated with a large family."[62] Since 1876, Elderton
decided, the birthrate had fallen substantially, if differentially, in every county
north of the Humber. Furthermore, the decline had sharply accelerated since
1901, though, unfortunately, not as much among the "unhealthy, careless and
thriftless."[63]

By 1914 such imprecise, qualitative euphemisms for the laboring poor
usually embellished supposedly objective, quantitative reports on the birthrate. Heron had contented himself with references to "the districts of least
prosperity and culture" where the "morally and socially lowest classes in the
community . . . are reproducing themselves with the greatest rapidity."[64] His
mentor Pearson increasingly located the notoriously prolific minority breeding
most of the next generation among the "unfit" denizens of low "civic worth"
who populated the squalid slums of the great towns. Comparatively few of the
people scientifically analyzing fertility data before the war were as virulent
as London neurologist Alfred Tredgold, who was sure that the declining
birthrate "is practically confined to the best elements" while "the whole parasitic class of the nation" continued to propagate "with unabated and unre-
stricted vigour."[65]

Elderton was more moderate in describing the aggressively fertile, hard-

drinking, unskilled, often unemployed people who lived in the dirty, overcrowded, low-rent, low-wage districts of northern England. She was, however,
no less certain that their differential rate of reproduction was "of the most
serious national gravity." If it continued for another forty years "racial degeneration" was inevitable, and with it "national disaster, complete and irremedi-
able, not only for this country but for Britain across four seas." [66]

Elderton, like Heron, was one of the principal assistants in the Galton
Eugenics Laboratory, where, given its primary interest in the statistical measurement of human heredity, many of the early studies on the differential
birthrate were carried out. But the inverse correlations made between fertility
and class quickly entered the public domain where they were anxiously debated by people who still had only the vaguest understanding of the new
science of eugenics. But the popular mind already possessed three of the basic
ingredients of eugenicist thought that made it readily comprehensible, if not
always acceptable, even to the mathematically illiterate. These were (1) a
fixation on class; (2) a simplistic assumption that "like begets like," or that
many physical, mental, moral, and behavioral human characteristics, qualities, and defects were hereditary; and (3) a belief in biological evolution with
its attendant notions of fitness and unfitness. Consequently, when Elderton
claimed that "no one who has even a feeble belief in the power of heredity can
regard [differential fertility] as anything but an unmixed evil," she was reflecting as much as formulating what many of her contemporaries were saying with
increasing frequency and disquiet. [67]

Newsholme and Stevenson in 1906 tried to discount some of the bleaker
interpretations of class fertility by recalling that differences had always existed. The revitalization of many aristocratic families on the edge of extinction, for example, depended upon the recruitment of fresh blood from their
more fecund social inferiors. Moreover, British accomplishments of the past
century alone clearly demonstrated the presence of talent and ability in all
classes. The two medical officers offered one final comfort that perhaps
intimated more of a sense of unease than they themselves recognized. Even if
the lowest classes were contributing a greater proportion to the population than
ever before, they concluded, it was a fairly recent development and there was
no assurance it would continue. [68]

After reviewing the returns for the 1911 *Fertility of Marriage Census*,
Stevenson, if not Newsholme, had second thoughts. He conceded the decline
in the birthrate in classes I–III was much greater than he had realized earlier.
Indeed, he concluded in his report, "Our population has been recruited . . .
under conditions fundamentally different from those of the immediately preceding and probably of any previous period. No appeal to English experience

. . . can indicate the probable effect of the change that has taken place." Stevenson could find nothing in the tabulations to quiet the misgivings about the future so widely felt in society. Whatever other interpretations might be put upon the *Fertility of Marriage Census*, there was no doubt in his mind that it had "much significance from the eugenic point of view."[69]

Two

Eugenics and the
New Population Question

T
he rise of the eugenics movement in Great Britain closely paralleled the emergence of the new population question which, unlike the old, focused not upon the Malthusian consequences of unchecked fertility but upon the implications of its differential decline. Arthur Newsholme and T. H. C. Stevenson recognized in 1906 that the surge of interest in eugenics was in large measure a response to fears that the "less fit" were reproducing themselves in greater proportions than ever before. Although the two medical statisticians were by no means persuaded this was so, or that fitness was a monopoly of class, they acknowledged the pervasiveness of contrary beliefs and the growing appeal of eugenic explanations.[1] Indeed, the fall in the birthrate was the catalyst that transformed eugenics from a relatively obscure, neo-Darwinist, statistically based science into an organized propagandist movement and, more important, into a credible biological way of explaining social, economic, political, and cultural change readily comprehensible to the educated public.

The recognition of inverse correlations between fertility and social and economic status long preceded the late Victorian decline in the birthrate. Malthus had been primarily concerned about the progenitive capacity of the poor, and even his critics conceded that poverty seemed to promote propagation. The smaller families of the rich were, however, widely believed to be a natural phenomenon that permitted the upper classes to be revitalized by the most talented of their more prolific social inferiors. Thus, the differential birthrate was not only a source of healthful replenishment but an important avenue of competitive social mobility.

Galton's Legacy

Francis Galton, the founder of eugenics, was far less sanguine about the consequences of differential fertility when, in the 1860s, inspired by his cousin Charles Darwin's recent revelations in *Origin of Species*, he turned his mathematical, classificatory mind to "the central topics of Heredity and the possible improvement of the Human Race."[2] Fertility was only one of the variables Galton sought to measure in his genealogical surveys of eminent men, first in an article in 1865 on "Hereditary Talent," and a few years later in the more comprehensive books *Hereditary Genius* (1869) and *English Men of Science* (1874).[3] Like many middle- and upper-class Victorians, Galton, who came from a wealthy Birmingham manufacturing and banking family, assumed that the characteristics and behavior of individuals, classes, and races were in large measure hereditarily determined. If the cautious Darwin gave wide berth to the subject of human inheritance, his contemporaries did not. Many were already certain of the existence of invariable, if incomprehensible, laws of racial inheritance. Galton, for whom *Origin of Species* marked a new epoch in "mental development" that demolished "a multitude of dogmatic barriers in a single stroke," undertook the daunting task of making these laws comprehensible.[4]

Basic to his subsequent inquiries was Galton's conviction "that a man's natural abilities are derived by inheritance, under exactly the same limitations as are the form and physical features of the whole organic world." Without understanding these limitations, or laws, men, on the basis of trial and error, regularly applied them to the breeding of desirable traits in animals. Galton contemplated the "galaxy of genius" within reach "if a twentieth part of the cost and pains were spent in measures for the improvement of the human race that is spent on the improvement of the breed of horses and cattle." One day it would be as practicable to produce a highly gifted race of men "as surely as we can propagate idiots by mating *cretins*."[5]

Underlying Galton's early explorations into human heredity were two personal concerns that a generation later gave eugenics a wider relevance than was yet possible in the palmy days of the 1860s and 1870s. The first was his conclusion that at some measurable point in the procreative history of eminent, talented families both the quantity and quality of offspring began to diminish. The second was his fear that the complexity of the modern world had outpaced the intellectual capacity and physical stamina of the race. Englishmen were, by his calculations, beginning to show themselves incapable of keeping pace with the continuous changes and trials of the age.

Galton's sensitivity to the declining fertility of accomplished families was probably accentuated by the sterility of his own marriage and those of his two brothers. By contrast they were members of a family of nine children; their father had been one of ten. Moreover, the family was not only financially successful but, more important to Galton, scientifically talented. Both his father and grandfather were respectable amateurs, while his mother, a daughter of the famous physician and naturalist, Erasmus Darwin, presumably reinforced the family's genetic propensity for outstanding accomplishment in the scientific field. The infertility of Galton's long marriage to Louisa Butler, the eldest daughter of the Reverend George Butler, former headmaster of Harrow and dean of Peterborough, was accentuated by the failure of any of her sisters in that previously large, academically distinguished family to have any children.[6]

Galton not only assumed fertility and infertility were hereditary traits, but strongly implied they were carried primarily by women. He derived his evidence from an examination of a number of extinct or near-extinct peerages as well as from the shrinking reproductive experience of statesmen's families. It suggested to Galton a close correlation between the marrying of heiresses and diminished fertility. Since heiresses themselves were usually the last representatives of families with weakened progenitive capacity, they were singularly unpromising stock for the perpetuation of distinguished lineage and talent. Yet the more successful a family, the more it was likely to attract wealthy heiresses. If younger sons failed to marry, or, as frequently happened, also married heiresses, "the side shoots of the genealogical tree are hacked off, and the leading shoot is blighted, and the breed is lost forever."[7]

Unlike some of his early readers, Galton was less concerned about aggregate class differentials in fertility than he was about marriage and reproduction within the ranks of the gifted, superior minority of outstanding men who populated the right end of the bell-shaped, normal distribution curve he constructed from his extensive genealogical surveys. They included hundreds of judges, statesmen, prime ministers, clergymen, military officers, scientists, university students, scholars, writers, poets, musicians, and even oarsmen and wrestlers of historical or contemporary prominence. What bound them together, in Galton's judgment, were natural abilities and "qualities of intellect and disposition" that stimulated them to overcome all obstacles and setbacks to "climb the path that leads to eminence" and "to perform acts that lead to reputation."[8] At best, these notables comprised no more than 250 men out of a million, or approximately 1 in 4,000. Otherwise, the population was comprised mostly of mediocrities whose varying levels of competency descended to the "true imbeciles and idiots" clustered at the extreme left of the distribution curve, and whose powers of reason and memory were even below those of dogs and other intelligent animals.[9]

In retrospect, Galton's criteria may seem ludicrously subjective and unscientific, but he was certain they proved that talent, ability, and, rarest of all, genius were hereditarily transmitted along a measurable scale. Regrettably, as the paucity of outstanding men in his own age suggested, "there is a regular average increase of ability in the generations that precede the culmination (of ability), and as regular a decrease in those that succeed it. In the first case the marriages have been consentient to its production, in the latter they have been incapable of preserving it."[10]

The key to eugenics, a term Galton coined in 1883 from the Greek word *eugenes*, meaning "good in birth" or "noble in heredity," was the modification of the haphazard customs of marriage and procreation currently practiced in English society.[11] It required the development of a "sentiment of caste among those who are naturally gifted" that would lead to a new and exclusive sense of class consciousness based not upon traditional social and economic values but upon the newly discovered laws of heredity. "If talented men were mated with talented women, of the same mental and physical characters as themselves, generation after generation," Galton pondered, "we might produce a highly-bred human race, with no more tendency to revert to meaner ancestral types than is shown by our long-established breeds of race-horses and fox-hounds." An increase in the average standard of the race by only one grade would, he calculated, raise the number of eminent men more than tenfold.[12]

Galton noted by contrast that prolonged checks on the fertility of the abler classes meant that as the less able continued to breed, the race could deterio-rate and become incapable of sustaining a higher civilization.[13] He did not, however, go as far as some of his early admirers, such as William Rathbone Greg, who complained of England already breeding disproportionately from "the poor, the incapable, the lazy, or the diseased," who were not allowed to die but were enabled, if not actually encouraged, "to propagate their incapac-ity, poverty, and constitutional disorders." Greg, a Darwinian cotton manufac-turer and, later, comptroller of the Stationary Office, was certain the "inge-nious" Galton, though concentrating upon the superior classes, had confirmed that "the tendency of advanced and complicated civilisations, to multiply from their lower rather than their higher specimens, constitutes one of the most formidable dangers which . . . if not counterworked in time, must bring about eventually the physical, and along with that the moral and intellectual deterio-ration of the race."[14] Darwin himself admiringly cited his cousin and Greg when, in *The Descent of Man*, he warned of the higher rate of increase among the "reckless, degraded, and often vicious members of society" who, com-pared to the "provident and generally virtuous," multiplied like rabbits.[15]

It was not, however, the procreative habits at the bottom end of society that inspired Galton's new science of eugenics, although they would preoccupy many of his twentieth-century disciples. What bothered him were the clear indications that modern civilization was evolving more rapidly than the race's

ability to comprehend the exigencies it confronted. "The needs of centralization, communication, and culture, call for more brains and mental stamina
than the average of our race possesses," he warned. "We are in crying want for
a greater fund of ability in all stations of life; for neither the classes of
statesmen, philosophers, artisans, nor labourers are up to the modern complexity of their several professions." Galton predicted that the "overweighted"
race was "likely to be drudged into degeneracy by demands that exceed its
powers," and compared to the past, "we are living in a sort of intellectual
anarchy, for the want of master minds."[16]

The consequences of an imbalance between environmental change and the
adaptive capacity of living organisms were evident in the determinant laws of
natural selection. As Darwin had demonstrated, if changes occurred slowly
enough, gradual adaptation, modification, and survival were possible. If,
however, the changes were rapid, only the fittest representatives of a species
would survive. Since to Galton the natural qualifications of "our race are no
greater than they used to be in semi-barbarous times," it was not surprising to
see "the foremost minds of the present day seem to stagger and halt under an
intellectual load too heavy for their powers."[17] Unless the number of men with
outstanding intellectual capacity, zeal, vigor, and determination was increased
and the overall level of ability raised before the pressures of modern civilization became overwhelming, the prognosis for Great Britain was very dim.

From its inception, then, eugenics was a manifestation of growing apprehension about the future and concern about change. It was also closely tied to
emerging post-Malthusian questions about the qualitative composition of the
population in an era in which new social, economic, and political relationships
were evolving under the pressures of industrialization, imperialism abroad,
and mass democracy at home. Certainly the Darwinian revolution was both
scientifically and symbolically an important part of the rapid transition to
modern civilization that fascinated and worried Galton and many of his late
Victorian contemporaries. The rapid translation of Darwinism from the contained, scientific world of the naturalist to that of the unharnessed social and
political theorist contributed greatly to the articulation of disquieting explanations of the present and alarming prophecies for the future. Galton was only
one of many for whom the question of natural selection and adaptation, with
its implications of fitness and unfitness, was a relevant, contemporary concern
with portentous possibilities.

The pessimistic prognostications often induced or confirmed by social Darwinism were in Galton substantially moderated by his certainty that most of
the intellectual, physical, psychological, and behavioral characteristics required to achieve the necessary salvation of the race were inheritable. Even if

the mechanism of their transmission was not well understood, the desirable qualities most closely associated with ability and success could be extracted from family histories and their frequency of occurrence in successive generations accurately plotted. These essential qualities consisted not only of intellectual power and robust health, but such traits as "tameness of disposition," "self-control," "labour-loving instincts," "great energy," "zeal," and "vitality," as well as a large appetite, good digestion, and, contrary to what many phrenologists believed, a smaller skull. Indeed, correlations between scientific achievement and cranium size revealed that "small-headed people" were endowed with remarkable energy.[18]

Despite his exaggerated tendency to see the determining hand of nature omnipresent in human behavior, Galton gave the word "heredity," which was not yet widely used, a special meaning by defining it as a physiological connection between generations that was open to research and quantification. In this sense he was trying to turn heredity into a concrete science, different from the imprecise "generalized tendency" or "force" implicit in the more commonly used expressions "inheritance," "hereditary," or "like begets like." It was an effort that led not only to eugenics, but less directly to the new science of genetics after 1900.[19]

The heritable qualities, instincts, and characteristics Galton extracted from his data would, he promised in 1883, if reinforced by selective marriages, "further the ends of evolution more rapidly and with less distress than if events were left to their own course."[20] One of his first discoveries was that, contrary to what his friend Herbert Spencer claimed in 1867 in *The Principles of Biology*, there was little conflict between intellectual advancement and physical reproduction, or "individuation and genesis" as Spencer described it.[21] Since most great men "are vigorous animals, with exuberant powers," Galton wrote, "there is no reason to suppose that, in breeding for the highest order of intellect, we should produce a sterile or a feeble race." Subsequent investigations only reconfirmed his initial supposition. Some forty years later, when many of his Edwardian contemporaries were uncertain, he reasserted, with slight modifications, "there is no reason to doubt that a very high order of intellect might be bred with little, if any, sacrifice of fertility or vigour."[22]

Galton's restless, nervous energy and growing confidence in his ability to comprehend the laws of heredity led him to spurn a passive acceptance of the irresistible power of natural and social forces in determining the quality of "future human stock." If nothing was done, he warned in 1883, and there was no attempt to interfere with natural selection, the British race would, like others before it, tend toward mediocrity and degeneration. According to Galton's law of hereditary regression, the descendants of exceptional individuals invariably reverted by measurable degrees toward the mediocre average as they were increasingly removed from the first degree of kinship. The law could, however, be amended and eugenic progress achieved by the continual infusion of new strains of talent. Whether, as more and more Britons wondered, those revitalizing strains were still available in sufficient quantity was, Galton acknowledged, questionable. Nevertheless, he warned, so long as the overall composition of the race remained as currently constituted, it was certain that no permanent improvement could take place. In time, the British people would become gradually weaker through inbreeding until, as we know from experience with plants and animals, reproductive fertility itself would be affected. The alternative, Galton proposed, consisted "in watching for the indications of superior strains of race and in so favouring them that their progeny shall outnumber and gradually replace that of the old one."[23]

Throughout history, Galton pointed out, man had interfered with natural selection by invasions, migrations, wars, massacres, deportations, and thoughtless social and religious customs. Races had, as a result, been altered in erratic and often harmful ways. Eugenics, by taking cognizance "of all influences that tend in however remote a degree to give the more suitable races or strains of blood a better chance of prevailing speedily over the less suitable" offered a systematic and scientific alternative for the formulation of new and progressive "racial policies." Conceding it would be difficult at present to achieve agreement on what constituted the most desirable eugenic qualities in a diverse population, Galton was nevertheless optimistic that after additional study a general consensus would eventually prevail.[24]

For his own part, Galton already had a fair idea about which desirable hereditary qualities would emerge from the multiplicative calculations, distribution curves, and anthropometric measurements extracted from the histories of past and present generations. In addition to intelligence, imagination, good looks, and a healthy physique, the eugenically fit were endowed with self-reliance, energy, determination, discipline, and patience. Their "nature, when left to itself, will, urged by an inherent stimulus, climb the path that leads to eminence" whatever the odds. Obstacles and setbacks were, for Galton, part of the "system of natural selection" that represses the mediocre, but proves the mettle of the truly able.[25]

There was little in this hereditarian exposition on the Victorian gospels of work and self-help that Samuel Smiles could not applaud. In a biological variation on the uplifting theme of that popularizer of nineteenth-century industrial, middle-class values, Galton promised "endowed" ability would eventually surface irrespective of social and economic advantage.[26] Equally important, the absence of the necessary inherited characteristics for success could not be compensated for by education or familial connections. Although Galton made general references to men of genius rising from the depths of social obscurity, he provided few specific examples. Instead he concentrated upon the offspring of the notable English families who populated the standard and specialized genealogies, encyclopedias, biographical dictionaries, and university alumni lists, or who, as in the case of prominent scientists, responded to his questionnaires.

Aware of the criticism he would receive for undervaluing the importance of social and economic position, Galton admitted that a beneficial environment could facilitate the development of talent, but could not create it. This explained why only a small proportion of men in the same family, sharing the same advantages, achieved distinction, and even then only for a finite number of generations. At the same time, however, the mathematical frequency with which ability emerged in the same families demonstrated the importance of heredity in establishing and maintaining their advantageous position and reputation in society. Bowing in the direction of the Victorian ideal of the self-made man, Galton added that if family, education, and patronage were insufficient to assure the success of the genetically mediocre, the absence of these advantages was ultimately no impediment to the genuinely well endowed. When "hindered or thwarted," their nature will rise to the challenge. It was almost "a contradiction in terms, to doubt that such men will generally become eminent."[27]

Galton's efforts to fend off expected criticism of his depreciation of environmental causation, or nurture, met with mixed success. Reviewers of *Hereditary Genius* for the most part acknowledged the importance of inheritance, or nature, without necessarily endorsing its author's quantitative generational distributions. But, as expected, they thought his dismissal of the importance of family, education, resources, and influence in the advancement of prominent careers flew in the face of reality. One of his sharpest critics, in the *Edinburgh Review*, insisted that for every person of low station who succeeded, a hundred no less able failed "for lack of circumstances." He found Galton's synonymical association of genius with popular reputation utterly simplistic and unconvincing. Everyday experience revealed the mediocrity of many eminent men, while people with much greater ability remained unnoticed.[28]

Such criticism was offset by the plaudits received from Alfred Russel Wallace, the codiscoverer of the theory of natural selection, and from Galton's illustrious, if hypochondriacal cousin Darwin who, after reading only fifty pages, had to "exhale . . . else something will go wrong in my inside. I do not think I ever in all my life read anything more interesting and original."[29] Emboldened by such praise, Galton, in *English Men of Science*, strengthened his initial findings that hereditary endowment was the most important variable in the cultivation of recognized ability. He defined nature as "all that a man brings with himself into the world" and nurture as "every influence from without that affects him after his birth" and found the latter to be at best a secondary consideration. Scientific accomplishment, for example, was frequently aided but not determined by nurture. It was the inheritance of natural energy, health, perseverance, business habits, independence of views, and a strong innate taste for inquiry that produced the successful men of science. Galton was not in the least surprised to find these characteristics distributed most heavily in the ranks of the middle and upper classes. Though "largely and continually recruited from below," he explained, they "are by far the most productive of natural ability." By contrast, the lowest classes were, in truth, "the residuum," lacking the necessary ancestral endowments to evolve from their inferior station.[30]

At the other end of the social scale the old aristocracy, weakened by primogeniture and protected from the laws of natural selection by wealth, privilege, and tradition, no longer had any claim to "natural gifts except so far as it may have been furbished up by a succession of wise inter-marriages." Galton became positively euphoric as he contemplated "the intellectual and moral grandeur of nature that might be introduced into aristocratical families," if their representatives took advantage of the rare privilege they had in winning wives to marry with "a view of transmitting those noble qualities to their descendants."[31] To Galton's way of thinking, that grandeur and even the survival of the old aristocracy enfeebled by its "morbific tendencies of body or mind" depended upon winning those brides from the new middle-class aristocracy of talent.

Galton's emphasis upon the primacy of nature over nurture and his belief that the richest genetic vein of talent and ability was to be found among the successful, educated middle classes, were fundamental to the early eugenics movement and remained an important if increasingly troublesome legacy throughout its history in the twentieth century. The qualities Galton and his followers admired most were to be found especially among the expanding ranks of the scientific, medical, legal, academic, political, military, and literary professions. The accomplishments of merchants, industrialists, bankers, and other entrepreneurs, however, found no place in the Galtonian hierarchy of family eminence. Without denying that the economic inventiveness, skill, energy, and courage of such people had played a vital role in Britain's rise to power, eugenicists from Galton on believed the preservation and extension of that power in a new era depended upon the intelligence, skill, imagination, and efficiency of educated, professional people very much like themselves. In this sense, eugenics from the beginning appealed to self-serving, professional middle-class interests who wanted a greater say in the building of a future in which they would play a role commensurate with their alleged abilities.

Far from being conservative or even reactionary, as later critics would charge, eugenics in its origins was in many ways radical and forward-looking. It was based upon the new, dynamic science of evolution and was defined by equally new mathematical techniques that became the foundations of modern statistics. Finally, it placed its faith and found its disciples in a new, so-called aristocracy of talent whose pretensions to replace the old were supported not by tradition, custom, or violent revolution but by coefficients of correlation, deviations, regression, frequency curves, and, with the rediscovery in 1900 of Gregor Mendel's remarkable experiments, by the selective arrangement of genes as well.

Whether there would be enough of the genetically elect to assume their critical role in raising the qualitative level of the race was on Galton's mind from the 1860s when he first began compiling his genealogical treasuries of family inheritance. As he himself acknowledged, few of his contemporaries found his arguments either compelling or, given their mathematical complexity, comprehensible. But anxieties about the declining birthrate in the opening decade of the twentieth century gave eugenics a new lease on life which was nurtured by the founding of Karl Pearson's biometric laboratory, the endowment of the Galton Laboratory for the Study of National Eugenics, and the establishment of the Eugenics Education Society in 1907.

Disciples and Evangelists

Pearson, along with his zoologist colleague at University College, Walter F. R. Weldon, was largely responsible for reviving Galton's eugenic work in the 1890s and for placing it on a much sounder mathematical and, they were sure, biological footing. The son of a taciturn, middle-class Quaker lawyer, Pearson, after study at Berlin, Heidelberg, and Lincoln's Inn, spurned his father's profession as well as his faith to pursue a career in mathematics, which he had studied as an undergraduate at Cambridge. As a young professor in the Department of Applied Mathematics at University College, London, he met and eventually formed a close friendship with Weldon, a brilliant biologist. Both men had been inspired by Galton's collection, *Natural Inheritance*, when it appeared in 1889 and, with the old man's encouragement, turned their talents to solving the "statistical problem" of evolution.[32] Pearson, in particular, felt like "an adventurous roamer . . . a buccaneer of Drake's days" as he boldly set forth to chart the statistical parameters delimiting the fractional distribution, or "particulate inheritance," of human conduct.[33] A "new kind of knowledge" was possible, Weldon enthused, that would go beyond Darwin and permit the measurement and classifications of populations within races or species, revealing not only average types but the degree and kind of deviation from that average.[34]

By the mid-1890s a biometric school, devoted to the statistical analysis of biological observations, had emerged under the tutelage of Pearson and Weldon with the support of Galton, who was nearly twice their age. It was a blending of the older Victorian tradition of the precocious, eclectic, self-supporting scientific amateur with the new institutionalized professionalism and specialization that increasingly characterized science in the late nineteenth and early twentieth centuries. After 1900 biometrics, supported by its own scholarly journal, *Biometrika*, rapidly become synonymous with Pearson's statistical laboratory at University College. Eugenics undoubtedly gained considerable authority and respectability in educated circles by its association with an important university and its promulgation by academicians and professional scientists.

Even the prolonged and bitter controversy over the physiology or mechanism of heredity that erupted between biometricians and Mendelian geneticists had the effect of alerting the learned scientific world to eugenic considerations. To the disciples of Gregor Mendel, the cardinal principle of heredity was the segregation of indivisible "unit characters" (genes) that either appeared completely or not at all. A person was either male or female, color blind or not—there was no intermediate blending of unit characteristics. Biometrics, with its actuarial approach to heredity, was based upon the assumption that traits were incremental variations from an intermediate norm which could be computed along frequency of distribution curves. Unlike the Mendelians, eugenicists did not ask questions to be answered by yes or no but by "to what extent?" and expressed the result numerically in a coefficient of correlation.[35]

Pearson's biometrical studies, under assault from prominent Mendelian geneticists such as William Bateson, who claimed that the understanding of heredity depended upon experimental breeding, not statistical inquiries, were put on a sounder financial footing in 1903 with the receipt of an annual grant from the Worshipful Company of Drapers.[36] More important, in the following year Galton himself, persuaded that the changing mood in the country would make the new century more receptive to eugenics than the old, endowed a Eugenics Record Office and fellowships to pursue the study of "National Eugenics," which he defined as "the study of agencies under social control that may improve or impair the racial qualities of future generations either physically or mentally." Two years later, in 1906, the office was merged with Pearson's biometric laboratory and renamed The Francis Galton Laboratory for the Study of National Eugenics. When its benefactor died in 1911, knighted and resplendent with scientific honors, he left an additional £45,000 from his considerable estate to endow a Galton Professorship of Eugenics. As his will suggested, the first recipient was his friend and disciple, Pearson.[37]

Galton went to his grave confident his new science was well established and on its way to becoming "an orthodox religious tenet of the future." His optimism was buoyed up by widespread concern in many sectors of society about the plummeting birthrate and the quality of the race. When, in 1904, the eighty-two-year-old Galton had been persuaded by Pearson to come out of retirement and address the recently established Sociological Society on "Eugenics: Its Definitions, Scope and Aims," he singled out as a principal goal the historical inquiry into the rates with which the various classes, based on their "civic usefulness," have contributed to the population. "There is strong reason for believing that national rise and decline is closely connected with this influence," he explained, "so the aim of eugenics is to bring as many influences as can be reasonably employed, to cause the useful classes in the community to contribute *more* than their proportion to the next generation."[38]

It was this interest in the problem of differential fertility and its effect upon the quality of the race that transformed eugenics from an abstruse, specialized area of scientific inquiry into a relevant, contemporary issue for Pearson and a great many of his less learned contemporaries. His warnings in the 1890s about the most fertile quarter of the population breeding more than half the next generation were manifestations of this interest and growing disquiet about recent population trends. Pearson pleaded with Galton in 1901 to use his prestige as a distinguished and honored scientist to help him bring home to thinking men "the urgency of the fertility question" before it was appropriated by cranks who understood little about heredity and relative fertility.[39]

The "fertility question" Pearson referred to was class specific. It involved the declining birthrate among the middle but not the lower ranks, which, he argued in 1900 in a consciously provocative lecture, "National Life from the Standpoint of Science," was approaching a very dangerous state of affairs. Like Galton, who he believed had first raised the issue, Pearson was also disturbed by the notable absence of highly intelligent, talented people in science, the arts, commerce, politics, and the professions, most of whom were once spawned by the able middle classes. The weaknesses of intellect and stamina exposed by the South African War were, to Pearson, obvious symptoms of the want of ability resulting from the more rapid multiplication of "the inferior stocks." Consequently, like the military, manufacturing, commerce, education, engineering, politics, law, and the colonial and civil service had all of late suffered from a lack of brains in the right places.

It would take much more than the creation of new universities, the introduction of competitive examinations, and the spread of technical schools, much touted by his fellow advocates of national efficiency in the 1890s, Pearson insisted, for Great Britain to compete with the Americans and the Germans, who seemed better able to bring their best brains to the top. Inferior people could not be trained to be superior, he warned; therefore, "Woe to the nation which has recruited itself from the weaker and not from the stronger stocks." Appealing to the middle classes and people in the skilled trades to marry earlier and breed more, Pearson added, "We cannot suspend the struggle for existence in any class of the community without stopping progress; we cannot recruit the nation from its inferior stocks without deteriorating our national character."[40]

Pearson's popular lecture went through several editions; it was frequently cited by proponents of national efficiency worried about Britain's dulled competitive edge in the world. Its author, however, was also interested in expanding the consideration of eugenics by established learned disciplines. Having failed repeatedly to persuade Galton's "thick-witted" colleagues, as Pearson described the members of the Anthropological Institute, to embrace eugenics formally, even after the old man came out of retirement to address them on the subject in 1901, the two men turned in 1904 to the Sociological Society.[41] There they received a much more sympathetic reception from its eclectic, open-minded membership still trying to define the parameters of a new discipline.

While many of these members were not convinced eugenics dealt with "the gravest problem which lies before the Caucasian races," most of them were willing to accept eugenics as an important sociological issue requiring serious consideration.[42] When Galton died in 1911, the society's young journal, the *Sociological Review*, observed with pride that the modern eugenics movement had been launched in 1904 with the presentation of Galton's paper, "Eugenics: Its Definition, Scope and Aims" to one of the new group's first sessions. It had excited considerable interest beyond the scientific community and led to the reception of eugenics by a much wider audience than ever before.[43] It also led directly to the founding of the Eugenics Education Society three years later.

Entering the Public Arena:
The Eugenics Education Society

For the aging Galton, eugenics was not just a new science but a new religion for the new century. It would be rooted not in the "paternalistic determinism" of established faiths but in the unselfish, noble, and sublime task of "the improvement of our stock," which he later described as "terrestrial . . . in its chosen theater, but celestial in its theme."[44] A clear if unstated positivist and utilitarian theme underlay much of Galton's thinking as he contemplated ways of rationalizing laws, customs, and institutions to advance his new "religion of humanity." The elite "Priests of Humanity" in his scheme of things were not the unselfish businessmen and enlightened administrators envisaged by Auguste Comte but genetically precocious scientists and other professional men whose accomplishments and eminence would assure them a guiding role in the formulation of policies designed to improve the hereditary quality of the race.

Galton had periodically considered the problems of spreading the eugenic gospels since 1873, when he first suggested the establishment of a society to study and promote human heredity.[45] His anthropometric laboratory, established in the 1880s to measure physiological attributes, had received some popular attention, but for the most part his eugenic revelations were shared primarily with anthropologists and biologists whose reception was at best cautious and mixed. For several years Galton contented himself with devising schemes to promote the keeping of family histories, the taking of premarital medical examinations, and the issuance of eugenically based marriage certificates. He envisioned utopian societies populated by carefully bred, highly intelligent, physically perfect specimens for whom eugenic reproduction was the highest ideal.

The surge of interest in the size and qualitative composition of the population at the turn of the century satisfied Galton that the time was right and enough was known about the laws of heredity to launch a major campaign of eugenic conversion among the educated and influential sectors of society. Differential fertility, he wrote in 1910, the year before his death, had become the "most important of all factors in Eugenics."[46] Pearson, who was repeatedly encouraged by his patriarchal mentor to make *Biometrika* a less technical, more popular journal to attract a wider audience, recognized but did not share Galton's eagerness for quick returns in the acceptance of eugenics. On the contrary, he was very suspicious of the glib, eye-catching studies and articles on the population question that filled the newspapers and magazines of the day. His own positivist instincts were reinforced by his flirtation with Fabian socialism in the 1880s and 1890s. Its advocacy of an elite of well-educated experts and civil servants guiding the state and overseeing its progress conformed with his own high opinion of the special talents and skills of middle-class professionals. Pearson was certain they would be needed more than ever to solve the difficult challenges the nation already faced at home and would face increasingly abroad. But like the early Fabians, he also shared the views of the positivist Frederic Harrison, that serious reformers must be willing to disregard demagogic rhetoric and short-term advantages for the long-term progress which could only come from social policies and legislation based upon careful, sound investigation. Eugenics, which only a small number of experts could pretend to understand, was a case in point. Unless it was built gradually on a solid foundation of biometric studies, he predicted, eugenics would never achieve the scientific credibility it required to become a powerful agency for social and racial improvement. Galton himself, Pearson complained, had not yet "fully differentiated [Eugenics] as a science from Eugenics as a creed of social action."[47]

Even though the warring Mendelians and biometricians agreed on the importance of obtaining through careful research an exact knowledge of the true principles of heredity, Galton was unconvinced of the need for a precise understanding of the mechanism before formulating a practical policy for racial improvement. Everyone conceded it was better to be healthy than sick, vigorous than weak, well fitted than ill fitted for a role in life, he reasoned. Only perverse cranks would deny that these characteristics, along with ability, manliness, and courtesy, were most likely to be found among the "best specimens" in the community.[48] All eugenics could do realistically, he wrote to Bateson, was try to raise "the fraternal mean" of the population by promoting an increase in the contribution of "the more valuable classes of the population and to diminish the converse."[49]

This was essentially the goal of the Eugenics Education Society when it was founded in 1907 to spread a knowledge of the laws of heredity, so far as they were known, "in order to modify public opinion and create a sense of responsibility in the respect of bringing all matters pertaining to human parenthood under the domination of Eugenic ideals . . . [to] affect the improvement of the race."[50] Many of its initial members were physicians, scientists, especially biologists, and academicians who participated in meetings of the Sociological Society and who were interested in the hereditarian implications of differential fertility. Not all of them were as sure as Galton and his more zealous advocates that a knowledge of human biology could or should provide the foundation of sociology or social policy. But as a founding member of the Eugenics Education Society, the biologist C. D. Darbishire, said at a Sociological Society meeting in 1906, "It is high time that some steps were taken to sweep away a state of affairs in which on the average a man's opportunity for reproduction varies inversely with his capacity for civilization."[51]

Although Galton had privately encouraged its creation, he at first declined to become honorary president of the Eugenics Education Society ostensibly because of his great age but more out of suspicion about some of the "fanatics" among the membership. He soon relented, however, when his friend and neighbor, the prominent barrister Montague Crackanthorpe, agreed to take the presidency, and William Ralph Inge, Lady Margaret Professor of Divinity at Cambridge and later dean of St. Paul's, joined.[52]

Despite Galton's assurances that the society "promises better than I could have hoped," Pearson refused several invitations to join, explaining his interests "lay more in accurate statistical work." In reality he thought the new organization was premature and feared for the acceptance of eugenics as a true science if a group of "high-strung, enthusiastic quacks" began advancing harebrained schemes unsupported by reliable evidence.[53] It was essential to convince the University of London and other academic and scientific institutions that eugenics was not a hobby but a quest for truth as valid as chemistry or physiology. To get mixed up with the likes of the sexologist Havelock Ellis, the temperance reformer Caleb Saleeby, or the playwright George Bernard Shaw, would alienate the scientific community and kill any chance of eugenics becoming a respectable academic discipline. While it might be justified to have propaganda societies to advocate such causes as teetotalism or votes for women, Pearson argued, our limited understanding of heredity precluded eugenics from entering the public arena for some time.[54] Although Pearson was himself not immune to extrapolative excess on occasion, Inge was not far wrong when he accused him of advocating that the Eugenics Education Society wait at least a half-century before making any recommendations.[55]

Pearson never wavered in his initial opposition and would permit no confusion of the work of his laboratory with that of the Eugenics Education Society. He clashed bitterly with members of the organization over whether tuberculosis and alcoholism were inherited defects, and whether biometry was more valid than Mendelian genetics as the scientific basis of eugenics. But ultimately the conflict was over who could best advance the eugenic cause. The split that developed while Galton was alive, and which he struggled to prevent, was irreparably widened after his death. As a result, the Galton Eugenics Laboratory and the Galton Professor remained, by choice, remote from the eugenics movement throughout much of its early history, despite their founder's hopes that the two would work in tandem to spread the new faith.[56]

Nevertheless, a substantial number of prominent academic scientists and social scientists, along with physicians, lawyers, clergymen, politicians, military officers, a smattering of aristocrats, and a variety of successful people from other walks of life, were quickly attracted to the new organization. While membership in the London society and in the ten branches established in the United Kingdom by 1914 was not large, hovering around 1,200, it was certainly prestigious. Most analysts of the society's membership lists agree that its natural constituency was the educated, scientifically oriented, professional middle classes, especially doctors and university people, who found in eugenics an ideology conforming to their social, economic, and political ambitions.[57] For some of them, like the president of the society from 1911 to 1928, Major Leonard Darwin, the second youngest and longest-surviving of Charles Darwin's five sons, eugenics gave life new meaning and purpose. After twenty years in the Royal Engineers, from which he retired at the age of forty, Darwin had entered public life, served as a member of Parliament for three years, and retired to the life of a country gentleman until, in his mid-fifties, he turned to eugenics. Perhaps burdened by the legacy of his eminent father, Leonard Darwin until that point had regarded his life "as more or less of a failure." Eugenics changed all of that, and when, at the age of sixty, he took over the new Eugenics Education Society, he at last felt he was doing work of great importance.[58]

Although professional men dominated the governing council of the society and the eugenics scene in London, their proportions were somewhat reduced in the overall ranks, where women, 40 percent of them unmarried, constituted half the membership before the war. The concentration upon London and the council in membership analyses has perhaps obscured the existence of a wider base of support, particularly in provincial towns such as Liverpool, Manchester, and Birmingham, where people in industry and commerce constituted a more important component of the bourgeois elite and were somewhat more prevalent in the eugenic ranks. In addition, several of the professional men who served on the Eugenics Education Society council before and after the war, including Darwin himself, also had substantial business interests, mainly as directors and trustees in banking, insurance, mining, and the railroads.

If Galton, Pearson, and a number of their followers did not necessarily hold the germ plasm of businessmen in high esteem and neglected to include them in the superior middle-class stock they wished to see reproduced in larger numbers, questions of economic efficiency, productivity, competition, and differential fertility absorbed affluent capitalists as well as eugenicist professors in the early twentieth century. Both were also concerned with managing the health, morals, social conditions, behavior, and even the very existence of the poor. Given these overlapping interests, it is not surprising that the eugenic approach would appeal to a broader spectrum of the middle class than just the professions. A recent study of the social hygiene campaign in Britain, while oversimplifying and exaggerating the procapitalist and antisocialist aspects of eugenics, particularly between the wars, is nevertheless not too far from the mark in its recognition that the eugenics movement was not as exclusive a stratum and group as depicted by scholarly analysts, but was rather "a social mix bound together by a set of ideologies about social health."[59]

Despite the presence of a minority of wealthy businessmen in the Eugenics Education Society, some of whom left it substantial legacies, for the most part people in the professions, particularly science and medicine, nonetheless guided and dominated the organization throughout its history. Moreover, if the membership was occupationally more diverse than has been recognized, it was still socially very homogeneous. No more than a fraction came from humble or very modest circumstances—before the war less than 3 percent, though this negligible number included a titled barrister and a bishop. They were curious exceptions to the self-serving eugenic rule, demonstrated by the composition of the Eugenics Education Society itself, that ability ran in families. The membership also cut selectively across political lines. Several of the society's more notable political figures, such as Arthur J. Balfour, Neville Chamberlain, and William Joyson Hicks, were Conservatives, but the organization drew members from the Liberal party as well, including John Fletcher Moulton, the Lord Justice of Appeal, and the economist John Maynard Keynes.[60]

By Galton's standards, the Eugenics Education Society represented a true "Treasury of Human Inheritance." Many of its members, including as they did eminent judges, scientists, doctors, churchmen, statesmen, headmasters, and university chancellors, were putative repositories of the favorable genetic traits he had plotted years earlier in his genealogical probings of hereditary talent and genius. But, like so many of their kind, they were not passing on their superior, heritable qualities to a sufficient number of progeny. One study made shortly after the war revealed that dedicated though they were to self-replication, officers of the Eugenics Education Society contributed on average no more than 2.3 children. Indeed, a quarter of the leadership had no offspring at all. A similar review of the fertility experience of the distinguished people who comprised the National Birth-Rate Commission and who, in their reports, singled out the racial dangers inherent in the small family, turned up an average of only 1.75 children. Sixteen of the forty-one commissioners had not yet deposited a farthing in the bank of racial health.[61]

The officers in the Eugenics Education Society and the Birth-Rate Commissioners were a microcosmic example of the dwindling fertility among the professional middle classes, documented so clearly in the 1911 *Fertility of Marriage Census*. Its author, T. H. C. Stevenson, was so struck by the phenomenon that in constructing his eight classes he set up a special sub-category, Ia, for the professions and compared their small families of 1.5 to 1.8 children with the 3.7 to 4.0 recorded for the more numerous unskilled manual workers at the other end of the scale. Depending upon duration of marriage, the fertility of the professional classes ranged as much as 25 to 30 percent below the national average for all classes.[62] These were exactly the sort of comparisons fledgling eugenicists, armed with Pearson's projections about the differential characteristics of the next generation, had been making with less precise data since the late 1890s. For many of them, like the Cambridge University physicist W. C. D. Whetham and his wife, Catherine, it was a compelling reason for the establishment of the Eugenics Education Society. They were charter members and were instrumental in organizing a Cambridge branch of the new group.

One of the Whethams' principal goals was to persuade politicians, economists, and other manipulators of public opinion who were worried about the nation's problems, to fret less about the erection of tariff walls and more about "the innate composition of the people, and the relative rate of reproduction in all ranks of life of the able classes." Since the "essential factor in the rise and fall of nations is the quality of their people," the key question for the age was "how quickly have the different strains which make up our people been reproducing themselves relatively to each other? What is the average character of the generation on whom the work of the country now rests? What of the future generations now in childhood or yet unborn?"[63]

The Whethams' own Galton-like examination of a sample of the most valuable classes, who were located in *Who's Who*, *Burke's Peerage*, and, of course, on the Cambridge faculty, illustrated the striking decline in the "racial contribution" of the aristocracy, the military, and the other professions during the past generation. In contrast to their own 6 children, for example, 70 of their married colleagues and acquaintances at the university produced on average no more than 2.8. Another 40 were childless, and when the celibates were added in, the adults on the faculty outnumbered children by a ratio of 3 to 2.[64] Despite their concentration upon the aristocracy and the professional middle classes, Whetham elsewhere insisted that class was not at issue since the selective birthrate "affects the most thrifty and far-seeing parts of each social class." That the "thoughtless and reckless" tended to be disproportionately distributed among the laboring poor was regrettable but a reality eugenicists felt had to be confronted. The alternative to promoting "conscious selection" on proven hereditary principles, Whetham warned, "will destroy a race more effectively and completely than fire and sword." Where, he asked in a question often posed by his Edwardian contemporaries, "is now the power that was Rome, or the glory that was Greece?"[65]

The Eugenics Education Society was in many ways the organized articulation of neo-Darwinian, educated, middle-class anxieties about the future. The prominent and not-so-prominent people who joined the new group saw themselves as the vanguard of a propagandist movement that could bridge the gap between the new science of heredity and popular assumptions and beliefs about what made individuals, and, more important, classes different from each other. It was as if in trying to define their own unsettled place in a fluid, intensely class-conscious society, the early eugenicists found it necessary to delineate as precisely as possible those qualities and characteristics that made them different from others and justified their pretensions to authority and leadership in the near future.

The formulation of hereditarian explanations in terms of class characterized what became a eugenic turn of mind, or mentality, in twentieth-century Britain. Like the Fabian mentality that always extended far beyond the small membership of the Fabian Society, the eugenic mentality transcended the limited ranks of the Eugenics Education Society. It was a variation on a biological way of thinking already endemic to a society long absorbed with lineage and breeding in man and animal. When Galton, to the embarrassment of his more sophisticated successors, made numerous allusions to the breeding of superior strains of cattle, horses, and dogs, he was speaking to an age that understood the references very clearly. Although the middle-class, urbanite professionals who in the next century shared Galton's interest in the quality of the race were less comfortable with stockyard and kennel metaphors, they were, in the final analysis, no less concerned about breeding from the right stock and, increasingly, avoiding overbreeding from the wrong stock. It was this, in the context of the declining, differential birthrate, that proved to be the vital stimulus to the establishment of an organized eugenics movement and, more significant, to the creation of a eugenic mentality.

Three

Deterioration and Decline

E dwardian anxieties about the declining birthrate were exacerbated by more generalized fears that the race was somehow physically and mentally deteriorating. Since the middle of the nineteenth century, numerous advocates of sanitary improvements and public health reforms had warned that England was "on the verge of a great calamity" unless steps were taken to reverse the physical deterioration of the lower classes. Descriptions of the appalling squalor and desperate poverty endured by millions of people in the industrial towns of the country were reinforced during the 1850s by reports of the high rejection rates of military recruits during the Crimean War. The patriotic bravado of a speaker at the Social Science Association in 1859 was tempered by his warning that although "the British soldier has never crossed bayonets with his equal," conditions in the large towns were already "enfeebling the nation" and threatening the sources of future recruitment. Others used the term "degeneration" interchangeably with deterioration and cautioned, "If degeneration should extend and large numbers of the English race be divested of its noblest characteristics, their reclamation would be an arduous if not impractical undertaking."[1]

While these observers, many of them physicians, described in grim detail the consequences of the physical and mental deterioration on successive generations of the urban poor, they were not really discussing hereditary degeneration. Cause and cure were primarily environmental, although like most Victorians educated in the Lamarckian tradition, they believed to varying degrees in the heritability of acquired characteristics. Their synonymous, often alternating use of such words as "deterioration," "degeneration," "decadence," and "decline" suggests the vagueness and confusion surrounding the interrelationship of environment and heredity. In 1857 the French physician Benedict-Augustin Morel attempted to clarify the terminology by defining degeneration as a hereditarily transmissible "morbid variation from an original type" that caused the tainted individual and his decadent posterity to become less and less capable of "intellectual and moral progress" as well as reproduction.[2] It was a definition which in no way challenged the assumption that environment could affect heredity, and reinforced growing concerns about the enervating results of congested city life on the health, morals, intellect, and procreative vigor of urban inhabitants.

Urbanization and the Race

The late Victorians and their Edwardian successors assumed few London families survived beyond the third generation. Consequently, the availability of a healthy, efficient working class required a steady influx of sound, energetic, physically strong recruits from the salubrious countryside.[3] When, from the 1870s on, that measured flow of racially reinvigorating migrants became a flood of immigrants fleeing agricultural depression, serious questions arose about future sources of revitalization.[4] Once the great towns took their debilitating toll on the new inhabitants, would there be sufficient healthy stock remaining to replenish their degenerating numbers? This was certainly one of the considerations that lay behind efforts in the 1880s and 1890s to stem the flow to the cities by reinvigorating the rural economy through industrial diversification, the preservation of skilled trades, and agricultural allotments.[5]

Noting in 1888 that the proportion of town dwellers to the rural population had increased by nearly half in the past forty years, the dean of Canterbury, F. W. Farrar, was reminded that the "great cities are the graves . . . of our race." In London, the most voracious consumer of racial vitality, the ratio was even greater and the consequences more magnified.[6] As another witness to the effects of urban life explained, "The child of the townsman is bred too fine, it is too great an exaggeration of himself, excitable and painfully precocious in its childhood, neurotic, dyspeptic, pale and undersized in its adult state, if it ever reaches it." There was no end to similar descriptions of the puny, effete, incapable "town type" whose only hope for avoiding extinction was a periodic replenishment of "fresh blood." Even then, however, the probability of his family surviving to a fourth generation was remote.[7]

As Gareth Stedman Jones has demonstrated, the widespread concern about urban degeneration that emerged in the last quarter of the century was closely associated with the revival of the Condition of England question. In an effort to explain the extent and persistence of chronic poverty in the midst of so much plenty, the late Victorians found biological and ecological answers in Darwinism and in urbanization. The squalor, vice, disease, irreligion, and idleness emblematic of the casual poor, or the "residuum," were increasingly seen as symptoms of poverty rather than causes. Their savage, sensual, and brutalized

condition, described in one study or report after another, was attributed less to
improvidence or misfortune than to a prolonged exposure to the demoralizing
and degenerating conditions of city life.[8]

The theory of urban degeneration and the racial dangers of rural depopulation rapidly came to color all social debate on the condition of the poor; it was
given authoritative backing by Charles Booth, Alfred Marshall, the statistician
G. B. Longstaff, Llewellyn Smith, and various official commissions and
committees of inquiry. More often than not, their conclusions reflected anxiety
and fear rather than sympathy or compassion.[9] Farrar was certain that "he who
bends down his ear low enough to listen may hear a murmuring of the ground-
swell in the lower deeps of humanity which at no distant date may burst into a
terrific storm."[10] The imagined threat for people in the 1890s and opening
years of the new century was, however, not from violent revolution but from
the continual deterioration and eventual degeneration of the imperial race.

The potent infusion of social Darwinism in the 1880s raised to cosmic
proportions the question of the relative contribution of town and country to the
vigor of the race. Darwin's guidance on the issue was at best indirect and
ambivalent. He had observed that when removed from their natural environment, animals and plants were often less fertile or entirely barren and eventually died out. At the same time, however, slight changes and crossbreeding
were often beneficial to a species.[11] His cousin Galton, as usual, tried to
quantify the phenomenon. A comparative analysis of rural Warwickshire
with industrial Coventry revealed that the rate of the town's contribution to the
next adult generation was already only three-quarters that of the country,
where infant and maternal mortality were lower and families were larger and
healthier. Without migration from the rural areas, Galton wrote in 1873, "this
decay, if it continued constant, would lead to the result that the representatives
of the townsmen would be less than half as numerous as those of the country
folk after one century, and only about one fifth as numerous after two centuries." But those "energetic members of our race, whose breed is most valuable
to our nation," who moved to the towns were threatened with deterioration as
well. Nearly thirty years later, when the question of race deterioration had
become tied up with the Boer War and the declining birthrate, Galton continued to warn that "those who come up to the towns may produce large families,
but there is much reason to believe that these dwindle away in subsequent
generations. In short, the towns sterilize rural vigour."[12]

Degenerative sterilization, the ultimate effect of deterioration, conjured up
images of depleted energy, vitality, and ability. Fears of urban degeneration in
the late nineteenth and early twentieth centuries were part of a more extensive
mental landscape within which broad sectors of the middle and upper classes

expressed in simplistic biological terms their concerns about the structure, stability, and endurance of British society and civilization. Translations in the 1890s of Max Nordau's sweeping, intemperate critique of fin de siècle art, literature, and popular culture as clear signs of germinal degeneration added another dimension to the pessimistic assessments of the period.[13] Social Darwinism was particularly important in providing an explanation and a vocabulary for the articulation of disquieting trends that really had much more to do with social psychology than with biology.

The Boer War and Race Deterioration

The country's inauspicious performance in the Boer War only confirmed what had been claimed for a generation. When in 1899 the journalist Arnold White, a strident Liberal imperialist and early eugenicist, questioned whether the British still possessed the "racial efficiency" to back up their jingoistic boast to teach the Boers a lesson, he paid particular attention to the 40 percent rejection rate reported for military recruits in the industrial towns. Two years later, his ratio had risen to three out of five and was supported by a variety of other alarmist estimates about the dwindling size of the pool of fit men in the populous towns.[14] Earl Grey, citing White's figures, wrote to the *Times* of his doubts about the survivability of this new, slum-reared race and called for an anthropometric study of school children to determine the true state of those "human reservoirs" needed to defend and replenish the empire.[15] Even anti-imperialists such as C. F. G. Masterman complained about the absence of balance and stamina in the stunted, small-chested, weakened "New Town Type" who, though voluble and excitable, lacked the strength and endurance of his Anglo-Saxon predecessors.[16]

All of this pointed to the provocative question, "Where to Get Men?" asked anonymously in 1901 by Maj. Gen. Sir John Frederick Maurice and then, a year later, under his own name. Maurice estimated that when the number of recruits found to be unfit within two years of enlistment was added to the initial rejections, the failure rate was indeed closer to 60 than to 40 percent.[17] Maurice's articles were prominent examples of what was fast becoming a genre of pessimistic commentary in Edwardian Britain. The depressing recruitment figures were often corroborated by other statistics demonstrating the diminishing size, weight, and health of the shrinking, narrow-chested misfits entering the ranks. When compared to the healthier, more efficient Germans, not to mention lesser breeds such as the Boers, Belgians, and Japanese, it seemed obvious that the race was not what it had once been.

Conscious of the debate stirred up by Maurice's writings, the Army Medical Services issued a memorandum in 1903 essentially confirming his assertions and supporting growing demands for a national inquiry, perhaps even a royal commission, to determine the extent of deterioration and offer corrective recommendations.[18] Politicians, physicians, and public health officials who claimed that the evidence was at best mixed and unreliable, nevertheless acknowledged that they were at odds with an expanding sector of public opinion. Contradictory positions taken by military leaders and, more important, doctors, contributed to the confusion. Both groups had often been on the defensive in previous decades when the question first arose. Citing declining mortality figures, higher recruitment standards, and the variable effects of the economy on the quality of available enlistees, they insisted that "the evil of decadence is more visionary than real" and that the "raw material of our recruits is as good as it ever was."[19] Such claims were met with a good deal of skepticism, leading the exasperated president of the Royal Statistical Society, T. Graham Balfour, to complain in 1889 that everyone these days felt competent to comment on the "supposed deterioration of the physique of our population." He was the first to admit, however, that in the absence of sound, comparative anthropometric data, it was difficult to make a conclusive judgment.[20]

The same problem remained more than a decade later when the Boer War reinvigorated the dispute. On balance, medical authorities were inclined to believe the high military rejection rates were a product of more stringent medical expectations being applied to a pool of applicants whose physical and mental attributes were traditionally below average. Even then, a report of the Royal College of Surgeons insisted in 1903, the problem was not one of irreversible decadence, but of environmentally caused deterioration correctable by better diet, cleaner air, less crowding, more exercise, and improved medical care. In concluding a royal commission was unnecessary, the report acknowledged that physical deterioration, which was remediable, was increasingly being confused in the public's mind with hereditary degeneration, which was not.[21]

Eugenicist physicians such as Alfred Mumford and G. Archdall Reid were particularly distressed by the sloppiness of thought and language adopted by many of their learned colleagues who, in their opinion, remained wedded to outmoded Lamarckian ideas of heredity. They did so in the face of increasingly compelling evidence supporting the newer theories of August Weismann, Gregor Mendel, Galton, and Pearson that seemed to disprove the heritability of acquired characteristics and to demonstrate the impermeability of the germ plasm to external influences. Indeed, Reid cautioned, since the issue of nature versus nurture has become "the burning question among students of heredity," it would be prudent for everyone to be exceedingly wary of presuming that the effects of prolonged exposure to life in the great cities had become hereditarily transmissible. [22]

People were so busy erecting a theory of the degradation of human nature "only . . . equalled in the teachings of the revivalistic religion," Mumford added, that they took to comparing biologically an unrealistic present with an idealized past. Without denying the physical toll urbanization had taken on a great many town inhabitants, it was, he insisted, imperative to delineate carefully among "deterioration," "degeneration," and "decadence." All described precise stages of "defective energy" marking a deviation from the norm, but deterioration, which was caused by an unhealthy environment, was clearly alterable. Degeneration was by contrast a direct consequence of uncorrectable inborn defects and would eventually lead to decadence, the last stage before extinction. The critical question for the nation, Mumford reasoned, was whether a substantial portion of the race was, as many people seemed convinced, in the second stage. He personally doubted it, but was reconciled to years of controversy and irresolution until the unfolding laws of heredity were fully understood and sufficient anthropometric data accumulated. [23]

The Inter-Departmental Committee on Physical Deterioration

The appointment in 1902 of a royal commission on physical training to examine the health of Scottish schoolchildren was the limited response of the Unionist government to mounting demands for an inquiry into the charges of race deterioration. Testimony before the commission represented a cross section of the diverse opinions on the subject. Most witnesses agreed that the weak frames, poor eyesight, stunted growth, rotten teeth, and low staying power afflicting the offspring of the urban poor constituted deterioration that was still reversible, but warned that unless the environment was improved, degeneration would soon follow. James Cantlie, a surgeon and lecturer in anatomy at Charing Cross Hospital, whose studies of degeneration amongst Londoners had been criticized in the 1880s, now noted with satisfaction that his findings were taken much more seriously. When pressed by the commissioners, many of the witnesses admitted that they were generalizing from limited experience, or were merely expressing a personal opinion. Moreover, they tended to confuse physical deterioration with hereditary degeneration and used the terms interchangeably. Several authorities who were more precise in their language nevertheless suspected that hereditary factors were more prominent in determining the deplorable conditions in the towns than was previously recognized.[24]

The commission's recommendations for the medical inspection and feeding of schoolchildren and the establishment of more provisions for physical exercise seemed inadequate, even ludicrous, to some of its critics. Deterioration, they complained, was far too extensive to be reversed by a few palliative measures in the schools.[25] Although the commission's deliberations were obscured by the excitement stirred up by passage of the much more comprehensive education act of 1902, the earl of Meath, who had given testimony, was determined in July 1903 to press the government for a broader inquiry. He wanted to know if the conditions revealed in Scotland also prevailed in England and, as many feared, constituted a "grave national peril." As chairman of the Lad's Drill Association and the London County Council Parks Committee, Meath was certain that British youth with their "weakened blood" were not up to the physical standard of their less urbanized German counterparts. In supporting Meath in the House of Lords, the bishop of Ripon, William Boyd Carpenter, agreed that with the rural "reservoirs of our national strength" drawn down while the towns continued "to burn up the population in numbers and vigour," an extensive investigation had become a question of self-preservation.[26]

The Inter-Departmental Committee on Physical Deterioration, established within the Home Office and Local Government Board a few months later, was the government's reluctant compromise with public and parliamentary demands for a royal commission.[27] "Deterioration" was carefully chosen to avoid any presumption of hereditary "degeneration"—a misunderstood word, the committee recognized, which had become even more confusing to the public since its popularization a few years earlier by the Paris-based journalist, writer, and physician, Max Nordau. Medical authorities, in pledging their cooperation, were particularly careful to deny that the appointment of the committee was in itself a confirmation that national vitality was on the wane. The *Lancet* feared that given the paucity of reliable data and the plethora of strong opinion, the proceedings would only add to the muddle and misconception surrounding the emotional subject.[28] Some of the testimony certainly justified its apprehension.

Much of the evidence presented focused upon military recruitment and conditions in the great towns. Efforts were made to correct exaggerated claims of rejection and failure rates and to put them in historical perspective. What was required, the director-general of Army Medical Services argued, was not a royal commission to listen to more unsubstantiated conjecture about the faltering of the race but a system for collecting and analyzing uniform data.[29]

Nearly everyone, however, agreed that the evidence of deplorable ill health and physical incapacity was indisputable but thought it was inadequate for resolving the conflicting diagnoses and prognoses offered to the public. Nevertheless, a minority of witnesses ranging from physicians to factory inspectors were convinced that city life had altered the course of evolution and created a smaller, weaker, laboring class whose declining physical and mental characteristics were part of a hereditary continuum. Some authorities took comfort in the thought that these degenerates would eventually die off in accordance with the laws of natural selection, but others were fearful that the proliferation of the unfit was already being facilitated by the more humane values and supportive institutions of modern civilization.[30]

The Inter-Departmental Committee's report of July 1904 expressed strong doubt that "the influence of heredity in the form of any direct taint . . . is a considerable factor in the production of degenerates." Most children, it concluded, were born healthy; whatever deterioration followed was the result of ignorance, neglect, malnutrition, poor housing, fetid air, polluted water, minimal hygiene, excessive drinking, and inadequate medical care. Moreover, the committee found, contrary to popular opinion, these conditions were by no means unique to the towns whose inhabitants, including many slum dwellers, were at least as healthy as the laboring poor in country districts. If the results did not add up to degeneration, they nevertheless posed a "grave menace to the community" requiring unprecedented state and voluntary intervention to preserve and improve the health of the young.[31]

Despite its limited mandate, the Inter-Departmental Committee's labors and recommendations were on a scale usually reserved for prominent royal commissions. They were not particularly welcomed by a Unionist government reluctant to commit resources to expensive, collectivist social programs already advocated by their Liberal opponents. But the strong endorsement the report received from the Royal College of Physicians and the British Medical Association undoubtedly emboldened the docile civil servants responsible for the investigation.[32]

Although the Balfour administration was openly hesitant about implementing the committee's recommendations, its Liberal successor quickly passed legislation in 1906 and 1907 providing for the feeding and medical inspection of schoolchildren. It proved to be the start of a pattern of social legislation that quickly overwhelmed the last barriers of nineteenth-century laissez-faire individualism, led to the National Insurance Act of 1911, and, eventually, to the welfare state.[33] More immediately, by reaffirming the claim that however deplorable conditions were for people the consequences had not yet become genetically fixed, the committee's much-publicized report also gave a strong boost to the efforts of the emerging Mothercraft movement in the early twentieth century to reduce infant mortality and improve maternal and child care.

Despite the committee's careful definition of the term deterioration and its rejection of hereditary determinants, within a week of its publication one of its most enthusiastic supporters, Sir John Gorst, referred to the "recent report upon the degeneracy of our race."[34] Like many of his contemporaries, Gorst, the M.P. for Cambridge University and a former member of Balfour's ministry, continued to confuse deterioration with degeneration. Galton, with whom he corresponded, found Gorst "keen and earnest" about the "degeneracy" of schoolchildren but largely ignorant of the mechanisms of heredity.[35] But the Inter-Departmental Committee's report itself was for Galton, Pearson, and other apostles of the new eugenics movement well meaning but fundamentally wrongheaded in its exaggerated confidence in environmental improvement. While eugenicists acknowledged the committee's deliberations and conclusions had done a great deal to alert Parliament and the country to the dangers of deterioration and degeneration, its failure to recognize that the problem was natural, or hereditary, rather than nurtural, or environmental, was regrettable. If anything, it was more important than ever that the public and the politicians understand the regeneration of the race was primarily a qualitative question of differential fertility rather than of ameliorative social programs, which would do little to stem Britain's decline.

Official efforts in the aftermath of the Boer War to measure the extent of race deterioration and degeneration reveal much more about the range of middle- and upper-class concerns in the opening years of the twentieth century than they do about physical and biological realities. The evidence collected seems to have had little effect on established preconceptions about whether or not the race was on a downward slope. While there was rarely disagreement about the accuracy of recruitment figures or of health statistics, there was considerable controversy over what they meant.[36] Medical authorities and public health officials, who questioned the extent of deterioration in the first place, were particularly sensitive to the implication that their efforts were inadequate or futile. But some of their own colleagues certainly supported such conclusions and often revealed how little they thought of their feckless charges when they complained of the Sisyphean task of trying to overcome the effects of accumulated germinal deficiencies. Many of them quickly gravitated toward eugenics where, along with others in different professions, they found hereditary explanations that more often than not conformed to what they already knew.[37]

Even those Edwardian critics who doubted that eugenics was anything more than a pseudoscientific rationalization for middle- and upper-class elitism nevertheless recognized it was also an increasingly important feature of the pessimism infecting their generation. So deep was the despair in some circles, the *Edinburgh Review* complained in 1911, that the press and public refused to be dissuaded by any evidence disproving the decline of the race. Our descendants, it predicted, will surely find it a marvel that in this age of great mechanical, scientific, medical, and philosophical progress, we were so obsessed with "the inveterate superstition of degeneration."[38]

Fertility and Biology

In explaining the debacle in South Africa that eventually led to the Inter-Departmental Committee, Karl Pearson insisted that the answer lay not with the living and working conditions of the urban poor but with the diminishing numbers of capable and talented people. The revivification of national life was dependent upon changes in the relative contribution of different classes to the reproduction of the race, which was being recruited increasingly from inferior stocks.[39] Both Meath and Boyd Carpenter took cognizance of the plummeting birthrate as a possible contributor to race deterioration when they moved the appointment of an investigatory body, and the Inter-Departmental Committee briefly acknowledged Pearson's demographic projections and call for the ablest classes to breed more. Witnesses gave conflicting views, however, about the causes and implications of declining fertility, and the committee contented itself with suggesting a need for further study.[40] The bishop of Ripon, who carefully followed the loudening debate about the birthrate, was one of many critics who regretted that the committee did not pursue the ominous implications of the differential increase in "the illiterate and ignorant classes" over the "cultured, or . . . intelligent classes."[41] In subsequent years, he joined with other prominent religious and lay figures, including several on the National Council of Public Morals, in urging a comprehensive inquiry into the population issue.

The question of the declining birthrate was a late intrusion into the prolonged debate over the deterioration or degeneration of the race, but in the heightened context of argument during and after the Boer War its importance was significantly magnified. Even before the Inter-Departmental Committee published its findings in 1904, demographic statistics were replacing military recruitment figures as the major source of quantifiable worry. Despite the efforts of Arthur Newsholme, T. H. C. Stevenson, Sidney Webb, and the biometricians in the Eugenics Laboratory to disprove the popular assumption that the declining birthrate was primarily an urban phenomenon, the belief in town-induced infertility died hard before the First World War. Galton, as Pearson knew when he wrote to the _Times_ in 1905, had contributed his considerable scientific weight to that unproven contention. But Pearson's own preliminary enquiries into the correlation between urbanization and reproductive degeneration caused him to doubt the old maxim that town life exterminated families after three generations or that very much was really known about the effects of an urban environment on the race.[42] Nevertheless, it was exceedingly difficult to dissuade those who believed that the declining birthrate was a consequence of some recent alteration in biological capacity.

The selective incorporation of social Darwinist ideas provided an evolutionary explanation for the fall to which the eugenically minded were especially vulnerable. All of the signs for the neurologist Dr. A. F. Tredgold pointed to "retrogressive variation" and the loss of the "inherent vitality" required for healthy, efficient reproduction.[43] As Sir James Crichton-Browne, a founder of the Eugenics Education Society, told the members of the Sanitary Inspectors Association in his 1906 presidential address, the falling birthrate meant the country was faced with race failure or race suicide starting at the wrong end of the social scale. In either case it was clear that England's "racial resistance" to degeneration was rapidly weakening.[44]

Not everyone who believed the falling birthrate was linked to a recent decline in biological capacity saw it as a manifestation of racial decadence. On the contrary, a number of analysts argued that the decline, after more than a century of "advanced germinal activity," was perfectly natural. It was part of a recurring cyclical pattern of diminished fecundity caused by everything from changing diet to the race's need for periods of "germinal tranquility." Others argued fertility was inversely correlated to the struggle for existence, which was why the poorer, less-nourished classes were so much more prolific than their well-fed betters. Consequently, the birthrate of a country could be considered a "natural and impartial test of the social condition and progress of its people." By this criterion, of course, the drop in fertility was to be welcomed, not feared.[45]

Eugenicists, however, were not really concerned about the overall decline in the birthrate but with its differential characteristics. The cause of race suicide was for them qualitative not quantitative. Logically, the sterilizing effects of urban life should have been reducing the swollen numbers of the degenerating residuum who, as Pearson and others calculated, contributed their tainted progeny disproportionately to the composition of the race. But in fact the statistics pointed overwhelmingly to an inverse correlation between socioeconomic status and family size. They raised serious questions about whether degeneration was really the final stage of environmentally induced physical and mental deterioration or a consequence of some other factor lessening the reproductive powers of the middle and upper classes. References to the failure of procreative energy as an explanation for the decline and fall of ancient civilizations and empires had been commonplace in educated circles since the eighteenth century. They were supplemented by the equally familiar if not always reassuring knowledge that it was natural for families among the higher classes to die out and for those below them to increase and take their place.

Galton believed this to be true in his early studies of ancestral inheritance but by 1904 thought it very probable that "types of our race" could be found who were highly civilized without losing their fertility.[46] He was in part responding to a revival of interest in his old friend Herbert Spencer's contention that as evolving organisms became more complex and differentiated, their reproductive energies diminished. The process as Spencer described it in 1867 was not cyclical but progressive; it was characteristic of an evolutionary continuum of "individuation and genesis" in which the absorption of energy to sustain heterogeneity and cerebral advancement came at the expense of more primitive procreative capacity.[47] This biological variation on the law of the conservation of energy meant that "each increment of evolution entails a decrement of reproduction" so that the progress of the race and its maintenance appeared to be mutually antagonistic. Spencer was aware of the implicit contradiction and explained it away by assuring his readers that since genesis decreased more slowly than individuation increased, the more highly evolved of the species would still be able to produce the minimum of two children needed to sustain the race. Furthermore, the fittest in society were not only more vigorous and intelligent, but they were also on average longer-lived and thus had more time to breed their replacements. In other words, he concluded, although "the more evolved organism is the less fertile absolutely, it is the more fertile relatively."[48]

Some of Spencer's contemporaries thought his theory would put an end to recurrent predictions of a "Malthusian crisis" because the age-old menace of overpopulation would gradually succumb to the natural population restraints of progressive evolution.[49] The idea of individuation and genesis, like Spencer's earlier formulation of the concept of "survival of the fittest," was quickly added to the canon of neo-Darwinism from which it was extracted a generation later by eugenicists and others to answer the new population question associated with actual rather than theoretical differences in the declining birthrate.

The more optimistic of their number, such as Havelock Ellis and Caleb Saleeby, saw the Spencerian calculus at work in their own time and took comfort in the knowledge that "the whole course of zoological evolution reveals a constantly diminishing reproductive activity and a constantly increas-

ing expenditure of care on the offspring thus diminished in number." Instead of
being a sign of incipient decline, Ellis argued, the current birthrate was, as
Spencer revealed, a manifestation of a more advanced, progressive civilization. Those who sought to restore the birthrates of a half-century ago, he
added, "are engaged in a task which would be criminal if it were not based on
ignorance, and which is, in any case, fatuous."[50]

Without denying that "the bearers of . . . culture and refinement die off as
naturally and inevitably as flowers in autumn," Ellis, continuing the seasonal
metaphor, described the "new and more vigorous shoots" springing up to
replace the old "dead roses of the summer that is past." It appeared, as Spencer
predicted, that as a family attained high culture and refinement, the "nervous
and intellectual force" required put such a strain on its nervous system that the
males in the line tended to die out. This was not a cause for despair; what man
gains on one side he loses on another. We should do well to remember that we
cannot have it both ways, Ellis wrote, when "we encounter those sciolists who
in the presence of the finest and rarest manifestations of civilizations, can only
talk of race decay." Ellis, in contrast to most eugenicists, also had little
patience with those who believed the best stock was always in the higher
classes. While in the main this was so, all classes, he insisted, were endowed
with desirable qualities to the extent that there was no justification for regard-
ing a greater net increase of the lower social classes as an unmitigated evil.[51]

Saleeby, a nonpracticing gynecologist who was perhaps the most energetic
publicist of eugenics before the war, was even more enthralled by the qualitative racial implications of Spencer's "masterpiece" of "philosophic biology."
He saw it as complementing Malthus whose famous theories had been formulated without benefit of a knowledge of evolution. As a result, although he
recognized the importance of differential fertility, Malthus had not seen that
in the struggle for subsistence the highest types would survive and the elevation of the race would contain a natural corrective to the danger of overpopulation. Today, Saleeby wrote in 1909, Malthus's call for preventive checks on
unrestrained multiplication was being followed not out of a fear of famine,
but because of progressive "individuation." Like Spencer, Saleeby believed
future evolution would take the direction of even higher intellectual and
emotional development marked by "*the supersession of the quantitative by the
qualitative*."[52]

Ellis and Saleeby had a much brighter demographic view of the future than
most of their eugenicist contemporaries, but neither was prepared to let nature
take its course without some help from the highly individuated, if comparatively infertile, personalities who were attracted to the eugenic cause. The
falling birthrate might well be a consequence of the struggle for existence and

at the same time a means for abating it, but a eugenics program to keep a better balance between the differentiated fit and the less-evolved unfit was necessary to offset the effects of modern civilization on natural selection. As the Regius Professor of Natural History J. Arthur Thompson explained in 1906, whatever Spencer implied, it was not true "that eagles need never fear the frogs who spawn." There was no assurance that quality was always safe against quantity, so that the best eugenicists could hope for until their new ideas caught on was the promotion of social and ethical variations which might improve biological conditions.[53]

Spencerian explanations ran up against three formidable barriers that strengthened the eugenic cause before the Great War: common sense, statistical correlations, and diminished confidence in the effectiveness of natural selection in advanced societies. Dr. W. Leslie Mackenzie, medical inspector to the Local Government Board of Scotland, was, like Arthur Newsholme, aware of how attractive the idea of individuation and genesis had become to people seeking a biological answer to the riddle of declining fertility among the better classes. But it strained scientific credulity and common sense to suggest that the rapid fall in the birthrate in the previous two or three decades was the result of some sudden surge in cerebral activity any more than it was a consequence of a change in eating habits. To Newsholme it seemed particularly unlikely that the halving of family size of peers and baronets recorded by the Whethams was somehow a consequence of intellectual individuation. Furthermore, the differences within classes and within regions of the country as well as in other nations made it extremely difficult "to justify *simpliciter* the conclusion that biological capacity has altered."[54]

Even though Galton continued to believe fertility was subject to the laws of evolution, he was persuaded by Pearson and his own observations that the causes were more numerous and less biological than he had once concluded.[55] As early as the mid-1890s, Pearson had tried without success to find correlations that would support a hereditary explanation for the declining birthrate.[56] He continued to search for the connection throughout the next decade, but found it extremely hard "to find any character whatever *which organically is markedly associated with fertility*." There was certainly no scientific evidence of a correlation between intelligence and reproduction. Spencer's popularity notwithstanding, Pearson found it difficult to understand how the proliferation of people with inferior mental and physical qualities could be viewed as a sign of racial progress. If low fertility was analogous to higher civilization, he added, the elephant will in the end supplant man.[57]

If reason and biometry undermined Spencerian explanations of recent demography, the rise of Mendelian genetics and the decline of confidence in the hereditary transmission of acquired characteristics made them even more improbable. It was difficult to believe that doctors, clergymen, scientists, barristers, university professors, and others of their class were so infertile because their germ plasm had somehow been sterilized by their education and professional activities. The other side of the genetic coin, however, was the possibility that intelligence and diminished reproductive capacity were complementary Mendelian unit characters, or genes, which had become dominant through intermarriage. Since the able offspring of small families tended to marry within or above their own station where small families were also the rule, infertility was genetically reinforced. Consequently, as one eugenicist physician, J. A. Cobb, explained shortly before the war, "society will tend . . . to become graded according to fertility—the more fertile at the bottom and the less fertile at the top." Social advancement therefore actually insured that small families would beget even smaller families.

In a variation on Galton's old theory about the sterilizing effect of marrying heiresses, Cobb wrote, "any able man who rises by his ability into a higher social class than that in which he was born will naturally marry into that class, and will be likely to have a less fertile wife and fewer children than his medium brother who remained in the class into which he was born." The tremendous expansion of opportunities for economic and social advancement in the past half-century or so had increasingly put in the same class "the children of comparatively infertile parents and the men of ability, and their intermarriage has the result of uniting sterility and ability."[58] It was an idea that was to gain much more prominence in the interwar years when advanced by the brilliant mathematical geneticist Ronald A. Fisher.

Civilization and Natural Selection

Whatever the biological causation, nearly all persons of a eugenic turn of mind agreed that the problem of differential fertility was compounded by the diminishing role played by natural selection in modern society. In denying "the physically inferior, the mentally slow are . . . naturally more fertile than the stronger in body and mind," Pearson stressed that "in our community today artificial interference assured that the less fit were the more fertile." As a result, "the process of deterioration . . . *is* in progress."[59] By artificial interference Pearson, like most eugenicists, meant all of the social, economic, political, educational, scientific, and cultural trappings of modern civilization affecting biological selection.

Although Darwin had himself generally avoided drawing social implications from his discoveries, he did complain in *The Descent of Man* about how "civilised men" checked nature's efforts to eliminate the weak. "We build asylums for the imbecile, the maimed, and the sick; we institute poor-laws; and our medical men exert their utmost skill to save the life of every one to the last moment. . . . Thus the weak members of civilised societies propagate their kind." It was in fact surprising, as animal breeders knew, "how soon a want of care, or care wrongly directed, lead to the degeneration of a domestic race." These were words to inspire a eugenicist a generation later. Despite his doubts, Darwin accepted that humane interference with natural selection was itself a necessary social instinct, "the noblest part of our nature" and the price we had to pay for civilization.[60] Nevertheless, at the end of his life, Alfred Russel Wallace reported, Darwin was gloomy about the prospect of a future in which natural selection had no play and the fittest did not survive. He talked about "the scum" from whom "the stream of life" is largely renewed, and of the grave danger it entailed in a democratic civilization.[61]

Wallace was himself much more optimistic about the course of social evolution, but many of his social Darwinist contemporaries saw the direst of consequences in the suspension of natural selection. Their anxieties were fueled by their fear and loathing of the urban poor whose deplorable condition and threatening numbers were allegedly perpetuated and encouraged by misguided charity, social welfare, and medical intervention. Spencer's harsh indictment in *Social Statics* of those who thwarted nature and assisted in the survival of the unfit, was repeated with variations by social Darwinists throughout the late nineteenth and early twentieth centuries.[62]

There were countless complaints about how the Poor Law, "tender-hearted" politicians and philanthropists, or Christian altruism had blindly combined to counteract and suspend the operation of the "righteous and salutary law" of natural selection. Social, scientific, and political progress too often provided a refuge for the criminal, the vicious, the incapable, and the hopelessly unfit.[63] Arnold White was among the more vituperative in describing the racial dangers spawned from "the imperishable fecundity of philanthropic and legislative ova." Lamenting in 1887 the blundering lack of foresight and "irregulated vitality" of earlier generations who had sown "the dark seeds of poisonous and eternal evil" that had now sprouted in the "Great City," he thought "we should attempt to harmonize our legislation and our public charities with the inexorable tendencies of natural law" while there was still time.[64]

A decade later White was still fulminating against the "sightless pity . . . enfeebling the British race, deteriorating our nation, and menacing the future of the Empire." There was no doubt in his mind that "hereditary intemperance" aided and abetted by hospital, sanitary, and Poor Law policies advanced a "cult

of infirmity" that was sustained by the new democracy. He recognized, perhaps regretfully, that it was nonsense to talk of lethal chambers to eliminate the
tainted degenerates who threatened the Anglo-Saxon race. Since there was
little chance "diseased Demos, half-conscious of his own physical unfitness,
but electorally omnipotent, would permit a curtailment of his pleasures or the
abridgement of his liberty," Parliament was not likely to provide relief. The
only hope that White could see was a change in public opinion.[65]

White's rages against the towns, the poor, the extension of the franchise,
and a host of other things articulated the feelings of an extremely conservative
sector of society overwhelmed by forces of social, economic, political, and
cultural change they could neither control nor understand. Others complained
about the loss of grit, discipline, and responsibility as well as the decline of
everything from individualism to literary, artistic, and theatrical taste. Problems with servants were sometimes bundled together with curmudgeonly attacks on trade unions, women, fashion, death duties, higher taxes, omnibuses,
and the rise of spectator sports as signs of the deteriorating times. There was
no end of nostalgic references to the "old days" when the British were more
like the hard-working Germans; even Prime Minister Balfour suggested in
1904 that the "de-Germanizing" of the population might be one of the insidious causes of degeneration.[66]

Hereditary biology in the form of social Darwinism at least provided an
explanation for these changes in terms many people could readily comprehend. It did not make the racial decadence or degeneration—code words for
change—they saw all around them any easier to accept, but a number of them,
like White, turned to eugenics for potential salvation. He, for example, went
on the council of the new Eugenics Education Society where he took his
responsibilities seriously and personally enough to refuse to attend his son's
marriage to a "eugenically unsuitable" woman tainted by some unspecified
hereditary flaw.[67]

Pearson, who was no less worried than White about the nation's racial
efficiency in an ever more threatening, competitive world, had nevertheless
long questioned the applicability of social Darwinism to eugenic improvement. A professed socialist and evolutionist, he had discovered Marx and
Lassalle and attended lectures on Darwinism while completing his education
in Berlin and Heidelberg. Deeply influenced by his German experience, he
blended socialism and biological evolution into a state form of social Darwinism different from that professed by those who, in the tradition of Herbert
Spencer, linked natural selection to the struggle of individuals within groups.
Pearson, by contrast, relegated such a process to primitive stages of develop-

ment long since past; for centuries natural selection had been far more appropriate to struggles between groups or, as in the modern world, nations.

As early as 1886 Pearson criticized the concept of the survival of the fittest as a misleading application of what occurred among prolific, simple organisms in a stationary environment to the much more complex evolution of men in civilized societies. Never a social Darwinist himself, Darwin avoided such a connection, he argued. The great majority of civilized men neither starve nor perish miserably before reproducing their kind, as even a slight acquaintance with vital statistics revealed. Infants and children in all classes, those least affected by individual struggle, were in fact the most vulnerable to mortality, indicating that hereditary physical weakness, not intragroup conflict, was the greatest weeder in the garden of natural selection. Whatever social Darwinists like Spencer, Benjamin Kidd, or the German Ernst Haeckel might claim, Pearson concluded, "There appears to be no direct relation between success in the rivalry of life and the extent of reproductivity in civilized man." Even Darwin eventually recognized this in the conclusion to *The Descent of Man*, where, influenced by Galton, he encouraged the better classes to have more children and the inferior classes to show more restraint. At best, Pearson insisted, we can talk about the "survival of the fitter," and this was determined much more by heredity than by some primitive struggle for subsistence.[68]

Though he was an adherent of Marxist economics, Pearson's rejection of class struggle and revolution inclined him toward Fabian socialism where, like the Webbs, Shaw, and H. G. Wells, among others, he denounced the use social Darwinists made of the idea of natural selection to defend laissez-faire individualism and attack the growth of collectivism. But his criticisms were not rooted in sympathy or compassion for the unfit, most of whom Pearson agreed were heavily concentrated in the overly fertile ranks of the laboring poor. Rather, they grew from his conviction, shared by the Fabians, that the implementation of eugenic policies would only be possible in a planned socialist state administered by efficient, scientifically trained professionals.[69]

Pearson privately groused to Galton in 1901 about the abuse one had to endure "to assert that the huge charities providing for the children of the incapable are a national curse and not a blessing," or that the widow whose husband died of consumption at age thirty-five and left her with seven dependent children "is really a moral criminal and not an object for pity."[70] If less warmhearted about the poor and far more skeptical throughout his life of the benefits of social and environmental reform than nearly all of the left-wing eugenicists who came after him, Pearson was, nevertheless, among the first of their number to see in eugenics the possibilities for building a better future by a merger of science and state socialism. It was an attractive prospect that appealed not only to Fabians in the late Victorian and Edwardian years but to a coterie of Marxist scientists and social reformers in the interwar years.

Despite Pearson's denial of the importance of natural selection within modern societies, he was as disposed as most of the eugenicists, whose perverted social Darwinism he condemned, to use the concept emotionally and imprecisely. He complained about how the suspension of natural selection was sapping national vigor, increasing the number of criminals and lunatics, and otherwise contributing to the deterioration of the race. In 1904 he recalled that "a hundred years ago you hung a rogue if you caught him. Nowadays you provide him with soup-kitchens and night shelters . . . and leave him to propagate his kin at will." And the next year in the preface to the second edition of his popular book, *National Life*, he begged his readers to consider the possibility "that while modern social conditions are removing the crude physical checks which the unrestrained struggle for existence places on the over-fertility of the unfit, they may at the same time be leading to a lessened relative fertility in those physically and mentally fitter stocks, from which the bulk of our leaders in all fields of activity have hitherto been drawn."[71]

From its inception the eugenics movement struggled with the applicability of natural selection to the differential birthrate. All but the most fanatical social Darwinists acknowledged the process had been dramatically modified with the advance of civilization so that the fit and the unfit had become social as well as biological categories. Galton's term "civic worth," which reflected the merging of the two, was used increasingly in the prewar years by those trying to redefine fitness in a modern eugenic framework. Dr. J. W. Slaughter, an American psychologist who was chairman of the Sociological Society and of the organizing committee of the Eugenics Education Society, went out of his way to explain that natural selection no longer meant a struggle for survival but involved the ability or inability to participate in group life.[72] His own participation and the future of the new organization were briefly imperiled in 1908 when he was arrested for indecent assault, though the charge was quashed on appeal.[73]

The recognition that natural selection was no longer as operative in society as it had been in earlier times was essential to the rise of eugenics. If, as eugenicists believed, the race was already being altered for the worse by human intervention, there was every reason to believe this intervention, when based upon sound, biological principles of rational selection, could be turned to the race's advantage. It also meant that the differential decline in the birthrate, which threatened to exacerbate the trend toward degeneration, was not the result of some cyclical or permanent loss of reproductive capacity but of human volition. The deliberate regulation of fertility, as Havelock Ellis insisted, was not a manifestation of organic degeneration but momentous evidence of progressive social and intellectual evolution.[74]

Indeed, the *Fertility of Marriage Census*, the National Birth-Rate Commission, the Fabian Society study of *The Decline in the Birth-Rate*, and the Eugenics Laboratory *Report on the English Birth Rate* all confirmed that the unrelenting if socially differentiated fall in fertility since the 1870s had nothing to do with depleted fecundity but was the direct result of the "artificial limitation" of conception. Moreover, there was general agreement in nearly all of the studies undertaken before the war that the adoption of "family limitation" or "Neo-Malthusian" practices was, as currently practiced, decidedly not eugenic. On the contrary, the National Birth-Rate Commission concluded, the current trends were actually "dysgenic"—a term coined by Saleeby—since restriction prevailed in the most "worthy" families rather than in those of the "unworthy." The latter, unfortunately, lived under hereditary and environmental conditions, "which are most adverse to the improvement or even maintenance of the quality of the population."[75]

Eugenics, its enthusiastic advocates claimed, could reverse this trend and with it the nation's slide toward racial decadence. To Saleeby it represented a new "Scientific Patriotism," the culmination of intellectual evolution. The eugenicist was obliged to use his highly individuated powers to aid and abet natural selection. Even if the laws of heredity were still subject to dispute, it was "well worth society's while that the genius and the saint, the athlete and the artist, should provide posterity, rather than the idiot, the criminal, the weakling, the Philistine." Despite the charge by repentant Darwinists such as Thomas Huxley that natural selection was incompatible with the ethical progress of society, Saleeby insisted eugenics could make them compatible. People failed to recognize that "fittest" was not a qualitative or moral term, but an objective adaptation to particular conditions. The eugenic ideal of "race culture . . . is *to ensure that the fittest shall be the best*." Nature cannot be thwarted, Saleeby warned, but it can be helped by increasing the contribution of the fit to the racial coffers, while "*extending to the unfit all our sympathy but forbidding them parenthood*."[76]

Eugenicists insisted that natural selection, as they interpreted it, was far from being the harsh, unfeeling doctrine critics claimed it to be. Galton himself stressed the humaneness of the eugenic approach to race reconstruction. He rather mystically described individuals as "partial detachments from the infinite ocean of Being," and the world as a stage on which evolution takes place, "principally hitherto by means of Natural Selection, which achieves the good of the whole with scant regard to that of the individual." Yet man, "gifted with pity and other kindly feelings . . . has also the power of preventing many kinds of suffering." Galton conceived of it falling well within the human province to replace natural selection by other processes "that are more merciful and not less effective."[77]

Similarly, the young Cambridge geneticist R. A. Fisher exulted in 1913 that eugenic understanding of Darwinian biology not only provided an explanation of the past and the present but the key to the future as well. Certainly this involved "the organisation and structure of the body, and the cruder physical impulses," but it also applied to "our ethical and aesthetic nature, all the refinements of beauty, all the delicacy of our sense of beauty, our moral instincts of obedience and compassion, pity or indignation, our moments of religious awe, or mystical penetration."[78]

Other converts asked, since the "stupendous process of evolution" was going to continue and the germ plasm, with its "great, expansive and creative energies" would continue to be altered by heredity, selection, and environment, did it not make sense to try to identify, extract, and promote that which was most beneficial? Such rhetorical questions were usually followed by the observation that we were already interfering with nature, so why not do it scientifically and intelligently so as to avoid fostering what we detest and destroying what we most admire. Employing a familiar nautical metaphor, A. F. Tredgold cautioned, "When man takes the helm from Nature it is essential for the safety of the vessel that he should be provided with a chart and understand the principles of navigation." After centuries of ignorance, neglect, and blind interference with nature, which had resulted in the "retrogression and extinction" of past civilizations and threatened our own, eugenics was the first attempt by man "to try and replace the interference with Natural Law with improving scientific policies."[79]

The most important of these policies, eugenicists recognized, was demographic. It involved the dramatic modification, if not reversal, of the differential class patterns of family limitation, or birth control, as it was called after 1914. Darwin had been shocked and embarrassed even to consider the subject when it was broached to him.[80] Pearson, a more modern man, recognized as early as the 1890s that its rapid adoption among the better classes, rather than some class-specific shift in generative capacity, accounted for the striking differences in the birthrate that he projected for the near future.[81]

Galton, despite his advanced age, realized that the issue of birth control and its effect upon differential fertility was in the long run closely tied to the acceptance of his new scientific religion. In the final lines of his autobiography, he singled out as the first objective of eugenics the checking of the birthrate of the "unfit, instead of allowing them to come into being. . . . The second object is the improvement of the race by furthering the productivity of the fit by early marriages and healthful rearing of their children." Natural selection, he concluded, "rests upon excessive production and wholesale destruction; Eugenics on bringing no more individuals into the world than can be properly cared for, and those only of the best stock."[82] The achievement of these goals required a precise understanding of where that "stock" could be found, and the promulgation of a new faith in which salvation was to be found not in the sacrifice of one eugenic man, but in the propagation of many.

Four

Class and the
Religion of Race Culture

C omparing the eugenics movement in Britain and the United States, Daniel Kevles has observed how in each country specific social, cultural, and economic anxieties determined what was proclaimed "in the name of eugenics."[1] In the case of the United States, tortured race relations and extensive alien immigration were the principal sources of eugenic worry; in Britain, where long-established ethnic and racial homogeneity prevailed, the relative contribution of indigenous classes to the population was the predominant concern. The influx of eastern European immigrants, mainly Jews, between 1880 and 1914 stirred up some ethnocentric, eugenicist fears about race adulteration, but the numbers compared to those crossing the Atlantic were comparatively minute.[2] Although there were occasional complaints in the *Eugenics Review* about "the scourings of Europe" compounding the existing problems of inferior procreation among the native population, immigrants ranked quite low on the eugenic scale of British racial apprehension.[3]

Eugenicists were much more troubled by the exodus of able, healthy, energetic men whose departure to the colonies at a time when the birthrate was no longer on the rise threatened to deplete the mother country of its best stock. As the number of emigrants rose in the decade before World War I from more than 200,000 to well over 300,000 a year, their departure focused more attention on the diseased, defective, aging incompetents who remained behind to breed their like and enlarge the already swollen relief rolls. Caleb Saleeby, for example, could imagine nothing more foolish or inevitably ruinous to the quality of the race than listening to Rudyard Kipling's disastrous advice to worthy men and women to go forth and populate the colonies. Indeed, he suggested that Britain's problems might soon become as insoluble as those of Ireland if, as in that unfortunate country, the worthiest people continued to leave.[4]

None of this meant that the eugenics movement was antiimperial. Many of its early adherents such as Karl Pearson, Arnold White, the Whethams, G. B. Shaw, the Webbs, and Leonard Darwin, among others, were social,

Liberal, or Conservative imperialists who believed that the prosperity, defense, and greatness of the nation were tied up with the empire.[5] They were no less interested in the breeding of an efficient imperial race, as Lord Rosebery vaguely described it, than were those of their contemporaries who worried about the declining birthrate in the white settlement colonies, particularly Australia and New Zealand, where the fall in fertility since the 1880s paralleled the losses at home. When compared with the much higher fertility of presumably inferior black and yellow races, the figures provided telling evidence for those who were prone to believe that the decline in reproductive vigor was an ominous sign of the decline of the West much discussed in the early years of the century. The bishop of Ripon, William Boyd Carpenter, for example, questioned whether the nations entrusted with the guardianship of the Christian faith were refusing their inheritance and by an inexplicable race suicide were surrendering their scepter to the East.[6]

Despite numerous references to the demographic problems of the empire as part of a general concern about declining, differential fertility and its likely impact on the race, British eugenicists were, nevertheless, decidedly insular. They were first and foremost interested in the demography of the British Isles and in the qualities and characteristics of the social classes into which its inhabitants fell. However much eugenicists talked about the race, what they were really describing was the aggregation of discreet social groups in Britain. The problems of empire were always secondary and tangential to domestic considerations; most eugenicists assumed that the vitality of the empire was, in the final analysis, dependent upon the qualitative vitality, not the size, of the race in the mother country.

Fears about the "Yellow Peril" were nonsense, C. V. Drysdale told the Royal Colonial Institute in 1914. The British were the best colonizers in the world because they were racially the most efficient; it took only a minority of them to govern the much more numerous but much less efficient races who peopled their empire. So long as Britain continued to produce healthy, virile, patriotic, and efficient people, the empire would be secure. Drysdale, like most eugenicists, assumed the mother country would remain a source for such people whose abilities rather than numbers were what mattered.[7]

In effect, the critical problem for eugenics was, as Galton explained, to identify and influence "the most useful classes in the community to contribute more than their proportion to the next generation." If they did so, Galton assumed, a portion of this adventurous "high human breed" which had already planted its stock all over the world would continue to be available to "lay the foundations of the dispositions and capacities of future millions of the human race." This is what lay behind the commonplace eugenic assertion, repeated with numerous variations, that "the nation which first subjects itself to a rational eugenical discipline is bound to inherit the earth."[8]

Such rhetoric aside, given its restricted focus upon the quality of the race at home, the eugenics movement in Britain was rarely concerned with the characteristics and qualities of other races abroad, particularly those presumed to be inferior. In this sense eugenics took its cue from Galton himself. Despite his extensive travels to Africa and the Middle East and his evaluations of the peoples he encountered there, when it came to formulating his eugenic ideas Galton concentrated exclusively upon the hereditary characteristics of different classes in his own country. The Eugenics Education Society council, for example, rarely discussed the empire except as it related to the eugenic consequences of emigration.

While the society as a general policy favored improving the white stocks in the colonies, it was troubled by the disproportionate number of fit men compared with fit women who left the country. Its council recommended to the Tennyson Commission on Emigration during the war that the family be the basic unit of emigration, and that some way be found to encourage more eugenically sound females unable to find a husband at home to try their luck elsewhere in the empire. Anticipating a resurgence of emigration after the war, the society also recommended to the Medical Research Council and the Royal Anthropological Institute that they consider undertaking an inquiry into the effects of racial intermarriage and climate on the fertility of those men and women who went out to the colonies. Though both groups expressed some interest in the project, nothing came of it, and the Eugenics Society did not pursue the subject after the war.[9]

Such diversions from the society's concentration on domestic demographic problems were exceptional. British eugenics as a product of late Victorian and Edwardian middle-class society remained fixed on the subject of class no matter how much its adherents talked imprecisely about race. Class in Britain was, in other words, as much a way of thinking and perceiving as it was a definable socioeconomic category. People consciously and unconsciously attached to it projective qualitative concepts of social and moral value, fitness and unfitness, or worthiness and unworthiness. These concepts often said more about the men and women sharing them than they did about objective reality.

Race regeneration, or "race-culture" as eugenicists often described it, was really an extension of their perceptions of class culture. Indeed, contemporary as well as later critics of eugenics assumed that its proponents were merely wrapping their middle-class fear and contempt of the working classes and ambivalent envy of the aristocracy in a self-serving, prejudicial mantle of pseudoscientific respectability. This, for example, was the thrust of Prince Kropotkin's charge at the first International Eugenics Congress in 1912 when (to cheers from the audience) he accused its sponsors of advocating their own form of class warfare.[10] Despite the protests of the Eugenics Education Society's new president, Major Darwin, that eugenics was not a class but a biological issue that had "no relation whatever to class prejudices," he knew perfectly well that much of the public thought otherwise.[11] It was a criticism that has if anything been reinforced by later study, and there is little doubt that it was to a large extent accurate.

Yet, in their regenerative campaign for race culture, eugenicists sometimes found it almost as difficult to agree upon what qualities and defects they wished to advance or eliminate as they did on the extent to which desirable or undesirable genes could be found at the various levels of the socioeconomic hierarchy. For a science initially so dependent upon locating where on the biosocial ladder the most valuable progenitive germ plasm was distributed, the problems were formidable and vexatious. More often than not they were solved not by biometry or Mendelian genetics but by a variety of class-based assumptions and wonderful leaps of faith.

Positive Eugenics:
Marriage and Selective Breeding

Early in his studies of heredity, Galton charted the course eugenic race culture was to follow until the interwar years. By that time it had become clear to all but the most entrenched old-liners that the selective breeding of the fit was socially and politically, if not scientifically, impossible. Although he did not become concerned with the issue of declining fertility until the turn of the century, Galton noted in the 1860s and 1870s the dangerous tendency of rising men of talent to marry later, if at all, and to sire fewer children than in the past. He attributed this phenomenon to the escalating costs of starting and maintaining a family, considerations that weighed lightly on the feckless and irresponsible who reproduced themselves with little thought of the future. Since, he calculated, no more than one-quarter of the children born to an able couple were likely to be as well endowed as their parents, it was important that desirable matches be made early and a sufficient number of children be bred to create a net increase in the proportion of the "naturally gifted" in the population.[12]

Galton was sure that such a system of positive race improvement, which he first called *viriculture* and, later, *eugenics*, was "perfectly in accordance with the moral sense of the present time." It would lead to a "new and exclusive class consciousness" rooted in merit rather than in custom, tradition, or inherited family wealth. In retrospect, it was a vision that proved to be particularly appealing to an expanding professional middle class seeking status and influence commensurate with its education, talent, and ability. Unlike the members of the old aristocracy who seldom made alliances out of their order except to gain wealth, Galton believed that the new nobility of talent would shrink from any misalliance that threatened to diminish the valuable hereditary gifts that justified their privileged place in society.[13] Gradually, as their numbers increased and their gifts were reinforced, the general qualitative level of the population would improve enough to reverse the slide toward degeneration and guarantee the continued advance of British civilization long into the future.

When in the new century Galton's visions began to attract a following and an organized movement, his notions of positive selective breeding were initially viewed as the most likely solution to the problems caused by the differential birthrate. Alleged increases in insanity, feeblemindedness, criminality, alcoholism, epilepsy, and a variety of supposedly hereditary diseases, as well as chronic pauperism, were added to the other stigmata of deterioration and degeneration to provoke angry demands that something be done about the unrestrained growth of the unfit. A variety of schemes to segregate, institutionalize, incarcerate, punish, deny the right to marry, and even to sterilize degenerates, as some American states were starting to do, were proposed throughout the Edwardian period. If all else failed, some people were prepared to entertain a "gentle, painless" policy of extermination.[14]

With the exception of the "lethal chamber," which only appealed to the rabid fringe, most eugenicists, including Galton, had little difficulty with the majority of these proposals. But other than the institutionalizing of the feebleminded, whose affliction was generally acknowledged to be hereditary and whose segregation was assured by eugenically inspired legislation in 1913, they recognized that the implementation of such restrictive measures was politically and logistically impossible for the foreseeable future. Even then, coercion was likely to have only a minimal impact on changing the qualitative composition of the population. Consequently, as Galton wrote in 1901, "the possibility of improving the race of a nation depends on the power of increasing the productivity of the best stock. This is far more important than that of repressing the productivity of the worst."[15]

If a number of eugenicists doubted it was feasible in current social, economic, and political circumstances to persuade the "superior stock" to marry younger and rear larger families, they nevertheless agreed with Galton's carefully formulated goal of bringing "as many influences as can be reasonably employed, to cause the useful classes in the community to contribute *more* than their proportion to the next generation."[16] To a person who believed human heredity was an incremental process, even a slight shift in the qualitative contribution to future generations would in time prove to be statistically and, consequently, biologically significant.

Over the years Galton concocted a variety of plans to identify worthy couples and promote eugenic marriages. As early as 1883 he suggested that localities throughout the country might provide endowments "in favour of those of both sexes who show evidences of high race and of belonging to prolific and thriving families." He pursued the plan some twenty years later, proposing that wealthy patrons and local authorities befriend promising youths and provide them the means for marrying. This might include racial dowries and healthy, convenient, inexpensive housing similar to the fellowships and lodgings colleges offer worthy scholars. Those representatives from each class with outstanding physique, ability, and character could be brought together by associations of the well born—the "Eugenes" as he called them. The example of a livestock fair was not remote from Galton's thoughts when he added, "It might well become a point of honour, and as much an avowed object, for noble families to gather fine specimens of humanity around them as it is to procure and maintain fine breeds of cattle, etc., which are costly, but repay in satisfaction." With annual contributions to public charities exceeding £14 million, Galton thought the money would be better spent on improving the race rather than maintaining its failures. Unlike cattle, of course, the unpredictable fancies of young people might not coincide with the hereditary desires of society, but Galton thought this was a superficial problem that could readily be overcome by social pressure and financial advantages.[17]

While to some the class thinking that was so fundamental to British eugenics appeared exceedingly old-fashioned, even reactionary, in its equating of desirable or undesirable hereditary characteristics with different sectors of society, to others, including Galton himself, eugenics seemed radically modern. In rejecting the traditional values of rank, privilege, custom, and legacy that would have excluded many of their number from positions of prestige, power, and influence, eugenicists fashioned new concepts of class in accordance with their estimation of talent, ability, and merit. Galton, for example, retained the Victorian concept of three broad classes but based it upon an evaluation of the genetically based "civic worth" of married couples. This fluid and imprecise term reflected Galton's view that people of recognized accomplishment were endowed with measurable hereditary qualities that largely determined their value to society. At the top stood "a small class of desirables," in the middle a "large class of passables," and at the bottom a "small class of undesirables."

Others thought the base was much broader and the curve less symmetrical with every passing year, but most agreed that civic worth would best be enhanced by increasing substantially the reproductive consciousness and activity of those at the top. "I can believe hereafter," Galton explained in his memoirs, "that it will be felt as derogatory to a person of exceptionally good stock to marry into an inferior one as it is for a person of high Austrian rank to marry one who has not sixteen heraldic quarterings."[18]

The identification of this select stock and, increasingly, its dysgenic opposite on the hereditarian social scale was at the core of eugenical thinking. It perplexed and frequently embarrassed the movement from its earliest years as supporters and opponents argued about what was and was not hereditarily determined and eugenically desirable. Galton naively believed that eventually learned people would be able to agree on "the several qualities of . . . goodness of constitution, of physique, and of mental capacity" they wanted to see reproduced. He favored the issuance of "eugenic certificates" based upon family history, educational accomplishment, athletic prowess, and medical examinations. Given the concerns about the quality of the armed forces, the medical reports on recruits could also be used in conjunction with those of insurance companies to identify potential candidates for eugenic selection. Galton thought that universities might also consider adding to the diplomas of outstanding eugenic prospects the letters "V.H.T. (Valid for hereditary transmission of qualities suitable to a citizen of an Imperial Country)." He recognized, however, that because similar comparative evaluations of women would be more difficult to come by, it would be necessary to lay even more stress on their medical examinations as well as on "hereditary family qualities, including those of fertility and prepotency."[19]

These proposals, which Galton hammered away on in the opening decade of the new century, represented an entrenched utopian streak in his thinking. In his first venture into the study of hereditary talent, he contemplated an ideal society in which a system of competitive physical and mental examinations would identify racially promising young men and women who would be led blushingly into each others' company and, six months later, to the altar of Westminster Abbey. There, in an enlightened gesture of royal approbation, Queen Victoria herself would give away the brides along with wedding gifts of £5,000 and assurances that the state would defray the cost of rearing and educating the "extraordinary talented issue" who would soon be forthcoming.[20]

Nearly fifty years later, in 1910, the aged Galton was still entertaining such eugenic fantasies when he tried without success to publish a utopian fable with the obvious title of "Kantsaywhere."[21] In it he described the trials and tribulations of an adventurous autobiographical hero, I. Donoghue, a professor of vital statistics from the distant land of Dunno Weir, as he wooed and, after rigorous tests and examinations, won the perfectly turned hand of the eugenically precocious Miss Augusta Allfancy. Instead of falling into social classes, the racially enlightened inhabitants of Galton's imaginary world were classified by the scores they achieved on tests administered and recorded by the Eugenics College that dominated Kantsaywhere. By following Galton's proposals to insure that family size was closely correlated with rank on a genetic scale, the academic Eugenes who guided the country were able to keep it prosperous, healthy, and racially vigorous. Since the well-built, handsome, intelligent, and athletic hero and his "thoroughly feminine, and . . . mammalian" race heroine scored in the superior range, they were free, unlike less well endowed couples, to replicate themselves at will.

The emphasis in "Kantsaywhere" as in all of Galton's work was on positive rather than negative eugenics. Nevertheless, in a utopian society where the propagation of children by the "Unfit" was a crime against the state, a range of penalties from social ostracism and fines to deportation or segregation in humane, though celibate, labor colonies was available to punish offenders. Such punishment was reserved for those who violated their quota of offspring or, in the case of those in the lowest grades of unfitness, who had any at all. So long as they observed the reproductive restrictions placed upon them by the Eugenics College, they would be treated kindly and supported by the state. Similarly, if a defective child were conceived in an approved marriage, the college would take responsibility for its benevolent but celibate upbringing. Galton, however, did not dwell on the consequences of dysgenic propagation which he believed would steadily diminish as the quality of the race improved.

Whatever the old man's literary fantasies, "Kantsaywhere" failed to find a place alongside such protoeugenic utopias as Plato's *Republic* and Campanella's *City of the Sun* or, more recently, Samuel Butler's satirical *Erewohn* and H. G. Wells's *Mankind in the Making*. Much to Galton's embarrassed family's relief, the manuscript for "Kantsaywhere" was rejected, and the frustrated author destroyed all but the most specifically eugenic parts shortly before his death. As the equally apprehensive Karl Pearson acknowledged, the crude story had been nothing more than a structure for Galton to spin out his ideas of selective breeding in a truly eugenic community.[22]

That these ideas in such a context might do more harm than good for the eugenics cause was very much on Pearson's mind when he complained about the quasi-utopian musings of nonscientific popularizers such as Wells, Ellis, Saleeby, and the scandalous George Bernard Shaw. The latter's insistence in 1904 that "what we must fight for is freedom to breed the race without being hampered by the mass of irrelevant conditions implied in the institution of marriage," seemed to confirm the long-held fears of some critics, like Alfred Russel Wallace, that eugenics might prove to be a threat to the monogamous foundations of civilized marriage. However shocked they might be by Shaw's notorious assaults on modern nuptiality, Edwardian eugenicists nevertheless shared his complaint that people today "select their wives and husbands far less carefully than they select their cashiers and cooks," which was perhaps why their bank accounts and their appetites were healthier than their offspring.[23]

Even the distressed Pearson had to admit that Shaw's *Man and Superman* did much to promote the public's awareness of positive eugenics. But the playwright's hilarious description of a robust, cheerful, "eupeptic British country squire" briefly mating with a clever, imaginative, intellectual, but otherwise uncongenial "highly civilised Jewess" to produce a superior son, was not likely to advance the movement's respectability with the public nor its credibility in the scientific community.[24] Beatrice Webb might have thought that the play raised the "most important of all questions, this breeding of the right sort of man," but she also knew that the time was not ripe for its answering.[25]

Caleb Saleeby, who joined Webb and Shaw in the Fabian Society in 1910, endorsed socialist proposals for the endowment of motherhood, state nurseries, and infant and maternal welfare centers. Unlike many of his colleagues in the Eugenics Education Society, he believed that "the eugenics century" must welcome all parties, factions, religions, and ideologies so long as they contributed to the furtherance of race culture.[26] But he strongly disagreed with Shaw that state programs could ever replace the care provided by the natural mother, or that sustained race regeneration could occur outside of the monogamous family. There was nothing inherent in marriage itself to thwart eugenic sexual selection, as Shaw seemed to think; all that was required was greater education and a change in social values. In emphasizing that "we desire to achieve race-culture by and through marriage," Saleeby insisted that "what we really need is not so much the abolition of Mrs. Grundy as her conversion to the eugenic idea."[27]

This same note was struck by nearly all eugenicist spokesmen before the First World War as they emphasized their commitment to a policy of eugenic marriage and reproduction free from the economic, religious, and social constraints that often led to dysgenic misalliance or a life of barren celibacy.[28] The core of the problem, Saleeby warned, was persuading "the worthy, the original, the autonomous, the responsible—the last men and women who will permit themselves to be married to order," of their racial and civic responsibilities.[29]

Despite his admiration for eugenics and its founder, Saleeby was exceedingly cautious about moving too quickly to implement the many schemes Galton and others proposed. The idea of marriage permits, eugenic certificates, and insurance company reports smacked of an interference in private affairs that would be resented in a free, highly individualistic society. Some of his colleagues called for the state regulation of marriage, insisting that licenses only be granted after a thorough check of family histories and a medical examination of the potential bride and groom. A. F. Tredgold, for example, looked to the centralization of educational records, the reports of medical inspectors of schoolchildren, Poor Law accounts, and prison and lunatic asylum lists to keep track of undesirables who might choose to marry.[30]

Saleeby thought eugenics was already suffering from a mistaken impression that it did not hold marriage to be a sacred and essential instrument of race culture. Talk about such impediments to undesirable nuptiality coupled to "intolerable" allusions to human stud farms only reinforced this image.[31] In fact, Saleeby insisted, eugenics was not trying to prevent marriage but to remove the artificial and unnecessary obstacles to the marriage and parenthood of the most worthy men and women. It was the reproduction within marriage, not marriage itself, that was of central concern. Even Galton, he suggestively recalled after the great man's death, married but left no offspring.[32]

Saleeby was being somewhat disingenuous. Galton himself had associated eugenics with the stud farm by his many examples of stock breeding, and his desire to impede the marriages of lunatics, the feebleminded, habitual criminals, chronic paupers, and others who were afflicted with extreme hereditary defects was widely shared by his followers. A number of these people, however, did think it premature to discuss any limitations on marriage since neither eugenicists nor anyone else really knew how to determine fitness or unfitness. Sir Squire Sprigge, the editor of the *Lancet*, who was otherwise sympathetic to eugenics, thought there was little chance the medical profession would endorse premarital medical examinations. It would be "an intolerable piece of social bullying" to screen prospective couples in hopes of averting a few tragedies. With characteristic class confidence, Sprigge claimed that in any event certification was not needed for people in the higher ranks, and not enough was known about heredity to apply it to the lower. Mendelism may some day be able to help, he thought, but not yet. Obviously profound imbeciles, degenerates, and syphilitics ought not to marry, but a medical veto would be a futile way of trying to keep them apart.[33] The Eugenics Education Society council

was under some pressure before the war to campaign for prenuptial medical
tests but decided in 1912 that it was an "extremely dangerous" issue in the
current climate of opinion.[34]

The council's reticence reflected the angry debate that eugenic ideas of
selective breeding had stirred up in Edwardian society. Stockyard and cattle
show metaphors that had been common in discussions of heredity in the 1870s
and 1880s made people uncomfortable a decade or so later. The *British Medical Journal*, for example, commenting on the fine breeds exhibited at the
Smithfield Cattle Show in 1880, suggested "that what we do with these poor
beasts we can do with . . . our artisans and labourers [to] yield the most
possible work with the least possible pain and injury to themselves." Admittedly the free will and rights enjoyed by human beings complicated the problem, but the writer did not consider them insuperable obstacles. Within a few
years they obviously were, however, and the journal dropped the subject
entirely. Commenting in 1901 on Galton's description in his recent Huxley
Memorial Lecture of the statistical possibilities for breeding civic worth, the
British Medical Journal contented itself with such adjectives as "ingenious
and suggestive."[35]

Even before the turn of the century, Thomas Huxley, Darwin's former
"bulldog" after whom the lecture series was named, had repudiated such
schemes as immoral, unnecessary, and impractical. Rebelling against the cruel
and selfish perversions of evolution he saw in the rise of social Darwinism,
Huxley insisted in 1894 that not only had the innate qualities of the race
remained unchanged in the past four or five centuries, but every age and every
society had different notions of fitness and unfitness. He was particularly wary
of those new "saviours of society" who, with their "pigeon-fanciers polity,"
would implement a system of "evolutionary-regimentation" that would endanger the ethical structure and free relationships of our highly advanced civilization. Unlike bees in a hive, he argued, men are not limited or predestined to a
single task or role. The species was so hereditarily complex—or polygenetic
as a later generation would say—that there was "no hope that mere human
beings will ever possess enough intelligence to select the fittest."[36]

Support for this point of view came in the next decade from such unlikely
sources as Benjamin Kidd and Max Nordau, who were otherwise far more
pessimistic than Huxley about the state of human evolution. Both thought that
eugenicists were wrong to compare human breeding with that of plants and
animals. For one thing, Nordau told the Sociological Society in a 1905 communication, the breeder knew what he wanted to breed and accepted that
certain qualities would be enhanced at the expense of others. It was doubtful
that we could agree on what points human beings should be bred for, even if

we knew how to do it. Kidd, addressing the same organization the following year, was not sure that society needed more intellectuals or men with higher grades of ability as eugenicists prescribed. There was a danger of confusing individual efficiency with social efficiency; Galtonian standards would have eliminated many great men of the past who lacked the physical and intellectual balance the founder of eugenics idealized. Are we really sure that fertility inducements to certain classes will have the result we expect? Kidd asked. In a swipe at the biometrical foundations of eugenics he added, "We cannot approach the study of these large questions armed only with a foot rule and a few biological generalizations."[37]

Nordau was less hostile to eugenics but thought its spokesmen were ludicrously simplistic when they talked about attractive physical and intellectual abilities as if they could readily be agreed upon and scientifically isolated. To say that people should marry beauty, health, and youth was to state the obvious; that was exactly what most young men and women tried to do within their range of acquaintances. "Eugenics, in order to modify the aspect and value of the nation," Nordau concluded, "must ameliorate not some select groups, but the bulk of the people, and this aim is not to be attained by trying to influence the love-life of the masses. It can be approached only by elevating their standard of life. . . . In one word: Eugenics, to be largely efficient, must be considered, not as a biological, but as an economical question."[38] To do so, of course, was to invalidate the fundamental premise of eugenics: that nature was a far more powerful agency of race deterioration or advancement than nurture. Eugenicists would eventually have to tackle the relationship, but few had doubts about it before the First World War.

The arguments raised by Huxley, Kidd, Nordau, and others were, as many eugenicists recognized, difficult to refute given the limited, often conflicting knowledge about the workings of human heredity. Despite efforts of eugenicist physicians to persuade their colleagues to the contrary, doctors either insisted that any proposals for sweeping premarital exams or certification were premature or that the problem was not the "raw material of the race" but the unhealthy environment in which the so-called unfit lived. In one medical meeting after another at which the question was discussed, a majority of the participants generally agreed with the eminent Dr. Henry Maudsley that far too little was known about inheritance to draw many conclusions. The great variety of personalities and talents existing even within the same family raised serious doubts about isolating hereditary causation. As the *Lancet* insisted on numerous occasions, before legislation could even be contemplated, the laws of heredity must be as firmly established as those of physics.[39]

A nonmedical critic, H. S. Shelton, commenting in 1912 on the debate, noted that despite the rhetoric on both sides, the actual proposals put forth by eugenicists to save the world were often very modest, if not "vague and minute." Opponents frequently went much further in spinning out the implications of positive eugenic proposals than did the eugenicists themselves. The latter appeared uncertain when asked who was to determine fitness and unfitness. What criteria would be applied and who would pay for eugenic marriages? What subsidies would be available for able children born of nonselective marriages? After all, Shelton noted, selective breeding was not the same as natural breeding; it did not produce permanent and stable varieties. Since the recognition of ability often came late in a person's life, as Galton himself had first observed, how was eugenic value to be identified in time to be transmitted through a eugenic marriage? Finally, Shelton asked, could positive selection really be separated from environmental conditions? If, for example, "the higher grades of men and women die childless is it because there is something in the structure of society which makes them do so?" Having launched his own barrage of provocative questions, Shelton, who described himself as a socialist, nevertheless concluded on a eugenicist note by conceding that there was indeed a genuine danger to the race because the "abler classes" were delaying marriage and restricting the size of their families. "The ages of Catholicism often sterilised their best in the convent," he recalled. "Do not we also sterilize our best? And can no remedy be found?"[40]

Spokesmen for the Eugenics Education Society were themselves divided over how to respond to their critics. Pearson, who deplored the society's campaign for race culture as premature and counterproductive, had his supporters within the organization. The young A. M. Carr-Saunders, the future director of the London School of Economics who had joined the society while a student at Oxford, agreed in 1913 that the state of biological knowledge was still too limited to support eugenic programs. While Pearson's opposition was met with charges that he was squandering Galton's legacy, Carr-Saunders was informed by several society members that incomplete knowledge had never precluded the advocacy of reform in other areas. In what became a standard reply, they insisted that all great changes entailed risk and speculation, and enough was known to warrant making a start before it was too late. No one had any illusions that public opinion was ready to embrace eugenic policies or the state so structured as to implement them, but the sooner the process of education and reform began the better.[41]

Defenders of the eugenics campaign were especially sensitive to the anger and ridicule that references to stock breeding stirred up in the popular press and scientific community. Pearson, in a 1913 letter to the *Times*, claimed that near the end of his life Galton himself saw that "the popular movement he had started was likely to outgrow its knowledge and feared that more evil than good might result from it." Indeed, since Galton's death, Pearson charged, this "science of race efficiency . . . has become a subject for buffoonery on the stage and in the cheap press. We are treated to 'eugenic' marriages and to 'eugenic' babies . . . which have nothing whatever to do with race welfare." The problem was compounded by Eugenics Education Society officials submitting to ridiculous interviews in which they made all sorts of foolish, unscientific pronouncements about breeding a new race.[42]

Pearson's angry criticism provoked a number of replies and assurances that eugenics recognized the complexity of the problem and did not advocate breeding an arbitrarily selected catalogue of human faculties. Its advocates did, however, believe certain characteristics, qualities, talents, and types of mind were desirable and could be found clustered in certain sectors of the population where they could be accentuated by selective breeding. They thought that there was more general agreement among the public, if not the scientific community, on what constituted fitness and civic worth than critics realized. Because of his narrow, restrictive concept of eugenics, Montague Crackanthorpe charged, Pearson was unable to see beyond his laboratory and recognize that eugenics involved people in all walks of life, not just in science. If the price to be paid for spreading the new gospel was a little humor or ridicule, it was one that all great movements encountered and would not, in the long run, prove harmful.[43]

Germ Plasm and Class

As eugenicists struggled to transform their elitist hereditarian theories into a science and an organized movement, they were well aware of the difficulties likely to be encountered in an age of expanding democracy and socialism. To many of them, the breeding of a new aristocracy free from the artificial limitations of class and wealth seemed on the surface to be the ideal eugenical outcome of a true democracy based upon ability and merit. But, as J. B. Haycraft warned, once people realized it was the few and not the many who would benefit "by a more complete and thorough sifting from all classes of the capable and intelligent," the results might not be acceptable to those who mistakenly equated democracy with social equality rather than equality of opportunity.

In raising this point in 1895, Haycraft pointed out that class relationships were already changing rapidly. He looked forward to the day when "class will . . . be separate from class by real organic differences, and the idea of social equality, ridiculous enough as it now appears to most of us, will then have become a demonstrated absurdity, as having contained the impossible idea that things that are unlike can be at the same time alike." Although even the laboring classes might advance in this biologically determined democracy, Haycraft was certain that as the position of the most capable members improved, the vast majority of workers would always remain relatively below their more capable superiors.[44]

This was an assumption that permeated the thinking even of the most democratic and socialist of eugenicists. No matter how much eugenicists insisted eugenic fitness was not a monopoly of any class and that their goal was to raise the hereditary level of all sectors of society, most of them before the war did not really doubt that the most desirable physical, mental, and moral qualities were concentrated primarily in the middle and upper middle classes. Some eugenicists were also prepared to extend the distribution curve into the ranks of skilled labor, but few ever descended much further into the social depths of germinal squalor, except to find the occasional deviation from the dysgenic norm.

At the same time, taking their cue from Galton, eugenicists spurned easy correlations between hereditary fitness and a hereditary aristocracy at the top of the social ladder. There was little obsequious tugging of the forelock on the part of people who wanted to replace not preserve the existing criteria of hierarchy. Darwin himself had warned in *The Descent of Man* of the evil consequences of primogeniture perpetuating the mental and physical weaknesses of elder sons while superior younger progeny were often unable to marry.[45] Galton added another dimension to this biological tragedy by demonstrating that younger sons were usually more intelligent and successful than their eldest brothers—a supposition reinforced by later biometric studies. They were used to buttress eugenic arguments for an aristocracy based, as Dean Inge put it, not on coats of arms or land but on genuine inbred superiority. His own utopian vision was of a Bushido-like new nobility dedicated to health, intellectual culture, heroic conduct, and the plentiful reproduction of children whose nobility would be severed from a need for any ancestral wealth.[46]

The prolonged struggle in 1910–11 to reform the House of Lords prodded Galton and Pearson among others to explain the biological contradictions in primogeniture and heredity. Concerned that the debate in Parliament failed to distinguish between the two, Galton wrote to the *Times* in March 1910 that since the latest research demonstrated that the eldest born were usually inferior to younger sons in natural gifts, primogeniture could not be defended on hereditary grounds. Consequently, "the claims of heredity would best be satisfied if all the sons of peers were equally eligible to the peerage, and a selection made among them." One cynical defender of the unreformed House of Lords reminded readers that Galton was himself a *third* son. Pearson, who was the second of two, detailed in a subsequent letter the greater tendency of the firstborn to be afflicted with tuberculosis, albinism, insanity, and criminality. Further biometric studies turned up additional weaknesses which were, in Pearson's judgment, compounded by the restrictive birthrate.[47]

The argument against the House of Lords, eugenicists were careful to point out, was not directed against a hereditary system. They believed, after all, enough in the inheritance of ability to feel certain that men who reached the peerage on their talents were very likely to produce superior offspring. Unfortunately, Pearson concluded, the House of Lords "has too often been recruited by mere plutocrats, by political failures, or by men who have not taken the pains necessary to found or preserve an able stock." What the Lords needed, then, was more, not less, heredity to justify its privileged role in the political system.[48] This would require the continual transfusion of new blood from proven stock, and most eugenicists were reasonably certain from which sector of society it would have to come.

W. C. D. Whetham, himself the son of a wealthy manufacturer, was fairly exceptional among eugenic scientists in his lament for the impending extinction of a peerage representing more than a thousand years of selection for character and ability. He described the dramatic decline in the size of noble families from 7.1 births in the 1830s to fewer than 3 in the modern age as "the systematic depletion of the best blood of the country." The dearth of talent in the military, the church, and in public service was a result of there no longer being enough younger sons of eminent families to enter these professions. Even if there were, however, their "well-ordered development of mind and body" was probably unsuitable to an era in which fevered precocity and specialization fostered by the competitive examination system had become the keys to success. Whetham likened the peerage to an endangered species when he complained of the people who devoted time, energy, and resources to preserve "low-grade aborigines," crocodiles, tigers, American buffalo, and the wild asses of Africa from extinction, but who acquiesced and even assisted "in the process of suppressing one of the finest manifestations of the human race, the well born, well bred, tried and trusted men and women of their own flesh and blood."[49]

No other defender of the Lords likened its titled members to aborigines and wild asses, though many of their critics certainly viewed them as archaic vestiges of an earlier time unable to accommodate themselves to a new, more democratic era. With the exception of the bishop of Ripon, who was determined to defend the principle, opponents of the reform of the Lords in both houses of Parliament did not themselves argue on the basis of heredity.[50] Instead, they emphasized history, tradition, continuity, and the need for preserving more than ever a system of constitutional restraint. But even as the old aristocracy was dying, eugenicists, including Whetham, were looking forward to the ascendancy of the new. Whatever gestures they might make toward the exceptional representatives of the lower classes, the eugenical Burkes and Debretts of Edwardian England knew that the "natural aristocracy" who would adorn the genealogical volumes of the future would come primarily from the ranks of the middle classes.

Using Charles Booth's ascending classification of the London population from A to X, Galton calculated in 1901 that the economic and civic worth of those in the top W and X middle-class categories was thousands of times greater than those at the other end of the alphabet. Babies in class X were likely to grow up to found major industries and create great wealth while others of their ability would guide and enlighten the nation. Recalling the impact of the French Protestants on the English economy in the seventeenth century, Galton promised that "the great gain that England received through the immigration of the Huguenots would be insignificant to what she would derive from an annual addition of a few hundred children of the classes W and X." He actually thought it was feasible to make an approximate estimate of the worth of a child at birth according to the class he is destined to occupy when an adult. Once the figure was known, it would be possible, he predicted, to determine how much it was worth spending to encourage early marriages among these offspring.[51]

Although Galton was somewhat reticent in singling out specific classes, his followers were not. In private correspondence in 1901 Pearson, whose earlier socialist predilections had perhaps made him reluctant to categorize specific classes in terms of their hereditary value, insisted that the middle classes were the key to race betterment. They had to be persuaded the stability of the nation depended upon their breeding fully while the weaker classes exhibited restraint.[52] Four years later, Pearson was much more open in his contention that the middle classes already formed a caste into which the bulk of the abler stocks in the community had drifted. Since exceptional parents, who numbered only about 0.5 percent of the community, produced exceptional sons at a rate more than ten times that of nonexceptional parents, he calculated elsewhere, their declining fertility was particularly alarming.[53]

The psychologist William McDougall, quoting Galton's scale of civic worth, thought the percentage of people with superior merit was higher than Pearson's estimate. He nevertheless agreed that they were "the product of a long-continued process of selection" now concentrated in "the upper middle class." Their continued progress was, however, jeopardized by their low fertility and the probability of their having to be revitalized by intermarriage with the more populous, mediocre classes.[54] Even those who, like Alfred Mumford, disputed that the overall level of civic worth was receding or that the race was in any way deteriorating still shared the conviction that the "best brains and most energetic natures" in the country were enjoyed by the upper middle classes who were ready to take the place of those members of the aristocracy who fell into deterioration and decadence.[55]

Despite repeated references to a new aristocracy, eugenicists insisted they were not consciously aristocratic or, more importantly, antidemocratic. They were not trying to turn the clock back, as their critics charged, but only make sure time did not run out on the race before it had an opportunity to regenerate itself.[56] The Oxford philosopher F. C. S. Schiller, who also dreamed of a "new and real nobility" based upon merit to replace "our present sham nobility, which has become a social institution that means nothing biologically," argued in 1912 and again in 1914 that the eugenical ideal was, nevertheless, not antidemocratic. It was "anti-egalitarian"—a distinction eugenicists often made—but so long as superiority and inferiority were acknowledged in society, the aristocratic principle, insofar as eugenics sanctioned it, was not wedded to any form of government.[57]

Eugenics then, as far as Schiller was concerned, had no quarrel with democracy so long as it did not commit the folly, knowingly or unknowingly, of trying to eradicate the best. Determining what was meant by the "best" was, even he conceded, a difficult problem eugenicists had not yet resolved. Schiller could offer little more of a rebuttal to their opponents than the reminder that "the human race has usually stumbled upon the truths it has achieved only after long wandering in the mazes of error." Having candidly admitted the "promised land" of understanding might only be reached after "many trials in the wilderness," Schiller insisted the eugenicist claim that ability was most heavily distributed in the upper ranks of society was not merely "a snobbish belief." On the contrary, it was a logical conclusion based upon the tendency of ability, even in the lower classes, "to be drafted off into the higher." What happened to this hereditary ability once it reached the superior classes was admittedly another question. One of the most pessimistic of the early eugenicists, Schiller feared that "the social machinery now proceeds to churn a great deal of the cream into scum."[58] Eugenics, of course, was trying to find a way to keep the cream from souring.

Schiller was not only responding to charges from eugenics opponents that the movement was riddled with class prejudices which made a mockery of its scientific pretensions, but he was also reacting to those within the movement who feared that much of the rhetoric emanating from the eugenic camp might warrant such charges. Saleeby, for example, in 1914 denounced the "poisonous growth" of "class eugenics" that had sprung up since Galton's death three years earlier. In an angry attack on Whetham, Schiller, and others who "are asking us to accept [some] social classes, and to reject others on eugenic grounds," he described as "absurd" and "ludicrous . . . wholesale generalizations about such infinitely heterogeneous aggregates of individuals as social classes." Saleeby charged class eugenics with being a pseudoscientific creation of biometry with its statistical notions of the distribution of germ plasm in different sectors of society. Its advocates, who usually had little biological or medical knowledge, seized upon the graphs, charts, and coefficient-of-correlation tables to justify attacks on the poor and to rationalize their unwillingness to aid the less fortunate. Modern genetics, by contrast, had shown how great the variations actually were within, not between, groups or stocks.[59]

As an early convert to Mendelism and a fierce opponent of Pearson, Saleeby repeatedly warned about the "mathematical divinations" of biometricians being used to justify the dominance of the so-called better classes over the lower classes. That the better classes were better looking, better fed, better rested, and better clad was true, he conceded, but these were hardly grounds on which to assert that race culture meant "keeping the lower orders in their place" and leaving the race to be recruited by their "betters—who are indeed rapidly ceasing to recruit the race at all."[60] Invoking the name of the great man himself, Saleeby warned, "directly the eugenist begins to talk in terms of *social* classes (as Mr. Galton has never done), he is skating on thin ice, and, if it lets him through, he will find the remains of his rash predecessors beneath it." The reason Galton in his later years had begun to use the more comprehensive term *civic worth* rather than *talent*, Saleeby explained in 1911, was his recognition of the complexity of good breeding and his emphasis upon positive parenthood in all classes.[61]

While it was true Galton generally avoided making class-specific references, Saleeby was stretching credulity to suggest that the founder of eugenics did not share the general belief of his followers that the greatest preponderance of civic worth was to be found among the professional middle classes. Certainly the rise of Mendelian genetics forced Galton to rethink some of his ideas about the mechanics of heredity, but it hardly resulted in his conversion to some form of biological democracy. He never acknowledged the criticisms of those moderate medical eugenicists such as F. W. Mott and L. N. G. Filon who, like the novelist H. G. Wells, believed brains and talent were socially ubiquitous and who doubted that Galton's concept of civic worth had any empirical validity. To Wells, "this idea of picking out high-scale individuals in any particular quality or group of qualities and breeding them, is not the way of nature at all. Nature is not a breeder; she is a reckless coupler and—she slays."[62]

None of these critics—some of them socialist, some Liberal, some Conservative—doubted that eugenic improvement would someday be possible, but they disagreed that the potent genetic material for this improvement was concentrated in any class. George Bernard Shaw could then argue that since "the bubble of Heredity has been pricked . . . and we know that there is no hereditary 'governing class' any more than a hereditary hooliganism . . . not only should every person be nourished and trained as a possible parent, but there should be no possibility of such an obstacle to natural selection as the objection of a countess to a navvy or of a duke to a char-woman."[63] Saleeby, who was otherwise offended by many of his fellow-Fabian's unconventional ideas, in this case had to agree.

Galton had no such democratic notions and shuddered whenever the extravagant Shaw chose to address the public on the subject of eugenics. But he also had little confidence in Saleeby's judgment and privately denied his unwanted acolyte's claim to be the true interpreter and keeper of the faith.[64] By the time of Galton's death in 1911, it was clear that a good many of Saleeby's colleagues in the Eugenics Education Society were displeased with his efforts to steer the movement away from the polarizing, class-conscious, elitist path it seemed to be taking. That was, after all, the direction a majority of them wanted to go. Nevertheless, Saleeby represented an important minority line of thought in the early eugenics movement which would become much more pronounced in the post–World War I period.

If a societal diagram were drawn dividing parental "sheep and goats," Saleeby hypothesized, it would not be horizontal at any level. Nor would it be vertical, as if the proportions of worth and unworth were the same in all classes. "Some would draw it diagonally," he knew, "counting most of the aristocracy good and most of the lowest strata bad; others would slope it the other way." For himself, Saleeby did not think it could be drawn at all since "the eugenic classification of mankind cuts right across the ordinary social classification." At every level of society, he concluded, "the quality of the germ-plasm which men and women carry is the supremely important thing."[65]

Whether desirable germ plasm was disproportionately clustered in the middle classes, as the majority of eugenicists instinctively knew, or distributed more randomly among all sectors of society, many true believers resolved their differences by agreeing that eugenic truth was an unfolding revelation. Though rooted in the biological and statistical sciences, it transcended them and, like religion, at some point had to be taken on faith. Given the contrast that early eugenicists saw between their actual knowledge and the awesome potential they envisioned in the control of heredity, it is not surprising that their propaganda was often suffused with biblical quotation and imagery. Eugenics was in many ways always more of a secular religion born of twentieth-century anxieties than a science fixed in provable natural laws.

Eugenics: A New Religion

Saleeby's advocacy of Fabian socialist programs and quarrels with unreconstructed social Darwinists made him increasingly uncomfortable in the Eugenics Education Society before the war. He wondered if many of the "unwary enthusiasts for Galton's views" recognized how much their implementation depended upon a profound alteration of existing beliefs, values, and institutions. There was something paradoxical about conservative, class-bound men and women, contemptuous of radical social welfare programs, advocating theories of eugenic race culture that were far more extreme in their implications than anything the dreaded socialists proposed. Their leap of faith was as great as, if not greater than, that of the most visionary of scientific socialists. However much Galton and his early disciples might have been offended by Shaw's lampooning of contemporary marriage and reproductive selection, they had to concur with the dramatist's warning that "there is now no reasonable excuse for refusing to face the fact that nothing but a eugenic religion can save our civilisation from the fate that has overtaken all previous civilisations."[66]

The agnostic Galton, for whom evolution was the final blow to his waning faith, was not unlike Shaw in his search for a new orthodoxy mired not in the fall of man but in his biological redemption. Sin, with its profound personal and social consequences, was for Galton and many of his followers not an eternal curse of spiritual or moral failure but a curable affliction of biological inadequacy. Their references to the healing effects of eugenic selection were filled with religious or quasi-religious allusions. "An enthusiasm to improve the race is so noble in its aim," Galton preached in 1901, "that it might well give rise to the sense of a religious obligation."[67] Like religion, the anthropologist A. E. Crawley added, eugenics "can have no higher duty than to insist upon the sacredness of marriage, but just as the meaning and content of that sacredness were the result of primitive science, so modern science must advise as to what this sacredness involves for us in our vastly changed conditions, complicated needs, and increased responsibilities."[68]

The merging of eugenics with religion was often vague, and Galton himself was not particularly lucid on the subject. Though he called for an "unambiguous and honest . . . revision of our religion to adapt it to the intelligence and needs of the present time," the Eugenes of his utopian Kantsaywhere worshiped a sort of fuzzy, omnipresent life force represented by judgmental ancestral spirits who closely watched the progress of selective breeding. This belief, or superstition, nevertheless inspired in the faithful a recognition of the smallness of actual life and the grandeur of potential life that was translated into "a unity of endeavour and a seriousness of action to the whole population."[69]

Churches were viewed as important potential allies in the promotion of eugenic marriages even if the faltering fertility of once bountiful clerical families, like that of the other professions, did not perhaps set the proper example.[70] Nevertheless, Galton was hopeful his gospel would be welcomed by every tolerant religion professing "far-sighted philanthropy, the acceptance of parentage as a serious responsibility, and a higher conception of patriotism."[71] Indeed, patriotism and religion were frequently interchangeable parts of the same argument. Saleeby, for example, in 1904 described eugenics as a new merging of religion and patriotism arising from "the practicable dream of this great biologist of the nineteenth century [Galton] who has been spared to preach a new gospel to the youth of the twentieth." The founder of Christianity said, "I am come that ye might have life, and that ye might have it more abundantly." This, Saleeby implied, was the message of the new messiah as well. The difference was that the modern creed turned the egoistic struggle for individual perfection toward the pursuit of racial perfection.[72]

A number of clergymen who, like the Reverend F. B. Meyer, were distressed by the differential birthrate and the absence of men of ability to lead the country, recognized the "symptoms of dry-rot in the foundation-timbers of the house of national well-being" and allied themselves to the eugenics movement. Meyer believed *eu* and genesis stood for "a high and holy conception" that went beyond science to merge religious and racial instincts necessary for true race regeneration. Reproduction of the race was, after all, of profound concern to eugenics and religion, he reasoned, so that the two were inextricably linked, like it or not.[73]

Other churchmen, such as W. R. Inge, Bishop Boyd Carpenter, and Edward Lyttelton, headmaster of Eton, also acknowledged the mutuality of interests between eugenics and religion but noted areas of conflict as well. For example, church support of charity and social welfare in the eyes of many eugenicists exacerbated the dysgenic consequences of the indiscriminate sanction of "loathly" marriages, as Arnold White described them. Nonconformists, as far as he was concerned, were no better than the national church where "incense and altar lights engage more of prelatical attention than the deterioration of our race."[74] Obversely, Galton often pointed out the lamentable effects on the race of religiously mandated celibacy in earlier generations, while Whetham, from his Cambridge vantage point, was sure that the legacy continued to hamper psychologically, though no longer legally, the marriages of eugenically desirable university dons.[75]

Despite some notable exceptions, eugenics was nevertheless associated in the minds of many clergy with a hard-hearted, scientific materialism derived from social Darwinist beliefs in the survival of the fittest. Some parsons resented eugenic implications that their care and ministrations were largely ineffective and even counterproductive when it came to improving the hereditarily determined condition of their inferior charges. By blessing the marriages of the poor, admonishing them to multiply, and, through indiscriminate charity, helping to preserve their dysgenic offspring, the clergy, eugenic critics suggested, actually did injury to the rest of society.

Clerical advocates of eugenics tried to overcome these inherent antagonisms by stressing what the two movements had in common rather than what separated them. Lyttelton, for example, insisted that even those eugenicists who spurned religion were basically Christian because of their reverence for the quality of human life. There was no doubt in his mind that the eugenic principle was "a living truth" that sprang from the nature of Christianity; its inculcation through education held out the promise of a reconciliation of scientific and religious faith.[76]

At the same time, Lyttelton, like most eugenicist clergy who discussed the issue, knew that the churches were at best ambivalent about their relationship to the new science. They were, as the Reverend James Peile, archdeacon of Coventry, warned in 1909, very conservative and cautious institutions. Since relatively few clergymen knew much about science, they found eugenics difficult to understand and feared its interest in selective breeding and race reproduction was somehow improper, even prurient. As a result, Peile explained, it took considerable courage for clergymen to support eugenics publicly, and he was not optimistic about the church's willingness to promote the cause until public opinion was sufficiently educated about the dangers of undesirable marriages and the proliferation of defective children.[77]

Montague Crackanthorpe hoped that Peile's appeal would help pave the way to a eugenic alliance with the clergy and prevent antagonism between the two complementary faiths. Both religion and eugenic science promoted "self sacrifice and beneficence to the whole of humanity, including generations to come." One emphasized pity and the other prevention, but both agreed that sufferers from "racial poisons . . . ought not to be allowed selfishly to lay their burden on their posterity. . . ." Pity had perhaps outweighed prevention in recent times, as reflected in the deteriorating quality of the race, but the pulpit, Crackanthorpe believed, could do much to redress the imbalance.[78] Even the lord mayor of London, in toasting the "Eugenic Ideal" at the opening banquet of the first International Eugenics Congress in 1912, assured his audience that he had often remonstrated with bishops and clergy to concern themselves more with the quality of the progeny resulting from the marriages they too readily solemnized.[79]

As Lady Margaret Professor of Divinity and, after 1911, dean of St. Paul's, Inge was the most visible and outspoken of eugenicist preachers, and there was no doubt in his mind about the deplorable effects of current marital fertility patterns on the race. The gloomy dean, as he was to be called by a later generation, launched the first issue of the *Eugenics Review* in 1909 by calling for the establishment of a "Christian-Biological morality." Since religion and eugenics shared a common ideal of individual perfection, Inge explained, they were, despite a somewhat different standard of values, indissolubly connected. Christian moralists and biologists might equally cite the Sermon on the Mount, "Be ye therefore perfect, even as your Father in heaven is perfect," or St. Paul's prayer, "that your spirit and soul and body may be preserved entire and without blame unto the coming of Christ." Perfection for Inge was manifest primarily in the "well-to-do classes" who were "on an average, among the finest specimens of humanity which have appeared since the ancient Greeks. It would be a dire calamity if they disappeared."

Unfortunately, the dean complained, a "half-hysterical humanitarianism" had, since the eighteenth century, corrupted social morality. Christianity suffered from a "fatty degeneration of the heart" that has diverted us from the perfection of the individual to the futile task of trying to perfect society. But, according to Inge, true Christian moralists and biologists agreed with Herbert Spencer that "you cannot get golden conduct out of leaden instincts" or, in the more homely aphorism frequently offered by eugenicists, "you cannot make a silk purse out of a sow's ear." Churches had to learn in the new century that instinct and superstition must give way to reason in the eradication of evil. "Be patient, my scientific friends, with us clergy," he pleaded, "for we are the natural custodians of various race-traditions which are by no means so absurd as they often appear in our homilies; but be quite firm with us in insisting that our common enemy must be met with modern weapons, and not with cross-bows and battle-axes for which most of us have such a sentimental affection."[80]

The *Eugenics Review* was grateful for any such signs of religious approbation before the war. The bishop of Bristol's suggestion to the local branch of the Eugenics Education Society in 1912 that the issuance of health certificates of life insurance might accompany the publication of the banns before marriage, was a welcome modification of nuptial customs, as was the archbishop of Canterbury's suggestion that if knowledge of a hereditary taint was withheld by either spouse the marriage should be annulled. But it was the bishop of Ripon, Boyd Carpenter, who was singled out by eugenicists as the most enlightened member of the episcopal bench because of his continual warnings about race suicide and diocesan appeals to diminish the proliferation of the unfit while encouraging an increase in the best classes.[81]

Boyd Carpenter, Inge, and a few other establishment dignitaries agreed with those lay eugenicists who believed the effectiveness of the church in the modern world depended upon its utilization of the sacraments of marriage and confirmation for purposes of racial selection. Whetham, a devout Anglican, for example, was sure eugenics was a new, divinely inspired variation on the old biblical injunction to multiply and replenish the earth. Its message was as relevant to the survival of a chosen people in a new age as the original mandate had been thousands of years earlier. Warning the church that its intellectual and spiritual evolution must keep pace with natural evolution, Whetham promised that enough was already known about heredity to warrant the preaching of a new evangel. A religion which only preaches to the failures of humanity, devoting its strength to mitigating their lot and increasing the probability of their racial survival, can never gain a hold on the abler classes. This was already evident, Whetham claimed, in the wave of materialism and unbelief spreading throughout the nation and affecting the birthrate of the worthy and more intelligent classes who no longer accepted the church's teachings on the sanctity and dignity of family life.[82]

According to Sir James Barr, president of the Liverpool branch of the Eugenics Education Society and, in 1912, of the British Medical Association, Nonconformists should have found eugenics particularly congenial to their beliefs. As a Presbyterian and a Mendelian, he saw how the teachings of Calvin and John Knox "on foreordination and predestination fits in exactly with modern views on inheritance from the germ plasm." Like a number of early converts to the eugenic faith, Barr tried to revitalize his old creed by mating it to the new. Character and ability were, in his judgment, just as predetermined or inherited as the shape of a nose, the color of hair, or the prospects for salvation. Where Knox and Calvin would have dealt very summarily with the unfit—the damned—the eugenicist, Barr claimed, was much more humane, but no less concerned about biological grace and genetic election.[83]

Although no religious denomination endorsed eugenics and many clergy were suspicious of its claims, eugenical considerations increasingly intruded into the demographic deliberations of church representatives. The National Birth-Rate Commission, cochaired by Inge and Boyd Carpenter and populated with clergy from each of the principal denominations, acknowledged the importance of eugenics to the question they were asked to investigate. But despite Inge's pessimistic convictions to the contrary, a majority of the members doubted the race was yet deteriorating and concluded that it was at present impossible to reach agreement on which human qualities and values were racially desirable.

There was, nevertheless, a general consensus among the commissioners that although the eugenic consequences of the decline in the birthrate were uncertain, the descent needed to be stopped and its differential features substantially altered. The villain, as far as the commission was concerned, was not some uncontrollable biological loss of progenitive vigor, but the deliberate and perhaps racially harmful adoption of neo-Malthusian or birth control practices by the ablest representatives of all classes.[84] It was a conclusion eugenicists endorsed. What to do about the spread of birth control was, however, another problem. If, as seemed likely in the changing moral, social, and economic climate of the new century, the deliberate restriction of family size was certain to increase, the possibility of endorsing birth control as a form of negative eugenics to curtail the disproportionately greater fertility of the unfit had to be addressed. Eugenicists were uncertain. The resolution of that uncertainty was central to eugenical thought and action not only before the First World War but, more important, in the decades that followed.

Five

Eugenics and Neo-Malthusianism

T he rise of the eugenics and birth control movements were parallel developments of the late Victorian and Edwardian years. Although Darwinism was not as central to the latter as it was to the former, supporters of both insisted that they were promoting policies of "rational selection" to compensate for the diminished effects of natural selection in the modern age. One of these effects was the persistence of a high rate of survival among people who in an earlier age would have seen their excessive numbers curtailed by disease and poverty. In the same vein, the two movements also shared a frustration with the failure of charity, the Poor Law, and increasingly costly social reforms to alleviate the ominous threat of poverty and halt the nation's slide toward supposed racial deterioration. Both were propelled into the public's consciousness around the turn of the century by the expanding awareness of the declining birthrate and the contentious debate about its causes and likely consequences. Despite explanations to the contrary, eugenicists and advocates of family limitation agreed the decline was primarily volitional rather than biological, and its differential characteristics were socially, politically, economically, and, ultimately, racially dangerous.

If, as the supporters of the two movements recognized, the fall in the birthrate was the result of a conscious change in the domestic strategy of married couples, the problems caused by existing patterns of reproduction could be solved by educating people to change those patterns. In effect, Neo-Malthusians and eugenicists were arguing from their different perspectives that the race was not caught in some irreversible, Malthusian dilemma or hereditarily deterministic biological vise from which there was no escape. Once the laws governing population growth and the distribution of inherited characteristics were understood, the exercise of rational selection would allow the Malthusian cycle of population outstripping subsistence to be broken or, in the case of eugenics, for enlightened, scientific race culture to take place.

As a result, the first birth control organization, the Malthusian League (founded in 1877 in the aftermath of the notorious obscenity trial of Charles Bradlaugh and Annie Besant), and the Eugenics Education Society (established thirty years later) were conceived primarily as agencies of education and propaganda.¹ Although the new, or Neo-Malthusians, as league members described themselves, looked to the old laws of classical liberal political economy, while eugenicists emphasized the newer laws of evolution and heredity, both were confident of their scientific and social scientific foundations. Indeed, they were convinced the future of the nation depended upon an alliance of the biological sciences with the social sciences to promote a talented, efficient population capable of coping with the complex challenges of the modern world. Nevertheless, the demographic lessons they tried to impart before World War I differed substantially in tactics and approach.

The Neo-Malthusians believed the population problem was fundamentally quantitative, and its solution was a negative policy of checking the excessive fertility of the laboring poor. Eugenicists, by contrast, thought mainly in qualitative terms and, in accordance with Galton's teachings, emphasized positive policies to encourage the fittest of all classes to bestow more of their rejuvenating progeny on the flagging race. In reality the two movements had more in common than they sometimes cared to admit, and Neo-Malthusians seeking respectability as well as credibility looked for an obvious alliance. Despite the care taken by the prominent, well-connected, middle- and upper-class men and women who took up the eugenics cause to steer clear of the somewhat disreputable Malthusian League, the two increasingly shared a number of the same members who believed their causes and methods were complementary rather than conflictual. Their conviction was not, however, to be translated into a formal alliance between birth control and eugenics until several years after The Great War.

Rational Selection: Selfish or Selfless?

Although most Edwardian analysts of the declining birthrate agreed by 1914 that it was primarily the result of the rapid spread of contraceptive practices since the 1870s, they differed widely in their explanations of people's motives. That the fall was sharpest among the middle and higher classes confirmed the belief of those who decried the selfishness and irresponsibility bred in an age of luxuriant materialism and secularism. Small families, as the unmarried bishop of London, A. F. Winnington-Ingram, complained in 1905, were the inevitable outcome of the "miserable gospel of comfort which is the curse of the present day."² His colleague Boyd Carpenter, whose eleven children perhaps compensated for the celibacy of several other censorious prelates, agreed that the shirking of parenthood in the "fashionable marriages" of the day was an "indulgence in unsubdued lust" that threatened the quality even more than

the size of the race.[3] Both men were instrumental in persuading the Lambeth
Conference in 1908 to denounce contraception as medically dangerous and
morally subversive. In calling for a return to the Christian ideal of a fruitful,
reproductive marriage, the bishops closed their deliberations with a eugenic
warning about race suicide and the "danger of deterioration whenever the race
is recruited from the inferior and not from the superior stocks."[4]

Similar condemnation of the "sins of cowardly but comfortable living"
added a subjective touch to the numerous medical diagnoses of contraceptively
induced diseases allegedly caused by thwarting nature. Even those physicians
who were divided over the physiological effects of family limitation recognized its eugenic implications. The *Lancet*, for example, like the *British
Medical Journal*, the *Practitioner*, and other medical publications, was cautious about taking sides in the often emotional debate over whether or not
contraception caused everything from mild palpitations to cancer, insanity,
and suicide. But they lamented the end of the large middle-class Victorian
family; its demise had seriously depleted the nation's stock of moral and
intellectual talent and allowed "increased room for a growth of tares by which
the harvest of a better humanity would be choked."[5] According to the medical
officers Arthur Newsholme and T. H. C. Stevenson, the more prosperous
classes, in their desire to preserve and enhance their "standard of comfort,"
had of late demonstrated "an almost pagan lack of communal responsibility."[6]

To others, however, such as Dean Inge, far from being a consequence of
wanton self-indulgence, the decline in the birthrate was a selfless and reasonable attempt by the "best men and women" to cope with the rising cost of
living so as to be able to provide adequately for those children they could still
afford.[7] As the economist J. A. Hobson explained, the middle classes were
more concerned with comfort, personal freedom, and the education of their
children. The rational control of fertility was a new and important weapon in
the pursuit of good health, opportunity, and improved status in society.[8] For
the more biologically minded Havelock Ellis, the smaller, planned families of
the middle and upper classes as well as those of the skilled artisans were
progressive manifestations of evolutionary intellectual individuation to be
expected in advanced societies. It was therefore natural that the most intelligent and rational classes were the first to respond to the changing economic
and social environment by taking control of their reproductive instincts. The
era of high fertility was over, Ellis predicted; it was only a matter of time
before the same rising expectations and more refined values of the middle and
higher classes would commend themselves to married couples further down
the social ladder.[9]

According to the Fabian Society's 1906 analysis of differential fertility, this was already happening among skilled workers who realized that another child would threaten their standard of living and would diminish opportunities for other members of the family. Hobson, who saw nothing threatening in the differential birthrate, told the National Birth-Rate Commission in 1914 that this realization was not surprising since most people were concerned with preserving the quality of life if they could. Workers were even more insecure than the middle classes whose prudence and forethought they had been admonished for nearly a century to emulate. Now some of them were responding and others would surely follow.[10]

Nearly all of the arguments in favor of family limitation before the First World War contrasted the growing importance of a thoughtful, qualitative, healthy activism in the domestic decisions of the younger generation with the passive acquiescence to reproductive fate accepted by their parents and grandparents. Opponents by contrast often tended to impugn the motives and morals of those who restricted their families. Selfishness was compounded by a want of patriotism, religion, and racial responsibility. Underlying the resistance was often a pervasive fear of unleashed sexuality and the dangers it held for a society whose institutions, values, morals, and beliefs, like its economic and imperial future, suddenly seemed uncertain and forbidding.

Cause and Effect

Whatever value judgments Edwardians made about the practice of family limitation, nearly all of them agreed its rapid adoption was generally associated with the depression in agriculture and trade that began in the 1870s and, more specifically, with the sensational trial in 1877 of Charles Bradlaugh and Annie Besant for republishing the American Charles Knowlton's long-forgotten birth control pamphlet, *The Fruits of Philosophy*.[11] The depression, they reasoned, convinced people Britain's extraordinary economic expansion was coming to an end and with it the seemingly limitless opportunities which had buoyed up earlier generations. It prompted the more intelligent and prudent classes to evaluate their status and to reassess the number of children they were able to support in comfort while maintaining or improving their families' status. The Bradlaugh-Besant trial thrust the issue of birth control before the public at this critical juncture, providing the means to facilitate, for better or for worse, an increasingly desired end. When in the 1890s and opening years of the new century Pearson, the Webbs, H. G. Wells, Shaw, and Ellis, among others, began to analyze the fall in the birthrate, they invariably connected it with the prosecution more than two decades before. Married couples, they assumed, were suddenly made aware of the possibilities for the "artificial sterilisation of matrimony" and the conception of children was transformed from an involuntary to a voluntary condition.[12]

Reviewing the profound effects of this transformation in her 1914 *Report on the English Birth Rate*, Ethel Elderton acknowledged that the impact of the Bradlaugh-Besant trial and the Neo-Malthusian movement it spawned was not recognized at the time. Within thirty years, however, "it legitimised the teaching of practical methods for the limitation of the family [and] revolutionised the sexual habits of the English people." One of the results had been a sharp reduction in the pressure "which carried an English population as the great colonizing force into every quarter of the globe, and it may be that coming centuries will recognize the Bradlaugh trial as the knell of the British colonial empire—and as the real summons to the Slavs, Chinese and other fertile races to occupy the spare places of the earth."[13]

The fusion of demography with imperial anxieties, economic worries, complaints about taxes, and the rising cost of living pervaded eugenical and noneugenical arguments about the declining birthrate and its relationship to the spread of neo-Malthusianism. Both the *Fertility of Marriage Census* and the National Birth-Rate Commission wove these themes into their tapestries of potential national deterioration. In rejecting biological explanations for waning fertility they recalled that the Neo-Malthusians first "showed the possibility of separating marriage and parentage." But their views would not have been accepted so quickly "had not the desire for children been much diminished owing to some social or economic cause." As the commissioners concluded, smaller families were the result of couples' trying to improve or preserve their position in an age of economic uncertainty, contracting opportunities, rising costs, declining profits, and soaring taxes.[14]

The reasons for the rapid adoption of family limitation were far more complex than the late Victorians and Edwardians recognized. Their simplistic association of the falling birthrate with the Bradlaugh-Besant trial and the rise of neo-Malthusianism failed to take into account that among the middle and higher classes the tendency toward smaller families appears to have started a generation earlier than the date of the prosecution, although it did not begin to have a noticeable impact on the aggregate vital statistics until the 1880s. Even Bradlaugh and Besant and the founders of the Malthusian League implicitly recognized this when they insisted that all they were trying to do was make available to the poor contraceptive information already accessible to couples in the higher ranks.[15]

In addition, the fertility decline was by no means limited to Great Britain. Most European countries, many of the colonies, and the United States experienced varying rates of decline unguided by birth control organizations, which generally appeared much later than in Britain. Nevertheless, zealous Neo-Malthusians over the years attributed the relentless drop in the crude and corrected birthrates after 1877 in their country to the trial and the subsequent propagandist activities of the Malthusian League. The more thoughtful of their supporters, however, agreed, sometimes with their opponents, that the appearance of their movement fortuitously coincided with a desire for limiting the size of families. Neo-Malthusianism was itself more a manifestation of a dramatic shift in private domestic values and objectives than a significant cause.

Many of the social and economic reasons offered for this shift—urbanization, the depression in trade and agriculture, greater longevity, the diminished economic value of children in an age of restrictive legislation and compulsory education, and the rising costs of their upkeep and schooling—seem to fit later models of the theory of demographic transition. But as Michael Teitelbaum recently concluded, after the construction of several alternative explanatory models based upon elaborate multiple linear regression analyses, subtle, unmeasurable cultural variables were probably as significant as the explanatory socioeconomic factors central to the theory of demographic transition. In other words, Teitelbaum found, perhaps not surprisingly, that the reasons for the fall in the birthrate in Britain were multicausal and were as qualitative as they were quantitative. Given the nature and complexity of the evidence and the difficulties of extracting viable reasons for the intimate behavior of individuals from aggregate statistics, Teitelbaum decided, with admirable humility and caution, that trying to disentangle them "is likely to be a fruitless task."[16]

The Edwardians were not so easily intimidated and rarely hesitated to offer explanations for the striking changes they witnessed in the reproductive behavior of their contemporaries. But the evidence for economic causation was, even then, particularly confusing and contradictory. Although the depression in agriculture was much more severe than in industry and trade in the last thirty years of the century, the decline in fertility occurred, with regional and occupational variations, in both rural and urban areas. At the same time profits and the availability of investment capital suffered during the recurrent trade slumps that marked the Great Depression of the 1880s and 1890s, prices fell while real wages and income rose somewhere between 17 and 25 percent a decade. Although the pattern began to reverse itself after 1896, resulting in the growth in real income being much less in the new century and the cost of living much higher, the fall in birthrate had already become statistically significant two decades earlier. During the late Victorian years, when people began to limit their families, industrial output doubled, the structure of employment actually became more stable, leisure and occupational opportunities multiplied, and the average standard of living improved substantially, particularly for those classes whose birthrates dropped first.[17]

To further complicate socioeconomic analysis, the restrictions on child labor and the introduction of compulsory education that kept children out of the workforce and, many believed, made them economically less valuable, appeared to have little effect on the relatively higher fertility of the unskilled working classes who should have most felt the impact on their domestic pocketbook. On the contrary, it was the middle and upper classes, those least affected by the new legislation, who first began reducing the size of their families. As a final irony, despite the claims of the Neo-Malthusians that their "crusade against poverty" was directed at improving the lives of the laboring poor by reducing their numbers, again it was couples at the other end of the social scale who most quickly adopted the contraceptive practices recommended to their social inferiors.

Galton had predicted just such an outcome a decade before the Bradlaugh-Besant trial when, in 1869, he warned that the Malthusian preventive check of late marriage might be tolerable if applied to all segments of the population, but "as it is put forward as a rule of conduct for the prudent part of mankind to follow whilst the imprudent are necessarily left free to disregard it . . . it is a most pernicious rule of conduct in its bearing upon race." Because Malthusianism was dependent upon such hereditary qualities as prudence and foresight, neither of which were much in evidence in the most fertile, impoverished classes, its implementation would mean the ruination of the "breed." Galton protested as "monstrous" the possibility "that the races best fitted to play their part on the stage of life, should be crowded out by the incompetent, the ailing, and desponding."[18] His cousin Charles Darwin expressed similar concerns in *The Descent of Man*, while advocating competitive sexual selection as the key to human progress. He agreed with Malthus that "all ought to refrain from marriage who cannot avoid abject poverty for their children," but invoked Galton's warning, "if the prudent avoid marriage whilst the reckless marry, the inferior members tend to supplant the better members of society."[19]

Despite the inflated posturing of the newly established Malthusian League, the falling birthrate in the 1880s and 1890s was often associated more with the age of marriage than with contraception. Several of the first inquiries into differential fertility explained variations in terms of the later age and reduced frequency of marriage experienced by the more prosperous classes. Early marriage, as Galton explained, meant larger families, the existence of more generations within a given period of time, and the prolific, geometric growth of the race. However much he admired Malthus, whose work he described as "the rise of a morning star before a day of free social investigation," Galton believed the "impulsive and self-serving" would continue to ignore all appeals to rational self-restraint. As a result, "those whose race we especially want to have, would leave few descendants, while those whose race we especially want to be quit of, would crowd the vacant space with their progeny" so that the race would actually deteriorate while growing larger. In substituting the positive eugenical policy of early marriage and vigorous procreation among the better classes for the Malthusian idea of marital restraint, Galton, like Darwin, believed that the laws of sexual selection would assure that the most vigorous and able stock would "breed down the others in a very few generations."[20]

More detailed studies by Newsholme, Stevenson, and others, soon demonstrated that it was not the age of marriage but the number of children born to those who were married that was statistically meaningful. The new Malthusianism, they recognized, with its emphasis upon contraception to control fertility within marriage rather than the avoidance of marriage itself, had changed the population question dramatically. Indeed, the Neo-Malthusians, like the eugenicists, decried, but for different reasons, the deleterious effects of prolonged celibacy. They proclaimed the physiological, psychological, and moral benefits of youthful marriage in which normal sexual relations facilitated by contraception assured domestic comfort and happiness. Their ideal "small family system" contained two or three carefully spaced children who would, like their parents, live healthier, longer lives free of vice, disease, anxiety, and chronic poverty.[21] Unfortunately from the eugenic standpoint, most of these desirable families were likely to be those favored with genetic grace, and their offspring were too few to assure the continued qualitative advancement of the race.

As early as 1886 Karl Pearson noted that "the Neo-Malthusians have by their teaching very sensibly lowered the birth-rate, but all the evidence I can collect seems to show that this lowering of the birth-rate is at the expense of national vigour, for it has taken place among the physically and mentally fitter." This was, of course, exactly what Galton had feared. Pearson had no quarrel with orthodox Malthusianism and quoted John Stuart Mill's premise in *Principles of Political Economy* that no one had the right to bring people into the world who will live at the expense of others. In a socialist society where the state guaranteed employment and an adequate wage, it might someday be possible, Pearson speculated, to mandate, as Mill implied, the size of families. But for the forseeable future "in our present capitalistic society," the only option appeared to be voluntary restraint on marriage and reproduction which, he thought, would not have much effect on the working classes. He was, however, certain "any doctrine which does not distinguish between the fit and the unfit is a grave national danger." This he claimed was the principal flaw in neo-Malthusianism.[22]

Turning down an invitation to address the Malthusian League's annual meeting in 1894, Pearson explained that while he too favored the rational limitation of the fertility of the poor, he thought it more important to increase selection among the better stocks. The unstated assumption was, of course, that the two could not possibly be one and the same. Neo-Malthusianism as far as Pearson was concerned was having just the opposite effect in being adopted by the thrifty, prudent, ablest members of society while the worst had more freedom than ever to replicate their deficiencies. He recommended to the league that it adopt a new motto: Limitation of population, but in the foremost place limitation of bad stock.[23] Though a socialist, Pearson was always far more critical of the lack of eugenic discrimination in Malthusian League propaganda than he was of its retrogressive, anticollectivist defense of classical laissez-faire liberalism.[24]

Quality versus Quantity:
Neo-Malthusianism and Negative Eugenics

Pearson and Galton's contention that there was an intrinsic conflict between voluntary family limitation and eugenics tenuously prevailed in eugenic circles before the First World War. Their charge was reinforced by the numerous official and unofficial tabulations of differential fertility and biometric studies demonstrating the greater distribution of physical and mental strength among younger sons in successful families. It was commonplace for critics of neo-Malthusianism to list the great men such as Shakespeare, Walter Scott, Tennyson, Lord Nelson, the Duke of Wellington, John Wesley, and countless others who never would have been born if the present limitations on children had been in force. The eminent gynecologist Dr. John Taylor, noting in 1906 the "absence of men of surpassing genius," suspected they had been "willfully prevented" from coming into being by the "vicious and unnatural habits of the present generation." He likened the "mischievous meddling with great natural forces" to "little children playing with edge-tools or with fire."[25]

The first "Studies in National Deterioration" undertaken by the Galton Eugenics Laboratory demonstrated the higher frequency of neurosis, insanity, tuberculosis, and criminal tendencies among the elder born of exceptionally small families. "If this special incidence on the earlier born be found to be true for other forms of pathological heritage," Pearson warned in 1910, "we have a very serious factor of national deterioration introduced by the growing limitation of the family." It was time to recognize, as human fertility changed from "the natural to the artificial phase," that similar changes in the past had led to the collapse of the great civilizations of the ancient world. In an age of political democracy, municipal hygiene, state support, medical progress, and unlimited charity, a selective death rate weeding out the incapables could no longer assure the dominance of the fit; the only hope was an increased, eugenically determined, selective birthrate.[26]

The weakness of the Neo-Malthusians, as far as most eugenicists were concerned, was their inability to recognize that the critical issue was not the size of the population but its quality. Family limitation as a form of negative eugenics directed against the unfit was not in and of itself undesirable. Like segregation, institutionalization, or even compulsory sterilization, which aroused growing interest among eugenicists before the war, contraception might help control the proliferation of inherited physical and mental defects. Unlike most restrictive plans, however, family limitation was almost entirely dependent upon the voluntary compliance of the sort of people who were least inclined to be educable and responsible. Moreover, as William McDougall wrote, none of the negative proposals would have much effect upon increasing the genetic contribution of that upper 10 percent of intellectual, highly cultivated people of "eminent civic worth" who had of late seized upon family limitation to facilitate the advance of their work and sustain their way of life.[27]

One eugenicist after another described Malthus's failure to see that economic, technological, and scientific advances would eclipse the growth of population and, for better or for worse, make it possible to sustain a much greater number of the poor and incapable than he ever would have thought possible. Throughout the first half of the nineteenth century, Whetham recalled, "Malthus and his school of economists cried out for some power to arrest 'this devastating torrent of children.' The flood has been stayed. And still we are not satisfied. We are coming to understand that it is the quality rather than the quantity of the population that is important." Although the race was ceasing to improve and beginning to deteriorate because of differential fertility, Whetham was comforted by the knowledge that the downturn had only been going on for about thirty years. Almost simultaneously, however, "by the blessing of Providence, our eyes have been opened, and we are become like gods, knowing good and evil. The future of our race is placed in our hands to mould as we will."[28] Many of the first generation of eugenicists were filled with a sense of transcendent power and destiny and talked much about the rational and conscious fashioning of the human race as a form of

sociobiological salvation. The alternative to solving the true population problem, they argued, was not famine, as Malthus predicted, but something far
worse—biological starvation.[29]

If leading eugenicists had serious doubts about the consequences of neo-
Malthusianism for their cause, the Neo-Malthusians were themselves ambivalent about eugenics as a potential ally in the fight against indiscriminate
breeding. Its origins in an obscenity prosecution of two radical secularists
and public advocacy of the joys of carefree marital sexuality linked neo-
Malthusianism in the minds of decent society to the prurient, the salacious,
and the atheistic. It was, as Neo-Malthusians were the first to admit, a difficult
legacy to shed. They were always eager for the approbation of the prominent
and well connected to give their movement credibility and respectability. The
Malthusian League coveted with only occasional requital the endorsement of
the doctors, lawyers, scientists, university academicians, peers, and prelates
who, along with other race-conscious middle- and upper-class ladies and
gentlemen, adorned the roster of the Eugenics Education Society. Sir James
Barr, one of the society's medical luminaries, declined to touch the contentious subject of contraception in a public lecture on eugenics in 1911, although, unlike many of his professional and eugenicist colleagues, he personally believed the practice to be harmless and potentially beneficial to the
improvement of the race.[30] As late as 1917 Major Darwin confessed to Havelock Ellis that most of the men and women in the Eugenics Education Society
still considered public discussion of birth control, as it was increasingly called,
distasteful.[31]

However much Neo-Malthusians might have envied the social and professional cachet of the Eugenics Education Society, they challenged the organization's positive Galtonian tactics of encouraging large families among the
select. The problem, as they saw it, was at the other end of the social curve
where the curtailment of overpopulation held out the only reasonable hope for
significant racial improvement. In spite of this fundamental difference, many
Neo-Malthusians believed eugenicists were natural if reluctant allies in the war
against racial and national deterioration. Both, after all, rejected the prevailing
belief that changes in the social and economic environment could by themselves permanently improve the condition of the poor and the unfit. Charity,
expensive welfare programs, expanded education, and extensive medical intervention were futile and frequently counterproductive.

For Neo-Malthusians poverty was the symptom of racial disease, overpopulation the cause, and contraception the cure. According to their liberal utilitarian economic philosophy, the more individual workers took responsibility for
themselves, reduced the size of their families and, as a result, the number of

surplus laborers, the higher their wages would rise, in accordance with the law of supply and demand, and their living conditions improve. The health of exhausted mothers and their frail offspring would get dramatically better and the quality of working-class family life would soar. These individual improvements would be translated into racial improvements by the elimination of millions of unwanted, undernourished, sickly children who were barely surviving on public and private charity. Eugenicists in particular should welcome such a scenario, Neo-Malthusians reasoned. Free from the sterilizing economic burdens of sustaining the genetically suspect, impoverished masses, responsible, taxpaying, middle-class men would be more inclined to take young brides and sire two or three promising children.

This eugenic dimension to what was to become the birth control movement was evident in the arguments of secularists such as Austin Holyoake, who figured prominently in the founding of neo-Malthusianism. As early as 1870 he was concerned about the better classes being overrun by the poor and saw the proliferation of children among the unhealthy populace as one of the many evils to be cured by family limitation.[32] At her trial seven years later, Annie Besant insisted the question of race quality could not be separated from that of quantity and cited Darwin, Spencer, and Galton as evidence. Neo-Malthusianism, she explained, was completely in tune with evolution, and she predicted the use of "artificial checks" as a form of rational selection would in three or four generations produce a "splendid race." These checks were more important than ever in modern societies where natural selection was no longer applicable because the weak, diseased, and incapable were being preserved to pass on their infirmities to the detriment of the race. She was as aware as Galton of the danger that only the "wise and prudent" would respond to Neo-Malthusian propaganda, leaving "the selfish and the foolish . . . more room to increase to the detriment of the race." But neither he nor Darwin offered a viable solution to the dilemma caused by the preservation of the weak and the sickly, she told the court. We do, and in a way that will not "interfere with the natural and healthy play of the feeling of mankind."[33]

Though the restless Mrs. Besant soon abandoned neo-Malthusianism for socialism and theosophy, others continued to urge a merging of Darwinism and Malthusianism to assure that the struggle for selection was qualitative, not quantitative. Neo-Malthusianism with its program of rational selection was not in conflict with natural selection, as critics charged, they argued, but complemented it in the quest for race improvement. While it was true that Darwin himself, the father of a large family, was reluctant to limit human increase, a writer in the Malthusian League's journal, the *Malthusian*, observed in 1882, the great naturalist was nevertheless aware of the need for intellect to prevail over blind sexual appetite and therefore strenuously asserted the importance of the careful selection of parentage.[34]

Much of the debate about natural selection and heredity within the Neo-Malthusian camp focused upon family limitation as an agency of what would later be termed "negative eugenics." In the second issue of the *Malthusian*, founded in 1879, a correspondent, G. A. Gaskell, entreated the Malthusian League to direct its energies "toward the destruction of the worst stock in the species." These were "the careless, the selfish and the foolish" within whose populous ranks the worst hereditary conditions were allowed to flourish because of our emotional and intellectual interference with natural selection. As a consequence, "the weak survive and the race degenerates." Several years later, in 1885, Gaskell alluded to the dangers of differential fertility and, inspired by the American Lester Ward's *Dynamic Sociology*, raised the possibility of selective breeding in conjunction with restrictions on the marriage and procreation of the diseased and incapable. Galton and eugenics were first mentioned in the *Malthusian* later the same year in the reprint of an article on "The Population Question" taken from the *Journal of Science*. The writer, fearful neo-Malthusian policies would compound the racial dangers of the differential birthrate, cited "the truths" recently given prominence under the name "Eugenism" by Mr. Galton to support restrictions on marriage.[35]

The Malthusian League was obviously under considerable pressure to pay more attention to qualitative issues. A resolution to speak out more forcefully against people with hereditary diseases having children was passed unanimously at the 1885 annual meeting.[36] In conceding the point, Charles Robert Drysdale, the Edinburgh-born physician who was the first president of the league and its principal financial supporter until his death in 1907, made sure that references to specific classes were avoided. Drysdale, who was more skeptical than many of his members about the relevance of natural selection and the validity of hereditary causation, always believed family limitation was "an infinitely better agent for producing an improved stock" than anything proposed by biologically minded social reformers.[37] Most disabilities afflicting the poor were neither inherited nor transmissible, he argued, but were the direct result of the endemic poverty caused by overpopulation. During the deliberations of the Inter-Departmental Committee on Physical Deterioration in 1904, Drysdale rejected the explanations of Darwinians such as Pearson and endorsed the testimony of those witnesses who claimed that intellectual and physical fitness as well as hereditary afflictions were to be found randomly distributed in stocks throughout society, not in specific classes.[38]

Drysdale was strongly supported from the 1880s on by the radical journalist and politician J. M. Robertson, who declined to play the eugenic variations on the neo-Malthusian theme that others found harmonious. Both men were strongly environmentalist in outlook, deplored as barbaric the misapplication of the idea of natural selection to contemporary society, and rejected the argument of positive eugenicists that the so-called fit should have much larger families. What is fitness? Robertson asked after reading Galton. It was non-sense in this age of "conscious progress" to claim that great brains came any longer from some primitive struggle for survival.[39] The eugenicist ideal of "*large* and thriving families," he argued in response to Galton's paper to the Sociological Society in 1904, was a contradiction in terms. The psychic, physiological, and economic costs of excessive childbearing were paid by people in all classes, not only the poor. Eugenicists, above all, Robertson said, should appreciate the positive correlation between quality and diminished quantity.

Drysdale's wife, Dr. Alice Vickery, also a physician, agreed, and added that population growth among the poor was a far more important problem at the moment than the quality of hereditary stock. Like her husband she was disturbed by the antidemocratic tendency of eugenicists to link favored racial qualities to particular classes. If qualitative breeding was possible at all, they countered, it would apply to all levels of society and involve reducing the number of incapable people who encumbered the progress of every class. Only in this sense could they concede that the "artificial control of the birthrate is a condition of eugenics."[40] These reservations aside, the Drysdales concluded, the Neo-Malthusians saw no barrier to cooperation with eugenic advocates of race culture and welcomed them as fellow reformers. To underline this cautious gesture, the Malthusian League adopted a new slogan, Non Quantitas Sed Qualitas, which remained emblazoned on its banners and publications until the organization's demise in 1927.[41]

It was a concession eugenicists scarcely welcomed, if they noticed it at all. Pearson, whom Drysdale described as a former Malthusian gone over to preaching to the upper classes about the need for more children to crush out the inferior progeny of the degenerate poor, wanted nothing to do with the disreputable league. He declined to dignify its accusations with a public response, but complained privately to Galton of the abuse that he and others had to endure whenever they challenged the "doctrine of limitation." At one point he denied ever suggesting the rich should have many more children than the poor, only that "the mentally and physically fit should not have a low fertility."[42] For his part, the elderly Galton in 1906 only vaguely recalled the Bradlaugh-Besant trial and was barely aware of the existence of "a certain Malthusian League" that apparently sent out pamphlets asking new parents, "Why have any more children?" Pearson began sending his friend copies of the *Malthusian*, one issue of which reminded readers that when solicited some twenty years earlier to help a physician, Dr. Henry Allbutt, struck from the medical register for publishing birth control instructions in *The Wife's Handbook*, Galton had not responded. The old man confessed to Pearson, "I almost wholly forgot the case of Dr. Allbutt."[43]

Despite repeated sniping at eugenicists and others, particularly physicians and clergymen, who spurned their overtures, an increasing number of Neo-Malthusians counted their success not in public approbation but in the plummeting birthrate statistics. They likened themselves to earlier vilified reformers who in the face of constant harrassment, occasional prosecution, and angry condemnation endured until their campaigns succeeded. Neither medical warnings, ecclesiastical denunciations, military anxieties, nor emotional, patriotic appeals were now likely to deter millions of married couples in the present or the future from restricting the size of their families. With the birthrate at the end of the century already some 30 percent lower than when the Malthusian League was founded, a longtime member wrote in 1899 it was perhaps time to examine additional questions about marriage and heredity raised by the league's success. The old and single rallying cry of "Reduce! Reduce! should now give equal place to a consideration of quality as well as quantity in human beings." He represented those in the movement who thought there was indeed some danger the fit were already reducing their numbers rapidly "in face of an equally mischievous multiplication of the proletariat," and who urged that the subject of eugenics have a permanent place in the columns of the *Malthusian*.[44]

So long as C. R. Drysdale controlled the journal it was open to eugenic considerations of the population question, but he insisted that not enough was known about heredity to propose qualitative answers. By contrast, there was no lack of solid evidence about the evils of overpopulation, and these, the editor explained, must remain the principal concern of the league.[45] While Drysdale's son and successor, Charles Vickery Drysdale, an electrical engineer, concurred, he was much more sympathetic to eugenics and interested in turning that movement away from its "futile and insane" promotion of larger families among the fit.[46] Although his mother, Alice Vickery, assumed the presidency of the league on her husband's death in 1907, the younger Drysdale and his wife, Bessie, a former schoolteacher, were firmly in control of the organization. They coedited the *Malthusian* into the war years until Drysdale's work at the admiralty and conflicts with socialists such as H. G. Wells and Eden Paul combined to force their temporary resignation. One of the attractions of eugenics for the virulently antisocialist heirs to what was largely a family-financed operation was their belief that the eugenic emphasis upon individual responsibility, competitive achievement, and the qualitative advancement of the race could help stem the tide of collectivist mediocrity which in their eyes threatened to overwhelm the nation.

The Unforged Alliance

When, after an initial coolness to its founding, C. V. Drysdale decided to join the Eugenics Education Society in 1909, it was with the hope that neo-Malthusianism would provide the practical direction needed to transform eugenics into a functional agency for social and racial improvement. Their collaboration would mark the start of a new era, he predicted.[47] While resenting the "cocksure and patronising tone" of such pronouncements, the *Eugenics Review* took note of the Malthusian League's assurances "that the question of restricting the birth of the unfit has always been a cardinal doctrine of Neo-Malthusianism." It was not, however, pleased with the league's commitment to the improvement of the environment by making it less crowded as a necessary first step to race regeneration, nor with its grossly distorted depiction of positive eugenics as some sort of unscientific reversion to a precivilized state of nature. Positive eugenics has always welcomed the discouragement of parenthood on the part of the "unworthy," the *Review* claimed. The two policies were not in opposition but mutually complementary and indispensable.[48]

In conceding family limitation had a complementary role to play in eugenic race culture, the *Eugenics Review* was responding less to the jibes of the Malthusian League than it was to pressures within the Eugenics Education Society itself. Drysdale, for example, was moved to join the Society by the election of the barrister Montague Crackanthorpe to the presidency in 1909. A neighbor and close friend of Galton, Crackanthorpe was a conservative, classical Malthusian who had, since the 1870s, been an advocate of smaller families for all classes. Under the family name of Cookson, which he later surrendered in return for a Westmoreland estate, Crackanthorpe in 1872 challenged the Victorian assumption that large families were intrinsically better than small. He called for some new Malthusian check on excessive fertility to alleviate the poverty of the poor and to improve the opportunities and quality of life for the middle classes. While it would be most beneficial for the "lowest strata of the English people it must begin . . . with those above them." Because of his concern with basic subsistence, Malthus never understood the importance of "regulative control" for the middle classes as well, Crackanthorpe reasoned. Yet these were the classes who could by their example lead "a social revolution of the highest importance . . . which would not be traced in blood or riot, but in man's moral, intellectual and material growth."[49]

Though Crackanthorpe firmly declined an invitation to appear for the defendants in the Bradlaugh-Besant trial and denied any sympathy for them, he was nevertheless quoted by Annie Besant and, occasionally, by other Neo-Malthusians in subsequent years as evidence of enlightened middle-class support for humane and rational curbs on human fertility. It was unwelcome recognition and probably contributed to his defeat as a Liberal candidate for Parliament in 1879.[50] If he refused to have anything to do with the Malthusian League, Crackanthorpe was, at the age of seventy-five, instrumental in the establishment of the Eugenics Education Society and in persuading the hesitant Galton to become its honorary president. Equally important, he tried, but with less success, to convince Galton that voluntary limitation was the new "D.E." or "Determining Element" that opened the way for eugenics to turn the nation from the path of race suicide to race regeneration.[51]

Jane Clapperton, whom Havelock Ellis credited with being the first person to see that national regeneration was dependent upon a merger of eugenics and birth control, recalled in 1904 how little impact the idea had had when broached twenty years earlier.[52] Unlike Crackanthorpe who was a Liberal Unionist, Clapperton, a friend of George Eliot's, was a moderate socialist who in 1885 welcomed neo-Malthusianism and eugenics as a cooperative solution to the terrible social conditions that afflicted the country. Together they held out the promise of the intelligent control of the reproduction of the lowest classes and the promotion of more births among the "social units that are generally *most fit*."[53]

The "scientific meliorism" of society's ills that Clapperton envisioned, though initially voluntary, would eventually require a socialist state to restrain the sexuality of individuals "who persist in parental action detrimental to society." Like many later negative eugenicists, Clapperton assumed that if the fertility of inferior types could be artificially restrained it would somehow lead to "a change which will in time procure the advent of a healthy, pure blooded race." For Clapperton the old Malthusianism was an outmoded product of a competitive, individualistic political economy. The new Malthusianism and the new heredity were products of the first stage of cooperative socialism. Together the two promised to become a great "social force tending to race improvement and general well-being."[54] That promise she felt in 1904 was on its way to being fulfilled. Family limitation was widely practiced and hereditary factors ignored a generation ago were now seen as essential to the improvement of society. Eugenicists were right to be concerned about the dangers to the race if the differential birthrate continued on its current path, but the only way to assure it did not was to be certain that the unfit, who were not likely to remain celibate, also knew how to avoid conceiving children.[55]

Socialist eugenicists such as Shaw, Webb, Wells, and Saleeby, among others, were joined by a number of nonsocialists in advocating family limitation in conjunction with the positive promotion of higher fertility among the fit of all classes. People as different as Crackanthorpe, Ellis, Drysdale, and Inge, for example, all agreed that the current dysgenic pattern of differential fertility was not likely to be substantially altered by positive eugenic breeding. However much they approved in principle the various schemes for medical examinations, eugenic certificates, educational allotments, tax reforms, selective family allowances, and albums of family inheritance to induce the fit to marry and reproduce, they knew that none of them would be remotely sufficient to offset the much greater fertility of those unworthy of such marks of genetic approbation. Crackanthorpe tried to convince Galton it would take several generations, if ever, before the offspring of eugenic marriages would be numerous enough to contain the racial harm caused by the multiplication of the biologically inadequate.[56]

Drysdale saw this as creating divisions within the eugenics movement which left the way open for a merger with his own. At a lecture at the Caxton Hall in 1908 he described the mounting tension between positive and negative eugenics and assured his audience that neo-Malthusianism had no quarrel with the latter, other than a desire to substitute contraception for sterilization or prohibition. In addition, he noted, Neo-Malthusians were not as persuaded that heredity was as unaffected by environment as positive, or neo-Darwinian, eugenicists like Pearson claimed. Indeed, Drysdale argued elsewhere, eugenics could make no more progress than any other movement for social betterment without the environmental changes brought about by the fall in the birthrate since 1877.[57]

In singling out neo-Malthusianism as the starting point for all improvement, Drysdale nevertheless assured the International Eugenics Congress in 1912 that the Malthusian League had, from its inception, favored negative eugenics. This meant "a *graduated* restriction of births from a maximum of four for the well off and fittest down to one in the case of the very poor, and to zero in the case of hereditary disease." Contrary to what critics charged, there was nothing in this to deprive the poor of the right to have children while placing no restrictions on the rich. "So long as the rate of increase is greater among the fitter than the less fit elements of society, progress is in the right direction, and a ratio of four to one or zero is sufficiently rapid progress."[58]

During extensive testimony before the National Birth-Rate Commission in 1913, Drysdale admitted when questioned by J. A. Hobson that he regarded wealth as an index of fitness and poverty of unfitness. Since most eugenicists shared this perception and recognized the current birthrate was already decidedly dysgenic, Drysdale could not understand why they did not support the Malthusian League's activities. He told the commission that the same educated classes who complained bitterly of the antieugenic effects of family limitation "took advantage of the knowledge of contraceptive methods for themselves and put every obstacle in the way of its extension to the people among whom it was most needed on humanitarian and eugenic considerations." If the educated classes have not and will not produce more children and modern humanitarianism has rebelled against the natural "killing-out process" among the less fit, what is to be done? he asked. "Mephistopheles himself could not have devised a better system for ruining the race," and there were but two alternatives. "Either the fit must increase their own multiplication and refuse all help to the unfit (with the spectre of the French Revolution to cheer them), or they must see to it that the unfit do not reproduce."[59]

In Drysdale's opinion, only the decline in the birthrate with its accompanying drop in the death rate had prevented the economic and social disintegration that might have led to revolution. If the positive eugenicists had their way, such a disastrous outcome was still possible, he believed. Experience in the Netherlands, where medical practitioners and trained midwives had provided contraceptive advice to the poor since the 1880s, demonstrated clearly there was no justification for the eugenics claim that "the less fit elements of society will reproduce faster than the fitter elements, if the knowledge of simple and hygienic methods of restriction becomes universal." Even at the current rate of progress, Drysdale predicted, "in seven or eight years . . . or in four or five years if the educated classes will co-operate, the quantity question will have been overcome, and Neo-Malthusianism will then become identical with negative eugenics."[60]

The Birth-Rate Commission was pulled in different directions. On the one hand, it was profoundly concerned about the interrelationship of the diminishing size of families to the crumbling moral and religious foundations of domestic life. On the other, it acknowledged the birthrate was "strongly selective, the net as well as the gross surplus of births over deaths varying (as a rule) inversely with the social position of the family." Although the commissioners claimed they had not considered "the eugenic question" in detail, it was nevertheless evident throughout their deliberations. While insisting the "physical and mental inferiority of the most fertile strata" was indisputable, they attributed it mainly to "bad environment" and deprecated "the tendency to identify the economic elite with the psycho-physical elite." The commission then went out of its way, however, to stress it "does not, of course, seek to deny the inheritance of both mental and physical characters, and it recognizes that legislation which ignores the facts of variation and heredity must ultimately lead to national deterioration." If on balance their teetering scales came down on the side of nurture over nature and they were unable to accept the hypothesis "that the broad distinctions between social classes are but the effects of germinal variations," they did not rule out the possibility that hereditary determinants might yet prove to be decisive.[61]

The commission was similarly ambivalent about the effects of family limitation which it associated with the rise of the Neo-Malthusian movement. Its willingness to receive testimony from Drysdale suggested the movement had become too important to be ignored by a prestigious board of inquiry, no matter how unpalatable the subject was to several of the members. Moreover, in spite of the contention of numerous witnesses to the contrary, the commissioners declined to condemn family limitation as selfish, immoral, unpatriotic, or medically harmful, but instead conceded the right of parents, whose motives were pure, to regulate their families by restricting intercourse to safe periods.[62] By "pure" they meant genuine economic stress or ill health, considerations which were much more likely to be relevant to the condition of the poor than to the rich.

Neo-Malthusians, whose campaign had been denounced only eight years earlier by the Lambeth Conference, now rejoiced in 1916 when, according to their inflated interpretation, the Birth-Rate Commission's report "wholly and finally cleared [their teachings] from the stain of being immoral and injurious to public decency and welfare." The commissioners' grudging acknowledgment was a compromise with reality rather than a confirmation of the Malthusian League's premature claim that the report marked the "great and final victory of our cause."[63] In fact, many of the bishops, clergymen, physicians, and other notables on the commission considered birth control to be a menace to the size and quality of the race and were only persuaded not to say so by their chairman, Dean Inge, who admittedly used his position "rather high-handedly" to get his way.[64]

With marital fertility half of what it had been a generation earlier, Inge argued it would be as foolish and as futile for the Birth-Rate Commissioners to denounce birth control as a physiological and moral atrocity as it had been for the bishops to do so in 1908. To insist blindly that marriage was in all cases ordained for the procreation of children was religiously questionable, scientifically doubtful, and racially irresponsible. Inge believed only an accommodation with demographic reality would halt the deplorable slide toward race degeneration propelled by the differential birthrate.[65] That accommodation, as he, Crackanthorpe, Saleeby, Ellis, and others argued, meant a willingness to add birth control to the arsenal of negative eugenics. They had persuaded the Eugenics Education Society council to consider it as early as 1909 when it was asked to send a representative to the First International Neo-Malthusian Conference at the Hague the following year. Although the council declined to do so, it did agree to provide the Malthusian League with the names and addresses of members who might be interested in attending and in 1912, after some hesitation, invited Drysdale to address the first International Eugenics Congress.[66]

These were very tentative overtures made more difficult by the repugnance that many society members felt for an organization linked in the public's mind to the seamy world of patent medicines, rubber shops, sexual quackery, and abortion. Although the Malthusian League was in fact strongly opposed to abortion as illegal and unnecessary and was exceedingly, sometimes frustratingly, circumspect when it came to recommending practical contraception, it remained very suspect in respectable circles. Despite decades of florid encomiums to marriage and domestic happiness, the league, by its own admission, was never able to dissociate itself entirely from the popular belief that it fostered a licentious "promiscuity, irresponsibility and irregularity" that imperiled the family.[67] Inge, for example, emphasized that while he shared many of the league's worries about the social, economic, and racial dangers of overpopulation in the large towns, he had no connection whatsoever with the organization. "I do not like their methods and should never recommend them," he wrote in 1913, "but at least they see where the shoe pinches."[68]

Saleeby and Ellis were rare among eugenicists in their willingness to link their names openly to the Neo-Malthusians before the war. Both were as concerned with improving the atrocious living conditions of the poor and decreasing the dreadful rates of infant mortality in the slums as they were with reversing the differential birthrate. Saleeby stressed this repeatedly in calling for the general diffusion of "Neo-Malthusian knowledge" to the poor and in condemning the churchmen, capitalists, militarists, and imperialists who for their various reasons wanted a continual surplus of compliant human fodder, no matter the cost to individuals and the race.[69]

Ellis, for his part, was more sanguine, certain that neo-Malthusianism was a new phase in the evolution of racial responsibility fully "consonant with the stage of civilization we are at the moment passing through." In contrast to previous eras, the voluntary control of numbers had now made it possible to create a new race through the regeneration of the old. This not only involved a higher breeding by the "sane and responsible classes but the elimination of those stocks which fail to help us in the tasks of our civilization today." Ellis concurred with the Neo-Malthusians that, at the present stage of knowledge, much more was known about how to accomplish the latter than the former. Eugenics, he thought, should be prepared to pursue both as the expansion of that knowledge allowed.[70]

In spite of such arguments, the Eugenics Education Society before World War I continued along the route to positive race culture mapped by Francis Galton. It was prepared to endorse such negative policies as segregation, sterilization, and the prohibition of dysgenic marriages and looked with envy on the "progress" being made in these directions in the United States. "Eugenic cranks," as one parliamentary opponent described them, did play an important role in agitating for the passage of the Mental Deficiency Act in 1913 with its provisions for the detention and institutionalization of the mentally deficient on a sexually segregated basis. Since the "defectives" subject to the act included not only certain categories of paupers and habitual drunkards but women on poor relief at the time of giving birth to an illegitimate child, the *Eugenics Review* welcomed the legislation as a first official step toward acknowledging the importance of heredity and curbing the multiplication of the unfit.[71]

Compromises to protect individual liberties and disagreements about what constituted mental deficiency made it highly improbable, as a number of eugenicists pointed out, that the act would have much of a statistical impact on the rapid growth of unfitness caused by the dramatic differences in the birthrate. Eugenic hopes that the 1913 measure was only a first installment were never fulfilled. Despite eugenic spokesmen in both houses, Parliament was unwilling to consider emulating those American states that aggressively sterilized, sexually segregated, or forbade the marriages of idiots, morons, the insane, alcoholics, the venereally diseased, and promiscuous paupers.

But the knowledge that parliamentary intervention was a distant prospect at best was an important consideration even before the war to those eugenicists who were trying to push the movement to adopt what was likely to be the only truly effective form of negative eugenics—birth control. They recognized correctly that the country's long tradition of individual liberties reinforced by the changing political, social, religious, and moral climate of recent years precluded any serious governmental intrusion into the most private areas of people's lives—marriage, sex, and childbearing. The only realistic chance to alter the race-decaying distribution of children from the different sectors of society first calculated by Pearson in the 1890s, they concluded, lay not in the direction of compulsion, but in education, persuasion, and inducement. As Ellis explained, "The only compulsion we can apply in eugenics is the compulsion that comes from within."[72]

Given the fear, resentment, and hostility a great many eugenicists felt toward the unfit, usually synonymous with the urban poor, whose hereditary capacity for thoughtful self-control was held in very low regard, a reliance upon voluntary restraint seemed to be an enormous risk. Leonard Darwin, citing the statistics of differential fertility, concluded neo-Malthusianism had already proven to be "racially devastating." Even in the face of mounting evidence after the war that the differential birthrate had appreciably narrowed, he never entirely abandoned his conviction that most of the working classes were constitutionally incapable of exercising the self-control needed for birth control to be eugenically effective. His opposition was instrumental in keeping the pages of the *Eugenics Review* uncontaminated by serious considerations of the subject until the 1920s. At the same time, Darwin recognized a decade earlier that a substantial minority of the Eugenics Education Society's membership did not share his adamancy and were increasingly open to exploring the eugenic possibilities of selective birth control. Unless there were a resurgence of large families among the more desirable classes, Darwin knew that the logic of the birth controllers would soon become all-persuasive.[73] The resurgence never came.

Despite their failure to forge a working alliance before World War I, eugenics and neo-Malthusianism nevertheless shared a common concern about the correlation of fertility to poverty and social class. The two movements were, like socialism or the "New Liberalism," responses to late Victorian industrialism, urbanization, and the Condition of England question. Both believed the correlation was determined by biological or demographic natural laws capable of amendment by rational intervention. However much their advocates flirted with the possibility of state-directed, mandatory controls to achieve their small- or large-familied utopias, they knew enough about the importance of public opinion to recognize that their only real weapon was education. While eugenicists and Neo-Malthusians agreed that the educators would be middle class, they disagreed about who they should be teaching, what should be taught, and the capacity of their pupils to learn.

The Neo-Malthusians, from their radical, secularist, democratic perspective, were certain the poor were fully able to absorb and apply the lessons of family limitation if only the middle and upper classes would facilitate rather than impede their dissemination. Eugenicists, from their educated, professional, middle-class vantage point, doubted their complex, scientific truths could be comprehended by the lower classes. In focusing its attention upon the universities, the scientific laboratories, the medical schools, the inns of court, and other bulging repositories of genetic wealth, the Eugenics Education Society made it clear who it thought should and could hear its progenitive message. These differences notwithstanding, eugenicists and Neo-Malthusians shared one final belief that proved to be a major source of division within each movement: so long as the fundamental demographic or genetic causes of race-sapping poverty and misery were ignored, charity, social welfare, and environmental social reform would prove to be futile and even dangerously counterproductive in breeding the healthy race family.

Six

Race-Motherhood

Perhaps nothing betrayed the Victorian bourgeois origins of the eugenics movement more than its idealization of the genetically precocious large family reared under the watchful guidance of the devoted "race mother." The Eugenics Education Society itself was in some ways, like the Moral Education League and the National Council of Public Morals, a descendant of an earlier social purity crusade committed to the motto: "The Foundations of National Glory are set in the homes of the people. They will only remain unshaken while family life of our race is strong, simple and pure."[1] The provisional council that drew up the constitution of the Eugenics Education Society in 1907 was drawn in part from these organizations, and the new group was initially called the Eugenic and Moral Education Society.[2]

The Victorian middle classes had invested the family with such exaggerated virtues and consolidating strengths and its guardian angel, the mother, with such unique and special qualities, that threats to domestic life could easily be amplified into multiple scenarios of disintegration and ruin. Ruskinesque images of the home as a "walled garden" or a besieged fortress in a hostile, competitive world were familiar enough to the Victorians. Many of the adjectival effusions describing the idyllic home as "a bright, serene, restful, joyful nook of heaven in an unheavenly world" were tempered by a complementary image of it as a "shelter, not only from all injury, but from all terror, doubt and division."[3] The deep sense of impermanence and insecurity evident in such language was, if anything, accentuated by the rise of the "Woman Question" in the late Victorian and Edwardian years.

Female demands for the vote, expanded education, greater economic, occupational, and professional opportunities, as well as control over property, children, and, less explicitly, sexuality, called into question the stability of the family, the nature of authority, the fundamental religious, moral, and scientific basis of gender, and the very future of the race. If in retrospect the cosmic, sometimes fantastical, leaps of imagination stimulated by the changing position of women seem ludicrous today, they say a great deal about the anxieties of people in the past.

The rise of the Woman Question, it should be remembered, paralleled the revival of the Condition of England question, the onset of the Great Depression, the first serious challenges to Britain's economic and imperial preeminence, the rapid extension of the franchise, and the swift emergence of the socialist alternative to bourgeois capitalism. In addition, the moral and intellectual foundations of British culture were under assault by a new generation of critics and writers from the 1880s on. They seemed to confirm Max Nordau's pessimistic assessment of the degeneration of Western civilization, while the Darwinian alternative to traditional religious explanations of the nature of life and human progress itself was profoundly altering basic structures of belief.

It is not surprising in this context that the Woman Question, which touched upon so many fundamental, even primal, areas of human relationships, became a magnet for a host of deep-seated fears, concerns, and sometimes hopes about the future. That its challenge to what many people believed were the sustaining strengths of Britain's favored place in the world—the patriarchal family, the division of labor, and the nurturing of a great imperial race—also paralleled the relentless decline in the birthrate was not lost on contemporaries for whom the connection was obvious and logical. Supporters as well as opponents of female emancipation quickly made that link, although they differed profoundly in their explanations and predicted consequences.

Eugenics, preoccupied with the hereditary worth of families and classes, originated in the same labile environment as the Woman Question. Although Galton himself was not initially concerned with that question, many of his followers recognized its importance for their cause. They were especially alert to the social characteristics of the women's movement and its close ties to the middle classes whose female representatives were presumably the best candidates for "race-motherhood."

Galton, Pearson, and the Nature of Women

Reconciling women's demands for greater legal, political, economic, and educational equality with the needs of the race was one of the most divisive contemporary issues to which eugenicists tried to apply their hereditarian calculus. In contrast to what a number of their feminist critics believed at the time, and more modern critics assume, eugenical prognosticators were as perplexed and uncertain about the implications of female emancipation as was the educated public at large. Despite broad agreement about the efficacy of biosocial causality, eugenicists, starting with Galton and Pearson, disagreed on everything from the relative genetic contribution of women to whether or not the satisfaction of their claims would advance or retard the progress of the race.

The mixed response of eugenics to the feminist agenda pointed up the difficulties that plagued so many of its efforts to try to explain complex social and political phenomena in biological terms. When it entered the public arena, science, as Pearson warned the first eugenicists, was in serious danger of becoming an agent of class and gender predilections reflecting the culture-bound values, biases, hopes, and fears of emotionally committed partisan interests. Though Pearson always believed others, including Galton, were prone to these lapses in scientific impartiality, he was no more able than other eugenicists to separate his personal feelings from what he believed to be objective evidence. The Woman Question was a case in point. However much the varying answers to it were buttressed with biostatistical data and volumes of scientific and medical testimony, from the eugenic perspective the biological imperative of race-motherhood in the final analysis defined the role of the "new woman" in society as it had the old. In this case, perhaps even more than in others, eugenics reinforced what most people were certain they already knew.

No obstacle was more difficult for feminists to overcome than the pervasive belief in a biological imperative decreeing that the female of the species had been created or had evolved for the primary purpose of reproduction and nurture. A woman's physical, moral, and mental characteristics were inevitably determined by these natural maternal functions as her activities, opportunities, and aspirations were circumscribed by them. Few people, including many supporters of at least some women's rights, questioned the existence of an inherent separation of spheres between the sexes. These were clearly marked by innate, distinct qualities designating specific roles and an ineluctable division of labor upon which depended the essential prosperity of the domestic economy.[4]

To dispute so obvious an imperative was not only an affront to experience, logic, and common sense but a challenge to what most people believed to be overwhelming theological and scientific evidence. Descriptions of the dreadful psychic and somatic penalties that awaited the individual woman who attempted to transgress the boundaries of biologically determined gender spheres constituted a virtual genre of medical literature. The more fortunate were only afflicted with minor gynecological and neurotic disorders; their less-favored sisters were visited with everything from masculinizing sterility and certifiable lunacy to a variety of terminal cancers.[5]

Eugenicists, whether physicians or not, were much more concerned about the consequences of female emancipation for the regeneration of the race than they were about its effects on individual women. What they were intent upon was calculating the impact of the vote, higher education, or the increase of middle-class women in the workplace on the age of marriage, the frequency of reproduction, and the quality of offspring. Given Galton's proof of the hereditary tendency of children to revert toward the mean, a eugenicist doctor, Arabella Kenealy, wondered in 1911 whether "the refined and highly-organised but neurotic mothers of our cultured classes" had sufficient "mother-power" not only to produce enough children to sustain the race but to assure that their genetic quality was up to the mark. On the basis of her own observations, Kenealy thought the evidence already demonstrated that the highly educated, fastidious, modern woman, "all nerves and restless activity" was begetting "offspring of the crude, rough hewn and unintelligent peasant type."[6]

Kenealy's disdain for the "crude, clownish and uncomely" children who seemed more suitable for a "gardener's family" than for the refined, intelligent classes who were breeding them was her highly impressionistic, class-conscious way of complaining about the decline of talent, ability, and appropriate behavior in the new century. While her comments radiated the commonplace social prejudices of the age that fed the eugenics movement, they also reflected deep-seated misgivings about the effects of modern civilization on the qualitative as well as the quantitative reproductive capacity of the new woman. Like most eugenicists, Kenealy was not interested in women in general but only in those exceptional representatives of the sex whose superior, inheritable qualities might not be passed on to future generations if they strayed too far from their biologically prescribed path. Eugenicists knew that these were often the same strong-willed, intelligent middle- and upper-class women who filled the suffragist ranks and whose low marriage and birth rates were continually cited as irrefutable evidence that the women's movement was a revolt against domesticity and maternity.

Although eugenicists were sure the desirable qualities of race-motherhood could be isolated and measured, they were hopelessly imprecise and invariably traditional in delineating the maternal hereditary contribution made to superior offspring. Despite a variety of biometric studies proving nature to be overwhelmingly more important than nurture, discussions of the race mother, such as that held at the Sociological Society in 1904, usually dwelt upon the "innate nurturing instincts" manifest in her gentleness, intuition, sensitivity, and emotional insight.[7] Little attempt was made to explain how these special, sex-

specific virtues were biologically associated with the propagation of genetically valuable progeny. More often than not, the connection was simply
assumed.

Galton had set the pattern himself in his extensive studies of eminent men in
various walks of life. His reliance upon genealogies, biographical dictionaries,
and surveys of contemporary scientists insured a concentration on male lineage and precluded his discovering much information about the maternal
contribution to hereditary talent. Galton recognized this limitation but nevertheless concluded that men of outstanding accomplishment derived most of
their ability from the male rather than the female side of their descent.[8] Like
Darwin, he reasoned that the absence of eminent women was itself evidence of
a different pattern of mental, moral, and physical evolution that diverted
female capacity and selectivity in the essential if more limited direction of
domesticity and race renewal. From their androcentric perspective, both believed the male of the species was physically, mentally, and genetically much
more variable and therefore superior to the female. This was demonstrated
outwardly in the great range of accomplishments achieved by men and in-
wardly in the larger proportion of genetic capacity they presumably transmitted to their sons. Women, chosen through a competitive, male-dominated
process of sexual selection, were to a very large extent submissive vessels for
conveying and nurturing the vital germ plasm provided by their mates.[9]

If in many areas Darwinian science challenged traditional beliefs, in the
case of the Woman Question it sustained them by imposing naturalistic limitations on feminist demands for greater equality. Indeed, Victorian science in
general tended to support culturally conditioned, socially contingent assumptions about the roles of men and women.[10] Much of the reason for the rapid
acceptance and popularization of Darwinism was its brilliant yet comprehensible articulation of what many people already believed or at least suspected.
This was especially true when it was used to refute as unnatural the egalitarian
claims of women from the 1860s on. Galton, like his reclusive cousin Darwin,
rarely challenged these claims publicly although he agreed they were biologically unsound. In numerically plotting the degrees of transmission of talent
through the ancestry of noteworthy men in law, science, religion, the military,
music, and the arts, Galton found the hereditary influence of women to be
statistically significant only in the case of clergymen (whom he generally
disliked) and, to a lesser extent, judges. It was obvious to the father of
eugenics that the popular notion that great men had remarkable mothers was
scientifically insupportable.[11]

One explanation for the more modest role of female heredity, Galton suggested, was the lower marriage rate for the female relatives and offspring of

prominent males. Women who were more talented, intellectual, and better educated than the general run of their sex often had elevated expectations that reduced the circle of men whom they found attractive. Equally important in the process of sexual selection, potential suitors were frightened off by the "dogmatic and self-assertive" or "shy and peculiar" personalities of such women.[12] Difficult as it was to explore female lineage, Galton thought the data nevertheless showed that many personality characteristics such as temper, disposition, and piety were probably inherited from mothers, but the more important attribute, creativity, was not.

All of this added up in Galton's tables to the feminine contribution to heredity being of significantly lesser value. He also seemed to suggest that germinal inadequacy was more likely to be manifested in women than men. In calculating the disproportionate number of marriages to infertile heiresses as the cause for the extinction of eminent families, the burden of failure was by inference clearly maternal rather than paternal.[13] Among the results of Galton's pioneering anthropometric studies of the 1880s was the discovery that not only were women physically inferior to men, but in contrast to received opinion, their sensory acuity and, consequently, their intellectual ability were less developed than previously believed.[14]

Galton's measured doubts about female capacity, though based upon a mixture of impressionistic observations and flawed genealogical surveys, were, like the pronouncements of learned physicians, given added credence by their scientific validation of popular perceptions of sex roles. The concurrent growth of the women's movement and social Darwinism combined to insure that feminist aspirations would be closely evaluated in evolutionary and hereditary terms. However much Galton shared the commonplace belief that women had not evolved as far as men and that biology determined a social destiny for them which was primarily reproductive, he did not necessarily agree with Herbert Spencer and evolutionary positivists, like the anthropologists Patrick Geddes and J. Arthur Thompson, that fertility was governed by the laws of individuation and genesis working in consort with the conservation of energy.[15]

Where Spencer argued progenitive capacity decreased as cerebral power increased, and Geddes and Thompson reasoned that a woman's fertility, like the process of evolution itself, was dependent upon the conservation and distribution of reproductive energy, Galton calculated that procreativity was an inherited characteristic distributed with measurable frequency in both sexes. Galton was no less fascinated by the expenditure of masculine energy in the evolution of the race than were Geddes and Thompson. He descanted at length about the importance of physical strength, vigor, and vitality as hereditary characteristics of the truly eugenic male. Moreover, his horror of homosexuality and of effeminate men has been noted by his most recent biographer with an appropriately restrained allusion to Freudian repression.[16] But Galton was less convinced by the Spencerian-inspired conclusion that the evolution of women and the race had depended upon females conserving rather than expending vital energy, nor did he believe for long that the differential decline in the birthrate was a natural consequence of the growing diversion or dissipation of that energy into non-reproductive areas.

Unlike many opponents of higher education or votes for women, Galton did not dwell on the sterilizing effects of such demanding activities. Although he assumed they were incompatible with a woman's role and doubted her intellectual abilities to benefit or contribute very much, it did not follow that her innate reproductive powers were diminished. Those powers, his distribution curves told him, varied widely but predictably among women in all walks of life. The belief that fertility was not an acquired but an inherited characteristic unaffected by environment was scientifically reinforced by the germ plasm theories of August Weismann in the late nineteenth century and by the rediscovery of Mendelian genetics in the early twentieth. But the logic and legacy of evolutionary Lamarckianism died hard, as eugenicists knew all too well. For them the problem was not one of preventing women from dissipating their finite reservoirs of "mother-power" in racially inappropriate diversions but of identifying the worthiest representatives of the sex and encouraging them to marry and have large families.

Some of the distinguishing characteristics of such women, Galton believed, were their physical attractiveness, excellent health, and robust energy, all of which were likely to be closely correlated with rich fecundity. Like many Victorian men, he had long assumed these heritable qualities would also correspond to the size of a woman's breasts, a part of the female anatomy to which he had first been attracted when a young explorer in Africa.[17] It was a connection reflected in Spencer's evocative image of "flat-chested girls who survive their high-pressure education [but who] are incompetent to bear a well-developed infant and to supply it with the natural food for the natural period."[18] In the Edwardian years these individuated though racially otiose creatures were reincarnated in the highly civilized, neurotic, spare-framed new woman who in trying "to beat the man at his game" had only managed "to get out of practice at [her] own game."[19]

The octogenarian Galton was himself not beyond noticing the unfortunate tendency toward a gaunt linearity in the female form which by his tastes was scarcely conducive to eugenic sexual selection. Yet only a few years earlier, in 1896, he had concluded, with some surprise, that secondary sex characteristics such as large breasts in women did not seem to be closely related to fertility. "In four large families that I know of," he wrote to Pearson, "the mother has *not* these characteristics, but all four mothers concur in looking youthful."[20] The uncertain correlation between fertility and mammary endowment notwithstanding, Galton's ideal women in his utopia, Kantsaywhere, were not only youthful but buxom, similar to those found frolicking in the paintings of Guido Reni. These comely maidens, their hair gathered in knots and (as befit Victorian sensibilities) their clothes more decorously buttoned and fastened than the fly-away garments in the paintings, were clearly "promising mothers of a noble race."[21]

Although Pearson did not see these pulchritudinous musings until after his elderly patron's death, he had tried for many years before to wean him from his romantic, Victorian illusions about women and their alleged biological attributes. In his struggle to separate scientific from popular eugenics, Pearson was contemptuous of much of the so-called objective evidence his neo-Darwinist contemporaries tacked on to their preconceptions about the nature of women and the likely consequences of female emancipation. He distrusted the emotionalism on both sides of the issue, doubting that the passionate invocation of the writings of Mary Wollstonecraft or John Stuart Mill was any more helpful than the unproven prognoses of self-serving, antifeminist gynecologists and their evolutionist allies.[22]

Like many Fabians, Pearson took a special interest in the relationship of the sexes in a socialist society. He was instrumental in the establishment of the Men and Women's Club in 1885 to discuss such questions, among others, and to explore the possibilities for equality and friendship among the sexes. It was there that he met a number of able, outspoken women such as Eleanor Marx, Olive Schreiner, Annie Besant, and his future wife, Maria Sharpe, who in 1889 reacted to his proposal of marriage, with its daunting prospect of physical as well as mental intercourse, by having a short-lived nervous breakdown.[23]

The founding of the Men and Women's Club was a consequence of Pearson's conviction that next to socialism the Woman Question was the most important issue of the day. Recalling his own mother's economic dependency and powerlessness in an unhappy marriage, Pearson questioned whether even in a socialist society an ill-educated and economically dependent woman could contribute her fair share of labor. Equally important, however, as feminist critics legitimately insisted, was the effect emancipation would have upon the future of the race. It was a serious matter, Pearson believed, requiring the scientific investigation of unprejudiced data not yet available. Even before he turned his considerable mathematical talents to the cause of Galtonian eugenics in the early 1890s, Pearson called for the careful evaluation of gender capacity and ability and tried to formulate accurate statistical procedures for measuring the hereditary contribution of each sex. He personally doubted the existence of any "rigid natural law of feminine inferiority" and suspected that a woman's physique and intellect were to a considerable extent environmentally conditioned. Anticipating the work of another member of the Men and Women's Club, Havelock Ellis, Pearson cited the need for a real "science of sexualogy" to resolve the passionate arguments for and against women's rights.[24]

Pearson's innovative calculations of statistical probability made him exceedingly suspicious of the representative validity of individual case studies cited by doctors, psychologists, and sexologists to support their generalizations about the nature of the "fair sex." He argued that only the accumulation and analysis of extensive data based upon a wide, scientifically determined sample would permit accurate correlations, for example, of the relationship between marriage and childbearing and intellectual, economic, and political activity. With some 20 percent of eligible English women never marrying, Pearson reasoned, it was important to determine if there were statistically significant physical and mental differences between spinsters and married women as well as between childless wives and mothers.

The central issue of female emancipation was not the franchise as suffragists would have us believe, he claimed. Even if women in the aggregate were physically and intellectually inferior to men, there were obviously many individual exceptions to this biological rule. Since weak and slow-witted men, who made up a large proportion of the electorate, were not excluded from the ballot box, "there must be some other disqualification which deprives a George Eliot of the vote that is granted to the dullest yokel."[25] He frankly doubted maternity by itself would justify continued disenfranchisement. It was far more important to discover whether females could inherit and transmit parental capacity to the same degree as males, to evaluate whether employment or prolonged study had "ill effects on women's childbearing efficiency," and to determine if the "physical degradation of the race" would inevitably follow the revolution in sexual relations that was under way. Pearson urged a moratorium until reliable answers were forthcoming.[26]

He was nevertheless fairly certain that evidence would show there is no rigid natural law of feminine inferiority and that after a generation or two in which the physical and intellectual education of girls was made equal to that of boys, women would achieve the economic equality allowing them the independence to form relationships based solely upon mutual sympathy and affection.[27] Pearson believed this was much more likely to happen in a socialist society in which men and women were free to marry on the basis of friendship and love. At the same time, he was no different from many of his Victorian contemporaries in his uneasiness about the effect sexual equality would have on the continued reproduction of the race. The long experience of subjection and restraint, he hoped, had imparted a "purer aim" and "keener insight" to the emancipated woman so that the self-control she had learned in the past would allow her to "be able to submit her liberty to the restraints demanded by social welfare and . . . the conditions needed for race-permanence."[28]

First among those conditions was the possibility that many of "the best women" might have to defer or set aside some of their aspirations if the continuation of the species was not to be left "to the coarser and less intellectual of its members." Female emancipation might raise "great racial problems" for the continued development of the middle classes in particular. Though strongly sympathetic to feminist goals, Pearson warned that if the alternative was the delegation of race reproduction to the diseased, the brutish, the reckless, and the idle who followed mere instinct without reason and who were presumably congregated in the working classes, it was possible that the "penalty to be paid for race predominance [would be] the subjection of women." It was not a palatable prospect, he admitted, but emancipation might only prove feasible for genuinely infertile women, or those beyond childbearing age.[29]

Whatever the alternatives, Pearson asserted in 1887, the problems of sex and population will come more and more into the foreground. Believing, as he did, that the natural struggle for survival had shifted from individuals to nations and peoples, he reminded his readers that "those nations which have been the most reproductive have, on the whole, been the ruling nations in the world's history; it is they who have survived the battle for life."[30] His own social imperialist views were a mixture of German idealism and Darwinism in which individuals were expected to subordinate themselves to the welfare of the evolving nation state. This in the final analysis would determine how far a woman's rights could be extended and in what ways she could contribute to "the common labour-stock of the community."[31] The only biological determinants affecting that contribution Pearson could foresee were associated with the role of the woman as race mother. Otherwise there was no scientific reason for denying her complete educational, economic, and political equality.

Pearson reinforced his argument with several correlative studies in the 1890s challenging a number of assumptions about the natural characteristics of the sexes. Contrary to what Darwin, Galton, Ellis, and other evolutionists believed, Pearson found that in general women were slightly more variable and therefore physiologically more complex then men. In addition, he concluded that while cranial shape and brain size varied significantly between advanced and less-advanced civilizations, the differences between men and women in a particular culture were not important.[32] Although Galton's own confidence in the correlation between skull size and inherited ability had begun to wane by the end of the century, many of his followers continued to agree with the medical director of the West Riding Asylum at Wakefield, James Crichton Browne, that women were inevitably less intelligent than men because the female brain was smaller and configured differently.[33]

Far more important from the eugenics standpoint were Pearson's findings from a survey of nearly 6,000 male and female correlations "that fertility is inherited both in the male and female lines" fairly equally. He suggested Galton might have to revise his old theory about the relationship of heiresses to sterility in aristocratic families. The statistics also indicated "that *the hereditary influence of the female is inversely proportional to her fertility*" and was therefore more evident in the offspring of smaller families. Is it possible, he asked Galton, that there is "a sort of quantitative limit to the amount of 'self' which a fertile animal can put into the world, and may be a check to the influence of reproductive selection, which has seemed to me so great?"[34]

Pearson's interest in trying to measure the capacity and hereditary potential of women derived not only from his feminist sympathies but from his growing eugenic concerns about differential fertility and its relationship to the perceptible decline in talent evident in the country. If, as he believed, reproductive selection had replaced natural selection so that "the survival of the most fertile" rather than the fittest now characterized modern patterns of reproductive behavior, the implications of the women's movement took on added importance.[35] Despite repeated complaints about the decline of ability being tied to the rise of feminism with its accompanying rejection of marriage and motherhood among the middle and upper classes, the true extent of female culpability could not be determined, Pearson decided, until much more was known about the hereditary contribution of women to their progeny.

For most eugenicists in the early twentieth century, the answer lay in the biometric analysis of family histories, not in basic genetic research. The only dimensions of the female contribution of particular interest to Galton when he publicly addressed the issue of eugenics again in 1901 was "fertility and prepotency." In agreeing that the plummeting birthrate had given a new relevance to eugenics, its founder noted the pronounced tendency among cultured women to defer marriage or to raise very small families. Given the difficulty of evaluating the race-enhancing potential of women, few of whom went to university or, compared to men, accomplished anything outstanding, it was probably necessary to lay even more stress on medical examinations and on the characteristics of the male members of their families since some of their heritable qualities were likely to be present, though less intensively, in their daughters and sisters.[36]

Unlike Pearson, Galton was not particularly concerned with providing women with greater opportunities to demonstrate their talents. He essentially ignored his disciple's egalitarian claims about the transmission of hereditary traits. When he had first broached the problem in the early 1890s, Galton thought that it would be sufficient for women who passed physical examinations to choose their husbands from the recipients of eugenic diplomas. In drawing up his questionnaires for "eugenic certificates" and "racial diplomas" a decade later, Galton decided to restrict them to men on the assumption that female inheritance was too unpredictable and in any event likely to be much less decisive than that of males.[37]

Although the female sex was supposed to lack much aptitude for intellectual endeavor, particularly the abstruse science of mathematics, Pearson reminded Galton in 1908 that five of the fourteen people attached to the Eugenics Laboratory were women. Not only was their work as good as if not better than that of the men, but one of them, Ethel Elderton, was the "real heart of the laboratory." It should therefore come as no surprise, he admonished Galton, that "they were a little tried . . . when your name appeared as on the Committee of the Anti-Suffrage Society." With characteristic courtesy, the unyielding Galton declined to point out that the five women in question were all unmarried, therefore depriving future generations of whatever special talents they might possess.[38]

Despite lending his name to the National League for Opposing Women's Suffrage, there is no evidence that the old man ever took any part in its campaign, nor was he assertively antifeminist. The geneticist William Bateson was, for example, surprised in 1897 when Galton voted against the granting of degrees to women at his alma mater, Cambridge.[39] He was perhaps misled in his expectations by Galton's resignation from the Royal Geographical Society four years earlier when it denied election to fifteen well-qualified women. But Galton's departure in that case had more to do with broader policy issues and was less an endorsement of female aspirations than it was an acknowledgment of rare merit in that sex.[40] He had grudgingly accepted the establishment of the women's colleges at Oxbridge but, like many of his contemporaries, always doubted the intrinsic intellectual ability and emotional and physical stamina of their students. As far as Galton was concerned, the colleges diverted the best women from their reproductive obligations and made them less attractive to the men of their class. He never relented in his opposition to their receiving degrees and died content with the knowledge that at least that mark of eugenic confirmation was still reserved for the most worthy representatives of the race.

Education, Feminism, and Fertility

Whatever their differences about the hereditary attributes of the female sex, Galton and Pearson agreed that in the final analysis the answer to the Woman Question had to be compatible with the demands of race-motherhood. The problem of reconciling those demands with other feminist aspirations bedeviled the struggle for women's rights from its inception, and though eugenicists were perceived as being hostile to emancipation, they were in fact far more ambivalent about it than contemporary and even more recent critics have appreciated. For people who saw themselves fashioning the future in a radically new way, it was not possible, as some of their number would have preferred, to put the lid on the progress and ambitions of half the species. As Montague Crackanthorpe warned in 1907, "Woman is now wide awake, her long slumber ended. To put her to sleep again is beyond human power."[41]

Crackanthorpe, like Pearson, had tried without much success to convince their mutual friend Galton of this reality in the hope that the new eugenics movement would not try to thwart inevitable social advances but would try to steer them as far as possible in the direction of progressive race culture. If neither man saw any biological reason to deny women the vote or an adequate education, they were no less concerned than many antifeminists both within and outside of the eugenics camp about the low marriage and birth rates of educated, middle-class candidates for race-motherhood. But spinsterhood and infertility, they recognized, were not consequences of higher learning, expanded professional opportunities, or political activity, as many of their contemporaries charged. One reason was the excess of nearly a million more women than men in Britain. But the prevalence of unmarried females and small families among those classes where the hereditary incidence of civic worth was supposedly most prevalent was also a reflection of changing marital values and domestic perspectives. Whatever the combination of reasons, however, differential fertility was in fact much more closely correlated to social class than it was to female education or other alleged antimaternal diversions.

Eleanor Mildred Sidgwick, a founder and principal of Newnham College, Cambridge, had first demonstrated this in an 1890 comparison of the health, marriage, and fertility experience of Oxbridge women since the 1870s with that of their sisters and first cousins who had not matriculated.[42] Sidgwick, the sister of the future prime minister Balfour, had been provoked to undertake such a survey by the charge of the journalist Grant Allen, among others, that the healthy girls who entered Newnham, Girton, or Lady Margaret and Somerville Halls became unattractive and unsexed, exhausted their "reserve fund of strength" and, if they married at all, were either sterile or made "physically inefficient mothers."[43]

Her analysis of nearly 600 questionnaires convinced Sidgwick that college-educated women, including those who took honors, were actually somewhat healthier and, when married, no less fertile than their sisters and first cousins who were spared the alleged masculinizing rigors of advanced learning. If on average fewer of those who attended university had yet found husbands, it had more to do with the later age at which they entered the marriage market than with any identifiable, educationally induced defect. Even then, however, only 10 percent of their number had wed, compared to 20 percent of their close female relations.

To some the figures confirmed that the exposure of women to science, philosophy, and mathematics was almost as sure a route to lifelong celibacy as were the vows of a medieval nun. For Sidgwick, however, the measurements clearly demonstrated that whether they attended university or not, only a minority of females in the more elevated classes were likely to marry. Their lack of success was not a result of frail health, deflated bosoms, or general unattractiveness any more than it was caused by a diminished desire to find a husband. On the contrary, the problem of surplus women had existed long before the advent of Newnham or Girton, and their need for alternative opportunities had contributed to the rise of the feminist movement in the first place. Their disproportionate numbers reflected the sexual imbalance caused by a higher survival rate of female children—a problem compounded in the middle classes by the later age at which eligible men chose to take a bride, if they did so at all.[44] When college-educated women did marry, which Sidgwick never doubted was the best career to which they could aspire, their fertility averaged 1.53 children. It was admittedly low but was not markedly different from their relatives and other women of their class married for the same period of time.[45]

Sidgwick's survey provided a foundation for several other inquiries before and after the First World War. All of them confirmed the low marriage and fertility rates of educated women but insisted these were characteristics of the social class to which they belonged. The Countess of Selborne, who welcomed the findings, was typical in blaming the problem on the reluctance of professional and middle-class men to marry and take on the burdens of a family. We might as well accept the fact, she argued, and see that girls receive a good education to prepare them to lead useful and fulfilling lives while waiting impatiently to be led to the altar.[46] With the 1911 *Fertility of Marriage Census* revealing that fewer than 46 percent of professional men were married, there was reason to think that the wait might take some time. Some comfort was found in the knowledge that although middle-class men in general married later than those in the working and agricultural classes, they eventually married nearly as often. Nevertheless, at any given time only about 56 percent of all adult males were actually married, and most of these were in the laboring ranks where, according to eugenic dogma, the genetic reservoir of hereditary talent was rather shallow.[47]

The growing militancy of the suffrage movement after 1905, coupled to the racial anxieties aggravated by the differential decline in the birthrate, greatly stimulated defensive arguments about the consequences of female emancipation. The *Englishwoman*, a moderately progressive publication, periodically acknowledged that the low marriage and fertility rates of educated, middle-class women should give even the most ardent feminist pause for thought. Nevertheless, one of its writers lashed out in 1909 at the ignorance of those who still believed education affected the marriage potential or reproductive potency of women any more than it did for men. The reason an educated woman of "a higher type" remained unmarried was not only because of a shortage of willing men, the contributor insisted, but because of her race-conscious obligation to wait for "a higher type of mate."[48]

Aware of the controversy surrounding the question, the National Birth-Rate Commissioners invited two medical statisticians, Dr. Major Greenwood and Dr. Agnes Saville, former students of Pearson, to compare Sidgwick's earlier findings with the more recent fertility experience of college women and their close relations, mainly sisters. Although their report on "The Fertility of the English Middle Classes" was not published until after the war, Greenwood and Saville informed the commission in 1915 that after correcting for age and duration of marriage of their nearly 800 respondents, "there is no physiological difference between the fertilities of the two classes." They married at close to the same age, around twenty-seven, and gave birth to the same number of children, approximately two. Whatever the reasons for fecund middle-class women missing out on years of potential childbearing, advanced learning, as Sidgwick had shown a generation earlier, did not hold up as a significant cause.[49]

Unlike Sidgwick, who in the 1880s never would have presumed to ask, Greenwood and Saville questioned women about why they had so few children. Of the 541 who responded to this intimate query, more than half admitted to some form of contraceptive practice, while only 25 percent denied it. College-educated women were more willing to respond to the questions than their sisters, and nearly 60 percent of their number admitted to deliberate restriction compared to only 40 percent for those who had never gone to university. Despite the differences and some confusion on the part of women in both categories about what actually constituted contraception, they still produced about the same number of children. The figures, Greenwood and Saville concluded, were barely sufficient to maintain the class if the fertility rate did not drop any further.[50] Although they declined to comment on the possible dysgenic effects of their findings, there was no shortage of people prepared to do so either before or after the war.

From the eugenic vantage point, the information was both reassuring and discouraging. Despite repeated claims to the contrary by physicians and others opposed to female emancipation, it seemed highly unlikely that modern women were any less capable of conceiving children and meeting "the demands of puerperium" than their mothers or grandmothers. Whether they were willing to do so was another question. Nevertheless, male and female doctors alike continued to recount the somatic and psychological punishment inflicted on their female patients by too much schooling, golfing, cycling, gymnastics, and of course, field hockey. Hearts atrophied, pelvises narrowed, and breasts shriveled while minds and muscles strained against the natural boundaries of gender.[51]

More often than not, medical evaluations of female emancipation were anecdotal and reflected the diagnostician's moral, social, and gender values instead of rigorous clinical research. In this doctors were not much different from the public at large. Particularly troubling to medical and nonmedical observers was the belief that masculinization had already altered the emotional nature of the modern female, destroying her maternal instinct and womanly ways. With the critical balance of sexual selection upset, it was not surprising, the eugenicist physician R. Murray Leslie complained, that marriage and fertility had declined while the rate of mental disturbance suffered by intellectual women had soared. Although the Lunacy Commissioners insisted that the increase in female commitments to asylums was a result of better diagnoses and the availability of more facilities to help the insane, Leslie knew that the more likely reason was the "sex starvation" and sterility fostered by the women's movement.[52]

Other doctors challenged their colleagues, insisting that physical activities and exercise actually facilitated childbirth and postpartum recovery. Moreover, as one Cheshire practitioner replied, the lower marriage rates of middle-class women had more to do with a paucity of clerks and professional men who could afford marriage than with any decline in femininity. When educated, active women did marry, two female physicians noted, they usually proved to be thoughtful, concerned, eugenically aware mothers devoted to advancing the quality of their family rather than its size. The comparatively low fertility of such women, as doctors and other professional men who sired on average the smallest families in the kingdom must have known, was not caused by any feminist-inspired loss of reproductive capacity. It was a rational rather than a biological response to the problems, opportunities, and challenges of the new age.[53]

From the eugenic perspective the missing factor in this response was its likely effect on the qualitative composition of the future generations who had to address those problems and meet the challenges. To the extent that the women's movement was at odds with increasing the hereditary quality of the race it was, like the Neo-Malthusian movement, a threat to the future. When in 1904 Galton laid out the definition, scope, and aims of eugenics to the Sociological Society, a number of listeners were immediately struck by the potential of eugenics to stimulate "the resumption of a lost power of race-motherhood," which among "refined and educated women" had of late shown distressing signs of partial paralysis.[54]

For the most unreconstructed antifeminist eugenicists, such as W. C. D. Whetham and his wife, Catherine, the recent demands of women were simply incompatible with strong family life and a direct menace to the future welfare of the race. "Woe to the nation," he warned in 1909, "whose best women refuse their natural and most glorious burden." The Whethams were certain that by "withdrawing its women from the home and . . . throwing them into the competitive struggle for existence or the political organization of the country," the fittest classes were heading down a path of self-destruction traversed by many great civilizations in the past.[55]

In the course of tabulating the dwindling fertility of the aristocracy and his academic colleagues at Cambridge, Whetham also noted that out of 3,000 students who had matriculated at the women's colleges during the past thirty years, only 22 percent had yet married. Moreover, the Whethams discovered, the incidence of marriage was highest among those who did not take their final examinations or honors, and it was lowest for girls who had studied mathematics. If the statistics reflected a conscious recognition on the part of university women that they were unfit for motherhood and family life and therefore consciously chose another career, the result, while regrettable, was not alarming. But if, as the Whethams suspected, "these figures mean that exceptionally capable women, attracted by the intellectual life of the Universities, are thereby rendered unfit or unwilling to discharge their natural functions, the whole matter requires very serious consideration." Analyses of the differential birthrate already revealed the notoriously low fertility of former elementary-school teachers, while the marriage rates for secondary-school teachers and women who had studied history, literature, and science assured that they would also contribute very few children.[56]

The Whethams insisted they had no objection to female education so long as it did not result in women leading careers outside of the home until they had raised at least four children. The low fertility and higher infant mortality experienced by working-class wives, particularly in the textile industry, was well known to the Whethams and their contemporaries and was discussed at length in the 1911 *Fertility of Marriage Census*.[57] Eugenicists were worried that the same dangers awaited middle-class women who became teachers, nurses, factory inspectors, physicians, office workers, or, as seemed possible in the near future, politicians. Combining a familiar economic variation on the law of the conservation of energy with organic imagery, the Whethams described men as income to be spent freely by each generation; women, by contrast, were considered capital to be depleted very sparingly in order to secure adequate resources for the future. Translated into the realm of separate spheres, "the natural duties of a man were directed to the maintenance of present-day conditions, while those of a woman infallibly lead her to take heed for the future welfare of the nation." The threat the women's movement presented to these critical roles was evident in "the spinster influence" and withdrawal from motherhood that characterized the feminist campaign.[58]

Eugenic Feminism

Despite Galton's doubts about the female brain, few of his disciples, including the Whethams, seriously argued that women were intellectually inferior to men. Rare even on the fringes of eugenics were extreme misogynists like Harold Owen, who, in *Woman Adrift*, asserted that with the exception of maternity, women were unnecessary and superfluous to the advance of civilization. His certainty that the "tyranny of Nature" condemned even the best female mind to perpetual inferiority might have been privately shared by many of his contemporaries, but few eugenicists were prepared to say so publicly.[59] Far more common was the warning that even if educated women were the intellectual equals of men, female success in the arts, sciences, or the professions would clash with what one physician described as a new "Law of Consonance," which decreed, "a woman should only develop intellectually along lines that are consonant with the natural development of her capacity for race creativeness." To a professor of chemistry, H. E. Armstrong, this meant, for example, that women with talent in his field should not develop it but marry and pass it on to their sons.[60]

Whetham was one of several eugenicists who agreed with suffrage advocates that women could be as astute as men in making political decisions. He was worried, however, that since mothers would not have the leisure or energy to participate in public life to the same degree as spinsters, they would be more vulnerable to the overweening influence and mischievous authority of single women. One solution which he and others proposed was that only mothers of large families be given the vote.[61] Frederick D'Arcy, the bishop of Down, Connor, and Dromore, thought a mimimum of four children was not unreasonable and tried to persuade the Eugenics Education Society council in 1914 to support the franchise on such a basis as a eugenic inducement.[62] The council, while sympathetic, was wary of becoming embroiled in the heated suffrage campaign and concluded that so exclusionary a measure might provoke more conflicts than it would resolve.

The society faced something of a dilemma. It was widely perceived by feminists as being hostile to their interests; yet half its membership and a quarter of its officers were women. Forty percent of this number were, like many other women of their class, unmarried, and some were active in the moderate wing of the suffrage movement. They were frequently the wives and daughters of successful professional men and, occasionally, peers, and a small minority, including Florence Willey, later Lady Barrett, Ettie Sayer, and Dame Ellen Pinsent, were statisticians, scientists, and physicians in their own right. For its part, the Eugenics Laboratory, under Pearson's direction, was a microcosm of female professional achievement. In addition the Eugenics Education Society was in its early years organized and run by a young widow, Sybil Gotto, the daughter of Admiral Sir Cecil Burney. It was Gotto who, inspired by Galton's writings, first approached him, as well as J. W. Slaughter and Crackanthorpe, with her ideas for an educational society. Galton found Gotto to be "particularly bright and energetic," and a half-century later one of the inaugural members, Lady Chambers, described her as the "real founder" of the Eugenics Society.[63] While endorsing the goals of higher fertility among women very much like themselves, female eugenicists were not especially inclined to remain ignorant or permanently disenfranchised as the price for achieving that racially desirable end. Even without the vote, they knew perfectly well that the women of their class were already among the least-married and least-fertile sector of the population.

Eugenics was continually pulled in two directions by the Woman Question. Starting with Galton himself, many critics of female emancipation feared its

beneficiaries would become unwomanly and unattractive to eugenically precocious men. Even more common, however, was the belief emancipated women
would have neither the time, interest, or capacity to attract such men or bear
their children, leaving the race to be recruited from the lower grades of society.
As Dean Inge asserted in his inaugural lecture to the new Cambridge University Eugenics Society in 1911, the women's movement encouraged a great
many of the ablest women to lead a single life devoted to politics and other
diversions while the worst examples of their sex married and bred with abandon.[64] He was enthusiastically applauded by both women and men in the
audience of 200.

Underlying much of this sort of rhetoric was an almost palpable fear of the
loss of power and control on the part of men if women did not need or want
them and declined to fulfill their biological destiny. Similarly, for many
women the loss of dependency was equally as frightening, and the defense of
their maternal role became an important weapon in guaranteeing them an
essential place in a rapidly changing world. When intemperate antifeminists
argued that women were superfluous outside of the home, unnecessary to
industry and trade, and of no consequence to science, art, and literature, they
played upon anxieties, insecurities, and low self-esteem embedded in the
culturally molded female psyche.[65] Time and again questions of economic
control and independence became confused with issues of sexual authority,
dependence, and race regeneration.

These various concerns and considerations ran throughout eugenic efforts to
reach an accommodation with the women's movement before the war. Those
who, like the suffragist Mabel Atkinson, believed such an accommodation
essential acknowledged the hostility many eugenicists and scientists felt toward feminism. Atkinson agreed it would be justified if the women's movement could not be reconciled with the requirements of race-motherhood.
Admittedly the advanced women of the first generation of feminists perhaps
seemed sexually neutral, unattractive, and indifferent to marriage and maternity. But it was necessary to remember, Atkinson recalled, that those women
represented the large surplus of unmarried females whose problems led to the
feminist movement in the first place.

Modern feminists, by contrast, were less hardened and more attractive than
the pioneers of the movement. Endowed with a "new beauty and grace" born
of greater independence, they had no aversion to love, marriage, and motherhood. More of them, she speculated, were probably married than their predecessors, but with spinsters still greatly outnumbering bachelors, finding a
suitable husband remained more of a possibility than a strong probability.
Eugenically, however, the situation had greatly improved. With her new-found

independence, the modern woman would no longer be forced to marry the wrong man and live as a sexual slave in dull, dependent drudgery. Feminism was, then, the true ally of eugenics, Atkinson rationalized: it allowed educated, independent women aware of the importance of good breeding to select their mates carefully.[66]

As in the response to neo-Malthusianism, a significant minority in both the feminist and eugenicist camps insisted their respective interests were not only compatible but logically lent themselves to some type of alliance. The guiding consideration was whether or not the arrangement would advance or impede the genetic improvement of the race. Those who thought it would, found an ally in the distinguished naturalist Alfred Russel Wallace, who as early as 1890 reasoned that in a truly equitable, socialist society where women were economically independent, intellectually active, and full participants in public life, they would meet a much wider range of able men from whom to select their husbands. When marriage was based upon mutual attraction, ability, and esteem, women would be in a position to reject the idle, selfish, diseased weaklings whom they were frequently forced by necessity to wed. Wallace thought Galton's recent discoveries about hereditary probability held out great possibilities for raising the average of the race from such freely selected alliances. He continued to make the same point nearly twenty years later, more convinced than ever that socialism provided the best environment for eugenic race improvement.[67]

Without necessarily agreeing with Wallace's political sentiments, several feminists agreed with his argument about women's rights and eugenic selectivity. In tying birth control to education and economic independence as the necessary ingredients of female equality, Alice Vickery Drysdale, who loathed socialism, promised a new "process of matrimonial social selection" based upon the sort of mental, moral, social, physical, and intellectual mutual attraction required to produce a truly "well-developed race."[68] Writing from a different perspective in the *Englishwoman*, the pseudonymous Eugenia Newmarch in 1910 assured her readers that the new woman would be instinctively attracted to the best sort of man and would choose him for her husband rather than the dullard or wastrel who had nothing but wealth or family connections to recommend him. Emancipated women, she continued, were devoted to the improvement of the race and "eminently fitted" to promote it through eugenic marriages. Like other eugenically conscious feminists sensitive to the charge that the struggle for women's rights was an unnatural revolt against marriage and motherhood, Newmarch countered that the truly eugenic woman was not against these institutions but rejected the drudgery, torpidity, and oppressiveness of stultifying alliances of convenience and dependency.[69]

The discovery of Mendelian genetics added another weapon to the feminist eugenics arsenal. Annabel Clark Gale, who had studied Galton and, more recently, Mendel and Bateson, presumably without suffering psychic trauma, found in the new patterns of dominant and recessive genetic transmission clear evidence that the hereditary contribution of the two sexes to their offspring was much more equal than previously believed. To Gale it meant that in denying women the vote and other opportunities to exercise their talents, the nation was depriving the public sector of an enormous amount of inherited talent at a time when ability seemed to be in short supply.[70]

This argument, which Pearson, among others, believed made biometric as well as genetic sense, raised implications eugenicists found difficult to reconcile with their positive objective of early marriage and procreation among the eugenically select. Many of the feminist sympathizers who expounded upon the racial benefits to be derived from the more egalitarian process of sexual selection implicit in the triumph of female emancipation accepted later marriages and fewer children as an inevitable consequence. Like Wallace, they were certain the quality of the diminished numbers of offspring born to these deferred but more selective unions would compensate for any quantitative disadvantages.

The Neo-Malthusians' recommendation that at least the first stage in the process, matrimony, need not be delayed while women and men expanded their horizons and opportunities was not particularly helpful in resolving the dilemma of reconciling feminist aspirations with the eugenic needs of the race. Without denying that modern, well-bred, well-educated, independent women were more observant about male character than their predecessors and better able to discern the eugenic qualities of their mates, Dr. Leslie still feared able women were declining the opportunity to produce "the finest race the world has ever seen." In sounding "The Alarm of Motherhood," another critic acknowledged that many of the most brilliant and creative women were suspicious of eugenics and feared that race-motherhood was inimical to their talent and individualism. Yet eugenics, in its demand for freedom of choice in marriage and its support of economic, educational, and social opportunities for women, "strongly reinforces all the rational claims of the emancipation movement." In its defense of the great creative work of women, eugenics only insists that the safeguarding and progress of the race be primary. Whether marriage or maternity was delayed while women pursued self-fulfillment, the result was the same, Leslie added: the best children, usually the third to the sixth, were not being born. "It thus follows," he concluded, "that not only is the race being mainly recruited from the lower grades of society, but the educated classes are not even producing the best of their kind."[71]

Feminism and neo-Malthusianism were, for many eugenicists, complementary perversions of the modern age. The two had emerged together in the last quarter of the nineteenth century and now jointly threatened the continued dominance of the British race in the twentieth. When intelligent, educated, fecund young women of the best classes chose to have as few children as possible, the outlook for the future was very bleak indeed. As in their evaluation of the impact of neo-Malthusianism, Saleeby and Crackanthorpe agreed that while there was mounting evidence feminism was on balance dysgenic, its acceptance by women was no more likely to be reversed than was the spread of family limitation. Eugenics itself, however, was part of the new age, they reasoned, and if it were ever to have any practical impact on society it needed to find a way to turn social forces in directions that would contribute to the hereditary improvement of the race.

In calling for a "eugenic feminism" rejecting sex antagonism and gender dominance, Saleeby acknowledged that Galton's open opposition to the women's movement left a difficult legacy to overcome. His excessive concentration on male ancestry alone distorted what modern genetics had now proven, Saleeby added: inheritance comes from both parents. In addition, Galton's emphasis upon masculine accomplishments, physical prowess, endurance, and energy ignored those civilizing qualities of maternal love, sympathy, intuition, and race responsibility which, along with intelligence, characterized the woman's contribution to her offspring. In the final analysis, the cardinal principle of eugenic feminism was the recognition that the modern woman was still impelled toward race-motherhood; "her body is the temple of life to come—and therefore . . . the holy of holies."[72]

Despite their distrust of the women's movement, eugenicists, Saleeby contended, understood its significance better than many of the best women in the feminist ranks who, hostile and ignorant of eugenics, did not know what was in their own best interests. Saleeby did not hesitate to tell them of the harm they were doing in "deserting the ranks of motherhood and leaving the blood of inferior women to constitute half of all future generations." Nor did he demur from reminding them that their individual development, higher education, and self-expression in works of art, thought, and practice could not safely be carried to the point at which motherhood is compromised.[73]

Crackanthorpe was only slightly more reticent in pointing out to the new woman her responsibilities now that "she has warmed her hands at the fire of life . . . [and] been permitted to eat of the tree of knowledge of good and evil." Since women were inclined to deal with superficial effects rather than contemplate serious causes, Crackanthorpe believed it was imperative they be encouraged to look beneath the surface to see their critical role in the destiny of the race during the coming century. No longer a mistress or a dependent wife, the new, eugenically aware woman "declines to give to her children for father the degenerate, the drunkard, the physically or mentally unfit. Marriage is for her a sacrament in the best sense of the word, and one to which only the shriven are bidden."[74]

Although the final destiny of the new woman in the eugenic century was not to be all that different from the old, she would nevertheless be physically and mentally healthier, more independent, better educated, and her germ plasm given the recognition it deserved. As far as Saleeby and Crackanthorpe were concerned, she should also have the vote, and the sooner the better. It was, as some of their colleagues proposed, more suitable for older women, who could also serve as members of Parliament, but too much energy had already been diverted from motherhood to the quest for the franchise. In urging its passage, which they believed to be inevitable, the two men thought it time to get back to the much more important issues of biology. They shared the prevailing feminist view that once enfranchised, women could bring their unique perspective to legislative reforms that strengthened marriage and the family.[75] Both anticipated, for example, that women would be especially helpful in achieving the difficult eugenic goal of changing the divorce laws to facilitate the termination of marriages in which couples proved to be genetically incompatible.[76]

Without minimizing the tension between the pursuit of women's rights and the progenitive requirements of the race, eugenic feminists did not really consider that having achieved their goals intelligent, educated women would be satisfied with them as alternatives to marriage and motherhood. After all, only the most militant of suffragettes, including their increasingly furious leader Christabel Pankhurst, obsessed with the belief that at least 75 percent of the male population was riddled with venereal disease, publicly welcomed the prospect of a life of celibacy.[77] Far more representative of even suffragette thinking was Emmeline Pethick Lawrence's assurance that the suffrage movement had never disputed the supreme importance of motherhood.[78] Confident this was indeed the case, Saleeby and Crackanthorpe spoke for most eugenic feminists when they predicted that once enfranchised, women would probably defer from casting their vote and participating in politics until after their children were grown or at least out of the nursery.

Eugenic opponents of women's suffrage were not prepared to make such a leap of faith, and several of them joined Galton in the National League for Opposing Women's Suffrage and signed occasional antisuffrage petitions against the pending Conciliation Bill in 1910 and the abortive Representation of People (Women) Bill of 1913. But eugenic considerations were more often implied than explicitly enunciated in the antisuffrage campaign. In none of the parliamentary debates before World War I about extending the franchise was eugenics specifically mentioned, although there were numerous descriptions of the biologically determined sphere in which women belonged and of the dangers that would befall the empire if their nervous, emotional, impressionistic sex strayed too far from what the Radical Liberal Henry Labouchere termed "the laboratory of nature."[79] Those dangers were rarely seen as demographic, however; it was not the new woman's low fertility that preoccupied M.P.s but her physical and psychological incapacity for statecraft, the uncertainty about how her vote would affect the political makeup of Parliament, and the inevitability of her demanding a seat in that ancient, male body.

Although a eugenic dimension was more evident in the organized antisuffrage campaign outside of Parliament, it was not a central theme in the propaganda put out by the National League for Opposing Women's Suffrage. Neither of its presidents, Lord Cromer or Mrs. E. L. Somervell, dwelt on the subject, though both were sympathetic to eugenics and alluded to the hereditary consequences of the women's movement for the family.[80] The league's principal journal, the *Anti-Suffrage Review*, only occasionally mentioned "unmarried" suffragists or referred to the falling birthrate and the breeding of the unfit. Even then it was often done obliquely, through favorable reviews of sympathetic books like the Whethams' *The Family and the Nation*, which linked declining fertility to the rise of the women's movement, noted the number of masculinized spinsters in positions of leadership, and accused emancipated women of allowing the race to be propagated from the worst stock. Similarly, attention was occasionally called to articles in the *Eugenics Review* and elsewhere that welcomed many of the advances that women had made but warned against the racial dangers of trying to emulate men and confusing the sexes.[81] A bold voice would periodically remind "the right sort of woman" that because there were things that only she could do, she belonged less to herself than to the race and needed to conserve her energy to avoid bringing additional degenerates into a society that already had more than its share.[82]

There were probably two reasons for the *Anti-Suffrage Review*'s reluctance to address the relationship of eugenics to the women's movement and the declining birthrate: differing views about women's roles and abilities and the tactical decision to remain focused upon the immediate question of the vote. As in the eugenics movement, opinions varied considerably among the antisuffrage forces, who only began to organize in the mid-Edwardian years when the extension of the franchise seemed to become a serious possibility. Some were adamant in their belief in the inferiority of women and were hopeful of reversing the changes that had occurred in women's lives since the 1870s. Many more, however, supported to varying degrees the improvements in women's education, occupational diversity, and their expanding participation in local government where, presumably, they could best address those issues appropriate to their sphere—infant welfare, maternal care, the establishment of milk depots, schools, nurseries, and poor relief. The one thing they could all agree upon was that if women were given the vote in national elections the balance of sexual power would be dramatically altered and the separation of spheres would be irreparably breached. The consequences for the future of the constitution, the nation, the empire, and the race were incalculable.

If in retrospect such apocalyptic imaginings seem excessive and strained, they reflect the sorts of doubts about the future that fed eugenical thinking as well. Given the exaggerated importance that the antisuffrage forces attributed to preventing women from obtaining the vote, they were reluctant to be diverted by other controversial issues, including eugenics or birth control, no matter how relevant these issues might seem to many of their supporters. Suffragist organizations such as the National Union of Women's Suffrage Societies and the Women's Social and Political Union adopted a similar strategy.[83]

A correspondent to the *Anti-Suffrage Review*, confused by contradictory predictions in the *Eugenics Review*, tried without success in 1913 to open a discussion about the likely effects of enfranchisement on the declining birthrate of the fittest classes. Many of the best women already resented marriage, the writer pointed out; would the vote increase this tendency, as some opponents claimed, or would it lead to a more eugenically conscious electorate endorsing legislation to stimulate the marriage and procreation of the "most valuable classes?"[84] She was not sure herself but thought it a grave question that should be answered. A poetic effusion elsewhere in the journal was at best a partial response:

Women, Makers of Nations,
Women, you know it's true,
Our Empire's greatest bulwark,
The Race depends on you.
Yet to the winds you are flinging
Motherhood's peerless right,
For the sake of a ballot paper,
Or a queered Election fight.
Thus do you war with Nature,

> Or the scheme of things entire,
> For a seat in the legislature,
> And the joy of pulling a wire.

Continuing in this lyrical vein for three more verses, the poet implored the "Makers of Nations" to build the race and people the empire while remaining "the womanly joy of man's desire."[85]

Not until 1917, when the battle was lost and legislation for the enfranchisement of women the following year was quickly making its way through Parliament, did the *Anti-Suffrage Review* first mention birth control and associate it directly with feminism and the dysgenic breeding of the race. Citing its favorite eugenicist, Whetham, one last time, the review bitterly lamented the "maternal atrophy" and passing of the well-bred child that must inevitably follow the final unleashing of sex competition in the country. What lay ahead was an even sharper decline in the birthrate followed by depopulation, decadence, and disorder which would continue until Britain's feminist community, like that of ancient Greece and Rome, was overthrown by more virile, God-fearing people who did not defy nature by mixing the sexes.[86]

Eugenicists attempting to reconcile the undeniable requirements of race-motherhood with the inevitability of enfranchisement, in the end fell back on their confidence in education and the compelling logic and scientific validity of their new-found faith. The best women, a number of whose outstanding representatives graced the rolls of the Eugenics Education Society, would somehow be drawn again to the rational regeneration of the race. In spite of all that might occur in the years ahead to distract and tempt her, Saleeby promised in 1911, woman was still "Nature's supreme organ of the future." Guided by the new light of eugenics, she would eventually yield to the biological imperative that shaped her in the first place.[87] Eugenic feminists and antifeminists disagreed about whether this meant traditional marriages of convenience to and dependency on men of good stock or emancipated marriages contracted freely on the basis of legal and economic equality, mutual respect, and compatibility. The outcome, however, had to be the same—full cradles in the nurseries of the fit. Whatever changes were occurring in the scientific, social, and political environment in which eugenics emerged, they were not about to displace the fundamental biological preconceptions about class and gender that gave eugenics its appeal in the first place.

World War I and the extension of the franchise to women in 1918 brought an end to the suffrage turmoil of the Edwardian years. From a eugenic standpoint it also destroyed the illusion that a sufficient number of potential race mothers could be persuaded to give birth to enough children to counterbalance the higher fertility of the more populous, genetically less-desirable classes. In spite of desperate recommendations that middle- and upper-class women marry and conceive as many heirs as possible before their warrior husbands were exposed to the risks of battle, eugenicists watched with grief for four terrible years as the birthrate of the fit, like that of the nation, fell to new lows and the proportion of young spinsters and widows of child-bearing age rose to new highs.

Seven

The Dysgenics of War

T he Great War was a eugenics nightmare. It allegedly destroyed the finest physical, mental, and social stock in the country and seriously disrupted family life and selective reproduction. A hopeful surge in the marriage rate from 15.9 per 1,000 to 19.4 during the first year of the war was short lived, and the rate quickly retreated to a low of 13.8. If men and women were eager to marry while they still had the chance, they were not particularly concerned with posterity. The birthrate never rose at all but instead dropped precipitously from around 24 per 1,000 in 1910–14 to 17.7 in 1918, a decline of 26 percent.[1] In aggregate terms the rates added up to a deficit of nearly 700,000 births in Britain when compared to the prewar figures, a loss not much below the 720,000 deaths suffered by men in the armed forces.[2]

From the eugenics perspective the combined destruction of the best representatives of the present generation, whose numbers were already diminishing before the war, and the irretrievable loss of their potential offspring constituted a genetic catastrophe exceeding the degenerative visions of even the gloomiest of Edwardian seers. For some it was a "vast holocaust" on the scale of the black death; for others it conjured up recollections of the French Revolution and the Napoleonic Wars, which many believed had started France on the path of race degeneration and demographic decline that had marked its history since Waterloo.[3] Biologically the British race stood to suffer for generations to come not only from the deprivation of hundreds of thousands of A1 or grade I young men, 75 percent of whom were between the ages of twenty and thirty-five, but from the survival of an even greater number of C3 and grade IV rejects who, unfit for combat or even recruitment, remained at home to reproduce their supposed heritable deficiencies.[4]

As if to compound this dysgenic disaster, the enormous battlefield casualties greatly intensified the demographic anxieties about the size and health of the population that had surfaced in the prewar years and had stimulated a rapid expansion of the pronatalist maternal and child welfare campaign. The introduction of local maternity and child welfare centers, professional health visitors, improvements in the notification of births, tighter regulation of midwives, the feeding and medical inspection of schoolchildren, and the general promotion of "mothercraft" in the Edwardian period were all designed to reduce the excessively high death rate of infants persisting into the early twentieth century despite a steady decline for more than a generation in general mortality.[5] This "wastage" of infant life hovered around 15 percent but was much higher in many overcrowded urban areas. The figures took on new, alarming significance in the Edwardian era when they were added to the millions of children who, because of the rapid adoption of birth control practices, had not been born in recent decades and were unlikely to be conceived in the future.

Calculations as to their number proliferated with each annual report from the registrar general and underscored the testimony and conclusions of official and unofficial inquiries throughout the prewar years. The outbreak of hostilities in 1914 and the staggering losses that soon followed invested the figures with portentous new meaning. James Marchant, the secretary of the National Birth-Rate Commission, estimated the reduction in the birthrate since 1877 had already cost the nation close to 11 million children, half of whom would have been born to the eugenically most valuable classes. If fetal deaths, only recorded since 1914, were extended back forty years, he added, the loss was nearly twice as large.[6] In the opening months of the war Herbert Samuel, the president of the Local Government Board, warned that Britain could only prevail if "backed by a sufficient mass of numbers" and lamented that "under existing conditions we waste before birth and infancy, a large part of our possible population."[7] By then, however, prodded by socialists, trade unionists, feminists, politicians, clergymen, physicians, philanthropic aristocrats, and businessmen, as well as a host of other social critics and reformers, local authorities had begun to pursue policies and programs to insure that the size and health of future generations would be adequate to the needs of the threatened nation.

Their efforts were predicated upon the growing recognition that most infant and childhood deaths were not the inevitable result of inherent defects, but were a consequence of environmental or nurtural conditions amenable to correction. During the war, predictions as to the number of babies who could be saved by the implementation and efficient administration of interventionist programs ranged from 1,000 to 3,000 a week.[8] When these unnecessary losses were added to the uncounted potential children who would have been born had the high levels of Victorian fertility persisted and to the horrendous casualty reports from the front, it was difficult, if not unpatriotic, to disagree with those who proclaimed as "a very urgent war measure" any piece of legislation designed "to meet the terrible depletion which has occurred in the ranks of the citizens."[9]

For the new eugenics movement, with its faith in biological determinism and class-specific, selective reproduction, the environmentally oriented pronatalist drive to increase the numbers of working-class children during the war created a major dilemma—to what extent was positive eugenics compatible with social welfare reform? It brought to a head for the first time serious disagreements about the relative contributions of nature and nurture which were endemic to eugenics and which plagued it throughout its history. Despite the pervasiveness of varying degrees of eugenical thinking in many sectors of society, the problem of reconciling imperfectly understood laws of heredity with the increasingly persuasive claims of environmental reformers always impeded the ability of the eugenics movement to have the impact upon social thought and policy its founders anticipated. If the exigencies of the war did not resolve the issue, they did prod many eugenicists and the Eugenics Education Society to consider a more inclusive theory of causation and to join with progressive social reformers to save the lives of as many children as possible, however questionable their pedigree. At the same time, eugenicists did not lose sight of the primacy of inheritance, and they carried on a separate pronatalist campaign to insure that the heritable qualities of British fighting men would be passed on to as many of the next generation as feasible.

"Skimming the Cream": *Eugenics and the Lost Generation*

Eugenicists assumed from the opening weeks of the war that it would be racially disastrous. The *Eugenics Review*, in its first issue after the outbreak of hostilities, observed, "Under modern conditions of mechanics and mobility [war] is almost entirely dysgenic." Although some militaristic social Darwinists believed the weeding-out effect of conflict enhanced natural selection, W. C. D. Whetham reminded them that Darwin himself had rejected its applicability to highly evolved civilizations. The argument was, however, now academic, the *Eugenics Review* lamented: "The horror of a great war—the greatest the world has ever known—is upon us, and the eugenic and dysgenic effects of war are about to be put to the supreme test of actual experience. All we can do is to put forward every endeavour to mitigate the racial injury to the utmost of our power."[10] In practice this meant increasing the birthrate of the depleted classes and assuring their valuable progeny reached maturity. It involved encouraging men to marry and sire children before leaving for the front, and providing for the wives and offspring of men in the forces, especially officers, while avoiding serious economic disturbances and high taxes that might further discourage the breeding of children.

Whatever rectifying policies were pursued, eugenicists were certain Britain's dependence upon a voluntary army meant it "must inevitably suffer racially more than other nations." The review's strategists predicted it would be the young men "of strongest character, possessing the most love of adventure, the greatest initiative, the keenest and fittest [who] will lay themselves out to be reduced in numbers." These physically and mentally superior specimens, whose rate of reproduction was already dangerously low, would be the first to flock to the colors so that the "sample of those killed will not be the average of the race, but the best type of the race." Although the system might ultimately result in victory, "the cream of the race will be taken and the skimmed milk will be left."[11] It was a theme and metaphor eugenicists repeated over and over, laying the foundation for their own biological version of the legend of the "lost generation."

Until the adoption of conscription in 1916, there seemed to be no way to avoid the disproportionate loss of the most "chivalrous, virile and courageous young men." Their deaths would certainly lead to what the Regius Professor of Natural History, J. Arthur Thompson, described as a "maternal depression" inevitably resulting in "some sort of race impoverishment."[12] Thompson, like many of his contemporaries during and after the war, was particularly sensitive to the social structure of enlistment which drew most heavily from the ranks of the non-manual occupations and the professions. They were shocked by the excessively high casualty rates suffered by young men from the elite public schools and universities who enlisted with enthusiasm in the first phase of the war. Major Darwin and Professor E. B. Poulton, Hope Professor of Zoology at Oxford, estimated that over 60 percent of the undergraduates from some Oxbridge colleges were in the forces, and there was unanimous agreement at the Headmaster's Conference in late 1915 that losses among former students of exceptional scientific and mathematical ability were already very grave.[13]

Whetham sadly reported that by the second winter of the war only the old, the physically useless, and the unsound in spirit were left in Oxford and Cambridge; they constituted "a true survival of the worst."[14] Nearly 20 percent of the more than 26,000 Oxbridge men who served in the war were killed; for those under twenty-five it was closer to one-quarter. Although the figures for several other colleges and universities in the kingdom were nearly as high, the loss of young men from the most elite educational institutions was especially painful to eugenic sensibilities. Students and junior faculty were joined by large numbers of volunteers from banking, finance, commerce, real estate, and the professions, who were twice as likely to join up as were manual workers. Working-class enlistments were in fact greater than commonly recognized and in absolute terms far exceeded those of the middle and upper classes. But their rejection rate was substantially higher while their casualties, however great, were proportionately lower than those inflicted on their social betters, who populated the exceptionally vulnerable junior officer corps in the line battalions.[15]

Eugenicists such as Leonard Darwin were early supporters of conscription in the hope "casualty lists would then more nearly represent a random sample of the population" instead of a preponderance of those from whom it was most desirable that "the stock of the future" be produced. It was a pity, of course, Saleeby complained, nations could not purge themselves of their "trash" by sending them to war—"God's medicine for the human race, as Treitschke calls it"—but conscription would at least dilute the exposure of the finest young men to destruction. While the level of combat in a conscript army was likely to be "less heroic," eugenicists found compensation in the knowlege that those who survived it would be available to impart "their manly qualities in the coming generations."[16]

With the passage of conscription legislation imminent in late 1915, Darwin urged the military planners in the War Office to reverse their policies and call up older men first to preserve as many of the younger as possible for the critical postwar task of race reconstruction.[17] By that time, however, and in the nearly three years that followed, the War Office was scarcely inclined to entertain such arcane demographic subtleties in its desperate rush to replace the thousands of young men slaughtered in one futile campaign after another. Indeed, the country had about exhausted its sources for manpower at the time of the armistice; by then more than 500,000 men under the age of thirty, most of them between the ages of twenty and twenty-four, had been killed, and nearly three times that many wounded.[18]

Reconstructing the Race

Months before the armistice it was already evident to the more pessimistic that the "cream had been skimmed off" and the ablest representatives of the generation lost. As Dean Inge wrote in his diary in the waning hours of 1917, "Whatever is the end of the war, Europe is ruined for my lifetime and longer. Nearly one-fifth of the upper and middle class of military age—the public school and university men, from whom the officers are chosen are dead."[19] It was a tragic confirmation of the qualitative assessment about the changing composition of society toward which his pessimism amd elitist, antidemo-cratic sentiments inclined him even before the First World War and from which he now never wavered. Many of his eugenicist colleagues, however, were less bleak in their assessments. Calculating the dysgenic consequences of the war, they concluded that although the "racial ruin" was likely to be greater and more prolonged than the economic and political ruin, it could be mitigated by assuring the reproduction of as many progeny as possible of the officer classes and the exceptional members of other ranks.

As the end of the first full year of the war approached, Ronald A. Fisher, who had recently been a student at Cambridge where he had joined the Eugenics Education Society, began projecting the number of children and length of time needed to recover an adequate stock of able men over the age of eighteen if, as already seemed possible, as many as half the men in the forces were killed. Even with this fearful prospect in mind, Fisher estimated the racial damage could be repaired in as early as three generations if "those strains and types which have borne the brunt of the fighting" had five children to every four sired by the less fit civilian population. The qualitative recon-struction of the race could in fact be speeded up, he argued, if the government were prepared to provide adequate pensions, marital bonuses, child allow-ances, special tax benefits, and other inducements to marry young and raise large families to the officer class in general and to those who have won military distinctions and honors in particular. It was reasonable to presume their courage and initiative were heritable qualities that should, like their other superior characteristics, be passed on to as many children as possible.[20] Though the fervidly patriotic and conservative Fisher's own poor eyesight had kept him out of the forces, he saw nothing in this defect to prevent him from marrying in 1917 the seventeen-year-old daughter of an evangelical preacher and setting about reproducing eight children to help redress the eugenic balance.

Others were less optimistic in drawing up their regenerative timetables, but agreed the sooner the process of reconstruction began the better. Realizing provisions would probably be made for the "industrial classes," and seeing "the urgent racial necessity of conserving the good stock that remains," repre-sentatives of the Eugenics Education Society arranged a conference in the early weeks of the war with the principal officers of the benevolent committees of several professional societies. The meeting resulted in the establishment of the Professional Classes War Relief Council, under the chairmanship of Major Darwin, to help the families of artists, actors, writers, and other professional and creative men who were at the front. These were the people likely to suffer the most from the war since they were used to a higher standard of living and, according to eugenic analysis, already inclined to sacrifice marriage and parenthood to maintain this standard.

The industrial classes by contrast were well organized, defended by their unions, and in times of necessity cared for by the state. Unlike the more intellectual, professional middle classes, who were unused to manual labor, the working classes could easily adapt to war work and would in fact find more opportunities for their physical talents. As a result, the professional middle class, "from which it is preeminently desirable that the largest number of children should be born, is, by the economic conditions arising out of the war, crushed down and dissuaded by circumstances from reproducing its kind."[21] By implication, of course, the working classes, whose contribution to the racial pool was already disproportionately large, would find even fewer impediments to their reproduction.

As members of the Professional Classes War Relief Council, eugenicists concentrated their efforts upon seeing to the delivery and care of racially valuable children born to the wives of professional men. In 1915 they prevailed, for example, upon J. Pierpont Morgan to make his London mansion available for a maternity home where nearly 250 children of doctors, lawyers, university teachers, and other people of "high civic worth" were delivered during the next two years.[22] It was the first time the new Eugenics Education Society had joined with another organization, and Darwin later admitted it was no more than a token gesture in the face of the terrible dysgenic elimination of hundreds of thousands of potential fathers.[23]

Equally ineffectual, though again reflective of the eugenic mentality during the war, was the society's morbid, three-pronged campaign (1) to persuade men to marry and conceive children before they went off to war; (2) to assure that in the event of their deaths their widows and posthumous offspring were provided with substantial allowances; and (3) to encourage the marriage of spinsters and widows to wounded or "broken soldiers" who, however maimed and disfigured, were still capable of propagating healthy heirs. Saleeby, who wanted the National Birth-Rate Commission to consider the dysgenic consequences of the war, told its members in 1915, "Some of us are trying to encourage the men as far as possible to marry before they go . . . for the definite eugenic end, as they are the pick of our men." He was certain the recent wave of marriages would soon crest and would be followed by a serious quantitative and qualitative decline both in nuptiality and fertility unless additional inducements such as guarantees to war orphans were forthcoming.[24]

The Eugenics Education Society's council, at the request of James Welldon, the dean of Manchester, agreed after some hesitation to promote publicly this wartime adaptation of positive eugenics. The organization's journal praised the archbishop of Canterbury's sensible decision to reduce marriage fees for men in the armed forces and urged the government to accede to the prelate's recommendation to wave the marriage license duty for the duration. Darwin hoped officers and noncommissioned officers in particular would be attracted by these positive gestures.[25] The society also petitioned the War Pensions Committee to guarantee that children already living or born after their father's death would be properly looked after and educated. In the same grisly vein, eugenicists led the way in trying to persuade the public, particularly women, that, however horrible, the wounds suffered by "broken soldiers" were not transmissible and most men were still capable of fathering splendid progeny.

Dr. R. Murray Leslie complained to the Institute of Hygiene in 1916 of the widespread belief that the physical and psychological deformities of the disabled soldier could be genetically passed on. However physically deformed and ill they might be, Whetham added, the hereditary aptitudes of such men were still well above those of the unskilled worker or agricultural laborer. Fisher reminded the noble women who chose to espouse these men "that the injuries of war last but for one generation, and that their children will receive, as a natural dower, a constitution unimpaired, and the power to become all that their father might have been. Their father's courage may grow again in a new and uninjured body."[26]

Eugenic spokesmen demanded medical boards weigh hereditary potential in determining disability pensions. They struggled in vain to persuade the beleaguered War Pensions Committee to grant generous tax allowances, tax rebates, and educational expenses to wounded men, particularly officers, to make them more attractive to hesitant women reluctant to take on the burden of marrying and bearing the racially valuable offspring of the disabled. At the same time, of course, no compensation was to be awarded to men invalided out of the forces for illnesses not connected to combat. To do so would only encourage "the reproduction of bad heritable tendencies."[27]

The council of the Eugenics Education Society discussed this issue at length amidst warnings from Saleeby and others that neither Parliament nor the public would tolerate the exclusion of enlisted men or their offspring from disability benefits. Since the battlefield had become the principal agency of natural selection it was imperative, Saleeby argued, that as many heirs as possible be produced, and leave the future to sort out their differing capabilities.[28] Few of Saleeby's eugenicist colleagues were as sanguine about the outcome of such a biological lottery, but given the scale of casualties suffered by people in all walks of life, most of them were sensitive enough to avoid overemphasizing the correlation between social class and military rank when they campaigned for veterans' allowances. Nevertheless, the interrelationship of class and racial worth was never very far from their thoughts. As Darwin argued in the Galton Lecture of 1917, eugenic selection fated superior men for the battlefield in the first place, and they or their heirs must now be given every chance to even the odds with those whose lesser racial value had spared them and their questionable posterity.[29]

These desperate, futile schemes to encourage the marriage and reproductive activity of A1 men in the forces would certainly have met with Galton's approval, as those who invoked his name frequently pointed out. Although he had never contemplated the extraordinary dysgenic crisis in which his followers found themselves after 1914, their call for early, selective nuptiality and the breeding of large families supported by special economic and educational inducements conformed to the canon of positive eugenics he had laid down in more peaceful times. Galton had envisioned such matches and the many healthy offspring they promised to spawn as qualitatively superior. Though less numerous absolutely, they were relatively sufficient to offset the higher fertility of the less fit and to raise incrementally the efficiency of the race over several generations.

To those disciples who hewed to the positive orthodoxies of the master's teachings, the Great War not only threatened to destroy the finest stock upon which the eugenic reconstruction of the race was dependent, but to replace it with the obviously inferior strains of a C3 and grade IV population. From the eugenic vantage point, this dysgenic disparity was in danger of being compounded by the expansion and intensification of the pronatalist campaign to preserve infant life to replace the terrible depletion of "the manhood of our country," as Walter Long, the president of the Local Government Board, explained in 1915.[30] The eugenics movement, in responding to that compelling campaign while promoting its own eccentric variation, faced for the first time the practical consequences of promoting a demographic strategy based upon qualitative assumptions of natural, hereditary fitness that ran counter to the predominant nurturing, environmentalist convictions of most social reformers in the early twentieth century.

Eugenics and Pronatalism

The problem of reconciling imperfectly understood, popularized laws of heredity with the persuasive claims of environmental reformers posed a serious dilemma for the emerging eugenics movement. If the declining, differential birthrate and concerns about the quality and efficiency of the race were important stimuli to that movement, the growing belief that the deterioration of the urban poor and the persistence of widespread squalor and misery could be corrected by social and economic programs was no less significant. At the core of eugenics, after all, was the certitude that these great and troubling problems were manifestations of individual weaknesses or unfitness primarily genetic, or natural in origin, rather than social, or nurtural. The social evils denounced by socialists and attacked legislatively by the "new liberals" after 1906 were to people of a eugenical bent an inevitable consequence of hereditarily deter- mined individual mental, moral, and physical inadequacies. Although some of the worst symptoms might be ameliorated by charity, philanthropy, and expen- sive social welfare programs, they would prove futile and counterproductive.

The emerging pronatalist movement in Britain, with its emphasis on the preservation of infant life, shared with the new eugenics movement before the war a concern with race deterioration and the falling birthrate. While many individuals and groups associated with pronatalism were interested in revers- ing, or at least slowing, the decline, they all agreed it was imperative to create an environment in which a far greater proportion of children born would survive and grow up healthy to fill the draining racial coffers. This meant the extension of infant protection legislation; the passage of an act mandating the training, registration, and medical supervision of midwives; the establishment of meals for elementary schoolchildren; and the creation of a school medical service. The 1907 Notification of Births Act, though not yet compulsory, facilitated the speedy registration of newborn infants and the early intervention of trained health visitors.

Many of these measures had initially been introduced by local authorities and volunteer associations in response to local conditions. They were sup- ported by a network of infant clinics, schools for nursing mothers, nurseries, and milk depots modeled on those in France and other European countries. The inauguration of annual conferences on infantile mortality in 1906 and the establishment of the National Association for the Prevention of Infant Mor- tality reflected the deep sense of urgency about the need to halt the physical deterioration of the race and offset the fall in the birthrate by improving antenatal and postnatal care. In addition, the introduction of grants from the Local Government Board and the Board of Education to encourage the estab- lishment of infant and maternal welfare centers and schools for mothers dem- onstrated a mounting, if belated, interest on the part of the government before 1914. By the outbreak of the war, infant mortality had fallen to an unprece- dented 95 deaths per 1,000 births, a decline of more than one-third from the deadly figure of 150 prevailing at the turn of the century. Supporters of the infant and maternal welfare movement were confident a rate of 50 per 1,000 was in reach.

Eugenicists, by their advocacy of early marriages and large families, were in their singular way more strictly pronatalist than many of their contemporaries active in the infant and maternal welfare campaign. However much people complained about the declining birthrate, evoked sad images of empty cradles, or uttered dire warnings about race suicide, comparatively few of them really favored as a solution an increase in the size of poor families. The correlation between working-class poverty and the number of children was well known; it had been established in Malthus's time and more recently corroborated by such widely read social investigators as Charles Booth and Seebohm Rowntree.

Socialist critics periodically accused capitalists or militarists of conspiring to assure themselves a steady supply of cheap labor or cannon fodder, and some Neo-Malthusians saw evidence of such a plot in the failure of greedy manufacturers and jingoistic politicians to endorse family limitation as the solution to poverty. But not even pronatalist bishops or doctors, whether intoning the biblical injunction "to be fruitful and multiply" while denouncing the moral evils of birth control or describing its dreadful psychic and somatic effects, endorsed the unchecked reproduction of the already too numerous laboring poor. On the contrary, when it came to the most populous classes, pronatalism had much more to do with the preservation of infant life than it did with encouraging its conception.

The relationship between eugenics and the burgeoning pronatalist movement before the war was tentative at best, weakened by serious ideological and political disagreements over the relative contributions of nature and nurture in the rebuilding of the race. Nevertheless, as the press cuttings books of the Eugenics Education Society suggest, developments in maternal and infant care and in mothercraft were carefully monitored by that organization as it struggled to formulate a policy allowing for the inclusion of a eugenic dimension.[31] For the orthodox or "mainline" eugenicists, as Kevles describes them, who believed in the overwhelming predominance of heredity and who dominated the movement in its early years, the virtual absence of genetic considerations in the rush to save and preserve infant lives only assured further deterioration of the race. Their position was fortified by the statistical studies emerging from Karl Pearson's biometric laboratory. Those who could not understand the complex coefficient correlations demonstrating Pearson's belief that the influence of the environment on individual and class formation was no more than one-tenth to one-fifth that of heredity, nevertheless readily grasped their significance for social reform.[32]

The popular press made much of such statistics and Pearson's dogged insistence that social and humanitarian programs, however well intended, were essentially futile. When critical papers like the *Manchester Guardian* accused eugenicists of misapplying evolutionary theory to justify their opposition to humane reforms, Pearson countered with warnings of the dangers modern Liberalism faced if it denied the seminal role of natural selection and neglected the laws of biology that must govern all sound social policy.[33]

Though he still considered himself a Fabian socialist, Pearson knew he was very much at odds with the dominant forces of environmental social reform in the country. Sidney Webb, who saw the task of eugenics as "deliberately to manipulate the environment so that the survivors may be of the type which we regard as the highest," tried to persuade Pearson that even if terrible social conditions do not affect germ plasm, there was no reason not to remedy them. "We don't live merely for posterity," he reminded him. Webb, as a eugenicist and a socialist, was worried about people in both camps jumping to the conclusion that the two ideologies were hopelessly incompatible, and he feared public recriminations would alienate eugenicists from radicals and progressives. Unlike Pearson, he saw nothing in eugenics that was at odds with improving care for the newborn and warned, "we will never get any collective measures on eugenics" until we have collective control over the environment and nurture.[34]

The problem of evaluating the role of biological determinism and social and economic opportunity had been implicit in Victorian ideas of individualistic self-interest and laissez-faire which reinforced the assumption that success or failure was a consequence of individual, even innate characteristics rather than environmental conditions. Victorian positivists, seeking the science of society, were, for example, divided over the relative contributions of nature and nurture to individual accomplishment, and their differing estimates provoked a significant disagreement between August Comte himself and John Stuart Mill, among others.[35] If the rise of Darwinism greatly reinforced the belief that biology was destiny, it also compelled those of a liberal and socialist persuasion to insist more emphatically on the creation of social and economic conditions that would permit individuals to maximize whatever endowed talents and skills they might possess.

A majority of mainline eugenicists in the early twentieth century questioned the costs and feasibility of trying to create such conditions, denied that social reforms would do much to increase the diminishing pool of genetic talent in the country, and feared such reforms would, by encouraging the proliferation of the unfit, actually prove counterproductive. But within the Eugenics Education Society itself, moderates with different political and social views—such as the Fabian Caleb Saleeby and the Conservative Leonard Darwin—recognized that the success of eugenics as a popular agent of racial improvement required accommodation with the dominant forces of environmental social reform. By adhering inflexibly to the hereditarian line of Pearson and his biometricians, eugenicists, they warned, were in danger of isolating themselves from more influential reformers whose collectivist propensities were for better or for worse likely to dominate Britain in the new century.[36]

The true eugenic reformer did not deny the primacy of "natural eugenics" over "nurtural eugenics," Saleeby explained in 1914, but under no circumstances did he hold that primacy out as an alternative to social reform. Rather, it complemented nurtural eugenics with its objective of rearing healthy, sound children and weeding out "race poisons" injurious to the germ plasm.[37] Saleeby, who had studied antenatal and neonatal pathology in Edinburgh with one of the leaders in that field, Dr. John Ballantyne, was the key figure before the war in trying to build a bridge to the maternal and infant welfare movement. His efforts were met with considerable suspicion by those eugenicists who could see little logic in assisting the survival of thousands of children in "the lowest types of careless, thriftless, dirty and incapable families."[38]

While admitting it would probably be better if some children were never born, Saleeby, who favored the neo-Malthusian solution to that problem, repeatedly denounced the "better-dead" school of "class eugenics" for perverting Darwinism into a justification for opposing the expanding struggle against infant mortality. To him advocates of crude natural selection were actually "pre-eugenic." True eugenics, he argued, was more humane, moral, and rational, and as such belonged in the ranks of the maternal and child welfare movement where it could promote an elevated idea of race parenthood based upon more thoughtful, selective conception.[39]

Pearson, no less than Saleeby, resented the charge eugenicists wanted weaklings killed off. Nevertheless, he had no doubt the intervention of medical skill, charity, and government legislation, coupled with the diminished fertility of the fitter stocks, had created a grave state of affairs. Since the majority of infant deaths were the result of innate frailties, the prolongation of tenuous lives would only extend suffering and shift mortality to a later stage of childhood. Statistical surveys, Pearson insisted, clearly demonstrated that "a heavy infantile death-rate does select the weaker individuals and leaves a stronger population physically to the later years of life." Even maternal ignorance and laziness, which was widely believed to be a major cause of infant mortality among the poor, was, for Pearson, a result of hereditary mental and physical impairments which were probably selectively advantageous for the race.[40]

If eugenicists felt ambivalent about Pearson's findings, important public health officials and statisticians like Arthur Newsholme, G. F. McCleary, and George Newman did not. With the assistance of one of Pearson's former pupils, George Udny Yule, they demonstrated that as many as one-half of all infant and childhood deaths were caused not by inherent weakness or natural susceptibility but by infectious diseases to which healthy as well as unhealthy offspring were vulnerable. Among the poor the disastrous consequences of these diseases were compounded by unhygienic conditions, incompetent midwifery, inadequate diet, and "inefficient" maternal care. All were correctable environmental dangers whose elimination was central to the infant and maternal welfare movement. Furthermore, in contrast to Pearson's prognoses, the statistics also showed that if delicate babies survived infancy they were, with proper rearing, no less likely to grow up strong and healthy.[41]

In spite of Saleeby's efforts to publicize these findings in support of his appeal to the Eugenics Education Society to play a more assertive role in the furtherance of social reform, many of its members and most of its governing council remained hostile at worst and skeptical or ambivalent at best. Their social Darwinist assumptions and Galtonian notions of heredity fed their deep misgivings about the proliferation of the unfit. These ideas also left them less than enthusiastic at the prospect of paying higher taxes to insure the survival of more of the genetically flawed types who already threatened the efficiency of the race.

Although Major Darwin himself expressed reservations about the eugenic value of social reform when he assumed the presidency of the society in 1911, the heated dispute between Mendelians and biometricians persuaded him that not enough was yet known about heredity to measure its relative contribution with confidence. What was certain, however, was there could be no heredity without environment and, like Saleeby, he feared eugenics would isolate itself from the mainstream of social reform where, with its unique perspective, it rightly belonged. He was also extremely sensitive to accusations that eugenics was merely a pseudoscientific rationalization for cruel class prejudice. In his first presidential address to the Eugenics Education Society, Darwin pointedly denied these charges and affirmed the organization's interest only in biology, not class. It was true, of course, that more "natural unfitness" was found among the lowest classes, whose high fertility was the cause of so much alarm, but, he assured his listeners, this was nevertheless a biological not a class problem.[42]

These efforts at accommodation perhaps explain in part the "ideological affinity" with eugenics of some socialist and Liberal progressives like Webb, L. T. Hobhouse, J. A. Hobson, and others before and after the war.[43] But for most eugenicists, particularly those in the Eugenics Education Society, the problem, however couched in biological terminology, was precisely class. They were unpersuaded that extensive social reforms and welfare programs would have much effect upon improving the quality of the population but felt these would probably exacerbate the problems that already existed. The much-vaunted campaign against infant mortality was a case in point. While the death rate of newborns admittedly fell by one-third between 1901 and 1914, it seemed ludicrous to divert pronatalist energies and resources from encouraging greater race motherhood among the genetically select in order to increase the number of genetically flawed survivors of a class whose excessive fertility, once checked by natural selection, was already a threat.

The mounting conflicts among eugenicists over the relative contributions of nature and nurture were moderated by the shattering impact of the war. The soaring casualty lists and manpower shortages, when added to the sharp plunge in fertility after 1915, were sufficient to convince the Eugenics Education Society that for the immediate future at least, prudence and patriotism required the preservation of quantity as well as the promotion of quality. It was prodded in part by Darwin's "Warning to Eugenists" that if they were to have any role in the shaping of social policy and postwar reconstruction they would have to come to terms with the new political and social realities.[44] The result was an uneasy, tenuous alliance of the eugenics movement with the diverse reform elements comprising the maternal and child welfare movement.

Initially the Eugenics Education Society joined with these other groups in lobbying for passage of such legislation as the compulsory Notification of Births (Extension) Act (1915), the Maternal and Child Welfare Act (1918), as well as for the establishment of a Ministry of Health (1919).[45] Following a prolonged, sometimes acrimonious debate among council members, the society also agreed in 1917 to join with some ninety groups in support of the first National Baby Week, with its laudable goal of securing "a birth right of mental and bodily health" for every child in the kingdom. Modeled on a similar undertaking in the United States, the meetings, exhibits, contests, and lectures were designed to focus attention upon the need for healthy children to fill the empty nurseries throughout the land.[46] Demographic anxieties about the future of the race merged with patronizing compassion and condescension in the wartime work of the National Baby Week Council, as it did in the even more fashionable Children's Jewel Fund for which wealthy ladies, proclaiming the incalculable worth of infant life, even among the "toil-driven" multitudes, raised some £70,000 to support the local welfare centers.[47]

Despite his own doubts about the racial consequences of such indiscriminate activity, Darwin struggled to contain the disagreements and occasional resignations among his members and to shield the Eugenics Education Society from charges of being unpatriotic as well as callous and undemocratic.[48] Only the foolhardy would challenge Long's assertion in 1915 that the fearful destruction of "young and lusty life" had made the preservation of babies and the filling of

racial cradles a form of patriotic war work.[49] In contrast to their repeated
prewar complaints about the cost and futility of expanding social welfare
services, eugenicists now quietly acquiesced in a tenfold increase in local
expenditures for such services. They had little to say about the doubling of
maternity and child welfare centers throughout the country—from 650 to
nearly 1,300—or the quadrupling of the number of paid health visitors to look
in on new mothers and their offspring.[50]

Skeptical mainline eugenicists found some solace in the rationalization that
since "the most intelligent parents will be those likely to avail themselves of
facilities offered for their help . . . particularly the mothers . . . their children
will tend to survive."[51] At the same time, however, even the most reform-
minded of their number acknowledged that the percentage of the "submerged
tenth," the lowest strata of society, was also bound to increase. They could only
hope efforts to encourage greater fertility among the dwindling A1 population,
whose numbers were severely depleted by the dysgenic effects of combat,
would in part offset the qualitative imbalance.

Darwin continued to be pulled in two directions by his mainline ideological
predilections on the one hand and his political instincts on the other. Even as
he led the Eugenics Education Society into alliances with such organizations
as the National Association for the Prevention of Infant Mortality, the Association of Infant Welfare Centres, the National Institute of Mothercraft, and the
working-class Women's Cooperative Guild, he insisted we must "keep harping
on the inequality of men as regards their inborn qualities, and we must keep
repudiating environmental reform as a practical method insuring racial progress in the future." But, he added, we must do so with moderation and an
understanding that the exigencies of the times dictate a balance between the
quantitative population requirements of the present and the qualitative needs
of the race after the war.[52]

If eugenicists were prepared to accommodate themselves to immediate
political and social realities, they also pushed ahead with their own long-term
pronatalist strategy of race reconstruction. Assisting the wives and children of
the professional classes and promoting the marriage and progenitive activities
of men in the forces was, as its proponents conceded, more symbolic than
substantive. What were needed were inducements to selective marriage and
fertility that would continue long after the war. Because economic considerations were widely believed to be at the core of domestic decision making
among the more thoughtful, better-educated classes, eugenic planners evaluated a number of possibilities, such as family bonuses or allowances, expanded maternity benefits, and most important, tax remissions.

Before the war, when these schemes were being proposed by pronatalist reformers, eugenicists had been particularly wary of any possibility they might encourage the poor to have more children. Proposals for the direct endowment of motherhood or basing wages upon family size received a particularly frosty reception in eugenic circles. Even Saleeby, who was more sympathetic than most of his colleagues, was worried about unworthy parents who might benefit the most. He agreed with those critics, many of whom were Labourites and trade unionists, who feared that by paying increased benefits directly to mothers, in order to insure that the funds were spent to help their children, paternal responsibility and family structure would be weakened. Unlike working-class opponents, however, Saleeby shared the eugenic belief that feckless, ignorant women would be even more inclined to get pregnant than they already were. Had it been possible to weight benefits in a way that encouraged only worthy parentage, eugenicist objections might have evaporated.[53]

In the absence of such assurances, it was more promising to recommend tax reforms for "potential parents of sound stock" whose income was sufficient to bring them under tax obligations in the first place. It was a strategy that conformed to the eugenic belief in the close correlation of economic success with innate ability, corroborated as recently as 1913 by the statisticians in Pearson's Eugenics Laboratory. Unfortunately, the numbers also proved "that size of family is related inversely to social value as determined by wages." Although they emphatically denied they were prejudiced against any class, biometricians were no less aware than other eugenicists that pronatalism based upon tax reform would, of course, exclude the majority of the laboring poor, whose income fell below the minimum rates, from any financial inducement to have more children. To encourage the fertility of the professional classes, who were both healthier and wealthier than general laborers, was not class prejudice but a rational response to scientific evidence pointing to a "chief factor of national deterioration."[54] Consequently when, in his contentious "People's Budget" of 1909, David Lloyd George introduced income tax child allowances of £10 for parents with income between £160, the exemption limit, and £500, Saleeby described him as "the first eugenicist amongst modern statesmen" and the precedent was not forgotten.[55]

Complaints about the burden of rising taxation on the better classes had become commonplace in the prewar decade when the rate rose from a modest eight pence in the pound to one shilling two pence. These costs, plus the increased expenses of rearing and educating children, were widely held to be major reasons for the later marriages and smaller families of the responsible, tax-paying classes. The huge costs of the war quickly magnified the problem and provoked continual pleas for meaningful relief for families with children. The National Birth-Rate Commission, which strongly supported the maternal and child welfare campaign, recommended in its 1916 report on the causes of declining fertility that joint incomes be taxed at a lower rate and educational bonuses and substantial tax remissions be given to families whose income was below £700 a year. With eugenic considerations in mind, it added that condemnation of the reckless poor, who had too many offspring, should be balanced with denunciations of the selfish rich, who had too few, and specifically urged the authorities to tax bachelors more heavily.[56] Walter Long assured a deputation from the commission that the Local Government Board was sympathetic and promised to support legislation to reduce taxation as a stimulus to larger families. The Finance Act of 1916 did provide some relief for families with more than two children and incomes under £800.[57]

However much the Eugenics Education Society welcomed the recommendations of the National Birth-Rate Commission, its council worried about the lack of selectivity in the many patriotic, wartime appeals for a general increase in the birthrate. With the Germans calling for 10 million more children, there was a danger the British might be panicked into indiscriminate reproduction. Even if humanitarian considerations required those above the average in all classes to bear the burden of those inherently incapable of caring for themselves, it was imperative, eugenicists repeatedly argued, to provide the fittest people adequate assistance to rebuild as much of the population as possible from their able ranks.

Shortly before the outbreak of the war, the society's council, at Darwin's urging, had begun calculating the effects of taxation on the low fertility of the professional middle classes with the intention of providing sympathetic politicians with its findings.[58] The war gave new urgency to the project, and between 1914 and 1918 proposal followed proposal urging the government to lighten the tax burden on people by such measures as dividing total family income by the number of family members and taxing each individually at the lower rate. People of substantial income would quickly seize upon the advantages of having more children, and many middle-class and skilled working-class families would fall into the same low or nontaxable brackets enjoyed by their economic, and, presumably, genetic inferiors. In addition, the council proposed that maternity costs and the total expenses for educating children be deductible from income and, in the case of the latter, from death duties as well.[59]

Discussions of tax reform during the war were frequently punctuated by the eugenically inspired grousing of people like Sidney Webb who complained of the rates falling most heavily upon the classes who should have the most children. They presented no impediment, however, to "the thriftless and irresponsible, the reckless and the short-sighted of all grades" with the result that "the community now breeds fastest from its socially least desirable stocks."[60] A decade earlier, in 1907, he had advocated the endowment of motherhood for "the best members of the middle and upper artisan classes" to offset the unrestrained breeding of Irish Catholics and Polish, Russian, and German Jews and the "thriftless and irresponsible largely casual labourers and other denizens of the one-roomed tenements of our great cities."[61] The situation, if not the rhetoric, had changed dramatically since 1914, and however much eugenicists applauded Webb's sentiments, they realized the war made it more unlikely than ever that any policy of direct, class-specific inducements to fertility stood a chance of being implemented. Tax reform as a part of reconstruction seemed to be the only hope.

Sir Hamar Greenwood, the Liberal M.P. and future chief secretary for Ireland, agreed. In 1918, at the urging of the Eugenics Education Society, he introduced an amendment to the Finance Act in Parliament allowing income for tax purposes to be divided into equal shares on the basis of family size.[62] "The frightful havoc of the War has compelled . . . every thoughtful person to think of the future of our race [which] is in the cradle," he told the Commons. "It is the first duty of the Government to encourage healthy men and women to multiply." Angered by men and women who delayed or did not marry at all when the race was in such peril, Greenwood also contemplated a regressive levy on bachelors and spinsters. His amendment was received sympathetically by the chancellor of the exchequer, Andrew Bonar Law, who acknowledged that while it would indeed "encourage healthy men and women to multiply" for the "future of the race," the loss to the treasury would be too great while the war was still being fought. He promised, however, to take it up in future considerations of financial legislation.[63]

Sex Ratios and Race Reconstruction

Whatever their impact upon correcting the qualitative and quantitative demographic damage of the war, neither tax reform nor any other financial incentives held out much hope for reversing the mounting imbalance in the ratio of females to males magnified by the deaths of three-quarters of a million men. Long before the war, Victorians interested in the role of sexual selection in evolution or concerned about the surplus of unmarried women in society contemplated the reasons for and consequences of the greater fragility of male lives evident in mortality statistics. Although on average 3 to 4 percent more males were born than females, male mortality was approximately 14 percent higher, and in some insalubrious areas the difference was closer to 30 percent.[64] The result, as worried observers of the nuptial habits of their country-men reported, was an excess of marriageable young ladies and a chronic shortage of suitable mates.

Alfred Russel Wallace was confident as early as the 1890s that with better maternal and infant care and improved medicines males would someday sur-vive as well as if not better than females, thereby improving the sexual selectivity currently denied women in choosing a husband.[65] Despite their impact upon infant mortality, the improvements Wallace anticipated had little effect on the comparative vitality of newborn males. As a result, in 1911 the ratio of 1,067 females per 1,000 males recorded for England and Wales represented the largest imbalance in Europe. The "vital superiority" of girls was further confirmed when, after 1915, the recording of stillbirths revealed that the mortality sex differential was as large as 40 percent.[66]

These figures greatly strengthened the position of those who argued that the wastage of life between conception and birth was not only greater than in infancy but constituted a scale of male mortality approaching that encountered on the battlefield.[67] As a result, antenatal care began to play a larger role in the thinking of pronatalists who, from 1915 on, increasingly recognized that the nine months before birth were perhaps as critical to the survival of children as the three months that followed. The prospect of saving thousands of valuable babies, half of them male, rapidly led to the better care of pregnant women as an adjunct to the main goal of child welfare.[68]

Saleeby, whose dismay at the casualty rates and continued fall in the birth-rate caused him to repudiate his prewar support of neo-Malthusianism as a form of negative eugenics, now stressed the positive eugenic importance of prenatal care in reducing the high rates of miscarriage, stillbirth, and infant mortality.[69] He knew from his own experience as a doctor and eugenicist how deeply ingrained the belief was in medical as well as eugenical circles that such losses were a "natural and healthy process . . . a rather merciful elimination of infants not fit to live." This "lie of lies," as Saleeby described it, had cost the nation millions of potential recruits who were now desperately needed and whose loss, coupled to those on the battlefield, would, even after victory, leave Britain with a more serious sex imbalance than ever.[70] There was already an excess of more than 1,300,000 females in 1914. Assessments varied about the disruptive effects of the war on this sex disproportion. The most accurate of them projected differences of around 3 million women, with more than half of them in the marriageable, fecund age brackets.[71]

Under such calamitous circumstances it is not surprising that so much of the rhetoric of the maternal and child welfare campaign singled out the importance of saving male infants. The deprivation of much-needed manpower resulting from the annual wastage of male infant lives since the 1870s was usually estimated to be at least a half-million.[72] Other gloomy calculations compared the number of babies who died hourly or daily with the losses during the same periods suffered at the front to demonstrate it was more dangerous to be an infant than a soldier. When the *Times* wrote about the "cult of the child," his gender was well understood by contemporaries.[73] One of the welfare campaign's strongest supporters, Sir Arthur Acland, a former president of the board of education, was typical in his mourning of the "waste of large numbers of fine, strong men-babies who are born splendidly healthy and ready to do their share for their country some day." In endorsing the Life Saving in War Time drive of the National League for Physical Education and Improvement, Acland hoped the infant mortality rate could be halved to about 50 per 1,000.[74] It might not alter what Sir Bernard Mallet, the registrar general, president of the Royal Statistical Society, and future president of the Eugenics Society, described in 1918 as "a rise in the sex proportion so marked and sustained over so long a period," but any reduction in the number of prenatal and postnatal infant deaths would at least diminish the absolute loss of male lives so precious since 1914.[75]

Many pronatalists assumed, despite the decline in infant mortality, that the surge in female employment from approximately 3,200,000 to over 4,800,000 during the war would endanger the advances made since the opening of the century. With married women constituting 40 percent of the swollen female workforce, there was a good deal of thoughtful consideration and, sometimes, hysterical rhetoric about the consequences for children and the race.[76] Dr. Arabella Kenealy continued to warn of the dangers of drawing down the limited "constitutional reserves" of her sex and exhausting "the constitutional resources of the generation to come."[77]

The lower fertility and higher infant mortality of the textile districts, where female labor was prevalent, had been observed for decades, and criticism of working mothers had intensified along with the infant welfare and mothercraft movements in the prewar years.[78] A temporary leap in infant mortality in 1915, though attributed to a severe measles epidemic, was immediately seized upon as evidence by opponents of mothers' joining the workforce. A closer examination of the correlation disproved any straightforward relationship; like the infant death rate itself, it varied from town to town. In mining districts, for example, where comparatively few mothers worked, infant mortality was higher than in many industrial centers where female employment was substantial.[79] During the war, three government committees and several unofficial bodies examined contradictory evidence and reached different conclusions about the seriousness of the problem.[80] It was an issue transcending political and social ideologies; Labour Party spokesmen and socialists were as concerned about the effects of female employment on "racial health" as were Liberals and Conservatives.[81]

With the exception of Saleeby and a few other Fabians, most eugenicists were not particularly bothered by the problem so long as it primarily affected the working classes.[82] Their colleagues were, however, wary about the impact of an expanded female workforce when it drew upon middle- and even lower middle-class women whose heritable qualities were presumed to be, on the average, well above those of their working-class sisters. Whatever the requirements of war, the place of able women, in their most fecund years at least, was still in the home. As the need for female workers increased, R. A. Fisher and C. A. Stock worried about the working-class model, with its "lower quality of marriage," becoming established among the eugenically better classes. They therefore urged a continuation of restrictive employment policies in teaching, government, and other areas to which women of higher civic worth were likely to be attracted. There was, after all, no evidence that a woman's earning capacity, unlike that of a man's, was a measure of eugenic excellence, they reasoned, nor was it especially useful in domestic life. Moreover, the elimination of barriers to the employment of non-working-class married women would discourage eugenic marriages by interfering with the different "spheres of capability and excellence" that had evolved over many generations to make such marriages valuable. If the eugenically superior classes began emulating the industrial classes where both husband and wife frequently worked, the ideals of marriage would deteriorate rapidly and the tendency toward a lower standard of domestic and racial responsibility already evident in the diminishing birthrate of the genetically select would increase dramatically.[83]

Given the elevated focus of their class preoccupations, eugenicists were not inclined to pay much heed to the fears of workers and union leaders of women being employed as blacklegs or cheap laborers who threatened to displace men permanently in the workforce. They did, however, share a concern about the preservation of a patriarchal society with the husband in the traditional role of breadwinner. Both eugenicist and non-eugenicist alike worried about the future of the family if gender roles continued to become confused, and they talked a great deal about the importance of the quality of motherhood in the rebuilding of the race. Though diehard antisuffragists, pointing to the achievements in reducing infant and childhood mortality, continued to insist that social improvements and race reconstruction could be accomplished without the extension of the franchise to women, their arguments seemed increasingly irrelevant and desperate and found virtually no echo in eugenic circles during the war.[84] Eugenicists had no quarrel with the *Anti-Suffrage Review*'s contention that women must "do women's work" first and rear children, but even socialist women who demanded the vote, such as Mary MacArthur, the most prominent female trade unionist, urged wives to stay home with their children. "Women have done some wonderful work," she conceded, "but a baby is more wonderful than a machine gun. I believe that the hand that rocks the cradle will still be a power when the other is only a hateful memory."[85] The problem for the eugenicist was how to increase the probability that the infant in that cradle would be genetically fit.

Although eugenicists continued to express reservations about the indiscriminate nature of the maternal and child welfare campaign, most recognized it was, for better or for worse, an inescapable and integral part of wartime pronatalism certain to remain an important feature of postwar reconstruction. But the war also forced all but the most unreconstructed of eugenicists to conclude that the race was perhaps stronger and more efficient than prewar diagnoses had revealed. Far from crumbling under the German onslaught, the population had proven to be extraordinarily resilient and productive. Moreover, despite persistent beliefs to the contrary, the health of the poorest and, presumably, most unfit sector of the civilian populace substantially improved. Infant mortality continued to fall, longevity rose, and with the exception of an increase in pulmonary ailments and the exceptional influenza pandemic of 1918–19, the incidence and fatal consequences of most infectious diseases declined.

Ironically, these advances in the physical well-being of men, women, and children on the home front paralleled a decline in the availability of some 14,000 doctors whose curative skills were needed by the armed forces. As J. M. Winter has persuasively argued, the dramatic improvements in civilian health had little to do with medical intervention or even with the many social programs so worrisome to eugenicists. They were, on the contrary, closely associated with the full employment, higher wages, and, despite shortages and rationing, generally healthier diet workers and their families enjoyed.[86]

Surplus labor was quickly absorbed into the economy, the workhouses were emptied, and the casual wards closed down. The First World War, as Robert Roberts recalled in his autobiographical recollections of Salford, marked the "great escape" from primary poverty. It also showed, as the Webbs later admitted, that the existence of the casual poor had not been the effect of some deviant mutation or hereditary taint induced by the degenerating influences of city life. The unfit poor were a social not a biological creation whose numbers rapidly disappeared as soon as regular employment with adequate wages was available. They had, in fact, never existed except as a "phantom army" called up by late Victorian and Edwardian social science to explain and legitimize social practices and economic realities.[87]

The eugenically minded continued to look for the hereditary component in the social and economic structure, but after 1918 they were willing to acknowledge that while inherited ability was still distributed more heavily among the successful classes it also extended to a wider range of the populace than had been realized before the war. It did not mean, however, that class eugenics with its invidious comparisons and "selfish opposition to social reform" was, as Saleeby predicted, unable to survive despite "the glory and devotion and endurance" demonstrated by all sectors of society.[88] On the contrary, though less prominent in eugenic propaganda in the interwar years, class considerations and qualitative evaluations continued to pervade eugenical thinking as they did British culture.

If the war forced the Eugenics Education Society to compromise with nurtural pronatalism and lend its support to official and voluntary programs for maternal and infant care, it remained an uneasy association. In the society's annual report for 1917–18, Darwin noted that eugenicists were for now at least generally in agreement on the need for improved social conditions. He welcomed efforts to promote infant welfare, better housing, and expanded maternity assistance to bring out the good qualities of the race once they were produced by parents of finer stock.[89]

Although the report tried to gloss over the conflict within eugenics over the comparative roles of nature and nurture that wartime considerations had obscured, it failed to reconcile the contradictions, and after 1918 the society quietly backed away from its uncomfortable alliances. Saleeby, who had played a major role in forging the fragile links of those alliances, remained, along with several others, committed to them and soon withdrew from the society's affairs with his predictions of a new "race hygiene" based upon a postwar merger of eugenics and socialism unfulfilled. Eight years after the end of hostilities, the society's council was still trying to reconcile the ambiguous mix of hereditarian and environmentalist ideologies that divided the faithful. It finally agreed in 1926 on a compromise "Practical Eugenic Policy" acknowledging that while many immediate benefits might be derived from changes in the environment, it was probably best if the society took no position on the matter. The council instead encouraged those members who wished to do so to cooperate as individuals with the "innumerable existing bodies already striving to improve human surroundings."[90]

Eugenic pronatalism, with its Galtonian dream of promoting higher fertility among the so-called fitter classes, had reached its peak during the war when the Eugenics Education Society, for largely pragmatic, tactical reasons, grudgingly added the preservation of infant life to its elitist agenda of race reconstruction. In reality, the enormous number of casualties to the A1 population in the war, coupled with the continued fall in the birthrate, convinced many architects of race renewal that no pronatalist scheme would ever succeed in reversing differential fertility enough to be able to halt the slide toward deterioration.[91] Consequently, as eugenicists became less confident in their ability to propagate a sizable racial elite from positive inducements, they increasingly turned from selective pronatalism to negative policies such as sterilization and, more important, birth control to curtail the proliferation of the unfit and gradually raise the qualitative level of the general population.

Eight

Eugenics and the Birth Control
Movement, 1918–1930

The Eugenics Education Society emerged from the war with its small numbers depleted and its direction uncertain. Its select membership had fallen to nearly 300 from a prewar high of 714—a figure not reached again until 1930.[1] Despite tenuous financial resources and reduced supplies, the organization had managed to publish a truncated *Eugenics Review* throughout the war, sustained by gifts and subscriptions as well as Major Darwin's personal generosity. Although in the slump of 1920–21 it had to dispense temporarily with its salaried staff, the society was rescued by a series of private donations from wealthy supporters and in 1923 received the first of several financial infusions from a previously unknown benefactor, Henry Twitchin, an eccentric, retired English sheep station owner in Australia.[2]

Twitchin's fear of an unspecified hereditary family affliction had convinced him to remain a bachelor and to devote his final years to the advancement of eugenics, a subject to which he had been drawn from sheep breeding. In 1922 he wrote an astonished but grateful Darwin that, as he had no heirs, he planned to send periodic donations anonymously to the society and upon his death leave it his estate, valued then at £160,000.[3] Throughout the 1920s Darwin cultivated this "queer being," as he described Twitchin to his presidential successor, Sir Bernard Mallet, and in 1930 the Eugenics Society (as it was renamed in 1926), struggling to cope with the financial exigencies brought on by the depression, was suddenly favored with a bequest of some £70,000 from Twitchin's reduced, but still very substantial, estate.[4]

The Twitchin bequest transformed the Eugenics Society into a moderately wealthy and potentially influential organization at the end of a decade in which the organization had struggled, with mixed results, to accommodate itself to the social, political, economic, scientific, and demographic realities of the postwar world. The biological permutations of eugenical thought had always been much more diverse than could be contained within the prevailing orthodoxies of the small and selective Eugenics Education Society. But the eclecticism and imprecision of eugenics was an important part of its appeal to social critics, reformers, and the educated public, for its fluid definitions and confusion of science and social science allowed it to be modified in different ways by people who believed to varying degrees in the importance of a "hereditary factor." They were free to explain as much or as little as they wanted to about social or economic conditions on the basis of heredity. The goal of organized eugenics was to persuade them that more rather than less was dependent upon inheritance and to see that this factor became an important consideration in whatever social planning was undertaken.

This was what was on Twitchin's mind in 1922 when he approached Darwin and offered him the means to turn the small Eugenics Education Society into an aggressive propaganda agency for race reconstruction. The problem, however, as Darwin already knew, was reaching agreement within eugenicist ranks on where to concentrate its propagandist activities. Many of his mainline followers were eager to extract the society from its unnatural alliance with the maternal and child welfare movement and return to the positive policies of eugenic pronatalism favored by Galton. Others, however, insisted even before the war that birth control had made it highly unlikely the fittest classes would ever reproduce themselves in sufficient numbers to halt the racial deterioration compounded by differential fertility. The loss of nearly a million A1 men between 1914 and 1918 made that prospect even more remote.

Vital Statistics and Demographic Strategies

Although the birthrate, stimulated by demobilization and the short-lived economic boom following the war, rose to 25.5 per 1,000, a figure last approached in 1909, it soon began falling once more. By 1921 fertility had receded to 22.4, the lowest peacetime level ever recorded, and by the end of the decade hovered around 16 per 1,000. The ratio of children born to women ages fifteen to forty-five was, at 65.8 per 1,000, even lower than the unprecedented wartime figure of 71.1. While the proportion of people married increased steadily in the 1920s, the size of their families continued to decrease to 2.1, a figure even lower than the 2.4 children born to the cohort married during the war.[5] Though Darwin was no less convinced of the dysgenic dangers in birth control than he had been before the war, he knew there was mounting sentiment within the Eugenics Society to reconsider its relationship to the expanding birth control movement.

Whatever moves the society had been making toward incorporating birth control into its strategies for race culture before 1914 had been abruptly halted by the war. Havelock Ellis and Dean Inge, both of whom sat on the organization's council, continued to argue that rational family limitation among "undesirable stocks" was a logical and necessary adjunct to a negative eugenic population policy; others such as Caleb Saleeby and Sir James Crichton-Browne, shocked by the swollen casualty lists and plummeting birthrates, repudiated their prewar sympathy for neo-Malthusianism. Both Ellis and Inge conceded to positive eugenicists that the social pattern of birth control had thus far proven to be dysgenic and acknowledged that the war would intensify the problem. But for the optimistic Ellis this was a temporary setback in the progressive evolution of the race, a major feature of which was the recent emergence of enlightened family planning among the more highly developed middle and upper classes. It was only a matter of time before the physical, economic, and social advantages of birth control would be grasped by those still a step down on the evolutionary ladder, he promised, and reasoned that it was more important than ever for eugenicists to accelerate its adoption as a great instrument for the elevation of the race.[6]

Inge, whose vision of the future was far bleaker, endorsed family limitation as the lesser of many evils. It would, he agreed with Ellis, be criminal to try to restore the birthrate of fifty years ago and unrealistic to think it was remotely possible. The great European population boom that had started in the eighteenth century was over, Inge warned; the problem now was not quantity but quality, the replacement of natural selection with rational selection.[7] Both Inge and Ellis deplored what eugenicists believed to be an indiscriminate campaign to increase the birthrate during the war, but neither endorsed the Malthusian League's tactless call to the working classes for a moratorium on children and its contemptuous dismissal of social welfare programs and improvements in infant and maternal care as futile and counterproductive.[8]

C. V. Drysdale's pleas on behalf of the Malthusian League, to recognize the long-term racial consequences of the unfit remaining at home siring the next generation while the genetically most valuable men were at the front, had little impact upon his eugenicist colleagues. However much they shared his worries about differential fertility, they were not persuaded the Malthusian League had either an answer or a reputation with which they wanted to be associated. When at the urging of Saleeby and Darwin the Eugenics Education Society decided to join with other organizations in 1915 in support of pronatalist programs, Drysdale and his wife, Bessie, angrily resigned from the organization.[9]

The departure of the Drysdales was cause for relief rather than disappointment, particularly for the cautious Darwin, who had carefully deflected recommendations that the society ally itself with birth control. He was not entirely successful and in 1917 was unable to prevent the publication in the

Eugenics Review of an article by Ellis advocating birth control as the most practicable and promising means for eugenic improvement. It was the first time a strong endorsement of birth control had appeared in its pages. Aware of the reluctance within the society's ranks to confront what many still believed was an unseemly subject, Ellis insisted that the time for "vain discussion" and "prudery and ignorance" was over. They belonged to the past; the Great War had sealed their fate. Birth control was "the magic formula . . . to stem the tide of unfit babies" threatening to overwhelm the superior stocks. The day for applying it had arrived; there was no turning back, for it would never dawn again, he warned.[10]

Shortly before Ellis's article appeared, Darwin wrote to him: "So far I have thought it politic with the audience I have to deal with to assume the existence of birth control, rather than emphasize it." He admitted, however, that the practice had come to stay, though it was not something that he especially wanted to deal with.[11] The *Eugenics Review*, for its part, prefaced Ellis's piece with a note assuring subscribers the Eugenics Education Society took no position on birth control.[12] When a year later the *Saturday Review* claimed the war had put the society in a quandary and forced it to turn from a policy of birth control to one of birth assistance, the editor of the *Eugenics Review* was quick to correct the mistake. The society, he assured readers, had always favored a limited and discriminating birth control to curtail the procreation of the unfit, but parenthood among everyone else was a national duty.[13]

The National Birth-Rate Commission, reactivated in 1918 under the pro-natalist chairmanship of Saleeby to study the demographic aspects of "national and racial reconstruction," basically agreed when it reported in 1920, though it was much more critical of birth control than the first commission had been. If Inge predicted the report would, because of its anti–birth control bias, be a "belated kick of the prewar mentality with its timid and reactionary ethics," no eugenicist disputed the commission's findings "that the classes which have demonstrated superior capacity for the struggle of life in the past by rising in the social scale, have, during the recent past, ceased to contribute anything like their fair share to the nation's capital of men and women." Some might have balked at the commission's recommendations for improved public housing, a minimum living wage, and expanded maternal and child welfare facilities, but its call for greater tax relief and extensive educational subsidies was like music to a eugenicist's ear.[14]

Though the second National Birth-Rate Commission report was suffused with eugenic assumptions and warnings about dysgenic breeding, racial obligations, worthy parentage, and the dangers of race suicide, reflecting

Saleeby's hand and the class suppositions of its members, it was cautious about explicitly describing its proposals as eugenic. Instead, the commissioners contented themselves with a brief, if obvious, paragraph near the end of their report suggesting "much more might be done from the eugenic point of view if parents would encourage and develop in their children higher ideals as to the racial aspect of marriage and parenthood, and the importance of character and fitness in the partner of their choice."[15]

There was little evidence to suggest such selectivity was at work in the sudden rise of the birthrate in 1920, which the geneticist William Bateson described as an occasion for rejoicing "on the part of the unthinking." Though not a member of the Eugenics Education Society, he shared its concerns about differential fertility and in the Galton Lecture of 1920 asked, "If we could see a parade of the parents who have made themselves responsible for this excess, I wonder if we should take so much pride in their performance, and whether we should not simply see in this output of spawn one more manifestation of the recklessness engendered by a period of spurious prosperity."[16] Two years later the economic boom had come to an end and the birthrate was falling once more. To Sir James Barr, however, so long as the C3 population, as the unfit continued to be called, remained disproportionately fertile, the final outcome of the war would remain unclear. Reviving Karl Pearson's old formula about the poorest quarter of society producing half the next generation, Barr lashed out at sentimental "pro-populationists" and "would-be philanthropists . . . crying upon those derelicts to produce more babies to replace the real nobility of manhood who perished in the war."[17]

Such angry, public vituperation over the differential birthrate was much less common in eugenic circles in the 1920s than it had been before the war. Darwin, who was concerned and embarrassed by the intemperate rhetoric of some of his more zealous colleagues, tried to temper it at the end of the war when he cautioned them that Galton's approach to race reconstruction was probably no longer feasible. The success of positive eugenics in the future would likely mean an increase not just in the highest types but also in the mediocre but self-supporting population of all classes whose ability to avoid dependency was probably inherited.

Even while urging eugenicists to avoid using offensive and outdated stock-yard metaphors, which were thrown back at them by their opponents, Darwin acknowledged he was departing from Galton's emphasis upon breeding "prize bulls" in proposing that the Eugenics Education Society concentrate in the future on raising the general level of "the herd." In the aftermath of a war in which the anthropomorphic imagery of slaughtered cattle was all too vivid, it was, he realized, politically insensitive, not to mention biologically inaccurate, to liken men, who were rational, moral creatures, to breeding stock. Perhaps not everyone would credit the species with these qualities in 1918, but Darwin was essentially a hopeful and optimistic man. He also thought of himself as a realist and calculated it was no longer possible in the more democratic climate of postwar Britain to expect either the state or most private institutions to provide pronatalist inducements specifically for the eugenically fit, as Galton had envisioned.[18]

As an enthusiastic supporter of family allowances, William Beveridge, the director of the London School of Economics (LSE), was more positive about the possibilities of encouraging selective couples through salary supplements and other endowments to increase the number of their offspring. He was also among the more notable of several eugenicists who, by the middle of the decade, recognized that the much-feared class differential in the birthrate was already diminishing and who questioned whether it had ever been as large as the influential Pearson had projected. In a paper delivered to the Eugenics Education Society in 1924, he claimed the *Report* of the 1911 *Fertility of Marriage Census*, which had finally been published the previous year, proved that the most fertile sector of the population produced at the most 30 percent of the next generation, not 50 percent as Pearson had long claimed.[19]

Beveridge was also responding to a series of regional analyses in the 1920s indicating that the differences in the fertility of various occupational groups and social classes were narrowing. London, as before the war, came under particular scrutiny. The birthrates in working-class districts such as Shoreditch and Poplar continued to be compared with the more fashionable boroughs of Hampstead or South Kensington. Although still well above the national average, fertility in the poorer, more populous areas was substantially below prewar levels and continued to fall more rapidly than in the prosperous districts of the city and in the country as a whole. By the end of the decade it stood at about 19 per 1,000 compared to 16.3 per 1,000 for all of England and Wales. Wide reproductive variations among districts and different socioeconomic groups still remained, but it was increasingly clear, as one analyst of the London figures noted, that the birthrate was down for all classes, and in many areas of the East End the two-child family had become far more common than the seven-child family so frightening to eugenicists in the past.[20]

In the absence of comprehensive data on differential fertility, however, people tended to find what they looked for in the available statistics. The *Fertility of Marriage Census* of 1911 dominated eugenical thinking about the birthrates of different occupational groups in the 1920s, despite evidence that the demographic trends described in that survey were already out of date. As early as 1925 the Eugenics Education Society began to agitate for another fertility inquiry in conjunction with the next census, scheduled for 1931. It discussed joining with a number of other groups, including the Royal Society, the National Population Committee, and the Medical Research Council, to petition the minister of health and the registrar general to introduce a policy of regular "human stock taking" to determine, among other things, the fertility of different social strata.

Eugenicists were confident the figures, if used in conjunction with intelligence tests, medical examinations, and anthropometric measurements, would reveal whether the individuals composing the nation were increasing or decreasing in average value so that the extent of deterioration and degeneration could be calculated more accurately from decade to decade. The society's council thought that another interdepartmental committee on national deterioration, like that which reported in 1904, or perhaps a royal commission, would be an appropriate forum for evaluating the data. Although the registrar general, S. P. Vivian, was concerned about budgetary constraints and the complexity of such an undertaking, he promised in 1929 to consult with the Eugenics Society and other interested organizations when plans for the 1931 census were drawn up. The economic crisis in which the country soon found itself precluded the taking of an expanded survey, although Vivian agreed to add a question about the age of new parents as a first step toward improving the gathering of vital statistics.[21]

The Eugenics Society's call for an updated fertility study was in fact not answered until after World War II when in 1946 a survey was taken on behalf of the Royal Commission on Population established two years earlier. That *Family Census*, the first since 1911, reaffirmed the perceptions of the 1920s and 1930s: reproductive variations among social classes were rapidly narrowing. The overall decline in family size, for example, was virtually the same for manual and nonmanual occupations. If the notoriously low fertility of the professional classes, which had so distressed the eugenically minded Superintendent of Statistics T. H. C. Stevenson in 1911, had continued to fall by another 25 percent, the decline was increasingly shared and sometimes exceeded by other sectors of the middle and working classes. Even the notoriously procreant miners and agricultural laborers marrying in the postwar decade sired nearly a third fewer children than their prewar cohorts. However, the numbers were still much too large and socially differentiated for birth control advocates and eugenicists. Their own observations confirmed later findings that despite the general decline in the fertility of the most prolific sector of society marrying in the 1920s, that group still produced twice as many offspring as couples in the least fertile categories.[22] Nonetheless it was becoming more difficult to single out family size as a distinctive socioeconomic variable.

Whatever the intellectual and economic value of the unskilled workers, miners, and agricultural laborers who, Pearson's exaggerations aside, continued to father a substantial minority of the next generation, they were certainly not deficient in stamina and physique, Beveridge recalled. Men in the latter two categories at least were, as wartime medical reports verified, among the fittest in the country. In addition, Beveridge, who had become a leading authority on the problem of unemployment before the war and the author of the standard work on the subject, pointed out to his eugenicist audience that, despite the current high levels of joblessness, the war had also shown only a small minority of the laboring population to be truly unemployable.[23] The so-called unfit were in fact much healthier than before the war, and there was no evidence their condition had deteriorated since 1918. On the contrary, the data all pointed in the other direction.[24]

Beveridge's argument was echoed by a number of noneugenicist critics in the 1920s and strongly reinforced in 1925 by A. L. Bowley and M. H. Hogg's answer to the question, Has Poverty Diminished? In responding positively, the two economists demonstrated the close correlation between improved wages and the health, vitality, and productivity of those who before the war were assumed to be congenitally incapable of escaping from chronic poverty.[25] To Sir Arthur Newsholme, who was both worried about the declining birthrate and skeptical of eugenic half-truths, the most important of Bowley and Hogg's discoveries was that "the effect of increased wages in producing this reduction in poverty was twice as great as that exercised by the diminution in the number of large families." Indeed, Newsholme insisted, the statistics did not support the view that the nation was endangered by an "avalanche of infants" in the slums of our towns, nor was it increasingly being replenished from "strata, which are characterized by inferior innate qualities."[26]

In the face of mounting evidence showing the differences in the birthrates of social classes moderating, eugenicists began to focus their analyses more closely on the reproductive experience of smaller sectors of society: (1) unskilled manual laborers and casual workers whose large families singled them out from other workers, and (2) chronic paupers whose practice of unrestrained, "assortive mating" with like types resulted in the begetting of a surprisingly large number of mentally, physically, and morally defective children and grandchildren. This Social Problem Group, as the second category came to be known after 1929, was first isolated in the East End of London before the war by E. J. Lidbetter, a relieving officer and member of the Eugenics Education Society. Astonished by both the poverty and fertility of his destitute charges, Lidbetter began what turned out to be a twenty-three-year study of "heredity and social inadequacy" detailed in thousands of "pauper pedigrees" collected in the East End and in Edinburgh.[27]

Whatever improvements full employment and higher wages brought to the working classes during the war, they did little in the following decade to stem the flood of destitute epileptics, mental defectives, lunatics, drunks, prostitutes, and criminals emanating from the tainted but unfailingly fecund stock of the Social Problem Group. Numbering an estimated 10 percent of the population, they constituted an interwar version of the old Victorian "residuum" or "submerged tenth." Lidbetter's research, supported by the London School of Economics and the Eugenics Education Society, was finally published at the society's expense in 1933 as *Heredity and the Social Problem Group*. But it had already gained considerable notoriety four years earlier when it figured prominently in the lengthy deliberations and report of a parliamentary Joint Committee on Mental Deficiency.[28]

The governing assumption in Lidbetter's book was that the defects he enumerated were hereditary and the source of most of the social problems in the country. A number of more progressive, reform-minded eugenicists such as A. M. Carr-Saunders, professor of social science at the University of Liverpool and Beveridge's successor as director of the LSE, Carlos P. Blacker, the Eugenics Society's general secretary and dominant figure after 1931, were wary of a number of Lidbetter's "questionable deductions." They worried about some of their unreconstructed, mainline colleagues seizing upon the Social Problem Group and recklessly widening it to include any poor person whom they assumed to be genetically defective.[29]

In practice this frequently happened as eugenicists simply equated high fertility with hereditary weakness and often confused the unskilled working classes with the indigent paupers. But eugenic analysts also biologically distinguished the unskilled from the skilled much more than in the past as the birthrate of the latter began to approach that of the middle classes, an obvious indication of higher genetic value. Byrom Bramwell, a prosperous businessman and treasurer of the Eugenics Society, complained in 1930 about the shortage of skilled, high-paid workers in his firm of printers, engravers, and box makers and compared their small families with the large number of children still being born to the redundant, unskilled workers. This differential raised very serious problems for the future, he wrote Blacker, when automation would require far more of the kinds of workers who were already in short supply while rendering the genetically less capable even more superfluous.

According to the standard eugenic scenario, the latter would fall on the dole where the cost of maintaining them would further discourage the more capable of their class, not to mention the higher ranks, from having more children.[30]

These hereditarian, demographic distinctions between workers were spelled out more clearly by Darwin in the Galton Lecture of 1929, the year after his retirement as president of the Eugenics Society. With characteristic understatement he submitted that the "ill-paid are on the average somewhat inferior in hereditary qualities to the well-paid" and contended race deterioration was now largely governed by their different rates of reproduction. If, as some claimed, differential fertility was smaller than it had been, then the rate of deterioration would be correspondingly slower. It would nevertheless continue, given the predominant power of heredity in human accomplishment. Darwin cited as evidence a recent American study calculating that it would require an increase of 48,000 offspring of unskilled laborers to produce one single additional entry in *Who's Who*. The same result would be obtained by an increase of only 1,600 children of skilled workers. The incidence of such acclaim would, of course, be much greater if the professional classes were included in the projections.[31]

In contrast to his more reform-minded colleagues, who were willing to concede the importance of environmental influences on human development, Darwin could find little comfort in the narrowing of class fertility differentials or in the improved economic, social, and physical condition of the poorer working families since the war. Instead of seeing hope in R. A. Fisher's estimates that every three years some 2 million people passed from the ranks of the worst paid to the better paid half of the nation, Darwin saw it as a threat to the genetic quality of the better paid. Unable to admit that the "inferior culture" of the poor was probably at least as environmentally conditioned as it was biologically determined, he described their upwardly mobile representatives as "inferior immigrants" whose entrance into the front ranks of our nation would inevitably result in further regression and decay.[32]

The Persistent Dilemma: Nature versus Nurture

Darwin's comments in his Galton Lecture were in large measure directed at a new generation of people in the eugenics movement who were trying to draw it closer to the mainstream of postwar social reform. Like Beveridge, they did not dispute that the differential birthrate was dysgenic, only that it was much less so than once believed and that many of the alleged hereditary defects of the poor were in reality environmentally induced. The attempt of these reform-minded eugenicists to weigh more accurately the balance between nature and nurture was not warmly received by the older generation of mainline, orthodox eugenicists. They continued to quote Pearson's quantified assurances that nurture was no more than 10 to 20 percent as important as heredity and to complain about the paucity of talent in the country despite a massive commitment to improving social conditions since the middle of the nineteenth century.[33]

More often than not, arguments about nature and nurture and the differential birthrate were closely associated with eugenic reactions to expanding social welfare programs and their costs. Even pragmatic supporters of the maternal and child welfare movement and other pronatalist programs during the war were uneasy. Not only would the schemes increase the proliferation of the unfit, but the spiraling costs of sustaining them and the dependent multitudes they spawned would further discourage larger families among the taxpaying middle and higher classes. When, after the war, the Eugenics Education Society began to pull back from its tactical alliances with pronatalist interests, Darwin assured them his organization continued to share their concern for the welfare of the poor and the elimination of poverty even if it remained unconvinced that improving environmental conditions was in and of itself very effective. Public assistance would probably continue to be futile and dysgenic and should therefore only be given to people in genuine distress who were not likely to have more children. How this was to be determined was left unresolved, but as Darwin admitted, the whole issue of nature and nurture promised to remain a serious dilemma and mounting source of conflict for eugenicists.[34]

A number of more moderate, scholarly eugenicists like Carr-Saunders sought an acceptable middle ground between nature and nurture. The son of a wealthy underwriter, Carr-Saunders was educated at Eton and Oxford where in 1908 he took a first in zoology. Though excited by Mendelian genetics, he briefly studied biometry with Pearson in 1910, joined the Eugenics Education Society, and served as secretary of its research committee. Unlike many of his colleagues, he had a good deal of firsthand experience with the laboring poor, having served before the war as a subwarden of Toynbee Hall and a member of the Stepney Borough Council.

In his important postwar study *The Population Problem* (1922), which combined his interest in eugenics and demography and led to his appointment in 1923 as the first Charles Booth Professor in Social Science at the University of Liverpool, Carr-Saunders questioned whether the hereditary differences among classes were anywhere near as large or as important as once believed. Mental testing, which had increased rapidly since the war, seemed to indicate that "children of a higher social status" enjoyed "some superiority of intelligence," and people no doubt inherited differences in "temperament and disposition." To what extent such qualities or others such as energy, recuperative powers, rapidity of response, self-assertion, or a "hopeful nature and healthy nervous tone" contributed to success was unclear, he wrote. Their possession did not vary much among classes, he argued, so that success, as a measurement of eugenic worth, may be more dependent upon sociological conditions or tradition than on innate abilities. Carr-Saunders was not challenging the importance of heredity, only the assumption that it was sufficient to explain differences in class accomplishment. In any event, he reminded his readers, because regression to the mean was always at work in a population, its effect over successive generations must tend to lessen innate class differences rather than increase them.[35]

The lean, ascetic Carr-Saunders was not a passionate, confrontational propagandist like the reform-minded Saleeby, many of whose Fabian socialist ideas he nevertheless shared. He was by contrast a thoughtful, balanced, respected student of biology and sociology with strong academic credentials. Though Saleeby angrily withdrew from the Eugenics Education Society after the war, convinced it was too mired in class prejudice ever to recognize that the poor were as much victims of their social and economic environment as they were of their genes, Carr-Saunders remained an active member throughout most of his long career. Like the other reform-minded, talented scientists and social scientists who gradually came to dominate the eugenics movement in the interwar years, he was certain that eugenics in the right hands had an important role to play in formulating sound social policy based upon an expanded understanding of the interrelationship between heredity and environment.

Darwin was painfully aware of the difficulties of holding eugenics to the narrow hereditarian course he preferred as more and more people like Carr-Saunders both within and outside of the society sought to expand the applicability of eugenics to major social movements. He continually spurned invitations for collaboration with various voluntary public health groups which frequently shared members with his own organization. Despite mounting pressure from within the ranks of the society, Darwin was able to persuade the council in 1926 to remain aloof from other bodies who might appear to have similar interests in improving the quality of the race but which were not avowedly eugenic.

Although to some the decision in that year to shorten the organization's name to the Eugenics Society indicated a turn away from education and propaganda toward a more cooperative and interventionist course, it was actually necessitated by a technicality in the tax laws governing the group's incorporation as a nonprofit company.[36] That no dramatic shift was in the offing was evident in the compromise "Outline of Practical Eugenic Policy" published in the 1925–26 annual report. The policy statement explained that if eugenic societies did not concern themselves with "the more immediate benefits to be derived from changes of environment" it was not because a great deal did not need to be done in this area but because it was best for Eugenics Society members as individuals to cooperate with the "innumerable existing bodies already striving to improve human surroundings."[37] What Darwin did not say was that he thought their efforts, however well intentioned, were, from the standpoint of eugenics, useless and expensive, and he urged his successor, Sir Bernard Mallet, to say "no thanks politely" to proposed mergers. While it might be appropriate to cooperate on specific issues if they discouraged the proliferation of the unfit, he added, it was much better if their organization continued to work separately.[38]

In fact, by the end of the decade the Eugenics Society had become deeply involved in one of the most important areas of social reform—birth control— despite Darwin's ineffectual opposition and his successor's shared skepticism about its eugenic value. The merging of the eugenics movement with the birth control movement in Britain was largely unplanned on both sides. It was a logical, if uncoordinated, drifting together of diverse interests who frequently shared little more than a concern for curtailing the fertility of the working classes, a fragile alliance of groups and individuals who, in other circumstances, would have had little to do with each other. One belief they all did share was that the decline in the birthrate since the 1870s was a result of the adoption of contraceptive practices, first by the middle and upper classes, and more recently but not sufficiently, by couples further down the socioeconomic scale.

Facing Reality: Birth Control Is Here to Stay

In the last wartime issue of the *Eugenics Review*, Major Darwin devoted a long article to the advantages of positive over negative eugenics. His extensive efforts to refocus upon the encouragement of larger families among the "self-supporting" population was in part a desperate attempt to head off demands that the society face the compelling truth: eugenically desirable couples were not about to reverse the well-entrenched reproductive habits of more than forty years to breed the four or five children required to counteract the higher fertility of their genetic inferiors. On the contrary, a number of his members contended, the continued spread of birth control was likely to keep that number at half the desired level. The only chance they could see of moderating, if not reversing, the existing dysgenic patterns of fertility was to assure that simple, reliable means of contraception were made available to the poor as soon as possible. Ernest W. MacBride, professor of zoology at the Imperial College of Science and one of the society's council members and vice-presidents during and after the war, still found it surprising years later that some eugenicists had not recognized early on that "all realistic eugenic proposals must come down to birth control in this country."[39]

Darwin feared the holdouts were a dwindling minority as he confronted insistent demands from a variety of interests for the society to provide some clear direction on birth control policy instead of diplomatically reiterating, as it had since 1917, that it was a "delicate and difficult issue" which the organization neither favored nor opposed. Behind the scenes, however, several members, who were also active in the Malthusian League, including Charles Killick Millard, the medical officer of health for Leicester, and Clifton Chance, a wealthy Manchester investment consultant, maneuvered the council into at least considering the question of birth control.[40] The council was in many ways more divided over the moral and political pitfalls of endorsing such a controversial policy than it was over possible racial consequences. But in their deliberations even the most critical members, including Darwin himself, seemed to accept the inevitability of having to come to grips with the problem in the near future.[41]

Although he privately continued to protest "that birth limitation will not be adopted voluntarily by the inferior types of the community to nearly the same extent as with the superior types, and that there is considerable danger of its remaining a dysgenic influence," Darwin conceded in his 1920 presidential address that it probably was time for the society to discuss the subject openly and take a stand. Birth control, as his critics claimed repeatedly, was here to stay, and no other negative policy such as segregation or sterilization could ever be applied extensively enough to alter the dysgenic birthrate. The result was a society-sponsored debate in October at Burlington House in which prewar Neo-Malthusian birth control advocates such as C. V. Drysdale and his mother, Alice Vickery Drysdale, joined with the newcomer Marie Stopes, the American Margaret Sanger, and others to try to assuage eugenicist fears and sensibilities and to demonstrate how birth control was an invaluable eugenic instrument to which the poor were far more receptive than commonly believed. In the final analysis, however, as Millard bluntly asserted, quantity would continue to be inversely correlated with quality, and birth control would remain the determining factor in the recruitment of the race. The Eugenics

Education Society could either face up to it and help reduce the fertility of the "less efficient classes" or be swept aside and remain irrelevant to the most important movement for social and racial improvement the world had ever seen.[42]

Some of the participants remained unpersuaded by such hyperbole; they continued to maintain that birth control was primarily a political and moral issue of debatable eugenic value, the adoption of which would alienate more people from the eugenic cause than it would attract. This being the case, one speaker reasoned, it would be best if the society continued to remain neutral on the controversial subject, although members were certainly free as individuals to express their views and support programs to limit the fertility of the unfit. As a society, however, he recommended a continuing emphasis upon improving the fertility of the fitter classes.

In theory this remained the society's formal policy for the next few years; but in practice, as the eugenic dimension of birth control became increasingly more important in the 1920s, it was forced to become more and more involved. Not to do so, as Millard and others warned, was to lose what many influential eugenicists believed was a golden opportunity to achieve their postwar goal of incrementally improving the quality of the population, though in ways never contemplated by Galton. As one convert to the new tactics, Dr. C. J. Bond, explained in a letter to the society's secretary, he did not know whether birth control would prove to be eugenic or dysgenic, but he did know that their organization had no choice but to become involved whatever the outcome. Even though Darwin continued to believe the key to eugenic improvement was the reduction of birth limitation among the fitter classes rather than the reduction of births among their genetic inferiors, he conceded that until the birth control question was resolved, eugenics could not expect to advance on a wide front.[43]

That resolution was not easy in the 1920s. Darwin's conciliatory efforts were often insufficient to prevent the society from being pulled in different directions by different members. C. V. Drysdale and his wife were encouraged enough to rejoin the Eugenics Education Society in 1921, persuaded it would have to adopt the tactics if not the philosophy of his own struggling Malthusian League.[44] Promising to direct birth control on sound eugenic principles, Drysdale was elected to the society's council where he served during most of the interwar period. He was frequently out of phase with the organization's evolving demographic policies but was probably correct in his 1925 assessment that most "modern eugenists" accepted birth control as a "great tool of negative eugenics."[45]

The Drysdales' growing involvement in the eugenics movement paralleled their declining role in the birth control movement where they, like the old-fashioned neo-Malthusianism they personified, were shunted aside by new populationist interests and personalities whose broader concepts of social reform, sexuality, and fertility control reflected more accurately the problems and values of the postwar era. A variety of new organizations, with different objectives and tactics, made neo-Malthusianism appear retrogressive and irrelevant, with its quaint Victorian ideas about laissez-faire individualism and periodic diatribes against socialism and collectivism. Not even the adoption in 1922 of a new, modern-sounding name, the New Generation, for the old Malthusian League and its journal, now edited by a Fabian socialist, R. B. Kerr, was enough to secure the survival of the first birth control organization to the end of the decade.[46]

Within the Eugenics Society a growing number of members wanted to move the organization more firmly into the birth control camp, including its secretary, Cora Hodson, an Oxford-educated physiologist and childless widow who was responsible for the organization's day-to-day operation throughout the 1920s.[47] The most obvious connection for the society, with its roster of distinguished physicians and research scientists, was the small network of voluntary birth control clinics founded in the wake of Marie Stopes's famous Mothers Clinic. That facility, "the first in the British Empire," as the self-aggrandizing Stopes never failed to remind her presumptuous imitators, was opened in 1921 under the auspices of her newly established Society for Constructive Birth Control and Racial Progress, or the CBC, as it was soon called.

A Scottish-born paleobotanist with doctorates from the University of Munich and the University of London, Stopes had been propelled to the forefront of the birth control movement after the war by the publication in 1918 of *Married Love*, her sensational and cloyingly romantic exploration of the emotional and physical joys she had failed to experience in her own unconsummated first marriage.[48] By contrast her second marriage, to Humphrey Verdon Roe, a wealthy member of the Manchester aircraft manufacturing family and, like her, a recent recruit to the Malthusian League, brought Stopes, temporarily at least, both wedded bliss and the economic resources to launch her best-selling book and controversial career in birth control.[49]

Readers of *Married Love* actually learned a great deal more about the ecstasies of conception than they did about how to prevent it. But since many of them were primarily interested in the mechanics of the latter rather than the delights of the former, Stopes's sequels, *Wise Parenthood* and *A Letter to Working Mothers*, were practical guides to contraception that emphasized female control of fertility. They also reflected her perceptions of class sexuality.[50] Unlike *Married Love* and, to a lesser extent, *Wise Parenthood*,

Stopes's advice to working mothers was unencumbered by the ethereal and erotic descriptions of rapturous foreplay and coupling savored by liberated husbands and wives in the higher ranks. Working-class women were instead bluntly reminded of the physical and economic consequences of having too many children and told in simple terms of the inexpensive alternatives available to them, such as vaginal caps, soluble quinine suppositories, or sponges saturated with soap powder.[51]

Although the Malthusian League endorsed and helped promote *Wise Parenthood* and *A Letter to Working Mothers*, Stopes was much more interested in the approbation of the cautious Eugenics Education Society. She manipulated friends to get both works reviewed in the *Eugenics Review*, despite its reluctance to consider birth control, and then angrily protested when the notices were more superficial and critical than she expected. They did not, however, prevent her from joining the society as a life member in 1921.[52] In doing so she had visions of transforming it into "the biggest and most successful Society in England today," an achievement dependent upon tying constructive birth control to racial progress and upon eugenicists following her lead.[53] According to one of her most vociferous supporters, the anthropologist George Pitt-Rivers, it was the preposterous conclusion of the narrow-minded officers of the Eugenics Education Society that there was little interest in birth control among the working classes that prompted the defiant Stopes to rent and fill the Queen's Hall in 1921 to launch her own organization.[54]

Both Stopes and her champion believed the Eugenics Society never forgave her her success and therefore declined to invite her to lecture or to publish any of her work in the *Eugenics Review*. Those who did not accord her the recognition she knew she deserved were usually accused by Stopes of being jealous and trying to steal or discredit her work. But the society's council, in the early 1920s at least, declined her persistent requests for a platform because they were unwilling to adopt birth control as a primary objective and were afraid that too close an association with the flamboyant Dr. Stopes would give an appearance to the contrary.[55] Moreover, although Stopes indicated she would have been content to work from within the Eugenics Society, she proved throughout her career to be constitutionally incapable of subordinating herself to anyone or of cooperating very long with other organizations.

If the society was always careful to keep her at a distance and feared being ensnared or smeared by her, eugenics nevertheless played an important role in Stopes's wedding of birth control to racial progress. As a member of the second National Birth-Rate Commission, she tried, with little success, to convince her colleagues that birth control was the best method to eliminate the hoards of weak, unhealthy, and tainted poor children whose dependence on tax-supported welfare programs prevented the overburdened middle classes from producing more children of good quality. Unlike the Neo-Malthusians, she did not think the size of the birthrate was the problem, only that it was too great among the poor and not large enough among the wealthy. What was required, she concluded, was not a further decline in fertility but a rearrangement of it to improve the quality of life for people in all classes.[56]

This mixture of negative and positive eugenics was at the core of Stopes's definition of constructive birth control. She spelled it out in 1920 in another of her popular books, *Radiant Motherhood*, which celebrated the delights of planned conception, healthy pregnancy, and the rearing of racially fit children in a eugenically conscious world. Her utopia was contrasted with the realities of a society that "allows the diseased, the racially negligent, the thriftless, the careless, the feeble-minded, the very lowest and worst members of the community, to produce innumerable tens of thousands of stunted, warped and inferior infants" who had to be maintained by "the better classes." Parenthood, she insisted, was not an individual right but a duty and privilege; it should be restricted to healthy, well-bred prospects. So long as the power of procreation continued to be exercised irrationally, "we as a race slide at an ever increasing speed towards the utter deterioration of our stock."[57]

With the exception of her prescription for a cure, there was nothing in this that even the most orthodox of mainline eugenicists could not applaud. The same theme was struck during Stopes's successful Queen's Hall rally the following year when she encouraged those of her speakers who were medical officers of health to recount their experiences in dealing with "the ruck, wastrels and throw-outs resulting from reckless breeding." As a number of the speeches demonstrated, it did not require much prodding to elicit a stream of emotional denunciations of the differential birthrate and the multiplication of the unfit whose unregulated increase threatened the future of the race and the Empire.[58] Sir James Barr was only one of several eugenicists who were inspired by Stopes's vision. He quickly agreed to accept a vice-presidency in the CBC and to be a patron of Stopes's Mothers Clinic. His acceptance was predicated upon the conviction that "until we get a selective birthrate there can be no general elevation of the human race. The nation which most effectually adopts eugenic ideals is bound to rule the world."[59]

Like most of the Eugenics Education Society members who lent their support to Stopes's new ventures, Barr was already active in the birth control movement. Although a number of them had endorsed neo-Malthusianism before the war, they were never very comfortable with the Malthusian League and welcomed an alternative so affirmatively eugenic in outlook. They had no success, however, in persuading the society's leadership that Stopes's organization, with its emphasis upon positive and negative eugenics, provided the perfect bridge to the birth control movement with its great potential for reducing the excessive fertility of the laboring poor. Major Darwin declined an invitation to attend the Queen's Hall meeting, and throughout the remaining seven years of his tenure as president of the Eugenics Society he avoided any formal association with the CBC.

When, in 1927, Stopes, who had not been invited, asked Cora Hodson to represent her organization as well as the Eugenics Society at the upcoming World Population Conference in Geneva, Hodson was not allowed to accept even though she promised not to wear a CBC badge. Darwin, who thought Stopes "an unscrupulous woman," was afraid she would publicly claim Hodson as a joint representative. Many on the council still wanted no association with the CBC because they remained opposed to birth control, he explained to Hodson. "Some do so because they dislike and distrust Dr. Stopes—as I do." She was not only rude to the Society at meetings, he added, but he preferred not to have the Eugenics Society dragged into her continual fights with the other birth control interests.[60] This was blunt talk for the old man, but he clearly loathed Stopes, whose love of publicity and shameless skill at self-aggrandizement made her the best-known advocate of birth control in the country. She would have said in the world.

Despite Darwin's opposition, Hodson, in hopes of reducing the friction between the CBC and the Eugenics Society, quietly represented the former group at the conference, which she described to Stopes as very disappointing.[61] Her doing so was part of an understanding within the Eugenics Society that members were free to associate as individuals with other movements or causes they believed furthered eugenics, even if the society did not formally affiliate with them. This was certainly evident in the number of eugenicists who continued on their own to support the National Association of Maternity and Child Welfare Centres, the National Association for the Prevention of Infant Mortality, the National Baby Week Council, the Family Endowment Society (FES), the British Social Hygiene Council, and a variety of other environmentally oriented organizations. Their involvement in the birth control movement initially followed the same pattern, but its importance to a realistic eugenic population policy was too compelling for the Eugenics Society to resist very long being drawn into a more formal association than Darwin and some others liked.

The Natural Alliance

Given the mounting pressure within eugenic and birth control circles after the war to acknowledge the complementary goals of the two movements and to work out some common race-enhancing strategy, it was sometimes difficult for the Eugenics Society to resist Stopes's enticements. Her concept of constructive birth control was, after all, strongly eugenic; she was herself a lifetime member of the society, and her organization attracted a sample of professional people in medicine, science, religion, politics, literature, and the arts, whom the Eugenics Society would have welcomed into its own successful ranks. In fact, several of them were already there arguing for the natural alliance between birth control and eugenics inherent in the idea of rational selection. Such an alliance, many increasingly believed, held out the only reasonable prospect of reversing the course of dysgenic selection the nation had been on for the past fifty years.

Much of the reason for spurning Stopes's overtures lay in the deep-seated distrust of some of the old-time eugenicists in the willingness or capacity of the feckless poor to check their animal instincts. In addition, an influential group in the Eugenics Society continued to regard birth control as an unsuitable subject for consideration, especially in an organization that attracted a substantial number of unmarried women. Considerations of propriety were reinforced by the medical testimony of some prominent council members, such as Lady Florence Barrett, who, like many other physicians, continued to believe that Conception Control, as she described it, was physically and psychologically harmful to her sex.[62] Stopes's quarrelsome personality and penchant for sensationalism undoubtedly reinforced the wariness of birth control felt by Darwin, Mallet, and other influential spokesmen for the society, and her open contempt for physicians did little to win the confidence of the medical people in the organization, who averaged somewhere between 15 and 20 percent of the membership.

If the Eugenics Society leadership was reluctant then to tie the organization to the CBC or any other birth control group, it was willing to explore some of the areas that might contain useful eugenic possibilities. The most obvious of these were the voluntary birth control clinics established in working-class districts around the country, most under the auspices of the independent Society for the Provision of Birth Control Clinics (SPBCC) founded in 1923. They numbered sixteen by the end of the decade. Of even greater importance from the eugenic standpoint was the possibility that the Ministry of Health, established at the end of the war, might be persuaded to allow local authorities to permit the dispensing of contraceptive information to married women who visited the 2,200 local welfare centers throughout Great Britain. This quickly became the unifying objective of the diverse groups making up the birth control movement in the interwar years, and eugenic interests, despite the initial reticence of the Eugenics Society, were prominently represented in the campaign.[63]

In contrast to Stopes, who declined to share her authority with doctors, who she insisted, with justification, knew far less about contraception than she did, the SPBCC insisted that all of its centers be under medical supervision, although it was often difficult to recruit physicians, particularly women, to take on the task. Both the CBC and the SPBCC attracted members of the Eugenics Education Society to their governing boards, and despite Stopes's efforts to discourage them from supporting her "rivals," they were frequently the same people. Cora Hodson, with the support of Dr. C. J. Bond, encouraged these associations and in 1923 persuaded the council to let her visit the clinics of both societies and to meet with sympathetic medical officers of health to explore the eugenic ramifications of their work. "I am very anxious," she wrote to Stopes, "to ascertain to how poor and incompetent a section of the community it may be hoped that Birth Control would penetrate if it were introduced into the Welfare Centres." A number of people in her society were very interested in this now, she explained.[64]

By the end of the year the Eugenics Education Society council agreed to establish a subcommittee to study contraceptive practices among the working classes in London, and a few months later, in early 1924, it accepted a recommendation to invite the medical societies to appoint representatives to a committee to consider birth control and to recommend what could be done for "social and racial" reasons to disseminate contraceptive information.[65] At the same time, the *Eugenics Review* began to open its columns to more discussions of birth control and regularly summarized information from Stopes's journal, the *Birth Control News*. The *Eugenics Review* also published reports of the activities of other organizations, such as the SPBCC and the Workers Birth Control Group, founded in 1924 to support the efforts of the Women's Section of the Labour Party to convince the minister of health to permit birth control instruction in the welfare clinics.[66]

Despite the mounting pressure from a few local authorities, birth control organizations, women's groups, and a small but vocal coterie of M.P.s, both Conservative and Labour ministers of health declined throughout the 1920s to face the political consequences of sanctioning family limitation in the welfare centers. Conservatives such as Sir Alfred Mond and Neville Chamberlain, who were personally sympathetic, were no more inclined than the Catholic Labourite John Wheatley, who was firmly opposed, to undertake such a "controversial and revolutionary" change without express directions from Parliament.[67] Until public opinion had changed substantially, they repeatedly explained, Parliament was unlikely to issue such orders. The unifying goal of the birth control movement became that of convincing the ministry and Parliament that the public's opinion was already evident in its plummeting birthrate. It was now only democratic and just, as well as racially prudent, to assure that the laboring poor were given access to the same information readily available to the middle and upper classes.

Although a few Neo-Malthusians, including Alice Vickery Drysdale, had recognized during the war the educational potential of the infant and maternal welfare centers and saw in the establishment of the Ministry of Health a potential agency for the nationwide promotion of birth control, it was certainly remote from the thinking of those who planned the new ministry.[68] The issue first came up for consideration in 1920. The Eugenics Education Society, eager to press the case for heredity, explained in a memorandum to the ministry that while in the interests of posterity there was general agreement about the importance of limiting inefficient families to avoid racial deterioration, there was considerable disagreement about the role of birth control in the achievement of this goal. Two years later, when urged by some of its members to join in another memorandum urging the Ministry of Health to authorize birth control instruction in the welfare centers, the Eugenics Education Society council was still badly split and only a minority were willing to sign. Even then the memorandum recommended that birth control only be allowed (1) for the spacing, not the prevention of childbirth, (2) for medical reasons, (3) to avoid hereditary defects, and (4) in the case of economic stringencies.[69]

By the middle of the decade these hesitant concessions had been transformed into "An Outline of Practical Eugenic Policy" that for the first time tried to spell out the eugenic position on birth control. Moreover, as the Eugenics Society struggled to catch up with eugenical opinion, it became a meeting ground for the diverse interests involved in the birth control campaign. Even Darwin conceded at the annual meeting in 1925 that it was probably time to issue a clearer and more definite program, perhaps even some sort of an endorsement, than had been possible earlier. Some long-time supporters might be driven away, he suspected, but others who believed that birth control was now the most important social agency for race culture would probably take their place.[70]

Darwin still harbored doubts that short of compulsion the "inefficient, the careless, the weak and the stupid" would limit their families enough and suggested sterilizing them as a safer alternative. But after intensive discussion with his council, it was finally agreed in 1926 to sanction birth control as a eugenic agent. In addition to the conditions contained in the society's earlier memorandum to the Ministry of Health, the new policy emphasized that the birth control campaign was to be directed primarily at the poor. The use of contraception by healthy couples was "immoral and unpatriotic," and though birth spacing might sometimes be employed to avoid a lowering of family living standards, it was never justified to safeguard against "a loss of social status."[71]

Darwin, who tried privately to get the council to include in its statement a description of birth control as "the greatest danger to the race," ran into opposition from new members such as the influential biologist Julian Huxley, and had to settle instead for "a potential danger." He nevertheless continued to object publicly to "any general or promiscuous propaganda" that might inadvertently discourage parents in the superior ranks from having the minimum of four children needed to keep up their numbers.[72] The Eugenics Society's anonymous benefactor, Henry Twitchin, responded sympathetically from his Mediterranean villa but pointed out that eugenicists could not afford to be overly scrupulous in the means they employed to combat race degeneration. "As Birth Control in some form is the only practicable way to this end," he thought it should be enforced by the authorities "regardless of the likes and dislikes of those who haven't the intelligence to know what is good for them or the Country."[73]

When in 1928 Darwin, nearing eighty, contemplated retirement, he joined with R. A. Fisher to persuade Sir Bernard Mallet, the former registrar general, who shared their reservations about birth control, to succeed him. They were particularly determined to thwart the claims of E. W. MacBride who was strongly committed to the growing alliance between eugenics and birth control.[74] Increasingly invested in the idea that the tendency to practice birth control was itself an inherited characteristic reinforced by social selection and economic advantages, Fisher believed the Eugenics Society would be better off promoting family allowances for the fit than contraception for the poor.[75]

Mallet hesitated to accept the presidency, fearing he might clash with the Eugenics Society council over its expanding involvement with the "fanatical birth controllers" who, he complained, assumed anyone interested in population or eugenics was on their side.[76] In the end Mallet came around and served as president of the society from 1928 until his death in 1932. He was, however, never comfortable with the proliferation of eugenically inspired birth control projects launched in the second half of the decade. Many of them grew out of a series of conferences called by the Eugenics Society in 1926 at the urging of Bond, Huxley, Hodson, and Lady Chambers to discuss various issues and possible research proposals with a number of birth control groups and clinics.

Of primary interest to the society's representatives was the prospect of gathering from the clinics a wide range of data about the use and effectiveness of contraceptives among "the more defective types in the Community."[77] Special meetings were arranged with physicians and medical consultants from the clinics. Stopes, whose book *Contraception* had become a standard work on the subject, was enraged when she was excluded because of her lack of a medical degree and refused her clinic's cooperation until the slight was rectified.[78]

Although *Dr*. Stopes, as she insisted on being addressed, doubted most physicians were either competent or necessary to advise women about birth control and correctly boasted, "I teach doctors," most birth control advocates recognized the political importance of medical support for their cause.[79] C. P. Blacker, who was beginning to emerge as an articulate medical spokesman for birth control and eugenics, was no less distressed than his colleagues that Stopes was preempting the field with her "flowery and highly-coloured" books. But, he reminded them in 1926, she had broken ground they had irresponsibly left untilled.[80]

Blacker, a psychiatrist whose pedigree included the Peruvian aristocracy on his father's side and a Union army general on his mother's, had studied zoology at Balliol College, Oxford, and, after the war, medicine at Guy's Hospital. He first wrote Stopes in 1924 in connection with a survey she had taken about the teaching (or, as was more common, absence of teaching) of contraception in medical school curricula. He described the indifference and hostility he had encountered when he offered to instruct the staff at Guy's on the subject and set up an outpatient clinic.[81] Although he soon found her to be as insensitive and uncooperative as many of his fellow physicians and fought with her off and on for thirty years, Blacker always admired Stopes's courage and vision even while he disapproved of her methods. But he also found it particularly irritating that much of her influence and notoriety was initially built upon the timidity and confusion of his own profession.[82]

In *Birth Control and the State* (1926), the first of his many books and pamphlets on eugenics and the population question, Blacker warned, "the human race is now passing through a biological crisis unprecedented in the history of life," and appealed to the Ministry of Health and his colleagues in the medical profession to take the lead in the study and regulation of contraception. At one stormy meeting of the society in 1927, he argued, until ruled out of order, that only doctors should be allowed to dispense birth control information and proposed that nonmedical propaganda, books, and sales should be made illegal.[83] Blacker was rarely so intemperate and impolitic, but his was one of a growing chorus of voices of younger physicians in the 1920s imploring doctors to recognize that birth control was a vital area of preventive medicine that should rightfully concern them but from which they were in danger of being excluded by default.[84] For his part Blacker was quick to urge the Eugenics Society in 1927 to support the founding and partial financing of a Birth Control Investigation Committee (BCIC) comprised of scientists and doctors to examine the medical and sociological principles of contraception and its effects upon physical, mental, and racial health.[85] In addition, Blacker played an important role in trying to recruit well-known physicians to the Eugenics Society and to its governing council where they were a decided presence in the next decade.[86]

For the Eugenics Society, involvement with the BCIC proved to be a controversial first step away from its primary role as a propagandist organization in the direction of the scientific research that was to mark its development in the next decade. The move reflected the growing influence of reform eugenicists, as Kevles has described them, such as Blacker, Huxley, Carr-Saunders, Fisher, J. B. S. Haldane, and others who recognized that human heredity and its relationship to environment was far more complicated than the old, mainline eugenicists appreciated. Like Blacker, the reformers believed biological criteria needed to be evaluated more carefully in a wider social or environmental context, and wanted to build closer ties to the expanding fields of demography and genetics.[87] Under the chairmanship of Sir Humphrey Rolleston, physician-in-ordinary to George V and Regius Professor of Physic at Cambridge, the BCIC brought together representatives from the birth control clinics, the Workers Birth Control Group, and the Eugenics Society to cooperate in the scientific collection of data and evaluation of existing birth control practices. Since Rolleston, who was also president of the Cambridge birth control clinic, and Blacker, who served as medical secretary of the BCIC, were both members of the Eugenics Society, there was little chance the eugenic aspects of birth control would be overlooked.

Even so, in 1928 the Eugenics Society agreed to contribute £200 only when it was assured that the new committee was an independent, investigative body uninvolved in any propaganda role on behalf of birth control.[88] In fact, the group represented a number of differing opinions about the desirability and consequences of family limitation, but all its members agreed that the practice was widespread and required impartial, scientific study. When Julian Huxley, who was an enthusiastic advocate of birth control, suggested the society might also want to appoint a delegate to another organization, the Birth Control Research Council (BCRC), run by Margaret Spring-Rice, a clinic representative to the BCIC, it declined to do so because the BCRC was too closely identified with evaluating and, what was more worrisome, recommending contraceptives.[89]

Despite the council's caution and even before the establishment of the BCIC, Eugenics Society statisticians issued a "Memorandum to Medical Officers and Superintendents" in the birth control clinics in 1926 asking them to provide detailed information about their patients. The eugenicists were particularly interested in the occupation of husbands as well as which harmless contraceptive methods were simple enough to be readily understood by "the stupidest and therefore the most undesirable members of society."[90] The BCIC took over much of this work the following year, but the Eugenics Society, through its representatives, remained involved.

Although Darwin continued to complain about the dysgenic effects of birth control, the opening of new clinics in working-class districts was increasingly welcomed by his colleagues. Hodson hoped the facilities might be used to teach simple lessons of heredity to the poor, while Twitchin contemplated financing several clinics until business difficulties with his sheep stations in Australia prevented his pursuing the scheme. Nevertheless, Twitchin, reinforcing his arguments with £1,000 donations, made it clear to Darwin that he thought the Eugenics Society ought to be pressing the government to permit the teaching of birth control in the "most populous, poorest" welfare centers.[91]

Twitchin did not live long enough into 1930 to savor the sudden reversal of the Ministry of Health's long-held position on the welfare centers. After a decade of continual pressure and with several local authorities openly challenging the ministry's directives against providing birth control instruction, the new Labour party minister of health, Arthur Greenwood, with the approval of the Labour cabinet, decided in the summer of 1930 to permit the practice.[92] His cautious Memorandum 153/M. C. W., which some euphoric birth controllers compared to the Magna Carta, reaffirmed that while it was not the function of the maternal and child welfare centers to provide birth control advice to married women, it was permissible "in cases where there are medical grounds" for doing so.[93]

These grounds were deliberately left vague, to be determined by the local medical officers. In emphasizing the role of medical authority, the ministry was also responding to an eruption of angry complaints and resolutions by doctors at the annual meeting of the British Medical Association who now insisted that contraception was a medical question which should be left to their judgment and discretion. The ministry declined to impose medical supervision on the voluntary clinics, as the British Medical Association also demanded; it contented itself instead with turning the sensitive issue over to local authorities, as the *Lancet* and others had suggested years earlier, leaving it up to the medical officers and their governing committees to work out their own policies.[94]

The various birth control groups were quickly organized into a National Birth Control Council (NBCC) in July 1930 to coordinate their efforts and, after issuance of the ministry's memorandum, to publicize its contents, to encourage local officials to act, and to monitor compliance. Its list of officers was a who's who of the birth control campaign. Although the Eugenics Society did not formally affiliate with the new organization, a number of its most prominent members, including C. J. Bond, Huxley, J. Arthur Thompson, John Maynard Keynes, Stopes, and even Leonard Darwin, accepted positions as vice-presidents or council members. In addition, the president of the NBCC, Lord Horder, the royal physician, and its chairman, Lady Denman, were both very active in the Eugenics Society, where Horder briefly served as president in the mid-1930s.

Eldon Moore, a statistician who had become the first paid editor of the *Eugenics Review* in 1927, described the Ministry of Health's memorandum as "a revolution of racial importance" and urged eugenicists to work closely with local health officials in advancing the eugenic potential of the new policy.[95] Similarly Stopes, who insisted she alone was responsible for the ministry's decision, concluded that the government's approval, however circumspect and restrictive, would move the struggle for birth control to a new level in which the genetic improvement of the race would prove to be far more important than limiting its numbers.[96]

By the end of the decade, in contrast to the prewar and immediate postwar period, eugenics was deeply enmeshed in birth control. Indeed, negative or preventive eugenics had almost entirely eclipsed the positive schemes for race culture so central to Galton's utopian vision. But even Darwin realized the prospects for selectively increasing the birthrate of the fittest classes enough to elevate the genetic quality of the race were remote at best. In addition, the recognition that heredity and its relationship to environment were far more complicated than previously understood drew eugenics after the war into a number of areas of social reform, of which birth control was clearly the most important. The old biometric calculations of the relative contribution of nature and nurture had been battered by the wartime experience when the working-class population had shown itself to be far more vital and energetic than pessimistic eugenicists would have predicted. The advances in health and longevity and the decline in chronic poverty continuing after the war made it difficult for all but the most fossilized of mainline eugenicists to deny that improved social and economic conditions had blurred the distinctions between fitness and unfitness which had seemed so obvious before 1914.

While agreeing with the stubborn Karl Pearson's long-held contention that heredity was much more decisive in human development than social environment, Beatrice Webb, like other socialist eugenicists, nevertheless argued in 1930 that the case would never be proven until that environment was more equitable. The Ministry of Health's new policy was an important step in that direction. "Changes in social environment appeal to the common man," she wrote Pearson, "whereas Eugenics is intensely repulsive, and will only be slowly accepted after preliminary birth control teaching has become a matter of course."[97]

Although Pearson, who continued to reject Mendelian genetics, was still confident he knew what constituted hereditary fitness and where in society it was most heavily distributed, his certitude was not shared by the new, more reform-minded generation of eugenicists who had become influential in the cause since the war. Their position was increasingly reinforced by the rapid strides being made in the study of human genetics which demonstrated, among other things, that like did not necessarily beget like, as mainline eugenicists, drawing upon Victorian notions of heredity and simplistic views of the distribution of Mendelian characteristics, had long assumed. On the contrary, inheritance was increasingly recognized by British and American geneticists to be polygenic; it involved a multiplicity of genes from both partners which combined in an infinite variety of unpredictable ways. Indeed, there were compelling reasons to believe that biological strength lay in the vast diversity of genetic makeup so that variety rather than uniformity was the essence of perfection. Not only were thoughtful eugenicists uncertain about what to breed for or even able to agree on the relative racial value of the characteristics they wanted reproduced, but the more the most advanced students of human heredity learned about the complexity of their subject, the more doubtful they became about predicting with any accuracy the outcome of selective breeding.[98]

The problem was, of course, further compounded by the unknown interrelationship of environment with the manifestation of heritable characteristics. Short of breeding humans like animals in carefully controlled conditions or, as some of the more radical scientists envisioned, a social revolution leading to the establishment of a socialist utopia, it might prove impossible to sort out the contributory factors. Darwin and Twitchin could still privately discuss man as a "domestic animal" for whom "some stockyard methods" of breeding were appropriate, but even they had to agree with Mallet's warning that in light of modern sensibilities and changing class attitudes, any public references to animals, stud farms, or stockyards would only lead to angry protests and do great harm to eugenics.[99]

None of these developments meant that the eugenical mind in the interwar years was purged by science and experience of its ideas of class-specific differential ability and fertility. Few who thought in eugenic terms really doubted that the most desirable social, physical, intellectual, and behavioral qualities, though perhaps molded considerably by environment, were still in large part hereditarily determined. Even if racial fitness could not be precisely defined and was distributed over a wider range of society than once believed, most eugenicists could still recognize it, as people could once recognize a gentleman. However modified by nurture, that fitness would manifest itself primarily in the skilled working class and in the middle and upper ranks of society. Similarly, if it had become more difficult to reach agreement about what precisely constituted fitness, there was far more of a eugenic consensus about what constituted unfitness—feeblemindedness, insanity, alcoholism, criminality, prostitution, deafness, dependency, and a growing number of transmissible diseases. These defects were most heavily clustered in the newly defined Social Problem Group, whose poverty and continued high fertility were seemingly inevitable consequences of its genetic makeup.

If the patterns of differential fertility convinced eugenicists that they really had no option but to ally with the birth control movement, their decision to do so also marked another important change in the direction of British eugenics in the interwar years. It reflected a growing awareness on the part of reform eugenicists, even within the Eugenics Society, that education and propaganda by themselves might slow the process of racial degeneration, but they would never stop it. That would require a much more thorough understanding of heredity, reproduction, and demography than was currently available, and this in turn necessitated a commitment to scientific research which could form the basis of a policy of sound social and, by definition, eugenic reform.

This, of course, was exactly what Pearson believed eugenics should have committed itself to when, in 1907, he opposed as dangerously premature the founding of a eugenics propaganda organization. He continued after the war to spurn Darwin's friendly overtures, refusing in 1922 an invitation to deliver the Galton Lecture on the centennial anniversary of the founder's birth. On other occasions he bluntly informed Darwin that he found the society's courting of eminent persons and influential support repellent. This effort to create "a priesthood and deities" was out of place in science, "which should be a democracy of intelligence, where the youngest may challenge the opinions of the oldest."[100] Pearson in fact rarely forgave those impudent enough to challenge him, but by the time he retired in 1934, still unreconciled to the existence of the Eugenics Society, it had moved briskly into scientific and social scientific research.

In the 1930s the society was propelled by its strong commitment to find an effective contraceptive that even the benighted degenerates in the Social Problem Group could use. The decision was freighted with difficulties and conflicts and it sharply changed the role of the Eugenics Society from that of a rather unfocused, casually run propaganda agency to an influential and innovative supporter of population research. The organization was already moving erratically in that direction by the end of the 1920s when, with the death and bequest of the reclusive Henry Twitchin in 1930, its fortunes and possibilities were suddenly changed. The still small but now wealthy Eugenics Society was, in the depression-wracked years of the thirties, one of the few organizations in the country with the will and the resources to support serious inquiry into the population question in general and into birth control in particular. The society's decision to do so gave eugenics a new purpose, a new lease on life, and an important role to play in the emergence of the modern family planning movement in Britain.

Nine

Reform Eugenics, Population Research, and Family Planning, 1930–1939

The majority of British birth control proponents in the interwar years believed 1930 was the turning point in overcoming the major barriers to the dissemination of birth control information. Not only did the government concede that public welfare centers could provide contraceptive information, and a number of physicians and some of their professional organizations indicate that they were prepared to furnish the medical guidance the Ministry of Health required, but that other bastion of resistance, the Church of England, also relented. The Lambeth Conference essentially reversed its earlier condemnation of birth control by conceding "in those cases where there is such a clearly felt moral obligation to limit or avoid parenthood, and where there is a morally sound reason for avoiding complete abstinence . . . other methods may be used, provided that this is done in the light of . . . Christian principles."[1]

None of this suggested that strong opposition to birth control disappeared within the government, the medical profession, and the church. The Ministry of Health was almost secretive in issuing its permissive memorandum allowing contraceptive information to be provided in welfare facilities; local authorities were slow to implement the new policy, and medical associations to endorse it.[2] A number of churchmen, including several bishops, tried without success throughout the decade to set aside the Lambeth Conference resolution, prompting one of their more realistic colleagues to assert, "Parsons must have some soft spots in their heads if they imagine any reasonable percentage of this country's population will take the slightest notion of their opinion as to whether birth control is right or wrong."[3]

In truth, the events of 1930 were a necessary and calculated response to demographic reality as well as to the profound changes that had occurred in public opinion and domestic behavior since World War I. Birth control had become a normal rather than an exceptional characteristic of marital relations in nearly all sectors of society. It was increasingly discussed in the popular press, in respectable women's magazines, and even in that new monument to cultural propriety, the British Broadcasting Company (BBC). Despite occasional harassment from offended local authorities, the proliferation of birth control literature, contraceptive advertisements, and "rubber shops" continued unabated. The decline in the birthrate, by contrast, began to moderate and level off at around 15 per 1,000 in the mid-1930s, a figure that translated into slightly more than two children per marriage.

Eugenic considerations were never very far removed from discussions of the birthrate. They were often evident in the arguments of physicians and local authorities, particularly medical officers of health who, throughout the depression years, complained that only the feckless and ignorant at the lower end of the hereditary scale continued to rear large families. Although eugenic presuppositions were not obvious in the deliberations of the Lambeth Conference, several prelates and prominent clergymen such as E. W. Barnes, the bishop of Birmingham, Percy Dearmer, canon of Westminster, J. E. C. Welldon, the dean of Durham, and, of course, Dean Inge, welcomed the bishops' ruling as racially enlightened. Many of them were also sympathetic to eugenic sterilization as a much more reliable way to arrest the alarming increase in people in the Social Problem Group unable or unwilling to exercise the foresight and self-restraint birth control required.[4]

The Eugenics Society, which for its own reasons had collaborated with the birth control interests to facilitate the spread of contraceptive information to the poor, joined with its allies in welcoming the "notable events" of 1930, as Marie Stopes exultantly described them.[5] In reality, the society's direct role in bringing them about was, as usual, much less important than the ideas it represented. But in part because of its growing involvement in the birth control movement, the organization, prodded by new members, was forced to re-evaluate whether following its traditional policies the eugenics movement would ever become a significant agency for biologically sound social reform. The result was a critical, often bitter struggle to move the society beyond its limited role as a propaganda organization to that of a supportive scientific research foundation with a primary interest in the genetic dimension of the population question.

The Eugenics Society had started to move in this direction in the later 1920s by endorsing and partially financing the work of the BCIC, a decision that brought it into closer contact with medical, biological, and social science research. Sir Bernard Mallet recognized the shift in direction when in 1928 he gave as one of the reasons for hesitating to accept the presidency of the Eugenics Society his concern that he was a statistician rather than a physician or biologist interested in birth control.[6] His successors in the next decade, Sir Humphrey Rolleston and Lord Horder, were both prominent medical authorities who fit that description and who strongly endorsed the new directions taken by the organization.

C. P. Blacker and New Directions

Critical to the survival and expanded influence of the Eugenics Society were the death in 1930 of the organization's eccentric benefactor, Henry Twitchin, the receipt of his substantial bequest of more than £70,000, and the appointment the following year of C. P. Blacker as general secretary. Twitchin's money kept the society alive, but it was Blacker, a medical psychiatrist at Guy's and Maudsley Hospitals, who transformed the group from a confused, unfocused, amateur organization dabbling uncertainly in the birth control movement, into a quasi-professional society committed to family planning and the serious study of population problems.

Blacker, a decorated war hero who had turned to psychiatry as a result of terrible experiences in the trenches, was thirty-five when he accepted his new position with the Eugenics Society. A liberal, reform-minded physician with socialist predilections if not commitments, he devoted the next twenty years of his life to trying to establish the scientific credibility of eugenics as an instrument of rational demographic planning and social improvement. The Eugenics Society, he realized, would never get very far by itself; it needed to broaden its base and reach out to other organizations if it was ever to have much of an impact on population policy. He believed the growing alliance with the birth control movement was particularly critical to the future of eugenics. When he applied for the position of general secretary, Blacker made it clear he planned to remain as medical secretary of the BCIC and to continue his work with the SPBCC.[7]

Leonard Darwin, who, like many of his generation in the society, clearly did not know the young psychiatrist very well, wondered whether the rather stern, aloof Blacker had the personality to deal with those pioneers of the movement troubled by the direction eugenics was taking. While Blacker was not his ideal candidate, the retired president privately admitted he could fill the gap for three years or so and then the whole matter could be reconsidered.[8] Although Blacker, as the architect of reform eugenics, found dealing with the old guard so frustrating he contemplated quitting on several occasions, he remained in office until 1952.[9]

The two most vexatious issues Blacker had to deal with in formulating a credible population policy were class prejudice and distrust of the role of nurture in race culture. They had plagued eugenics from the beginning and still lay at the core of eugenic thought. Opponents of eugenics, especially Labourites and socialists whose numbers increased dramatically in the interwar years, had hammered away on these offensive aspects of the movement. They were joined by countless social reformers, critics, medical officers of health, and scientists who challenged or ridiculed eugenic claims of scientific accuracy and social evaluations of fitness and unfitness.

The most devastating and, for eugenicists, worrisome of their critics was the prickly, controversial biologist Lancelot Hogben. A radical, socialist professor in the newly founded Department of Social Biology at the London School of Economics and an effective popularizer of left-wing causes in the 1930s, Hogben launched an unremitting assault on the scientific pretensions and social prejudices of eugenics in his inaugural address at LSE. Hogben's sarcastic references to eugenic notions of heredity and reproduction were made more offensive by his "thin, scornful voice," as Blacker described it, and by his "pink tie and . . . hair arranged in such a way that three curls dangled down over his forehead, rather like what you see behind the counters in Selfridges." Hogben's writings and speeches were considered particularly damaging by eugenicists such as Carr-Saunders who complained to Blacker that there was a widespread belief that they had "knocked the bottom out of eugenics" and created a good deal of skepticism among educated people.[10]

Blacker, who worked with Hogben on the BCIC, was encouraged by Julian Huxley and J. B. S. Haldane, among others, to be patient with their brilliant if awkward, erratic, and ill-bred colleague. The poor man had struggled to overcome a narrow, oppressive upbringing in a fundamentalist Methodist family and had only escaped by winning a scholarship to Trinity College, Cambridge, where he discovered both Quakerism and Fabianism. Imprisoned as a conscientious objector during the war, Hogben's facility for making enemies had for years after made it difficult for him to secure a permanent appointment. He had finally migrated to posts in Canada and then South Africa when, on Harold Laski's recommendation, he was invited to LSE.

Though often angered by the provocative Hogben, Blacker privately admitted he shared a good many of that "angular and difficult" character's attitudes toward eugenics. Hogben's hostility had little to do with any denial of the importance of hereditary selection, Blacker wrote to Carr-Saunders, but lay in the not-unfounded fear that eugenics had perverted genetics and become identified with "ancestor worship, anti-semitism, colour prejudice, anti-feminism, snobbery and obstruction to educational progress."[11] None of these objections, however, prevented the brazen Hogben, with his "highly developed sense of humour," from applying to the Eugenics Society for funds later in the decade when his Department of Social Biology was dismantled for financial reasons and he had to move once again, this time to the University of Aberdeen. He did so even while colorfully denouncing eugenicists for "decking out the jackdaws of class prejudice in the peacock feathers of biological jargon" and describing Eugenics Society leaders as "childless rentiers" who as "twentieth century Bourbons . . . have earned nothing and begotten nothing."[12]

Hogben was perhaps both the most vituperative and amusing of eugenic opponents in the 1930s, but however irritating Blacker found him to be, his own opinion of many mainline, old-guard eugenicists was hardly more complimentary.[13] Moreover, other accomplished biologists were no less critical of the reactionaries in the organization and of the questionable, class-ridden, hereditary theories they tried to pass off as science. Notable among these critics were Huxley, Fullerian Professor of Physiology at the Royal Institution and secretary of the London Zoological Society, and Haldane, professor of genetics at the University of London, who joined the Eugenics Society because of their interest in birth control and population genetics.[14]

In contrast to Hogben, both Huxley and Haldane came from distinguished intellectual and scientific families whose pedigrees justified their enshrinement in any eugenic "Treasury of Family Inheritance." Their eclectic careers in zoology, physiology, and genetics brought them great distinction in scientific circles and a substantial public following as well. Huxley, in particular, was one of the most influential popularizers of science between the wars. His coauthorship with H. G. Wells of *The Science of Life* (1929) and his role as a member of the BBC brain trust made him a national figure whose ideas about heredity and demography strengthened the hand of reformers like Blacker and Carr-Saunders in the Eugenics Society. Although Haldane was unable to reconcile his expanding knowledge of genetics and his increasingly more radical socialist views with the eugenics he had embraced when a student at Oxford and in time became a severe critic of the movement, Huxley remained a supporter. With his help, Blacker was able to enlist the aid of other reform-minded scientists and physicians in his efforts to turn eugenics into a responsible, socially neutral research discipline before it lost whatever credibility it might still enjoy in influential scientific and social scientific circles.

Blacker was convinced that whatever its scientific credentials eugenics would never play a critical role in the formulation of population policy so long as it was tied to class prejudice. One of his main objectives since becoming general secretary, he wrote on numerous occasions, was to break that knot and to combat the perception of eugenicists as wealthy people who think themselves superior and who want to prevent the poor from having children whom the rich have to support.[15] This, of course, is exactly what a great many people of eugenic persuasion believed and wanted, and the Eton-educated, rather patrician Blacker himself was not entirely immune. When the Oxford biologist John Baker was invited in 1933 to discuss birth control and eugenics on the BBC, Blacker urged him to play down the class question at all costs, and suggested he say that "social status is a very inadequate index of eugenic merit and the eugenic worth of the artisan, and *probably* [italics added] also of the working classes, was just as great as that of the professional classes and leisured rich." As an afterthought, he sensibly reminded Baker that "since our eugenic proposals are all voluntary, it seems to me to be in the highest degree necessary to enlist the cooperation and support of dysgenic people. . . . You are not very likely to enlist their sympathy if you speak about them disparagingly as dregs and scum."[16]

Baker, whose search for a cheap, effective contraceptive was being financed by the Eugenics Society, was among the least likely of eugenicists to use such language. He and several other Oxford members of the society had angrily threatened to resign two years earlier because of the "untruthful and scurrilous" people who were attracted to the organization and who felt nothing but contempt for the unfortunate poor.[17] On that occasion, as on several others, it took all of Blacker's considerable powers of persuasion to keep Baker from resigning, an effort he had to make with other socially conscious members throughout the decade.

In addition to trying to contain the damage caused by the indiscretions of the dwindling representatives of mainline eugenics in the society, he had to remind his more progressive allies, one of whom was writing a leaflet on birth control for working-class women, to avoid using the term "eugenically inferior" as if it were synonymous with "lower classes" or "uneducated classes." The poor, he found, tended to be particularly "class-conscious" and take offense easily.[18] Blacker, in a 1935 internal memorandum, complained that the worst enemies of eugenics were not socialists and Catholics but people "who expound eugenics in terms of class and language which shows contempt for the depressed classes."[19]

As a way of demonstrating the alleged social neutrality of eugenics, Blacker tried to entice Labour party members into the movement. He arranged interviews with a number of Labour candidates and M.P.s, and at the urging of several socialist eugenicists invited them to participate in a series of debates on "Eugenics and Party Politics" during the 1931 election. In light of the pervasive belief within the Labour party that eugenics was nothing more than a camouflaged system of social and political prejudices "masquerading as a pseudo-science," it is not surprising that few Labourites were prepared to discuss the topic.[20] One of the few willing to do so was Ellen Wilkinson, who even suggested the establishment of an advisory committee to the Eugenics Society council consisting of people with Labour party sympathies. Blacker himself personally believed eugenics "harmonize much better with the Socialist Party's conception as to the proper distribution of wealth, than with the corresponding conception of the Conservative Party." By depriving the "incompetent rich of the financial life belt of inherited wealth," socialism would equalize opportunities for natural ability to emerge. While several members of the society shared his views, Blacker knew many more did not. He found it hard to visualize Labour representatives on the same council with "a retrograde menace" like Dean Inge, whose visible identification with the movement "goes far to explain why Eugenics is so unpopular with Socialists."[21]

In reality, the dislike many left-wing scientists and social scientists expressed for eugenics in the interwar years had less to do with a rejection of qualitative hereditarian assumptions and biological inequities than it did with eugenic justifications for the prevailing social order. Hogben, Haldane, and Huxley, for example, were hardly biological egalitarians. On the contrary, although they recognized that individuals were genetically much more diverse and complicated than was commonly known, they nevertheless still believed strongly in the dominance of heredity in determining the intellectual, psychological, and moral traits of people. Despite their scientific sophistication they were, in this, no less immune to the pervasiveness of hereditarian causation assumed by most eugenicists and much of the public.

In addition, a number of socialist biologists were as enthusiastic about the eugenic possibilities of selective breeding as the most ardent Galtonian. Several of them fantasized about the race-enhancing possibilities of artificial insemination, and at least one, Haldane, who turned to communism in the 1930s, was prepared to contribute his name, money, and valuable sperm to the cause. Indeed, the most ardent eugenics advocate of artificial insemination in the 1930s was a mentally unstable socialist postal clerk and trade unionist, Herbert Brewer, who hoped to arrange an improbable marriage between eugenics and the Labour movement. Though he shocked the aged Darwin and other remnants of the old guard, Brewer's visions of a selectively bred, classless "eutelegenetic" future were not only encouraged by Eugenics Society leaders, but by distinguished left-wing geneticists such as Huxley, Haldane, and the American communist, Hermann Muller, who had introduced Huxley to genetics when the two were at Rice University before and during the war. The eighty-one-year-old Fabian George Bernard Shaw in 1937 sent the grateful Brewer £100 and a plaintive thought about all of the ova he, Shaw, might have inseminated in his younger days.[22]

Unlike the mainline, old-guard eugenicists whom they held in contempt, most left-wing eugenicists saw little evidence of genetic superiority among nations, races, or classes whose characteristics were believed to be culturally and environmentally rather than biologically determined. But some advocates of a pure socialist eugenics such as Haldane and, to a lesser degree, Huxley, disagreed. Themselves the products of the Victorian intellectual and scientific aristocracy, they were more inclined to believe races and classes differed substantially in their proportional endowment of highly gifted people. Haldane, for example, despite his communist predilections continued to believe that the upper classes from which he sprang were innately more able and intelligent than their social inferiors. However often he condemned the faulty science and social prejudices of right-wing eugenicists, he was no less worried than they about the racial consequences of the higher fertility and declining intelligence of the poor. "In short," as a recent study of eugenics and the left concluded, "wherever one looks—among right-wing geneticists, left-wing geneticists, and political moderates; amongst those conventionally associated with an environmentalist position as well as those considered hereditarians— one finds agreement on the fact (though of course not the extent) of substantial genetic determination of intellectual, psychological, and moral traits and the advocacy of some kind of eugenics."[23]

Where socialist eugenics differed most sharply from the mainstream, and from moderate reformers such as Blacker, was in its advocacy of a state-regulated, egalitarian environment in which true hereditary talent would not be stifled by a privileged, class-ridden, capitalistic social order. To many of them, the Soviet Union was the obvious place to test and apply eugenics. Despite Blacker's cautious expressions of sympathy for socialism, he was far too political, pragmatic, and in the final analysis, socially conservative to go to such extremes. Talk as he did about the necessity of building bridges to Labour, he was never very comfortable with the prospect and admitted after the 1931 election that eugenics was likely to fare much better in the short run at least with the Conservatives dominating the coalition government. He agreed with the assessment of Maurice Newfield, the new, reform-minded editor of the *Eugenics Review*, that even if Labour had won it would have had to concentrate on economic problems exclusively for the next few years. A few prominent Labourites, like Harold Laski who as a precocious teenager before the war had met Galton and embraced eugenics, might support it in conjunction with birth control, but most would not. Effective political help would have to come from the Conservative party which was not burdened with a large Catholic electorate and had not yet "saddled itself with the belief that all men are born equal." But with Labour attracting more than 6 million votes even in defeat, Blacker reminded members, it would remain a powerful political force in the country whose support would still be necessary in the long run if eugenics were ever to win the approbation of the working classes.[24]

Newfield, a physician who wanted to transform the *Eugenics Review* from "a parish magazine" into a national organ for the study of population problems, human genetics, and birth control, described himself as a "liberal socialist" who, in contrast to the Marxists, did not believe in the inevitable collapse of capitalism. While on balance he thought eugenics was more compatible with socialism, he did not believe it was necessary to "shut up shop until a social revolution creates the environment in which it will . . . be possible to see the role of heredity." He, like Blacker, knew however of the strong opposition of "individualist eugenists" to an accommodation with socialism and struggled to keep the review open to diverse opinions while deflecting the letters and articles of the lunatic fringe who were drawn to its pages.[25]

No matter how often eugenicists insisted they were only interested in hereditary characteristics, not in social classes, the distinction was lost on contemporary critics. Repeated assurances that eugenics was neither biased nor socially prejudiced were not helped by Lord Horder's reasoning, "if a certain class, *qua* class, produces through heredity, as distinct from environment, a better race, then we have got to accept that, be it the poor, the middle, or the upper class."[26] The problem for reform eugenics was the old one of trying to sort out that elusive distinction and to determine the relative contributions of nature and nurture which, Huxley argued in his Galton Lecture of 1936, could only be accomplished through the equalization of social conditions, a notion guaranteed to horrify mainline eugenicists.[27]

With socialist biologists within and outside of the Eugenics Society agreeing openly or privately with Hogben and his equally radical wife, the economist Enid Charles, that they much preferred the eugenics of Lenin to the eugenics of Dean Inge, the question of a standardized environment was pressed on eugenic reformers throughout the decade. While not every left-wing critic shared Charles's conviction that true eugenics could only be evaluated and achieved in the Soviet Union, where the promise of genuine environmental equality existed, several did. Many more concurred with the basic thrust of her argument that an "acquisitive society" could not create the conditions for developing or applying scientifically the knowledge of man's inborn nature.[28] This belief in the fundamental incompatibility of capitalism with the construction of a eugenic utopia was on the minds of most, if not all, of the twenty-two British and American scientists who signed Muller's "Geneticists Manifesto" in 1939.[29] It was the last of a series of blows before the war challenging the increasingly defensive contention of eugenicists that even if human genetics proved not to be immune to the effects of social services and environmental reforms, there was already enough agreement about hereditary causation to permit the formulation of eugenic policies even while social and economic opportunities for people remained unequal.

Lord Horder, in making this argument in 1940, nevertheless admitted that the separation of genetic from environmental factors was the major problem in establishing eugenic credibility. Blacker agreed, and though he personally doubted environmental improvements would enhance the innate genetic capacity of the race very much, he conceded that until some equitable base for all classes was established, the difficulties of proving the claims of heredity would remain formidable.[30] Two decades later, looking back on the depression years, Blacker recalled how the attack on eugenics by socialist critics was part of a wider assault on the social and economic inequities of capitalism. In that context, the nature-nurture argument was energetically revived by antieugenic biologists who contended that heredity could not be correctly assessed when such enormous disparities in social conditions prevailed.

Blacker remembered how difficult it was to separate the question of eugenic policies from class, because "*inter*-class differences were . . . so prominent in people's minds that many were reluctant to examine *intra*-class differences."[31] At the time it was not easy to take the stinging abuse of scientists such as Hogben, but in a 1939 review of his adversary's important new book *Political Arithmetic*, Blacker nevertheless praised him for having profitably stimulated the study of eugenics and for making "many of us . . . more critical than we were of some traditional postulates as to the importance of heredity, and more diffident in generalizing about the genetic effects of certain eugenic measures."[32]

This was what had happened to the thoughtful, reform eugenicist Clifton Chance, who was an investment consultant interested in birth control rather than a scientist knowledgeable in the intricacies of genetics. The more he learned, the more confused he became. In a revealing letter to Blacker in 1940, Chance recalled how simple and seductive the idea of hereditary quality and selective breeding once seemed. But the closer one gets to human problems, he continued, the more elusive and complex the issue becomes. While the extremes of "good and bad" traits are usually clear, when we try to separate them from environmental and hereditary factors we face a question of scientific analysis we are not really able to answer. This is the "joint in our armour as fighting eugenicists" which leaves us vulnerable to attack, Chance complained, and "it is the inability to give satisfying answers about what to do to improve the quality of future generations that makes me soft-pedal propaganda and always advocate financial support to research of . . . quality."[33]

Eugenics and the National Birth Control Association

In many ways the turn toward population research and birth control taken by reform eugenics in the interwar years was an implied acknowledgment of the failure of Galton's positive evangelistic vision. Negative, preventive policies such as birth control and sterilization increasingly dominated the thinking of those devoted to race regeneration. The Eugenics Society's expensive, controversial, and ultimately futile campaign to persuade Parliament in the 1930s to legalize voluntary sterilization of the alleged defectives who comprised a substantial portion of the Social Problem Group drew a good deal of support from a wide range of organizations and individuals. Two bills introduced on the society's behalf in 1931 and 1932 failed to get very far, but they contributed to the authorization of a special government inquiry on which several eugenicists served under Laurence G. Brock, the head of the Joint Committee on Mental Deficiency.

The Brock report in 1934 denied there was any "sound scientific basis for sterilization on account of immorality or character defect" and claimed that human conduct and character were too complex and "too interwoven with social conditions . . . to permit any definite conclusions to be drawn concerning the part which heredity plays in their genesis." Eugenicists were nonetheless encouraged by its endorsement of voluntary sterilization in cases where disorders were indisputably hereditary.[34] Many of them saw in the recommendation an important first step that would eventually lead to a more comprehensive sterilization program. But only an enthusiastic minority seriously believed that even if sterilization were eventually legalized it would ever have much of an impact on reducing the less severe but more pervasive dysgenic problems resulting from differential fertility. Indeed, a number of Eugenics Society members vigorously opposed the controversial sterilization campaign with its focus on the very poor as unnecessarily provocative and, when compared to the much greater eugenic advantages to be derived from the spread of birth control, wasteful of the organization's resources and energies. Some, like Professor F. M. A. Marshall of Christ's College, Cambridge, resigned over the issue, while others, like Huxley, prevailed on the society to keep the two questions entirely separate so as not to undermine the birth control campaign when it was on the verge of success.[35]

Blacker had to reassure skeptical critics that the society's involvement with sterilization legislation in no way diminished its growing support of birth control. While he and other champions of sterilization believed the two were complementary, they acknowledged that in the arsenal of negative eugenics, birth control would remain the most effective weapon for the foreseeable future. Only the "real genetic unteachables" who were too "stupid, lazy or shiftless" to learn birth control, and who stood out by virtue of their unchecked reproduction, were obvious candidates for sterilization. In this sense birth control was increasingly seen by eugenicists as a sort of screening program for the sterilization of the most "inferior stock, which, like dregs have silted down to the bottom of society."[36] This had been on Cora Hodson's mind when in the 1920s she had first encouraged the collection of data from birth control clinics and visited a number of sterilization programs in the United States.

However much Blacker and other reform eugenicists tried to separate population policies from the appearance of class prejudice, there was no escaping their primary concern with reducing the birthrate of the unskilled and semi-skilled working classes and, of course, the unemployed poor whose numbers increased dramatically once more in the depression. At the same time, birth control was also seen by reform eugenicists as an effective method of moderating the sharp environmental inequities masking the true contribution of heredity to the development of social classes. It did not mean they were prepared to concede the old neo-Malthusian argument that poverty was a consequence of too many children rather than too many defective genes, but they were much more willing to consider the extent to which it was true.

Recalling the "extremely nebulous" attitude of the Eugenics Society toward birth control when he joined in 1926, Blacker was struck by how quickly that attitude had changed by the end of the decade. Although a minority of the membership continued to insist that birth control was hopelessly dysgenic and clung to the hope that the best stocks would one day start rearing large families again, the overwhelming majority, including the society's council, had no such illusions. They were nearly unanimous in favor of advancing "the discriminating and selective employment of birth control."[37] Some, like Carr-Saunders, were positively rapturous about the possibilities. "I am more and more impressed with the fact that birth control is the greatest thing that has come over our species," he wrote Blacker. "The ultimate result will be . . . that the society of the distant future will be recruited from self selective philoprogenitive groups."[38]

If, on balance, Carr-Saunders's eugenicist colleagues were rather more restrained in their assessment, they were no less committed to supporting the BCIC, the SPBCC, and the National Birth Control Council which, in 1931, changed its name to the more inclusive National Birth Control Association (NBCA). Under the leadership of Margaret Pyke, who had not previously been prominent in the birth control movement but who, after separation from her husband, needed employment, the NBCA absorbed the Workers Birth

Control Group and amalgamated with the BCIC, the birth control clinics, and their parent organization, the SPBCC.

For two years the NBCA was even able to harness the formidable Marie Stopes who, with some trepidation, had been invited to affiliate her Society for Constructive Birth Control and to sit on the governing board of the new group. It was a strained relationship which ended in 1933 when Stopes withdrew, angered by the election of Newfield in his capacity as editor of the *Eugenics Review* to the executive committee of the NBCA. Like several other physicians, he had infuriated her by questioning the reliability and safety of some of the contraceptives she prescribed. But Stopes also quit because she resented the credit the NBCA enjoyed for the Ministry of Health's 1930 memorandum and subsequent directives and complained repeatedly that her own accomplishments as the self-styled "pioneer of the birth control movement" did not receive enough recognition from the new organization.[39]

Stopes's relationship with the Eugenics Society was not much better despite the growing intensity of her desire to rid the country of the "diseased, C3 and potentially rotten members of society" who continued to proliferate. She was an ardent supporter of *compulsory* sterilization which she claimed to have been quietly promoting since 1921. Unfortunately, as she saw it, the Eugenics Society had butted in with its disastrous, ill-conceived tactics to get a useless parliamentary bill legalizing ineffectual voluntary sterilization. All the campaign did, as far as she was concerned, was stir up the opposition of sentimental Labour politicians, reactionary Catholics, and retrograde doctors.

Though Stopes continued her membership in the organization and eventually left it her considerable library and a handsome legacy, she quite rightly felt "cold-shouldered."[40] Like Huxley, who found her to be "rather terrible," Blacker, Horder, Lady Denman, and others on the society's council always managed to have another engagement when she invited them to something. Finding her "quite impervious to reason" and continually trying to ensnare them in one of her causes, they decided the less they had to do with her the better. At the same time, they succeeded in avoiding an acrimonious break by periodically stroking her ego with such assurances as "whatever . . . we may feel about the personality of Dr. Stopes, and some of the methods by which she has achieved her ends, we can but admire such courage and such attainments."[41]

In complaining as she frequently did to the editors of medical journals and to officers in the British Medical Association of her differences with the NBCA, Stopes was indirectly acknowledging the success the new organization was having in winning over important physicians to the birth control cause.[42]

Unlike Stopes, whose relations with the medical profession remained thorny and adversarial, the NBCA deliberately cultivated medical officers, hospital officials, and public health organizations in which doctors played a predominant role. Much of this important activity was guided by the BCIC and its secretary, Blacker, who, with the assistance of the royal physician, Lord Horder, pressed eugenic claims on the medical profession. Together they overcame the resistance of the Royal Society of Medicine to the establishment of a study section on morbid inheritance, and Eardley Holland, a Eugenics Society fellow and president of the Obstetrical and Gynaecological Section of the Royal Society of Medicine, was instrumental in promoting the case for genetic instruction among students in his specialty.[43]

The campaign to attract doctors to eugenic birth control was in part a recognition of where the power to advance hereditary considerations in society really lay. It was far better to teach eugenics to senior medical students than to mothers' meetings all over the country, the University of Edinburgh biologist F. A. E. Crew wrote to Blacker. If the medical profession took it up, he believed, the future of eugenics would be assured. Unless this happened and eugenics was shown to have some direct, practical application to people's lives, others warned, there was a danger the Eugenics Society would become nothing more than an academic debating society for geneticists.[44]

In arguing for the study of genetics as an important part of a doctor's education, Horder claimed eugenics was really a branch of preventive medicine "fraught with a deeper and more lasting effect than any other." He warned the members of his profession not to make the same mistake they had made with birth control. For too long they had refused to take it seriously as an area for medical inquiry and only recently admitted its relevance to the health and happiness of their patients. As in the case of birth control, Horder added, if doctors were unwilling to provide scientific leadership and direction in the application of eugenic procedures, others less qualified were prepared to do so.[45]

The response of the medical profession was careful and mixed. The *Lancet*, which had always been sympathetic to eugenics and which was the first of the medical journals to acknowledge the importance of birth control, repeatedly endorsed a triple alliance of medicine, eugenics, and sociology. Enthusiasm for eugenics in *Nature*, the most authoritative scientific periodical in the interwar years, was even more emphatic. Its editor, Sir Richard Gregory, who became a vice-president in Stopes's Society for Constructive Birth Control, went beyond the *Lancet* in his call for compulsory birth control and, if that failed, mandatory sterilization of the grossly unfit.[46] The *British Medical Journal*, like its parent organization the British Medical Association, was far more cautious in its treatment of eugenics as it had been in its coverage of birth control.

Blacker realized the Eugenics Society was still regarded "by many scientific men—among whom is emphatically included the Editor of the British Medical Journal—as a propagandist society which derives its main inspiration from enthusiastic lay women."[47] While it was true a substantial minority of the membership still fit this description, the percentage of doctors in the organization steadily rose so that they filled nearly a third of the seventy-five officer positions and council seats. Several of these physicians served on the BCIC, which remained an autonomous medical and scientific arm of the NBCA. Others were among the fourteen officers and council members in the Eugenics Society who also held official positions in the NBCA.[48] These included the NBCA's president from 1930 to 1936, Horder, who was also a vice-president of the Eugenics Society throughout most of these years. Sir Humphrey Rolleston, who succeeded Mallet as president of the society in 1932, was chairman of the BCIC and, along with Blacker, C. J. Bond, and Newfield, sat on the executive committee of the NBCA. They were joined there by two more recent additions to the Eugenics Society ranks, the economist Eva Hubback, principal of Morley College, and Lady Denman, both of whom were instrumental in the founding of the NBCA.

Even the retired Darwin, whose fears about the dysgenic effects of birth control had not entirely been laid to rest, agreed to lend his name to the new organization though questioning the extent to which the Eugenics Society should become involved with any group not totally committed to its objectives. He was placated to some extent by the willingness of NBCA lecturers to stress that birth control was still dysgenic and only appropriate for those who were too poor, ill, or genetically unsuited for parenthood. Otherwise the best stock in all classes should have more not fewer children. But in emphasizing as they did that the birthrate of married miners and unskilled workers was still nearly twice that of the middle and upper classes, the class-specific, eugenic thrust of the NBCA guidelines was obvious.[49]

Despite lingering doubts in both camps about the appropriateness of the relationship, the multiple ties between the Eugenics Society and the NBCA grew stronger throughout the decade. Without planning or in many cases even recognizing it, a substantial sector of the organized birth control movement became increasingly enmeshed with and to a large extent dependent upon the much smaller but much richer eugenics movement. The birth control cause was particularly vulnerable for two reasons: (1) it was extremely difficult in the economic depression to raise adequate funds to carry on an ambitious campaign to persuade local authorities to establish more birth control facilities, to encourage the Ministry of Health to liberalize its guidelines, to lobby for legislative reforms, to support scientific research, and to educate medical students and practitioners, all with the goal of making birth control an essential part of the public health system in the United Kingdom; and (2) the problem was compounded by widespread fears from the mid-1930s of the birthrate falling so far that the population would soon begin a geometric decline which in a few generations would leave the country dangerously underpopulated and grossly overaged.

While the connection between birth control and eugenics was not universally welcomed by proponents in either camp it was increasingly accepted, sometimes grudgingly, as logical and necessary. To coordinate its burgeoning role in the birth control movement, the Eugenics Society council, at Blacker's request, established a special Birth Control Committee in 1933 which recommended, among other things, that the organization use some of its now considerable wealth to finance the activities of the NBCA. Initial grants of £50 were provided to lobby sympathetic M.P.s to press the minister of health to broaden his guidelines so that local health authorities could give birth control advice to any married woman who requested it. In addition, £125 was made available to help the NBCA persuade medical officers to take advantage of the permissive directives already available, while smaller awards were given to the voluntary birth control clinics administered by the SPBCC. By 1935 about 10 percent of the Eugenics Society's annual expenditures of nearly £5,000 were being used for such purposes.[50]

After 1931 the Ministry of Health gradually expanded the permissible medical reasons for giving birth control information and in 1934 extended them enough to include those women "who are suffering from other forms of sickness, physical and mental, which are detrimental to them as mothers."[51] Although the Birth Control Committee complained that the ministry's new circular should have included transmissible illnesses and economic conditions, its members thought the new designation of mental illness could be eugenically interpreted by sympathetic doctors and proceeded to subsidize the distribution of copies of the regulations to medical officers around the country.[52] Three years later the ministry, worried about an increase in maternal mortality even as the infant deathrate continued to decline, yielded to arguments for more gynecological services in the welfare centers and agreed birth control could be a legitimate part of postnatal care where the health of a new mother was in question.[53] Lord Horder and Lady Denman usually represented the NBCA in the deputations that met periodically with the minister of health, Sir Kingsley Wood, to urge the opening of more clinics and the expansion of gynecological care in poorer districts. As far as the eugenicists were concerned, the poorer the better, but as Wood rightly pointed out at one of these meetings in 1937, it was really up to the local authorities to decide.[54]

The problem of getting medical officers and their councils to act was often extremely difficult in the face of organized local opposition, usually Catholic, economic stringencies, and lingering doubts about the safety and propriety of contraceptives. By 1939 only 77 of the 414 maternity and child welfare authorities in England and Wales had established their own clinics, but more than 280 of them, mostly in populous urban areas, provided some way for women to receive birth control instruction in public or private health facilities. Their activities were supplemented by nearly 70 voluntary clinics, all but 5 of them affiliated with the NBCA, or the Family Planning Association (FPA) as it was renamed a few months before the war, and supported in part by Eugenics Society grants.[55] Only Marie Stopes's clinics stood apart, and though they were not recipients of the society's largesse, eugenic counseling, sometimes bluntly delivered by Stopes herself to the unwary degenerate, was taken very seriously. She did after all disinherit her only son for the dysgenic folly of marrying a woman tainted with poor eyesight.[56]

Despite the Eugenics Society's providing about 10 to 15 percent of its operating costs, the NBCA ran a substantial deficit throughout the 1930s with expenses at times exceeding income by 20 to 40 percent. Newfield, who worked very closely with Margaret Pyke, made the pages of the *Eugenics Review* available for the publication of NBCA materials on a regular basis to help reduce costs. The NBCA was the largest and most comprehensive birth control organization in Great Britain with nearly fifty branches and a dozen or so affiliated organizations—some of them, like the Women's National Liberal Federation or the National Union of Societies for Equal Citizenship (NUSEC), much larger. Its own membership, though studded with luminaries from different walks of life, was, nevertheless, at around 250 in the later 1930s, very small. Ten percent of these were also in the Eugenics Society, whose own limited numbers were still three times those of the NBCA. More important, the society's investments and property holdings, which despite the depression still totaled nearly £70,000, were more than thirty times the resources of the constantly strapped NBCA.[57]

By the fall of 1936 Blacker, with the approval of his Birth Control Committee, was discussing the possibility with Pyke of a merger between the NBCA and the Eugenics Society in order to save the former organization.[58] Troubled by alarming predictions of impending population decline and eager to change the negative connotation of eugenics and birth control, Blacker contemplated consolidating the two groups into a more positive, family-oriented institute. He had raised the possibility the previous year in a memorandum to the society's council and even suggested, more hesitantly, that the name of the organization be changed to the Institute for Family Relations. Under the new rubric it would dedicate itself to advancing the quantitative as well as the qualitative composition of the population. Despite Carr-Saunders's endorsement of the idea in his 1935 Galton Lecture, several of the society's officers were, as Blacker predicted, less than enthusiastic. They feared such a change would of necessity lead to the support of more social welfare schemes, family allowance programs, additional maternal and child care facilities, and other plans likely to encourage the fertility of the working classes.[59]

Despite the setback, Blacker continued to pursue the plan.[60] Most of those Eugenics Society officers who also served on the NBCA's governing board welcomed the proposal, but many others in both organizations were skeptical or opposed. Nevertheless, a joint committee was established to consider the possibility and in April 1937 recommended that the NBCA be absorbed into the Eugenics Society as its Birth Control Committee, with representation on the executive committee and governing council. The BCIC and Medical Sub-Committee, heavily engaged in the evaluation of contraceptives, would remain attached to the new group as its scientific advisory board. To placate expected opposition from Labour members and several branches in working-class districts, supporters of the NBCA would not be required to join the Eugenics Society until they were convinced that eugenics was not hostile to their interests.

The principal advantages to be derived by the birth control group were financial and operational. With the NBCA chronically in debt, harassed by opponents, and unclear as to the direction to take in the face of an impending decline in population, the Eugenics Society promised economic security and a more comprehensive role in family planning. A section of the *Eugenics Review* would be devoted exclusively to birth control news, and the NBCA would be provided office space in the society's building at 69 Eccleston Square, near Victoria Station. In return, the Eugenics Society would gain "an unrivalled opportunity" for drawing attention to its principles and for demonstrating the importance of selective birth control in influencing population measures "in a biologically desirable direction."

The society's representatives particularly coveted the NBCA's affiliated network of branches and clinics throughout the country. Its own efforts to build and sustain branches had peaked before the First World War when most of them collapsed. Since then it had been content, mostly out of necessity, with remaining a small, London-based propaganda society. A merger with the NBCA raised the prospects of a larger membership and even held out the hope of a better understanding with the Labour party which, despite strong Catholic resistance, generally supported birth control.[61]

Reaction to the proposed merger was less than enthusiastic. A number of eugenicists, including Dr. Stella Churchill, who was involved in the negotiations and active in both organizations, questioned months earlier whether the NBCA branches and clinics were prepared to offer eugenic teaching. Her own visits to a great many of them provided few reasons for confidence and none to suggest that any clinic would even consider the sterilization procedures some Eugenics Society planners hoped could be introduced.[62] Major Darwin, who had reluctantly approved the negotiations, was not alone in his fears that the NBCA would take the society's money and divert it to noneugenic ends. He was worried that the broader concepts of family planning such as marital counseling, problems of sterility, sex education, child guidance, and women's welfare would prove expensive and divert the society from its primary goal of advancing the "*inborn* qualities of future generations." While Darwin conceded the validity of Eugenics Society support for birth control and even birth spacing, which seemed to be having the effect of reducing the size of larger, less intelligent families more than those of the smaller, more intelligent families, he spoke for many of his active colleagues who wanted greater assurances of a eugenic commitment from the NBCA.[63]

Such assurances, NBCA officials recognized, were out of the question. After considerable discussion of the joint committee's report, they concluded it would be a mistake to submit the proposals to the branches. Not only were they "unlikely to accept or work for the diversity of objects outlined by the Eugenics Society [but] the present name, aims and objects of the Eugenics Society were unacceptable to the Association." An alternative approach to local authorities, it added, would probably not be any easier "as there was a tendency in the country to regard the Eugenics Society as highbrow and sometimes dogmatic on insufficient data."[64]

Rejection of the amalgamation scheme put the NBCA in something of a dilemma. Its leaders knew that despite the recent efforts of Blacker and other reform eugenicists to refute charges of class prejudice and of wanting to sterilize the laboring poor, many Labour party members and socialist supporters of the NBCA, as well as a substantial number of its clientele, would never accept the idea of a eugenic clinic. At the same time, within the upper reaches of the governing body and executive committee the financial advantages of working closely with the Eugenics Society were candidly admitted. Although some members would have preferred to sever all formal ties with the society, more practical heads prevailed. It was agreed the joint committee should continue to explore how the two organizations could cooperate and how the interest of the NBCA branches in the work of the Eugenics Society might be aroused. The most likely area was a joint study of social aspects of the population question rather than the implementation of practices, and the NBCA held out the hope of presenting a resolution to this effect at a future annual meeting. Until there was a drastic alteration in the stated aims and objectives of the Eugenics Society as well as a change of name, there was, however, little chance that the branches could be brought around.[65]

None of this came as any surprise to Blacker who had made similar recommendations two years earlier and who had hoped a change of name would help make a merger more palatable to the NBCA rank and file. He was content to continue recommending annual grants of from £100 to £300 to the NBCA and its affiliates and permitted the organization to occupy at low rent the second floor of the society's premises. It was the one specific recommendation of the joint committee accepted by the NBCA's board. Otherwise, by 1939 the prolonged negotiations had achieved little more than a vague acknowledgment by the executive committee of the birth control organization that it might be able to recommend to the larger body identification with one or more objectives of the Eugenics Society but not with its general program.[66]

In the end it was the National Birth Control Association that changed its name and its aims and objectives rather than the Eugenics Society. Although most of its efforts were directed at providing clinics for the poor, the NBCA always insisted that unlike the Malthusian League it did not advocate smaller families as the solution to poverty but as a humane and rational way of reducing the physical, psychological, and, in many cases, economic strain of excessive childbirth that would benefit people of all classes. It was a positive end even if the means appeared decidedly negative. Advocates of reform, like Margaret Spring-Rice, reminded NBCA members, "birth control has come to imply in the minds of those who work for it, in the minds of those who use it, and in public opinion,—the *limitation* of births rather than the *regulation* of births, which is a far more exact connotation of the term, more really approximates to the ethical basis of the movement, and is . . . a far more valuable concept."[67]

The effort to associate birth control with constructive population planning rather than only with the prevention of conception was, as Spring-Rice pointed out, closely linked to mounting concern that "the seed of birth control knowledge" had been scattered "without accepting responsibility for its harvest." Eugenic critics had always made this point in complaining about the dysgenic consequences of differential fertility, but now a much wider public was alerted to the more serious prospect of a general population decline threatening not only the quality but the quantity and age distribution of the nation's dwindling demographic resources. Despite its reliance upon such negative programs as birth control and sterilization, the Eugenics Society under Blacker's direction was by the mid-1930s becoming alarmed by population projections and exploring more positive alternatives. The NBCA was encouraged by both its eugenicist and noneugenicist members to do the same. Its efforts to respond were reflected in executive committee suggestions as early as 1937 to change the organization's name to the National Association for Family Planning or the National Association for Maternal Health and Family Planning.

The consensus of the committee, which comprised such diverse people as the aristocratic Lady Denman, the Ministry of Health official Dr. Janet Campbell, the Labourite Mrs. Hugh Dalton, and the physician Dr. Helena Wright, among others, was that they were really looking for a name connoting a more comprehensive program of planned parenthood. Nevertheless, when two years later in May 1939 the NBCA adopted from several nominations the more abbreviated title Family Planning Association, the decision was hotly resisted by several individuals and clinics opposed to the abandonment of the term birth control after so many years of struggle to get it accepted.[68]

Supporters admitted the change was regrettable, but it had to be undertaken to "simplify both money-raising and organising work, owing to the widespread identification of 'birth control' with birth prevention."[69] By way of placating opponents, individual branches and clinics were assured they were free to emphasize those aspects of family planning with which they were most comfortable. A major consideration throughout the NBCA's deliberations in 1939 was the worsening international situation and fear of a backlash when the population began to decline. Spring-Rice warned, "The tide of public opinion which has been steadily rising in our favour will inevitably turn when the threatening disaster is fully realised, a disaster which at any moment may be hastened by the ravages of war."[70]

The Family Planning Association's commitment to a more expansive, positive program was evident in its objectives of advocating and promoting facilities for scientific contraception so that married people could space or limit their families and thus mitigate the evils of poverty; advancing the establishment of women's health centers at which women could get not only contraceptive advice, but help for involuntary sterility, minor gynecological ailments, and difficulties with their marital relationship; and examining and assisting in the solution of any other relevant problems.[71] Conspicuously absent in this statement, as several eugenicists were quick to note, was any reference to eugenics.

Margaret Pyke, whose enthusiasm for eugenics had always been more tactical than ideological, lamely explained even before the objectives were formally approved that she forgot to include it and assured Blacker there was nothing in the impending name change or the stated objectives to preclude closer affiliation with the Eugenics Society in the future. In fact, she suggested rather disingenuously, the FPA's wider scope may make it more acceptable to those society members who were still not anxious to be "closely allied with undiluted birth control propaganda."[72] Others, such as Spring-Rice, were more convincing in their claim of a "eugenic principle at the bottom of all birth control doctrine." Though still in its infancy, eugenics contained "infinite potentialities" for birth control so that "in principle . . . the birth control movement should take part in, or rather be part of the wider one of eugenics."[73]

Despite the grumbling of some old, mainline eugenicists like Inge, who continued to oppose any environmental reforms that might "subsidise the teeming birth-rate of the slums," the Eugenics Society formally approved of the new name and new directions.[74] Welcoming the changes, the *Eugenics Review* explained that birth control was much misunderstood in the current demographic context. Alive to contemporary realities, the FPA was, quite rightly it went on, as equally concerned with problems of low fertility, infertility, and the healthy spacing of children as it was with excessive childbearing.[75] Its new name and orientation notwithstanding, the survival of FPA was still very tenuous at the outbreak of the war a few months later. The organization was more than £700 in debt, was forced to lay off staff, and with many of its volunteers called into the forces or other wartime occupations, was in danger of collapse. In addition, with the future so uncertain and anxieties about the size of the population so high, birth control and family planning seemed rather inconsequential, if not a direct threat.

The Eugenics Society, though financially sound, was itself uncertain about trying to carry on during the war with Blacker and many others quickly called into service. Before his departure, the general secretary arranged for another £100 grant to the FPA and invited it to remain in its offices rent free. If the society closed down for the duration, he explained to its financial adviser, Chance, its funds would grow rapidly anyway so the rent would not be needed. Lady Denman volunteered to pay off the FPA's remaining overdraft to keep it from folding, and when an emergency council of the Eugenics Society was established, it agreed to lend income and staff to the FPA on the understanding that it would encourage the teaching of eugenics in its welfare centers.[76] There is no evidence it ever did and nothing to suggest that the affiliated branches were any more inclined to do so than they had been before the war. Worried about its own survival, however, the society decided it had little choice but to look to the FPA to help keep the eugenic idea alive. Blacker and Horder encouraged the FPA to associate with other organizations, such as the Marriage Guidance Council, to which the society also gave money, in what proved to be a vain hope that after the war eugenics would somehow be carried along as part of a centralized comprehensive plan for the reconstruction of the family.[77]

Research and Voluntary Parenthood

Despite the more positive thrust of eugenic family planning ideas in the 1930s, limitation of the reproduction of the unfit remained at the core of eugenic birth control policy. Moreover, however much reform eugenicists insisted they were interested not in class but in biology and conceded the importance of environment in determining the course of people's lives, they never really doubted that, on average, intelligence, ability, and even physical attractiveness were more heavily distributed among the upper, middle, and skilled working classes than among the laboring poor. The social range of eugenic fitness steadily expanded in the more democratic atmosphere of the interwar years, but at some unspecified point down the social ladder it narrowed quickly.

Although one of the "aims and objects" of the Eugenics Society was to determine if afflictions such as "insanity, mental defect, epilepsy, occupational instability, recidivism, inebriety and social dependency" were hereditary characteristics of the Social Problem Group, most people of a eugenicist turn of mind already knew the answer. They also believed the high fertility of the Social Problem Group explained the dramatic increase in mental defectives reported from the early years of the century.[78] The inverse correlation between cerebral capacity and reproduction rates first calculated by Karl Pearson in the 1890s and generally accepted without question by eugenicists, was given a mathematical certitude with the expansion of intelligence testing in the interwar years.[79] For example, the educational psychologist Raymond Cattell confirmed the worst fears of those inclined to have them in the first place when, in his controversial *The Fight for Our National Intelligence* (1937), he estimated that as a consequence of the differential birthrate, IQ was falling by 1 percent a decade and would in 300 years leave half the population mentally defective.[80]

Although Cattell's study was in part financed by the Eugenics Society, some of its members, including Blacker and Huxley, agreed with critics who charged that the sampling methods were inadequate, the language intemperate, and the conclusions exaggerated.[81] Sensational newspaper headlines such as "English Children Getting More and More Stupid!" and "Ban Balmy Babies!" did little to further the cause of dispassionate science the Eugenics Society purported to advance, Blacker complained.[82] But relatively few of the eugenically inclined who questioned Cattell's testing methods and projections doubted a decline of some sort in intelligence was under way, and Huxley's sensible hypothesis that it might have as much to do with dietary deficiencies as with heredity was not especially convincing to his eugenicist colleagues. While many critics disputed Cattell's assertion that it was foolish to provide more medical and social services without first restricting the birthrates of the mentally inadequate, few challenged the logic of his appeal to lower the fertility of those in the bottom quarter of the IQ scale and increase it among those in the top half.

Despite the simplistic attraction of such a solution, the correlation of intelligence with social class was, as reform eugenicists were compelled to acknowledge in light of new research, not so obvious. One of their number, the geneticist J. A. Fraser Roberts, principal investigator to the Burden Mental Research Trust at the Stoke Park Colony for the Mentally Defective in Bristol, concluded from the testing in 1934 of 3,400 Bath school children born between 1921 and 1925 that class, while a factor, was much less a variable in family size than intelligence. He found, for example, that at all levels of society the brightest children came from small families averaging 1.6 offspring, while the dullest were in homes where the number was nearly 4. Indeed, 33 percent of children at the lowest end of the IQ spectrum had 5 or more siblings, while fewer than 4 percent of those at the highest level fell into this fertile category.

It was clear to Roberts that the families of children in the brightest group were virtually complete, while those in the dullest continued to increase throughout the reproductive life of their mothers whose childbearing had begun earlier and lasted longer. While on average there tended to be a marked association between the number of siblings in the dullest groups and their fathers' manual occupation, no such association could be delineated in the brightest groups. This led Roberts to the worrisome conclusion that the decline in intelligence was not only more rapid than previously shown, but the dying out of the very gifted in the higher social categories could not partly be compensated by the greater reproduction of the very gifted poor who were themselves just as infertile as their betters.[83]

If such studies demonstrated that the correlations between intelligence and class were too slight to be significant and showed that since intelligence classes were not social classes it was fruitless to hunt for social and occupational groups whose parenthood should be encouraged or discouraged, they did not alter eugenical thinking on the subject very much before the war.[84] For the most part eugenicists continued to hold to the assumption that intelligence, like other desirable hereditary qualities, was less than it had once been. It would diminish further unless something was done to check the fertility of the most fertile and, by definition, dullest sectors of the population while seeking reasons why the ablest people were unwilling to have more children. The need to find an answer to these perennial problems was a major factor in the Eugenics Society's controversial decision to move away from its origins as a propaganda organization in the 1930s to become a scientific population re-search foundation. It was a new direction not easily taken or approved because it raised fundamental questions about loyalty to the Galtonian gospel and the future of the eugenics movement.

To the discomfort of a number of the old guard, the Eugenics Society council from the mid-1920s on was being pushed by R. A. Fisher, Blacker, and others to reach out to research geneticists, zoologists, and biologists as well as to physicians.[85] Affiliation with the BCIC in 1927 was the first step in the direction of a research role reformers wanted to take but which many of the mainliners, including Major Darwin, believed threatened the society's primary mission to preach the eugenic cause through education and propaganda. By 1930 the organization was already badly divided between scientists and propa-gandists. Darwin, in his Galton Lecture of that year, reminded his listeners of what the founders of the organization intended in naming it the Eugenics *Education* Society. He agreed with Eldon Moore, the editor of the *Eugenics Review*, that the society should not undertake research; there were already plenty of people to do it but only one organization to explain eugenics to the public.[86]

If the Twitchin bequest brought financial salvation to the Eugenics Society caught up in the throes of the depression, it also brought to a head many of the stresses building up in the movement since the war. Personal rivalries exacer-bated fierce disagreements over how the suddenly affluent organization should use its considerable resources when they became available. Huxley, for exam-ple, who was appalled by the scientific ignorance and class prejudices still prevalent among the membership, threatened to quit if the society could not even agree to fund something as obviously eugenically valuable as contracep-tive research.[87] With scientists and propagandists clashing on the council, Darwin wrote to his successor Mallet, "I hope you are not beginning to curse the Society and all its works!"[88]

Despite Fisher's personal efforts to persuade the former president that eu-genics would never make serious progress until it had the widespread endorse-ment of professional science and to convince him of the importance of sup-porting scientific research in achieving this goal, Darwin was afraid the propaganda function would be swamped by the needs of the scientists whom he suspected of being jealous of the society's good fortune.[89] As far as he was concerned, the further their influence could be reduced the better.

Having patiently cultivated the reclusive Twitchin for years, Darwin feared that now, when his beloved organization was at last in a strong position to influence public opinion, it would be inundated with requests to support projects having only a tangential relationship to eugenics. He knew that many of the newer, reform-oriented members would be inclined to honor them. Always open to compromise, however, Darwin was attracted to suggestions that the organization be divided into two discreet sections—one devoted exclusively to research and the other to active propaganda. The second would continue to be called the Eugenics Society and would have exclusive access to the Twitchin money, which was specifically designated for eugenic education. The first might be called the Population Society and, though endowed by the Eugenics Society, would remain an independent scientific branch with its own journal.[90]

When in 1933 Fisher was nominated to succeed the hostile Pearson as the Galton Professor at University College, Darwin hoped the Galton Eugenics Laboratory would prove more cooperative than in the past and take over all scientific research functions while the Eugenics Society remained content to be the proselytizing organization Galton and Twitchin intended.[91] Though the society grudgingly subsidized publication of Fisher's remarkable scientific journal, the *Annals of Eugenics*, in which much of the most important pioneering work in mathematical population genetics appeared before and after the war, personal animosities and irreconcilable objectives precluded, by mutual agreement, collaboration between the research laboratory and the more eclectic Eugenics Society.[92]

It was testimony to Blacker's patience and skill as general secretary that he was able to transform the society into a population research foundation without completely alienating all of the old-time supporters. Nevertheless, a number of them, including Cora Hodson, E. W. MacBride, Eldon Moore, George Pitt-Rivers, Sybil Gotto, and eventually even Dean Inge, resigned for various reasons in protest over the new directions the organization was taking. Many others remained, however, joined by scientists, social scientists, and birth control reformers attracted to the society's multiple interests in demographic problems. In the course of the decade, funding was provided not only for the BCIC, the NBCA, the FPA, and the SPBCC, but for the newly established Population Investigation Committee (PIC) and Population and Economic Planning (PEP), the Galton Laboratory, the Bureau of Human Heredity, the British Social Hygiene Council, the Marriage Guidance Council, the Joint Committee on Voluntary Sterilization, and various mental health organizations as well as for preliminary inquiries into the eugenic possibilities of artificial insemination, or eutelegenesis as it was described. In addition, the society also underwrote the costs of publication for several books and pamphlets and the quarterly *Annals of Eugenics*, whose heavily statistical, theoretical articles, as a string of complaints to the council indicated, were totally beyond the comprehension of much of the membership.

Each new grant stirred up conflicts over priorities and identity. Some members groused about the society being too cautious and moving too slowly; many others believed things were changing too quickly and warned of the dangers of becoming overextended. Even Lord Horder, who was usually a reliable supporter of Blacker's reformist policies, reminded him in 1936, "We can't stand for *everything*. . . . Why not stand for eugenics as Galton defined it?" He then added what was often on the minds of eugenicists, "*Is* there any evidence that environmental improvement will/would improve the race?"[93] Blacker often felt battered between a minority of able and distinguished, reform-minded scientists and social scientists and a majority of members who had no scientific pretensions or qualifications. The editor of the *Eugenics Review*, Maurice Newfield, shared the same problem; readers continually complained about the journal becoming more of an outlet for scholarly, scientific research, while others protested it was not scientific enough.[94]

Despite his own anxieties about some of the society's new ventures, Darwin sympathized with the problems Blacker was having in keeping the council intact, getting agreement on a statement of aims and policies, and holding the organization together. Eugenicists had never been of one mind, he wrote to Mallet, and without compromise and flexibility they would tear the society apart. Though he continued to use his still considerable influence to mollify some of the resentment directed at Blacker, in private Darwin complained of the absence of a clear eugenic purpose in many of the research projects the council approved. He was particularly agitated by the absence of a strong eugenic thrust to some of the recent Galton lectures, including that of John Maynard Keynes in 1937.[95]

There was no confusion about the eugenic purpose of what was perhaps the society's most contentious research undertaking—the development of the contraceptive Volpar, a contraction of voluntary parenthood. In its quest to find a solution to the dysgenic effects of differential fertility, manifested now in the alleged decline in national intelligence, the Eugenics Society was drawn to supporting, among other things, the search for a cheap, safe, effective contraceptive capable of being used by all but the most incompetent of couples. Despite a profusion of quack preventives and poorly manufactured appliances on the market, several existing methods and devices, including condoms, occlusive vaginal pessaries such as Marie Stopes's Pro-Race Cap, or the more widely recommended Mensinga diaphragm, were reliable enough. Unfortunately, the clinics reported, many working-class men and women were too ignorant or impulsive to use these appliances correctly, or they found them cumbersome, unpleasant, and expensive. As a result, couples frequently failed to take precautions when engaging in sexual intercourse or reverted to the notoriously unreliable but widely employed practice of coitus interruptus. If this was true among the small sample of 21,000 women who by the end of the postwar decade had received instructions at one of the voluntary clinics, the problem was obviously much greater among the population at large, especially its poorest members.[96]

The willingness of the Ministry of Health to permit birth control advice in local welfare centers promised to increase substantially the number of women instructed in the prevention of further pregnancy. Nevertheless, as several birth control advocates argued, until an economical, trouble-free, simple, self-administered contraceptive was available for use without difficulty or shame by the most ignorant of women, the poor would continue to breed larger families. It was primarily the absence of such a contraceptive, the author of a report on the Cambridge clinic wrote in 1930, and not, as many people believed, a surfeit of animal lust and unchecked passion that still condemned lower-class women to a physically and economically debilitating cycle of pregnancy and childbearing.[97] From the eugenics outlook, of course, it also doomed the nation and the race to continued deterioration.

When, in the mid-1920s, the Eugenics Society agreed to support the BCIC as an independent and neutral scientific body of inquiry, it hoped for the discovery of some contraceptive "magic bullet" to stop the proliferation of the unfit. This was particularly important to Blacker whose questioning of working-class mothers in his student days at Guy's Hospital had convinced him that, if the right contraceptive were available, no more than 40 percent of his poor patients would have additional children.[98] The best hope for such a eugenic breakthrough lay in the work of the Oxford zoologist John Baker, whose decade-long search for a cheap, powerful, but harmless spermicide was initially funded by the BCIC in 1928, and later by the NBCA and, more important, by the Eugenics Society.

At first the society's contribution to this venture in pure, scientific, laboratory research was small and indirectly funneled through the BCIC. With the receipt of the Twitchin endowment, however, and with Baker's quest for the "perfect" chemical contraceptive beginning to show promise, the society, under Blacker's direction, took a more direct and costly role in supporting his experiments. It was driven to do so in 1934 when a three-year grant from the Bureau of Social Hygiene in the United States ran out and the BCIC turned to the Eugenics Society for help. At issue was not only Baker's research, which seemed close to fruition, but that of his fellow zoologist Solly Zuckerman's important primate studies to determine the still uncertain female menstrual cycle as well as the lifespan of sperm and ovum.

Although Blacker assured Baker "there is a keen demand on the part of certain members of the Council . . . that we should spend more money on birth control," the resistance of others, such as the philosopher F. C. S. Schiller, led to what the general secretary described to Huxley as an "unspeakable dog fight."[99] Schiller, who bitterly resented the growing influence of scientists in the Eugenics Society, argued that the organization should not support any pure research but return to its function as a propaganda agency. Even the most foolproof of contraceptives, he insisted, would never be used by the dysgenic populace. Sterilization was the only form of negative eugenics that would ever diminish the differential birthrate.

In a rare moment of anger Blacker, defending grants for Baker and Zuckerman, penned a blistering four-page rebuttal in which he warned that even if, as he hoped, voluntary sterilization legislation were passed in the near future, as the special blue-ribbon government Brock committee had recently recommended, no appreciable genetic results could be expected for a long time. Given the mentality and habits of the poor, he went on, it would be a thousand times better for eugenic purposes to produce a cheap, effective, soluble contraceptive that would dramatically reduce, if not eliminate, differential fertility.[100]

Blacker found a strong ally in Sir Humphrey Rolleston who, in a memorandum to the Eugenics Society council, promised that a simple, foolproof contraceptive would, "as an achievement of negative eugenics . . . have racial consequences thousands of times more important than the legalizing of voluntary surgical sterilization." Rolleston was in part responding to those critics who, excited by the sympathetic report of the Brock committee, which had included several leading eugenicists, believed that the society should concentrate upon publicizing its findings and lobbying Parliament for passage of a voluntary sterilization bill. Because even some of the most ardent advocates of sterilization acknowledged that its impact on the aggregate quality of the population would remain fairly minimal for many generations, he could not understand why they did not embrace with equal enthusiasm the search for a contraceptive, which would have an immediate effect on the differential birthrate.[101]

In many ways the battle was not over which form of negative eugenics would best improve the inherited qualities of the race but over the control of the eugenics movement itself. Much of the resistance came from those who believed every step in the direction of scientific research was a retreat from the eugenics evangel as preached by Galton. Many of them saw the issue of science versus propaganda as a variation of the nature versus nurture controversy and feared the reform-minded scientists would continue to undermine faith in the overwhelmingly dominant role of the former. Cora Hodson, who as secretary of the Eugenics Society in the 1920s had initiated contacts with the birth control clinics and favored the establishment of the BCIC, now complained in the mid-1930s that eugenics had become too closely involved with the birth control movement and had lost its unique moral purpose and goal.[102]

Despite such opposition, the council in 1934 approved a £400 grant for Baker recommended by its Birth Control Committee, the first of several such awards over the next few years. Although Zuckerman's first request for support was rejected by the council, it agreed the following year by a narrow vote of eleven to ten to provide him the same amount.[103] In the end, the majority of the members were persuaded by Zuckerman's argument, formulated with Blacker's guidance, that his research on the periodic fertility of primates was directly related to determining the reliability of the "safe period." Since this was the only method the Catholic church was prepared to sanction for those "Irish-Catholic families . . . thought by many to constitute a eugenic problem in certain parts of England and Scotland," it was in conformity with the Eugenics Society's revised aims and objects. That Zuckerman was also interested in serological sterilization utilizing hormones helped his case when, in 1936, he was awarded another £160.[104]

The main hope, however, remained Volpar, as Baker's successful contraceptive suppository was named in 1935. His discovery of the spermicidal qualities of phenyl mercuric acetate followed the testing of dozens of chemicals provided by British Drug Houses, Ltd., and came when he was under considerable pressure from the BCIC and NBCA for results. Pushed out of his zoology laboratory for pursuing birth control research, Baker, who finally found a home in the pathology laboratory at Oxford, was convinced his career had suffered because his work on contraception was not considered scientifically important. Blacker continued to assure him that it was eugenically of great significance and discussed with Chance and Horder the possibility of raising £50,000 to establish an institute for human biology under Baker's direction.[105] Although nothing came of it, Chance, who as treasurer successfully managed the Eugenics Society's investments throughout the depression, thought that in the present parlous state of Western civilization it was "caution verging on insanity" not to go into capital, which amounted to about £75,000 in 1937, to solve the country's serious population problems.[106]

As controversial as support for the development of Volpar was, the problem of what to do with it when the testing was completed raised even more problems for the Eugenics Society. These included questions of commercialism and the publication of Baker's scientific research. Certain her own patented Pro-Race rubber cap and Racial Solubles, as she called the birth control suppositories she provided at cost, were virtually 100 percent effective, Marie Stopes thought Baker's research was unnecessary. In protesting Eugenics Society support for Baker's experiments, she warned Blacker that the Oxford zoologist, who she intimated had not given her sufficient credit for her accomplishments, was not a "true scientific worker" and that all laboratory tests on sperm were unreliable. Her own notions of research were to some extent summarized in the practical advice she gave to doctors about chemical contraceptives at a British Medical Association meeting: "Never put in the vagina what you would not put in your own mouth."[107]

In addition to self-interest and personal pique, Stopes opposed Baker's experiments because they were partially underwritten by a commercial firm which obviously expected to benefit economically from the results. Her own clinics, as she never tired of reminding listeners and readers, were totally nonprofit, and she never hesitated long to unleash her finely honed litigious wrath against anyone attempting to make money from her name or that of her Society for Constructive Birth Control. In trying to get the Eugenics Society to withdraw its support of Baker's work and later its endorsement of Volpar, she argued repeatedly that any commercial involvement would call into question the selflessness of the birth control cause and the scientific impartiality of its proponents.[108]

Blacker, who bore the brunt of Stopes's indignant protests, tried to keep her informed about Baker's progress and assure her, without much success, of the safety of Volpar, but otherwise he paid little attention to her complaints. Yet she raised important points that the society suddenly had to confront in the mid-1930s when decisions had to be made about who owned the rights to Volpar and where and in what form Baker's experiments were to be made known to the scientific community and the public. For his part, Baker was emphatic in eschewing any desire for payment or profit from his discovery. All he wanted was the right to publish his research and continued support from the BCIC and the NBCA for his experiments. He decided those two groups should own the rights to the product and reinvest the royalties from its sale in further research.

Unfortunately, British Drug Houses, Ltd., which had contributed more than £700 to Baker's study in return for the right to manufacture the results, insisted he refrain from publishing his findings for two years to give it a lead over its competition. Several other drug companies protested this special arrangement and argued that the NBCA and Baker should be willing to help them as well. Of more serious concern, many of the physicians on the Medical Sub-Committee of the NBCA, the BCIC, and the Eugenics Society who had monitored Baker's work believed his arrangement with British Drug Houses was an unscientific and potentially dangerous way to proceed. When in 1935 it came time to register Volpar in the NBCA's name, its medical advisers refused to arrange for clinical tests until they knew what was in "methexyl" as Baker first labeled the contraceptive jelly. Several members of the Eugenics Society council were so upset by the controversy and fearful they would be likened to the sleazy proprietors of tawdry rubber shops who peddled "preventives" that Baker's grant was put in jeopardy. Only after a stormy meeting did the group vote another £400 for the trials to continue.[109]

In the end, a compromise was worked out preserving some degree of secrecy for the formula while the tests went ahead, but it was an arrangement all parties found frustrating, including Baker, who was eager to publish his results. The controversy blew up once again in 1938 when, with the trials completed, there were sharp disagreements among doctors and scientists about how to announce the results without appearing to endorse a commercial product whose ingredients could not yet be fully revealed. A number of physicians, including such longtime supporters as Horder, Bond, and Rolleston, feared the reaction of their medical colleagues, many of whom were still suspicious of contraceptives and the taint of commerce. Rolleston was so worried the General Medical Council might intervene that he resigned as chairman of the BCIC rather than lend his name to a cautiously worded letter of announcement finally published in the *Lancet* after weeks of prolonged arguments over multiple drafts.[110] Others simply refused to sign. When several scientific journals declined Baker's more extensive but still restricted exposition of his discovery, the *Eugenics Review*, which had become a major organ of the birth control movement, agreed to publish it in two parts.[111] A few months later, in February 1939, Baker announced that having established a scientific basis for contraception upon which others could build, he was turning to other research interests. The BCIC, which had supported his work for more than ten years, also decided it was time to bow out and voted to dissolve and reconstitute itself as a scientific advisory committee to the NBCA.[112]

If Volpar did not prove to be the racial magic bullet its Eugenics Society patrons anticipated, their involvement in its development symbolized how deeply the eugenics movement had become enmeshed with the birth control movement in the interwar years. Without its evolving interest in birth control, eugenics probably would have been relegated to the fringes of the prolonged debate over social policy throughout the 1920s and 1930s. The Eugenics Society's ticket to that debate continued to be the declining birthrate, which had led to the society's establishment in the first place. However much people welcomed, deplored, or ridiculed their contribution, eugenicists were instrumental in keeping hereditary considerations of the population question before both the public and the medical and scientific community. Moreover, after 1930 they had the economic resources to do so and, despite bitter differences, used them to support a wide range of demographic inquiries, of which birth control, though most important, was only one.

Eugenicists, however, were never entirely at ease with the negative thrust of birth control. They embraced it out of necessity, not out of conviction that it would by itself improve the genetic quality of the race. Unless there were an increase in the fertility of abler stock, birth control, like sterilization, could only slow, not reverse, the rate of hereditary deterioration. The opening of the welfare clinics, the development of Volpar, and other measures to curtail the higher fertility of the poor and less intelligent could only moderate the dysgenic consequences of birth control until a more favorable social and economic environment for the breeding of children was created and a new sense of racial responsibility imparted. C. J. Bond, who had been an early advocate of birth control in the Eugenics Society and an important medical supporter of the development of Volpar, had this in mind when he recommended as part of the plan to announce the new contraceptive a campaign "to urge upon healthy married citizens, of sound stock, the imperative duty to beget and rear a moderate-sized family of healthy children, according to the social conditions and financial circumstances of the home."[113]

This anticipated revival of positive eugenics, closer to what Galton had envisioned, was tied up in part with the more constructive idea of family planning that emerged shortly before the war. It was stimulated in large part by dire prophecies of an imminent decline in population reminiscent of the terrible warnings of race suicide inspired before the First World War by less-sophisticated demographic projections but equally complex anxieties about an uncertain future.

Ten

Race Suicide Revisited:
The Menace of Underpopulation

E ugenic anxieties about differential fertility and race degeneration altered considerably in the interwar years. The insistence of apologists
that eugenics was concerned not with socioeconomic classes but with
biological stocks in all sectors of society was a significant if not entirely
convincing concession to political as well as scientific realities. Uncertainty
about what constituted hereditary fitness and unfitness, coupled with the
dramatic narrowing of the differing birthrates within the social and occupational hierarchy, forced a greater caution on those who, on the basis of prewar
experience, were inclined to forecast the rate at which deterioration and decay
would occur. But the recurring disquiet about the future sparked periodically
by demographic revelations took a new turn in the 1930s when, with the nation
struggling to recover from the depression and the possibility of another great
war looming on the horizon, the oft-repeated warnings of experts that the
fittest classes were not reproducing themselves were extended to include most
of the rest of the population as well.

The so-called depopulation scare or panic that followed revived the old fears
of race suicide felt so strongly by early opponents of birth control, fears which
were never very far beneath the surface of eugenical thought. Once again
demography—as it had off and on since Malthus's time—provided a measurable structure or framework within which people could fit their apprehensions,
hopes, and increasingly, worries about the future when in fact they were really
reacting to their perceptions of the present.

"Are Our Children Today As Good As Their Grandfathers?"

When the *Report* of the 1911 *Fertility of Marriage Census* was finally published in 1923, it was already seriously out of date. One critic after another
argued on the basis of a series of new small-scale studies that the wide
variations among occupational groups it depicted had obviously been tempo-

rary; the gap was rapidly closing. If the birthrate of the middle classes was still distressingly low, working-class fertility was also now plummeting and in some cases had fallen beneath that of couples in the educated, professional middle and higher ranks.[1] The young demographer and sociologist David Glass followed David Heron's 1906 model comparing gross reproduction rates in the poorest and richest districts of London. He found that as of 1931 the average decline since before the war in areas such as Bethnal Green, Bermondsey, Shoreditch, and Stepney was, at 51 percent, nearly three times greater than the 18 percent recorded for fashionable Kensington, Hampstead, and Chelsea and 11 percent more than the average decline for London as a whole.[2] Glass, a recent graduate of the London School of Economics and a research assistant to its director, William Beveridge, was urged to work on the statistical aspects of population problems by Lancelot Hogben and others in the new Department of Social Biology.

While Glass's study was admittedly crude, it confirmed other surveys demonstrating that although the inverse correlation of fertility with economic status had increased in the years 1851 to 1911, it had substantially moderated since the outbreak of World War I. Several people, including reform eugenicists, added to their prophetic calculations the recent experience of Sweden to demonstrate that the birthrate of the higher classes might soon exceed the figures for some sectors of the working classes.[3] Armed with such data, they tempered or confidently dismissed hereditarian alarms about differential fertility. One critic of eugenics was sure "the picture of a sterile middle class and a rapidly multiplying proletariat is becoming as mythical as the Nordic race"—a link to Nazi ideology few eugenicists appreciated in the political climate of the 1930s.[4]

The University of Liverpool sociologist D. Caradog Jones's influential social survey of 7,000 Merseyside families taken in 1930 and published in 1934, did little to support such skepticism. His preliminary reports were published in the *Eugenics Review* which welcomed his findings and continued to rely upon them throughout the decade. Although he agreed the birthrate for all classifications ranging from the lowest slum dweller on public assistance to the middle classes had fallen since the 1880s, Jones demonstrated that the inverse correlation between fertility and social status still remained very marked. B. Seebohm Rowntree found this to be true in York as well in his second social survey of that cathedral town. When age, duration of marriage, and mortality were taken into account, people in the lowest of Jones's seven categories continued to produce nearly twice as many children as those in the highest, while in York the differential was even greater. In a variation on Karl Pearson's prewar formula, Jones calculated that while infant mortality remained higher among the poor, it had fallen dramatically since the turn of the century. As a result, the unskilled would likely provide 20 to 25 percent more of the next generation than semiskilled and nonmanual workers and an even greater proportion than the middle classes whose total numbers would probably soon start to diminish rapidly.[5]

Jones's sample also portended a continued decline in national intelligence since the birthrate among families with one or more mentally retarded children was found to be appreciably greater. Indeed, the correlation between unskilled occupations, high fertility, and defective offspring posed a social problem "of peculiar gravity." Without trying to calculate the relative contributions of heredity and environment, Jones warned a Eugenics Society audience in 1936 that "unless the present differential class fertility can be reversed . . . we are inevitably piling up for ourselves trouble in time to come."[6]

The Eugenics Society had been eager throughout the preceding decade to determine "whether the individuals composing the nation are increasing or decreasing in average value." It had joined with the Royal Society, the Royal Statistical Society, and the National Population Committee, among others, to urge the registrar-general and the minister of health to undertake another fertility review or "national stock-taking," as Darwin infelicitously described it, in conjunction with the 1931 census.[7] From the eugenic standpoint, however, it was not only important to see what had actually happened to fertility among the different social strata but to correlate the findings with physical and mental data collected on a regular basis. As Darwin explained in 1927 to the Conservative minister of health, Neville Chamberlain, the greatest differential statistics were probably to be found now in the mental ability of classes rather than in their fertility.[8] While Chamberlain was not unsympathetic he balked at the possible economic and political costs of a national, eugenically inspired demographic survey.

Darwin was no more successful in persuading the influential Medical Research Council (MRC) to petition the government to establish a permanent system for measuring the intelligence and health of the population to determine if the higher birthrate of inferior types was still contributing to race deterioration. The secretary of the MRC, Sir Walter Fletcher, considered the Eugenics Society's plan for "human stocktaking" too imprecise, unmanageable, and beyond the functional sphere of his organization.[9] Though similarly put off by the complexity, expense, and, after Labour returned to power in 1929, the potential political consequences of Darwin's scheme, the registrar-general, S. P. Vivian, was nevertheless not indifferent to other appeals for a more extensive gathering of vital statistics bearing upon the differential birthrate. The economic crisis, however, killed any chance for a comprehensive fertility survey as part of the 1931 census.[10]

To those eugenicists still convinced differential fertility was a prescription for racial disaster, the 1911 census, with its nine occupationally determined classes, remained the demographic gospel, and they relied upon it heavily. The *Eugenics Review* even printed a summary of its out-of-date statistics in 1927 to assist lecturers and writers who needed evidence to refute those who disputed the dangers inherent in the birthrate.[11] These figures were reinforced in the 1930s by the higher fertility of the Social Problem Group identified by Lidbetter and the Joint Committee on Mental Deficiency and of the mental defectives whose numbers, according to some of the intelligence testers, had doubled since before the war.

The alleged decline in national intelligence came as no surprise to people who saw in the differential birthrate the reason why sufficient brains and talent were no longer available to cope with the crises of the 1930s. R. A. Fisher's response to the desperate situation in which Britain found itself in June 1940 was to recall that it was only two generations since Galton had begun to point out the rarity of men endowed with the gifts needed to "make a success of administrative responsibilities in difficult times. A crude prediction made at the time *Hereditary Genius* was published might well have been that in 1940 three posts out of four involving important decisions would be held by incompetents."[12]

Fisher believed the inclination among the most intelligent classes to want the benefits of smaller families was in part hereditarily determined and culturally reinforced by the economic and social advantages enjoyed by couples with few children. Contrary to popular belief, birth control, Fisher insisted, did not start among the upper classes and spread downward. Birth control propaganda was always aimed at the poor, not the rich, but the practice was adopted by the most intelligent and far-seeing people in all classes who were genetically inclined to appreciate the benefits of reducing their fertility as social and economic conditions changed. As a result, the limitation of families "spread quickly and far among the well-to-do, and slowly and not so far in the poorer groups." This explained why, despite the diminution of the birthrate in all classes, the decline of talent and intelligence which had alarmed Galton in the first place was so apparent and dangerous.[13]

Although political attitudes and scientific skepticism made it more difficult between the wars to proclaim too loudly the genetic superiority and higher civic worth of the middle classes, the assumption was still evident in the continued comparison of the size of their families with those of various sectors of the working classes. Some eugenic enthusiasts continued to talk about the need for "breeders clubs" to build up the "reservoirs of race replenishment" and occasionally reverted to inflammatory condemnation of the "unregulated parasitic degenerates" who were allowed "to suck the life-blood from the healthy and responsible sections of the community." But such rhetoric, common before the war, was increasingly avoided as an embarrassment to the eugenic cause.[14]

A more subtle, but no less familiar, way of expressing eugenic anxieties about degeneration was seen in a revival of the debate over the fitness of military recruits. While it never came close to reaching the scale and intensity of the dispute prevailing at the turn of the century, many of the same old arguments about interfering with natural selection and the hereditary causes of 60 percent rejection rates were raised once again.[15] In the context of the 1930s, however, much more emphasis was placed upon the increased incidence of feeblemindedness and mental illness among aspiring enlistees. Eugenicists were quick to point out that in some areas the level of failure was even higher than in 1900 despite nearly thirty years of social welfare programs and a dramatic improvement in the standard of living. The cause then as now was not truly environmental but the result of "inborn degeneracy" compounded by differential fertility, they explained, and warned, "We have not yet touched bottom."[16]

Not even the worsening international tensions of the 1930s and comparisons with the much lower rejection rates of German recruits were sufficient to give much credence to the revival of eugenic jeremiads. Critics reminded the public that peacetime recruits were not any more representative of the general manpower pool now than they were before World War I which Britain, after all, had won. Moreover, although no national accounting of fitness had been taken since that conflict, the preponderance of evidence indicated that the populace today was much healthier than it had been before 1914.

In spite of such assurances, the eugenicist physician C. J. Bond, appearing on a BBC broadcast in 1933 to discuss the question, "Are our children today as good as their grandfathers?" was certain they were not. Their life expectancy had undoubtedly increased dramatically as infant and childhood mortality plummeted, but they were physically less vigorous and capable and not as intellectually acute as earlier generations. This was the result of degeneration, and it could only be reversed by the scientific introduction of a system of eugenic culture. Unlike previous civilizations faced with "national degeneration and racial decay," Bond confidently assured his listeners, we know what to do.[17]

In his efforts to change the direction of eugenics in the 1930s, Blacker tried to tone down the rhetoric of race degeneration which he doubted had much scientific validity. Moreover, he knew the public associated the eugenic idea of decay with proliferation of the laboring poor, an impression he was eager to dispel in trying to widen the Eugenics Society's sphere of influence. Replying to John Baker's complaints about snobbish zealots who kept many desirable people from joining the society, Blacker divided the organization into two groups. The first were the "eugenic alarmists" Baker described, who believed that unless eugenic measures were instantly adopted "the race will forthwith toboggan downhill into decrepitude and extinction." On the other side were those like him who, while they believed some degeneration might be taking place, did not "necessarily think the race will become extinct in a short period unless the principles of eugenics are put into practice."[18]

By the middle of the decade Blacker was pleased that a majority of the council agreed there was still plenty of scope for eugenics even if everyone did not believe, "as an article of faith, in our present racial decay."[19] The general secretary knew perfectly well, however, that for many members of the society such an "article of faith" remained central to their eugenic beliefs, and in 1939 he had to overcome considerable opposition in order to exclude a reference to "race deterioration" in the revised *Aims and Objects of the Eugenics Society*. Its place was taken by an expression of concern about "the preservation and even the relative increase of biologically unfavoured types, which improvements in the environment alone cannot check."

The modified guidelines retained the traditional plea for "rational eugenic selection." But they also contained a new statement on "The Practice of Eugenics" reflecting the society's growing involvement with a vitally important new facet of the population question erupting in the few years preceding the outbreak of World War II—the imminent start not of a differential but of an absolute decline in the population. It required eugenic policymakers to reconsider the negative strategy, particularly birth control, they had pursued for over a decade to achieve their goals. "The chief aim of eugenics," the revised document proclaimed with a bow in the direction of Galton, "is to promote the fertility of persons who possess inborn qualities above the average. This aspect of the subject will become increasingly important if, as is anticipated, recent trends in fertility continue and the population begins to decline."[20]

For eugenicists, whose support of birth control was predicated upon moderating the dysgenic effects of differential fertility, the prospect of the nation unable even to maintain its existing numbers revived in a new way latent, pessimistic anxieties about race suicide suppressed in the aftermath of the Great War. But it also touched a wider, more pervasive dimension of popular concern about the future which "scientifically determined" population numbers helped concretize and articulate. Though fortified by more sophisticated statistical analyses and a less inflammatory and less hysterical vocabulary, the fear of depopulation which erupted in the 1930s was another phase in the recurring continuum of pessimistic demography which had started with Malthus when the birthrate was soaring. It revived a century later when fertility was discovered to be falling, and again shortly before the Second World War, when the population was predicted to begin to shrink at an accelerating rate. Some believed within a century or two Britain would have even fewer people than the 10 million or so who had alarmed Malthus in the first place.

Many of the most widely quoted prophets of race suicide—or depopulation, or underpopulation, as it was more commonly described in the 1930s—were not eugenicists and consciously ignored or rejected controversial class comparisons. But given the socioeconomic patterns of reproduction which, despite the spread of birth control in all classes, still continued, eugenicists were especially disturbed by the forecasts, and eugenical considerations clearly permeated much of the debate.

Net Fertility and the Twilight of Parenthood

Fear of an absolute decline in population had been an important feature of the race suicide panic a generation or two earlier when the fall in the birthrate first became an issue of national concern. Then, as in the 1930s, many demographic projections cited Professor Edward Cannan's 1895 predictions that the population of England and Wales would reach a peak of 37,376,000 in a hundred years and then begin to fall. His slight underestimation of maximum size (which was already approaching 40 million in 1931) and overestimation of the length of time it would take before the decline started did not change the basic thrust of Cannan's prophetic warning: underpopulation rather than overpopulation would dominate demographic problems in the next century.[21]

The ability of the less fertile British to defeat the more populous Hun, coupled with the temporary surge in the birthrate after the war, added considerable credibility to those who had long denounced the "myth of race suicide." Though they usually conceded the rate of increase would diminish substantially from the unprecedented levels of the nineteenth century, they were confident a parallel decline in deaths as well as births would assure that the population would continue to grow. A. L. Bowley's challenge to this assumption in 1924 and prediction that the population would indeed soon begin to decline spurred William Beveridge to apply to the Rockefeller Foundation for a grant to establish the Department of Social Biology at the London

School of Economics to study all aspects of the population problem, including eugenics.[22]

Bowley's cautious projections and Beveridge's concern were strengthened by Registrar-General S. P. Vivian's observation in his *Statistical Review* for 1926 "that since about 1923 the birthrate in this country has entered upon a stage which, if no future improvement takes place, must eventually result in a declining population." Although he concluded that even in the most extreme circumstances decline could hardly be expected for some decades to come, he acknowledged the prospect was already the occasion of extensive "vexed comment."[23] A year later Vivian, while deliberately avoiding any value judgments, went a bit further in projecting continued population growth for several years. The current birth and death rates were not, however, sufficient to insure a continuous increase in the national population both now and in the remote future. At some point the balance would be disrupted, he warned; deaths would exceed births and the population would begin to fall. He estimated slow, sustained growth required a crude birthrate of about 19.5 per 1,000; the current rate of 16 resulted in a replacement rate which was only about 85 percent of what was needed to maintain even a stationary population. By 1931 the rate was down to 81 percent and the only viable source of replenishment appeared to be an increase in the birthrate.[24]

In his preliminary report on the census of that year, Vivian calculated the population would reach its maximum size of 41.5 million about 1951, followed by a small but increasing decline. He observed that he had been pressed from several quarters, including the Eugenics Society, to repeat the 1911 inquiry into differential fertility, but having been unable to do so he hoped to set up a separate mechanism for gathering more vital statistics to permit a continual and more comprehensive analysis of the birthrate in the future. What was certain about the current figures was what they revealed about "the conscious collective desire of the people to procreate themselves." Though he declined to say whether present trends should be "applauded or deplored," and the tone of his report was considerably less alarmist than other projections already inspired by his department's figures, the registrar-general was nevertheless obviously concerned about the "profound changes" in the growth and structure of the population which the country would eventually have to face. "Our Swarming is over," the *Observer* responded to the census, "the expansion of England . . . is at an end." With only Sweden and Austria showing a smaller birthrate and with a further reduction in mortality unlikely to do much more than delay the start of the decline, it was time to begin to anticipate consequences and make plans.[25]

Others had already begun to do so. Under the direction of Hogben, the short-lived Department of Social Biology attracted a number of able people including his wife, Enid Charles, Glass, and Robert Kuczynski to explore the myriad social, economic, and political implications of the continued fall in the birthrate. All played a major role in alerting the public to "the *menace of under-population*" as Charles described it in her alarmist description of *The Twilight of Parenthood* published in 1934.[26] Indeed, in subsequent editions she adopted *Menace of Under-Population* for the title. It proved to be only the first of a series of scholarly and sensational popular tracts and articles contributing to what contemporaries described as a "Depopulation Panic." Nearly all of the literature of demographic prophecy in the 1930s, whether serious or popular, was based to some extent upon the important formula for determining net reproduction worked out by the German-born Kuczynski while he was at the Brookings Institution in Washington the preceding decade and published in 1928 in the first of his three volumes analyzing *The Balance of Births and Deaths*.

Though Kuczynski insisted he was only interested in a dispassionate presentation of the facts, his evaluation of fertility and mortality in western and northern Europe convinced him that at their current rates of reproduction France, Germany, and England were "doomed to die out." In reaching this conclusion, which made one reviewer's "flesh creep," Kuczynski stressed the importance of the reproduction and survival rates of female children who could alone grow up to bear the replacements the population required.[27] Students of demography had long been sensitive to the number of women of reproductive age in a society when assessing population trends. Bowley, for example, had determined that the maximum number of females theoretically able to conceive children would be reached in 1931, after which the birthrate would decrease even further.

In elaborating his projective methodology, Kuczynski concluded that the most reliable predictor was the "net reproduction rate" which showed the number of women by whom the average woman of reproductive age in a community would be replaced a generation hence. It was determined by subtracting age-specific mortality from fertility rates of female cohorts up to the age of fifty to ascertain the size of the pool available for reproduction. If 1,000 female infants survived to produce 1,000 or more daughters, Kuczynski reasoned, the population would either remain the same—at "unity"—or increase. In reality, however, about 900 of every 1,000 girls born reached their sixteenth birthday and about 790 their fiftieth. If they failed at least to reproduce themselves and additional children to compensate for those of their sex who did not survive to a reproductive age or did not have children, the population would inevitably die out.[28] This, he argued, was what lay ahead for Europe if current trends were not reversed.

Kuczynski had first learned about fertility tables as a student in Berlin, and in a paper presented in 1907 to the International Congress on Hygiene and Demography held in that city, he stressed the importance of female births to the determination of reliable population projections. Because mortality was so much lower than fertility at the time, he recalled, his paper attracted little interest. The rapid decline in birthrates during and after the war had made the problem of accurate computation much more critical.[29] In the 1880s, for example, the number of girls born to women in European countries varied from 2.0 to 2.5 in average families of 4 to 5 children. By 1926 it ranged from 1.05 to 1.43 in families of 2.15 to 2.95. England and Wales had the lowest gross reproduction rate of all with only 1.05 girls being born in families averaging a total of 2.1 offspring. When the number of females who failed to reach maturity, died before their childbearing years were over, or had no children was subtracted to yield net fertility, it was evident that reproduction in recent years had fallen below replacement.[30]

Kuczynski demonstrated from his extensive analysis of quinquennial age groups and life tables in different countries since the early nineteenth century that although the proportion of girls who survived to the fecund ages fifteen to fifty improved dramatically and contributed to the rapid growth of population, their fertility was now so low that their greater longevity was no longer a vital factor. While there were more women of childbearing age than in earlier generations in northern and western Europe, their net reproduction as of 1926 stood at 0.93, which meant that 100 mothers gave birth to only 93 daughters to bear the children of the future. In England and Wales the rate stood at 0.88, the smallest in Europe.[31]

When the "bulge of women over men" exacerbated by the war started to diminish, Kuczynski predicted, the number of potential mothers would begin to fall even more rapidly. Moreover, as the population aged and was not replaced by the young, the lower death rates experienced in recent years would start to rise once more and would soon exceed the birthrates. Since further reductions in the mortality of women under fifty were not likely to be very great, the future "depends mainly on the trend of fertility." Unless it was reversed and the demographic pattern prevailing in earlier years revived, "the population . . . is bound to die out."[32]

Kuczynski contented himself with presenting evidence and giving a warning. He deliberately eschewed offering any explanations for the trends he described and thought they would not in any event reduce the population to half its present size for several centuries.[33] A number of analysts who adopted or modified his methods in the next decade were not so restrained in their assessments. Estimates as to when the population would begin to shrink and the size it would ultimately reach multiplied rapidly. Glass counted at least twenty-eight different sets of projections in addition to his own by 1940, and these did not include many more offered to the public by a wide variety of learned and not-so-learned speculators.[34] Nearly all showed declines which ranged from 10 million to 35 million people during the next two centuries, depending upon long-term fertility trends.

Among the more cautious of their number was Bowley, who calculated in 1932 that the number of children needed to maintain a stationary population was already barely adequate. It was likely to diminish further in the next twenty years so that the population would only be older, not larger, in 1951, after which date it would begin to "dwindle."[35] His warning that only an increase in the birthrate of the populous working classes could make a significant difference was not what some of his eugenicist readers wanted to learn. Both Huxley and Haldane thought the decline would begin sooner and be more precipitous. In much-publicized reports they anticipated it would start in 1940 and could be down as much as one-quarter ten years later. Even Haldane, though increasingly skeptical of eugenic claims, agreed with his scientific colleague that the population promised to be both smaller and inferior unless the government and science combined to study and solve the problem before it was too late. The British Association meetings in 1931 were preoccupied with population questions, and there was a great deal of discussion involving several prominent Eugenics Society members about when growth would cease entirely and the numbers of people would begin to decrease.[36]

But it was Enid Charles's anti-Malthusian specter of the menace of underpopulation in a society losing the power to reproduce itself that first attracted widespread attention. The daughter of a Welsh Congregationalist minister, Charles had taken an economics degree at the University of Liverpool before marrying Hogben with whom she shared a passion for socialism and an interest in the problems of population in a capitalistic society. She praised Kuczynski's index of net reproduction for revolutionizing the science of demographic measurement. Aware that the replacement rate of female children had fallen by 1933 to about 0.75, or only three-quarters of the offspring needed to sustain the population, Charles warned, "The population of Great Britain may or may not at any future time be halving itself in a generation. Our present knowledge makes such a possibility less incredible than any of the 'nightmares of population' which Malthus depicted." If no further change in fertility and mortality rates occurred, a stable age composition would eventually be reached, she reasoned, and the population would be reduced by three-quarters in each subsequent thirty-year generation. At that rate the 45 million people currently living in England and Wales would be reduced to 6 million in about 200 years. Although this figure was frequently cited by demographic pessimists describing the worst-case scenario, Charles's extrapolative fantasies were actually carried to the end of a third century in which only 45,000 Britons would remain.[37]

Like all of the prophets of depopulation in the 1930s, Charles emphasized she was describing what would happen in a given set of demographic circumstances rather than predicting those circumstances would continue and her calculations come to pass. Obviously any alteration in net fertility would be reflected in the size of the population. But, she reminded her readers, it had taken many years to fall to a replacement rate of only 0.75, and there were more reasons than not to believe it would continue down rather than remain static or start back up. While it was perhaps comforting to think the nation was merely in a cyclical phase characteristic of advanced industrialized, urban societies, as early theorists of the demographic transition claimed, it was nevertheless unprecedented in its extent, and there was no assurance the reproductive curve would again turn in the desired direction. To assume population would gradually tend toward stability in such societies was to rely upon older, unreliable statistical methods which did not accurately measure reproductive realities. A new law of population based upon new data was needed, Charles insisted; it was very possible such a law would disclose that modern industrialization tended not toward demographic stability, as some economists and biologists promised, but actually induced "biological failure."[38]

Charles recognized how difficult a concept this was for a society which had long assumed too many people not too few were being born. She blamed Malthus and latter-day Malthusians like Keynes for creating a false antithesis between sex and resources and for perpetuating a rationalization of reproduction that had now "produced a social problem of first magnitude." Malthus's static views of nature precluded his understanding that biology and science would allow man to control his own reproductive behavior as well as regulate the evolution of the animal and plant economy to feed an expansive population. Nevertheless, despite his fears of overpopulation, even Malthus had never intended to enthrone sterility as the cardinal virtue it had become in the twentieth century in the minds of the prosperous classes seeking to control the lower orders. Charles found it particularly ironic that "in seeking to mitigate poverty by preventing the poor from reproducing they [the rich] have moulded the destiny of a civilisation which has lost the power to reproduce itself."[39]

Eugenics, with its unfounded obsession with the differential birthrate, was, as far as she was concerned, no less culpable in promoting the "philosophy of sterility." Again, ironically, that philosophy had been enthusiastically adopted by the professional middle classes whom eugenicists most wanted to replicate. Many of them used "imagined eugenic skeletons in their closet" to rationalize having few or no children. Like her acerbic husband, Hogben, she slashed away at the snobbishness and prejudice motivating eugenicists as well as the questionable genetic assumptions determining their demographic policies. One of the few comforts to be found in the statistics of net reproduction was that they were "by no means propitious to eugenic proposals which aim at restricting births. The infertility of civilised communities is now so low that any policies tending to lower fertility still further will be prejudiced by the fear of racial extinction, when the facts become widely known." What was alarming, as people would soon realize, was not differential fertility, which would continue to become even less pronounced, but net reproduction in general. Indeed, Charles added ominously, "As a socially organized whole, the human species has the power to seal its own doom in a way that has probably never happened in the history of any extinct species."[40]

As was so often the case in the prolonged debate over the declining birthrate, Charles used supposedly objective demographic statistics to support and help articulate a social, political, and intellectual agenda which reflected contemporary perceptions of experience and fears and hopes for the future. In her case, the agenda was obvious: capitalism had not only failed economically and socially, but biologically as well. The ultimate condemnation of the acquisitive society was its inability "to accommodate the biological machinery by which any form of society can be perpetuated." At the same time twilight descended on parenthood in the capitalistic West, the sun was rising on children and their families in Communist Russia. There, collective planning with its elaborate network of social services to mitigate the most serious handicaps to parenthood had "reinstated the child as a functional unit in a planned ecology." The young were not viewed as parasitic, a poor investment in an inequitable acquisitive society, but were valued as an "integral part of the communal productive machinery." Unlike the industrialized West, where an "ideology of sterility" had arisen amidst the inefficiency, despair, and hopelessness created by laissez-faire capitalism, the USSR held out the hope and support which could alone induce people to bring children into the world with confidence and pleasure.[41]

Without for a moment sharing her rosy and romantic view of reproduction and family life in Stalinist Russia—which was itself a demographic variation on the anger, frustration, and disillusionment in the 1930s that turned many of

Charles's contemporaries eastward for salvation—even eugenicists conceded the seriousness of the problems she described. Blacker, who was already concerned about the implications of Kuczynski's measurements for the Eugenics Society's negative policies of sterilization and birth control, respected Charles's statistics if not her politics and contempt for his organization. Moreover, the correlations she posited between capitalist culture and depopulation reinforced questions about causation Blacker was increasingly interested in exploring. Glass, reviewing Charles's book in the *Eugenics Review*, agreed with her that underpopulation was likely to become more of a problem than overpopulation and described the work as an "extremely valuable analysis of a very urgent problem."[42]

Like many others who were to cite her findings over the next few years, Glass concentrated upon Charles's data, grounded in Kuczynski's methodology, rather than her simplistic, ideological explanations and utopian solution. He shared her view that the new techniques of population analysis had ended "the Malthusian spectre" haunting the West for 140 years. With nine of sixteen countries already below unity, or replacement, and the prospect of losing nearly a quarter of the population each generation on the horizon, Malthus's hypothesis was obviously no longer relevant.[43] *The Twilight of Parenthood* was followed by a number of books and articles with similar projections. They ranged from the brief, scholarly, but widely quoted "Estimate of the Future Population of Great Britain" by Grace Leybourne at the University of Liverpool, to G. F. McCleary's more subjective *Menace of Depopulation*.[44] Blacker and Glass published jointly and individually their own analyses on behalf of the fledgling Population Investigation Committee and the Eugenics Society, in which they explained Kuczynski's indexes of net reproduction, brought them up to date, and examined the various projections of decline.[45]

Conceding their estimates were much more reliable for the near rather than the distant future, Blacker and Glass nevertheless charted a possible line of descent that put the population at 26 million in 1985 and around 4.5 million in 2035. It was predicated on the assumption fertility would continue to diminish. Blacker believed the birthrate would fall below the death rate for the first time in 1942 and by 1945–49 would at 9.21 per 1,000 be appreciably less than the 12.3 mortality rate he anticipated for those years. Even if the birthrate stabilized at current levels of around 14 per 1,000, which it appeared to be doing by the mid-1930s, they agreed with Charles that in 100 years there would still only be half the number of people—20 million—as in England and Wales today.[46]

The problem, as nearly all of the oracles of depopulation emphasized, was not only the dwindling reproductive potential of women but the inevitable aging of the populace resulting from fewer children and greater longevity. They emphasized that the long-term consequences of the retreat from parenthood under way since the 1870s had been partially obscured by the dramatic improvements in mortality after the turn of the century. But, as the population grew older and an increasing proportion of its members succumbed to the infirmities of the elderly, the death rate would begin to climb once more and eclipse the shrinking birthrate. Blacker saw this beginning early in the next decade when the population would cease to grow and would start its absolute decline. Assuming the birthrate continued to fall and longevity improve, he and Glass envisioned that within a hundred years the percentage of children in the population under the age of fourteen would fall from 23.2 to 2.9 percent, while people over the age of sixty would increase from 12.5 to 57.7 percent. Moreover, after a small rise in the next generation to about 66 percent, the distribution of people in the reproductive age brackets could be expected to drop by more than a quarter by the year 2035.[47]

It did not require a sophisticated knowledge of economics, politics, or international relations to imagine the impact of such an age distribution on British agriculture, industry, and trade as well as on virtually every institution in the country, not to mention, of course, the empire abroad. If there was ever a demographic formula for race suicide, this was it. That it was not unique to Great Britain was of little comfort to those who saw in the net reproduction rates of northern and western Europe the demise of white, Western civilization. Though only Austria's and Sweden's replacement rates of 0.71 and 0.72 were lower than England's rate of about 0.73 in 1935, Germany and France had also fallen below unity with figures of 0.91 and 0.87. These contrasted with the higher rates of 1.68 and 1.54 available for Japan and the Ukraine. Kuczynski had predicted in 1929 a great rise in the Slavic and Asian populations while the Teutonic, French, Scandinavian, and Anglo-Saxon peoples diminished.[48]

In the context of the depression and the mounting international tensions of the 1930s, the menace of underpopulation stimulated revived fears of the "Yellow Peril" and countless warnings about the "shadow of race suicide" descending on the white races and, more directly, on the British Empire. Who would do the work, buy and consume the products, and preserve the size and quality of the breed around the globe and at home a generation from now, the distinguished physiologist Sir Leonard Hill asked, unless English women were prepared to have three or four children each?[49] Introducing the budget in 1935, the chancellor of the exchequer, Neville Chamberlain, expressed the "considerable apprehension" with which he viewed the continued diminution in the birthrate and wondered whether the country could any longer supply the citizens of "the right breed" needed in the empire.[50]

Such comments reinforced by the grim assessments of other politicians, economists, physicians, and notable clergymen usually provoked sensational headlines in the daily press about the "Crisis of Population" stemming from "The Peril of the Empty Cradle," "The Menace of the Falling Birth-Rate," or, as was announced in the midst of the Munich crisis of 1938, "British Wives Help[ing] Hitler!"[51] The stories that followed often described the dull, dreary, aged, and pitifully small remnant of the once-great empire Britain would be reduced to in a century if net reproduction estimates were correct.[52] The torrent of articles, commentaries, and sermons unleashed by the prospect of depopulation in the second half of the decade led one skeptical critic in the *Glasgow Sunday Mail* to imagine some writer in 1986 looking back with amusement and disbelief at "the panic in Europe before the famous Baby Boom of '65' set in."[53]

The Depopulation Panic

Blacker believed the depopulation scare turned into a depopulation panic on a specific date, 28 September 1936. On that day the *Times*, motivated by the Oxford University Press's nearly simultaneous publication of books by Carr-Saunders, Glass, and Kuczynski, discussed in the first of a two-part article what it described as "The Dwindling Family."[54] In reality the scare had already come close to panic earlier in certain sectors of society where Kuczynski's calculations and Charles's extrapolations had stirred up a good deal of apprehension and hyperbole. Sir Josiah Stamp, the eugenicist and statistician, had, for example, in October 1934 called for an emergency fertility census. "By the closest calculations," he wrote to the *Times*, "we are now on the eve of the greatest event in the population history of this country, for we reach our maximum population in two or three years, and thereafter a gradual decline is anticipated, with some most far-reaching changes in the age-distribution."[55]

It was not, however, until two years later that the *Times* caught the attention of newspapers all over the country with its portentous prediction that unless something was done soon to reverse the net reproduction rate, our "numbers will certainly fall, perhaps catastrophically, during the next 50 years." The paper alluded to the severe economic and social consequences implicit in such a development but took some heart in Chamberlain's reference to the problem during his budget speech the previous year. It at least indicated the start of some official interest in the impending crisis which the Germans and Italians were already addressing by merging patriotism and pride with a variety of pronatalist inducements.[56]

When, according to Blacker, the *Times* articles were seized on by other London papers and the provincial press, "overnight a muted over-population scare was changed into a strident depopulation scare."[57] Within a few weeks of the appearance of "The Dwindling Family," several other newspapers and journals launched their own series on the population question with such jarring titles as "Birth-Control is Leading to Disaster," "Our Tumbling Birth-Rate," "The Menace of the Empty Cradle," and rhetorically, "Does Britain Need More Babies?" Some publications commissioned Glass, Blacker, McCleary, Carr-Saunders, and economists such as Roy Harrod and T. H. Marshall, among others, to explain the mysteries of net fertility and to consider the multiple consequences of a much smaller, much older population in a post-Malthusian world in which the danger was "a famine of babies" rather than of food.[58] The articles invariably unleashed a rush of letters which sometimes bordered on the hysterical. More often, however, they expressed the correspondents' views of the social, political, and economic problems of the day, offered a variety of explanations, called for a government inquiry, and demanded something be done to encourage people to have more children.

The term *demography*, which the *Evening Standard* called a new word connoting the statistical methods employed to forecast future population trends, began to appear frequently in the popular press in 1936–37.[59] On a more elevated note, in April 1937 the BBC broadcast a series on "Population" arranged by T. H. Marshall two months after the subject had been considered in a much-publicized debate in Parliament.[60] In London alone the *Daily Telegraph*, *News Chronicle*, and *Morning Post* were only a sample of the papers to comment on the "extraordinary increase" and "remarkable preoccupation with the matter" evident in "the volume of public discussion." A *Times* leader proclaimed, "It has become one of the topics of the hour."[61]

Forecasting the size, age, and gender composition of the population appeared for a while to be as important to people in the later 1930s as predicting developments in the depressed economy or estimating the likelihood of another world war. It also stirred up a host of grim conclusions as a sizable body of public opinion saw in the demographic statistics a concrete articulation of many of the fears, frustrations, and despair they felt about the present and the future. During a conference of University Liberal Societies held in London in March 1937 many speakers, including several who considered the decline in the birthrate to have been beneficial initially, expressed their apprehension that it had gone on too long and had now become a clear sign of weakness, and even decadence, in English society.[62] The publisher Geoffrey Faber, citing

Charles and McCleary, warned in a letter to the *Times* that the menace was real and the "days of our greatness are numbered and our civilization is under sentence of death."[63] As an antidote to the gloomy prognoses implicit in so much of the demographic prophecy of the era, many papers often ran uplifting features on large, happy families which were usually embellished by a picture of a smiling mother surrounded by the youngest members of her sizable brood.

The medical press, though more restrained, was no less caught up in the depopulation mania than the public at large. The *Lancet* was only one of several medical journals to cite Leybourne's projections and to review Charles's book favorably in 1934.[64] In the aftermath of the *Times*'s provocative description of "The Dwindling Family" two years later, most of the leading medical publications examined the writings of Glass, Blacker, McCleary, Carr-Saunders, Kuczynski, and lesser prophets and ran series of articles on what nearly all agreed was a genuine "national menace." Even more cautious observers, who acknowledged there was reason for disquiet, were not above reminding their readers of the fate of Greece and Rome.[65]

The subject was also increasingly on the agenda of professional meetings and even when it was not it came up for discussion as doctors debated the various reasons for the continued fall in the birthrate and the consequences of a smaller population. They wondered, for example, about how the country could sustain its industry, feed its people, and find a sufficient number of workers and consumers. Medical officers of health complained of the disappearing families in their districts, frequently emphasizing the need for at least three to four children, particularly among the better-off classes who had replaced the pram with the motorcar. They frequently applied the net reproduction formula to their own communities to demonstrate how in fifty or a hundred years towns such as Ripon or Eastbourne would be virtually moribund, while counties such as Gloucestershire or Cumberland would have only a fraction of their present populations.[66]

Doctors were no less aware than economists and politicians that wages would rise sharply as the labor supply diminished, social welfare expenses would soar as the number of elderly multiplied, and it would become increasingly difficult, if not impossible, to maintain an adequate army, navy, and merchant marine.[67] As the royal physician, Lord Dawson of Penn, told a medical group in 1939, while no one wanted a return to the high birthrates of the Victorian period, the strength and survival of the race was nevertheless dependent upon a steady infusion of youthfulness and vigor which for several years had not been forthcoming.[68]

Newspapers from the mid-1930s on discussed regularly the complaints of educational authorities throughout the country about empty places in the schools. The London County Council in 1936 predicted a decline of 40,000 schoolchildren for the following year, while many other communities confronted similar problems on a much smaller scale.[69] In Mountain Ash, Wales, the school population had fallen by 3,000 in recent years, while in the tiny Sussex village of Ashurst only 21 pupils were enrolled, one-quarter of the number who attended a generation earlier. The local parson was unable to recruit more than two boys for the church choir. Although the lack of opportunity for young people caused them to leave, the principal reason for the crisis, according to the schoolmistress, was that there was only one marriage a year in the village and even then, "women here don't seem to want babies."[70]

On a national scale, however, where there were already 681,000 fewer elementary-school children than in 1910, the problem was not a want of marriages—the proportion of people marrying steadily increased in the interwar years—but the reluctance of couples even to replace themselves in the population pool. Their unwillingness to do so inspired one bardic demographer to proclaim:

> The Birthrate has fallen *again*!
> The Statement's accepted as written—
> It falls with the grimness of rain
> In an average summer in Britain:
> And parents grow shyer and shyer
> Of progeny newer and newer,
> For expenses grow higher and higher
> So babies grow fewer and fewer.

The consequences were poetically summed up in the concluding verse:

> Though the wheels of the future it clogs
> When the Birthrate approaches cessation
> Though the Nation must go to the dogs
> If the babies won't come to the Nation.[71]

Educational authorities, citing population projections for the next generation, predicted a decline of more than 3 million schoolchildren by 1965 even if mounting demands to raise the school-leaving age were met. The Incorporated Association of Headmasters was especially sensitive to Glass's prediction that 200,000 of that number would be at the secondary level where the loss would be on the order of 40 percent. Some politicians of an egalitarian bent, such as Duncan Sandys, thought the situation propitious for putting an end to expensive private schools and the class snobbery they perpetuated. He hoped their demise would lead to an upgrading of public education and a willingness of middle- and upper-class parents, no longer burdened with the expenses of exclusive instruction for their offspring, to have larger families. But, as educational statisticians pointed out, with the number of children under the age of fifteen expected to fall from 23 to only 4 percent of the population in two generations, if current trends continued, it would take more than a surge in middle-class fertility to save the nation from catastrophe.[72] Indeed, Glass had warned in *The Struggle for Population*, "If there is to be any significant increase in the birth-rate, the major part must come from the working classes."[73]

Nearly all of the prognostications, whether from Communist social scientists such as Enid Charles or Conservative imperialists such as Winston Churchill, who worried about the fecundity of Russians and Asians, concluded that governmental planning and intervention were essential.[74] Expressions of concern in Parliament about depopulation first surfaced in 1935 when the minister of health, Sir Edward Hilton Young, was asked to confirm estimates and projected consequences of a 50 to 60 percent decline in the number of children under fifteen over the next forty years. In his brief reply, he emphasized that the forecasts were based upon highly problematical demographic assumptions, and assured the Commons the registrar-general would continue to monitor developments carefully.[75]

Despite prodding from M.P.s and the press, neither members of the government nor civil servants were swept along by the depopulation panic. Vivian's reaction to the occasional parliamentary inquiry was typical: he acknowledged there might be reason for concern, as he had pointed out in his annual reports, but little could be done to stimulate the birthrate until the causes of low fertility were better understood. His attitude was shared by the Cabinet, which only discussed the population question once, in January 1935, when it rejected for economic reasons another proposal for a special census to help develop a national plan.[76]

Government efforts were designed to head off a full debate in the Commons which might lead to demands for an expensive program of pronatalist inducements or, as was more likely, to the appointment of a royal commission whose recommendations in the current climate might prove irresistible. These efforts, with one significant exception, were largely successful. In February 1937, during the height of the depopulation panic, the Conservative M.P. Ronald Cartland managed to introduce a motion calling for an official examination of the dire social, economic, and imperial consequences extrapolated of late from the shortage of "girl babies." The nation, he warned in a confusion of alpinist metaphors, was already on a "slippery slope" leading to the "edge of an abyss" from which it was imperative to climb back before tumbling over the brink. No more than twenty years remained to reverse the slide or prepare for the consequences.

Acknowledging that the PIC, recently established with Eugenics Society support, had provided him with much of his evidence, Cartland emphasized that the problem was of such a scale it required government involvement. It should start, he reasoned, with an inquiry into why people were unwilling to have more children, followed by the introduction of programs to encourage them to change their minds before it was too late.[77] Some skeptics and much of the press found it ironic and amusing that many of those who endorsed the motion and who spoke enthusiastically on its behalf, including Cartland himself, were among the 200 bachelors who populated the House of Commons.

While an occasion for humorous comment and recommendations for a "bachelor tax," their marital status also sparked numerous eugenic references to the disproportionate sterility of intelligent people throughout society, but especially among the middle and upper classes. Sandys, for example, in proposing to the Conservative party conference later in the year a resolution calling for the support of measures "to encourage the increase in the numbers of healthy children on which the future of the nation depends," stirred up a good deal of discussion about the quality of the population and the dangers to the race if government programs facilitated an increase in the "lowest types." The *Eugenics Review* was especially satisfied with the tone of the debate and with Minister of Health Sir Kingsley Wood's cautions about indiscriminate pronatalism. Indeed, the unanimous passage of Sandys's resolution, endorsed by numerous delegates citing differential fertility statistics derived from eugenically influenced PIC studies, was welcomed by the *Eugenics Review* as evidence that an understanding of the qualitative as well as quantitative implications of depopulation was taking hold in the majority political party.[78]

Eager to dissociate eugenics from class prejudice and to tie it closely to objective demographic research organizations like the PIC, Blacker was pleased to see how much support there was across the political spectrum for a governmental inquiry. Despite the lingering hopes of a minority that birth control might somehow be legislatively curtailed, most M.P.s recognized that the essential issue was not the means employed by people to avoid having children but the reasons why they deliberately chose to do so in the first place. As inducements to fertility, pronatalist advocates of government intervention proposed extensive programs for maternity care, leaves, nursery schools, better housing, marriage loans, larger child tax rebates, family allowances, and equalized educational opportunities. Whether these schemes would make any difference was the critical question which only a thorough national, and even international, investigation could answer.[79]

The PIC and "The Nosey Parkers"

The outbreak of the war in 1939 temporarily put an end to repeated demands for a royal commission or similar investigation. They had come from many quarters and were invariably met with government assurances that many demographic projections were exaggerated and based upon questionable statistics.[80] Without discounting the importance of the problem and the intensity of feeling it aroused, the Ministry of Health's Parliamentary Secretary R. S. Hudson, though opposed to the appointment of a royal commission, reluctantly agreed in the aftermath of the debate over Cartland's motion to a more modest collaborative inquiry with the registrar-general's office and the new Population Investigation Committee.[81]

That collaboration led to the introduction in October 1937 of the Population (Statistics) Bill designed to improve and extend the collection of vital statistics to better understand demographic trends and permit more accurate planning for the future. Glass, on behalf of the PIC, had submitted a detailed memorandum outlining possible directions for research if additional information could be gathered about the age and occupation of parents, the date and duration of their marriage and previous marriages, the number, sex, and birth order of their children, and the marital status of deceased males. Though some of these questions had been asked in the 1911 *Fertility of Marriage Census* and Sir Bernard Mallet had tried to make some of them permanent additions before the war, they represented the first significant change since civil registration had been introduced and the registry office established a century earlier. The 100th anniversary of those events in 1936 had stimulated a number of articles in the press in which writers noted that the Malthusian fears contributing to the passage of the first Births and Deaths Registration Act had proven to be unfounded and the nation was threatened not with overpopulation but underpopulation.[82]

When established in 1936 to study this new threat, the PIC emphasized its demographic interests were purely scientific despite the important role played by Eugenics Society personalities and resources in the new organization. The society's council, at the urging of Carr-Saunders in his 1935 Galton Lecture, had taken the initiative in bringing the committee together. In spite of some serious doubts, the members accepted Blacker's condition that although the PIC would, in return for financial support, report to the council, it was to be an independent agency free to explore the population question as it saw fit and to co-opt whomever it wanted.[83] Glass, for example, though paid by the Eugenics Society, was responsible to the PIC and, despite his moderate eugenic leanings, did not at first even bother to join the organization. The Eugenics

Society was, nevertheless, heavily represented on the committee: Blacker was secretary and Carr-Saunders chairman, while Lord Horder, Eva Hubback, and Julian Huxley served as formal representatives. In addition, many of the other members representing such groups as the British College of Obstetrics and Gynaecology, the Medical Research Council, and the Society of Medical Officers of Health were also Eugenics Society members while some, including Kuczynski, were fellow travelers. Hogben was one of the few avowed critics of eugenics on the committee.

Until the PIC was placed on a sound financial footing by the Nuffield Foundation in 1945 and moved to the London School of Economics the following year, it was subsidized primarily by the Eugenics Society or one of its members, the chocolate and biscuit magnate, L. J. Cadbury, with grants ranging from £200 to £1,000 a year. Along with the National Birth Control Association and, later, the Family Planning Association, it was also housed in the society's headquarters in Eccleston Square.[84] The new research organization did not even have its own bank account until 1938 when it began to raise additional funds from other sources, and the Eugenics Society agreed to transfer its contribution.[85]

The Eugenics Society's near-symbiotic relationship with the PIC was even more important evidence than its involvement with the National Birth Control Association of Blacker's success in turning the eugenics movement in the direction of research and reform. By using the society's ample endowment to link it to the rapidly expanding fields of population research and control, he and his reform-minded allies gave eugenics a new lease on life and a louder voice in considerations of social reform than it otherwise could have anticipated in the changing political climate of the interwar years. It had not been easy, as Blacker knew all too well, and the changes left a trail of withdrawals and resignations of the old guard. Many of them not only resented the use of society funds to support research rather than propaganda but resisted giving the PIC the independence that Blacker, Carr-Saunders, Huxley, and others insisted was essential to establishing the credibility of the new committee as a unique, purely scientific population research agency uninterested "at present" in the advocacy of social measures. Too close an identification with the Eugenics Society would, they recognized, compromise their vision of the PIC evolving, as it did, into a respected, permanent institute helping to formulate population policy on the basis of sound historical, contemporary, and projective evidence.

In urging the support of such a facility, Carr-Saunders warned eugenicists that with depopulation on the horizon it was no longer possible to be only concerned with the quality of population to the exclusion of numbers. By remaining wedded to negative programs of sterilization and birth control while failing to consider the possibilities of positive eugenics, he cautioned in his Galton Lecture, the organization will soon earn the nickname, The Society for the Detection of Persons Undeserving of Posterity. Unless eugenics was prepared to change and enlarge its vision, the initiative for developing a realistic population policy would be left to those who had little concern with the problem of quality. Blacker assured the membership that eugenics had nothing to fear from the scientific elucidation of population problems; once they became a matter of general interest, "it will be obvious that the people to be helped are those that are worthy to be parents."[86] This assumption, or faith, that a eugenic dimension was implicit in the development of any effective population policy, underlay the willingness of the Eugenics Society to invest so heavily in demographic research in the 1930s.

The establishment of the PIC met with wide acclaim in the popular and medical press. Many papers agreed research should precede the appointment of a royal commission and praised Blacker and Glass's *The Future of Our Population* as an example of the sort of work needed to be done to alert the country. Neither author particularly appreciated such scare headlines as "A Britain of Empty Townships!" which often accompanied the front page treatment of their modest book, but they welcomed the publicity it brought the PIC.[87]

The *Times*'s endorsement of the new committee provoked an extended controversy in its columns about whether a private group like the PIC was the appropriate body to conduct an extensive inquiry into the falling birthrate. Sir James Marchant, who had been instrumental in the establishment of the National Birth-Rate Commission in 1913, when an earlier government also declined to appoint a royal commission, believed more than ever that the problem required a comprehensive, official investigation. Citing the familiar consequences of waning net reproduction which threatened to leave the country with a birthrate of only 3 per 1,000 and a deathrate of 30 per 1,000 in a hundred years, he reminded readers he had been warning of such a possibility since World War I.[88]

The controversy died down when it became apparent that the registrar-general's office was working with the PIC to study the problem and that the government intended to introduce legislation to modernize the gathering of demographic information which could lead in the future to a royal commission and proposals to encourage people to have more children. Blacker, who worked behind the scenes with several sympathetic M.P.s, including Cartland, to advance the Population (Statistics) Bill, was concerned it went beyond what the PIC suggested in the number and content of the questions asked and feared it would arouse substantial opposition in the Commons.[89] He was correct.

Despite the minister of health's efforts to anticipate opposition and to defuse it in advance in a public interview on the day of its second reading, the "Nosey Parker" bill, as it was quickly labeled, was fiercely denounced by Labour party members. They resented its prying into the private lives of working-class people and threatening them with a £10 fine if they failed to answer questions that could reveal evidence of illegitimacy, adultery, and even bigamy.[90] Nearly all opponents were offended by a catchall provision which allowed the registrars to inquire about "any other matter with respect to which it is desirable to obtain statistical information with a view to ascertaining the social or civil condition of the population."[91]

To critics this smacked of bureaucratic meddling at best and Nazi police state tactics at worst. There were repeated references to the insulting, inquisitorial, self-incriminating tone of the bill. A cartoon in the Labourite *Daily Herald* depicted a spider web in the shape of Great Britain with Kingsley Wood, Statistics Bill in hand, standing in the middle surrounded by black widow spiders labeled Unemployment, War, and Want, and giving the Nazi salute. Off to the left a naked child standing on a rising cloud called The Population Problem was being asked by the menacing insects, "But *why* will you not walk into our Parlour?"[92]

Aneuran Bevan, himself one of fourteen children of a Welsh miner, had an answer as to why the offspring of large families like his had few or none of their own: it was their way of practicing "silent, secret sabotage" against a Conservative-dominated society. The Statistics Bill, as far as he was concerned, was typical Tory cant; it attempted to divert attention from the social and economic conditions sterilizing the populace. "The human race is physically as fertile as ever it was," he insisted. But there was "social and economic infertility. . . . This private and secret sabotage will continue until a kind of society is created in which they themselves can get pleasure and delight."[93] The fiery Welshman did not explain why those in the higher classes, including many wealthy Tory M.P.s, were even less inclined to sire children than were his working-class colleagues.

Nevertheless, Bevan's effort to turn the debate into an attack on the government was seconded by several of his Labour party supporters who emotionally recounted the hardships and anxieties they and their large, exploited families had endured before and after the war. But the most telling criticism came from the Independent member for Oxford A. P. Herbert, the novelist, playwright, satirical humorist, and, as he pointedly noted, father of four children. In a hilarious, limerick-punctuated speech, he ridiculed the Nosey Parkers for going about it all in the wrong way. If the government was really interested in finding out why there were so few babies, he reasoned, it made no sense to ask questions of a woman who has just had one. On the contrary, the prying registrars should be badgering those women who had none.[94] Herbert's skeptical humor contrasted with dark prophecies about the peril to the race and questions about whether some "involuntary unconscious factor" was at work "undermining the fertility of the people generally in either sex." In the end a majority by a vote of 197 to 125 sided with those speakers who reminded the House the basic issue was the impending decline in the population and the need to begin to address it.

The passage of the second reading of the Population (Statistics) Bill unleashed a wave of public criticism that rolled across the political and religious spectrum. Catholics as well as Protestants protested the incursion into family life, and though Conservatives and Liberals were on the whole supportive of the measure, a number of them raised doubts about its wisdom. Labour remained the most adamant in its opposition. There was a good deal of sensational talk in the left-wing press about government plans to keep secret registers for reasons which were ominously unclear. The London Labour Women's Advisory Committee denounced the legislation as a trick to provide more children for the low-wage labor force and cannon fodder for the militarist warmongers and urged the Labour Party to oppose it at all costs.[95]

Marie Stopes, for her own reasons, called the bill "idiotic" and suggested the minister of health would be much wiser if he instead subsidized her constructive birth control clinics with large grants. She was incensed that as the founder of the birth control movement she had not been asked to help in the fashioning of the questions or in the establishment of the PIC. Its chairman, Carr-Saunders, who had recently succeeded Beveridge as the director of the London School of Economics, was commonly believed to be the author of most of the provisions of the bill. Stopes was also irritated that men rather than women had dominated the debate, since women and women alone could provide the answers to the population question.[96]

Despite explanatory articles and letters to the press by Roy Harrod, Stella Churchill, and Carr-Saunders, among others, who warned that the population problem was of "great urgency (some would say the most serious which confronts the present generation)," the *Daily Mail* reported with characteristic pungency, "Outcry Killing Nosey Parker Bill!"[97] To save it, the minister of health agreed to a number of amendments restricting the questions to the new mother's age, her date of marriage, and the number of children living or dead she had conceived with her current partner or previous husbands. The controversial provision allowing "any other matter" to be raised at the discretion of the registrar was also dropped from the final bill, and stronger assurances of confidentiality were added. Wood accepted a ten-year limitation on implementation, after which time the legislation would be reviewed.[98] Even Herbert, who had become a favorite of the popular press, though still skeptical the problem was as great as some claimed and doubtful the legislation would make any difference, now agreed it was relatively harmless. The act, he wrote in an article headlined "Population Panic!" "will be an enjoyable tool for civil servants and economists and will increase the number of Blue Books, but not, I fancy, the number of babies."[99]

Most of the opposition, which was really over the breadth of the questions asked and the possibilities of punishment, not over the need for an inquiry into declining fertility, quickly melted away and the Population (Statistics) Act passed its third reading easily on 17 February 1938. Two weeks later the House of Lords, after a brief debate in which the seriousness of depopulation was stressed, added its approval. In contrast to the deliberations in the Commons, where the issue of eugenics was carefully excluded from the deliberations out of fear of further alienating Labour, the bill's supporters in the Lords cited the Eugenics Society's endorsement and the need for a eugenic-scientific analysis of the birthrate which improvements in civil registration would facilitate.[100]

Eugenicists were in fact delighted with the outcome. The new act not only permitted the gathering of more refined data about differential, age-specific patterns of childbirth, something the Eugenics Society had been advocating since the war, but greatly enhanced the visibility and credibility of the PIC as the first population research organization in the country. Neither the registrar-general nor the minister of health, who, after some initial doubts, had worked closely with the PIC, were insensitive to the popular perception that the latter group rather than their offices was most responsible for the improvements.[101] Because the Eugenics Society was instrumental in its creation and support and intimately involved in its activities, the successes of the PIC could only enhance eugenic interests in demographic planning. If the questions permitted in the final version of the Population (Statistics) Act were limited to describing in more detail what was happening to the birthrate but not why, the PIC was in the unique position of being able to explore the latter question through more detailed, intimate inquiries that eugenicists were certain would address their particular concerns.

Depopulation Doubted

The Nosey Parker Bill, as the Population (Statistics) Act continued to be described by critics, was the government's one concrete response to the depopulation panic before the Second World War. Although it partially satisfied long-standing eugenic demands for more sophisticated methods to calculate trends in differential fertility, it made no distinction between quality and quantity, as mainline eugenicist critics pointed out. This had been an issue since the mid-1920s when the possibility of depopulation had begun to arise. F. C. S. Schiller complained in 1925 of the "vast amount of nonsense" about depopulation being talked about by people clamoring for an increase in the birthrate without considering its impact on the already questionable quality of the race. Even if the population were stationary for awhile, the fertility of the species was too great for a static or declining condition to last for very long. Schiller was irritated by hysterical references to the ancients which invariably accompanied ruminations on the atrophy of reproductive vitality and intellectual energy. The prime minister, Stanley Baldwin, was among the more noteworthy perpetrators of this classical demographic myth when in 1926, with allusions to Rome, he expressed fears that the Great War and the plummeting birthrate had combined to deprive the nation of enough of the breed to carry on the work of empire.[102]

For most eugenicists in the 1920s the danger was not from a stationary or declining population but from the overpopulation of the most dysgenic classes. Even Blacker, who a decade later was to ally the Eugenics Society with those trying to ward off the menace of underpopulation, in 1926 believed the country had too many people, especially of the wrong sort, and looked to more birth control, not less, to solve the population question.[103] The Eugenics Society, already moving closer to the birth control movement, declined to take a position on the dangers of a diminishing population, though urged to do so by some of its members, including R. A. Fisher who was deeply impressed by Kuczynski's projections. In acknowledging in 1929 that an imminent halt in the rate of population increase was becoming an issue, the *Eugenics Review* nevertheless claimed the Eugenics Society had no corporate views on the question, though there was nothing to disprove that a slowly increasing or stationary population "may be quite compatible with national health and virility."[104]

To underline its skepticism, the journal permitted the Neo-Malthusian C. V. Drysdale to review Kuczynski's new book, *The Balance of Births and Deaths*, and to publish a refutation. Kuczynski, as far as Drysdale was concerned, was merely the latest in a long line of prophets predicting the decline and extinction of the race. The problem, he argued, was not the low fertility of women but their surplus numbers, their low incidence of marriage, and an economy that did not encourage young people to wed. There was no reason to believe the decline in the number of women born for replacement purposes would continue as conditions changed. "During the war an outcry went up concerning the loss of men and increase of 'superfluous' women," Drysdale recalled, "and now that nature is beginning to redress the balance, Mr. Kuczynski raises the cry of diminishing womanhood and impending race extinction." In the meantime, Drysdale was sure births would continue to exceed deaths, and greater longevity, which Kuczynski underestimated, would keep the numbers up.[105]

Neo-Malthusians proved to be the most trenchant, if not particularly influential, critics of the depopulation panic in the 1930s. Far from worrying about the population declining, they complained it was still growing by 200,000 people a year when millions were already unemployed, underfed, poorly housed, and badly clothed. Moreover, Britain was now the densest and most urbanized of great nations and unable to produce more than 30 to 40 percent of its own food. Neither Drysdale nor R. B. Kerr, who defended the old Malthusian position, denied the population was aging slowly or that numbers were being sustained by a temporary bulge in women of childbearing age. At some point in the next generation or two the rate of increase would very possibly cease and decline would set in. As far as they were concerned, however, Britain would be stronger with half its current population, which, given differential patterns of fertility, would likely be of higher eugenic quality.

It was a position reinforced by the American geneticist Raymond Pearl, who, in a lecture at the University of London where he had once studied with Karl Pearson, repeated his controversial theory that population decline was a natural and racially beneficial result of urban overcrowding.[106] Without endorsing Pearl's biological explanation, Neo-Malthusians and others who welcomed the idea of a less-crowded Britain emphasized the improvements in the quality of life that would accompany the decline. The one example of depopulation that usually came to mind was Ireland which, the *New Generation* argued, was much more prosperous and better off with a population of 4 million than it had been with twice that number a century earlier.[107]

Despite hysterical prophecies to the contrary, Neo-Malthusians regretted there was little chance, however desirable, the same opportunity would be offered Britain. Continued improvements in longevity, which depopulationists tended to discount, meant the birthrate required to sustain the population could be lower than the 19 per 1,000 claimed by the registrar-general, and with marriages on the rise, as they were in the mid-1930s, the likelihood of more women replacing themselves increased. Drysdale calculated that with a birth-rate of 14.3 or 15.4 per 1,000 and an average longevity of seventy or even sixty-five—all obtainable ratios in the near future—the population would continue to grow at a modest rate supplemented, if necessary, by immigration, a source of replenishment seriously underestimated by Kuczynski, Carr-Saunders, Enid Charles, and other experts.[108]

The most telling argument the Neo-Malthusians used, however, was the unpredictability of the variables depopulationists relied upon for their projections. Because family size had fallen from four or five to two children in the last sixty years, Kerr wrote the *Eugenics Review* in 1936, there was no reason to believe that in another sixty years people would prefer to have none.[109] Indeed, the birthrate had stopped falling in 1933 at 14.4 and instead of sliding to the 12.4 predicted by the PIC for the years 1936–39 had actually increased slightly. As a result, the *New Generation* reported, the population of England and Wales was in 1938 already 571,000 above the figure forecast by Blacker and Glass and constituted the largest natural increase since 1931.[110] Government spokesmen, working to head off the appointment of a royal commission, were quick to make the same argument from the registrar-general's annual statistics.

The prophets of depopulation countered in the press and elsewhere that the increase in the birthrate and larger-than-expected growth in population were probably temporary phenomena brought on by a swell of some 300,000 immigrants between 1931 and 1935 and a surge of over 40,000 more marriages a year celebrated when the worst of the depression was over. As Carr-Saunders explained in 1937, the small increase in the birthrate reflected the first births of newlyweds, but there was no reason to believe they would have many more. Moreover, despite fluctuations in the recovering economy, the average size of families would continue to fall as the distribution of population shifted away from the bulge in women in their childbearing years.[111] Kuczynski, for his part, discounted the impact of more marriages. About 85 percent of all women married at some point in their lives, he told the Congress of the Royal Sanitary Institute, but because there were only 88 males for every 100 females over the age of twenty it would never be a universal experience and the percentage was unlikely to go much higher.[112]

Neo-Malthusian critics remained unconvinced, pointing out the proportion of women married in their most fecund years, twenty to forty, was closer to 56 percent, and only a minority of these were having more than two children. Even a modest increase in both numbers could quickly transform the demographic outlook from one of decline to unity or continued growth. Such a change could be anticipated with improvements in the economy, more opportunities for working mothers, better maternity benefits, or adequate family allowances. If all else failed, natural selection itself would inevitably raise the birthrate, Kerr added, by weeding out those women who are sterile or hate having children and leaving the fertile and philoprogenitive to perpetuate their type.[113] A simpler neo-Darwinism was implied in the confidence many people expressed in the power of "Nature" or the "Life Force" to readjust any race-threatening imbalance in the population.

Without necessarily following or even being aware of the permutations of the neo-Malthusian argument, a great many people agreed that their country was overpopulated and believed that its economic problems would diminish and efficiency would rise if there were fewer people to feed, house, and employ. Lord Raglan, for example, made exactly this point in reply to a series of Carr-Saunders's articles in the *Daily Telegraph*. Raglan was unable to understand why a smaller population, healthier and better educated, was a threat to British civilization, considering other countries faced the same problem. Far from being worried about the dreaded 5 or 6 million people projected in a century or two, he thought they might even exceed the accomplishments of the Elizabethans who got by on that number. Others recalled what Wellington and Nelson had done with only 9 million two centuries later and observed that the British Empire was built and governed by a much smaller number than that. Carr-Saunders reminded such critics that the Elizabethans and their descendants who triumphed at Waterloo and Trafalgar or who led Britain to imperial greatness in the eighteenth and nineteenth centuries were the products of a young, vigorous population rather than of an aged society certain to develop if the contemporary pattern of net reproduction continued.[114]

A good many of the same arguments punctuated the meetings of the Eugenics Society council as the leaders of the organization struggled to respond to the depopulation panic. Blacker, who had "*no* great sympathy for Neo-Malthusianism," described several acrimonious clashes between Drysdale and Fisher. While he tried to follow a middle road and urged the editor of the *Eugenics Review* to do the same, Blacker nevertheless estimated that three-quarters of the council members would welcome a decline of at least 5 million people providing, of course, they were from the lower end of the social ladder.[115] Blacker recognized the difficulties in trying to turn the society's officers around. Eugenicists had just about accommodated themselves to the negative policy of birth control and thrown in their lot with individuals and organizations seeking, through scientific research and propaganda, to control the growth of population, when they were suddenly told that things had perhaps gone too far.

The menace of underpopulation was to be relieved by a delicate blending of negative eugenics, primarily birth control, with a new policy of positive eugenics based upon scientifically determined, pronatalist schemes for altering the dangerous net reproduction rate. The problem of promoting birth control for genetically selective reasons on the one hand and population growth on the other posed formidable scientific, ideological, and practical dilemmas for the eugenically minded as it did for their allies in the family planning movement. Both were trying to advance their mutual causes at a time when the nation, already in economic crisis and facing the horrendous possibility of another war, was allegedly tottering on the edge of a demographic disaster first predicted by prophets of race suicide a generation earlier when the relentless fall in the birthrate was first noticed.

As in that earlier period, the concentration upon, even obsession with, population statistics provided an authoritative language in which educated middle- and upper-class people could express the multiple, often inchoate anxieties and sense of insecurity they felt in their rapidly changing age. When merged with eugenics, these statistics provided a compelling scientific explanation which appeared compatible with common sense, observation, and social experience. That the figures so often added up to decline and degeneration only reinforced the deep sense of pessimism many people obviously felt in the first half of the century. In retrospect, the disillusioning experience of the Great War and the powerful, explanatory myth of the Lost Generation, when added to the collapse of the economy and the deteriorating international situation, further confirmed, for those who were inclined to interpret them that way, what the population statistics appeared to be telling them about the grim future ahead.

Many people undoubtedly laughed at the menace of underpopulation, as A. P. Herbert found to the advantage of his popularity during the debate over the Population (Statistics) Act. One wag, speaking for the "Population Prophecy Society of Astrological Rot, Ltd.," predicted a population in the year 2374 of somewhere between 27 and 74,348,926—not including a Mrs. Bathurst, who will have moved to Nigeria to take the waters.[116] What is perhaps more revealing, however, is the number of intelligent, educated, comparatively well-off people who found nothing humorous in the depopulation scare. They were for the most part neither fools nor fanatics perched on the fringes of society, but serious, thoughtful, well-respected, and admired individuals of considerable accomplishment who were deeply worried about the future and for whom the evidence for decline was logical and compelling. As incomprehensible as it might seem to us today, the eugenics movement continued to attract such people throughout the 1930s as it had from its beginnings. Like the authoritative seers whom they quoted, they carefully acknowledged the difference between projections based upon a given set of statistical parameters on the one hand and unscientific prophecy on the other. Then, more often than not, seemingly oblivious to the real threat to their civilization from abroad, they insularly dwelt upon the scariest, worst-case scenarios in a pseudodemographic never-never land.

Eleven

Family Planning and the
Fear of Population Decline

I f the Eugenics Society's equivocal decision to support the expanding birth
control movement in the interwar years was an important first step to
assure its voice would be heard in the formulation of a "racially-sound"
population policy, its response to the fear of population decline completed the
convergence of eugenics with the emerging field of demography. As in the
case of birth control, it was the society's wealth and C. P. Blacker's determination to use it to foster the inclusion of eugenic considerations in the
development of social and economic planning that governed the organization's
response to the depopulation scare. The Eugenics Society's success, he recognized, would never be reflected in the size of its membership and would, for
some time, be difficult to measure. By comparison, he recalled, all the agitation for women's suffrage did not get them a single vote until the law was
passed in 1918; it did, however, help create the climate in which enfranchisement was ultimately accepted.[1]

The key to creating a eugenic climate, Blacker believed, was influencing
other agencies and organizations, the most important of which were those
concerned with the interaction of demography with social reform. The Eugenics Society helped establish some of them and infiltrated and permeated
others. As a consequence, its influence greatly transcended its small numbers
and helped eugenics to survive in an era when it was increasingly battered by
the confluence of democracy, left-wing science, advances in genetics, and the
growing fear of Nazism with its punitive, authoritarian policies of "race
hygiene." To the annoyance of old guard mainliners who complained about
supporting research projects and groups over which the society exercised little control and whose eugenic objectives seemed secondary if not obscure,
Blacker, Carr-Saunders, Huxley, and other reformers insisted that in the political environment of the 1930s the more unobtrusive the society's involvement,
the more effective it would be in the long run.

This was certainly evident in the eugenicists' struggle to work out an effective demographic policy reconciling their emphasis upon the negative program

of selective birth control and sterilization with positive plans for confronting the impending decline in population. With the beginning of the descent expected in the next decade, the issue of quantity once again loomed larger than that of quality. Moreover, ideas of degeneration and race suicide were increasingly defined in terms of gender and age-specific numbers rather than in the context of class-specific differential fertility. The impending decline in population created a tactical and ideological dilemma for the eugenics movement as it did for the birth control movement, with which it was so closely intertwined. In both cases the approaching danger inspired a redirection of activities and policies which attempted to transform the restrictive, negative concept of birth control into a more comprehensive, positive program of family planning.

Birth Control and the Depopulation Scare

At the same time they became closely allied with the birth control interests in the country, many eugenicists, paradoxically, remained critical of the dysgenic effects of contraception. The Eugenics Society continued to hold officially that on balance birth control had been harmful to the race and should "be practised by persons of superior biological endowment only with a view to spacing births."[2] A minimum of four children from such couples would still be required to offset the higher fertility of those at the other end of the genetic scale for whom birth control was entirely appropriate.

In light of the nearly universal premise that the size and composition of the population were closely correlated with the voluntary adoption of contraceptive practices, it is not surprising that the depopulation scare was a cause of major concern to people active in the birth control movement. Opponents, such as the bishop of Oxford, Charles Gore, who had vigorously resisted the Lambeth Conference's softening of its position on contraception in 1930, forecast an outbreak of panic when the population started to decline.[3] Huxley, by contrast, welcomed the Lambeth resolutions as another step toward the democratization of birth control. Once it was available to everyone, "the real genetic unteachables" who continued to produce defective children could be more readily identified and targeted for other eugenic measures to preserve "the integrity of the racial stock." But, he cautioned in 1932, the approaching danger to the race was not overpopulation but depopulation, which would require a major reconsideration of the sociological impact of birth control.[4]

Not everyone, however, was persuaded the fall in birthrate and the impending decline in population were directly attributable to the voluntary adoption of birth control. A legacy of biological causation persisted throughout the interwar years. Some people continued to argue that diminishing fertility, not only in Britain but in other advanced Western countries, was the predictable result of Spencerian evolutionary individuation reaching further down the social ladder, while others insisted the decline was merely a repetition of cyclical reproductive patterns determined by environmental conditions. Charles Edward Pell, for example, in the early 1920s resurrected old nutritional theories proving population rose and fell in inverse correlation to prosperity and a more nutritious, protein-rich diet.

Though he had no objection to birth control and agreed it was widely practiced in certain circles, Pell nevertheless insisted that the dietary manifestations of growing prosperity had reduced fecundity dramatically since the 1870s, not self-control exercised by married couples. So long as people were better paid and better fed, the problem of differential fertility would continue to diminish, Pell reasoned, to the applause of social reformers who agreed that the best way to get rid of the "slum types" was by bettering their home life.[5] It was not an approach that recommended itself either to Neo-Malthusians or eugenicists.

Without necessarily accepting Pell's dietary correlations, others, such as the statistician G. Udny Yule and the animal geneticist F. A. E. Crew, also agreed fecundity and fertility were, like mortality, cyclically affected by social and economic environmental changes. Crew shared the belief of the American geneticist Raymond Pearl that the biological capacity for reproduction was curtailed by overcrowding and diminished opportunities for the conquest of nature. Contraception, like migration, did not really reduce the gross size of a population, Crew argued, but only altered the proportions in different sectors of society. The same number of babies would continue to be born if birth control did not exist, only more of them would be in slums than in suburban homes. Indeed Crew, like Yule, was convinced in 1928 that their overcrowded country was reaching the end of an expansionary cycle started in the eighteenth century. The birthrate, which ultimately reflected reproductive capacity, would not begin to rise again until population density was reduced and new opportunities for growth emerged.[6]

Though a number of critics, including T. H. C. Stevenson, were critical, even contemptuous, of such "high brow" theories of cyclical infertility and insisted the fall in the birthrate was overwhelmingly the result of the volitional adoption of birth control, a number of leading eugenicists continued to wonder if this was the case.[7] Eldon Moore, the editor of the *Eugenics Review*, decided contraception was probably a secondary factor to some basic Darwinian law regulating the density of population by increasing sterility. Did not the notorious unreliability of contraceptives and the gradual, rather than abrupt, fall in

mean family size from four to three to two not suggest some natural, evolutionary process at work? he asked. Moreover, birth control had been known at least
since the 1820s; why had its impact not come earlier? Perhaps this was all
farfetched, he admitted in a long, private letter to Sir Bernard Mallet, but he
doubted birth control was as much the answer to waning fertility as most
people assumed. He thought it probably had more to do with population
density, food supply, sanitation, and the effects of prosperity on reproductive
vitality.[8]

Moore's suggestion that there were tangible, discoverable natural forces at
work which were in need of investigation was reiterated by Carr-Saunders and
Blacker in the early 1930s when they also questioned whether the birth control
explanation was "too readily accepted as sufficient." Neither man could understand why the decline in the birthrate was so much greater than the proportion
of people using contraceptives, which, even when employed, were frequently
defective or ineffectual. Blacker, for example, in referring to Pearl's inquiries
into birth control practices in the United States, was puzzled as to why fertility
had dropped so precipitously in that country when only a third to a half of the
populous laboring classes made any attempt to limit conception. Even among
the professional, educated upper classes in England, Carr-Saunders observed,
perhaps no more than two-thirds or three-quarters used birth control methods;
yet small families were nearly universal in their ranks. The steadily increasing
delay of first births in all classes, a stage of marriage when contraception was,
logically, least likely to be used, added to the possibility of involuntary sterility
being far more prevalent than it had once been. With the birthrate already
below replacement levels and the population in danger of falling by one-fourth
in a generation, it was obvious to Blacker and Carr-Saunders that a great deal
more needed to be learned about the relative contribution of birth control and
other factors.[9]

Their colleague R. A. Fisher's ingenious attempt to link environmental
conditions, social aspirations, and birth control to a genetic predisposition to
limit family size offered an explanation which some people, including Enid
Charles, found plausible. As early as 1920, during the debate in the Eugenics
Education Society over birth control, Fisher expressed his belief that those
types, currently the fittest, whose "innate qualities of temperament" inclined
them, often for high-minded and conscientious reasons, to limit their progeny
would gradually be eliminated. Their loss, he predicted, would eventually
provoke a moral revulsion against contraception as people in previous ages
turned against infanticide.[10]

Critics countered that the adoption of birth control was a result of opportunity, education, and environment, not heredity, but Fisher continued to insist

throughout the interwar years that the temperament to restrict fertility was inherited and reinforced by the social and economic advantages of smaller families.[11] This process of social selection explained the differential birthrate eugenicists found so alarming. As the ablest, industrious, "most beautiful" people made their way into the upper classes in a more plutocratic, Liberal Britain, they carried with them their tendencies to reduced fertility which had facilitated their rise in the first place. The menace to civilization, Fisher explained in 1926, "arises solely from the social advantage which our economic system gives to families of low fertility." It resulted in a vicious circle maintained by a "stream of infertile promotions by which the fertility of the upper classes is continually forced down" while that of the lower classes becomes relatively larger.[12]

Fisher's attempts to construct a biological explanation for the inverse correlation between fertility and social mobility met with a mixed response in eugenic circles. Huxley, a fellow geneticist, found it plausible while Blacker, a psychiatrist, did not. The restraint of parenthood, he wrote Huxley, had much more to do with attitudes, ideas, values, and the experience of couples in certain environmental conditions than it did with some hypothetical infertility gene activated by social ambition.[13]

The depopulation scare kept the question of an increase in a hereditary predisposition to natural sterility alive throughout the remainder of the decade and on into the Second World War, when occasional voices were still heard insisting that women were simply less fecund than their mothers and grandmothers.[14] By the late 1930s, however, a consensus had emerged among expert physicians, demographers, biologists, and eugenicists that biological factors were responsible for no more than 5 to 10 percent of the sterility threatening the population. Carr-Saunders, Kuczynski, and Blacker joined with some twenty different speakers at a meeting of the Obstetrics and Gynaecology Section of the Royal Society in 1938 to consider the multiple causes for depopulation. Regardless of their differing emphases upon diet, psychology, economic conditions, eugenic concerns, and the effects of contraceptives, nearly all agreed that the dwindling family resulted from conscious decisions deliberately made by fertile couples.[15]

It was a perfectly obvious conclusion to most of the public, as it was to the registrar-general in his *Review* of 1938, the first based upon the new age-specific data gathered under the recently passed Population (Statistics) Act. He calculated that the fertility of women in all reproductive ages had fallen by 42 percent since 1911. Moreover, as the duration of marriage increased, their fertility remained lower than in the first two or three years of wedlock which, the registrar-general concluded, had nothing to do with biological capacity. On the contrary, it meant that women who were able to do so were just not having children.[16]

Whatever the ends, and there was no shortage of pronouncements on the subject, few people now doubted the means—birth control. Those who had long considered it immoral, selfish, unchristian, unhealthy, unpatriotic, dangerous, a sign of degeneration, or a prescription for race suicide saw vindication in the approach of depopulation. Many others, however, some of them prominent supporters of the birth control movement, agreed that perhaps they had been too successful and thought some restraints on the sale and use of contraceptives might be prudent. Enid Charles, herself the mother of four children, was sympathetic to Fisher's contention that infertility was not only physiologically but socially determined. She questioned whether birth control was as responsible for the decline as Carr-Saunders, Beveridge, and others believed and doubted if enough was yet known about sexual physiology and human fecundity to really isolate causation.

She did not, however, mean to underestimate the prevalence and importance of birth control in maintaining low fertility, even if it did not explain very well why the birthrate declined in the first place. But, Charles emphasized, she did not agree with those who attacked birth control; not only was the continued disassociation of parenthood from sexual companionship necessary for happiness, but it was futile to think the clock could be turned back. Contraceptives would, if anything, become cheaper, more reliable, and more readily available. What, she asked, would be the effect on the birthrate then? The point Charles wished to make was that the social and economic failure of capitalism, not birth control, was the cause of the impending population crisis. She feared the depopulation panic would lead to a retrograde assault on one of the most important instruments of "a rationally planned ecology of mankind" while ignoring the real causes for the twilight of parenthood in the West.[17]

Charles's concerns about a resurgence of anti–birth control rhetoric and of demands for greater restrictions on contraceptives were shared by leaders of the birth control movement. The National Birth Control Association was already aware of the resistance of many local authorities to implementing the Ministry of Health's memorandum. Religious opponents were especially quick to add the threat of depopulation to their litany of the evils of contraception. By the mid-1930s Catholic denunciations of birth control were as likely to emphasize race suicide as they were theological pronouncements and papal encyclicals. The authority of the registrar-general was frequently added to that of the ecclesiastical hierarchy to support the assertions of Cardinal Bourne, the archbishop of Westminster, or Dr. Downey, the archbishop of Liverpool, that "we are a vanishing race."[18]

Catholics were, admittedly, vanishing more slowly than the population at large, but the low birthrates in Austria, France, and even Ireland, as well as in some of the predominantly Catholic states in Germany and America, indicated their faith was less of a barrier to family limitation than it had once been. The hierarchy was clearly worried at home as well that many of the 13 million people who Bourne predicted would disappear over the next thirty years, when the population fell from 45 million to 32 million, might come from the approximately 2.4 million who made up the small Catholic community in Britain.

Most of the proponents of birth control, including their eugenicist allies, took Catholic denunciations of their activities in stride. Reinforced by papal edicts, the Catholic church had become increasingly ferocious since World War I in its condemnation of birth control and eugenics as crimes against God and nature. Although Marie Stopes kept up an incessant counterattack in print and in court against the "malevolent and perfidious R.C.s" and went so far on one occasion as to chain a copy of her book *Contraception* to the altar railing of Westminster Cathedral, most people in the movement were more restrained in their response and resigned to Catholic opposition.[19] Neo-Malthusians, for example, always assumed that in the long run economic and social considerations would have a much greater impact on the domestic strategy of Catholics than the pronunciamentos of celibate clerics.[20] Blacker, himself a lapsed Catholic, was firmly convinced it was good policy, though not always easy, to be scrupulously polite to his former coreligionists in hopes of encouraging the more reasonable of their number and perhaps reducing the fevered hostility of the twenty-five or so Catholics in Parliament.[21]

The problem was not only Roman Catholics but their Anglican allies, several of whom like Lord William Cecil, the bishop of Exeter; Charles Gore, the bishop of Oxford; A. F. Winnington-Ingram, the bishop of London; and Edward Lyttelton, the former headmaster of Eton, continued to repudiate the Lambeth Conference resolutions of 1930 and cooperated with the interdenominational, but mainly Catholic and Anglo-Catholic, League of National Life in its campaign against birth control. The league's president, Dr. F. J. McCann, a gynecologist who a few years earlier had discovered a contraceptive-induced malady he described as "Malthusian uterus," praised the work of Kuczynski, Carr-Saunders, and others for confirming the league's warnings of looming race suicide. Only the fall in the death rate and the increase in longevity had masked the enormous danger implicit in birth control; he hoped the "spectre of depopulation" so graphically illustrated of late would at last alert the public and its government to the loss of empire and the race extinction which lay ahead.[22]

Religious opposition, particularly from the Catholic church or a minority of establishment prelates, was not about to end the spread of birth control any more than it was able to prevent it in the first place. In the absence of an explicit scriptural injunction, most Nonconformist denominations continued to leave the decision to the individual conscience of the faithful, while some, like the Methodists, actually deprecated "the careless, improvident and unde-signed begetting of children . . . as wrongful to children and injurious to the social order."[23] Not all Christians agreed, but more worrisome to birth control enthusiasts than prelatical anathemas and conflicting biblical interpretations were the warnings of distinguished demographers like Carr-Saunders that the birth control movement would have to act more responsibly in the face of a reproduction rate already 25 percent below replacement. With the develop-ment of a perfect contraceptive on the horizon, he saw in 1936 a potential catastrophe in the making.[24]

To some other supporters of the birth control movement, such as the royal physician and notable churchman Lord Dawson of Penn, existing contracep-tives were already enough of a menace. His surprising public conversion at a church congress in 1921 to the birth control cause had given it an enormous boost. Distressed by the Lambeth Conference's reaffirmation of its prewar opposition to family limitation a few months earlier, Dawson had rejected both ecclesiastical and medical arguments as obscurantist and futile and asserted that birth control was a moral, safe, and desirable manifestation of a more elevated concept of love, marriage, and the family.[25] Although he was more cautious about taking a public stance the remainder of the decade and declined numerous invitations to join birth control organizations and attend interna-tional congresses, Dawson remained one of the heroes of the birth control campaign. It was therefore particularly distressing and ominous when, near the end of 1933, without consultation or warning, he introduced legislation in the Lords to restrict the sale, display, and advertisement of contraceptives.[26]

Dawson, who had always believed doctors should approve and regulate the dispensing of these appliances, emphasized he was not renouncing his support of birth control. He still thought small families were in many cases appropriate and continued to believe that it was ludicrous and futile to preach sexual restraint and abstention to young couples. Moreover, he resented the efforts of prelates who trumpeted the legislation as an anti–birth control bill and, in the case of the bishop of London, contemplated the terpsichorean delights of dancing around a bonfire of condoms. All Dawson wanted to do was to halt the unregulated advertising, hawking, and soaring sales of the devices on the streets, in public places, and even through automatic dispensing machines. He likened his proposals to the restrictions on cinemas and the liquor trade, which were designed to protect immature youth. Far from injuring the birth control movement, Dawson argued, his proposed regulations would give it more respectability.[27]

A number of peers countered that since contraceptives were not harmful they should be readily available, especially to the working classes who were most in need of curtailing their families. Others thought the bill useless or a legal hornets' nest impossible to enforce. Much of the debate was really over the increase in sexual promiscuity since the war, and even the government's spokesmen, who were otherwise neutral, agreed that the real issue was not birth control but the protection of youthful morals. After considerable modification to protect doctors, nurses, midwives, and birth control clinics, Dawson's Folly, as the *Birth Control News* labeled the measure, ultimately passed and was sent on to the Commons where it promptly died.[28]

Without denying that the "Leicester Square rubber shops," sleazy street hawkers, and unscrupulous quacks who peddled contraceptives were offensive, defenders of birth control worried that Dawson's bill might threaten reputable shops and outlets and shackle honest people without stopping the disreputable trade. The failure of a similar measure in France was noted by several critics. Although some in the birth control camp, including C. V. Drysdale, were willing to give Dawson the benefit of the doubt in return for his important help in the past, most saw the bill as an opening wedge to undo the advances of recent years. Private sales, they recalled, especially to the working classes, had done far more for the spread of birth control than had the medical profession whose support was at best still cautious and cool.[29]

Lord Horder, as president of the NBCA and a vice-president of the Eugenics Society, was under considerable pressure to lead the opposition to Dawson's bill in the House of Lords. Despite his strong disapproval of the legislation, however, he said nothing during the debates. The sight of two medical peers, both acknowledged supporters of birth control, squabbling with each other would, he concluded, have been professionally unseemly and grossly misunderstood.[30]

Nevertheless, the NBCA saw in Dawson's abortive bill evidence of a changing attitude toward birth control as fertility rates remained low and anxieties about replacement rates began to rise. Dawson himself had cited the diminishing birth control figures for all classes since the war and noted the growing interval between births.[31] The publication of Charles's book *Twilight of Parenthood* followed by the *Times*'s articles based on the works of Carr-Saunders, Glass, and Kuczynski not only reinforced his arguments but, as worried birth control advocates observed, aroused the passions of people who were virulently opposed to their efforts. Where in 1934 Dawson had used birthrates to support his case for restricting the sale of contraceptives, a few years later he employed net reproduction and age-distribution figures to make the same point and to urge the adoption of policies to encourage motherhood. Although he insisted he did not want to return to the high birthrates of Victorian times, he was reminded by critics that the ideal, carefully spaced family of four children he recommended would of necessity require exactly such a return.[32]

Margaret Pyke spoke for many of her colleagues in the NBCA when in 1936 she expressed some nervousness about the impact the depopulation scare might have on their birth control activities. In response to the charge that their campaign had the greatest appeal to couples who wanted no children, she pointed out that in many of the organization's clinics the women who came for advice already had on average four or five offspring.[33] Despite such assurances and repeated assertions of the NBCA's opposition to an indiscriminate reduction in births, the approaching population decline was viewed as a very serious threat within the birth control camp.[34] Though Edith How-Martyn emboldened her colleagues not to be panicked by Kuczynski and the new prophets of doom while Dr. Margaret Jackson told the Bristol Mother's Welfare Clinic, "We could use some underpopulation for a change," ominous warnings by the well-known maternal and child welfare specialist G. F. McCleary that "the countrymen of Shakespeare are ceasing to reproduce themselves" were difficult to ignore.[35]

McCleary was considered a friend to birth control. Some of his medical colleagues, who bombarded the *British Medical Journal* and the *Lancet* with letters about "birth extinction" and demanded strict government regulation of contraceptives for medical reasons only, obviously were not. Their lamentations for "a shrunken people which has lost faith in itself" and "passed its zenith" reflected the despair the depopulation panic triggered in some sectors of educated society from the mid-1930s on. Much of their unhappiness focused on "the falling away being from the top, or most fit," and they frequently directed their anger at "the unchecked growth and commercialization of birth control [which] has attacked the strength of our race, and threatens the destruction of our ideals and our empire." One agitated gynecologist condemned the "insidious surrender of our racial strength" to the birth control societies and contraceptive manufacturers who threatened to leave Britain an "empty empire."[36]

Defenders of birth control retorted that they were concerned with the health, welfare, and quality of people's lives, not with the size of the population. Indeed, their arguments were often emphatically eugenic, emphasizing that "the wrong people" are still producing themselves, and "the dominant race of the future will be that which succeeds in eliminating the unfit and degenerate."[37] Evelyn Fuller, the secretary of the Society for the Provision of Birth Control Clinics, went so far as to complain to Blacker that his book *The Future of Our Population*, coauthored with Glass, did not discuss race quality though the SPBCC thought it an important argument in deflecting criticisms stirred up by the fear of population decline.[38]

Blacker and the Eugenics Society were by no means certain at first how to reconcile their support of birth control with the dangers they saw in existing patterns of depopulation. The *Eugenics Review* was not unsympathetic to the moral objectives in Lord Dawson's contraceptive bill but concluded that, while it would not prevent intelligent, determined couples from obtaining preventive devices, it would make them less accessible to those whose fertility "is a doubtful social blessing." These questionable people, the review's editor Maurice Newfield reasoned, were not likely in any event to turn from the rubber shops to the medical profession to procure contraceptives. As a doctor himself he knew that the vast majority of people limiting their families did so without medical instruction and would continue to do so.[39]

By 1936, however, with Malthusianism in full retreat and depopulation dominating the headlines, the *Eugenics Review* was more cautious in its support of the birth control movement. Reviewing Carr-Saunders's *World Population*, it expressed the hope that birth control proponents would act responsibly in the light of newly revealed demographic realities. If they continued to maintain that overpopulation was a problem, they would do a disservice to their cause and rightly lose the influence they had gained since the 1870s. The small family system, according to the writer, had become a dangerous dysgenic force. To survive, the birth control movement needed to formulate a program of positive eugenics favoring the restriction of births among the physically and mentally ill-endowed, the spacing of children for health reasons, and in accordance with Eugenics Society teachings, promote many more births among the eugenically desirable. In the case of the latter, it meant the investigation of the physical, psychological, and social causes of infertility and the inculcation of a new, positive attitude toward parenthood.[40]

Blacker's prolonged negotiations with the NBCA about a possible merger with the Eugenics Society was in direct response to the difficulties the depopulation scare was creating for the birth control movement. His own society's journal, while professing its support of the NBCA's activities and welcoming the opening of new clinics and local welfare centers, grew increasingly critical of the negative image burdening birth control recommendations and the refusal of its leaders to acknowledge that declining population, not overpopulation, was now the issue. With some eminent biologists forecasting a population of fewer than eight people in 400 years' time, it was wrong to believe any longer birth control was the answer to social and international problems.[41]

One birth control enthusiast, Frank White, in 1937 warned his colleagues in the Eugenics Society that depopulation hysteria had gotten completely out of hand. It would be cruel and dysgenic if the silly assumptions of a few expert statisticians playing with numbers led to a cutback in what was the only feasible way of dealing with the fertility of the Social Problem Group. In the real world, White wrote, people left descendants in accordance with reproductive patterns that swung to and fro and were rarely very predictable. He appealed to his fellow eugenicists not to allow "statistical shadows" to obscure the real sufferings of the poor, for whom birth control was the greatest blessing, and on no account to give support to any policy based upon those "shadows, which may antagonize their brethren of the birth control movement." Disunion, at this critical juncture, would, he believed, be a catastrophe for society and the future of the race.[42]

It was disunion Blacker was trying to avoid when in 1937 memorandums to the NBCA and the birth control clinics he expressed the conviction "that the anticipated decline of the population requires a reorientation in the birth control movement" and recommended merger with his organization. As he explained to Margaret Jackson and others on numerous occasions, the Eugenics Society council was by no means unanimous in its support of birth control in the country's "present demographic position." He himself regarded the decline in fertility "of the normal couple today as one of the most ominous and sinister features of contemporary social life." Something would have to change. In accordance with the positive image the times required, he recommended that the movement no longer stress lowering the birthrate nor in any way suggest the suppression of parenthood. It should instead emphasize the advantages of birth spacing and planned parenthood as being in the best interests of "the mother, the children and the race." Furthermore, he suggested, because birth control was obviously only a means, not a cause, the clinics ought to become as interested in the sociological reasons or motives for limiting families as they were in the medical aspects of the subject. Efforts to restrict the availability of contraceptives were no better a solution to the threat of depopulation than was a return to unplanned parenthood.[43]

That there was little support for either, despite the frantic rhetoric, was brought home in the refusal of Parliament in 1938 to consider a revised version of Lord Dawson's anticontraceptive bill sponsored by the Public Morality Council.[44] In *Cavalcade* and British Institute polls taken the same year and in 1939, 70 percent of those surveyed who were willing to express an opinion answered affirmatively the question, "Are you in favour of birth control?"

When those respondents who expressed no opinion were factored in, the positive responses fell to 52 percent, but the figure among those under age thirty stood at 64 percent. The response to the British Institute's query as to whether there should be free public centers to provide birth control information to married couples was even more decisive, with 73 percent saying yes, while the remainder were nearly evenly divided between those saying no or expressing no opinion on the question. Though men were slightly more inclined to respond positively than women (76 to 70 percent), opinions tended to run fairly consistently across age and class lines.[45]

The polls confirmed what Blacker, Carr-Saunders, Huxley, and their eugenicist colleagues had argued in persuading the Eugenics Society to support the establishment and demographic research activities of the PIC while funding and working closely with the NBCA and its various affiliates. Birth control had become an entrenched part of modern life for a multiplicity of economic, social, physical, and psychological reasons which had long ago transcended simplistic neo-Malthusian assumptions about the relationship of large families to poverty. If it was naive to believe any longer that birth control was the cause of low fertility and delusional to think it could be eliminated or restricted effectively by legislation, it was not only possible but essential to discover why successive generations of healthy men and women were determined to limit their families so severely. Only then would demographic planners and eugenicists be able to devise policies and programs to persuade all but the least racially efficient couples to modify their restrictive procreative habits. What the reformers in the eugenics movement were recommending in their dual alliance with the PIC and an NBCA committed to a wider concept of family planning was a return to positive eugenics on a scale never envisioned by Galton and his elitist acolytes earlier in the century.

"And Everybody Wondered Why the Population Fell"

With depopulation imminent and advances in genetic research challenging traditional beliefs in the innate differences between classes, Carr-Saunders, in his 1934 Galton Lecture, emphasized the importance of formulating new eugenic policies. It was time, he insisted, to pay more attention to quantity than quality through positive programs designed not "to breed a race of supermen," but to raise at least to replacement levels the fertility of the great majority of people in all classes who were not definitely subnormal. Negative eugenics appeared increasingly repressive and unconstructive, he complained, its advocates seen by the public as "scolds and prophets of disaster."

Though birth control would remain an important eugenic weapon, Carr-Saunders agreed, its accelerating adoption by the poorer classes would soon bring their fertility into line with that of the rich so that the loss of population would probably be even greater than currently projected. When this began to occur in the next decade, "everyone [would] be asking what can be done" and demands for action would become overwhelming. One way or the other, a national population policy would have to be constructed; now was the time "to ensure that it will be a policy in which eugenic considerations are not omitted." Carr-Saunders believed that in practice this meant research and planning for a coherent, biologically sound program of birth promotion as well as birth control. It was not enough to talk about "the retreat from parenthood" or to set about removing obstacles to childbearing, he insisted, until they first discovered what factors influence fertility decisions. Only then did it make sense to propose a positive population policy that would lead to a change in domestic values, attitudes, and strategy.[46]

The Eugenics Society, under Blacker's direction, had been moving in this direction since 1933 when its council began deliberating a response to predictions of population decline at the same time the organization was becoming heavily involved in contraceptive research and the advocacy of population control. One of the immediate consequences of Carr-Saunders's influential address was the council's agreement in 1935 to establish a Positive Eugenics Committee to study ways to promote fertility before "intensive and largely panicky" demands were made "for something . . . to be done about the decline in total volume and net reproduction rate of our population."[47]

Despite the "anti-semitic leanings" of some of the council members, especially the anthropologist George Pitt-Rivers, Blacker, on William Beveridge's recommendation, hired David Glass, the son of a Jewish East End journeyman tailor, as a research assistant instead of another "pleasant and intelligent Jew" to undertake a study of family endowments and other pronatalist schemes for the new committee.[48] When, in the following year, the PIC was established at the instigation of the Eugenics Society, Glass, whose work for the Positive Eugenics Committee culminated in the publication of *The Struggle for Population*, went to work for the PIC where his salary continued to be paid by the Eugenics Society.

To insure that the Eugenics Society would continue to support the turn toward more positive policies, Blacker, threatening resignation if necessary, engineered radical changes in the bylaws of the organization and the composition of the council. In conjunction with the restructuring of the society and the addition of more progressive voices on the council, Blacker successfully advocated the election of Lord Horder, who generally supported his objectives, as president.[49] The changes confirmed the worst fears of several old-guard members such as Cora Hodson, F. C. S. Schiller, Lady Askwith, and Dean Inge. They soon resigned despite Horder's assurances in his presidential address that qualitative considerations and favorable differential fertility remained the principal province of eugenics as it had since Galton's times. Inge, who thought the depopulation projections were rubbish and recalled when people a few years earlier were predicting "we would all be packed like sardines in a tin," did not believe Horder's protestations that the alarm over falling numbers was not of central concern to the newly structured council. On the contrary, the dean complained, some of its members were trying to "stampede the society into panicky agitation that has little to do with eugenics."[50]

The *Eugenics Review*, like the society itself, was pulled in different directions. Echoing the new president, it stressed repeatedly that "the primary concern . . . is with the quality of population, not with its numbers." Unless something was done, however, no power on earth would be able to stop the population falling to one-eighth or one-tenth its present size, provoking prescriptions for repopulation which, from a eugenic standpoint, might prove even worse. This was a point supporters of positive eugenics made over and over in defense of the new policies. As Lady Chambers put it in a letter to Blacker, "If we don't tackle it scientifically all sorts of scared people posing mad, ill-considered remedies [will do so] which will do more harm than good." Negative programs such as birth control and sterilization would have to continue, the *Eugenics Review* explained, but we must develop positive plans as well if the term "race suicide is to remain a timely warning and not descriptive of an event taking place under our eyes."[51]

In addition to its involvement with the PIC, the Eugenics Society, in accordance with its tactics of affiliation and infiltration, also established in 1938 a Population Policies Committee (PPC) in conjunction with PEP, the political and economic planning group established in 1931 to plan scientifically for the recovery of the economy. Their various proposals for state intervention in the modernization and efficient rationalization of corporate Britain included an interest in the control and manipulation of population that attracted a number of prominent eugenicists over the years, including Blacker, Carr-Saunders, Huxley, Sir Basil Blackett, Josiah Stamp, and Sybil Neville-Rolfe.[52] The primary purpose of the joint Population Policies Committee was to employ PIC data to survey the social and economic conditions which discouraged the replacement of eugenically sound stock and to report on proposals for raising the fertility of healthy stocks in different occupational groups. Despite its pronounced eugenic interests in the work of the Population Policies Committee and willingness to underwrite financially much of its research, Blacker thought it unwise to advertise the connection so as to avoid the prejudice against eugenics of many left-wing intellectuals who had otherwise supported PEP since its inception.[53]

Moreover, partly to placate the Left and partly as a favor to Havelock Ellis, Blacker recommended Ellis's unemployed stepson, Francois Lafitte, a young Oxford-educated Labour radical, for the position of secretary to the Population Policies Committee. Given Lafitte's negligible enthusiasm for eugenics and strong belief in the primacy of environmental causation, the importance of extensive family allowances, social support policies, and expanded welfare programs to alleviate poverty, it was not an especially happy relationship. Both Carr-Saunders and Blacker had to remind him on various occasions that inheritance and differential fertility, not the effect of environment on physical quality, was what was of primary importance, and Clifton Chance found Lafitte's obsession with the word "equal" particularly alarming. The strained association finally ended by mutual agreement in 1945 when Lafitte, in spite of repeated proddings and reminders of the Eugenics Society's years of subsidies, failed to deliver a long-awaited report on the eugenic possibilities of family allowances after the war.[54]

Some of Blacker's supporters, including Horder, were less than enthusiastic about his desire to make such sharp distinctions between positive and negative eugenics and wondered if the Eugenics Society really needed the assistance of other organizations to figure out how to raise the fertility of those above the biological average. Since compulsory methods of birth promotion and restriction such as those employed in Germany were unacceptable in Britain, Blacker reasoned, they were dependent upon research into the reasons why the vast majority of perfectly sound couples declined to breed and upon educating and encouraging them to change their minds. In the absence of a royal commission, which eventually would have to be appointed, this could best be accomplished through groups and organizations such as the PIC, PEP, and NBCA that already had the confidence of large sectors of the public as well as a number of M.P.s.[55]

A great many people, however, thought the answers to why the birthrate was so low were obvious, and some found it odd or laughable that anyone could seriously ask why the population was about to decline. During the debate over the Population (Statistics) Act in 1937, A. P. Herbert launched into a poem listing the various causes and ending most of the verses with the sarcastic line, "And everybody wondered why the population fell."[56] His rhyming explanations encompassed economic conditions, housing, tax laws, the cost of education, the love of luxury, the intrusion of modern technology, the fear of war, and general despair about the future. All of these were commonplace reasons, many of them dating back to the first alarms about the birthrate at the turn of the century.

Equally familiar were countless analyses of the diminishing value of children and, more importantly, the changing position of women in society which took on particular significance in the context of their much-heralded unique role in determining the vital net reproduction rate. Less prevalent, but still discussed in press and Parliament, was the effect of the servant problem on the willingness of the modern woman to accept the drudgery of raising children or maintaining a house or flat large enough to accommodate more than one or two of them. Quoting a "woman of means," Captain G. S. Elliston, M.P., in his presidential address to a Conference of the Royal Institute of Public Health in 1937, proclaimed, "Give us maids and we will soon fill our nurseries."[57] The eugenically sensitive bishop of Norwich, in endorsing parliamentary proposals in 1939 to encourage unemployed women to go into domestic service in lieu of unemployment compensation, was especially worried about the deterrent effect the lack of servants had on the willingness of "women in the better classes" to have larger families.[58]

Economic motivations of one sort or another dominated the multiple reasons adding up to the menace of underpopulation. Lady Rhys Williams, a member of the PIC, discovered in 1939, to no one's surprise, that of 3,000 people questioned in a Welsh survey taken for the Joint Council of Midwifery, 60 percent gave economic justifications for declining to have more children.[59] Working-class people, as other studies illustrated, had learned the correlative lessons of poverty and fertility; equipped with the knowledge of how to limit their families, they had no intention of threatening the marginal standard of living they were able to sustain on what were already inadequate wages, if they were fortunate enough to be employed at all. One Fabian investigation revealed that 40 percent of adult males could not possibly provide for a family of three children, and for many of these men even one or two severely strained their limited domestic resources.[60]

Much of the discussion about economics and the birthrate, however, did not focus upon the poor. Indeed, a number of critics argued that despite the narrowing of class and occupational fertility differentials, the persistence of an inverse relationship between income and family size demonstrated that the fear of poverty was probably not as significant as other considerations. One of these was the lack of adequate, affordable housing for young couples with children. As Herbert rhymingly told the Commons:

They pulled down all the houses where the children used to crowd
And built expensive blocks of flats where children weren't allowed;
So if father got a job there wasn't anywhere to dwell,
And everybody wondered why the population fell.

More important, many popular analyses suggested, was a rational and under-
standable or, depending upon the analyst's perspective, a selfish and short-
sighted desire on the part of married people to improve their standard of living
and enjoy more of the material advantages of life. This often translated into a
choice between "prams or cars" and inspired numerous press descriptions of
"Empty Cradles and Full Garages!" The eugenic consequences of what the
minister of transport labeled in 1929 as the "car purchasing class" buying ten
motorcars for each baby they produced, were obvious. One writer in the early
1930s noted that of 1,050,000 automobiles in Britain, 250,000 belonged to
childless couples who left the multiplication of the race to the unfit.[61] As the
zoologist D. Ward Cutler told the British Social Hygiene Council in 1933,
only the most "thriftless" classes were still replacing themselves while "the
better classes prefer to invest in motor-cars instead of baby citizens." It was a
certain prescription for racial deterioration.[62] To Herbert the demographic
consequences of the craze for automobiles were not so much eugenic as they
were Malthusian in contributing to feelings of overcrowding in a deteriorating
environment:

Five hundred brand-new motor cars each morning rode the roads,
And flashed about like comets or sat motionless as toads;
Whichever course they took they made the public highway hell,
And everybody wondered why the population fell.

There were no end of accusations of middle-class selfishness and of appeals
to the young and to their parents and teachers to adopt values in which children
were seen as far more important to the quality of life than cars, motorcycles,
and the cinema. Those of a classical bent were, as usual, quick to recall the
consequences of twisted priorities for ancient Greece and Rome.[63] Many
critics denounced modern advertising for depicting the small family of one or
two children as the ideal instead of three or four. Others deplored the humor
and lightly veiled contempt attached, in popular culture, to the unfashionable
minority who still reared a large brood of offspring. Reminding her contemporaries of the intensive campaign to increase the birthrate in Nazi Germany and
of the sizable advantage in population that dangerous nation already possessed, Lady Rhys Williams wondered three months before the outbreak of
the Second World War who would have the last laugh. In a reference many

hoped had disappeared with the last war, she recalled Napoleon's famous confession of faith that "God is on the side of the big battalions." Those battalions, she pointed out, currently belonged to Dr. Goebbels and Field Marshall Goering.[64]

As of 1936, the press reported from the most recent *German Army Year Book*, Germany contained 313,700 twenty-year-old men compared to England's 296,900 and France's 171,000. If current trends continued, the registrar-general's figures suggested, by 1950 the Germans would have over 4 million more men ages twenty to forty-five than Britain and nearly twice as many as the rapidly dwindling French.[65] Indeed, some demographically conscious strategists warned, more lives had been lost to birth control every year since 1918 than in the worst year of the war, which was a far graver threat to the nation's security than were the Nazis.[66]

Socialists and left-wing feminists were especially persistent in the 1930s in their claims that the fear of war was nearly as important in its sterilizing effects as the defective economic and social system. Vera Brittain, whose poignant memoirs of the shattering effects of the First World War, *Testament of Youth*, gave her a wide audience, reiterated the refusal of women to provide cannon fodder to be slaughtered in another great conflict.[67] Labour M.P.s made the same point during the depopulation debates, while other critics argued that, hysterical pleas notwithstanding, working people were unlikely to follow the lead of the militaristic Germans and Italians in their push for more and more people to feed their war machines.[68] As a commentator in the *Daily Herald* asked, is it a "Battle for Babies or Babies for Battle" we are engaged in? Women knew the answer, he believed; it was evident in the small size of their families.

Although the correlation between the fear of war and a reluctance to bring more children into the world was widely assumed, it did not go unchallenged. There was plenty of evidence to demonstrate that the birthrate began to fall when the danger of war was fairly remote, and the decline was especially sharp in the relatively peaceful 1920s. Furthermore, as an analyst in the *Times* reported in 1937, the birthrate had actually stopped its slide and had shown signs of recovery since 1933 despite the mounting war scare.[69]

The myriad of explanations only confirmed the contention of Blacker and others on the PIC that the reasons for the declining birthrate were complex and interrelated, even if the mix of considerations varied within different sectors of society. In broad terms they seemed to fall into three general categories: (1) medical, (2) socioeconomic, and (3) psychological. Despite the persistence of biological theories of diminished reproductive capacity, sterility and the incidences of miscarriage, physical abnormalities, ill health, or the fear of hereditary disease (all of which came under the first category) were generally considered responsible for no more than a small portion of the total infertility in the country. Nevertheless, the transformation of the birth control movement into the family planning movement was based upon the need to address these problems and to give "the parental instinct" a new meaning as part of a positive response to the menace of depopulation.[70]

If most students of the subject were disinclined to accept R. A. Fisher's thesis of a genetic predisposition to family limitation, the association of economic well-being and social promotion or the preservation of status with small families was generally acknowledged to be a major factor in family planning. Enid Charles described this as the growth of a "social tradition in favour of sterility" which spread from the more prosperous classes to the rest of the community. For the first group social promotion was involved; for the less prosperous it was a response to restrictions on child labor, the introduction of universal education, and the declining economic value of children. People learned they could be better off with fewer children, she explained. The result was a paradox in which couples limited their families because they were prosperous or because they were not.[71]

Charles disagreed with her colleague at the London School of Economics, William Beveridge, who doubted that economic conditions and material motivations were as important as the discovery of birth control itself in explaining the plummeting birthrate. He recalled how Britain, Germany, Australia, and France were all at different stages of economic development in 1881; yet all experienced a heavy decline in fertility. Moreover, the economic experience and needs of people in different occupations and classes within countries varied dramatically; yet the adoption of birth control was fast becoming universal. Beveridge's point—that irrespective of their differing economic surroundings, people everywhere were to varying degrees eager to limit their families and leaped at the chance when it came—was challenged by Charles. She claimed birth control methods, though not widely employed, were well known before the decline in fertility began. What changed was the socioeconomic structure in the capitalist West which created an environment inimical to reproduction in all classes. As a consequence, although the socialists and radicals first preached birth control to the working classes as a cure for poverty, it was the middle and upper classes who first chose to practice limitation on a large scale.[72] On the one hand, Charles seemed to be defending the centrality of economic motivation in all classes, though for different reasons, in the adoption of birth control; on the other, however, she conceded the complexity of the problem and thought a great deal more needed to be learned about changes in social habits as well as the physiology and psychology of reproduction before it would be possible to dogmatize about the relative importance of causative factors. At the same time she, like her husband, Hogben, was sure of two things: eugenics did not have the answers, and when they were found, they could never be successfully applied in an unplanned, laissez-faire capitalist society in which people, left alone, did not really know what was good for them. The solution to the population problem was not simply higher wages and a more equitable distribution of wealth, as many socialists assumed; it required the centralized application of the sort of planned "social bio-technology" being studied in the Soviet Union to refashion a social environment in which the value and enjoyment of parenthood was central.[73]

The Russian model, as filtered through the selective demographic vision of socialist state planners, was no more appealing to much of the British public than the authoritarian pronatalism advanced by the Germans and Italians in their fevered efforts to increase the birthrate. According to an extensive body of middle- and upper-class opinion, it would have been far simpler to achieve this goal within the framework of the existing socioeconomic and political structure by revising the tax system to allow larger and more extensive exemptions and rebates for children and their educational expenses.

Eugenicists had been in the forefront of selective, pronatalist tax reform since before the Great War and continued their efforts in the interwar years to persuade the government to increase the allowances given taxpaying parents while raising the assessment on the childless and unmarried. Believing as he did in the probable correlation of larger salaries and incomes with superior genetic endowment, Major Darwin was particularly assiduous in recommending proposals to grant parents with larger incomes greater allowances. Like most of his colleagues in the Eugenics Society who to varying degrees endorsed his argument, he was less certain about the eugenic value of inherited wealth and therefore less inclined to advance the claims for lower inheritance taxes other property owners demanded.[74]

As early as 1925 the Eugenics Society used taxation as a recruiting slogan, noting that the cost of social services, excluding war pensions, had increased twelvefold since the 1890s and pointing out that 50 percent of the budget was being paid for by 5 percent of the population at an average rate of £180 per head.[75] Two years later Darwin, in working up resolutions to be presented by supporters in Parliament calling for a doubling of child rebates and exemptions for school fees and the costs of confinement, calculated that the replacement rate of taxpaying parents was already only half of what was needed. Though the desired changes in the finance bill to stem this "grave national danger" were not made in 1927, the Eugenics Society was pleased when in the follow-

ing year the rebates for children were raised from £36 to £60 for the first child
and from £27 to £50 for subsequent offspring. While some eugenicists, including Blacker, were uncertain as to whether high taxes and the cost of living were
as significant motives for avoiding children as a selfish desire for luxury,
personal comfort, vanity, fear of childbirth, or a quest for pleasure, they did
agree that the larger allowances were a welcome official acknowledgment of
the problem of differential fertility.[76]

The combination of the depression and the depopulation scare reinforced
the Eugenics Society's conclusion in its 1929 statement of practical policy that
the problem of differential fertility required "an economic rather than a moral
remedy."[77] In practice this meant birth control and sterilization for the poorest,
least capable classes, and tax rebates, weighted family allowances, educational
scholarships, and other graded economic inducements for everyone else who
was not on the dole and was healthy, married, and willing to have children.
The skeptical Neo-Malthusian R. B. Kerr, who doubted high taxes were the
reason for middle-class infertility, reminded those subject to "eugenic delu-
sion" that the earned income of a married man with three children was already
totally exempt from taxes up to £462. This was an advantage unavailable to
people in Gladstone's time, when the income tax was not graduated, there
were no allowances for wives and children and when, nevertheless, the birthrate was much higher. To Kerr it seemed obvious that the middle classes, like
an ever-increasing number of working-class people who were not taxed at all
or at much lower rates, were declining to reproduce for reasons having little to
do with the rates they had to pay.[78]

Eugenicists largely ignored Kerr's arguments and those of his Neo-Malthusian colleague in the Eugenics Society, C. V. Drysdale, and continued
throughout the 1930s to push for greater tax deductions, separate assessments
on husbands and wives, and educational rebates to encourage the fertility of
those who would presumably benefit the most. Some even proposed pegging
death duties to the number of heirs, with all payment forgiven if there were
three or more to carry on the family pedigree.[79] But however popular the
economic explanations for the low birthrate and the faltering net reproduction
rate, they seemed to a number of reform eugenicists overly simplistic and
fraught with incongruities and inconsistencies.

The PIC was created to consider all of the possible causes: medical, economic, and, perhaps the most nebulous of all, psychological. Blacker appropriated William James's term, the "tender-minded," to describe the "sensitive,
conscientious and far-seeing persons" who were particularly distressed by the
possibility of another war and especially troubled by the consequences of
economic slumps and social upheaval. They were, he suggested, the most

eugenically valuable of their class and, like the characters in Oliver Baldwin's novel *My Unborn Son*, especially susceptible to a pessimistic view of the future. Another war would make their feelings predominant and have an even more devastating effect upon the willingness of thoughtful, intelligent young couples to have children.[80] Although Herbert made no such fine distinctions in the concluding verse of his unique explanation to the House of Commons, his argument summed up the apprehension many of his contemporaries felt about the past and the future:

The world, in short, which never was extravagantly sane,
Developed all the signs of inflammation of the brain;
The past was not encouraging, the future none could tell,
But the Minister still wondered why the population fell.

The tender-minded were, according to Blacker and Glass, perhaps also more aware of privation and suffering than others and, in the case of women, feared the pain and dangers of childbirth. A puzzling, worrisome, and much-publicized increase in maternal mortality from 3.91 per thousand births in 1921 to a peak of 4.41 in 1934 contrasted with the continued decline in the infant death rate and reminded women of the higher risks they continued to run in bearing children. Though much to the relief of the Ministry of Health the rate fell by nearly a third during the remainder of the decade, public and official concern about maternal deaths continued, and eugenicists were not alone in wondering how much it contributed to the reluctance of women to expose themselves to the dangers of childbearing when they knew how to avoid them.[81]

Contraception had given people more control over their lives, Blacker and Glass wrote in 1936. Couples found that the parental instinct could be satisfied with one or two children, the risks of more eliminated, and the size of their families adjusted to their sensitive perception of a changing, dangerous world in which the future was increasingly uncertain. The two men speculated that improved contraceptives might exacerbate even more the inverse correlation between tender-mindedness and fertility. But until the reason why people did not want children was really known, they concluded, it would be extremely difficult to know how to change their minds.[82]

In his ambitious proposal in the later 1930s to merge the Eugenics Society and the National Birth Control Association into the core of a federated Institute for Family Relations, Blacker hoped to remove the obstacles, whether physical, economic, or psychological, to the "free expression of [the] reproductive impulse" which was, at the time, weak and in need of nurturing. His concept of family planning within the institute went far beyond birth control in its emphasis upon reducing the pain and risks of childbirth, investigating the causes of involuntary sterility, lobbying for family allowances, tax rebates, improved housing, medical, dental, and nursery care. In addition, he envisioned a network of psychological counseling centers and child guidance clinics to encourage people to have children when they should and to help them when they did.

Blacker, who sent an advanced copy of his plan to the sympathetic Carr-Saunders, anticipated correctly the protests it engendered from those in the Eugenics Society who charged such an undertaking would be too indiscriminate and would betray the eugenicists' goal of improving racial quality rather than quantity. If eugenics was to have a meaningful voice in solving the population problem, Blacker countered, it would have to address both dimensions of the issue. They were not incompatible; the institute he proposed would be as interested in helping the minority of people who should not have children as it would the majority of those who should have them but, for one reason or another, did not.[83] In the majority of cases, Blacker was convinced, the "psychology of infertility" was far more important than physiology and probably weighed more heavily on women than on men. Indeed, much of the debate over the causes of depopulation focused on the changing role of women in modern society and the critical role their replacement played in determining net reproduction.

Twelve

Feminism and Family Allowances

Although the women's movement had not been prominent in the struggle for birth control before World War I, in the public's mind the two were closely connected. Not a few observers recalled that the Bradlaugh-Besant trial and the emergence of neo-Malthusianism in the late Victorian period paralleled the beginning of concerted efforts on the part of feminists to expand their educational and economic opportunities and, more important, get the vote. Even if the women's organizations pursuing these objectives deliberately avoided confusing them with the highly contentious issue of family limitation, their aspirations were nevertheless frequently interpreted as a "revolt against motherhood." The relentless decline in the birthrate and the notoriously low incidence of marriage and fertility among active, educated, new women provided the statistics for whatever case the opponents of the feminist cause wished to make.

The association between the control of fertility and the enjoyment of newly achieved rights and opportunities, improved health, and a higher quality of domestic life was of course obvious to many feminists in the late Victorian and Edwardian era. It was not, however, until the interwar decades, when popular attitudes toward sexuality had substantially changed to permit more open discussion of the subject, that birth control became an integral, if not necessarily central, part of their campaign. In nearly all of the major feminist groups it was still more often an implicit understanding than an explicit policy except where it involved making birth control facilities available to the poor or persuading the minister of health to permit the giving of contraceptive advice in the local welfare centers.

As the practice and theory of birth control became morally, culturally, and politically acceptable in postwar British society, its specific links in popular thought to feminism were diluted—particularly as it spread to working-class women who, with some exceptions, had been ancillary rather than central to the women's movement. Indeed, critics of feminism and birth control, whether eugenicists or not, thought mainly in terms of middle- and upper-class women rather than their lower-class sisters whose higher fertility was generally assumed to be in inverse correlation with their genetic endowment. The depopulation scare in the 1930s blurred such qualitative distinctions as the question of quantity became predominant.

While in earlier years the plummeting birthrate provoked cries of race suicide, the issue now was not only one of sufficient manpower to sustain the nation and the empire but of "motherpower" as well. The quest for an answer to the problem gave considerable stimulus to the old prewar socialist idea of family allowances paid directly to mothers who would, presumably, be more inclined to use them for the benefit of their vulnerable offspring. Then the idea was not to stimulate the fertility of the laboring classes, which was high enough, but to improve their health and standard of living which tended to deteriorate with each successive child.[1] Coupled with other child and maternal welfare programs designed to improve the skills of mothercraft and reduce infant mortality, family allowances were viewed by their advocates as an important weapon in the fight against poverty, disease, and the high death rate of the young.

It was a weapon of dubious eugenic value from which most eugenicists before the war recoiled. Their conviction that people in the armed forces were genetically superior to the C3 misfits unable to endure the rigors of combat made them less hostile to the introduction of separation allowances on the basis of rank and family size during World War I, but they could not accept the extension of similar benefits to the mass of the laboring poor in the years after the conflict. As much as the leaders of the eugenics movement would have preferred to steer clear of the family endowment question, their growing involvement with birth control and other population issues made it impossible from the mid-1920s on to avoid the subject. When, in the following decade, with depopulation on the immediate horizon, family endowment schemes were advanced not only as a solution to poverty but also as a way of replenishing the dwindling supply of children, particularly females, they were permeated with eugenic views. As usual these views represented not a single-minded ideological position but a compromise, tortuously evolved out of the endemic conflicts among eugenicists with widely differing perspectives on the population problem.

The "Female Famine"

Among its various effects, the depopulation scare had the curious result of reversing the deep concerns about sex ratios that prevailed during World War I and in the years immediately after. The loss of three-quarters of a million men, coupled with the sharply declining birthrate and the higher mortality of male children, raised serious anxieties about the availability of adequate manpower for the reconstruction of the race. To many people the wartime rise in the ratio of male to female births from an average of 1,039 per 1,000 in 1914 to a high of 1,060 in 1919 was nature's way of compensating for the destruction of young men and the increase in the already troublesome surplus of a million women. In reality the ratios before, during, and after the war varied widely throughout the country, suggesting something other than nature was influencing prenatal and postnatal mortality, but the aggregate figures were what caught the public's attention.

Some analysts hypothesized that the postponement of marriage and the absence of husbands during the war increased the spacing of births, allowing weaker males in utero to benefit from the diminished stress on their mothers and so survive. Others wondered if the availability of servicemen's allowances, higher wages, less crowding, better diet, and improved prenatal care made fragile males more viable. Julian Huxley, by contrast, thought the strains of wartime conditions might have somehow altered or converted zygotes which would otherwise have been females. If the normal sex ratios resumed in the postwar generations, it would, he reasoned in 1922, give credence to his theory.[2]

Though the figure soon returned to the 1,040 or so male births per 1,000 females many people regarded as normal, the ratio fluctuated and in some quarters of 1934 and 1935 approached the World War I numbers, occasioning a resurgence of scientific and popular speculation.[3] This was especially true in the midst of the depopulation scare when most analysts agreed with William Beveridge that "boy babies matter very little now; it is only necessary to count girl babies."[4] Whereas a decade or two earlier the excessive numbers of female children were largely irrelevant or even a burden to planners of demographic reconstruction, they suddenly became extremely valuable in the 1930s and the reasons why modern women were not producing more of them a subject of national concern and inquiry.

Robert Kuczynski had demonstrated the central importance of girl babies to the net reproduction of the race and set a generation of amateur and professional demographers to explaining his formula and charting the dwindling supply of potential mothers. "Net reproduction" quickly became part of the language of public discussion; even people who had no idea how to calculate it knew it added up to a "famine of females," as the *Daily Express* described the shortage of young women already evident in 1934 in a number of occupations. The head of a large employment bureau who advertised for 1,000 typists received 4 replies, an experience reported by many other businesses despite the high unemployment of the depression. A similar shortage of young women willing to go into domestic service was particularly vexatious and, many believed, compounded the reluctance of more prosperous women to have larger families. The immediate cause, the *Daily Express* concluded, was the low birthrate of the war years and the subsequent shortage of eighteen-year-old girls.[5] Since then the birthrate had fallen even lower and the nation was facing not only a shortage of female workers but, more ominously, a dearth of future mothers. In a frequently quoted article in the *Sunday Times*, the secretary of the Scottish Association of Insurance Committees predicted in 1936 that in thirty years the number of mothers in the country would be only two-thirds of the current figure and would produce nearly 230,000 fewer offspring.[6]

Where a few years earlier, concerns about the sex ratios had centered on the proportion of male to female births, by the mid-1930s they focused on the number of female children per 1,000 women. This net reproduction rate of 0.76, at 25 percent below the 1.0 or "unity" needed for women merely to replace themselves, was already substantially lower than the rate of 0.88 Kuczynski had calculated less than a decade earlier. It was also half the 1.5 figure that had obtained in 1871 when the average number of children per marriage stood at 4.78 and the population was growing briskly.[7] Beveridge did not think it unreasonable to expect the rate to fall soon to 0.50, a figure already reached in Saxony and some other German states where half the population of the next generation would probably disappear.[8] The *Evening Standard*, recalling the pity felt for the million surplus women after World War I, noted in 1935 that the figure had been cut in half and the country would instead soon have to contend with a surplus of eligible men. Not only would relations between the sexes be altered, the paper warned, but the smaller, older society of the future would be "less a man's world."[9]

Allowing for the mortality of women and the failure of about 17.6 percent of those who reached the ages of forty to forty-nine ever to marry, demographic prognosticators estimated that those women who did reach maturity and wed needed to have at least 2.87 children to sustain the population, rather than the 2.05 prevailing in the 1930s. Glass calculated the country would need 764,000 live births a year merely to stabilize the existing number of women ages fifteen to forty-nine and to hold the population of the United Kingdom at about 46 million. In 1934, however, the figure was only 597,642, enough to maintain a population of no more than 36 million, some 4.5 million fewer than currently existed in England and Wales alone. In order to sustain even these levels as the number of fertile women declined by more than 2 million during the next fifty years, Glass estimated, the ratio of live births per 1,000 women would have to increase from 57.1 to 68.7. This was no more likely to happen, he predicted, than was a sharp cut in armaments and a massive outlay of financial allowances to induce people to have more children. He admitted, however, that even if the government were to take such action, there was no guarantee it would be successful because the reasons for people limiting their fertility remained obscure.[10]

Occasional voices were still heard blaming the decline on the sterilizing effects of evolutionary individuation, female education, and the expenditure of women's vital procreative energy in the pursuit of modern fads and fashions. But despite the intensity of feelings stirred up by the fear of depopulation and the broader anxieties about the future it represented, denunciations of feminism or of the modern woman for revolting against "life, motherhood and domesticity" remained less common and much more subdued than they had been before the war.[11] Typical of most critics was the popular novelist A. J. Cronin, who did not go much beyond denouncing modern women for selfishly preferring cars to babies, defying nature's laws, and threatening to turn Britain into "a forsaken tribe."[12]

Yet for every criticism of the selfish, flat-chested, slim-hipped, beautiful degenerates who would not bear children or burden themselves with their care, there were many more rebukes of men who nowadays spurned "short, strong, big-waisted, young women capable of hard work and bearing healthy children."[13] Even commentators who might have wished otherwise conceded that women were much better educated, had wider interests, and were more concerned with the quality of life for themselves and their children than they were with the size of their families. In many of the countless articles on "Wives Who Shirk Motherhood" or "Britain Needs More Babies!" writers alluded to the selfishness of wives but frequently noted that it was encouraged by husbands. The pleasures of motherhood, the papers judiciously observed, had to compete with many other pleasures today which were not available to the previous generation. An obvious answer was to make motherhood more attractive.[14]

Whenever criticism exceeded judiciousness it triggered a flood of rebuttals like that from a twenty-four-year-old typist who reminded the male politicians who called for "More Babies! Increase England's Manpower!" of the risks to health and happiness the members of her sex ran if they heeded such thoughtless injunctions. Women wanted more out of life now both for themselves and their children. Feminists like Florence Key, president of the Open Door Council, were quick to see in the depopulation scare "a new weapon with which to attack the freedom of women" and to deny them equal opportunities and employment. She was joined by Cicely Hamilton and others at the council's annual meeting in 1938 in passing a resolution calling upon investigators of the population problem to treat women as human beings to be respected, not as means to an end.[15]

Similar resolutions from other women's organizations called attention to the dangers to recently won political and economic gains implicit in efforts to increase the birthrate. The National Union of Societies for Equal Citizenship emphasized that no "stud mentality" would be permitted to prevail in Britain as it did in Germany and recommended that the present population be taken care of before a larger one was contemplated.[16] Indeed, women, often supported by men, predicted the birthrate would continue to fall until women were satisfied the environment was conducive to raising children. But in any event, they invariably added, families would never again be as large as they once were now that birth control was available to permit the spacing of children and to keep the size of families compatible with economic opportunities.

Another source of women's complaints throughout the decade was the dominance of men in discussions of the birth control issue and in the formulation of population policy. Lela Florence, who had helped establish the first birth control clinic in Cambridge, complained in 1930 that the debate was academic because it ignored "the one essential and vital factor in the population question—the woman who has to bear and rear the children." Instead of calling legions of men to testify, she asked, "Would we not reach sound facts sooner if women themselves were summoned?"[17]

Although many people agreed that women should be much more involved in the study and formulation of population policy, female voices were comparatively quiet. A female correspondent to the *Manchester Guardian* in November 1937 complained about the reluctance of women to speak out on a subject they knew a good deal about and to which they could bring both their experience and their special insight.[18] During the debate over the Population (Statistics) Act later in the month, one of its opponents, R. W. Sorenson, the Labour member for Leyton West, wondered why none of the eleven women in the House had even bothered to attend and explain why their sex refused to have more children. Several of them, he recalled, were in fact unmarried or had very small families. Was it, as he suspected, because they viewed maternity as a voluntary function, not a tyranny, and wanted to live their own lives and have more freedom? "Probably the eleven of them are in their own little drawing room in the corridor giggling and saying to themselves in their feminine privacy, 'What fools these men must be.' " Sorenson's own informal questioning of several hundred women convinced him that irrespective of economic conditions, women wanted on average no more than 2.5 children.[19]

Marie Stopes was not giggling; she was furious that women in general and she in particular had not been asked for their views. Convinced that a male conspiracy was afoot to take advantage of the current panic in order to denigrate the birth control movement, she denounced the hysteria stirred up by the press and the "claptrap" put out by Carr-Saunders and the M.P.s who cited his statistics. Her own inability to get letters published in many newspapers was evidence of the press's collusion in "cooking up" the depopulation crisis despite the birthrate having been stable for the past four years. When history asked, "Where were the women in 1937?" the answer, Stopes predicted, would be an emphatic, "gagged!"[20]

In reality, a minority of women were active and highly visible in the population debate of the 1930s. The self-aggrandizing Stopes, in spite of her complaints, never lacked for an audience. Those who spoke for the NBCA were largely women, as were many of the public lecturers who, like Cora Hodson and Hilda Pocock, worked for the Eugenics Society and were active on its behalf in the National Council of Women. The wealthy, Oxford-educated, Liverpool philanthropist Eleanor Rathbone and several of her female colleagues were unrelenting in their public and private pursuit of family allowances as a way of halting the slide in the birthrate. Furthermore, the *Manchester Guardian* reminded its readers in 1937, three of the seventeen members of the new PIC, established to discover the reasons for the decline and propose ways to reverse it, were indisputably women.[21] Of this formidable trio, which included Stella Churchill, Lady Rhys Williams, and Eva Hubback, all eugenicists, Hubback, as president of one of the largest women's groups, NUSEC, was particularly active in alerting her sex to the importance of the population issue.

Although the nearly simultaneous publication in 1936 of three books by men—Kuczynski, Carr-Saunders, and Glass—triggered the depopulation panic in the press, the work of two women, Grace Leybourne and, more important, Enid Charles, had first called attention to the problem two years earlier. The demographic projections in Charles's *Twilight of Parenthood*, though derived from Kuczynski's vital net reproduction formula, were in fact cited in the extensive debate far more than were those in his more restrained studies. Only Carr-Saunders, perhaps, enjoyed as much authority in public and political discussions of the declining population in the late 1930s, but his analyses were unencumbered by Charles's glowing descriptions of Soviet central planning and the approaching domination of women in underpopulated, capitalist societies.

In their concentration upon her much-quoted net reproduction figures, reviewers, critics, and advocates overlooked the strong feminist component to Charles's thesis. Women, she argued, knew that children were no longer an economic asset, necessary for support in old age, but were in fact impediments to an improved standard of living. In addition, motherhood was simply not a very satisfying career, Charles added, and it was not surprising that as opportunities opened up and family limitation made it possible to take advantage of them, women would seek occupations and pursue interests outside of the home.[22]

Despite these gains, however, Charles insisted men still dominated society to the point of determining the rate and extent of female reproduction. Her study of birth control practices convinced her that husbands in all classes were actually more inclined than their wives to perceive the advantages of limitation and to use or encourage the use of contraceptives.[23] Charles's assumptions were in part confirmed by the experience of some of the birth control clinics. The Cambridge facility, for example, reported that, middle- and upper-class beliefs to the contrary, working-class men were not endowed with an excess of lust and a paucity of self-restraint. Most of the men whose wives came to the clinic were "extremely moderate and self-controlled" and frequently persuaded their spouses to seek advice when other methods of limitation had failed.[24] Charles thought the stage might not be far off when births were either accidental or initiated by wives who wanted children.

In shifting the blame for the dwindling family from women to men, Charles was trying to illustrate the sterilizing effects of a male-dominated capitalist system and advance a notion of companionate marriage in which there would be equality of interests, decision making, and responsibility, particularly in the area of family planning. At the moment, she concluded, women were more interested in spacing the birth of children; their husbands, motivated by profit-driven socioeconomic aspirations, in preventing it entirely.[25] Unless men and women made the necessary emotional adjustments and joined in the building of a new cooperative society, such as in the Soviet Union where children fulfilled a true social function, the nation could face a fierce and destructive sex war when the population crisis finally came. Not only would women have great power to demand changes, dominate government and the professions, and even relegate men to the home, but to complete this misogynist nightmare she predicted that with sex determination and artificial insemination not far off, sufficient girl babies of high genetic quality would soon be able to be produced with only a small serf-like class of men needed to carry on the race.[26]

Rather than abandon capitalism or the male sex, most people were inclined to explore less extreme solutions to the depopulation problem such as tax rebates, marriage loans, baby bonuses, improved pre- and postnatal maternity care and benefits, better infant and children welfare schemes, nurseries for working mothers, housing subsidies, and wage-supplementing family allowances. This was the position taken by most of the important women's groups such as the Women's Institutes, the Mother's Union, NUSEC, and the National Council of Women. Even some members of the Women's Cooperative Guild, who were suspicious of any efforts to increase the birthrate, nevertheless conceded that the plea for more daughters to halt the nation's slide toward race suicide was too compelling to ignore.

Eva Hubback, the influential principal of Morley College, had the Eugenics Society's blessing when in 1937 she appealed to NUSEC and the National Council of Women not to "let our race become extinguished as is today foreshadowed." She succeeded in persuading their executive councils to pass resolutions, probably drafted by Blacker, favoring family planning instead of birth control and investigating "whether the time had come to consider what means should be taken to encourage the increase in the birth-rate among the physically and mentally fit."

In carrying the resolutions, Hubback had to contend with the strong opposition of Helena Normanton, the senior female barrister in England. Like a number of more militant feminists in the interwar years who feared that women were abandoning the prewar struggle for equality and acquiescing in the old idea of separate spheres that relegated them to domesticity and motherhood, Normanton warned that passage of the resolutions would undermine women's gains and serve as an invitation to provide cannon fodder for the next war. Conflicts within feminist ranks over what constituted a woman's "natural sphere" had led to a split in NUSEC in 1927. A minority of older, egalitarian advocates of complete sex equality had rejected the claims of Rathbone, Hubback, and other new feminists that the endowment of motherhood and family allowances should become the central goal of women's organizations and that there was no fundamental incompatibility between the attainment of equal rights and a woman's place in the home. A decade later, Hubback, herself the mother of three, pointed out that if current population trends continued much longer the issue would be irrelevant: there would not be enough women around to preserve and enjoy those rights and to win more of them.[27]

The Eugenics Society was less concerned with women's rights than with support for eugenic family planning when it decided to pay for a membership in the National Council of Women as a way to keep eugenics under consideration in the women's movement and to be in a position to advance resolutions of interest. In this the society worked closely with those members who, like Hubback and Lady Denman, were also active in the major women's groups. Though these organizations welcomed Eugenics Society lecturers and heredity exhibits at their meetings, on balance they proved to be less receptive to most controversial eugenic issues than the society hoped. The one notable exception was their willingness to endorse sterilization plans to contain the proliferation of the mentally retarded and others with serious hereditary afflictions who were incapable of or unwilling to regulate their own fertility. Despite the opposition of the Labour party, even the Women's Cooperative Guild agreed. Like other women's groups, it was emboldened to do so by the alarming revelations contained in the Wood report on mental deficiency in 1930 and the Brock committee's approval of voluntary sterilization four years later.

Women's organizations were, however, like feminists in general, much more interested in the 1930s with improving opportunities and living and working conditions for the members of their sex than they were in preventing the genetically suspect from breeding too often. Birth control, as Blacker discovered when he contemplated merging the Eugenics Society with the NBCA, was valued by its female proponents for the ability it gave women to space pregnancies and to plan and regulate their lives in accordance with economic, social, and personal considerations. Even support for sterilization was couched in terms of eliminating the dreadful burden of mental illness and feeblemindedness that the mothers of tainted children, primarily in the Social Problem Group, had to bear generation after generation.

The response of feminists to revived accusations of a rebellion against motherhood and of selfish couples preferring cars to prams, stirred up by the depopulation scare, was, more often than not, to argue that women were not repudiating marriage and children but responding rationally and responsibly to an environment they found increasingly inhospitable to family life. In their eagerness to find out "Why Girls Say No"—as one newspaper put it—demographic investigators needed to pay more attention to what it would take to get them to say yes.[28] For most women's groups, as for an increasingly larger number of people in general, part if not all of the answer lay in the area of family endowments. It was a conclusion eugenicists also reached very reluctantly, and one with which many of them were singularly uncomfortable.

"Yea, I Have a Goodly Heritage!":
 Eugenics and Family Allowances

From its beginnings the eugenics movement favored selective inducements to marriage and parenthood among the genetically fit while opposing interventionist measures likely to encourage the reproduction of their hereditary opposites. Galton's utopian community of privileged Eugenes who married young and bred often was a crude example of a pronatalist paradise some eugenicists dreamed of before the Great War. Despite the negative thrust of eugenic policy in the postwar years directed against the recklessly philoprogenitive poor, the ideal of the favored eugenic family remained, supported by race-enhancing marriage bonuses and scientifically crafted maternity and child endowments. Proponents might disagree about who should receive the benefits and quarrel over definitions of hereditary fitness and the methods for determining it, but most of them still believed the ablest stock, at least, was as identifiable as the worst. The most favored types were graphically portrayed in the pronatalist eugenics iconography of the 1920s and 1930s. Handsome, virile men and attractive, buxom women in classical dress, or sometimes nude, were depicted lifting up the torch of life or a chubby baby, while surrounded by four healthy offspring in various stages of undress, exuding confidence in the knowledge, "Yea, I Have a Goodly Heritage!"[29]

In reality, as eugenicists knew, the number of children in eugenically desirable families was on average no more than half that in the illustrations adorning their propaganda. Selectively reconciling the real with the ideal in an era when social reformers were increasingly demanding a universal system of family allowances to alleviate poverty and halt the fall in the birthrate created political, tactical, and ideological problems for eugenicists which were compounded by the depopulation scare. In contrast to its growing accommodation with the birth control movement, the Eugenics Society, despite many overtures from the Family Endowment Society founded in 1924, remained much more ambivalent about what its relationship should be to that organization and family allowances as a way of increasing the "goodly heritage" of future generations.[30]

The ideas of family endowment that had emerged before the war contained a strong eugenic component. Socialist eugenicists in particular, such as Caleb Saleeby, H. G. Wells, and Sidney Webb, stressed the importance of improved maternity services and grants, pensions, free milk, nurseries, and other inducements to fertility as likely to encourage the best representatives of working-class society to have more children. They would in all probability still not have as many as "the thriftless and irresponsible—largely casual laborers and other denizens of the one-roomed tenements of our great cities," as Webb described the unfit, but these allowances would help reduce the differential.[31] If most orthodox eugenicists were wary of such arguments, they did join with their socialist colleagues in welcoming Lloyd George's introduction of modest income tax child allowances in 1909 as a particularly important precedent to be extended in subsequent budgets.[32]

What most eugenicists found appealing in the income tax legislation was, however, the class-specificity of such an approach, rather than the precedent it might set for less discriminate allowances to the millions of couples whose income fell below the taxpaying minimum. This was of less concern to such professed eugenic sympathizers as Eleanor Rathbone, Eva Hubback, Mary Stocks, Maude Royden, and other leaders of the family endowment movement, when they promised maternal and child maintenance allowances would help redress the problem of differential fertility. The allowances, they and their socialist supporters in the eugenics camp claimed, would do so by raising the birthrate of the artisan and professional classes while dramatically lowering that of the poorest classes whose high level of unplanned reproduction was presumed to be a consequence of low economic status and a lack of self-respect.[33]

In making her case to the Eugenics Society in 1924, Rathbone, who believed fertility declined as the standard of living improved, reasoned that since lower-class couples were already having as many children as their physical capacity allowed without cash allowances, there was nothing to be lost in trying them and everything to gain. Moreover, if they took into account varying family needs, which the present wage structure in the country did not, and were graded on family size and the parents' standard of living, the allowances, to be paid by employers and the state, would probably have the salubrious effect of at least moderately increasing the birthrate of "brain workers" and skilled workers.[34]

Rathbone's arguments, laid out in her influential book *The Disinherited Family* (1924), were rooted in her strong feminist and socialist conviction that family allowances, determined by the number of children in the home and paid directly to their mothers, were a logical extension of the vote and necessary for the achievement of economic and social equality in a male-dominated society. As a student of the economics of motherhood, she believed the problem women faced was less one of equal wages than of the undervalued, dependent position of the housewife who should be paid directly and fairly by the state for her special contribution of certifiably "sound" children to the community and race. Rathbone, in seeking the support of the Eugenics Society for the recently established FES, knew it would take more than a promise of certification and references to the experience of other countries, such as France, to overcome skepticism and fears that family allowances, far from diminishing the birthrate of the "wrong people," would have just the opposite effect.[35]

Major Darwin, for example, had expressed grave reservations about the endowment of motherhood as a eugenic weapon when it had been raised in 1917 by the Equal Pay and Family Committee, the wartime forerunner of the Family Endowment Society. Convinced as he was of the close correlation between earned wealth and natural eugenic fitness, Darwin believed the artificial raising of family income would have little appreciable effect on the quality of offspring. It might instead make low-paid husbands even less responsible if their wives received allowances. Because economic pressures weighed more heavily on the domestic considerations of the better classes, Darwin reasoned it would make much more sense to reduce the costs of rearing and educating children through tax benefits, scholarships, and inheritance laws prohibiting full estates from going to children if there were fewer than four in the family. The costs of family allowances, by contrast, threatened to increase the tax burden on the fittest classes and exacerbate rather than alleviate the dysgenic patterns of differential fertility. Endowments would do nothing to alter the earlier marriage age of manual workers and the longer exposure of their wives to pregnancy. Moreover, he warned, by improving conditions without improving racial quality, the allowances would reduce even further the selective death rate in large, impoverished families.[36]

Despite R. A. Fisher's strong support of Rathbone's efforts, Darwin remained skeptical. Fisher claimed that allowances, if graded according to income and need, would assure that the fittest candidates for parenthood would receive the benefits of rearing larger families. Perhaps equally important, they would also lose the social and economic advantages they now enjoyed by having only one or two children. In spite of his respect for the young geneticist, Darwin simply did not believe it possible in the postwar political climate for the better classes to receive equity. The demands of the poor would, if anything, become more insistent, he predicted, and in response the government would shift even more of the sterilizing burden of maintaining them onto the backs of the fit. At the same time, however, Darwin once again saw the inevitability of change and, however much he disliked it, conceded "the eugenist must consider whether in place of mere opposing this reform, it would not be wiser to endeavour to insure that the tiller of maternity is turned in the right direction." The tack he was prepared to consider, largely at Fisher's urging, involved proportional allowances based upon parental income and financed in part by contributory occupational pools in different professions to insure that the best stock would receive the most.[37]

Beveridge's pioneering introduction in 1925 of such a system for teachers and senior administrators in the London School of Economics was a model eugenicists hoped could be extended to other desirable professions.[38] Without putting aside its belief that qualitative distinctions in family allowances would be impossible to legislate, the Eugenics Society emphasized from 1926 on that while it favored the provision of family allowances "by the establishment of graded equalization pools and other systems calculated to have a eugenic effect," it regarded as "wholly dysgenic the provision of allowances through flat-rate payments by the State."[39]

Fisher, who was largely responsible for drafting the society's statement and, later, for seeing that the eugenic advantages of selective occupational allowances were included in the FES's testimony before the Royal Commission on Civil Service in 1930, thought Rathbone and some of her other colleagues in the FES overestimated eugenic hostility to their proposals.[40] This was only true, he wrote in a review of *The Disinherited Family*, so long as advocates thought in terms of a flat rate as adopted in France rather than in terms of payments proportional to the salaries of groups receiving them. Trying to assuage the doubts of trade unionists and Labour politicians who feared family allowances might be used to justify reducing or keeping wages low, Rathbone was perhaps less appreciative of these eugenic distinctions than Fisher might have wished. He knew, however, from his own experience in the FES that others agreed with him: if based upon proportional, graded payments, family allowances "might constitute the most effective social achievement yet devised for benefiting the human race."[41]

The family allowance system was, for Fisher, an antidote to the dysgenic effects of birth control which Galton himself had recognized. In an FES memorandum to the Royal Commission on Civil Service, Fisher warned, "In about thirty years, more or less . . . whatever is worth keeping in the genetic potentialities of the upper and middle classes in England and Scotland will have been reduced to half its present quality."[42] His hypothesis that the economic determinants of family limitation became genetically fixed when practiced over generations led him to tell a French eugenics conference in 1926, "The fertility of the upper classes is only maintained at its low level by the selective promotion of the least fertile members of the lower classes." Family allowances proportional to the father's income and covering the "full net cost of children" could nullify or reverse the social and economic advantages of having fewer children and gradually tend to raise the fertility of the superior classes. The economic advantages enjoyed by "the less fertile stock" may seem a small thing, he told his Gallic hosts, but their abolition may determine whether a civilization survives or perishes.[43]

Not all of Fisher's Eugenics Society colleagues in the FES shared his certainty that economic motives and the social advantages wealth brought them were the main reasons wealthier couples practiced birth control more than their poorer contemporaries. Hubback, like Rathbone and a number of others whose feminist arguments Fisher discounted as "unscientific sex antagonism," believed the diminishing birthrate had much more to do with the quality of life, the growth of leisure, and the expanding opportunities available to women. Family allowances, they predicted, would bring more of these benefits to the poor, along with better health; rather than induce them to have more children, maternal grants would encourage women to have smaller families to sustain and enjoy their improved standard of living.[44]

Though Rathbone, in *The Dishinherited Family*, claimed to disagree with eugenicist concepts of "bad stock," her language was often permeated with references to the excessive fertility of "those who have sunk into the lowest strata because they are physically, mentally or morally degenerate." She compared the thrifty, ambitious artisans and professional classes, who should have more children, to the unskilled "dregs of society," who already had far too many. Family allowances, by making possible "those higher standards with regard to housing, orderly living, and the status of women . . . are the best antidote to excessive and dysgenic breeding."[45] For the most part, however, FES propaganda was restrained in its use of eugenic arguments that might antagonize much larger socialist and feminist constituencies.

Despite Rathbone's occasional rhetoric and the presence of several Eugenics Society members in the small FES, the association, at Darwin's urging, remained tentative at best throughout the 1920s. While willing to concede a good deal to Fisher, who was the most emphatic champion of family allowances in the Eugenics Society, Darwin was obviously uncertain and at times confused by his young friend's convoluted reasoning. The inclusion of Fisher's questionable family endowment arguments in his most important book, *The Genetical Theory of Natural Selection* (1930), did little to assuage Darwin's fears that the poor might receive yet another fertility subsidy.[46] His anxieties were shared by many members of the Eugenics Society council when in 1929 they struggled to work out another statement on family allowances deploring flat rate payments and more taxation for social services. They instead endorsed equalization pools among employing bodies or salaried professions and skilled occupations.[47]

Eugenic interest in family allowances, so long as they were protected by proper safeguards, was substantially increased in the 1930s by the fear of depopulation and the observed need for more positive eugenic policies. With the birthrate at its lowest point in 1933 and the prospect of the population falling by one-quarter in a generation, it was difficult, even for the most unreconstructed of eugenicists, to talk very convincingly about reckless breeding. Some of them continued to try, however, as Blacker discovered when he began to introduce an expanded idea of family endowment into Eugenics Society deliberations. Fisher, in his eagerness to persuade the organization to embrace family allowances, accused the new general secretary of stirring up trouble by being overly cautious in bringing the issue before the council. He was unpersuaded by Blacker's increasingly angry assurances that while the two of them might find Rathbone's *Disinherited Family* compelling, many of their colleagues who saw it as another dysgenic scheme of state paternalism did not and would have to be shown alternatives.[48]

Fisher was frustrated in part because of his success in getting the FES to pay more attention to eugenic fears by directing some of its pronatalist campaign at people in selected professions and white collar groups as well as the poor. In addition to civil servants, teachers and clergymen, whose mental, moral, and social qualities were presumably above the average and would "enrich the race," were targeted for special consideration.[49] The *Eugenics Review* nevertheless worried about the depth of the FES's commitment to qualitative selection.

Eldon Moore, its editor, who agreed family endowment was the most practicable scheme for positive eugenics, complained in 1932 that Fisher was the only person to have anything eugenic to say at a recent family endowment conference where the impact of the depression on the poor was discussed. Persuaded, nevertheless, that selective family allowances in conjunction with sterilization and birth control offered the best hope to prevent the "further degradation of the race" and to take some "small steps forward to develop a slightly finer, sounder, saner man or woman," Moore offered a £10 prize for the best essay outlining how family allowances might contribute to this end.[50]

As Blacker knew all too well, many of his colleagues considered such undertakings an exercise in futility. They did not believe that any program seeking to preserve the eugenic value of desirable sectors of society, such as the salaried and professional classes, was politically possible even if selective enough to be conceptually valid. Darwin's successor, Bernard Mallet, for example, warned that the experience of family allowances in France and Belgium indicated that only a flat rate payment that was too small to have any effect on the fertility of the better-off had any chance of parliamentary approval.[51] The whole scheme "smacked of economic egalitarianism" and socialism as far as some eugenicists were concerned. They nevertheless recognized, as one medical officer of health predicted, the impending fall in population would probably result in the government subsidizing parenthood along with agriculture. He only hoped it would not result in the production of "more half-wits in the sacred name of equality," but knowing the times, he thought the country would be fortunate to escape with a compromise to subsidize only "three-quarter wits."[52]

Belief that the fear of depopulation, when added to the demands to help working-class families impoverished by the depression, would inevitably lead to the implementation of some type of family endowment program, strengthened the hand of those who argued it would be prudent and political for the Eugenics Society to try to play a role in designing the plan. One member, in urging the organization to lead the way in lobbying for the restoration of the cuts made in children allowances in the 1931 emergency budget, looked to the advocacy of family subsidies as a way of bringing eugenics "straight into the centre of the political limelight." William McDougall, who had first described the eugenic potential of family allowances in 1906, expected in 1933 to see them universally adopted in the near future and spoke of the political advantages to be gained by joining with humanitarian social reformers and feminists in expediting their adoption.[53]

Blacker, whose strategy of reform eugenics was based upon linking the Eugenics Society to other groups and causes that could advance at least some of its aims, did not need much convincing, though his council, which was deeply divided, certainly did. A two-year effort from 1932 to 1934 by a family allowance subcommittee under Fisher's chairmanship failed to reach agreement on a plan to present to the society, or a pamphlet to publicize its position. The meetings, which were frequently held with representatives of the FES, were often stormy, taking their cue from the strained relationship between Blacker and Fisher. Unable to agree on whether to prepare a short leaflet simply stressing the eugenic potential of family allowances or a more elaborate pamphlet describing Fisher's complex system of graded equalization pools, the two men maneuvered behind the scenes to force the resignation of the other.[54]

Despite the prolonged quarrels and his brief departure from the committee, Blacker managed to draft a succinct statement on "Eugenics and Family Allowances" calling upon "all men and women who possess good health, good character and good brains" to leave at least four children. It outlined how employers might pay a fixed proportion of their wage bill into an equalization pool to be distributed to employees on the basis of the number and ages of children they had. The psychiatrist Lionel Penrose, though increasingly skeptical of eugenic efforts to unite biology, medicine, and society, added his own memorandum recommending allowances be paid on a sliding scale determined by the father's income while mothers were to be given bonuses in inverse correlation to their age and in direct correlation to their mental ability.[55]

In the end, however, the Family Allowance Sub-Committee could not agree on any statement. Moreover, Blacker's pointed rejection of any state-aided, flat-rate schemes to be employed in conjunction with variable occupational pools was not enough to convince a majority of the Eugenics Society council that such indiscriminate payments could be avoided in any family allowance plan likely to find acceptance. Unwilling to endorse the general secretary's desire to support a more active campaign, the council contented itself with a reassertion of its earlier carefully phrased statement on the subject. By way of compromise, however, it agreed to Blacker's and Carr-Saunders's recommendation that in light of "the approaching steady and deep decline in the population, which threatens to become a menace to white civilization and especially to the Anglo-Saxon races," family endowment programs in other countries and the replacement rates in various occupations in England should be studied by a new Positive Eugenics Committee.[56]

Though Blacker was especially interested in the pronatalist efforts of Germany and Italy to stimulate marriages and fertility, David Glass, who was hired to undertake the inquiry, found little to encourage proponents of marriage bonuses and family allowances wherever they were tried. In some countries, such as France and Belgium, where family allowances had the longest history, the system was never really designed to increase the birthrate but to ease the burdens of married workers. But no country offered enough benefits to overcome the economic reservations young couples had about having children.[57] Even in fascist Italy, Kuczynski noted in a follow-up analysis, the number of births actually fell from 1,095,000 in 1926, when allowances were introduced, to 955,000 ten years later.[58] The major flaw Glass and other investigators discovered in every scheme was a failure to understand the complexity of factors which influenced the fertility strategies in all social classes. If economic motives appeared on the surface to be predominant, many other considerations such as housing, attractions and opportunities outside of the home, changing aspirations, ambitions, and perceptions of the future also had an effect on how the costs of raising children were calculated by different people.

Only Nazi Germany, which Glass visited in 1935 on behalf of the Positive Eugenics Committee, had seen a sharp rise in the birthrate, but a close evaluation of the reasons suggested it might be a temporary result of a surge in nuptiality stimulated by some 700,000 marriage loans. Once the pool of potential couples who had delayed marrying in the 1920s and early 1930s was exhausted, the birthrate, Kuczynski suspected, was likely to level off and begin to fall once again. He also observed that despite an increase in births from 970,000 in 1933 to 1,280,000 in 1936, the net reproduction rate in Germany was at 0.89, still below replacement.[59]

Eugenicist defenders of the FES, such as Hubback, acknowledged that more substantial payments from public and private sources, graded to the economic standards of different sections of the community, would probably be required to stimulate eugenically desirable fertility. But, she added, it was still too soon to know if the Germans and Italians, who were especially determined to increase the birthrate, would prove successful.[60] Even if family allowances failed to stimulate or sustain the general birthrate in England, the *Eugenics Review* concluded, the Positive Eugenics Committee must continue to explore how far family allowances may succeed in raising the fertility of "biologically well-endowed persons."[61] It was a task passed on in part to the Population Investigation Committee as well in 1936, which gave the Eugenics Society council another excuse for putting off taking a firm position on family allowances for at least another year or two.[62]

Nazis and Eugenicists in a "Baby Mad" World

With prophecies of declining population proliferating and Germany, Italy, and now Great Britain advocating marriage loans, baby bonuses, and all sorts of endowment schemes, the Conservative paper *John Bull* wondered if the whole world was going "baby mad." The linking of Great Britain to the fascist powers, especially Nazi Germany with its compulsory, punitive sterilization laws and virulent anti-Semitism wrapped in the eugenic mantle of race hygiene, was particularly embarrassing and extremely troublesome for Eugenics Society demographers. Within a few months of the Nazis' coming to power in 1933, Blacker began to receive reports about the dangers to the eugenics movement implicit in Hitler's policies. Aubrey Lewis, the psychiatrist and senior medical officer at the Maudsley Hospital, examined the new German sterilization laws announced in July and described Nazi eugenics as a "queer mixture of orthodox eugenics and racial hate-stuff, undisguised," which eugenicists would have to avoid. Writing from Cambridge where zeal for the eugenics cause among undergraduates was fast waning by the end of the year, Michael Pease complained to Blacker, "Hitler . . . has been largely responsible—he has made eugenics stink in the nostrils of any decent folk."[63]

Even before the publication of the new sterilization laws, Huxley suggested to "Pip"—as Blacker's close friends addressed him—that the *Eugenics Review* publish an article distancing the British movement from the "so-called eugenic policy" being developed in Germany. "It is mere pseudo-science," he wrote in May, "and it would be a great pity if we were tarred with that brush."[64] Blacker responded at once with a letter to the *Lancet* in which he emphasized the Eugenics Society's strong disagreements with the compulsory features of German eugenic sterilization laws, the breadth of what were classified as "hereditary defects," and the attempt to direct the legislation against a particular race, mainly the Jews. "If the German nation as a whole decides to discourage the propagation of Jews, that is its affair," he wrote. "But let it not be alleged, on the most dubious scientific grounds, that such a measure has a eugenic justification." Blacker was especially worried that Nazi policies might turn the British public against the modest, voluntary sterilization proposals being evaluated by Laurence Brock's interdepartmental committee. The general secretary assured readers that if adopted in Britain they would be very different from those introduced in Germany.[65]

The same point was emphasized repeatedly in the *Eugenics Review* which deplored the racial and anti-Semitic dimensions of Nazi sterilization legislation as well as its punitive application by "eugenic courts" to a number of criminal offenses. The Eugenics Society council quickly passed a resolution deprecating "the use of the term Eugenics to justify racial animosities," and in another letter to the *Lancet* and other journals Blacker stressed that English eugenicists would never permit sterilization to be misused "as an instrument of tyranny by racial or social majorities." For its part, the *Lancet* endorsed Blacker's assurances and regretted the support of so many learned scientists and eugenicists in Germany for the "odious racial and nationalistic" policies of their government.

Opponents of eugenics, however, were not about to accept the *Lancet*'s assurances that English eugenicists were more restrained, critical, and scientifically honest. Detractors were quick to use the Nazi experience as an example of the sort of "eugenic dictatorship" Britain would face if the Eugenics Society ever had its way. Blacker was only one of several eugenicists who recognized early on the threat such an argument posed to eugenics and urged the members to take every opportunity to emphasize the differences between Germany and their own country.[66] The general secretary was also advised in 1933 by a eugenicist M.P., A. W. H. James, to steer clear of the British Union of Fascists whose representatives had expressed an interest in compulsory sterilization and suggested the possibility of working with the Eugenics Society on the question. Not only was its endorsement unneeded and unwanted, James warned, but any hint of fascist support would antagonize Labour and ruin whatever progress had been made among the rank and file. Already encumbered by charges of being prejudiced and antidemocratic, the further eugenics could be separated from the Nazis and the fascists the better.[67]

In the decade before the war there were always a few individual eugenicists of some visibility, such as the Conservative M.P. Sir Arnold Wilson, who were open admirers of Hitler or, like Sir Josiah Stamp, of Mussolini. In his Galton Lecture of 1934, Stamp praised the Italian dictator as the kind of "genius-leader" the nation needed to save it from degeneration and likened him to Newton and Faraday.[68] But there were many other respectable people in politics, science, journalism, the church, and elsewhere who were no less attracted to the vigorous efficiency of the fascist states and, perhaps, some of their racial policies, but had no eugenic affiliation.

Blacker, not surprisingly, was most worried about the assorted "cranks, misguided enthusiasts and irresponsible propagandists" who were drawn to eugenics where some of them tried to "out-do Herr Julius Streicher in vilipending the Jews" and other dysgenic aliens who they imagined were threatening to take over the country. Many of these zealots were antidemocratic, deploring the corruption and weakness of the British government and praising the fascists for their sense of racial responsibility. Though they were, as Blacker claimed, at most a small, embarrassing minority on the fringes of the eugenics movement, they were nevertheless considered to be exceedingly dangerous to the cause by the leaders of the Eugenics Society, who tried to keep them at bay.[69] Blacker hoped his program of positive reforms planned and carried out in conjunction with less suspect organizations and movements, many of them peopled with socialists, would help distance British eugenics from the stigma of totalitarian fascism. But in the end, he acknowledged after World War II when eugenics had lost whatever credibility it had achieved in the 1930s, the movement had been overwhelmed by events and the horrific, nightmarish consequences of the Nazis' grotesque racial theories.[70]

If eugenicists denied any direct ideological ties to fascism and Nazism, and publicly deplored the racial theories propounded in the Third Reich to justify compulsory sterilization, anti-Semitism, and the persecution of allegedly inferior peoples, they were keenly interested in the pronatalist campaigns launched in Germany and Italy to increase the marriage and birth rates. In this they were not alone; the press was filled with accounts of German and Italian efforts to stimulate population growth, frequently emphasizing that declining fertility was characteristic of the white races everywhere. What made the fascist powers' endeavors to raise their birthrates so important was the potential threat they posed to Great Britain and the powers of compulsion they could supposedly employ.

Though some papers envied the centralized planning and efficiency Hitler and Mussolini could bring to the problem, most were critical of compulsory methods and skeptical they would really work. Their doubts were confirmed by much-publicized reports showing that despite more than ten years of inducements and appeals the birthrate in crowded Italy had by 1937 fallen to 22.7 per 1,000, some 25 percent below the rate that prevailed when Mussolini came to power in the early 1920s. Even the Nazis' heralded successes in raising fertility during their first three years from under 18 per 1,000 to 19 per 1,000 appeared to falter in 1937 when 5,000 fewer births were recorded.

The nearly moribund *New Generation*, reviving pre-1914 neo-Malthusian arguments that overpopulation caused war, favored giving the Germans the territorial concessions they demanded in order to buy more time to allow their birthrate, which was already half what it was in 1900, to fall even further. Not only was the editor, R. B. Kerr, certain "Hitler bears us no ill will," he was sure that with German parents rearing on average only about two children, they were not about to permit them to be used as cannon fodder in another war.[71] It was a demographic variation on the theme of appeasement which few others played, although the association of fascist population policies with the production of cannon fodder was familiar enough. In the end, most analysts of vital statistics suspected, couples in Berlin or Rome would or would not have children for many of the same reasons influencing their contemporaries in Paris and London.

However much reform eugenicists complained of the damage the Nazi sterilization laws had done to the English cause, some of them thought it important to pay close attention to German programs. "What will happen in Germany in four years is problematical," one council member wrote Blacker. "If the present people remain many interesting eugenic changes will have occurred and they will have an effect on their moral outlook." The Positive Eugenics Committee agreed that aside from compulsory sterilization Nazi eugenic policies were still unclear and arranged to send Glass to Berlin for the 1935 International Population Conference to gain a better understanding of German demographic planning.[72] Like Huxley, who had visited earlier, Glass found that most of the Nazi eugenic exhibits were little more than anti-Jewish diatribes or shrines for the worship of the Nordic cult. As a result Blacker, who described Germany as suffering from a "collective psychosis," was reluctant to accede to the request of another member, Ursula Grant Duff, to call a special meeting of the Eugenics Society to discuss Nazi eugenics. It would, in his judgment, only antagonize Labour and create associations in the public's mind English eugenicists needed at all costs to avoid.[73]

Like her husband, Duff had joined the society shortly after it was founded in 1907; she had served as honorary secretary for seven years and was also active on behalf of the eugenics cause in the National Council of Women. Fluent in German and a frequent visitor to that country, she was impressed with its potential for eugenic innovation even while critical of the "Aryan race non-sense" its leaders spouted. At her recommendation the Eugenics Society purchased a set of photographs on "Rassenkünde" from the Reichsmuseum für Gesellschafts und Wirtschaftskünd in Dusseldorf, and on other occasions she sent along examples of Nazi race propaganda, though she repeatedly insisted she was not sympathetic to Hitler. On the contrary, she was certain in 1936 that he was preparing for war and suggested to Lord Horder the start of a campaign to remind the Germans of the dysgenic consequences of international conflict. The French after all had been suffering from them since the revolution had destroyed its aristocracy and Napoleon "the flower of its manhood."[74]

Blacker was himself ambivalent about how the Eugenics Society should respond to Nazi population policies, particularly when the German birthrate began to increase under the short-lived stimulus of marriage bonuses and family allowances. Though it began to fall again slightly in 1937, the rate, at 18.9 per 1,000, was still significantly above the 14.9 per 1,000 in England, and with a net reproduction rate of 0.934 in 1939 was approaching unity or replacement. Blacker was forced to conclude that the German reversal was "substantial and remarkable"; it showed something could be done about the birthrate.[75] On the one hand, the general secretary wanted to dissociate English eugenics as much as possible from its Nazi variety, but on the other, he was impressed by German accomplishments. At one point in 1938 he thought it would be helpful for the *Eugenics Review* to have a regular correspondent in the Third Reich but worried it might be seen as showing sympathy for that country's authoritarian methods.

Under Blacker's direction, the Eugenics Society helped a number of German refugees, some of them Jewish, who had been active in the birth control movement, but he was reluctant to permit them to address society-sponsored meetings out of a fear of being drawn into the bitter political disputes in the country over how to respond to the fascist threat.[76] It is less clear how much he was worried about conflicts within his own ranks where a minority, at least, looked to the fascist powers as possible architects of the eugenic utopia that seemed further away than ever in Britain.

It was the menace of underpopulation rather than fascism that Blacker believed should preoccupy the time and resources of his organization. Whatever solutions were recommended, however, they would have to be free of qualitative tests and avoid any hint of compulsion. When in 1938 Lionel Penrose proposed a eugenic sliding scale of family allowances based upon parental income, age, and tested mental capacity, the general secretary expressed strong doubts that the awarding of benefits conditional upon any physical, mental, or moral examinations had any chance of acceptance. They would justifiably be seen as authoritarian and "savoring of dictatorship." As a result, Blacker concluded, any system to promote childbearing would, as in France, have to be implemented without discriminating tests on a statutory basis.[77]

Despite Blacker's caution, prominent advocates of family allowances such as Lord Dawson recommended to the Royal Society of Medicine the introduction along German lines of medically approved marriage loans of up to £200 to raise the quality of stock in the country. The obligation to repay would be reduced with each child and forgiven entirely after the fourth. The press, as Blacker feared, immediately responded with headlines blaring, "State Stork Bribes to Race. A1 Couples!" This, the *Sunday Pictorial* reported, was what was really behind the Nosey Parker bill permitting the government to require more information from the parents of newborn children.[78]

Though many accounts of the proposed "Loans to Aid Cupid" made wary references to the Nazis, more often than not they were viewed favorably as part of a larger plan for family allowances. The Labour party's *Daily Herald* was apprehensive that marriage loans and "baby bounties" might be used as racial and political weapons as in Germany to intimidate workers but was in part reassured by reports that the government would soon receive recommendations urging flat rate allowances of five shillings a week for a first child in a family and three shillings for each of the others. There was even talk of the payments being increased for children of the unemployed. Much of the discussion was not over whether family endowment was a good idea, but, as the economist Roy Harrod argued, whether it would be large enough to attract people before the spectacular decline in the population became unstoppable.[79]

For eugenic reformers who had increasingly tied the movement's fortunes to wider population interests, it was necessary to walk a narrow line between those who were prepared to accept family allowances as a way of increasing the overall birthrate in the country and those who continued to insist that unless selectivity could be assured, family allowances were inappropriate if not actually inimical to their interests. Their dilemma was evident in L. J. Cadbury's assertion in 1939 that eugenicists, after thirty years, now recognized they could not only be concerned with quality but with quantity, and could no longer "confine our research to those aspects of our population problem which interested Darwin and Galton, but must also pay attention to those raised by Malthus." He had already started to do his bit to halt the population slide by giving the employees of his large chocolate manufacturing company five shillings a week for each of their children.[80]

In response, the *Eugenics Review* acknowledged a much greater awareness of the importance of numbers, but only insofar as net reproduction could be brought up to unity in qualitative, eugenic terms. "We know," the editor wrote, "that the present differential fertility, though not biologically as disadvantageous as it has been, is still on the dysgenic side." This bow in the direction of a wider social distribution of hereditary fitness was translated on the eve of World War II into a modified revision of the Eugenics Society's statement on family allowances which cautiously allowed, "these might be provided by graded Equalisation Pools or other methods which would provide relief for parents in the higher occupational groups as well as in the lower."[81]

The tentativeness of the concession reflected the strong doubts about the wisdom of family allowances persisting within eugenic ranks. Some years earlier these doubts had driven Fisher to withdraw in frustration from Eugenics Society activities. Despite his efforts and those of other eugenicists in the FES, his colleagues continued to have much more confidence in the racial value of large tax rebates for children and the more extensive award of scholarships to "ease the financial burdens of parents producing children of superior ability."[82]

The Eugenics Society's wariness about family endowments was consistent with its coolness to any scheme it feared might increase the numbers of the poor. Its council, for example, was even more reluctant to support the work of the National Association of Maternity and Child Welfare Centres or its parent body, the National Council for Maternity and Child Welfare, though it was urged to do so by pro-Labour members like Stella Churchill. Individual members of the Eugenics Society regularly attended maternity and child welfare conferences, but the council did not formally agree until the mid-1930s that maternal mortality probably had a bearing on eugenics and "the prevention of infant mortality comes rather more into our province now that we are looking at population problems from the quantitative as well as the qualitative standpoint."[83]

It was prompted to do so by mounting concerns in the health community and in Parliament about the puzzling rise in maternal deaths and growing anxieties about the approaching shortage of potential mothers evident in the much-publicized net reproduction rate. Blacker recognized the fear of dying in childbirth might inhibit the willingness of thoughtful, tender-minded couples, who were probably eugenically well suited for reproduction, from having many children. But, he admitted in 1935, the Eugenics Society had no "formulated views on maternal mortality" despite the pressure of some members to develop a position in conjunction with the Obstetrics and Gynaecological Section of the Royal Society of Medicine.[84]

Any attempts perceived to interfere with natural selection, however, still elicited complaints from such people as the deputy medical supervisor of the Lancashire Medical Hospital about saving those with "the weakest and poorest blood." Too much intervention would only result in the further impoverishment of the "quality of our breeding mothers," George Pitt-Rivers reminded the softhearted, and would result in higher infant and maternal mortality a generation later. These contentious observations, made unblushingly at the World Congress on Population Problems in Berlin, only reinforced Blacker's dim view of the provocative anthropologist's "unrivalled aptitude for rubbing people the wrong way" and of turning them against the Eugenics Society.[85]

Blacker was painfully aware of the damage caused by having to deny repeatedly that eugenicists were crude Darwinists or heartless neo-Nazis who welcomed the deaths of poor mothers and their genetically flawed offspring. But the general secretary was himself in no rush to bring his organization into the infant and maternal welfare camp. Although the National Council for Maternity and Child Welfare had issued several invitations to affiliate in the past, Blacker was not convinced to accept them until 1939 when he did so as a way of deflecting criticism and as a potentially useful facet of the Eugenics Society's recent endorsement of a more comprehensive and positive view of family planning. Like many other eugenicists, however, Blacker was never very comfortable with the link and tried to keep the society's involvement to a minimum.[86] Some of his influential allies wanted the society to do more, but Blacker knew that a number of his less than tactful colleagues could see little advantage in preserving the fragile lives of dysgenic children. Even worse, he was constantly fearful they might say so in public and "do us much harm."[87]

His own opinion, however, was evident in his response to Ursula Duff's request during the war for the Eugenics Society to take up the problem of infant mortality and use the organization's considerable resources to support maternal and child welfare activities. "Do you yourself," he asked almost rhetorically, "consider that the lowering of infantile mortality is, in general, desirable on eugenic grounds? Clearly it is desirable on purely quantitative demographic grounds, but what about the eugenic?"[88] It was essentially the same neo-Darwinian question eugenicists had been asking since before the First World War when they had first confronted the issue. They had made a temporary tactical accommodation with the infant and maternal welfare movement during that conflict, but had never really resolved the ideological doubts and disagreements about natural and artificial selection their decision engendered.

Family allowances, with their threat of nonselective flat rate payments to the poor, raised many of the same problems for eugenicists, including reformers like Blacker. However much they talked about the importance of nurture as well as nature and agreed that hereditary quality was distributed more widely throughout the social spectrum than their predecessors recognized, at the core of their thinking the conviction remained that genetic deficiency, manifested in physiological and mental capacity and in socioeconomic behavior, was more heavily distributed among the lower classes.

There is no evidence that decades of eugenic propaganda had any influence one way or the other on the government's indifference to family endowment schemes before the Second World War. Though there were undoubtedly many people in official positions who shared, to varying degrees, eugenic assumptions about different classes, most civil servants and members of Parliament probably viewed it as a rather esoteric science which, even if to some extent true, aroused too much controversy.[89] In addition, with the exception of the Population (Statistics) Act, the government in the 1930s did not legislatively respond to the depopulation scare and even then it was in support of the argument that more information was needed before any pronatalist policies could be recommended.

Cabinet rejection of special fertility censuses and of vociferous demands for the appointment of a royal commission suggests the government had far fewer concerns about the menace of underpopulation than the dire projections of demographic experts and frantic stories in the press might have been expected to stir up. Indeed, during the debates on the subject in Parliament the government's spokesmen were, like the registrar-general, invariably skeptical or cautious. While admitting since the mid-1920s that the birthrate was below replacement, he was not persuaded it would remain so and could see no justification for taking remedial measures until the trend was clearer and the reasons for it understood. This position was if anything strengthened when in 1934 the relentless fall in the postwar birthrate stopped and in subsequent years showed at least slight signs of being reversed.

As a result, although there was a good deal of parliamentary rhetoric about the adoption of family allowances to stimulate fertility, the government was never in danger of being stampeded into accepting expensive pronatalist programs it did not want. A majority of members in both houses were dubious of demographic arguments for family endowment, however else they felt about the advantages or disadvantages of baby bounties. Neville Chamberlain's expressed anxieties in 1935 about the approaching shortage of "citizens of the right breed" to sustain the empire were interpreted by eugenicists and family allowance enthusiasts as the reason for his restoring the 1931 cuts in tax rebates for children, but there is no evidence that he or the government expected the birthrate of the hard-pressed, taxpaying classes to soar as a result. They had not had that result in the past and though by 1939 the total annual rebates exceeded £87 million, more than twice what they were a decade earlier, the families of rate-paying couples steadily shrank further and further below replacement.[90]

The evidence from other European countries where family endowment measures were introduced was no more encouraging to the pronatalist cause. Contemporaries tended to extract different meanings from vital statistics depending upon their varying demographic strategies and comparative analyses of economic and military dangers. Although the Eugenics Society was far less sanguine about the birthrate than was the government, it agreed with those political leaders who insisted that substantial research into the causes of declining fertility was necessary before concrete demographic policies could be adopted.

Behind the strategy of supporting and influencing what were purportedly neutral, scientific demographic research organizations, such as the Population Investigation Committee and Population and Economic Planning, lay the reform eugenicists' dream of achieving what they feared they could never accomplish on their own—the inclusion of qualitative, hereditary criteria in whatever population policies future governments advanced. Demographic realities, these eugenicists believed, would in the near future make the demands for official action irresistible. Whether they would be met through the appointment of a prestigious royal commission, as most analysts believed, or some other institutional mechanism, sound, reliable data in which the public could have confidence would have to provide the foundation of those policies. Such data, eugenicists believed, would by definition involve the creation of a "eugenic or racial conscience" which would open the way to the fulfillment of Galton's dream of "improving the inborn qualities of future generations" by promoting the fertility of "superior, healthy and useful stocks" while restricting, "through voluntary measures, the multiplication of those who suffer from hereditary disabilities and infirmities."[91]

At the outbreak of World War II, Eugenics Society spokesmen predicted that the conflict would be even more dysgenic than World War I in the destruction of persons "above the average in physique and courage" and in its deterring from parenthood "persons who take into account the well-being of their children." Some of them nevertheless saw the war as a last opportunity for their cause.[92] According to their scenario, the birthrate would drop dramatically as it had in the last war, thereby accelerating the predicted decline in population and intensifying public demands for the introduction of pronatalist measures to secure first the preservation and then the reconstruction of the race. The appointment of commissions with great powers could not be put off for long, and eugenicists needed to be ready to serve on them and to demonstrate the importance of qualitative as well as quantitative considerations in the rebuilding of what promised to be a much-depleted population. It was this objective that held the Eugenics Society together in the darkest months of the war and which gave it the motivation to keep the PIC and PEP as well as the FPA struggling along as well. The expected commissions were in time appointed and eugenicists got their chance to make their point. By then, however, it mattered very little, and nothing turned out as they had hoped.

Thirteen

World War II and the Population Question

For more than two years after the outbreak of war in September 1939, the population question was pushed into the background of political, economic, and social concern. Not until 1942, when the Battle of Britain was over, America had entered the conflict, and there was reason to believe that the country would survive and eventually win the war, were the unresolved demographic issues of the 1930s revived. With a future, however uncertain, to look forward to, arguments over the birthrate, net reproduction, age distribution, and, of course, the quality of the population again accented discussions of the demographic needs of the new, postwar society to be built on the rubble of the old.

In 1942, in an effort to continue to minimize the population problem and ward off extensive debate in Parliament, the government issued as a white paper a cautiously optimistic prewar assessment by the registrar-general of current demographic trends. But the specter of an aged, diminishing, inefficient populace was not so easily exorcised.[1] For one thing, Sir William Beveridge's sensational report later that year on social insurance and allied services specifically warned, "with its present rate of reproduction, the British race cannot continue." Indeed, Beveridge's blunt assessment that unless the birthrate were promptly raised in the near future the population would begin to fall precipitously was a major stimulus to the revival of the population question during the war.[2] Even Winston Churchill, who would have much preferred to defer consideration of the report until after victory was achieved, expressed his own "somber anxieties" about the "dwindling birth-rate" in a radio broadcast. Whatever disagreements he had with the Beveridge report, they did not extend to its author's conclusion that "in the next thirty years housewives as mothers have vital work to do in ensuring the adequate continuance of the British race and of British ideals in the world."[3]

Though Beveridge was in part using the depopulation scare to rally support for his many pronatalist recommendations, he was genuinely worried about differential fertility and the size and age composition of the population.[4] His anxieties were increasingly shared by many members of Parliament who challenged the registrar-general's and minister of health's reassuring evaluations of population trends and accused them of trying to whitewash the problem with the 1942 white paper. These challenges led in 1943 to an extensive debate in both houses of Parliament and, after nearly a half-century of repeated demands, to the appointment of a royal commission to investigate the birthrate and trends of population.

Paradoxically, the revival of the population question in World War II was accompanied by a surprising turnaround in the birthrate. After an initial drop in the first two years of the war to a recorded low of 13.9 per 1,000 in England and Wales, fertility, in contrast to the First World War, unexpectedly began to rise dramatically. Buoyed by a surge of new marriages, it reached a wartime high of 17.7 in 1944, and three years later hit a postwar peak of 20.5, a figure not seen since the early 1920s.[5] The figures baffled some demographic prognosticators, were explained away as a temporary phenomenon by others, and prompted several defensive commentators, including the editor of the *Eugenics Review*, to remind critics that the net reproduction statistics were not prophecies but hypothetical estimates based upon available data and subject to continual revision.[6]

Keep the Eugenic Flag Flying

When the war broke out and Blacker was immediately called up and sent off to France, his colleagues in the Eugenics Society at first seemed uncertain about continuing operations. Major Darwin recalled that during the last war, when the same considerations arose, he was determined "to keep the Eugenic flag flying all the time, even if only a small one." After considerable debate about the wisdom of trying to keep going, the council agreed with those who, like Julian Huxley, reasoned that since the conflict was likely to be decidedly dysgenic in its consequences and would generate many social and economic measures having a serious bearing on eugenics, it was essential to carry on, even on a reduced scale.[7]

The threat of war had for years deterred "provident, tender-minded couples with a highly developed social sense" from having children, the *Eugenics Review* warned. Now that war had come, it "must widen the gap between the fertility of less and that of more desirable parents." Whatever lay ahead, the editor, Maurice Newfield, added, it must be "our constant endeavour to create such post-war conditions as will result in a reversal of this deplorable trend in the differential birth-rate." It was the key to securing a better world with "biologically better . . . people to live in it."[8]

As in the First World War, eugenicists thought the sooner they got started preserving and rebuilding sound stock the better. When, as an economy measure in the early days of the war, the government temporarily cut back on income tax allowances for married people and their offspring and proposed only very modest grants for servicemen's dependents, Newfield strongly complained of the "biological wastage" in such shortsighted policies. He was particularly offended to learn that while only the first three children of totally disabled officers and men, whose genetic endowments were presumably above average, would get the miserly five shillings offered, mental defectives, by contrast, were budgeted at thirty shillings. Those responsible for our policy must realize, he warned, "we have on our hands both a dysgenic war and a population problem." Although the scales were soon improved, especially for dependents of men in the forces, the Eugenics Society continued to press for even higher allotments.[9]

In a throwback to the morbid campaign of 1914–18 to persuade men to marry and sire children before they left, eugenic demographers stressed the importance of young couples having at least one child before the husband was killed. When by 1941 the anticipated slaughter of World War I had not been repeated, eugenic calculations focused upon the disproportionate losses of men in the two most selective services, the air force and the navy. Appeals were sent to the press urging it to entreat all ranks of chivalrous men to marry as quickly as possible so that "if they leave a widow, they should also leave a mother." Byrom Bramwell, the chairman of the Eugenics Society's council, suggested that the state could do its part by being more generous to war orphans than to widows. But as the latter had the vote and the former did not, he thought it would take a good deal of persuasion to bring politicians around.[10]

If eugenicists did not take credit for the surge in marriages in the early years of the war, they were nevertheless surprised and delighted. To Walter Langdon Brown, professor emeritus of physic at Cambridge, the splendid performance, militarily and reproductively, of the "War Babies of 1914–1918" who were defending the country in 1941, demonstrated that heredity had won out over adverse conditions. They were not decadent, as many feared; few of the social problems of World War I and after had been transmitted. There was every reason to believe their offspring would prove to be as eugenically valuable. Whether there would be enough of them was another question.[11]

As one way of insuring the survival of adequate representatives of the next generation, the Eugenics Society in 1940 proposed to send several thousand "suitable" children under sixteen and their mothers to Canada. This was a more ambitious variation on the organization's World War I Professional Classes War Relief Council scheme of securing a supply of eugenically desirable children for rebuilding the race by providing maternity services to the wives of officers at the front. Working in conjunction with the Canadian Eugenics Society, a Homes in Canada Service Committee was established to provide for "certain eugenically important groups" not included in government evacuation schemes to remove poor, urban slum children from the East End of London and other large, manufacturing centers targeted for heavy bombing by the Germans. The Eugenics Society proposed to save "from the Nazi clutch many of the finest children from the Motherland" irrespective of class or region so long as they had won scholarships to non-grant-aided schools. Mothers with offspring under five were also eligible if they and their children were intelligent, in good health, and hereditarily sound. These valuable qualities were to be determined by a panel of doctors who would certify the genetically elect for shipment to host families across the Atlantic who promised to care for them without reimbursement.[12]

Although the Canadians offered to take 500 mothers and children the first year, only 23 children and 5 mothers were actually sent. The problem of booking passage in the critical summer and fall of 1940, coupled with Canadian regulations and restrictions, forced the Eugenics Society in that country to abandon the plan early in 1941.[13] By then, however, the worst of the blitz was over, the threat of German invasion had substantially diminished, and many of the evacuated children were returning to their homes.

The central problem for eugenics during the war was not, however, the preservation of selective stock for the reconstruction of the race but the very survival of the movement and the preservation of what remained of the nation's "eugenic conscience." Nazism had put both in peril, Newfield was certain, and he insisted that unless the Eugenics Society and its journal somehow continued to function, if only to show that German and British eugenics were opposed doctrines, eugenics would be so vilified by the end of the war it would have no chance of recovery. It was imperative to demonstrate that "our eugenics is based upon and implies freedom and respect for the individual; theirs is based upon compulsion and puts the political needs of the Militarist State before the biological needs of the people [by emphasizing] blood rather than genes."[14]

Blacker emphatically agreed and was particularly concerned while in France that the *Eugenics Review*, which had long been financially solvent, be kept going at all costs. In his judgment, it was the cement holding the movement together, and its demise would, he feared, be followed by a flood of resignations from which the Eugenics Society might never rebound.[15] Adequate personnel to keep the operation afloat, rather than finances, constituted the society's major problem. The organization still enjoyed assets worth nearly

£70,000, and though some members thought it would be prudent to suspend all activities to preserve capital until after the war, the council decided that with cutbacks and a policy of care and maintenance the society could probably survive a protracted conflict. In fact, its assets actually increased modestly during the war, and it was able to provide rent-free facilities and a subsidy for the struggling Family Planning Association as well as for the Population Investigation Committee when that investigatory committee was revived in 1943 after temporarily suspending activities.[16]

Once there was agreement to try to keep things going and "to save what we can from the wreck," as Ursula Grant Duff described the society's task, a nine-member War Emergency Committee under Lord Horder was established to govern the Eugenics Society.[17] It did so until 1943, when the council was able to resume meeting. By then Blacker, who had been evacuated at Dunkirk and later decorated for heroism, had returned to resume the secretaryship while working on a survey of mental health services for the Ministry of Health. In his absence a good deal of the slack had been taken up by Richard Titmuss, a largely self-educated clerk and bookkeeper who, despite the absence of a formal degree, had developed impressive statistical and analytical skills during his sixteen years in an insurance office.

A former Liberal attracted to Fabian socialism and Labour, the thirty-year-old Titmuss was introduced to the Eugenics Society in 1937 by R. R. Kuczynski, who was impressed by the young clerk's quantitative skills. The publication the following year of Titmuss's book *Poverty and Population*, written with the encouragement and assistance of his new wife, Kathleen, who shared his social and political sentiments, made its mark in Liberal and socialist intellectual circles where it attracted the attention of a number of reform eugenicists including Lord Horder, Eleanor Rathbone, Newfield, Carr-Saunders, and Blacker, among others. Titmuss's expert use of social statistics to examine social problems, particularly the population question, prompted Blacker to recommend his appointment to the Eugenics Society council in 1939.

Though appalled by some of the reactionaries he found there, Titmuss was able to bring significant new insights to the relationship of environment to heredity.[18] He insisted it was no longer possible to dogmatize about nature and nurture as the Victorians had done. State services, he reasoned, including the cooperative rationalization of social welfare and family allowances, could go a long way toward establishing the environmental equalization that would make it possible to isolate more accurately the role of heredity. Such indiscriminate, collectivist propositions were hardly designed to endear him to some of the council members as well as the mainline remnants of the rank and file.[19] Chance and Bramwell, both businessmen, particularly resented Titmuss's egalitarian emphasis upon the importance of nurture and his criticisms of the sterilizing effects of acquisitive capitalism on "economic man."

Despite continual complaints, Titmuss firmly resisted recommendations to suspend Eugenics Society activities for the duration, and with the assistance of Ursula Duff and several other women, he largely ran what remained of the organization from 1939 to 1942. When Newfield fell ill in 1941, he also edited the much-leaner *Eugenics Review* for a year.[20] There was something ironic about Titmuss, the "High Priest of the Welfare State," as he was later described when professor of social administration at the London School of Economics, struggling to preserve an organization that had long deplored the racial consequences of the humane, egalitarian social programs he promoted so effectively.

Newfield's defense of the importance to eugenics of a progressive, liberal mentality and the willingness to confront a diversity of social, political, and economic views, contributed to the council's bitterly disputed decision to subsidize secretly the publication in 1943 of Titmuss's important book, *Birth, Poverty and Wealth*.[21] Unlike Titmuss's critics, Newfield saw not a rejection of qualitative hereditary determinants in his work but the restoration of a balance permitting us to "contemplate the problems of nature and nurture in explicit terms, not as antithetical factors but as variables within conditions that can be defined with increasing precision." The infant Eugenics Society, he implied in Darwin's obituary in 1943, had perhaps gone overboard in its emphasis on "the role of heredity as a determinant of phenotypical characters." Had it not done so, however, "the prevailing assumption that the differences between men reflected merely the differences in the circumstances of their lives might have continued to hold the field."[22]

Reflecting on the wisdom of the Eugenics Society's decision to keep the flag flying, as Darwin had urged, Duff described after the worst of the blitz was over how the evacuation of slum children, "many of whom were difficult in character and subnormal in intelligence and behaviour," had brought home to their hosts the recognition that "heredity and environment were the warp and woof of life, so inextricably woven together that we were bound to regard not only applications of heredity but all social service as part of our domain." The recipients of such children could not avoid asking themselves, "How much of this evil, affecting people of our own stock was due to bad housing, bad nutrition and faulty education, and how much to inborn defects?" The Eugenics Society stood ready to try to answer these vital questions.[23]

In language reminiscent of World War I, Duff, like the more optimistic of her colleagues, talked a good deal about the opportunities the war provided for eugenicists to position themselves for an important role in the qualitative and quantitative reconstruction of the race. The appointment of a government interdepartmental committee under a eugenic sympathizer like Beveridge to consider the need for social services was an encouraging sign to reform eugenicists that the planning process was under way and in good hands. At the same time, they recognized that any impact their ideas might have on reconstruction programs was still in large part dependent upon resolving the dilemma over nature and nurture in a way that would make it politically and socially as well as scientifically acceptable.

Blacker's return in 1942 was followed by a slow revival of Eugenics Society activities oriented toward assuring that policies of demographic reconstruction would contain a significant eugenic dimension. The War Emergency Committee was disbanded in 1943, the council restored, and the annual Galton Lecture revived with Beveridge as the speaker. The following year Newfield, Blacker, and Duff combined to draft a revised statement of the Eugenics Society's aims and objects stressing its commitment to democracy and emphasizing the voluntary basis of its recommendations. While the fundamental goal remained of trying to improve the inherited qualities of mankind by encouraging the natural increase among "well-endowed persons and discouraging propagation among inferior and sub-normal stocks," much more importance was placed upon building a solid foundation in scientific and social scientific research upon which a campaign of moral persuasion could be based.

In a determined effort to distance true, scientific eugenics from the Nazi perversion of *rassenhygiene*, eugenics was explicitly defined in the revised statement as a study and a practice, not an ideology dedicated to the creation of one type of person over another. Even if sometime in the future it became genetically possible to breed a particular type, it should not be done, the document emphasized. Genetic diversity was welcomed in all sectors of society so long as it resulted in a great majority of healthy, intelligent, long-lived, moral types free of transmissible defects. This meant in practice ascertaining the rates of reproduction of different social elements, examining the distribution of eugenically desirable hereditary characteristics among the community, and discovering the deterrents to early marriage and parenthood operative in those groups considered to be most valuable.

The elimination of these deterrents to the best citizens' giving "full expression to the instincts of parenthood" would in all likelihood require maternity and graded family allowances, tax rebates, educational assistance, larger houses, and economic facilities for employed women who wanted children. On the negative side, the revised document concluded, birth control would remain the principal weapon against defective breeding, but where it was unsuitable, sterilization should be readily available.[24]

Differential Birthrates and Population Policy

In contrast to World War I, demographic analysts were much less preoccupied with the sex ratio of reproduction. For one thing they had come to realize that for any number of possible reasons the relative distribution of male to female births had fluctuated over the past hundred years and varied considerably from region to region.[25] But earlier concerns about male births had also been altered by the depopulation scare and the centrality of girl babies to the net reproduction rate upon which population growth depended. By World War II it was widely understood that the availability of a sufficient number of children to populate the country, whatever their sex, was dependent upon an adequate number of mothers to bear them. Though male children remained more vulnerable than females, the continuing decline in overall infant mortality throughout the interwar years, to around 55 per 1,000, also helped diminish anxieties about differential sex ratios.

Despite the assumption that the new war would, like the previous conflict, be dysgenic in its killing off the fittest male stock, there was much less discussion of the subject than there had been a generation before. One reason was the immediate implementation of conscription, which from a eugenic standpoint was statistically far more favorable than voluntary recruitment because it exposed a cross section of the race to danger rather than just "the flower of young manhood." Similarly, the loss of more British civilians than combatants in the first three years of fighting suggested that total war, as dreadful as it was in the destruction of people of all sexes and ages, at least offered similar eugenic compensation.[26] Indeed, one eugenicist squadron leader in the early days of the blitz seemed positively pleased that the bombing was so nonselective in inflicting casualties. Looking on the bright side in those dark days of 1940, he concluded that the war would ultimately prove eugenic because the nation with better brains and a higher standard of physical fitness would best be able to design, construct, and use the modern weapons necessary for survival.[27]

Few eugenicists, however, believed that war in the modern world somehow weeded out the unfit and that certain peoples were endowed with a special inherited capacity for international conflict. Newfield, for example, thought it ludicrous to think that the French were somehow biologically stronger in

1914–18 than they were in 1940 but that the advantage now belonged to the Germans who had just conquered them. War, he insisted, was universally dysgenic. The birth and marriage rates in every country plummeted in World War I, resulting in a tremendous loss of potential children sired by men above the average in physical fitness, courage, and sense of responsibility. Since then, he recalled, resistance to parenthood had grown stronger especially among "imaginative, sensitive, far-sighted persons, who in a happier society would be among the first to fulfill their responsibilities to posterity." It was the final indictment of the current war, with its great but socially selective pessimism, that both its direct and indirect casualties fell most heavily on the best people. Britain would ultimately win this dysgenic war as it won the last, Newfield predicted, but again not because its people were genetically superior but because of its material resources, diversity, capacity to destroy, and determination to preserve its freedom.[28]

What debates there were about the likely dysgenic effects of the war were largely confined to the early years of the conflict, before it became evident that there would be no repeat of the staggering losses of World War I and that both the marriage and birth rates were rising rather than falling. Although there were still occasional references to the C3 population or their defective equivalents remaining at home to breed the postwar generation, eugenic analyses of differential fertility tended to avoid the invidious class distinctions that had often accompanied evaluations of the relative contribution and sacrifice of social classes during World War I. All but the most crass of eugenicists were sensitive now to the damage such obvious social prejudice did to their cause. With the poor clustered around the docks, railroad yards, and industrial plants of the great cities suffering disproportionately heavy casualties from the relentless bombing, condemnation of their excessive fertility sounded particularly churlish, if not irrelevant.

Victory in the First World War also made it much more difficult to dredge up the old anxieties about racial degeneration. Titmuss speculated that the early eugenicists were so pessimistic because of the deplorable social conditions they had witnessed in the late Victorian period. But, he asked, had their predictions come true? Were people poorer today in intelligence, health, and capacity for citizenship than fifty years ago? Had the differential fertility of the rich and poor led to a decay in the inborn endowment of the nation? Had the rise of state provisions for health, education, welfare, pensions, etc., undermined individual responsibility and pauperized the nation? Though Titmuss warned it would be a mistake to think the questions had been answered conclusively, he was fairly certain of the outcome once the great inequalities of opportunity and experience still prevailing in the country were eliminated.

Only then could "the biological fruits" of a slowly improving environment be reliably harvested.[29]

This was exactly the kind of thinking that caused some of Titmuss's more Victorian colleagues to question his eugenics credentials. Nevertheless, his supporters believed the harvest of which Titmuss wrote had in fact started and provided lifesaving nourishment in the darkest months of the war. The population, they thought, was obviously far more efficient than once believed and, by nearly every measure, had grown healthier as the environment had improved in the interwar years. This was critically evident in the much lower rejection rates of military recruits when they were called up in World War II, as well as in the demonstrably better health of civilian workers.

Perhaps in some cases the medical exams were hurried or lower standards accepted, the *Eugenics Review* commented in 1941, but the results more likely reflected decades of improved child and maternal care. Nature and nurture had combined in a "great toughness of mind, body and spirit under stress," thwarting Nazi assumptions that under constant bombardment inherent defects, especially among the laboring poor, would surface, destroy the workers' fragile health and morale, and cause them to break. With a fine eugenics touch, the review added, "Our adverse differential birthrate may have resulted in a lowering of some of our standards—indeed with respect to some qualities, intelligence for instance, there are reasons to believe that it has; but the stocks are still sound and the standards still high. . . . The biological endowment of the masses has been tested and not found wanting." It did not mean negative eugenics could be neglected, the journal cautioned, though most people would prefer methods less drastic and more discriminating than those favored by the Luftwaffe. It did mean, however, that in encouraging the fertility of the generality of the people, eugenicists were on safe ground.[30]

Though eugenic wartime strategy was on balance decidedly pronatalist and focused more on the overall birthrate than its differential characteristics, curtailing the fertility of genetically unpromising people remained a constant preoccupation. In continuing to provide rent-free facilities and a subsidy to the FPA throughout the war, the Eugenics Society explained that although birth control had on balance been dysgenic, the ever-widening use of contraceptives among the less gifted and less intelligent members of the community was probably starting at last to bring more eugenic advantages than disadvantages. A differential pattern in which family size was more proportional to educational status was still desirable, the *Eugenics Review* added, but attempts to place tighter controls on birth control, as some physicians still suggested, would prove counterproductive. Better-endowed citizens would always find a way around them, while the "irresponsible and incompetent" would just go ahead and breed.[31] In any event, modern family planning, Blacker emphasized at the end of the war, was as interested in increasing the fertility of "well-fitted" couples as it was in preventing the conceiving of more children by that minority of people who were physically, economically, or genetically unsuitable.[32] He suspected, of course, that all too often the first two shortcomings followed from the third.

Although public anxiety about depopulation still inspired occasional demands throughout the war for the strict control of contraceptives, the FPA was relieved when no serious attack on the principle of birth control was launched. "Family spacing," as its spokesmen usually described it, was generally accepted as necessary and right, and there appeared to be little chance that the clock in the much-cited metaphor would be turned back.[33] Among those who wanted to reverse the hands a bit at least was, again, Lord Dawson of Penn, who in 1942 predicted a loss of 3.5 million people by 1965. He was supported by the psychiatrist A. Spencer Paterson, whose 1943 analysis of entries in the 1940 *Who's Who*, along with other contemporary biographical directories and genealogies, convinced him of the importance of denying contraceptives to people under the age of thirty-five unless dispensed by a physician or marriage clinic.[34]

Paterson supplemented his research into the fertility of the business, professional, and titled classes with questionnaires to discover that with the exception of industrialists, peers, and old public-school boys, who had on average somewhere between 2.4 and 2.7 children, no other group met David Glass's 2.37 estimate required for replacement. Professors, doctors, lawyers, scientists, and military officers were particularly nongenerative, failing even to father a mean of 2.0 offspring. Some 10 percent of their number had none at all. A less complete tally of parliamentary fertility revealed that about one-third of all M.P.s were unmarried. Among those who were married, however, Conservatives, with nearly 2.0 future Tories to their credit, were somewhat more productive than their less numerous Labour colleagues, who begat only 1.44. Paterson discreetly avoided any comment on the eugenic advantages of this political differential, but was certain the aggregate figures, laid out at length in graphs, charts, and tables, added up to the demographic failure of the best classes and their inevitable extinction.

English society, Paterson annnounced, was afflicted with a malady that made it fear or shun an abundance of healthy children. It was, he insisted, a psychological condition rather than some biological weakening of the germ plasm possibly brought on, as Lord Geddes suggested in Parliament, by everything from changing diets, prosperity, urbanization, and industrialization, to coffee, electrical currents, and an overindulgence in sexual intercourse. None of this probably explained why Lord Iveagh's herds of cattle suddenly stopped breeding for a while in the 1930s, an analogy elicited by Geddes's speculation and discussed for a time by their fellow peers. But it did suggest, a number of them agreed, that the government, perhaps through an interdepartmental committee or a royal commission, should undertake animal and human studies to determine if, in fact, "the germ plasm has ceased to be actively reproductive."[35]

To Paterson who, like most students of the subject, believed infertility was primarily volitional, not biological, the solution lay in getting people in the better classes to marry much earlier and to restrict their access to contraceptives.[36] But doubts that birth control was the problem continued throughout the war, and a number of people, including the prominent expert on mental testing, J. A. Fraser Roberts, offered variations on "the Fisher effect," questioning how voluntary the decline in fertility really was. So long as infertility facilitated social advancement, Fraser Roberts argued, the birthrate of the ablest stock—those who were perhaps hereditarily predisposed to think in socially qualitative terms—would continue to diminish. Given the proven correlations between intelligence and fertility, he warned in 1944, the 4 most intelligent of every 100 people will only be replaced by 3 in the next generation, while the 4 dullest will be replaced by 5.[37]

The late Victorian belief that biological factors had been at work to reduce fecundity at least since the middle of the nineteenth century persisted in public as well as in scientific circles at the end of the war. The polling organization Mass Observation found in a 1945 survey many people who still thought some form of Spencerian evolution was at work reducing the fecundity of modern couples so that even when contraceptives were not used, women had fewer children than their mothers. There was, of course, at present no way to prove it, the pollsters observed, but something had to be done to increase the birthrate.[38]

Actually, the birthrate had risen by more than 20 percent since reaching its low point of 13.9 per 1,000 in 1941. The steady increase appeared, however, to have had little effect on depopulation fears but in fact, as Titmuss noted, seemed to revive prewar anxieties and stimulate discussion. He was himself surprised the birthrate did not fall as far in 1940 and 1941 as it had in the first two years of the Great War. The rate for the first quarter of 1942, for example, was higher than in any similar quarter since 1931, which was especially remarkable because it revealed that many conceptions took place during the heaviest bombardment and when the outcome of the war was most in doubt. By way of explanation, Titmuss referred to the unusually large number of nineteen- and twenty-year-old women in the population owing to the larger birthrate after World War I. They helped swell the overall number of women ages nineteen to thirty by 60,000 compared to the same cohort in 1938. He speculated that their availability in the marriage market, which increased the number of nuptial registrations by 220,000 in 1939–41 compared to the previous two years, coupled with the swift introduction of war allowances and less marital separation than in 1914–16, kept fertility from falling by more than 10 percent.

Although the *Eugenics Review* found some comfort in the existence of 300,000 more children than might have been expected to be born because of the war and the almost continuous bombing since 1940, it grieved for an estimated 41,000 who were not conceived because their parents were more sensitive, farsighted, imaginative, and intelligent. The review based its qualitative calculation on Titmuss's findings that a great many of the younger women who had given birth since the outbreak of the war had already been pregnant at the time of their marriage, and their offspring were in all probability unplanned. This conclusion was reinforced by his discovery that the abnormal number of first births recorded contrasted markedly with a substantial decline in second and subsequent births by couples who were now planning more carefully. Titmuss did not have to dwell on the likely relative eugenic value of the children produced in each category, but his emphasis on the qualities to be found in sensitive, thoughtful, and farsighted, if socially pessimistic, couples had class connotations few of the readers of the *Eugenics Review* were likely to miss.[39]

The Revival of the Depopulation Scare

Titmuss was provoked to his analysis of the recent birthrate statistics by the publication in 1942 of the registrar-general's memorandum on current population trends and by a running debate in the *British Medical Journal* over whether or not the population was really in danger of declining. Though originally drafted in 1939 for a Royal Commission on Geographical Distribution of the Industrial Population, the memorandum was submitted to Parliament as a white paper by the minister of health and secretary of state for Scotland because of revived interest in the population question. While the memorandum confirmed that the current number of annual births was some 300,000 fewer than the million or so recorded for the years 1876 to 1914, it was enough to sustain the population at its current level for a while if the mortality rates remained constant rather than continued to decline. But, the registrar-general admitted, even if the death rates stabilized and the birthrate, which hovered around 15 per 1,000, remained unchanged, the number of women in their childbearing years would gradually fall as the population aged. Unless the replacement rate rose from the present 75 percent, the total number of children born annually would slip to about 640,000 in 1951 and 570,000 ten years later. Fertility was, however, notoriously volatile and unpredictable, the memorandum noted optimistically, and there was no reason to conclude that things would go one way or the other. If, for example, more women married a little earlier and increased their fertility about 19 percent above what it was in 1938, there would be no problem.[40]

In issuing the white paper, the government believed it was offering a moderate correction to the exaggerated forecasts that began to appear again in 1942. While some people were assuaged, a good many demographers, economists, physicians, and politicians were not. They disputed the registrar-general's claims that the war had probably not greatly altered the conclusions found in the memorandum and claimed the figures were outdated, misinterpreted, or deliberately manipulated to avoid having to introduce costly pronatalist programs. The Keynesian economist Roy Harrod was particularly critical in a letter to the *Times* which prompted the registrar-general to explain that the memorandum had been written for experts, not the public, and to express his perplexity that anyone could find its contents comforting.[41] The *Eugenics Review* agreed with Harrod: the document was far more optimistic than the evidence warranted, and the public should be told unequivocally of the seriousness of the problem.[42]

Efforts by Percy Stocks of the registrar-general's office to defend the white paper and to challenge many of the facts about population decline thrown about in letters to influential publications, such as the *British Medical Journal*, met with mixed success. The *BMJ*'s editor was inclined to agree that the threat of depopulation was greatly exaggerated and pointed to the recent, sharp increase in both marriage and the birth rates as portents of an even greater rise in reproduction after the war. The demographic consequences of war were hard to predict, Stocks warned, and questionable prophecies about an inevitable decline only contributed to discouragement and "to that lamentable sense of national inferiority from which a large section of the population now seems to be suffering."[43]

A substantial number of the *BMJ*'s correspondents were unconvinced. The most pessimistic of them expected massive casualties to drain the racial reservoirs beyond recovery this time and saw the "devitalisation" of Western societies as the final stage of inevitable decline. Some specifically raised the issue of eugenic quality and wondered if what was called the British race was really worth perpetuating. One particularly bizarre offering from a eugenicist female physician to the *Lancet*, which an embarrassed Blacker urged be rejected, claimed that after the war the depopulation of Europe would be so great that European women would have to be inseminated by selected American donors. Those of a less cosmic disposition merely complained once again about the sterilizing effects of luxury, materialism, high taxes, rising education costs, the loss of religious values, and the shortage of servants. More common, however, were the usual demands for pronatalist inducements to motherhood such as better housing, family allowances, maternal and child care facilities, tax rebates, and educational allowances. Whatever their explanation or solution, the various correspondents generally assumed the population was bound to start falling soon.[44]

Interpretations of the white paper and the statistics showing that the birthrate was on the rise by 1942 tended to correlate with the degree of optimism or pessimism felt by individual analysts. Titmuss, for example, replied that had it not been for the temporary increase in available women, the high marriage rate, and the surge in the number of first, unplanned children, the population might have already begun to drop. Though there were nearly 250,000 more marriages in the years 1939–41 than in the last two years of peace, they actually produced 31,000 fewer children. Indeed, though the birthrate was again on the upswing, the number of children, 645,000, was still lower than in the worst year of World War I, and there were nearly 1 million more potential mothers now.

Despite the much-noted jump in the marriage rate in 1940 to an unprecedented 22.7 per 1,000, the number of marriages had actually been rising over the past ten years, Titmuss pointed out, depleting our marriageable stocks but having a trifling effect on the birthrate. This was already reflected in the decline in the marriage rate to 17.8 in 1942. As the eligible female stock born in the post–World War I boom was married off, as were those women who had delayed marrying during the depression of the 1930s, the low fertility of the 1920s would begin to take effect. Even if the birthrate rose to 20 per 1,000, Titmuss concluded, the country would soon recognize it had been borrowing marriages and births from the future and advancing "on the last wave of a tide of high fertility" which was now rapidly ebbing.[45]

In contrast to those who seized upon his analyses to confirm their portentous expectations of race suicide, Titmuss and his wife Kathleen were basically optimistic. As far as they were concerned, man, not nature, had made the problem, and man could solve it by creating a more equitable, nonacquisitive, cooperative environment in which couples could economically and psychologically afford to have more children. People, they wrote in *Parents in Revolt*, needed to divest themselves of the competitive, materialistic, intensely individualistic Victorian legacy that had turned them into economic men. Behind the parents' revolt lay a deep, inarticulate protest of common men and women against the whole idea they were primarily economic creatures amenable to no higher motives than personal gain. Birth control was, in other words, a twentieth-century protest against the social and economic order created in the nineteenth. It reflected a loss of faith in progress and a desire for security in a competitive, increasingly insecure world in which even biological survival was now in doubt. Only in a free, cooperative community, where children were welcomed and desired for the value they brought to individual dignity and communal happiness, would the population problem ultimately be resolved.[46]

If the white paper failed to satisfy Titmuss and his eugenic colleagues, some of whom were dismayed by his socialist solution to the problem, it also failed to satisfy those in Parliament who feared a whitewash and demanded a debate on the subject. From the time of the document's appearance, M.P.s repeatedly queried the minister of health, Ernest Brown, about the gloss put on the figures and whether the government intended to take additional steps to maintain the population. On one occasion a member pointedly asked if the authorities planned to inform the people that there was not much point in winning the war if "the British race is to cease to exist through committing racial suicide."[47] It was a question a good many worried people had been asking one way or another since the outbreak of the war.

Brown attempted, with mixed success, to explain away the white paper as a preliminary, informational report and to defend the government's pronatalist policies of tax rebates, child and maternal care grants, education, school meals, medical services, and a number of special wartime allowances. His announcement that the net reproduction rate, calculated from more accurate data gathered under the 1938 Population (Statistics) Act, was actually 0.80 rather than 0.75 did not exactly electrify the Commons.[48] On the other hand, publication of the Beveridge report at the end of 1942 did, and in its aftermath a motion with nearly ninety signatures was submitted proclaiming the House's alarm at the approaching decline in the population and the menace it posed to the future security and prosperity of the British nation and race. Taking note of the government's approval in principle of the allowances and improved social services recently proposed in the Beveridge report, the motion urged their rapid implementation as well as other economic and educational measures. After some additional prodding, both Clement Attlee and Anthony Eden agreed on 6 June to a full debate in the near future.[49]

Taking their cue from the Commons, several members of the House of Lords attacked the white paper as "misleading and dangerous" and asked what the government planned to do about the threatened decrease in population. In demanding a full inquiry, they revived all of the old fears about the decline of the West and the loss of empire and added to them the prospect of the eventual disappearance of the race.[50] Nearly all of them agreed that "salvation from extinction" lay in creating a climate or culture in which larger families were "the fashion" or "the thing." Lord Nathan and Viscount Samuel, who recalled their own efforts in 1939 to get a royal commission appointed while the government tried then, as now, to paper over the problem, believed the Beveridge report was a major step in the right direction. Its emphasis upon family allowances, maternity and child benefits, small marriage grants, improved housing, rental assistance, and better health care could, they contended, go a long way toward changing people's attitudes.

Some eugenically sensitive peers faulted Beveridge's social insurance schemes for failing to address the exceptionally low fertility of "the most healthy and prosperous families" who required much more generous tax deductions and educational subsidies to induce them to reproduce the fabled four or five offspring needed to assure the qualitative as well as quantitative recovery of the race. Other members doubted that in the absence of any sense of a wider obligation the complex reasons that motivated young couples to spurn parenthood would not easily be overcome by economic benefits and new social insurance services.[51]

Although the government was obviously not keen for the debate, it went on for five hours, often degenerating into rambling personal digressions in which the issue at hand became sidetracked or obscured. Not everyone was convinced that a smaller population was such a bad thing, but they were clearly in the minority. Nearly all of the arguments, statistics, and prognoses that had attached themselves to the population question in the interwar years were repeated. The most recent figures on the marriage and birth rates were interjected to prove the danger was receding or to demonstrate that the surprising wartime rise was temporary. Most participants were genuinely anxious about the possibility of decline, even if they disagreed about causes and solutions and were confused by the various demographic projections bandied about.

Despite several references to peopling the empire with representatives of the "advanced races" and the domestic population with more of the "valuable stock" of the middle- and higher-income groups, blatantly eugenic statements were rare. Only Wing Commander A. W. H. James, a member of the Eugenics Society, complained about the submerged tenth and the Social Problem Group whose numbers nobody wanted to increase. His suspicions about the responsibility of the working classes in general, however, were evident in his recommendation that if the flat-rate eight shilling family allowance scheme recommended by Beveridge was approved, the payments should be in kind and go directly to the children rather than to their irresponsible mothers who would squander any cash awards.[52]

While there were repeated references to demographic race suicide during the prolonged debate, there was virtually no mention of race deterioration or decadence. No one was prepared to challenge the Labour M.P. James Griffith's assessment of the high quality of British stock. He recalled the many charges of race degeneration made before the war, but these had obviously been disproven once again. This did not mean the population was not growing older and in danger of numerically declining; it did signify, however, that in a new, more equitable society the desire and the capability to breed and raise healthy children would quickly revive.[53]

In contrast to the population debates before the war, women this time took a more direct, though still comparatively subdued, part. Lady Astor complained of this in a feminist diatribe against the insensitivity and ignorance of men who continued to dominate discussions about women, motherhood, and the population issue. As the mother of seven, she knew a good deal more about it than the "superior hypocrites" in Parliament who kept the members of her sex from positions of power and influence where they might be able to advance policies which would induce women to want children. If her blistering comments were hardly designed to endear her to her male colleagues in the Commons, Lady Astor was in part directly provoked by Dr. Francis Freemantle's fossilized denunciations of female emancipation and birth control, which he associated with the utter breakdown of Christian morality. They were sentiments which, if privately held, were rarely expressed any longer in Parliament, and Freemantle's call for legislation to "control the sale of Conservatives," as he inadvertently put it when denouncing contraceptives, provoked a good deal of laughter but no support.[54]

But Lady Astor's rhapsodizing about the joys of large families, even among the poor, did not elicit much enthusiasm either, though it did generate some very different recollections from Labour members. Dr. Edith Summerskill, conceding the falling birthrate was indeed the result of female emancipation and, she added, enlightenment, was sure that women in modern, literate societies would never go back to the dependency and powerlessness associated with having too many children. Some increase in family size was possible in a truly socialist society where marital equality existed and women were provided with adequate prenatal and postnatal care, Summerskill argued, but she thought for the near future at least, the population would become older and smaller until the country began to address the severe problems that made childbearing so unattractive.[55]

Despite assurances of concern and promises of further study, skepticism about the government's intentions ran high in both houses of Parliament. Though the minister of health, who supported his position with statistics demonstrating improved fertility, infant mortality, and longevity, was himself nowhere near as gloomy about the trend of population as many of those he listened to, he knew even before the debate that nothing less than a full national inquiry would put an end to the recurrent depopulation scare. He therefore announced plans to establish a number of expert committees preliminary to the appointment of a royal commission to investigate the population problem.[56] Brown and the cabinet had finally been brought to it, not only by the revival of panic the previous year, the failure of the white paper to assuage M.P. concerns, and the prime minister's own worries, but also by the deep demographic concerns that underlay the influential Beveridge report.

Beveridge, Family Allowances, and the Eugenicists

In making his case for noncontributory, flat-rate children's allowances of at least eight shillings a week for all offspring after the first, Beveridge boldly played the depopulation card. Unless the birthrate were raised very materially in the near future, he stressed at various places in his report, "a rapid and continuous decline of the population cannot be prevented," and the British race would inevitably falter. It was therefore "imperative to give first place in social expenditure to the care of childhood and to the safeguarding of maternity." Unlike most of the other social insurance schemes and services he proposed, children's allowances for financial, practical, and symbolic reasons were to be paid from the national exchequer, not from the contributory Social Insurance Fund.

Beveridge had no illusions about allowances or other economic incentives by themselves inducing people to have children they did not want. But they could help restore the birthrate to at least a replacement level by making it possible for parents who desired more children to bring them into the world without damaging the chances of those already born, and by helping to set the tone of public opinion by sending a signal of national interest in larger families. These goals could be in part accomplished by providing all children with guaranteed benefits and allowances which would continue and even increase until they reached the age of sixteen.[57]

To the distress of a good many of his present and former colleagues in the Eugenics Society, Beveridge's recommendations were entirely non-eugenic—indeed, to some they were positively dysgenic. When the interdepartmental committee made up of civil servants from various interested governmental agencies was appointed in 1941, Titmuss had urged Beveridge, as its chairman, to consider eugenic factors and tried to get Blacker, who was still in the forces, to prepare a memorandum to submit on behalf of the Eugenics Society. In begging off the task, Blacker disclaimed any expertise in the area of social insurance, nor had he thought much about eugenics in the past two years. "The peace-time world is as different from the one I now live in," he replied, "as is another historical age."[58] But neither Beveridge nor his committee of careful, neutral civil servants were about to enrage Labour party interests by including eugenics or anything else that might inflame class feelings, and no effort was made to bring into their deliberations the usual balancing testimony from groups and individuals outside the government.

Beveridge knew that his flat-rate allowance scheme to be paid from the national coffers was anathema to many eugenicists. He tried to explain his thinking in his 1943 Galton Lecture on the "Eugenic Aspects of Children's Allowances." He came to the Eugenics Society's podium fresh from hearing the opening debate on his report in the House of Commons and told his audience of the constraints felt by the committee to concentrate exclusively upon the economic facets of children's benefits, not the biological. This did not mean that he was unconcerned about differential fertility or the eugenic possibilities of family allowances. But he did not believe they would have much effect one way or another on the size of the population or on the reproductive habits of the thoughtless. Allowances might, however, induce the more thoughtful members of the working class to have additional children, he reasoned, which should eventually prove eugenically beneficial.

Although he did not necessarily share Fisher's belief that the tendency to have small families was an inherited characteristic reinforced by social success, Beveridge did agree that fewer children facilitated economic and social promotion. In all classes "ability and infertility rise together and infertility tends to kill the ability of our race." By equalizing conditions between large and small families, as Fisher recommended, "the premium on infertility" would be removed and thoughtful parents would be more inclined to beget more children.

Beveridge admitted his flat-rate proposal would only mean equalization among the poorest families, not between classes. Because the cost of children rose with family income, parents with incomes of £500 would find each child a greater expense than those with £100 so that the allowances would do nothing to check the premium on infertility for families above subsistence. To solve this problem, Beveridge recommended supplemental, contributory vocational and occupational programs, particularly for the professions, in which the allowances would be proportionate to salary. If he had his way, such programs would be compulsory in the civil service and in education, though voluntary schemes would probably be better in some other occupations. There was nothing antidemocratic in any of this, he insisted; differential fertility was not simply between rich and poor. It extended throughout the social scale, making children's allowances democratic in their neutralizing of family size as a liability or advantage. The argument, Beveridge added, was in some ways actually "left-wing" in its opposition to the inheritance of wealth being concentrated through infertility on a small number of heirs and heiresses. Moreover, none of these recommendations, he emphasized, dictatorially interfered with human breeding and individual liberties, including the freedom to choose mates and rear children.

Along with these superallowances for the higher grades, Beveridge, in accordance with long-standing eugenic policy, also recommended larger income tax rebates to stimulate the fertility of all of the taxpaying classes, including skilled workers who possessed "the greatest store of unused intellectual ability in the country." The easier you make it for them to rise by their infertility into the "frigid, unfertile atmosphere of the social classes above them, the more you are going to breed out that ability," Beveridge maintained. So long as the small family remained an important strategy for the ablest in any class to advance, he warned, it would be racially harmful.

Though he had not made the point in his report, Beveridge believed his proposals were an important first step in bringing economic and biological tendencies into line with one another. By covering the whole of the population, children's allowances constituted a start to neutralizing the premium on infertility. He was first and foremost concerned with getting a fair, minimal payment for all classes which would lay the foundation for other, more selective schemes later on. Flat-rate allowances of eight shillings, which he expected to pass with some modifications, were obviously only suitable for the poor, but the principle was established. The next step, supplementary, occupational allowances and income tax rebates would, he predicted, be decidedly more eugenic.[59]

The response of eugenicists to Beveridge's lecture was, like the reaction to the report itself, mixed. Upon learning Beveridge was to give the Galton Lecture, Dean Inge, who had for years complained about the council's surrender to the environmentalists, resigned his thirty-six-year membership in the Eugenics Society with a parting shot: "To subsidise the teeming birth-rate of the slums is not the way to improve the quality of the population."[60] Despite his strong emphasis upon children's allowances as a pronatalist measure to help reverse the net reproduction rate, Beveridge, like Glass and others who had studied such inducements in different countries, doubted they would have much impact on the decision of couples to conceive more children. To eugenicists who agreed with Inge or who asked what would prevent poor mothers from using the eight shillings to get "perms" or go to the pub or the cinema, Beveridge responded that the amount was too small to encourage anyone who thought about it to have more children. Obviously there were no guarantees some people would not abuse the allowances, but he thought most recipients needed them and would use them as intended to help relieve existing poverty.[61]

Some of Beveridge's supporters, such as Titmuss and Eva Hubback, noted that the birthrates of all classes had fallen dramatically, in some cases much more among skilled, unskilled, and semiskilled workers than in the middle ranks. Whether Beveridge's proposals would promote "fertility of persons who possess inborn qualities above the average" was unclear, Hubback admitted, but they might give a greater sense of security to thinking people when they were contemplating having children. As the lowest group in society was already breeding as fast as it could, allowances should not make any difference to it.[62]

Lidbetter, who opposed any Eugenics Society endorsement of the Beveridge report, argued against the inclusion of the Social Problem Group in the insured population. They should have no access to any services or payments that might even indirectly encourage their fertility. In light of the enthusiasm with which the Beveridge report was received by the public, Newfield only reluctantly agreed to publish an article by Lidbetter in the *Eugenics Review* condemning social security as dysgenic. "It would be calamitous," the editor wrote to Blacker, "if eugenics became associated again in the public mind, as it was in the past, with comfortable middle-class opposition to social reform."[63]

Much of the hostility to Beveridge's plan centered on the expected costs to the already infertile, allegedly overburdened taxpaying classes. It was a complaint by no means unique to eugenicists. Cecil Binney, who thought Beveridge was "an incompetent and self-advertising old humbug" whose socialist schemes to make babies would fail, noted that the birthrate had started falling in the first place as social services increased in England. Population was invariably largest in countries where there were the least number of such services, he argued, and the Beveridge provisions with their heavy tax costs were the least likely to increase the population.[64] Like a number of his colleagues in the Eugenics Society, Binney recoiled at the £86 million Beveridge estimated his plan would cost. As far as they were concerned, it constituted only the first installment on a package of dysgenic services whose demands on the exchequer would effectively sterilize the remainder of the taxpaying classes who had not already given up on trying to bring more children into the world.

Publication of the Beveridge report, followed by his Galton Lecture, brought to a head the difficulties family allowances posed for reform eugenicists trying to keep their tattered flag flying during the war. If the voices of reform were far more dominant in the eugenic movement than they had been during the 1914–18 conflict, they were, as then, forced to confront tactical, political realities as well as varied, but strongly held, feelings by the faithful. Although in January 1940 the society's Emergency Committee agreed to Blacker's suggestion that family allowances offered the best opening for the organization to carry out a constructive wartime policy that would keep it in the mainstream of social reform, the committee members were far less confident of the support they would find among the rank and file.[65] Family allowances, with their alleged subsidy of dysgenic breeding, potentially sterilizing tax burdens, and inflation of nurtural rather than biological considerations, touched a number of exposed nerves in the eugenic mind. This was particularly evident in the extensive published articles and letters in the *Eugenics Review* and private correspondence between Eugenics Society members in the first two years of the war.

Repeated efforts by reformers to get eugenicists to accept a flat-rate program as a nucleus upon which to build graded allowances later were strongly resisted, as the response to Beveridge indicated. C. V. Drysdale, still trying to sustain the implausible alliance of neo-Malthusianism with eugenics, was so angered by the Emergency Committee's preoccupation with family allowances rather than birth control that in 1942 he wrote a provocative letter to the *Eugenics Review* claiming that, despite its wealth and distinguished membership, eugenics had failed to achieve most of its goals and was no longer taken seriously by the public. It had become too academic and scientific and, by accepting Kuczynski's wrongheaded prophecies and diverting its attention to the myth of depopulation rather than the continued reality of dysgenic overpopulation, had ruined its last opportunity to awaken the nation's "eugenic conscience." The birth control movement, by contrast, was, with far fewer resources, an enormous success. Family allowances to Drysdale were the last straw; they smacked of a policy of "social appeasement" which would prove no more successful than had political appeasement in the 1930s.[66]

Though Titmuss wrote Drysdale off as a wrongheaded, unscientific "mid-Victorian reactionary" who should be ignored, some others, including Chance and Bramwell, thought there was something in what the old Neo-Malthusian had to say.[67] J. M. Keynes, a Eugenics Society council member, life fellow and former Neo-Malthusian, was astonished and embarrassed when his name turned up the next year listed as a vice-president on an outdated Malthusian League letterhead opposing family allowances and other pronatalist measures. "The whole thing, I should say, is complete fudge," he wrote a worried Blacker. "The Malthusian League does not really exist to-day and is merely a piece of note-paper in the possession of Mr. Drysdale and one or two friends."[68]

Aside from an occasional lecture or article, Keynes was not very active on behalf of the eugenic cause; Blacker, however, was once more deeply engaged and knew that Drysdale's complaints about the Eugenics Society having diluted its hereditarian principles and lost sight of its goal were not unique. Following the Beveridge report and the much-publicized debate in the House of Commons, the *Eugenics Review* provided some solace to skeptics by pointing out that none of the advocates of flat-rate allowances seriously believed the small payments, which it correctly predicted were likely to be closer to five rather than eight shillings, would have any appreciable effect on the birthrate. Indeed, as Beveridge and Titmuss made clear, flat-rate allowances were designed to relieve poverty, not solve the population problem.[69] A reading of the report, however, could and did permit another interpretation.

The *Eugenics Review* was clearly reluctant to criticize and eager to find something of clear eugenic value in a document which quickly found so much public approbation and promised to be one of the foundations for postwar social planning. But the best the editor could do was to hold out the feeble hope that the small number of people who would be moved to have more children by Beveridge's schemes were probably more conscientious and responsible than the majority of those who would benefit and were therefore "more likely than not to belong to eugenically desirable stocks."[70]

Nevertheless, there was no denying that the Beveridge report and the social insurance system it proposed was a disappointment from a eugenic standpoint despite its author's efforts to describe his recommendations as an essential first step toward race reconstruction. Not even Beveridge's eugenic defenders, however, had expected his largely internal, interdepartmental inquiry to do much to solve the qualitative aspects of the population problem that preoccupied their thinking. They looked instead to the Royal Commission on Population, whose investigation promised to be far more extensive and its deliberations open to a much wider range of interests, including those of the Eugenics Society, which directly and indirectly was well positioned to make sure its voice was heard.

Fourteen

From Baby Boom to Birth Dearth

The prolonged deliberations of the Royal Commission on Population, which reported in 1949, and the detailed fertility surveys made on its behalf, resulted in the most comprehensive review of British reproductive behavior since the *Fertility of Marriage Census* taken in 1911.[1] The commission's official inquiries, the last of which were not published until 1954, were seized upon by eugenicists as a long-awaited opportunity to achieve Galton's dream of scientifically improving "the inborn qualities of the race" so as to "raise the average quality of our nation to that of its better moiety." In trying to refashion the Victorian founder of eugenics to fit modern, postwar realities, Blacker assured the royal commission in 1945 that Galton's "principles are as apposite today as they were sixty years ago," even if "they need to be re-stated in terms of the present demographic situation and of current social standards."[2]

Eugenicists were deeply involved in the commission's proceedings either directly or indirectly through the Population Investigation Committee, the Family Planning Association, and Population and Economic Planning. With the first chairman of the commission, Sir John Simon, the lord chancellor, a strong supporter of both the Eugenics Society and the PIC, and with Carr-Saunders as one of the commissioners and head of its Statistics Committee, there was good reason to believe that the prestigious body would be sympathetic to Galton's admirable goals. Blacker was, however, exceedingly dubious about the British public. Even before the war the social and political climate, the detestation of authoritarianism, the outspoken scientific skepticism of a new generation of geneticists exploring the complexities of molecular biology, and the growing doubts about isolating the hereditary components of intelligence or other human characteristics from the environmental, had already made it extremely difficult to spread the eugenic gospel very widely. In the aftermath of the Nazis, ethical considerations had if anything compounded the problem enormously. The only hope Blacker and others still wedded to the eugenic dream could see for the rehabilitation of their movement was continued anxiety over the threat of depopulation and the endorsement of a qualitative solution by a prestigious national group such as the royal commission.

The "Unique Opportunity":
The Royal Commission on Population

In 1937 Blacker was privately informed that both the registrar-general and the new prime minister, Neville Chamberlain, favored the appointment of a royal commission in the near future. As a result, Blacker began planning for the "unique opportunity" it would provide to make the case for the promotion of fertility on eugenically favorable lines. When that day came he hoped that through alliances with other organizations, such as the PIC and PEP, and by avoiding the use of the word "eugenics," which he feared had become a liability in the political atmosphere of the 1930s, the Eugenics Society would have significant influence in shaping the study and in the formulation of demographic policies while avoiding stirring up prejudices.[3]

These concerns were behind the secretary general's attempt to cover up the Eugenics Society's role in the establishment of the Population Policies Committee in 1938 to work with PEP and other medical, economic, and sociological organizations studying the population question. The potential was too exciting, however, for the *Eugenics Review* not to mention the arrangement. With the PIC concentrating exclusively on the gathering of data and PEP formulating policies for raising the fertility of healthy stocks in all grades and classes, the approaching appointment of a royal commission, which would rely on the information and recommendations of these important groups, could, according to the review, only enhance the influence and prestige of the Eugenics Society.[4]

The war at least temporarily put an end to these wishful expectations. Despite Eugenics Society efforts to prop them up with financial subsidies and facilities, those collective Trojan horses of eugenic infiltration, the PIC and PEP, were soon unable to function and closed down. In addition, the London School of Economics, which was the center of PIC activity, moved to Cambridge, and its invaluable library was so dispersed as to make it inaccessible for continued population research.[5] The revival in 1942 of interest in the population question spurred the Eugenics Society Emergency Committee, at Richard Titmuss's urging, to establish a small population committee to watch the birthrate figures, correct misinformation being put out in some publications, and keep the essential facts before the public.

Carr-Saunders expressed serious reservations about the appropriateness of the Eugenics Society taking on this role, given that it was a propaganda organization whose ideas were not universally applauded. He feared it might do more harm than good to the demographic cause and was only persuaded to go along with the proposal on the understanding that the Population Committee was temporary and would cease to exist as soon as the PIC or PEP were able to function again as scientific bodies. A central task of the new committee was to identify potential topics for investigation by those groups when that day occurred. Kuczynski, Lafitte, Keynes, Beveridge, Huxley, Carr-Saunders, Cadbury, and G. D. H. Cole, among others, agreed to help in the selection.[6]

By the spring of 1943, with Blacker at the Ministry of Health and David Glass back from a posting in America as deputy director of the British Petroleum Mission and now working in the Ministry of Supply, the Emergency Committee decided, in light of the revived interest of Parliament and the public in the population problem, to resurrect the PIC and, as promised, close down its own committee. The decision, taken at Titmuss's request, was augmented by a willingness to give the PIC £500 a year as well as rent-free space, like that provided the FPA, in the Eugenics Society's offices in Eccleston Square. Despite Horder's preference that the PIC stick to its original task of concentrating exclusively on investigative research, the revived group added to its original purpose "the study, in light of her special needs, of such population policies as may be advocated in Great Britain." At the same time, the PIC reaffirmed it was not a propaganda agency for any particular policies its research might generate.[7]

Though it would take nearly a year for the PIC to be fully reactivated, the decision to start, as far as the Eugenics Society was concerned, did not come a moment too soon. In November 1943 the minister of health, as promised, announced the appointment of the long-anticipated Royal Commission on Population. Blacker was positively jubilant. He was certain that the PIC would play a major role in the commission's investigation and that several prominent eugenicists, including the commission's chairman, would be involved in the deliberations and the writing of the report. He had, after all, already been consulted about the work of a number of preliminary committees established, following the debate in the Commons, to examine various medical, scientific, political, economic, and religious aspects of the problem prior to the announcement of the royal commission. Not surprisingly, the Eugenics Society and the PIC were strongly represented on these committees, and the latter organization was quick off the mark in submitting memorandums recommending various lines of investigation to the minister of health and others.[8]

Once the commission was established and launched its prolonged inquiry, eugenicists, either as members of the main body or its many investigatory subcommittees, had substantial influence, as Blacker anticipated.[9] The PIC's chief investigator, David Glass, at the request of Blacker and Carr-Saunders, had been released from the Ministry of Supply in 1944 to assist in the great undertaking. Blacker described Glass's return as research secretary to the PIC as being of the greatest importance not only to that committee but to the Eugenics Society and "to the world of demography in this country."[10] He arranged for L. J. Cadbury to put up £1,000 to pay Glass's salary for two years or, as it turned out, until the research secretary, with Carr-Saunders's endorsement, was appointed to a readership in demography at the London School of Economics in 1945, a position that led three years later to Glass's elevation to professor of sociology. By then the PIC, placed on sound financial footing by a £5,000, five-year grant from the Nuffield Foundation, had itself moved from its rent-free Eugenics Society offices to the LSE, where, despite some uncertainty in the early years, it has remained ever since.[11]

Blacker was delighted with the PIC's success. It was not only a credit to the good judgment of its "generous godparent," as he described the Eugenics Society, but he was rightly confident that the offspring would survive the royal commission to become an enduring center or institute for population studies. He had, in fact, urged the establishment of such a facility at the LSE to its director, Carr-Saunders, a year before the war ended.[12] As always, the politically astute Blacker was more than satisfied to have the eugenic cause carried in the baggage of less controversial travelers along the road to race improvement.

But the royal commission also provided a "golden opportunity" for the Eugenics Society to stand on its own and begin the process of rehabilitating its science from the disparagement suffered in the interwar years at the hands of Hogben, Haldane, and other critics. In drawing up a lengthy memorandum on behalf of the society to submit to the commission, Blacker spoke of the cloud the word "eugenics" was under and feared some of the commissioners might be unconsciously prejudiced if not openly hostile. He planned, therefore, to begin with Galton's original and still relevant definition of eugenics and then to deal frankly with the criticisms and perversions which had become more severe since the advent of the Nazis and the outbreak of the war.[13]

The memorandum stressed that while the founder of eugenics "believed that the different branches of the human race were unequally equipped with the inborn characters that produce and sustain highly organized civilizations, it was no part of his outlook that biologically inferior races should be persecuted or suppressed." Blacker denounced the German preachers of race hygiene with their fanatical message of Aryanism, anti-Semitism, and aggressive national-ism for having done great harm to the cause of eugenics. The damage, he added, had been compounded by the analogous views of Americans "actuated by colour prejudice" as well as by the perversions of other cranks who had contributed to eugenics' becoming "politically and biologically suspect" in certain quarters.[14]

Blacker believed the way to rehabilitate eugenics was to redirect attention to Galton's "standpoint which, fortified by advances in the science of genetics, has gained in cogency and in relevance to affairs of the present day." He admitted that the founder of eugenics was less concerned with the problems of differential fertility that had preoccupied his successors since the opening of the century and agreed that, like the master, some of his early disciples had underestimated the complex interrelationship of heredity and environment and the difficulties of reaching agreement on what constituted eugenic standards. Nevertheless, nearly everyone now conceded the importance of (1) sound physical and mental health, (2) intelligence, (3) social usefulness and moral integrity, (4) freedom from genetic taints, (5) fondness for children and membership in "a big, united, and well-adjusted family."[15]

Only the fourth of these criteria, Blacker noted, was solely concerned with genetic qualities; all the others included environmental factors that were difficult to measure. In fact, with all of the advances made in genetic studies and population statistics, only intelligence could be quantifiably demonstrated. Even if no single test to measure total eugenic value were ever devised and only a simple biological index constructed, a social index, evident in the five qualities, already existed. The more the environment was improved, the more evident this would become as voluntary eugenic selection operated unimpeded by external considerations that interfered with our "philoprogenitive instincts." In the final analysis, however, Blacker was quick to add, differences among people would always exist for hereditary reasons no matter how uniform their environment.[16]

Though Blacker defensively reasserted that eugenics did not equate social classes with rigid biological castes and denied that the reversal of differential fertility was its sole aim, he reproduced the standardized birthrates of the eight classes described in the 1911 *Fertility of Marriage Census* and admitted eugenicists "hold it desirable that our population should be more largely recruited from the first four . . . than at present." It was more important to secure the largest number of births from the most intelligent families whatever their social and economic status. Unfortunately, "careful surveys have shown that the least intelligent families have on the average some three times as many children as the most intelligent," which correlated fairly closely with the registrar-general's social scale.[17]

Even the socially conscious, politically sensitive Blacker, desperately trying to establish the liberal, democratic credentials as well as the scientific validity of eugenics, was unable to see how much his criteria reeked of subjective, middle-class values and deep-seated social prejudice. However much he went on about the distribution of hereditary quality in all levels of society, he, like eugenicists since Galton's days, time and again found the physical, mental, and moral qualities he most admired distributed disproportionately in middle-class genes.

Ironically, in preparing the memorandum and his testimony, Blacker had to be reminded by Carr-Saunders not to overemphasize the importance of environment in explaining the correlations between eugenic qualities and class. It was imperative, the commissioner coached the witness to appear before him, to prepare "a really careful exposition of the need to keep the quality problem of the population question in mind." He urged Blacker to draw upon the best minds to show why the genetic makeup of the population was so important in the formulation of demographic policies to reverse the birthrate in such a way as to halt the "deterioration in the genetic heritage of the race." Carr-Saunders was concerned that in their eagerness to show how much eugenics appreciated the importance of nurture in explaining the differences between social groups, Blacker and other Eugenics Society spokesmen might not emphasize enough the determining role of nature.[18]

Not only did Blacker and the other Eugenics Society witnesses, Fraser Roberts and Aubrey Lewis, agree to stress the qualitative aspects of the population problem, leaving the quantitative to others, but they were carefully led through their oral testimony before the commission by Carr-Saunders. The evidence presented by the latter two on the correlations of intelligence with family size and the dangers posed by the Social Problem Group readily supported such an emphasis, and Blacker made certain that the eugenic possibilities of pronatalist schemes such as family allowances were understood.[19] Certain potential witnesses such as Lidbetter were ruled out by Carr-Saunders and Blacker for being too extreme and likely to provoke Labour, while Horder was rejected as too old, confused about the facts, and unlikely to take the time to prepare carefully.

Both Blacker and Carr-Saunders were very concerned that the Eugenics Society witnesses project an image of youthful vigor, intelligence, and expert authority in their subjects. Titmuss, they felt, would have best fit the bill, but because of other obligations he was unavailable to testify. "In short," the general secretary wrote, "I should like them [the commissioners] to think that the Society is active and progressive." If in its final report, he added, the royal commission used "eugenics" in a favorable demographic context, it would do much "to reinstate the word in general favour and popular usage" and help prepare society for the benefits Galton had dreamed of when he coined the term.[20]

The hope this might occur was strengthened by the important role played by modern, scientifically expert eugenicists on the various specialist and technical committees that provided the evidence upon which the commission would base its critical report. Eardley Holland was able to assure the presentation of a eugenic perspective in the inquiries undertaken by the Royal College of Obstetricians and Gynaecologists into the causes of involuntary sterility and childbearing, while another Eugenics Society member, the physiologist Alan Parkes, headed a Medical Research Council study of the medical and scientific facets of human fertility. Their various reports, replete with hereditarian allusions and explanations, were often everything the leaders of the Eugenics Society could have wished for.

Although the society had placed less emphasis upon birth control since the depopulation issue had arisen, it remained closely involved with the FPA and firmly endorsed its recommendations to the royal commission so long as they were couched in terms of "birth spacing" and took into account the socioeconomic status of those encouraged to use birth control methods to regulate the size of their families. Officially the society continued to warn of the dysgenic dangers of birth control when practiced by the genetically sound majority but linked it to sterilization as an important weapon of negative eugenics when the reproduction of additional offspring was physically and racially unwise. Eugenicists also welcomed the growing interest of the FPA in problems of sterility, and their hereditarian hand was especially evident in the addition of genetic counseling to the FPA's expanding list of services it wished the commission to endorse as part of comprehensive population planning.

Eugenic anxieties about differential fertility and declining intelligence were also well represented in the pessimistic assessments of Godfrey Thomson, Cyril Burt, E. O. Lewis, Fraser Roberts, and other experts in intelligence measurement and mental deficiency. Much of their evidence repeated the worrisome findings of the 1930s and reinforced the importance of hereditary causation. Though a more up-to-date, postwar survey of Scottish intelligence in 1947 did not discover the unbroken lines of descending brain power and ascending fertility eugenicists drew on their correlative charts, it failed to dislodge very much the belief in decline permeating the data received by the commission and analyzed by contemporaries at the time.

The influence of the PIC in many of the collateral studies was considerable. Among the most important was the 1946 *Family Census* taken on behalf of the royal commission by Glass and his colleague at the LSE, Eugene Grebenik.[21]

Based on sophisticated sampling techniques and revised social classifications, it not only confirmed how much the size of families had fallen in the twentieth century, particularly in the interwar years, but how pervasive the decline was in all sectors of society. Some eugenic comfort could be taken in the confirmation that although wide reproductive variations still existed among different occupational groups, these variations were no longer expanding and were in many instances rapidly narrowing.

Since the 1920s, for example, some of the most prolific groups identified in the 1911 census, such as miners, had reduced their fertility by more than a third, while the overall decline in family size in a number of manual and nonmanual occupations was virtually the same. The democratization of birth control meant that the notoriously low birthrates of the professional classes were in many instances being matched and sometimes exceeded by other sectors of the middle, skilled, and even semiskilled working classes.[22] Unlike T. H. C. Stevenson's report on the 1911 data, Glass and Grebenik's did not speculate on the possible eugenic implications of the differences discovered among the various occupational classifications. For one thing, the trend and pattern of fertility they described indicated there was less reason to worry about differential reproduction than there had been a generation earlier. But for another, Glass was always exceedingly cautious about drawing subjective, qualitative, eugenic conclusions from the demographic evidence he examined, and was even less likely to do so in the postwar world of the welfare state.

Before undertaking the survey, Glass told Carr-Saunders he could see no way to tackle the issue of differential fertility other than by collecting the statistics on its obvious reversal and publishing them. He knew the Eugenics Society had its own specific interests and suggested it might want to recommend a Darwin Scholar to the royal commission to look into them.[23] Glass, however, had no hesitation in evaluating reproductive experience in terms of the problem of depopulation, and there the *Family Census* could offer little encouragement. It instead precipitated more studies and anxieties about the decline in the birthrate as well as even more sophisticated techniques to measure net reproduction rates.[24]

The Population and the Polls

In 1945, a year before the Family Census was taken and nearly a decade before the findings of Glass and Grebenik were published, the independent polling organization, Mass Observation, reported in its own survey, *Britain and Her Birth-Rate*, on "the coming problem" for England and the rest of western civilization—the approaching decline in the population. Despite its claims of objectivity in examining social change, political trends, and public opinion, Mass Observation admitted that in this case it was "frankly partisan" in lining up with those "who do not want the English people to disappear." Its interviews, questionnaires, conversations, and observational studies in sample regions and neighborhoods in different parts of the country were designed to find out why men and women, but particularly the latter, did not want more children.[25]

After summarizing the net reproduction projections of the 1930s and describing their predicted effects on the economic and social structure of the country as the population aged and grew smaller, the authors of the Mass Observation report expressed their surprise at discovering that approximately 40 percent of their sample either had no idea the birthrate had been falling for the past fifty years, or thought it had been going up. Even more distressing to the worried pollsters was the knowledge that people were evenly divided over whether the decline in fertility and the population was good or bad. Those who favored decline gave the usual reasons: uncertainty about the future, fear of war if cannon fodder were readily available, improvement in living standards, and more opportunities and a decline in unemployment. Economic considerations were certainly paramount in the responses but, the report argued, fallacious. The authors candidly admitted that in setting up public opinion as an "Aunt Sally" and refuting it they were departing from objectivity. But they felt that since the problem of declining population was so important and on its way to becoming the "most burning social issue" within a generation, it was imperative to get the facts straight.[26]

Mass Observation found a good deal of ignorance about birth control and variance in its use but concluded its adoption was the principal means if not the cause of the problem. The willingness of couples either to plan in advance or to leave the conception of children to chance varied with the length of marriage and, not surprisingly, with the size of families. The more recent the marriage, the more likely husbands and wives were to plan carefully, which was also strikingly true in marriages of longer duration where there were fewer than three offspring. With only 25 percent of people with more than three children claiming they did not leave matters to chance, compared to 54 percent with less than three, it seemed evident to the Mass Observation analysts that larger families were generally unplanned.

When higher educational and social status levels were taken into account, planning increased dramatically, indicating that middle-class parents with a secondary education were far less likely than those in the working classes, with only an elementary education, to take any chances they would have more children than they wanted. The report added, however, that probably half the women with more than three children would have fewer if they knew how to prevent getting pregnant. This finding suggested that as the spread of birth control information continued, the decline in fertility would accelerate. It was a prospect that "only those who do not like the English race could look forward to."[27]

The problem, the pollsters reasoned, was not the availability of birth control but the role children played in modern thinking about marriage and the family. For example, although a majority of every group, irrespective of class and education, said children were very important to their happiness, only 10 percent of women gave children as a reason for marrying in the first place. Love and a desire for a home of one's own were much more important. "Children are one of the least adequately foreseen and planned-for sides of married life," the report claimed. A desire for them did not loom large in marriage decisions; it usually came later as a way to strengthen a relationship or hold a home together. They were not conceived for their own sake or for the country, but for their parents. With the exception of some Catholics, who felt an obligation to their faith, children were wanted for purely personal reasons and these could be sufficiently satisfied with one or two. The point of the argument was that unless the fundamental motivation for children changed, no social programs or improvements could be expected to increase family size. In fact, the decline in fertility had paralleled the great rise in such programs. They might make it more pleasant to give birth and raise children, but they did not create a desire for them.[28]

While demographers were struggling to devise statistical formulas and models to predict family size, Mass Observation investigators employed a technique that has tended over the years to prove more reliable—they asked people how many children they wanted. They found that most couples married more than five years wanted the number they already had and this was usually two or three. Sixty percent of those married for less than five years, however, wanted only two children, the number preferred by about half of all respondents and usually described as "ideal." Taking into account the minority of couples who wanted more than three—they were usually married more than ten years and already had more than three children—the average came out to about 2.7.

A British Institute of Public Opinion poll based upon interviews with unmarried as well as married men and women and published early in 1944 had found the ideal number of children to be closer to three than two, and as many as one-third of the respondents expressed a desire for four.[29] Mass Observation's concentration upon the reproductive plans of married women a year later found very little sentiment for families of such size. Indeed, the investigators turned up a good deal of hostility toward people with large families. They were somehow considered old-fashioned, indecent, and immoral, especially if a wife had children after age thirty-five. With women marrying on average at age twenty-five and likely to delay getting pregnant for a couple of years before spacing childbearing so as to complete their reproductive activity in their early thirties at the latest, the trend pointed forcefully to no more than two or three offspring at best. None of this added up to a middle-class "revolt against parenthood," as was frequently charged, the report concluded. On the contrary, couples in all families continued to want children. They just wanted fewer of them, and as contraception became more reliable and readily available, they would satisfy their limited goals whatever their class or locale.[30]

In analyzing the primacy of economic reasons and inadequate housing for the reluctance of English men and women to go beyond the norm of two or three children, the investigators found it paradoxical that only about half of working-class respondents said payment of family allowances might alter their decision. Improved housing would have more of an impact, but nearly 40 percent still claimed it would make no difference. Initially, the pollsters observed, 60 percent of those asked could not spontaneously think of what would induce them to have more children and had to be presented with concrete choices to which to respond.

Eugenicist complaints about family allowances, however, seemed to be confirmed, the report noted. The wealthiest and best-educated people already had the fewest number of children, and two-thirds of their number questioned said the addition of family allowances, unless they covered all of the basic costs of child rearing, would not be a factor in changing their minds. Even if the allowances were graded, as Mass Observation thought they should be, rather than flat rate, the net gain was still likely to be small. Nevertheless, since only the very poor seemed inclined to respond to flat-rate, cash payments, it was essential, for eugenic reasons, that allowances be pegged to income and be in goods and services that would guarantee children received the benefits directly.[31]

Mass Observation was convinced something else which could not be easily quantified was at work inhibiting the reproductive instinct. It was not a loss of religious faith, as some claimed. With the modest exception of Catholics, there was not a great deal of difference in the reproductive aspirations of religious, vaguely religious, and irreligious women. In practice, those of a strong spiritual persuasion only averaged one more child than their more numerous, if less zealous counterparts. Not even the decline of servants, much complained about by the middle and upper classes, explained the determination to keep families small, though for some it was a sign of the passing of a more comfortable, attractive way of life. While 37 percent of middle-class women admitted that the availability of domestic help would have some effect on the number of children they had, 61 percent said it would make no difference whatsoever, a figure not markedly below the 74 percent of working-class women who had the same response.[32]

All of the tables and percentages measuring the reasons for the birthrate problem added up to a "forest of question marks." Finding the answer, Mass Observation conjectured, might depend upon determining "to what extent is the will, even the ability, to perpetuate the race linked deep with the sense of life's purposefulness and point." It was led to this imprecise conclusion by the discovery of a striking inverse correlation between fertility and the pessimism or, as was less common, optimism of the people surveyed. Despite the approach of victory, only 22 percent of women in the low birthrate, mainly middle-class areas sampled were optimistic about the postwar world, while 46 percent were decidedly pessimistic. Though gloom in the high birthrate areas, which were more likely to be working class, was, at 26 percent, substantially less, only a third of respondents expressed much confidence in the future. Approximately 40 percent of the women conceded that a secure future would encourage them to have more children—the figure was 55 percent for women married less than five years—but half the couples expected another war in fifteen to twenty-five years. These statistics added up to "feelings of insecurity and purposelessness" against which the "maternal instinct today is fighting a losing battle."[33]

Much of what the Mass Observation poll revealed confirmed Blacker's prewar opinion that the explanation for the failure of the British people to replace themselves lay in the realm of psychology where tender-mindedness, fear, and pessimism had taken hold. The effects were unfortunately more pronounced among the more intelligent, educated, thoughtful, and farsighted sectors of the populace. Mass Observation essentially agreed, and the more subjective and intuitive its evaluation of the data, the more eugenic its report became. Noting the tendency of the more fertile sectors of the working classes in their sample to be more optimistic than the middle and upper classes, it attributed the difference to the inability of the less-informed and less-interested workers to see the long-term implications of things.

Commenting on the "sad truth today that children are distributed in inverse ratio to knowledge and the ability and desire to assimilate facts," the report asked, "have we to rely on the improvident and the wishful-thinking for the perpetuation of the race?" Without questioning the beneficial effects of social programs and legislative efforts to improve the standard of living, the authors were nevertheless leery of schemes that did not take into account qualitative results. "If it is desirable to perpetuate the don't knows, and the don't cares and the can't thinks while the others gradually become extinct, well and good," they wrote. "Let's get ahead with numbers, and to hell with eugenics."

The key to quality as well as quantity, according to Mass Observation, was the stimulation of a desire for children among those sectors of society where the practice of limitation was strongest. Because legislation was more likely to raise that desire most where it was already highest, "for the eugenic future, something deeper is needed." The authors were vague as to what this might be, but it involved convincing parents that Britain would be a fit place for babies to live. "Legislation should plan towards a purposeful future for tomorrow's unborn citizens," their report concluded, "and maybe the birth-rate, numerical and eugenic, will take care of itself?" They were not, however, confident that the social insurance measures and flat-rate family allowance programs contemplated or already passed by Parliament would have this effect.[34]

The strong eugenic tone of *Britain and Her Birth-Rate* served to inflate further the hopes of the Eugenics Society that the royal commission would endorse many of their ideas. The "special motivation" that the Mass Observation report claimed was needed to induce desirable young couples to want more children was not very different from the "eugenic conscience" Galton had proposed as a new religion at the turn of the century when the plummeting birthrate had first generated widespread alarm. If the avowed number of his apostles remained small, they were sustained by the knowledge that their assumptions and ideas permeated the social beliefs and attitudes of millions of their countrymen who did not explicitly think of themselves as eugenicists. Although their legislative achievements were still negligible, Eugenics Society leaders expected this would change as they joined cause with other population groups and pursued their plan for rehabilitation and vindication through influencing the recommendations of the royal commission. Like the Jesuits of the past, they were primarily interested in converting the princes; the people would follow.

In Blacker's judgment, the final report of the royal commission after five years of inquiry and the expenditure of £250,000 substantially vindicated this policy. While it was not an explicitly eugenic document, the report addressed, at least indirectly, most of the qualitative issues surrounding the population question eugenicists worried about. The commission's strong endorsement of the availability of free birth control advice and contraceptives as a right of every patient enrolled in the new National Health Service held out the promise at last of effectively restricting the fertility of the very poor. With the establishment of a national system of family planning clinics in the offing, eugenicists relished the prospect of requiring premarital examinations to screen out defectives, helping the worthy overcome sterility problems, and providing genetic counseling.[35] In addition, the commission's ambitious recommendation of family allowance schemes and other proposals to reduce the social, economic, and physical burdens of bearing and raising children took into account the need to assist families at all income levels, something that the flat-rate payments finally introduced in 1945 had failed to do.[36]

Despite the enormous amount of time and cost that went into producing the report, it made little impression on the public or Parliament, whose collective anxieties about the menace of underpopulation had led to the appointment of the royal commission. No political party took it up, it was never debated, and no population policy was ever implemented. By the time the report and several of its supporting studies were published, the birthrate, though never as robust as it had been earlier in the century, was still above the perilously low figures that had brought on the depopulation scare in the first place. Indeed, the birthrate had already begun to turn upward before the commission had been appointed, but the momentum for an inquiry had been building for decades and, by 1943, was too strong to arrest.

Instead of being well on its way to losing a quarter of its population in the next generation or two, the country was discovered to be growing at a slow but steady rate. By 1951, the population was nearly 4 million larger than it had been when the projections had been made two decades before.[37] More than half the increase were females who, if the postwar trends continued, were not only more likely to marry than in the past but to replace themselves. The talk after 1945 was not of a baby shortage but of a baby boom, and the young couples responsible for it were not much inclined to notice the report of a commission established to determine how to keep the population from falling rather than rising. They were probably even less aware of the vigilant efforts of eugenicist propagandists to make sure that hereditary quality would not be discounted in the pursuit of numerical quantity.

If eugenicist aspirations were in part thwarted by the unexpected baby boom, they were unlikely to have found much satisfaction in the postwar political and social climate even if the population had begun to decline. The Labour party, which had never been as fearful of the prospect as the Conservatives, and whose members strongly resented the class prejudices that continued to permeate eugenic discussions of the subject, was not inclined to pay much attention to any schemes in which hereditary quality was a factor. The welfare state it was attempting to construct out of the wreckage of the postwar economy was based upon egalitarian premises that still ran counter to eugenic sensibilities no matter how much reformers acknowledged the importance of nurture.

Similarly, whatever eugenic presumptions they harbored, the Conservatives after returning to power in 1951 were not about to commit political suicide by trying to dismantle the welfare state however much many of their number questioned the egalitarian assumptions upon which it was built. Although Conservatives had been the most vociferous parliamentary prophets of demographic disaster in the 1930s and early 1940s and had led the way in demanding the appointment of the royal commission, they too could see no compelling reason after the war for tackling a complex and controversial problem that people seemed to be solving well enough in the privacy of their bedrooms.

The Failure of the Eugenic Dream

In a brief history of the eugenics movement published in 1952 to coincide with his resignation after twenty-one years as general secretary of the Eugenics Society, Blacker acknowledged that the movement, as Galton had envisioned it, had essentially failed. He attributed the failure, however, not to any alteration in the birthrate or to new breakthroughs in the study of human genetics that challenged basic eugenic dogma, but to Nazi racism. Although the perverted "Nietzschean eugenics" of the Third Reich were a far cry from those of Galton, Blacker complained, the entire eugenics movement had been discredited.[38]

Eugenicists had become used to prominent left-wing scientists and the occasional Labourite denouncing eugenics as a subversive, racist, antidemocratic, pseudoscientific doctrine practiced by the Nazis and advocated in Britain as a way of dealing with the supposedly inferior working class. But even those most inured to such attacks were shocked by Hogben's assertion at a scientific meeting in November 1945 "that the official creed of the 3rd Reich permeated our own eugenics—from Galton to Dean Inge." He went on to charge that the same "intellectual sewage" of "*Rassenhygiene* or Eugenics— call it what you will," was as responsible for British class relations as it was for the extermination camps. Though Blacker tried to shrug it off as being "in accordance with what we all now expect of him," he knew how devastating such linkages were to the credibility of eugenics in the postwar world.[39] When in 1947 he evaluated for an international scientific commission the scientific value of eugenic sterilization experiments carried out by doctors in the German concentration camps, Blacker not only concluded that the appalling experiments were cruel, unnecessary, and of no scientific use whatsoever but ended with the assurance, "None of these experiments have any bearing on eugenics as the subject is understood in this country."[40]

Such defensiveness characterized much of eugenic propaganda after the war as its advocates struggled to separate their battered faith from that of the Nazi heretics. The fear and hatred of tyranny, as well as distrust of power and authority, made it more imperative than ever, Blacker wrote a few years later, that "personal liberty should therefore be specially treasured when demographic policies are devised." He was certain there were "few eugenists to-day who are not conscious of how this principle should be specially safe-guarded and cherished."[41]

These sentiments notwithstanding, eugenics, to the vast majority of Britons who knew anything about it, seemed after 1945 more incompatible than ever with personal liberty if not with modern science. The old Comtean notion that biology was destiny had never blended very well with British secular concepts of free will and individual liberty as eugenicists knew. Moreover, despite nearly two decades of trying to reconcile eugenics with environmentally based social reform, determining the relative contributions of nature and nurture, which had troubled the eugenics movement from its beginnings, had in many ways become more difficult. While most people in the middle and upper classes probably continued to believe that heredity was to some extent a significant factor in the qualitative composition of society, they were less and less persuaded that it was especially critical and doubted anything should be done to manipulate the gene pool even if it were possible to do so.

In 1962 the Eugenics Society commissioned the Gallup organization to survey a thousand people listed in *Who's Who* about their hereditarian beliefs. Although the society had by that time ceased publishing the *Eugenics Review* and largely abandoned its propagandist role to become a small research organization primarily interested in human genetics, family planning and population problems, nearly 90 percent of this elitist sample could define the term "eugenics" and knew that it was concerned with race improvement, limiting problem families, and to a lesser extent, with encouraging some people to have more children than others.[42] Of the 50 percent who responded to the questionnaire, 93 percent were male, primarily scientists, academics, civil servants, government officials, businessmen, and engineers. Most of them, 83 percent, believed in evolution and natural selection. Though nearly 60 percent of these people thought heredity had more effect than environment on intelligence compared to 30 percent who believed the factors were equal, the figures were reversed for social behavior.

In general, older respondents placed more emphasis upon heredity than their younger colleagues, and 80 percent of the total number favored more research in human heredity. Only one-third of them, however, believed such research should be encouraged to improve the quality of the human race and even fewer of them supported financial allotments to encourage selected people to have more children. Indeed, the overwhelming support for birth control contained in the questionnaires primarily reflected a desire to control population growth in general rather than the fertility of particular sections of society. About 63 percent of the respondents did, however, endorse the additional advantage of deterring "certain people" from having any more children. Perhaps the Eugenics Society's sensitivity to the issue of class prejudice prevented its asking about the criteria for deterrence.[43]

The sampling method used in the Gallup poll would have appealed to Galton himself; it demonstrated the Eugenics Society's continued preoccupation with the successful, educated elite. That most of the respondents from *Who's Who* were very familiar with the general principles of eugenics and shared a belief in the efficacy of Darwinian selection and hereditarian causation was undoubtedly satisfying to eugenicists, as was the strong support the questionnaires revealed for genetic research. But the reluctance of those queried to translate their beliefs into a policy of positive eugenics promoting the reproduction of selective sectors of society reflected a recognition of the still unmeasurable importance of environment and a deep distrust of sociobiological engineering and the authoritarian threat it posed to democracy and individual liberties in a "brave new world."

None of this meant that eugenical, hereditarian presuppositions about class and, increasingly, race, as immigrants came into the country from India, Pakistan, Africa, and the West Indies, did not continue to permeate the thinking of a great many successful, well-placed Britons. They were, however, like members of the Eugenics Society themselves, more cautious and restrained in expressing their beliefs and were in any event uncertain as to how they could be implemented in some concrete way without stirring up charges of class prejudice and racism. When the wealthy, Conservative politician and later minister for education and science, Sir Keith Joseph, ventured in 1974 to offer his eugenic opinion of those of his less prosperous fellow countrymen who were breeding to excess and threatening Britain with degeneration, he quickly learned how provocative and politically embarrassing the open expression of such ingrained assumptions could be.[44] Similarly, although the mounting obsession of another Tory luminary, Enoch Powell, with the immigrant birthrate and its mongrelizing threat to the British race won him considerable applause in the 1960s and 1970s from the nativist Right in Britain, he soon became an embarrassment to the Conservative party and saw the prospects for his political career quickly fade.[45]

The unacceptability of eugenical argument in the public arena after World War II probably had less to do with eugenics' devalued scientific credentials, which were to some extent always suspect, than it did with the profound change in the social and political climate. The breakdown of the "eugenic consensus" that pervaded scientific and educated popular thought across the political spectrum for several generations was ultimately rooted in political events rather than in any dramatic scientific discovery. Polygenic inheritance, gene-gene interaction, and gene-environment interaction, which undermined the scientific foundations of eugenics, were all known before the war. Reform eugenicists themselves acknowledged the much larger genetic variability that existed in populations than the pioneers of the movement had recognized, and accepted the biological advantages of diversity through natural selection without losing their faith in the critical importance of heredity. However, unlike their more rigidly deterministic predecessors such as Pearson and even the genial Galton, they rejected the proposition that the salvation of the race was exclusively, or, in many cases perhaps, even primarily bound up with an improvement in its genes.[46]

Confronted with changing scientific evidence coming out of the genetic laboratories about the nature of heredity and its uncertain relationship to environment reform, eugenicists in the 1930s had begun to retreat, reconsider, and regroup. But they were prodded to do so as much by the social and political environment of the interwar years as they were by the lessons of Huxley, Fisher, Haldane, Muller, Hogben, and the other architects of modern genetics who were themselves stimulated to varying degrees by this environment. The often stormy process of reevaluation and reformulation of eugenic principles and policies was not forced by the rise of Nazism but paralleled it. It would have happened without Hitler, or, for that matter, without Stalin, whom some left-wing scientists and social scientists regarded for a while as their eugenic "man on horseback."

In the aftermath of World War II the loathsomeness of authoritarian science and racism, as Blacker and most eugenicists recognized, made it extremely difficult to win new recruits to their cause. While the process of readjustment and accommodation to scientific and political realities continued, the fading away of eugenics from the public scene was inevitably linked to more fundamental changes in British society. The eugenics movement had always been a product of its times. Rooted in the imprecise popular Victorian observation that like begets like, ideas about the biological foundations of social class were given credibility by the growth of positivism and social Darwinism. Eugenics, as formulated by Galton, was inspired by this mixture of popular social assumption and observation, positivistic confidence in science, and the *Origin of Species*. It was moved in the early twentieth century from the realm of mathematical, neo-Darwinian esoterica, which few people could understand, to the public arena by something most people could comprehend and were increasingly concerned about—the declining birthrate.

The transformation of eugenics into a movement, and, more important, a popular way of thinking about heredity, was directly connected with fundamental social, economic, and political changes occurring in the late Victorian and Edwardian years which, for many people trying to come to terms with them, were reflected in precisely measurable demographic statistics. Indeed, as this book has argued, eugenic patterns of thought, like the eugenic movement itself, remained closely linked to the population question throughout its history. That link contributed to the movement's attracting a more eclectic political and intellectual following than has generally been acknowledged. Enthusiasm for the class-based, hereditarian tenets of eugenics varied widely, and people tended to find in them what they wanted. In the interwar years, by becoming deeply involved in the birth control movement and then in the expanding area of population research stimulated by the depopulation scare or panic of the 1930s, eugenicists sought to expand their base of support and influence the formulation of social policies in such a way as to improve "the inborn qualities of the race," as Galton described the goal of eugenics in 1904.

That it was becoming more difficult and controversial to try to define those qualities, or even to discuss them publicly in the altered social and political surroundings of the prewar years, was obvious to the reform-minded leaders of the eugenics movement in the decade before the Second World War. Their efforts to deflect criticism of what many opponents charged was an antidemocratic, anti–working class agenda included supporting not only the major birth control organizations, the NBCA, and later, the FPA, but also respected social scientific research groups such as the PIC and PEP. These alliances were, to a large extent, pragmatic, tactical responses to assure that qualitative, hereditarian considerations would be included in any formulation of a national population policy.

Blacker knew that these organizations embraced a broad range of able liberal and socialist analysts. Some of them were Eugenics Society members who acknowledged the importance of heredity even if they were unprepared to give it the prominence in their deliberations and proposals the society, which was often paying their salaries or expenses, might have wished. The tradition of Fabian socialism within the eugenics movement had, despite the conflicts it provoked, helped open a narrow path to some Leftist social reformers even before World War I, and reform eugenicists consciously tried to widen it in subsequent years. Only the pervasive uncertainty and ambivalence about the scientific validity of eugenics, combined with external social and political pressures that threatened its ability to survive as an organized cause, allowed the reformers to do so and the movement to encompass as wide a range of ideologies as it did. That eugenics could attract a Richard Titmuss and, despite protests, even permit him to speak for it while repelling an Enid Charles or Lancelot Hogben, whose explanations of the population problem were very similar to his, says a good deal about the fluidity of eugenic thought by World War II. It was especially ironic that the Eugenics Society, which justified its establishment on a very different reading of the demographic evidence, should become allied with social reformers whose utopias were in many ways inimical to the intellectual heritage and sociobiological assumptions of Galton's "New Jerusalem."

Because anxieties about the birthrate and social patterns of reproduction had fueled the rise of the eugenics movement in the first place and dominated its history, it was perhaps appropriate that as those anxieties rapidly diminished after World War II, eugenics rapidly faded into comparative obscurity. Already weakened by the new genetics, tainted by the horrors of Nazism, and battered by the emergence of Labour and the welfare state, its hereditarian message was not only scientifically suspect and politically and intellectually unpalatable, it was irrelevant to postwar demographic realities.

Eugenicists had gambled their rehabilitation on influencing the recommendations of the long-awaited Royal Commission on Population for turning the fifty-year decline in the birthrate around. But contrary to what all of the experts expected, the rate started to reverse during the war, even before the commission was appointed and, compared to the interwar years, constituted a veritable baby boom by the time the commission reported. All of the Eugenics Society's efforts to persuade the commission of the continued efficacy of Galton's principles, and the influence of the many eugenicists involved in the preparation of the report and its supportive inquiries, had little effect. With the birthrate in Great Britain averaging nearly 20 per 1,000 since the end of the war and the population growing briskly, the Labour government saw no reason for allotting time to debate the findings of a commission set up to examine the causes and consequences of population decline. The problem the government faced was not one of stimulating the growth of a larger population, but of housing, educating, and caring for its present one, which showed every sign of continuing to increase.

Although the birthrate declined to an average of 17 per 1,000 in the next decade before rising again to nearly 19 per 1,000 in the early 1960s, the Conservative government, whose wartime members had never wanted the commission appointed in the first place, was not inclined to resurrect its report from the obscurity to which it had been consigned. The interests of demographic planners and population-minded politicians switched rapidly to the international scene where the Malthusian dangers of a population explosion in the underdeveloped world appeared far more ominous. At home the complaints were not about empty cradles but about the social and environmental consequences of overcrowding and diminishing resources.

The Eugenics Society was well aware of how out of favor its principles were in the postwar atmosphere. Sensitive to the extent to which the term "eugenics" had become a lightning rod for charges of racism, class prejudice, and bigotry, it moderated its ambitions for rehabilitation, replaced the propagandist *Eugenics Review* with the scholarly *Journal of Biosocial Science*, and issued in 1961 a revised statement of aims stressing equally the study of hereditary and environmental aspects of human qualities. Some longtime reform eugenicists such as John Baker found the statement to be "so feeble as scarcely to be eugenic at all." He had wanted the new charter to proclaim: "Eugenists believe that certain persons are genetically better qualified than others to be the parents of the next generation: The Eugenics Society exists to investigate this subject, to devise practical measures that will yield the results desired by eugenists and to convince the public of the need for such measures."[47] It was an objective that the mainline founders of the organization a half-century earlier would have applauded.

As far as Baker was concerned, since Blacker's departure to work on international population problems and become the first chairman of the Simon Population Trust, the society had lost sight of its goal; it was becoming "too sociological and cautious" in its desire to find acceptance in the postwar world.[48] Like Blacker, he had moved decidedly to the right since 1945 and worried about the pronounced Leftist sentiments of many in the scientific community. While many of the questions about the biological determinants of social class that had driven English eugenics earlier in its history had been resolved, Baker thought that the mounting racial difficulties in the country and around the globe offered new opportunities for eugenic evaluation. "Is the Society so convinced that everyone in the world is exactly equal," he complained, "that a lecture [on inequality] would be indecent?"[49]

Baker's criticisms reflected an assumption that was probably correct: a far greater number of influential, educated people continued to believe in hereditarily determined, qualitative differences among peoples, races, and even sectors of society than were prepared to admit it publicly in the political atmosphere of the 1950s and 1960s. They were, in other words, crypto eugenicists, intimidated by the times in which they lived. The Gallup poll commissioned by the Eugenics Society in 1962 was designed in part to determine the extent of eugenic belief among a sample of the nation's elite, and though only half those approached returned the questionnaires, those who did certainly shared a good many eugenic perceptions, if not strong eugenic convictions.

If a legacy of biological-hereditarian ways of thinking about class and race persisted in the educated, elitist realms of British culture after the war, people were much more circumspect about expressing it in eugenic terms. Perhaps nothing demonstrated more clearly how far eugenics had been removed from public discourse than the revival of the current debate over the birthrate in the 1970s. After reaching its postwar high of 19.2 per 1,000 in 1964, fertility in Great Britain began a steady decline which by the mid-1970s approached 12.5 per 1,000. This rate, which has persisted more or less to the present day, confirmed that the baby boom was, as some demographers predicted, but a temporary reversal of the downward pattern that began a hundred years ago. As early as 1971 the press, not only in Britain but in the United States, began writing about the baby boom giving way to a birth dearth and contemplating once again the multiple consequences of zero population growth or worse, population decline.[50] When in 1973–74 deaths nearly equaled births, headlines proclaimed "Population Rise at Record Low." By the middle of 1975, the *Times* thought it possible that for the first time since records were kept, emigration might be enough to tip the close balance between births and deaths so as to record a net decline.

In subsequent years when the birthrate occasionally slipped beneath 12 per 1,000 and deaths actually exceeded births in some quartile periods, the press was quick to calculate the daily loss in the population.[51] With headlines waving "Bye Bye Baby Boom!" and asking rhetorically, "Are Babies Going Out of Fashion?" concerns about the future of the economy, educational requirements, and the likely demands for social services in an aging population became commonplace once again. While some authorities predicted a drop in the school population of at least 25 percent in the next fifteen years, others warned that if current reproductive practices continued that long, there would be no births at all in some parts of England.[52]

These renewed anxieties, redolent of the depopulation scare of the 1930s, were reinforced by net reproduction or replacement rates showing that whereas in the 1960s women were having on average 2.3 children, more than the 2.1 now estimated by postwar demographers as necessary to sustain the population, the rate fell to 1.8 in the 1970s and to 1.77 in the mid-1980s. In some countries such as Denmark and West Germany, where the replacement rates were around 1.45 and 1.30 respectively, declining population was already a reality. Some prophets calculated that over the next forty years the population in parts of Britain would fall to pre–World War I levels.[53]

Demographers determined in the early 1970s, when the drop in fertility again became a topic for public notice, that a birthrate of approximately 13.5 per 1,000 was required just to maintain the present population. Their assurances that the rate would soon begin to rise again when the children of the postwar baby boom reached maturity, married, and began to have families, proved not to be correct. As a result Britain in the 1970s, when the population barely increased by .03 percent, moved into what *New Society* described as "the years of zero growth."[54] If they continued, a new generation of prophets calculated, the population in the year 2000 would remain at around 56 million instead of rising to the 76 million some planners had anticipated in the comparatively fertile years of the 1950s and 1960s. The British people would also be much older and less productive so that plans for schools, roads, jobs, hospitals, early retirement, and social services would have to be reevaluated and, in many cases, scrapped.[55]

The knowledge that the rates of reproduction were substantially lower in many other European countries was of little comfort to those who saw Britain's future after 1973 tied to that of its Common Market neighbors. There were already one-third fewer "Eurobabies" in 1981 than in the 1960s, and with every country in the European Economic Community, with the exception of Ireland, recording fertility figures well below replacement, the "decline of the west" took on another quantifiable dimension.[56]

Contemporary analysts who favor zero growth or even a smaller population for economic, environmental, and ecological reasons enthusiastically approve of these trends. They hope the government will not only resist pressures to encourage people to have more children but will actually promote family planning programs that lead to a slowly declining population. While welcoming the return to lower fertility, several of them nevertheless have tempered their optimism by recalling how similar predictions made earlier in the century about population decline have proven to be unfounded. Even the "stupidest couple," to quote the *Economist*, knows how and how not to make babies, so reproductive patterns could change again depending upon social, economic, and political conditions.[57]

But as numerous critics point out, since the current decline began, "babies have gone out of fashion" and are likely to remain that way for the foreseeable future. With women far more independent and integrated into the workforce, contraception and abortion readily available, divorce commonplace, the fear of chronic economic problems and unemployment, and the widespread belief that the country and the world are already overpopulated and straining against available resources, few commentators in the 1970s and 1980s have found much reason to expect another baby boom anytime soon.[58] The small family system which had started to gain acceptance among the middle and upper classes, and some sectors of the working classes a century earlier, now appears too deeply entrenched among all sectors of society to be displaced without some dramatic alteration in social and cultural values and expectations.

What is striking about this latest chapter in the British response to the declining birthrate is the virtual absence of eugenic considerations. Even if it were still politically possible to discuss the decline in class-specific, eugenic terms, the nearly universal adoption of birth control makes it exceedingly difficult to analyze reproductive behavior in socially qualitative, differential ways. Although there have been occasional suggestions that "college girls," who on average have only about 1.8 children, are more responsible for the falling birthrate than less-educated women, little has been said about the qualitative implications of the data. In any event, the aggregate fertility of women lacking higher education, though slightly higher, is at 2.06, also below replacement. Similarly when the unemployed are singled out as having more children—"for lack of anything else to do," as the *Sunday Times* suggested— no invidious class distinctions are made. On the contrary, nearly all of the social analyses of the low birthrate in the 1970s and 1980s have noted that, in general, working-class couples are actually having fewer children than their middle- and upper-class counterparts, prompting the *Times Educational Supplement* to contemplate with satisfaction the continued production of "better class babies" to sustain the enrollment of independent schools worried about the supply of future pupils.[59]

When in a 1974 speech to the Conservative Birmingham Association Sir Keith Joseph publicly endorsed the promotion of birth control as an antidote to the degeneration that he saw implicit in the greater fertility of "the deprived classes," where the "least fitted mothers—the unmarried, deserted, divorced, those of low intelligence and low education" were producing one-third of the nation's children, many of his angry critics pointed out that his social prejudices aside, he simply "got it wrong." As one of them retorted, the figure of one-third Sir Keith quoted referred to babies born to mothers under the age of twenty irrespective of class. Moreover, he went on, "there is now evidence that . . . the birthrate . . . appears to be declining so fast, particularly among the working classes, that . . . the prospect of the next generation may be too few families of any class—rather than too many."[60]

Joseph's warnings about the threat to the quality of "our human stock" implicit in the differential birthrate, and his certainty that "the worship of instinct, of spontaneity, the rejection of self-discipline, is not progress—it is degeneration," brought applause from a few of his listeners, one of whom was "delighted that someone has the courage to utter a genetically based opinion."

Like a number of Conservative backbenchers, he shared Sir Keith's conviction that if nothing was done about the birthrate of the people in the registrar-general's classes IV and V, "the nation moves towards disintegration, however much resources we pour into preventive work and the overburdened educational system." It is a sign of the times, however, that nothing was said about increasing the fertility of the prosperous and, presumably, genetically superior middle- and upper-class people in classes I and II.

Far more common were denunciations, particularly from Labour spokesmen, of Sir Keith's revival of "the master race concept" associated with ideas of human stock breeding, castration, or compulsory contraception. Representatives of the FPA were quick to dissociate themselves from his eugenic reasoning even while welcoming anything "which draws attention to the need for classes four and five to effectively control their own fertility when they cannot afford children." But, they added, there was no evidence that birth control could improve the quality of Britons, and they emphasized their opposition to "selective birth control."[61] Old time Eugenics Society members might well have wondered why they had invested so much in the birth control movement and the FPA before, during, and even after the war.

No one was more astonished by the "tinderbox of reaction" his comments ignited than the often maladroit Sir Keith himself, who had been saying such things for years and recalled when they were perfectly appropriate. He only mentioned them in passing in his Birmingham speech to demonstrate his support for the inclusion of birth control services in the national health service, a progressive policy recommended by the Royal Commission on Population twenty-five years earlier. He insisted he had been grossly misrepresented, denied advocating "a master race," and was baffled as to why his views were now so controversial. A *Times* editorial tried to explain it by pointing out that "Sir Keith Joseph's brief excursion into eugenics was bound to raise the roof since he introduced into it distinctions of social class."[62]

The furor over Joseph's remarks indicated how sensitive the subject of eugenics had become in public considerations of the population question since the war. This was one of the few times eugenics had been raised in conjunction with the birthrate, and even Sir Keith, despite his eugenic demographic assumptions and worries about degeneration, steered clear of any direct mention of the relevance of eugenics to his argument. The same reticence was evident in the often explosive debate over race triggered by the influx and fertility of commonwealth immigrants, particularly blacks. Complaints by Enoch Powell and others on the Tory Right about the disproportionate number of "coloured births" making up anywhere from 20 to 30 percent of the diminishing total, despite blacks comprising only about 2.5 to 3 percent of the population, certainly achieved a good deal of notoriety in the 1960s and 1970s and contributed to deteriorating race relations in the country. But even Powell's warnings about the racial consequences of immigration and the high fertility of mothers from India, Pakistan, Bangladesh, and the West Indies were couched in economic and cultural rather than genetic terms and did nothing to revitalize a eugenic movement concentrating this time upon race rather than class. It was not that Powell and many other Britons did not fear for the quality of the race and complain on occasions about "bastardization" and "mongrelization," but more often than not, their eugenic presuppositions were (and perhaps still are) implicit in their analyses of the birthrate rather than specifically articulated.

Whether a prolonged continuation of the birth dearth combined with an extensive economic crisis, frustrations with welfarism, and endemic class and racial antagonisms could at some point in the near or distant future stimulate a revival of some new kind of protoeugenic plea for qualitative reproduction, lies, of course, in the realm of speculation, not history. But it is still a question perhaps worth posing at the dawn of a new age of genetic engineering in which, experience would suggest, the potential for generating new, even more sophisticated scientific and pseudoscientific panaceas for racial salvation remains a distinct possibility. Has the long-held, eugenic assumption that people in certain classes (or races) with definable social, intellectual, and economic qualities are genetically better qualified than people in other classes to be the parents of the next generation really been discredited? If supported by comprehensible scientific evidence and a different political climate, could it not again become an important and respectable avenue for the expression of educated fears in the event of some future real or imagined demographic crisis? That crisis, according to the American author Ben Wattenberg's recent account of the birth dearth, is perhaps fast approaching not only for Britain but for all industrialized western countries whose population relative to the rest of the world has declined precipitously from 22 percent in 1950 to around 15 percent today.[63]

The use of population data as a concrete way of articulating often inchoate anxieties about change which go far beyond whether birthrates are rising or falling has, as we have seen, a well-established tradition since the nineteenth century. At the moment, analyses of the impending birth dearth have focused upon the social, economic, military, and international implications of zero population growth or, if current low reproduction rates continue to prevail, population decline. But in contrast to the alarms of degeneration and race suicide set off by eugenically inspired demographic analysts nearly a century ago, qualitative, biological factors have yet to play much of a role in the contemporary debate.

When Galton and his eugenic apostles first addressed the problem they proposed solving it by rudimentary schemes of sociobiological engineering, even if they never used this modern term. Nevertheless, their visions of selective breeding, whether positive or negative, transformed by the Nazi fantasies of *rassenhygiene*, haunt contemporary considerations of the possible moral and ethical consequences of genetic engineering. The scientific and political failure of eugenics in Britain was obvious even before the war, though many of its hereditarian presuppositions, nourished by a long tradition of social Darwinism, remain latent in modern culture.

At least one scholar has already speculated that the controversy stirred up in scientific and educated lay circles in recent years by sociobiology and, it could be added, by the revival of arguments about the hereditary determinants of intelligence, talent, and ability, signifies the fading of bitter memories that did not for a generation permit open discussion of such emotionally charged, value-laden subjects.[64] Consequently, it follows that if eugenic demography was submerged by political and social change rather than permanently defeated in the scientific and social scientific arena and therefore remains latent in modern culture, it would not be surprising to see it reemerge in a different political and socioeconomic environment, perhaps under a different name, sanctified by a modern science that is itself in large part a product of that same culture and environment. But low birthrates and the prospect of an aging, dwindling, and ethnically more heterogeneous population notwithstanding, in Britain at least, that environment does not yet seem particularly inviting for a eugenic revival.

Notes

FPA   Family Planning Association
NBCA   National Birth Control Association
NBRC   National Birth-Rate Commission
NCPM   National Council of Public Morals
PEP   Population and Economic Planning
PIC   Population Investigation Committee
PRO/MH   Public Record Office/Ministry of Health
SPBCC   Society for the Provision of Birth Control Clinics

Introduction

1. For a list of participants and their publications as well as a summary of findings see Coale and Watkins, eds., *The Decline of Fertility.*

2. For a succinct survey of the project's conclusions see Knodel and van de Walle, "Lessons from the Past," pp. 390–414; Watkins, "Conclusions."

3. See Notestein, "Economic Problems of Economic Change."

4. Knodel and van de Walle, "Lessons from the Past," pp. 397–98.

5. Watkins, "Conclusions," pp. 434–35.

6. Teitelbaum, *British Fertility Decline*, pp. 192, 218.

7. Ibid.; Knodel and van de Walle, "Lessons from the Past," p. 392.

8. See, for example, Wattenberg, *The Birth Dearth.*

9. See, for example, Haller, *Eugenics*; Pickens, *Eugenics and the Progressives.*

10. Farrall, *English Eugenics Movement.*

11. See, for example, Searle, *Eugenics and Politics*, and Searle, "Eugenics and Politics in Britain"; Freeden, *The New Liberalism*, and his "Eugenics and Progressive Thought." For a different view see Greta Jones, "Eugenics and Social Policy," and her *Social Hygiene*; MacKenzie, "Eugenics in Britain," and MacKenzie, "Karl Pearson and the Professional Middle Class," also his *Statistics in Britain, 1865–1930.* A useful if increasingly outdated bibliographic review can be found in Farrall, "The History of Eugenics.

12. See Forrest, *Francis Galton*; Cowan, *Sir Francis Galton.* See also Cowan, "Francis Galton's Statistical Ideas"; and Cowan, "Nature and Nurture."

13. Kevles, *In the Name of Eugenics.*

14. Ibid., p. 392.

15. See, for example, Chase, *The Legacy of Malthus.*

Chapter 1

1. *Parl. Debates* (Lords), 4th ser., 25 January 1901, vol. 89, col. 10; (Commons), 25 January 1901, vol. 89, cols. 20–21. See Hynes, *Edwardian Turn of Mind*, pp. 15–17.

2. Blunt, *My Diaries*, pt. 2, p. 1; pt. 1, p. 377.

3. *Times*, 23 January 1901.

4. *Fortnightly Review* 69 (January 1901): 20–34; *Westminster Review* 155 (June 1901): 604–13; Read, *England 1868–1914*, pp. 379–80.

5. Glyn, *Romantic Adventure*, pp. 97–98.

6. Gilbert, *Evolution of National Insurance*, p. 60.

7. Masterman, *The Condition of England*, p. 304; Read, *England 1868–1914*, pp. 380–81.

8. Malthus, *Essay on the Principle of Population*, chap. 1.

9. *Economic Review* 1 (April 1891): 152–70.

10. Mitchell and Deane, eds. *British Historical Statistics*, p. 6.

11. Wrigley and Schofield, *Population History of England*, chaps. 6–7.

12. Official registration was not introduced into Scotland until 1855, but the overall crude birthrate was approximately the same as in England and Wales.

13. The underregistration of births remained a problem until 1874 when parents, rather than the local registrar, were made responsible for notifying the authorities. See Glass, "Under-registration of Births in Britain"; Teitelbaum, *British Fertility Decline*, pp. 56–68.

14. Teitelbaum, *British Fertility Decline*, pp. 48, 75–76.

15. For the founding of the Malthusian League see Ledbetter, *Malthusian League*, pp. 25–55; and Soloway, *Birth Control*, chap. 3.

16. *Malthusian* 50 (April 1883): 407; 68 (November 1883): 558.

17. *Economic Review* 2 (July 1892): 380–84.

18. *Daily Mail*, 10 August 1903.

19. *Daily Telegraph*, 17 July 1905.

20. *Fortnightly Review* 81 (January 1907): 102–6.

21. *Lancet*, pt. 2 (1906): 1290–91.

22. *Nineteenth Century* 71 (March 1912): 483–96.

23. *Fortnightly Review* 69 (June 1901): 968.

24. Ibid., pp. 966–68.

25. *Times*, 11 October 1906.

26. Parl. Papers, *Registrar-General 65th Annual Report*.

27. Newsholme and Stevenson, "Decline of Human Fertility."

28. *Times*, 15 September 1906; also Newsholme and Stevenson, "Decline of Human Fertility," pp. 57–58, 63–64.

29. Sidney Webb, *Decline in the Birth-Rate*, p. 4; Elderton, *Report on the English Birth Rate*, pp. 10–11, 19–20. For a modern analysis of variations in regional fertility see Teitelbaum, *British Fertility Decline*, chaps. 4–6.

30. *Malthusian* 32, no. 7 (1908): 55.

31. Ibid. 30, no. 5 (1906): 33.

32. Ellis, *The Task of Social Hygiene*, pp. 136–48.

33. *Fortnightly Review* 69 (1901): 966.

34. Karl Pearson, "Reproductive Selection," pp. 78–80.

35. *Times*, 31 May 1911.

36. Ibid.; Ellis, *The Problem of Race Regeneration*, p. 8.

37. Hynes, *Edwardian Turn of Mind*, p. 289.

38. *Times*, 31 October 1913.

39. NCPM, *Declining Birth-Rate*, pp. v–x.

40. Parl. Papers, *Census of England and Wales, 1911: Fertility of Marriage*, pt. 2, p. xcix (hereafter cited as *Fertility of Marriage*).

41. See, for example, Glass and Grebenik, *Trend and Pattern of Fertility*, pp. 87–88; Tranter, *Population since the Industrial Revolution*, p. 98.

42. *Fertility of Marriage*, pt. 2, pp. lxxvi–lxxxvii, 27–73, 98–143, tables 30, 35. For detailed analyses of the 1911 census classifications see Szreter, "The Decline of Marital Fertility"; Innes, *Class Fertility Trends*, pp. 38–41, 65; and Glass and Grebenik, *Trend and Pattern of Fertility*, pp. 98ff.

43. NCPM, *Declining Birth-Rate*, pp. 16, 358–65.

44. *Fertility of Marriage*, pt. 2, pp. ci–civ, cix.

45. Teitelbaum, *British Fertility Decline*, pp. 98–106.

46. *Fertility of Marriage*, pt. 2, pp. lxxviii–lxxx.

47. Ibid., pp. xci, xcviii; Stevenson, "The Fertility of Various Social Classes," p. 417.

48. *Fertility of Marriage*, pt. 2, pp. cxviii–cxxi.

49. Ibid., p. cxviii; NCPM, *Declining Birth-Rate*, p. 365.

50. Booth, *Life and Labour of the People in London* 17:17–30; Rowntree, *Poverty: A Study of Town Life*, pp. 119–21, 134–35.

51. Karl Pearson, "Reproductive Selection," pp. 78–83.

52. Galton to Pearson, 26 March 1896, Galton Archives, 245/18B. On social imperialism and Pearson see Semmel, *Imperialism and Social Reform*, pp. 24–42.

53. Karl Pearson, "Reproductive Selection," pp. 97–99, 101–2.

54. For the national efficiency movement see Searle, *The Quest for National Efficiency*.

55. Karl Pearson, "On the Inheritance of the Mental and Moral Characters."

56. Karl Pearson, *The Groundwork of Eugenics*, pp. 27–30.

57. Heron, *On the Relation of Fertility in Man to Social Status*, pp. 11–20.

58. Yule, "Changes in the Marriage and Birth-Rates, pp. 118–21.

59. Sidney Webb, *Decline in the Birth-Rate*, pp. 5–13; *Times*, 16 October 1906.

60. *Times*, 23 October 1906.

61. Elderton, *Report on the English Birth Rate*, pp. 231–32.

62. Elderton et al., *On the Correlation of Fertility with Social Value*, pp. 2–4.

63. Elderton, *Report on the English Birth Rate*, pp. 19–20, 231.

64. Heron, *On the Relation of Fertility in Man to Social Status*, p. 15.

65. *Eugenics Review* 3, no. 2 (1911): 111.

66. Elderton, *Report on the English Birth Rate*, p. 237.

67. Ibid., p. 223.

68. Newsholme and Stevenson, "Decline of Human Fertility," pp. 69–70; Newsholme, *The Declining Birth-Rate*, pp. 43–46.

69. *Fertility of Marriage*, pt. 2, pp. xci, xciv.

Chapter 2

1. Newsholme and Stevenson, "Decline of Human Fertility," pp. 69–70.

2. Galton, *Memories of My Life*, pp. 287–88. Galton, who had studied medicine and mathematics, traveled extensively in Africa and the Middle East under the auspices of the Royal Geographical Society and was also an accomplished mountain climber and meteorologist before he turned to the study of heredity. For Galton's early life see Karl Pearson, *Life of Galton*, and Forrest, *Francis Galton*.

3. Galton, "Hereditary Talent," pt. 1; Galton, *Hereditary Genius*; Galton, *English Men of Science*.

4. Galton, *Memories of My Life*, pp. 287–88.

5. Galton, *Hereditary Genius*, p. 1; Galton, "Hereditary Talent," pt. 1, p. 158.

6. Forrest, *Francis Galton*, pp. 84–85.

7. Galton, *Hereditary Genius*, pp. 131–40.

8. Ibid., pp. 17, 37–38, 316; Galton, "Hereditary Talent," pt. 1, pp. 162–64.

9. Galton, *Hereditary Genius*, pp. 7–11, 35–36.

10. Ibid., p. 123.

11. Galton, *Inquiries into Human Faculty*, pp. 24–25. Previously Galton had used the word "viriculture" but wanted a "neater word" to describe his ideas.

12. Galton, "Hereditary Talent," pt. 2, p. 319; Galton, *Hereditary Genius*, p. 343.

13. Galton, *Hereditary Genius*, pp. 361–62.

14. Greg, *Enigmas of Life*, pp. 67–69, 116–18.

15. Charles Darwin, *The Descent of Man*, pt. 1, chap. 5, p. 505.

16. Galton, *Hereditary Genius*, p. 345; Galton, "Hereditary Talent," pt. 1, pp. 165–66.

17. Galton, "Hereditary Talent," pt. 1, p. 166.

18. Galton, "Hereditary Talent," pt. 2, p. 326; Galton, *Hereditary Genius*, p. 38; Galton, *English Men of Science*, pp. 56–59, 74–75.

19. Cowan, *Sir Francis Galton*, pp. 201–3, 256.

20. Galton, *Inquiries into Human Faculty*, p. 1.

21. Spencer, *The Principles of Biology* 2:427.

22. Galton, "Hereditary Talent," pt. 1, pp. 157, 164; Galton, *Memories of My Life*, p. 314.

23. Galton, *Inquiries into Human Faculty*, pp. 198–99.

24. Ibid., pp. 24, 25, 200, 211.

25. Galton, *Hereditary Genius*, pp. 38–39.

26. Ibid., pp. 42–44.

27. Ibid., pp. 38, 63–64.

28. *Edinburgh Review* 132 (July 1870): 110–13.

29. *Nature* 1 (1870): 501; Forrest, *Francis Galton*, p. 101; Galton, *Memories of My Life*, p. 290. See also Charles Darwin, *Descent of Man*, pt. 1, chap. 2, p. 414.

30. Galton, *English Men of Science*, pp. 9–10, 16–17.

31. Galton, "Hereditary Talent," pt. 2, pp. 326–27; Galton, *Hereditary Genius*, pp. 86–87.

32. Galton, *Natural Inheritance*. In this work, which contained several earlier articles as well as his latest ideas, Galton tried to appeal to a wider audience.

33. E. S. Pearson, *Karl Pearson*, pp. 18–19.

34. Farrall, *English Eugenics Movement*, pp. 60–69.

35. *Biometrika* was founded in 1901 after the Evolutionary Committee of the Royal Society refused to publish the results of biometric research. Pearson had to be dissuaded by Galton from resigning from the society on several occasions. See Pearson, *Life of Galton* 3:241–50, 282–88. On the conflict between biometry and Mendelism see Provine, *The Origin of Theoretical Population Genetics;* Farrall, "Controversy and Conflict in Science"; Froggart and Nevin, "The 'Law of Ancestral Heredity' "; MacKenzie, "Sociobiologists in Competition"; Field, *Essays on Population*, pp. 161–62.

36. Sociological Society, *Sociological Papers* 1:64–65 (hereafter cited as *Sociological Papers*).

37. E. S. Pearson, *Karl Pearson*, p. 46; Karl Pearson, *Life of Galton* 3:222–24, 437–38.

38. *Sociological Papers* 1:45–50.

39. Pearson to Galton, 10 January 1901, Galton Archives, 233/E.

40. Karl Pearson, *National Life*, pp. 27–35; *Times*, 25 August 1905; Karl Pearson, "On the Inheritance of the Mental and Moral Characters."

41. Karl Pearson, *Life of Galton* 3:226, 259; Galton, "Possible Improvement of the Human Breed."

42. *Sociological Papers* 1:53. See also Karl Pearson, *Life of Galton* 3:259.

43. *Sociological Review* 4, no. 2 (April 1911): 143.

44. *Sociological Papers* 1:50; see *Eugenics Review* 1 (April 1909): inside cover.

45. Galton, "Hereditary Improvement," p. 124.

46. Galton to Leonard Darwin, 1 September 1910, Galton Archives, 245/8.

47. Galton to Pearson, 2, 16 March 1903, Galton Archives, 245/18F; Pearson to Galton, 22, 25, 29 October 1906, 2 March 1907, ibid., 293/G. Also Karl Pearson, *Life of Galton* 3:296–97.

48. *Sociological Papers* 1:45–47.

49. Galton to Bateson, 12 June 1904, Galton Archives, 245/3.

50. See "Objects," *Eugenics Review* 1 (April 1909).

51. *Sociological Papers* 3:83–84.

52. Galton to Pearson, 25 January 1908, Galton Archives, 293/J; Eugenics Education Society, *Minute Books*, Council Meeting Minutes, 12 February, 3 June, 8 July 1908.

53. Eugenics Education Society, Council Minutes, 12 February 1908; Pearson to Galton, 24 January, 29 February 1908, Galton Archives, 293/J.

54. Karl Pearson, *Life of Galton* 3:363, 371–72; Pearson to Galton, 14 October 1908, Galton Archives, 293/J; 7, 10 February 1909, ibid., 293/K.

55. *Eugenics Review* 1 (April 1909): 29.

56. Ibid., pp. 1–2.

57. Farrall, *English Eugenics Movement*, pp. 212–29; MacKenzie, "Eugenics in Britain"; MacKenzie, "Karl Pearson and the Professional Middle Class"; Searle, "Eugenics and Class."

58. See Darwin to R. A. Fisher, 29 March 1932, in Bennett, ed., *Natural Selection*, pp. 12, 152.

59. Greta Jones, *Social Hygiene*, pp. 19–21.

60. Membership lists were published in the annual reports of the Eugenics Education Society until 1916 when they were suspended for the duration of the war.

61. Pell, *The Law of Births and Deaths*, pp. 17–24, 30–31.
62. *Fertility of Marriage*, pt. 2, pp. lxxxv–lxxxvii, cxx–cxxi.
63. Whetham and Whetham, *The Family and the Nation*, pp. 130–31.
64. Ibid., pp. 131–42.
65. *Eugenics Review* 3 (July 1911): 139–40.

Chapter 3

1. Wohl, *Endangered Lives*, pp. 260, 274, 331.
2. Morel, *Traité des dégénérescenses*, pp. 26–46.
3. See, for example, Cantlie, *Degeneration amongst Londoners*; and Cantlie, *Physical Efficiency*.
4. Saville, *Rural Depopulation*, pp. 128–29.
5. Ibid., pp. 158–60; Spenceley, "The Lace Associations."
6. *Fortnightly Review* 49 (March 1888): 354–55; *Nineteenth Century* 21 (May 1887): 673–74.
7. Gareth Jones, *Outcast London*, p. 127; See also *National Review* 10 (October 1887): 167–70; *Fortnightly Review* 53 (March 1893): 388–91.
8. Gareth Jones, *Outcast London*, pp. 282–87.
9. Ibid., pp. 128–30.
10. *Fortnightly Review* 43 (March 1888): 354.
11. Charles Darwin, *The Variation of Animals and Plants* 5, chap. 18.
12. Galton, "The Relative Supplies"; Galton, "Possible Improvement of the Human Breed," p. 664.
13. Nordau, *Degeneration*. See also Jackson, *The Eighteen-Nineties*.
14. Arnold White, "The Cult of Infirmity," pp. 239–41; Arnold White, *Efficiency and Empire*, pp. 101–2. See also Rowntree, *Poverty*, pp. 216–21.
15. *Times*, 26 November 1901; See also Gilbert, *Evolution of National Insurance*, p. 121.
16. Masterman, "Realities at Home," pp. 7–8.
17. *Contemporary Review* 81 (January 1902): 78–86; 83 (January 1903): 41–56. For a fuller discussion see Skelley, *The Victorian Army at Home*, chaps. 1, 5–6.
18. Parl. Papers, *Memorandum by the Director-General, Army Medical Service*.
19. See, for example, *Lancet*, pt. 2 (1887): 342, 768; pt. 2 (1888): 1257; Don, "Recruits and Recruiting."
20. *British Medical Journal*, pt. 1 (1889): 201–2. The Anthropometric Committee of the British Association had found many examples of environmental deprivation when, earlier in the decade, it had examined people in several factory towns but could find little evidence of progressive deterioration in their condition. See "Report of the Anthropometric Committee."
21. *Lancet*, pt. 1 (1903): 315–17; *British Medical Journal*, pt. 2 (1903): 1338–39; pt. 1 (1904): 86.
22. *Sociological Papers* 1:68–72.
23. Mumford, "Some Considerations on Physical Degeneration."
24. Parl. Papers, *Report on Physical Training* 2:20–21, 31, 206–10, 257–60.

25. See, for example, Vines, "The Physique of Scottish Children."

26. *Parl. Debates* (Lords), 4th ser., 6 July 1903, vol. 124, col. 1324–26, 1331–32, 1344–46. Also *Report on Physical Training* 2:338–42.

27. Gilbert, "Health and Politics"; also Gilbert, *Evolution of National Insurance*, pp. 88–89.

28. *Lancet*, pt. 2 (1903): p. 768.

29. Parl. Papers, *Report on Physical Deterioration* 2:4–9, 11–15, 95–96.

30. Ibid., pp. 85, 450–51.

31. Ibid. 1:13–17, 46–47.

32. Ibid., pp. 10–11.

33. Gilbert, *Evolution of National Insurance*, pp. 157–58.

34. *Parl. Debates* (Commons), 4th ser., 10 August 1904, vol. 140, col. 47.

35. Galton to K. Pearson, 30 May 1904, *Galton Archives*, 245/18F. See also Gilbert, "Sir John Eldon Gorst."

36. Soloway, "Counting the Degenerates."

37. See, for example, *Lancet*, pt. 2 (1909): 1332–33; *British Medical Journal*, pt. 2 (1910): 452–53; *Eugenics Review* 1, no. 3 (October 1909): 196–200.

38. *Edinburgh Review* 214 (July 1911): 153–64.

39. Karl Pearson, *National Life*, pp. 26–33, 45.

40. *Parl. Debates* (Lords), 4th ser., 6 July 1903, vol. 124, cols. 1336–43; *Report on Physical Deterioration* 1:38–39; 2:102, 141.

41. *Parl. Debates* (Lords), 4th ser., 20 July 1905, vol. 149, cols. 1306–12.

42. *Times*, 5 September 1905.

43. *Quarterly Review* 217 (1912): 44–48.

44. *Times*, 14 September 1906.

45. See Soloway, *Birth Control*, pp. 11–14.

46. *Sociological Papers* 1:47–8.

47. Spencer, *The Principles of Biology* 2:427–31.

48. Ibid., pp. 501–5.

49. Greg, *Enigmas of Life*, p. 84.

50. Ellis, *The Task of Social Hygiene*, p. 185.

51. Ibid., pp. 19–23.

52. Saleeby, *Parenthood and Race Culture*, pp. 98–103.

53. *Sociological Papers* 3:182–83.

54. Ibid. 1:67; Newsholme, *The Declining Birth-Rate*, pp. 32–33. See also Whetham and Whetham, *The Family and the Nation*, pp. 109–21.

55. Galton, *Essays in Eugenics*, pp. 47–48.

56. Karl Pearson, "Reproductive Selection," pp. 77; also Galton to Pearson, 23 January 1896, Galton Archives, 245/18B; and Pearson to Galton, 30 October 1901, ibid., 293/E.

57. Karl Pearson, *The Groundwork of Eugenics*, p. 32; *Nature* 91 (March 1913): 84–85.

58. *Eugenics Review* 4, no. 4 (April 1913): 379–82.

59. Karl Pearson, *The Groundwork of Eugenics*, p. 32.

60. Charles Darwin, *The Descent of Man*, pt. 1, pp. 501–2.

61. *Fortnightly Review* 48 (1890): 325.

62. Spencer, *Social Statics*, pp. 414–15.

63. See, for example, Greg, *Enigmas of Life*; Clapperton, *Scientific Meliorism*; Kidd, *Social Evolution*; and Haycraft, *Darwinism and Race Progress*.

64. Arnold White, *Problems of a Great City*, pp. 260–64.

65. *National Review* 34 (October 1899): 236–43.

66. See, for example, Meath, "Have We the Grit of Our Forefathers?"; Petrie, *Janus in Modern Life*; *British Medical Journal*, pt. 2 (1904):454–55.

67. Aldersey White to Arnold White, 4 September 1913, Arnold White Papers, WH1/82.

68. Karl Pearson, "Socialism and Sex," p. 411; Karl Pearson, "Socialism and Natural Selection," pp. 123–26, 129. For an analysis of Pearson's special variety of social Darwinism see Semmel, *Imperialism and Social Reform*, pp. 35–52.

69. Karl Pearson, "Socialism in Theory and Practice," pp. 345–50. See also Freeden, "Eugenics and Progressive Thought."

70. Pearson to Galton, 10 January 1901, Galton Archives, 233 E.

71. Karl Pearson, *National Life*, 2d ed., pp. ix–x, 101.

72. *Eugenics Review* 1, no. 3 (October 1909): 155.

73. Karl Pearson, *Life of Galton* 3:335–36.

74. Ellis, *Essays in War-Time*, pp. 225–27.

75. NBRC, *Report*, pp. 71–72.

76. Sociological Papers 1:82–83; Saleeby, *Parenthood and Race Culture*, pp. 30, 50.

77. Galton, *Memories of My Life*, p. 323.

78. *Eugenics Review* 5, no. 4 (January 1914): 309.

79. *Eugenics Review* 1, no. 3 (October 1909): 155; 2, no. 1 (April 1910): 11, 13; 4, no. 1 (April 1912): 76; *The Quarterly Review* 219 (July 1913): 383.

80. *New Generation* 12, no. 10 (October 1933): 109.

81. Karl Pearson, "Socialism and Sex," pp. 423–24; Karl Pearson, "The Moral Basis of Socialism," p. 322.

82. Galton, *Memories of My Life*, p. 323.

Chapter 4

1. Kevles, *In the Name of Eugenics*, chaps. 6–7.

2. On alien immigration see Garrard, *The English and Immigration*; and Gartner, *The Jewish Immigrant in England*.

3. *Eugenics Review* 3, no. 2 (July 1911): 111–12.

4. Saleeby, *Parenthood and Race Culture*, pp. xi–xii; *Times*, 2 April 1914; *Fortnightly Review* 95 (1914): 253–62.

5. See Semmel, *Imperialism and Social Reform*, chaps. 1, 3.

6. *Times*, 29 September 1910.

7. Drysdale, *The Empire and the Birth Rate*, pp. 2–9.

8. Galton, *Essays in Eugenics*, p. 34; *Eugenics Review* 2, no. 2 (July 1910): 150. See also Searle, *Eugenics and Politics*, pp. 34–36.

9. Eugenics Society, Minute Books, 13 November 1917, 1 October 1918, 11 March 1919; Eugenics Society Papers, Eug./D.103.

10. *Times*, 30 July 1912.

11. Eugenics Education Society, *Fourth Annual Report*, pp. 6–7.

12. Galton, "Hereditary Talent," pt. 1, p. 164; Galton, *Hereditary Genius*, p. 86; Galton, "Possible Improvement of the Human Breed," pp. 659–60.

13. Galton, "Hereditary Improvement," pp. 116, 119; Galton, *Inquiries into Human Faculty*, pp. 215–16.

14. See, for example, Arnold White, *Problems of a Great City*, pp. 48ff; *National Review* 34 (October 1899): 243–44; McKim, *Heredity and Human Progress*, p. 188; Masterman et al., *Heart of Empire*, p. 246; Parl. Papers, *Report on Physical Deterioration* 2:431; *Sociological Papers* 2:19, 24–25; Rentoul, *Race Culture*, pp. vii–viii, 31–32, 72–77, 144–50, 173–80; *Quarterly Review* 210 (January 1909): 174; *Eugenics Review* 2, no. 1 (April 1910): 75–76; no. 3 (November 1910): 177; *Lancet*, pt. 2 (1910): 816; pt. 2 (1911): 1702.

15. Galton, "Possible Improvement of the Human Breed," p. 663.

16. *Sociological Papers* 1:47.

17. Galton, *Inquiries into Human Faculty*, p. 214; Galton, "Possible Improvement of the Human Breed," pp. 663–64; *Nature* 78 (22 October 1908): 646–47; Karl Pearson, *Life of Galton* 3:350–53.

18. Galton, *Memories of My Life*, pp. 311, 322.

19. *Sociological Papers* 2:17; Galton, "Possible Improvement of the Human Breed," pp. 663–64; Galton to Pearson, 1 July 1901, Galton Archives, 245/18E; June 1906, ibid., 138/10.

20. Galton, "Hereditary Talent," pp. 164–65.

21. See Galton Archives, 138/5, 138/6. Also Karl Pearson, *Life of Galton* 3:414–23.

22. Karl Pearson, *Life of Galton* 3:413.

23. *Sociological Papers* 1:74–75; Alfred Russel Wallace, "Human Selection," in *Fortnightly Review* 48 (1890): 331.

24. Shaw, "The Revolutionist's Handbook," in *Man and Superman*, part 2.

25. Beatrice Webb, *Our Partnership*, pp. 256–57.

26. Saleeby, *Methods of Race Regeneration*, pp. 14–15.

27. Saleeby, *Parenthood and Race Culture*, pp. 179–80, 183, 231–32.

28. See, for example, Whetham and Whetham, *The Family and the Nation*, p. 178; *The Manchester City News*, 6 November 1909; *The Manchester Despatch*, 3 November 1909; Ellis, *The Task of Social Hygiene*, pp. 209–12.

29. Saleeby, *Methods of Race Regeneration*, p. 22.

30. *Eugenics Review* 4, no. 1 (April 1912): 82–84.

31. Saleeby, *Parenthood and Race Culture*, pp. 192, 199.

32. Saleeby, *Methods of Race Regeneration*, p. 22.

33. *The Contemporary Review* 96 (November 1909): 580–86.

34. Eugenics Education Society, Minute Book, bk. 1, 14 February 1912.

35. *British Medical Journal*, pt. 1 (1880): 28–9; pt. 2 (1901): 1363–64.

36. Thomas Huxley, *Evolution and Ethics*, pp. 21–33, 39–40.

37. *Sociological Papers* 2:27–28; 3:82–83.

38. Ibid. 2:32–33.

39. Ibid. 1:53–58; *Lancet*, pt. 1 (1907): 960–61; pt. 2 (1910): 1553.

40. *Contemporary Review* 101 (January 1912): 88–94.

41. *Eugenics Review* 5, no. 3 (October 1913): 223; no. 4 (January 1914): 316–42.

42. *Times*, 15 October 1913.

43. Ibid., 23 October 1913. See also *Eugenics Review* 4, no. 1 (April 1912); Ellis, *The Task of Social Hygiene*, pp. 196–98; Barr, *Aim and Scope of Eugenics*, p. 20.

44. Haycraft, *Darwinism and Race Progress*, pp. 130–34.

45. Charles Darwin, *The Descent of Man*, pt. 1, chap. 5, p. 503.

46. *Eugenics Review* 1, no. 1 (April 1909): 31–32.

47. *Times*, 21 and 31 March 1910; *Western Morning News*, 22 March, 1910; Karl Pearson, *On the Handicapping of the First Born*, pp. 67–68.

48. *Times*, 31 March 1910.

49. *Nineteenth Century* 66 (July 1909): 97–108.

50. *Parl. Debates* (Lords), 5th ser., 22 May 1911, vol. 8, col. 666.

51. Galton, "Possible Improvement of the Human Breed," pp. 660–61.

52. Pearson to Galton, 10 January 1901, Galton Archives, 293/E.

53. *Times*, 5 September 1905; Pearson, *National Life*, pp. 70–71, 76–77.

54. *Sociological Papers* 3:63–67.

55. *Fortnightly Review* 76 (1904): 337.

56. *Nineteenth Century* 72 (1912): 555–56.

57. Eugenics Education Society, *Problems in Eugenics* 1:170–71.

58. *Eugenics Review* 5, no. 4 (January 1914): pp. 331–33.

59. Saleeby, *Progress of Eugenics*, pp. 163–64, 177.

60. *Pall Mall Gazette*, 10 May 1910; Saleeby, *Methods of Race Regeneration*, pp. 11–12.

61. Saleeby, *Parenthood and Race Culture*, p. 119; *Methods of Race Regeneration*, pp. 17–19.

62. *Sociological Papers* 3:85–89; Wells, *Mankind in the Making*, pp. 39–48.

63. Shaw, *Man and Superman*, preface.

64. For Galton's problems with Shaw and Saleeby see Galton Archives, 245/18K; 293/K.

65. Saleeby, *Parenthood and Race Culture*, pp. 119, 135.

66. *Sociological Papers* 1:74–75.

67. Galton, "Possible Improvement of the Human Breed," p. 664.

68. *Sociological Papers* 2:21.

69. Ibid., p. 13; Karl Pearson, *Life of Galton* 3:423–24.

70. For clerical fertility see *Fertility of Marriage*, pt. 2, pp. cv–cviii, table 48; Soloway, *Birth Control*, p. 103.

71. *Sociological Papers* 2:52.

72. Ibid. 1:84; Saleeby, *Parenthood and Race Culture*, pp. 351–52. See also Houghton, *National Ideals and Race Regeneration*, p. 33.

73. Meyer, *Religion and Race Regeneration*, pp. 7–10, 22–23.

74. *National Review* 34 (October 1899): 240–41.

75. Galton, *Hereditary Genius*, pp. 357–58; *Sociological Papers* 2:12–13; Whetham and Whetham, *The Family and the Nation*, pp. 131–42.

76. *Nineteenth Century* 74 (1913): 156–63; *Eugenics Review* 5, no. 1 (April 1913): 42–43.

77. *Eugenics Review* 1, no. 3 (October 1909): 163–73.

78. *Fortnightly Review* 92 (1912): 746–47.

79. *Times*, 25 July 1912.

80. *Eugenics Review* 1, no. 1 (April 1909): 26–36.

81. Ibid. 4, no. 2 (July 1912): 218; no. 3 (October 1912): 326; 1, no. 4 (January 1910): 221–22; 2, no. 1 (April 1910): 1; no. 3 (October 1910): 162.

82. Ibid. 1, no. 3 (October 1909): 158–59; 2, no. 3 (November 1910): 162–63; Whetham and Whetham, *The Family and the Nation*, pp. 225–30; Whetham, *Heredity and Society*, pp. 53–55.

83. Barr, *Aim and Scope of Eugenics*, p. 15.

84. See NBRC, *Report*, pp. 20–21, 42–43.

Chapter 5

1. For the founding of the Malthusian League see Soloway, *Birth Control*, chap. 3, and Ledbetter, *Malthusian League*, chaps. 2–3.

2. Winnington-Ingram, *A Charge*, pp. 31–33.

3. *Daily Express*, 27 April 1904.

4. Lambeth Conference, *Conference of Bishops*, pp. 38, 147. See also Soloway, *Birth Control*, chap. 5.

5. *Nineteenth Century* 59 (February 1906): 224–25; *Lancet*, pt. 2 (1907): 170–71.

6. Newsholme and Stevenson, "Decline of Human Fertility," p. 69; also Newsholme, *The Declining Birth-Rate*, p. 42. For a discussion of medicine and Malthusianism see also Soloway, *Birth Control*, chap. 6.

7. *Daily Telegraph*, 28 October 1913.

8. NCPM, *Declining Birth-Rate*, pp. 282–84.

9. Ellis, *The Task of Social Hygiene*, pp. 170–76.

10. Sidney Webb, *Decline in the Birth-Rate*, pp. 17–18; NCPM, *Declining Birth-Rate*, p. 284.

11. Knowlton, *The Fruits of Philosophy*. For the trial itself see *In the High Court of Justice*.

12. *Malthusian* (December 1894): 90; Webb and Webb, *Industrial Democracy*, p. 638; Shaw, *Preface to Three Plays by Brieux*, p. 39; Drysdale, *Small or Large Families*, p. 15.

13. Elderton, *Report on the English Birth Rate*, p. 234.

14. NCPM, *Declining Birth-Rate*, pp. 41–42; *Fertility of Marriage*, pt. 2, p. xci; Newsholme, *The Declining Birth-Rate*, pp. 39–40; Stevenson, "The Fertility of Various Social Classes," pp. 417–18.

15. *In the High Court of Justice*, pp. 149, 237.

16. Teitelbaum, *British Fertility Decline*, p. 218. See also chaps. 1, 7–9. See also Coale and Watkins, *The Decline of Fertility*, p. 446.

17. Coale and Watkins, *The Decline of Fertility*, chap. 2.

18. Galton, *Hereditary Genius*, pp. 356–57.

19. Charles Darwin, *The Descent of Man*, p. 618.

20. Galton, *Hereditary Genius*, p. 353; Galton, *Inquiries into Human Faculty*, pp. 207–10.

21. *Malthusian* (October 1880): 166–67; (January 1880): 95; (May 1880): 122; (August 1880): 147; *In the High Court of Justice*, pp. 107–9; Besant, *Law of Population*, pp. 28–29. See also Soloway, *Birth Control*, pp. 60–61.

22. Karl Pearson, "Socialism and Sex," pp. 423–24; Karl Pearson, "Moral Basis of Socialism," p. 322.

23. *Malthusian* 21, no. 12 (1897): 90.

24. Soloway, *Birth Control*, pp. 77–79.

25. *Nineteenth Century* 59 (1906): 226.

26. Karl Pearson, *Problem of Practical Eugenics*, pp. 19, 38–39; *Eugenics Review* 2, no. 1 (April 1910): 3; Karl Pearson, *Statistics of Pulmonary Tuberculosis*.

27. *Sociological Papers* 3:64–65.

28. Whetham and Whetham, *The Family and the Nation*, pp. 133, 228, 230.

29. *Hibbert Journal* 12, no. 2 (1914): 244. For other examples see *The Westminster Review* 178 (March 1912): 348–52; *Eugenics Review* 1, no. 4 (January 1910): 290–91.

30. Barr, *Aim and Scope of Eugenics*, p. 4. Also Searle, *Eugenics and Politics*, pp. 102–3.

31. Darwin to Ellis, 17 January 1917, Havelock Ellis Papers.

32. Holyoake, *Large or Small Families?* p. 7.

33. *In the High Court of Justice*, pp. 96–99.

34. Aveling, *Darwinism and Small Families*; *Malthusian*, no. 19 (August 1880): 145; no. 42 (July 1882): 333–34.

35. *Malthusian*, no. 2 (March 1879): 16; no. 79 (October, 1885): 642; no. 81 (December 1885): 658–59.

36. Ibid., no. 75 (June 1885): 613.

37. Ibid. 36, no. 1 (January 1912): 8.

38. Ibid. 28, no. 10 (October 1904): 73–74; 27, no. 12 (December 1903): 89.

39. Robertson, *Overpopulation*, pp. 13–14; *Malthusian* 12, no. 1, (January 1890): 4–5.

40. *Sociological Papers* 1:60, 73; 2:21–22; *Malthusian* 28, no. 10 (October 1904): 73–74.

41. Ledbetter, *Malthusian League*, p. 206.

42. *Malthusian* 27, no. 12 (December 1903): 89. Pearson to Galton, 10 January 1901, 30 October 1901, Galton Archives, 293E; 5 January 1907, ibid., 293H.

43. Galton to Pearson, 20 December 1906, Galton Archives, 245/18G; 1 June 1907, ibid., 245/18H. For a brief résumé of the Allbutt case see General Medical Council, *Minutes*, p. 309. The complete transcript was published in the *Malthusian*, January 1888.

44. *Malthusian* 23, no. 3 (March 1899): 20.

45. Ibid.

46. Ibid. 32, no. 9 (1908): 66.

47. Ibid. 34, no. 5 (1910): 33–34.

48. *Eugenics Review* 1, no. 3 (October 1909): 146–47.

49. Cookson, "The Morality of Married Life."

50. *In the High Court of Justice*, p. 114; Besant, *Law of Population*, p. 26; D'Arcy, "The Malthusian League and the Resistance to Birth Control Propaganda," p. 436.

51. Crackanthorpe to Galton, 1 March 1907, Galton Archives, 226; *Fortnightly Review* 80 (1906): 1004–16.

52. Clapperton, *A Vision of the Future*, p. 114; *Eugenics Review* 9, no. 1 (April 1917): 35.

53. Clapperton, *Scientific Meliorism*, p. 96.

54. Ibid., pp. 102, 118.

55. Clapperton, *A Vision of the Future*, pp. 114–15, 129–30, 150–52.

56. Crackanthorpe to Galton, 1 March 1907, Galton Archives, 226.

57. *Malthusian* 32, no. 7 (1908): 52; 35, no. 8 (1911): 62–63.

58. Ibid. 36, no. 8 (1912): 57–58; no. 1: 8.

59. NBRC, *Report*, pp. 90, 124–26, 131–32.

60. Ibid., pp. 90–91.

61. Ibid., pp. 44–45.

62. Ibid., pp. 40–41; *Malthusian* 40, no. 8 (August 1916): 67.

63. *Malthusian* 40, no. 8 (August 1916) 68; no. 10 (October 1916): 90–91.

64. Inge to H. Ellis, 1 July 1918, Havelock Ellis Papers.

65. *Malthusian* 36, no. 3 (March 1912): 22.

66. *Eugenics Review* 1, no. 3 (October 1909): 146–47; Eugenics Education Society, Minute Book, bk. 1, 7 June 1910.

67. Soloway, *Birth Control*, pp. 56–57.

68. *Eugenics Review* 5, no. 3 (October 1913): 261–62.

69. *Sociological Papers* 3:81; *Parenthood and Race Culture*, pp. 110–11; *Malthusian* 34, no. 5 (1910): 35.

70. Ellis, *The Problem of Race Regeneration*, pp. 51, 55–59, 70; Ellis, *The Task of Social Hygiene*, pp. 25–27.

71. Kevles, *In the Name of Eugenics*, pp. 98–100.

72. Ibid., p. 90; Ellis, *The Task of Social Hygiene*, pp. 45–46.

73. Darwin to Ellis, 25 September 1920, Havelock Ellis Papers; Leonard Darwin, *What Is Eugenics?* pp. 74–75.

Chapter 6

1. *Eugenics Review* 1, no. 1 (April 1909): 51–54; *Times*, 31 May 1911.

2. Eugenics Society Papers, Eug./B.11.

3. Ruskin, "Of Queen's Gardens"; Brown, *Young Men and Maidens*.

4. Harrison, *Separate Spheres*, p. 56

5. Burstyn, "Education and Sex." For examples of the persistence of these ideas into the Edwardian years see Clouston, "The Psychological Dangers to Women in Modern Social Developments," pp. 111–12; *British Medical Journal*, pt. 1 (1904): 578, 757; Wright, *The Unexpurgated Case against Woman Suffrage*.

6. *Eugenics Review* 3, no. 1 (April 1911): 44–45.

7. See, for example, *Sociological Papers* 1:76–77.

8. Galton, *Hereditary Genius*, pp. 328–29.

9. See Richards, "Darwin and the Descent of Women," pp. 64–66.

10. Ibid., pp. 59–60. For a strong feminist assault on Darwin see Hubbard, "Have Only Men Evolved?"; also Mosedale, "Science Corrupted: Victorian Biologists Consider 'The Woman Question.'"

11. Galton, *Hereditary Genius*, pp. 36–62.

12. Ibid., p. 329.

13. Ibid., pp. 131–40.

14. Forrest, *Francis Galton*, pp. 226–27.

15. Conway, "Stereotypes of Femininity," pp. 48–51.

16. Forrest, *Francis Galton*, pp. 227–28.

17. See Galton, *Tropical South Africa*.

18. Spencer, *The Principles of Biology* 2:511–13.

19. See, for example, *Lancet*, pt. 2 (1910): 816; *Eugenics Review* 3, no. 1 (April 1911): 44.

20. Galton to Pearson, 23 January 1896, Galton Archives, 245/18B.

21. Karl Pearson, *Life of Galton* 3:422.

22. Karl Pearson, "The Woman's Question," p. 356.

23. Kevles, *In the Name of Eugenics*, pp. 24–26; Walkowitz, "Science, Feminism and Romance," pp. 37–60; First and Scott, *Olive Schreiner*, pp. 144–72.

24. Karl Pearson, "The Woman's Question," pp. 355–57, 360–61; Karl Pearson, "Socialism and Sex," p. 425.

25. Karl Pearson, "The Woman's Question," p. 361.

26. Ibid., p. 359.

27. Karl Pearson, "Socialism and Sex," p. 425.

28. Ibid., pp. 415, 426–27; Karl Pearson, "The Woman's Question," pp. 377–78.

29. Karl Pearson, "The Woman's Question," pp. 373–75.

30. Karl Pearson, "The Moral Basis of Socialism," pp. 322–23.

31. Karl Pearson, "Socialism and Sex," p. 421.

32. Pearson to Galton, 10 July 1896, Galton Archives, 293/B; Karl Pearson, "Variation in Man and Woman," pp. 315, 350–75.

33. *Lancet*, pt. 1 (1892): 1011–18.

34. Pearson to Galton, 29 August, 27 December 1896, Galton Archives, 293/B.

35. Pearson to Galton, 1 February 1896, ibid.

36. Galton, "Possible Improvement of the Human Breed," p. 663.

37. See "Eugenic Certificates" in Galton Archives, 138/10, June 1906; "Notes" 1893, 138/4.

38. Pearson to Galton, 15 December 1908, Galton Archives, 293/J.

39. Bateson to Galton, 5 February 1897, ibid., 198.

40. Forrest, *Francis Galton*, pp. 225–26.

41. Crackanthorpe, *Population and Progress*, p. 116.

42. Sidgwick, *Health Statistics*.

43. Grant Allen, "Plain Words on the Woman Question"; also Linton, "The Higher Education of Women."

44. Sidgwick, *Health Statistics*, pp. 14, 19, 56–59, 90.

45. Ibid., pp. 62–66, 91; also Sidgwick, *University Education for Women*, p. 18.

46. *Englishwoman*, no. 54 (1913): 257–62; no. 55 (1913): 105–6.

47. *Fertility of Marriage*, pp. lxxviii–lxxx, table 34.

48. *Englishwoman*, no. 10 (1909): pp. 16–22.

49. NCPM, *Declining Birth-Rate*, pp. 18–20, 322–28. Also Greenwood, Brown, and Wood, "The Fertility of the Middle Classes."

50. NCPM, *Declining Birth-Rate*, pp. 20–21; *Eugenics Review* 12, no. 10 (October 1920): 205; *British Medical Journal*, pt. 2 (1920): 672–73.

51. See, for example, *British Medical Journal*, pt. 1 (1904): 578, 757.

52. *Eugenics Review* 2, no. 4 (January 1911): 284–90.

53. *British Medical Journal*, pt. 1 (1904): 636; *Lancet*, pt. 2 (1910): 817.

54. *Sociological Papers* 1:76–78.

55. Whetham and Whetham, *The Family and the Nation*, pp. 198–99; *Nineteenth Century* 66 (1909): 106.

56. Whetham and Whetham, *The Family and the Nation*, pp. 143–45.

57. *Fertility of Marriage*, pt. 2, p. xciii.

58. Whetham and Whetham, *The Family and the Nation*, pp. 199–200; *Hibbert Journal*, 10, no. 1 (1911): 188–94, 197–98.

59. Owen, *Woman Adrift*, pp. 160–62.

60. *Eugenics Review* 2, no. 4 (January 1911): 290; *Chester Chronicle*, 13 November 1909; *Sociological Review* 3, no. 1 (January 1910): 51.

61. Whetham, *Heredity and Society*, p. 100–2.

62. Eugenics Education Society, Council Minute Books, bk. 2, 17 June 1914.

63. Chambers, "Notes on the Early Days of the Eugenics Education Society," Eugenics Society Papers, Eug./B.11.

64. Stock, "Notes, Papers Read," Cambridge University Eugenics Society, 23 May 1911, C.1, Eugenics Society Library.

65. Owen, *Woman Adrift*, pp. 70–76.

66. *Sociological Review* 3, no. 1 (January 1910): 51–56.

67. *Fortnightly Review* 48 (September 1890): 333–37; 89 (January 1908): 1–24.

68. *Sociological Papers* 1:60; 2:21–22.

69. *Englishwoman*, no. 28 (1910): 36–38.

70. *Westminster Review* 172 (August 1909): 186–88.

71. *Eugenics Review* 2, no. 4 (January 1911): 293–95.

72. Saleeby, *Parenthood and Race Culture*, pp. 106, 173–76; Saleeby, *Woman and Womanhood*, pp. 7, 18.

73. Saleeby, *Woman and Womanhood*, pp. 8–14.

74. Crackanthorpe, *Population and Progress*, p. 116.

75. Ibid., p. 117; Saleeby, *Woman and Womanhood*, pp. 22–24.

76. Despite the objection of some members, the Eugenics Education Society council voted in 1910 to cooperate with the Divorce Law Reform Union in its efforts to liberalize the law, and several of the society's officers, including Crackanthorpe, testified before the Royal Commission on Divorce and Matrimonial Causes. See Parl. Papers, *Royal Commission on Divorce*, pp. 85–87; Saleeby, *Woman and Womanhood*, pp. 291–95.

77. *Suffragette* (9 May 1913): 503; (29 August 1913): 797; (9 January 1914): 289; Pankhurst, *The Great Scourge*.

78. *Votes for Women* (23 September 1910): 829.

79. *Parl. Debates* (Commons), 4th ser. 12 May 1905, vol. 146, col. 146.

80. *Englishwoman*, no. 10 (1909): 163–64; *Anti-Suffrage Review*, no. 29 (April 1911): 72. For an account of the league see Harrison, *Separate Spheres*.

81. See, for example, *Anti-Suffrage Review*, no. 30 (May 1911): 94–95; no. 31 (June 1911): 111.

82. Ibid., no. 43 (May 1912): 108; no. 44 (July 1912): 150–51.

83. See Banks, *Feminism and Family Planning*, pp. 24–25; Soloway, *Birth Control*, chap. 7; McClaren, *Birth Control*, chap. 11.

84. *Anti-Suffrage Review*, no. 60 (October 1913): 216–17.

85. Ibid., p. 212.

86. Ibid., no. 107 (September 1917): 68–69.

87. Saleeby, *Woman and Womanhood*, p. 14–16, 25, 47.

Chapter 7

1. Parl. Papers, *Registrar-General 82d Annual Report*, pp. 5–6.

2. For the difficulty of estimating the number of war-related deaths suffered by Great Britain see Winter, *The Great War*, pp. 66–76.

3. Ellis, *Essays in War-Time*, pp. 35–36; *Quarterly Review* 227, no. 450 (January 1917): 25; *Eugenics Review* 10, no. 3 (October 1918): 134–35.

4. Ibid., pp. 48–64; See also Parl. Papers, Ministry of National Service, *Report upon the Physical Examination of Men of Military Age*.

5. For the most recent studies of the infant and child welfare movement see Lewis, *Politics of Motherhood*; Dwork, *War Is Good for Babies and Other Young Children*.

6. Marchant, *Cradles or Coffins?* p. 79; Marchant, *Birth Rate and Empire*, pp. 39–41.

7. Davies, *Maternity: Letters from Working Women*, p. xii.

8. See Parl. Papers, *Forty-fifth Annual Report*; and Carnegie United Kingdom Trust, *Report on the Physical Welfare of Mothers and Children*, 1:1–4. Also *Parl. Debates* (Commons), 5th ser., 14 November 1917, vol. 99, cols. 386–87; 19 November, col. 862; 22 July 1918, vol. 108, cols. 1450–51; (Lords), 1 May 1919, vol. 34, col. 448.

9. *Parl. Debates* (Lords), 5th ser., 7 July 1918, vol. 30, cols. 942–45; (Commons), 26 February 1919, vol. 112, cols. 1328–32.

10. *Quarterly Review* 227, no. 450 (January 1917): 21; *Eugenics Review* 6, no. 3 (October 1914): 197.

11. *Eugenics Review* 6, no. 3 (October 1914): 197–98.

12. Ibid. 7, no. 1 (April 1915): 2–4.

13. Ibid. 8, no. 1 (April 1916): 34–49.

14. Ibid. 7, no. 2 (July 1915): 97; 8, no. 1 (April 1916): 38–39; *Times*, 24 December 1915; *Quarterly Review* 227, no. 450 (January 1917): 26–27.

15. Winter, *The Great War*, pp. 32–39, 83–99.

16. *Eugenics Review* 7, no. 2 (July 1915): 96; *Contemporary Review* 107 (March 1915): 333–34.

17. *Eugenics Review* 7, no. 3 (October 1915): 201–2.

18. Winter, *The Great War*, pp. 76–83.

19. Inge, *Diary of a Dean*, p. 43.

20. *Eugenics Review* 7, no. 3 (October 1915): 206–7.

21. Ibid. 6, no. 4 (January 1915): 288–89.

22. Eugenics Education Society, Council Minute Book 1914–1918, 15 September, 21 October 1914; *Eugenics Review* 6, no. 3 (October 1914): 200–201; 8, no. 4 (January 1917): 359.

23. Darwin to Sir Bernard Mallet, 1932, Eugenics Society Papers, Eug/I/3.

24. NCPM, *Declining Birth-Rate*, pp. 414–15.

25. Eugenics Education Society, Council Minute Book 1914–1918, 23 March 1915; *Eugenics Review* 6, no. 4 (January 1915): 286; 7, no. 2 (July 1915): 101.

26. *Times*, 5 April 1916; *Eugenics Review* 7, no. 2 (July 1915): 202; 9, no. 1 (April 1917): 15; *Quarterly Review* 227, no. 450 (January 1917): 30–32.

27. Eugenics Education Society, Council Minute Book 1914–1918, 16 May 1916. See also the *Times*, 5 April 1916, and *Eugenics Review* 9, no. 1 (April 1917): 2–9.

28. Eugenics Education Society, Council Minute Book 1914–1918, 16 May 1916; NCPM, *Declining Birth-Rate*, p. 415.

29. *Eugenics Review* 9, no. 1 (April 1917): 4–9, 15.

30. Palmer, *Life-Saving in Wartime*, p. 85.

31. See Press Cuttings (General) 1907–10, Eugenics Society Library.

32. Pearson, *Nature and Nurture*, p. 27.

33. *Manchester Guardian*, 19, 22 March 1910. See also the *Glasgow Herald*, 9, 16 December 1909.

34. S. Webb to K. Pearson, 16 November 1909, Pearson Papers, 888/2.

35. See, for example, Semmel, *John Stuart Mill*, chap. 2.

36. Saleeby, *Methods of Race Regeneration*, pp. 11–12; *Eugenics Review* 5, no. 2 (July 1913): 154.

37. Saleeby, *The Progress of Eugenics*, pp. 28–31.

38. Saleeby, *Parenthood and Race Culture*, p. 25.

39. Ibid., pp. 25–28; also Saleeby, "The Nurture of the Race."

40. Karl Pearson, *Darwinism, Medical Progress and Eugenics*, pp. 13–17. See also Pearson and Elderton, "Further Evidence of Natural Selection in Man." On the alleged "ignorance and fecklessness" of working-class mothers see Lewis, *Politics of Motherhood*, chap. 2.

41. Parl. Papers, *Forty-second Annual Report*; *Forty-fifth Annual Report*; Newman, *Infant Mortality*; Palmer, *Life-Saving in Wartime*, pp. 15–17.

42. Eugenics Education Society, *Fourth Annual Report*, pp. 6–7.

43. See Freeden, "Eugenics and Progressive Thought."

44. Leonard Darwin, "Heredity and Environment."

45. See Eugenics Education Society, Council Minute Book 1914–1918, 13 November 1917; 14 May, 8 June 1918. Also *Parl. Debates* (Lords), 5th ser., 7 July 1918, vol. 30, cols. 928–29.

46. *Contemporary Review* 112 (July 1917): 97–100; *Times*, 2, 3 July 1918. Also Eugenics Education Society, Council Minute Book 1914–1918, 16 January, 13 February, 17 April 1917. The society allotted £100 for exhibits.

47. *Eugenics Review* 10, no. 1 (April 1918): 53; McCleary, *Maternity and Child Welfare*, pp. 19–20; Braybon, *Women Workers*, pp. 130–31.

48. *Eugenics Review* 8, no. 4 (January 1917): 306–7, 314; also NCPM, *Declining Birth-Rate*, pp. 127–31.

49. *Parl. Debates* (Commons), 5th ser., 8 July 1915, vol. 73, cols. 617, 625.

50. Expenditures for these services rose from £10,500 in 1914–15 to over £122,000 in 1917–18. The number of health visitors increased from approximately 600 to nearly 2,600. See, Palmer, *Life-Saving in Wartime*, pp. 85, 95–97; McCleary, *Maternity and Child Welfare*, pp. 12, 18–19; Lewis, *Politics of Motherhood*, p. 34. Also *Parl. Debates* (Commons), 5th ser., 2 May 1918, vol. 105, cols. 1742–43.

51. *Eugenics Review* 9, no. 2 (July 1917): 107.

52. Ibid., 8, no. 2 (July, 1916): 112.

53. See, for example, *Sociological Review* 3 (1910): 278–9.

54. Elderton, *On the Correlation of Fertility with Social Value*, pp. 1, 40–43. For further discussion of this before the war see Hamilton, "The Relation of Eugenics to Economics."

55. Saleeby, *Methods of Race Regeneration*, pp. 31–32. Eugenicists were more critical of the modest maternity allowances provided in the 1911 National Insurance Act for being too indiscriminate and threatening paternal responsibility.

56. NCPM, *Declining Birth-Rate*, pp. 77–80. The NCPM followed up its report with a petition in 1917 calling for tax relief based upon educational allowances for parents of middle and higher incomes.

57. *Times*, 29 June 1916. The exemption for children was raised from £10 to £25, and a man with a wife and two children was not taxed on income below £200.

58. Eugenics Education Society, Council Minute Book 1914–1918, 15 May, 17 June 1914.

59. Eugenics Education Society, Council Minute Book 1914–1918, 6 July 1916, 9 October, 3 November 1917.

60. NBRC, *Report*, p. 65.

61. Sidney Webb, *Decline in the Birth-Rate*, pp. 16–17.

62. Eugenics Education Society, Council Minute Book 1914–1918, 14 May 1918. The council first tried to get Sir John Simon, the former Liberal attorney general and home secretary, to introduce the measure.

63. *Parl. Debates* (Commons), 5th ser., 4 June 1918, vol. 106, cols. 1513–16. See also *Eugenics Review* 10, no. 2 (July, 1918): 85–87.

64. Parl. Papers, *Registrar-General 82d Annual Report*, p. 5; Palmer, *Life-Saving in Wartime*, p. 18; *Eugenics Review* 10, no. 2 (July 1918): 79.

65. *Fortnightly Review* 48, no. 285 (September 1890): 336–37.

66. *Child Study* 9 (1916): 22–23.

67. Ibid.

68. Lewis, *Politics of Motherhood*, pp. 16, 33–35, 40, 50

69. *Daily Chronicle*, 14 December 1915; *New Statesman* 6, no. 148 (February 1916): 419; *National Health*, no. 5 (April 1918): 39; *Malthusian* 11, no. 1 (1916): 78; no. 2 (1918): 12.

70. *Child Study* 9 (1916): 25, 27–28.

71. Marchant, *Birth Rate and Empire*, pp. 138–39; *Eugenics Review* 10, no. 2 (July 1918): 136.

72. *Daily Telegraph*, 28 May 1917; Carnegie United Kingdom Trust, *Report on the Physical Welfare of Mothers and Children*, p. 1.

73. *Times*, 3 July 1917; Winter, *The Great War*, p. 193.

74. *Times*, 7 April 1916.

75. *Eugenics Review* 10, no. 2 (July 1918): 78. Mallet joined the Eugenics Education Society after his retirement as registrar-general and succeeded Darwin as president in 1928.

76. Braybon, *Women Workers*, pp. 47–49, 118–25.

77. *Daily Mail*, 11 February 1916.

78. Dyhouse, "Working Class Mothers and Infant Mortality in England." See also *Report of the Proceedings of the National Conference on Infant Mortality*, 1906.

79. Palmer, *Life-Saving in Wartime*, pp. 31–32.

80. Parl. Papers, *Final Report of the Health of Munition Workers Committee*; *Report of the Women's Employment Committee*; *Report of the War Cabinet Committee on Women in Industry*. See also Palmer, *Life-Saving in Wartime*, pp. 31–32.

81. Braybon, *Women Workers*, pp. 122–23.

82. Ibid., p. 119. See also Soloway, "Feminism, Fertility and Eugenics."

83. *Eugenics Review* 6, no. 4 (January 1915): 313–15.

84. See, for example, *Anti-Suffrage Review*, no. 79 (June 1915): 40; no. 86 (December 1915): 90, 96; no. 87 (January 1916): 3–4.

85. MacArthur, "The Woman Trade Unionist's Point of View," pp. 18–19; *Daily News*, 15 August 1917; Lewis, *Politics of Motherhood*, p. 80; Braybon, *Women Workers*, pp. 120–25, 149.

86. Winter, *The Great War*, pp. 186–87, 213–45. See also Roberts, *The Classic Slum*, chap. 9.

87. Gareth Jones, *Outcast London*, pp. 335–36; Sidney and Beatrice Webb, *English Poor Law History*, pt. 2, 2:667–69.

88. *New Statesman* 6, no. 147 (January 1916): 395–96; no. 148 (February 1916): 418–19; no. 149 (March 1916): 516–17.

89. Eugenics Education Society, *Tenth Annual Report*, p. 4.

90. Eugenics Society, *Annual Report 1925–26*, p. 6. The Eugenics Education Society changed its name to The Eugenics Society in 1926.

91. *Eugenics Review* 16, no. 1 (April 1924): 96–97.

Chapter 8

1. Membership lists were published in the society's annual report until the war, then again in 1919–20 and from 1936 to 1939. See Eugenics Society Papers, Eug./A.85.

2. Eugenics Education Society, Council Minutes, 12 February 1918, 8 April 1919. Also Constance Green to Marie Stopes, 6 December 1920, Stopes Papers, Add. MSS. 58644.

3. For the correspondence between Twitchin and Darwin, 1922–30, see Eugenics Society Papers, Eug./C.87 and C.43. Twitchin had joined the society in 1911 during a stay in England. He returned from Australia in 1926 but lived much of the time in a villa in Nice.

4. Darwin to Sir Bernard Mallet, 1 March 1930, Eugenics Society Papers, Eug./I.2. Also C. F. Chance, "Draft Report, Treasurers Page no. 2 February 1937," ibid., Eug./C.64.

5. Mitchell and Deane, *British Historical Statistics*, pp. 29–30, 36–37; Rollett and Parker, "Population and Family," p. 31, table 2.2; Tranter, *Population since the Industrial Revolution*, p. 98.

6. Ellis, *Essays in War-Time*, pp. 188–93, 205–8, 215–17; Robinson, ed., *Small or Large Families*, pp. 75–89.

7. *Edinburgh Review* 225 (January 1917), pp. 71–80.

8. Soloway, *Birth Control*, pp. 174–76.

9. *Malthusian* 43, no. 12 (1919): 91.

10. *Eugenics Review* 9, no. 1 (April 1917), pp. 35–41.

11. Darwin to Ellis, 17 January 1917, Havelock Ellis Papers.

12. *Eugenics Review* 9, no. 1 (April 1917), pp. 33–34.

13. Ibid. 10, no. 1 (April 1918): 42.

14. Inge to Havelock Ellis, 1 July 1918, Havelock Ellis Papers; NBRC, *Report*, pp. v–viii, xxxviii–xxxix, xli–li.

15. NBRC, *Report*, p. clvi.

16. *Eugenics Review* 13, no. 4 (January 1921):334.

17. *New Generation* 1 (5 May 1922): 5–7. See also Barr's introductory note in Stopes, *Contraception*, pp. xv–xvi.

18. *Eugenics Review* 10, no. 3 (October 1918): 145–59.

19. Beveridge's paper was also submitted as testimony to the National Council of Public Morals, *The Ethics of Birth Control*, pp. 169–71.

20. *New Generation* 3 (December 1925): 143; 11 (May 1932): 56. See also Teitelbaum, *British Fertility Decline*, pp. 75–89.

21. Eugenics Education Society, Council Meetings, January 1915–October 1926, 14 January 1925; Council Meetings 1926–1930, 13 July 1926, 24 July 1929, 27 May 1930 (Vivian to R. A. Fisher). See also Darwin to Sir Walter Fletcher, Secretary, MRC, 1925; Fletcher to Darwin, 23 June 1925; Registrar-General to Darwin, 1 February 1928, Eugenics Society Papers Eug./I.1; *Eugenics Review* 18, no. 4 (January 1927): 336; 19, no. 2 (July 1927): 137–39.

22. Glass and Grebenik, *Trend and Pattern of Fertility*, p. 110, table 40; pp. 112–13, table 42; Halsey, ed., *Trends in British Society*, p. 56, table 2.36.

23. See Beveridge, *Unemployment*; Harris, *William Beveridge*, pp. 108–43.

24. NCPM, *The Ethics of Birth Control*, pp. 169–71. See also Winter, *The Great War*, pp. 48–65.

25. Bowley and Hogg, *Has Poverty Diminished?*

26. Newsholme, *Health Problems in Organized Society*, pp. 231–32, 235.

27. Lidbetter, *Heredity and the Social Problem Group*.

28. Parl. Papers, *Report of the Mental Deficiency Committee*.

29. Carr-Saunders to Blacker, 20 April 1930, and Blacker to Carr-Saunders, 20 November 1933, Eugenics Society Papers, Eug./C.209.

30. Bramwell to Blacker, 13 December 1930, ibid., Eug./C.36.

31. *Eugenics Review* 21, no. 1 (April 1929): 16.

32. Ibid., p. 19.

33. Inge, *Outspoken Essays*, p. 257; *Eugenics Review* 60, no. 2 (July 1921): 94–95.

34. Leonard Darwin, *Organic Evolution*.

35. Carr-Saunders, *The Population Problem*, pp. 469–82.

36. Eugenics Education Society, Council Minutes, 26 May 1926, 13 October 1926.

37. Eugenics Society, *Annual Report 1925–26*, p. 6.

38. Darwin to Mallet, 10 June 1930, Eugenics Society Papers, Eug./I.2.

39. *New Generation* 1, no. 6 (June 1922): 4–5.

40. *Eugenics Review* 12, no. 1 (April 1920): 71–73; Binnie Dunlop to Marie Stopes, 6 February, 23 March 1920, *Stopes Papers*, Add. MSS. 58564.

41. See, for example, Eugenics Education Society, Council Minute Books, Executive Committee Meeting, 13 April 1920.

42. *Eugenics Review* 12, no. 3 (October 1920): 156–57; no. 4 (January 1921): 289–98.

43. C. J. Bond to Cora Hodson, 16 November 1922, Eugenics Society Papers, Eug./C.31; *Eugenics Review* 12, no. 4 (January 1921): 289–90.

44. Cora Hodson to Bessie Drysdale, 19 July 1922; Drysdale to Hodson, 24 July 1922, Eugenics Society Papers Eug./C.92.

45. *New Generation* 4, no. 9 (1925): 102–3.

46. Soloway, *Birth Control*, pp. 193–97, 206–7; Ledbetter, *Malthusian League*, pp. 223–30.

47. For Hodson see Eugenics Society Papers Eug./C.158.

48. Stopes, *Married Love*.

49. For Stopes's early career see Soloway, *Birth Control*, chap. 10. For a fuller biographical treatment see Hall, *Passionate Crusader*.

50. Stopes, *Wise Parenthood*; Stopes, *Letter to Working Mothers*.

51. Stopes, *Letter to Working Mothers*, pp. 5–13.

52. Archdall Reid to Stopes, 5 November 1919; Stopes to Reid, 30 August, 1 October 1920; Reid to Stopes, 3 October 1920, Stopes Papers, Add. MSS. 58565.

53. Stopes to Constance Green, 8 December 1920, Stopes Papers, Add. MSS. 58644.

54. George Pitt-Rivers, "Birth Control and the Eugenics Society," undated memorandum [1930s], Stopes Papers, Add. MSS. 58645.

55. Lady Chambers to H. V. Roe, 3 May 1922, Stopes Papers, Add. MSS. 58644.

56. NBRC, *Report*, pp. 252–54.

57. Stopes, *Radiant Motherhood*, pp. 221–27.

58. Stopes to C. Killick Millard, 10 May 1921, Stopes Papers, Add. MSS. 58564. See also *Queen's Hall Meeting on Constructive Birth Control*.

59. Barr to Stopes, 26 May, 30 June 1921, 24 January 1922, Stopes Papers, Add. MSS. 58566.

60. Stopes to Hodson, 10 June 1927; Hodson to C. J. Bond and Bernard Mallet, 14 June 1927; Darwin to Hodson, 24 June 1927, Eugenics Society Papers, Eug./K.1.

61. Stopes to Hodson, 10, 27 June 1927, and Hodson to Stopes, 21 June, 8 September 1927, Stopes Papers, Add. MSS. 58644.

62. Barrett, *Conception Control*, p. 31.

63. For an account of the establishment of the voluntary birth control clinics and the Ministry of Health campaign see Soloway, *Birth Control*, chaps. 9–10, 13; and Leathard, *Fight for Family Planning*, chaps. 7–8.

64. Stopes to C. J. Bond, 19 April 1923, and Hodson to Stopes, 11 December 1923, *Stopes Papers*, Add. MSS. 58644.

65. Eugenics Education Society, Council Minutes, 6 November 1923, 29 January 1924.

66. For the origins of the Workers Birth Control Group see Soloway, *Birth Control*, pp. 285–86.

67. *Parl. Debates* (Commons), 5th ser., 30 July 1924, vol. 176, col. 2050; 6 August 1924, cols. 2908–9.

68. *Malthusian* (May 1917): p. 2.

69. Eugenics Education Society, Minute Books, Executive Committee, 13 April 1920; 4 April, 13 June 1922. *Eugenics Review* 12, no. 2 (July 1920): 109.

70. *Eugenics Review* 16, no. 1 (April 1924): 101–04; 17, no. 2 (July 1925): 141–43.

71. Eugenics Society, *An Outline of a Practical Eugenic Policy*, pp. 3–4; *Eugenics Review* 18, no. 2 (July 1926): 95–97.

72. Darwin to Twitchin, 30 January 1927, Eugenics Society Papers Eug./C.87; Darwin to B. Mallet, 11 March 1928, ibid., Eug.I.2; Leonard Darwin, *What Is Eugenics?* pp. 76–77.

73. Twitchin to Darwin, 30 October 1928, Eugenics Society Papers, Eug./C.87.

74. Mallet to Darwin, 21 March 1928, ibid., Eug./C.233; Fisher to Mallet, 5 April 1928, ibid., Eug./I.2; C. P. Blacker to Carr-Saunders, 7 November 1932, ibid., Eug./C.56.

75. *Eugenics Review* 18, no. 2 (July 1926): 133–34; 20, no. 3 (October 1928): 183–84.

76. Mallet to Darwin, 21 March 1928, Eugenics Society Papers, Eug./C.233.

77. Eugenics Society, Council Minute Books, 21 July 1926; Hodson to Stopes, 14 December 1925; Eugenics Education Society to Stopes, 18 February, 16 June, October 1926, Stopes Papers, Add. MSS. 58644.

78. Stopes to Hodson, 1 March 1926; Stopes to Bond, 2 March 1926; Hodson to Stopes, 27 March, 1 April, 16 June 1926, ibid.

79. For Stopes's strained relationship with the medical profession see Stopes Papers, Add. MSS. 58568, 58569. Also Soloway, *Birth Control*, chap. 12.

80. *Guy's Hospital Gazette*, 11 October 1924, p. 463. See also Peter Fryer, *Birth Controllers*, p. 227.

81. Blacker to Stopes, 10 August 1924, Stopes Papers, Add. MSS. 58655.

82. See Blacker's obituary for Stopes in *Eugenics Review* 1, no. 4 (1959): 228–30.

83. Marie Stopes, Notes of Eugenics Society Meeting, 29 March 1927, Stopes Papers, Add. MSS. 58644.

84. Blacker, *Birth Control and the State*, pp. 6–7, 85–88, 94.

85. "Birth Control Investigation Committee" (1927). Pamphlet in Eugenics Society Papers, Eug./D.13.

86. Eugenics Society, "Meetings 1920–1929," Council Minutes, 23 February 1927, 24 July 1929.

87. Blacker, *Birth Control and the State*, pp. 85–86; Eugenics Society Meetings 1920–1927, Officers Committee, 23 February 1927. On reform eugenics see Kevles, *In the Name of Eugenics*, chap. 11.

88. Eugenics Society, Minutes, 11 July 1928; Huxley to Marjorie Farrar, 1 March 1928, Eugenics Society Papers, Eug./D.11.

89. Hodson to Huxley, 27 March 1927, ibid., Eug./C.185.

90. Stopes Papers, Add. MSS. 58644; *Eugenics Review* 17, no. 3 (October 1925): 195.

91. Hodson to Darwin, 27 January 1927, Eugenics Society Papers, Eug./C.86; Twitchin to Darwin, 20 December 1926, 25 January, 10 April 1927, ibid., Eug./C.87.

92. The Memorandum, CP 201, was sent to the cabinet on 6 June 1930 and approved 2 July. PRO/MH 55/289.

93. Soloway, *Birth Control*, p. 311.

94. Ibid., pp. 313–14; *Lancet*, pt. 1 (1927): 1141; pt. 2 (1930): 258.

95. *Eugenics Review* 22, no. 4 (January 1930): 237.

96. Stopes to Dr. F. D. Saner, 3 June 1930, Stopes Papers, Add. MSS. 58570.

97. Beatrice Webb to Pearson, 17 September 1930, Pearson Papers, 888/1.

98. Kevles, *In the Name of Eugenics*, pp. 145–47.

99. Leonard Darwin, *What Is Eugenics*? pp. 21–23; Twitchin to Darwin, 14 December 1927, Darwin to Twitchin, 6 January 1928, Eugenics Society Papers, Eug./C.87; Mallet to the Bishop of Exeter, 16 July 1931, ibid., Eug./I.3.

100. Pearson to Darwin, 14 April 1921, Eugenics Society Papers, Eug./C.268; Pearson to Darwin, 22 July 1924, Pearson Papers, Cab. 1, Drawer 8.

Chapter 9

1. For the changing position of the medical profession and the church on birth control see Soloway, *Birth Control*, chaps. 11–12, 14.

2. A year after the memorandum was issued only 35 out of more than 400 local authorities had elected to authorize birth control instruction. Although the Royal Institute of Public Health in the fall of 1930 began providing instruction in birth control practices for physicians and senior medical students and the British Medical Association opened its meeting rooms to medical officers from the voluntary birth control clinics, it was another three years before any local branch of the BMA (Dundee) formally gave its approval to one of the clinics. Moreover, the first regular course on contraception was not added to the curriculum of a British medical school until 1936.

3. *Birth Control News* 11 (July 1932): 48.

4. See, for example, C. S. Hodson to the Rev. C. Tovey, 21 October 1930, Eugenics Society Papers, Eug./C.360; J. E. C. Welldon to Hodson, 1 July 1927, and Welldon to Miss Collyer, 21 August 1933, ibid., Eug./C.350; C. P. Blacker to R. Hussey, 7 March 1934; Hussey to Blacker, 11 March 1934; Hussey to Lord Horder, 2 January 1937, ibid., Eug./C.181; *Birth Control News* 11 (December 1932): 197, 207–8.

5. *Birth Control News* 11 (September 1930): 73.

6. Mallet to Darwin, 21 March 1928, Eugenics Society Papers, Eug./C.87.

7. Blacker to Mallet, 28 September 1930, ibid., Eug./I.2.

8. Hodson to Bond, 1 November 1927, ibid., Eug./C.31; Darwin to Mallet, 26 September 1930, ibid., Eug./I.5.

9. See, for example, Blacker to Clifton Chance, 25 January 1935, ibid., Eug./C.64.

10. Blacker to Julian Huxley, 24 October 1930, ibid., Eug./C.185; Carr-Saunders to Blacker, 17 February 1932, ibid., Eug./C.56.

11. Huxley to Blacker, 4 November 1930, ibid., Eug./C.185; Blacker to Carr-Saunders, 23 February, 6 June 1932, ibid., Eug./C.56; Blacker to Herbert Brewer, 18 April 1932, ibid., Eug./C.42.

12. Blacker to Lord Horder, 14 January 1938, ibid., Eug./C.172; Hogben, *Dangerous Thoughts*, pp. 53–54, 57.

13. See, for example, Blacker to John Baker, 15 February 1933, Eugenics Society Papers, Eug./C.10.

14. Kevles, *In the Name of Eugenics*, pp. 122–28.

15. Blacker to Baker, 15 February 1933, Eugenics Society Papers., Eug./C.10; Blacker to J. Hatch, 4 November 1935, ibid., Eug./C.144.

16. Blacker to Baker, 14, 15 February 1933, ibid., Eug./C.10.

17. Baker to Blacker, November 1931, ibid., Eug./C.1D.

18. See, for example, Blacker to Bramwell, 22 June 1936, ibid., Eug./C.37.

19. "Memorandum on the Formation of An Institute of Family Relations," (1935), ibid., Eug./C.57.

20. Blacker to Lady Askwith, 2, 6 November 1931, ibid., Eug./C.7; M. S. Pease to Blacker, 29 August 1931; Blacker to Pease, 6 November 1931; Pease to Mallet, 27 March 1932, ibid., Eug./C.269.

21. Blacker to Stella Churchill, 30 April, 17 December 1931, ibid., Eug./C.68; Blacker to Chance, 24 August 1935, ibid., Eug./C.64.

22. J. B. S. Haldane to Brewer, 13 November 1935; Brewer to Blacker, 20 January 1937, ibid., Eug./C.43. See also Kevles, *In the Name of Eugenics*, pp. 184–92.

23. Diane Paul, "Eugenics and the Left," p. 587.

24. Newfield to Blacker, 20 December 1931, Eugenics Society Papers, Eug./C.243; Blacker to Askwith, 2 November 1931, ibid., Eug./C.7.

25. Newfield to Blacker, 11 October 1935, 5 March 1936; Blacker to Newfield, 6 March 1936; Newfield to Blacker, 9 June 1938, ibid., Eug./C.244–45.

26. *Eugenics Review* 32, no. 1 (April 1940): 6.

27. Julian Huxley, "Eugenics and Society."

28. Charles, *Twilight of Parenthood*, pp. 222–23.

29. "Social Biology and Population Improvement." See also Kevles, *In the Name of Eugenics*, p. 184.

30. *Eugenics Review* 32, no. 1 (April 1940): 5–6; Blacker to Horder, 8 June 1936, Eugenics Society Papers, Eug./C.171.

31. Blacker, *Eugenics: Galton and After*, p. 145.

32. *Eugenics Review* 30, no. 4 (January 1939): 290.

33. Chance to Blacker, 12 February 1940, Eugenics Society Papers, Eug./C.64.

34. Parl. Papers, *Report of the Departmental Committee on Sterilisation*, pp. 17–18, 37–40. See Kevles, *In the Name of Eugenics*, pp. 166–67.

35. Marshall to Blacker, 11 December 1930, Eugenics Society Papers, Eug./C.226; Huxley to Blacker, 21 February 1930, ibid., Eug./C.185.

36. *Eugenics Review* 24, no. 1 (April 1932): 61. See also SPBCC, *Birth Control and Public Health*.

37. See Blacker, "Memorandum on the Present Position of the Eugenics Society," 6 March 1936, Eugenics Society Papers, Eug./C.27; Blacker to Marshall, 3 March 1932, ibid., Eug./C.226.

38. Carr-Saunders to Blacker, 10 June 1932, ibid., Eug./C.56.

39. See, for example, Stopes to NBCA, 17 November 1933, Stopes Papers, Add. MSS. 58643; Blacker to Newfield, 7 March 1932, Eugenics Society Papers, Eug./C.243.

40. *Birth Control News* 11, (May 1932): 3; *New Generation* 14, (10 October 1935): 119–20; Stopes to Hodson, 24 March 1936, *Stopes Papers*, Add. MSS. 58645.

41. Blacker to M. Pyke, 24 February 1932, Family Planning Association Archives, A14/67; Huxley to Blacker, 27 February 1931, Eugenics Society Papers, Eug./C.185; Blacker to Horder, 19 October 1936, and Denman to Horder, 13 February 1938, ibid., Eug./C.171–72.

42. See, for example, Stopes to the *Medical Times*, 24 February, 29 February 1936; M. Stallard to Stopes, 21 February, 1936; Stopes to BMA, 2 February 1938, Stopes Papers, Add. MSS. 58643.

43. Eugenics Society Council Minutes, 3 February 1932, Eugenics Society Papers,

Eug./C.36; Blacker to Royal Society of Medicine, 1931, ibid.,Eug./D.192; Holland to Blacker, 22 July 1934, ibid., Eug./C.164.

44. Crew to Blacker, 6 May 1930, ibid., Eug./C.79; Bramwell to Blacker, 24 July 1931, ibid., Eug./C.36.

45. *British Medical Journal*, pt. 2 (1933): 1057–60; pt. 2 (1935): 694.

46. See, for example, *Lancet*, pt. 1 (1934): 1344; pt. 1, (1938): 503; pt. 2 (1939): 1373–74. Also Werskey, *Visible College*, pp. 30–33.

47. Blacker to R. Ruggles Gates, 22 February 1933, Eugenics Society Papers, Eug./C.120.

48. Harrison, "Women's Health," pp. 61–62.

49. See NBCA, "Speakers Notes," Eugenics Society Papers, Eug./D.19; *Eugenics Review* 28, no. 2 (July 1936): 127.

50. See "Recommendations of Birth Control Committee," 23 November 1934, Eugenics Society Papers, Eug/C.36; "Memorandum for Members of the Parliamentary Group on Birth Control" (1933), ibid., Eug./D.30, C.177; C. V. Drysdale to Blacker, 24 November 1934, 4 November 1935, ibid., Eug./C.92.

51. See PRO/MH Circular 1208 (1931), Ministry of Health Papers; PRO/MH Circular 1408 (1934), ibid.

52. Eugenics Society Council Minutes, 11 April 1934, Eugenics Society Papers, Eug./C.170. *Eugenics Review* 26, no. 2 (July 1934): 102–3.

53. PRO/MH Circular 1622 (1937), Ministry of Health Papers; NBCA, "Quarterly Letter," June 1937, Eugenics Society Papers, Eug./D.20.

54. *British Medical Journal*, pt. 1 (1937): 340–41; *Eugenics Review* 29, no. 1 (April 1937): 6–7.

55. Family Planning Association, *Report 1939*; Leathard, *Fight for Family Planning*, p. 66; *Eugenics Review* 29, no. 4 (January 1938): 234–36. For the origins of the grants see Blacker to Evelyn Fuller, 27 March 1932, 2 January 1935, Eugenics Society Papers, Eug./D.32.

56. Hall, *Passionate Crusader*, pp. 300–304.

57. "Recommendations As to the Future Relations of the National Birth Control Association to the Eugenics Society," April 1937, Eugenics Society Papers, Eug./D.18; Minutes of the Joint Committee for the Eugenics Society and the National Birth Control Association, 8 July 1937, ibid., Eug./D.23; FPA Archives, FPA/A/13/21.

58. Blacker to Horder, 15 September 1936, Eugenics Society Papers, Eug./C.171.

59. See "Memorandum on the Formation of An Institute of Family Relations," ibid., Eug./C.57; Blacker to Carr-Saunders, 11 January 1935, ibid., Eug./C.57; Blacker to Huxley, 17 May 1935, ibid., Eug./C.185.

60. See "The Eugenics Society and the National Birth Control Association," Memorandum, 22 September 1936, ibid., Eug./D.18.

61. "Recommendations As to the Future Relations of the National Birth Control Association to the Eugenics Society," April 1937, pp. 13–22, ibid.

62. Ibid., p. 21; Churchill to Blacker, 10 November 1936, ibid., Eug./D.23.

63. Darwin to Blacker, 28 April 1937, ibid., Eug./D.23; Blacker to Horder, 3 May 1937, ibid., Eug./C.172.

64. NBCA, "Minutes of the Governing Body, National Executive Committee and Sub-Committees, 1933–1937," 23 June 1937, FPA Archives, FPA/A5/2, 2A.

65. Ibid. See also 21 July 1937, 23 March 1938, ibid., FPA/A5/3.

66. Ibid., 23 June 1937, 22 February 1939; Eugenics Society, "Executive Committee Minutes", 3 November 1937, 1 November 1938, FPA Archives, FPA/A5/3.

67. M. L. Spring-Rice, "Memorandum from Mrs. Spring-Rice. The National Birth Control Association," February 1939, FPA Archives, FPA/A1/2.

68. NBCA, "Executive Committee Minutes," 27 October 1937, 26 October 1938, 22 March 1939, ibid., FPA/A5/3. For protests see ibid., FPA/A1/2.

69. See NBCA letter "To Members and Branch Secretaries," 16 May 1939, Eugenics Society Papers, Eug./D.20.

70. "Memorandum from Mrs. Spring-Rice. The National Birth Control Association." February 1939 FPA Archives, FPA/A1/2.

71. NBCA letter "To Members and Branch Secretaries," 16 May 1939, Eugenics Society Papers, Eug./D.20.

72. Pyke to Mrs. Clifford Smith, 25 March 1939; to Blacker, 27 March 1939, FPA Archives, FPA/A1/2.

73. "Memorandum from Mrs. Spring-Rice. The National Birth Control Association," February 1939, ibid., FPA/A1/2.

74. Inge, *Diary of a Dean*, p. 14.

75. *Eugenics Review* 31, no. 2 (July 1939): 87.

76. Blacker to Chance, 29 August 1939, Eugenics Society Papers, Eug./C.64; Denman to Blacker, 5 October 1939, ibid., Eug./C.89.

77. "Minutes of the Emergency Council," 11 June 1940; Blacker to Horder, 8 July, 30 September 1943, 31 March, 5 May 1944, ibid., Eug./C.173.

78. *Eugenics Review* 26, no. 2 (July 1935): 134; MacNicol, *Family Allowances*, p. 79.

79. For the rise of intelligence testing see Sutherland, *Ability, Merit and Measurement*.

80. Cattell, *The Fight for Our National Intelligence*.

81. *Lancet*, pt. 1 (1937): 1475–76; Blacker to Bramwell, 15 December 1937, Eugenics Society Papers, Eug./C.37. Cattell was the first recipient of a Leonard Darwin Research Fellowship established by the Eugenics Society as part of its growing involvement in research.

82. *Birth Control News* 14 (February 1936): 69. *Bristol Western Daily Press*, 2 January 1936; *West Yorkshire Pioneer*, 4 January 1936.

83. *Eugenics Review* 30, no. 3 (October 1939): 237–47.

84. See, for example, Penrose, *A Clinical and Genetic Study*; *Eugenics Review* 33, no. 3 (October 1941): 67–70; Kevles, *In the Name of Eugenics*, pp. 148–63.

85. See, for example, Eugenics Society, "Meetings 1920–1927," Officer's Committee, 23 February 1927, Eugenics Society Library.

86. Leonard Darwin, "The Society's Coming of Age"; Darwin to Mallet, 19 April 1930, Eugenics Society Papers, Eug./I.2.

87. Huxley to Blacker, 29 July 1930, Eugenics Society Papers, Eug./C.185.

88. Darwin to Mallet, 19 April 1930, Eugenics Society Papers, Eug./I.2.

89. Bennett, *Natural Selection*, pp. 170–71.

90. Bennett, *Natural Selection*, pp. 129–32; Moore to Mallet, 15 April 1930, Eugenics Society Papers, Eug./I.2.

91. Bennett, *Natural Selection*, p. 168.

92. *The Annals of Eugenics* had been founded by Pearson in 1926 "for the scientific

study of racial problems." Fisher changed the quarterly's orientation and subtitle to a journal "devoted to the genetic study of human populations." Kevles, *In the Name of Eugenics*, pp. 210–11.

93. S. Neville-Rolfe (Gotto) to Horder, 18 November 1938, Eugenics Society Papers, Eug./C.64.

94. Blacker to Huxley, 30 July 1936, ibid., Eug./C.185.

95. Darwin to Mallet, 27 March 1932, ibid., Eug./I.3; Bennett, *Natural Selection*, p. 174.

96. Florence, *Birth Control on Trial*, pp. 30, 35–36; *British Medical Journal*, pt. 2 (1928): 634; *Public Health* (October 1929): 11–12.

97. Norman Haire to Stopes, 24 October 1929, Stopes Papers, Add. MSS. 58567; Florence, *Birth Control on Trial*, p. 119; Mrs. Fanella Paton to Hodson, 4 July 1928, Eugenics Society Papers, Eug./C.265. See also Soloway, *Birth Control*, pp. 277–79.

98. Blacker, "The Practice of Contraception."

99. Blacker to Baker, 18 July 1934, Eugenics Society Papers, Eug./C.10; Blacker to Huxley, 5 December 1934, ibid., Eug./C.185.

100. Blacker to Schiller, 6 December 1934, and Schiller to Blacker, 8 December 1934, ibid., Eug./C.306.

101. Humphrey Rolleston, "Memorandum on Grants Recommended by the General Purposes Committee," March 1934, ibid., Eug./C.295–96.

102. *Eugenics Review* 28, no. 1 (April 1936): 80–81.

103. Blacker to Zuckerman, 10 December 1934; Zuckerman to Blacker, 15 December 1934; Blacker to Zuckerman, 2 January 1935, Eugenics Society Papers, Eug./C.358.

104. Blacker to Zuckerman, 6 January 1936; Zuckerman to Blacker, 23 October 1936, ibid. See also Zuckerman, "Research on Factors Concerned in the Control of Fertilization," ibid., Eug./C.296; Eugenics Society, *Annual Report 1936–1937*, p. 9.

105. For the progress of Baker's research and his relationship to Blacker and the Eugenics Society see Eugenics Society Papers, Eug./C.11–13.

106. See "Draft Report" and "Treasurer's Page no. 2, February 1937," ibid., Eug./C.64.

107. *Lancet*, pt. 1 (1938): 577.

108. Stopes to Blacker, 17 February 1931, Eugenics Society Papers, Eug./K.1.; See also H. V. Roe to Blacker, 13 June 1944, Stopes Papers, Add. MSS. 58645.

109. For the conflict over Volpar see Eugenics Society Papers, Eug./D.17, particularly J. A. Gillian, M.D. to Blacker, 11 July 1935; Pyke to Blacker, 8 October 1935.

110. Rolleston to Blacker, 21 February, 22, 26 July 1938, ibid., Eug./C.296; *Lancet*, pt. 2 (1938): 882–85, 970, 1030, 1381.

111. Blacker to Baker, 28 November 1938, and Baker to Blacker, 29 November 1938, Eugenics Society Papers, Eug./C.13. *Eugenics Review* 30, no. 4 (January 1939): 261–68; 31, no. 1 (April 1939): 23–31.

112. Baker to Blacker, 21 February 1939; Blacker to Baker, 22 February 1939, Eugenics Society Papers, Eug./C.13.

113. Bond to Blacker, 16 August 1938, ibid., Eug./C.32.

Chapter 10

1. *Eugenics Review* 20, no. 3 (October 1928): 157. Also Himes, "Birth Control for the British Working Classes."
2. *Eugenics Review* 19, no. 2 (April 1927): 137; 30, no. 2 (July 1938), pp. 117–24.
3. Ibid. 20, no. 1 (April 1928): 23; *Birth Control News* 10, no. 12 (April 1932): 196.
4. Charles, *Twilight of Parenthood*, p. 127; *Public Opinion*, 4 May 1934.
5. D. Caradog Jones, *The Social Survey of Merseyside*; *Eugenics Review* 24, no. 3 (October 1932): 178–90; Rowntree, *Poverty*.
6. *Eugenics Review* 28, no. 2 (July 1936): 103–13.
7. Eugenics Society Council Minutes, 14 January 1925, 13 July 1926, 24 July 1929.
8. *Eugenics Review* 19, no. 2 (July 1927): 137–39.
9. Darwin to Fletcher, 1925, and Fletcher to Darwin, 23 June 1925, Eugenics Society Papers., Eug./I.1.
10. Registrar-General to Darwin, 1 February 1928, ibid.; S. P. Vivian to Fisher, 27 May 1930, in Eugenics Society Council Minutes.
11. *Eugenics Review* 18, no. 4 (January 1927): 336.
12. Bennett, *Natural Selection*, p. 267. See also *Time and Tide*, 12 February 1938.
13. Bennett, *Natural Selection*, pp. 233–34, 240–41.
14. See, for example, Stopes, *Contraception*, p. 222; Ayling, *Retreat from Parenthood*, pp. 8, 86–87, 138; *Birth Control News* 12, no. 4 (October 1933): 54; 14, no. 8 (April 1936): 87–88; Frank White, *Posterity in the Light of Science*, pp. 19–21, 48–49; Hodson, "Contra-Selection," pp. 373–74.
15. *Parl. Debates* (Commons), 5th ser., 10 February 1937, vol. 320, cols. 517–21.
16. *Times*, 29 March, 4 April 1930; Hodson, "Contra-Selection," pp. 375–76.
17. Bond, "Are Our Children To-day As Good As Their Grandfathers?" 20 October 1933, Eugenics Society Papers, Eug./C.32.
18. Blacker to Baker, 15 February 1933; Baker to Blacker, 18 February 1933, Eugenics Society Papers, Eug./C.10. See also Blacker to C. J. Stoney Archer, 16 May 1935, ibid., Eug./C.2.
19. Blacker to Paul Espinasse, 13 February 1934, ibid., Eug./C.99.
20. Eugenics Society, *Aims and Objects*, pp. 2, 4.
21. Cannan, "The Probability of a Cessation of the Growth"; Glass, *Struggle for Population*, pp. 8–9.
22. Bowley, "Births and Population in Great Britain"; Beveridge, *Unemployment*, p. 398. See also Harris, *William Beveridge*, pp. 286–90.
23. Parl. Papers, *The Registrar-General's Statistical Review 1926*, pp. 157–58.
24. Parl. Papers, *The Registrar-General's Statistical Review 1927*, pp. 131–33; and *The Registrar-General's Statistical Review 1931*, p. 134.
25. Parl. Papers. *Census 1931: Preliminary Report*, pp. i–xii, and *Census 1931: General Report*, pp. 24–26; *New Generation* 10, no. 8 (31 August 1931): 86.
26. Charles, *Twilight of Parenthood*, p. 36.
27. Kuczynski, *Balance of Births and Deaths*, pp. 1–4, 54; *Eugenics Review* 21, no. 2 (July 1929): 130–31.
28. Kuczynski, *Balance of Births and Deaths*, pp. 16–19. See also Blacker and Glass, *Population and Fertility*, pp. 23–24.

29. Kuczynski, *Balance of Births and Deaths*, pp. 40–44.

30. Ibid., pp. 35–37.

31. Ibid., pp. 47–54.

32. Ibid., pp. 58–62.

33. Ibid., p. 62.

34. *Eugenics Review* 35, no. 3–4, (October 1942, January 1943): 71–84. Glass's list was originally prepared as an appendix to his *Population Policies and Movements in Europe* but was not published.

35. Bowley, "Economic Aspects," pp. 48–50.

36. See, for example, reports in the *Morning Post*, 28 September 1931; the *Birmingham Post*, 8 August 1933; the *Sheffield Daily Independent*, 13 December 1934; *Birth Control News* 12, no. 7 (January 1934): 109.

37. Charles, *Twilight of Parenthood*, pp. 45, 70–76.

38. Ibid., pp. 105, 147, 150, 161.

39. Ibid., pp. 1–2, 8–9, 31, 35–36.

40. Ibid., pp. 143–45, 161.

41. Ibid., pp. 214–23.

42. *Eugenics Review* 27, no. 1 (April 1935): 53–55.

43. Ibid. 29, no. 1 (April 1937): 39–41.

44. Leybourne, "An Estimate of the Future Population"; McCleary, *Menace of Depopulation*.

45. See, for example, Blacker and Glass, *Future of Our Population*; Blacker and Glass, *Population and Fertility*; and Glass, *Struggle for Population*.

46. Blacker and Glass, *Future of Our Population*, pp. 12, 15–16; *Eugenics Review* 28, no. 3 (October 1936): 211.

47. Blacker and Glass, *Future of Our Population*, pp. 14–15.

48. Kuczynski, "The World's Future Population."

49. Hill, "My Warning to England"; *Birth Control News* 10 (6 October 1931): 81–82; *Manchester Guardian*, 2 September 1936.

50. *Parl. Debates* (Commons) 5th ser., 15 April 1935, vol. 300, col. 1634.

51. *News Chronicle*, 24 October 1938.

52. See, for example, *Morning Post*, 1 July 1935; *Daily Mirror*, 1 September 1937; *Daily Sketch*, 21 September 1937.

53. *Glasgow Sunday Mail*, 30 August 1936.

54. Blacker, "The Confluence of Psychiatry and Demography," p. 496. The three books reviewed were Carr-Saunders, *World Population*; Glass, *Struggle for Population*; and Kuczynski, *Population Movements*. See also Leathard, *Fight for Family Planning*, pp. 60–62. For a brief survey of depopulation fears see Teitelbaum, Michael S., and Winter, Jay M., *The Fear of Population Decline*, chaps. 1–3.

55. *Times*, 27 October 1934.

56. Ibid., 28, 29 September 1936.

57. Blacker, "The Confluence of Psychiatry and Demography," p. 496.

58. See, for example, *Daily Dispatch*, October 1936; *Northern Mail and Newcastle Chronicle*, 2, 4, 6 November 1936; *John Bull*, 9 December 1936, 20 March 1937; *Spectator*, 18, 25 December 1936; 8, 15 January 1937.

59. *Evening Standard*, 11 March 1937.

60. See *Parl. Debates* (Commons), 5th ser., 10 February 1937, vol. 320, cols. 482–537. The BBC programs were published in 1938 under the title *The Population Problem.*

61. *Daily Telegraph*, 30 November 1937; *News Chronicle*, 1 April 1937; *Morning Post*, 11 March 1937.

62. *Liverpool Daily Post, Nottingham Journal*, 9 March 1937.

63. *Times*, 23 March 1937.

64. *Lancet*, pt. 2 (1934): 760, 765.

65. See, for example, *British Medical Journal*, pt. 2 (1936): 715–16, 721–22; *Lancet*, pt. 1 (1937): 933–34, 944–45; *Medical Press and Circular*, 14, 21, 28 July; 1, 8, 15, 22 September 1937.

66. See *Medical Officer*, 22 October 1938; *Western Daily Press*, Bristol, 3 May 1937; *Liverpool Daily Post*, 7 August 1937; *Ripon Gazette*, 15 December 1938; *Eastbourne Herald*, 18 February 1939.

67. See for example *Medical Officer*, 27 March 1937; *British Medical Journal*, pt. 1 (1937): 470–72.

68. *Lancet*, pt. 1 (1939): 1279–80.

69. *Daily Herald*, 13 February 1936.

70. *Western Daily Mail, Cardiff*, 6 May 1936; *Sunday Chronicle*, 18 April 1937.

71. *Birth Control News* 11, no. 3 (July 1932): 47.

72. *Daily Telegraph*, 13 April 1937, 5 January 1938; *Sheffield Daily Telegraph*, 5 January 1938; *Pulman's Weekly News*, 6 April 1937. See also Leybourne and White, *Education and the Birth Rate*.

73. Glass, *Struggle for Population*, p. 91; *Eugenics Review* 28, no. 2 (July 1936): 97–98.

74. *News of the World*, 25 September 1939.

75. *Parl. Debates* (Commons), 5th ser., 6 June 1935, vol. 302, cols. 2056–57.

76. MacNicol, *Family Allowances*, p. 91.

77. *Parl. Debates* (Commons), 5th ser., 10 February 1937, vol. 320, cols. 482–90.

78. See *Observer*, 3 October 1937; *News Chronicle, Daily Telegraph*, 8 October 1937; *Eugenics Review* 29, no. 3 (October 1937): 169–70; no. 4 (January 1938): 253–56.

79. *Eugenics Review* 29, no. 1 (April 1937): 11–12; *Parl. Debates* (Commons), 5th ser., 10 February 1937, vol. 320, cols. 491–97. See also Blacker to C. J. Bond, 8 April 1937, Eugenics Society Papers, Eug./C.32.

80. See, for example, *Parl. Debates* (Lords), 5th ser., 21 June 1939, vol. 113, cols. 600–626, 642–47.

81. *Parl. Debates* (Commons), 5th ser., 10 February 1937, vol. 320, cols. 527–33.

82. Mallet, "The Organisation of Registration"; *Eugenics Review* 29, no. 1 (April 1937): 12. See also *Daily Herald*, 17 August 1936.

83. Blacker to Carr-Saunders, 12 June 1936, PIC Archives, VIa; *Eugenics Review* 31, no. 1 (April 1939): 47.

84. See Blacker, "Memorandum: Future Activities of this Society" [1937], Eugenics Society Papers, Eug/C.27; *Eugenics Review* 35, no. 1 (April 1943): 6–7; Glass to Carr-Saunders, 12 December 1944, 21 February, 1 March 1945; Carr-Saunders to Glass, 29 March 1945; Cadbury to Blacker, 6, 8 September 1944; Blacker to Carr-Saunders,

8 September 1944, PIC Papers VIa. Much of the money was used to pay Glass's salary. See Wise, "David V. Glass."

85. Eugenics Society, Council Minutes, 14 February 1938. Among the new contributors to the PIC was the Carnegie United Kingdom Trust which in 1939 and 1940 matched the Eugenics Society's annual £500 donation. The Carnegie Corporation had also helped finance the establishment of the committee with a £1,155 grant in 1936.

86. *Eugenics Review* 31, no. 1 (April 1939): 47. See Blacker, Memorandum, 26 April 1937, *Eugenics Society Review*, Eug./C.172.

87. For example, *Reynold's Illustrated News*, 27 June 1937.

88. See, for example, *Times*, 17, 19 April 1937; *Bournemouth Daily Echo*, 4 May 1937.

89. Tufton-P.H. Beamish, M.P. to Blacker, 30 November 1937; Blacker to Beamish, 1 December 1937; Beamish to Blacker, 4 December 1937; Blacker to Beamish, 6 December 1937, Eugenics Society Papers, Eug./C.16.

90. *Daily Express*, 29 November 1937.

91. The bill was introduced on 28 October 1937. See *Parl. Debates* (Commons), 5th ser., 28 October 1937, vol. 328, col. 259. For the extended debate over the second reading on 29 November 1937 see vol. 329, cols. 1717–1835.

92. *Daily Herald*, 30 November 1937.

93. *Parl. Debates* (Commons), 5th ser., 29 November 1937, vol. 329, cols. 1775–79.

94. Ibid., cols. 1760–63.

95. *Daily Herald*, 13 December 1937.

96. *Daily Mirror*, 10, 11 December 1937; *Time and Tide*, 18 December 1937; *Birth Control News* 15, no. 7 (December 1936): 74.

97. *Times*, 3, 19 December 1937; *Observer*, 5 December 1937; *Daily Telegraph*, 7 December 1937; *Daily Mail*, 1 December 1937.

98. *Parl. Debates* (Commons), 5th ser., 1 February 1938, vol. 331, cols. 105–41.

99. *Sunday Pictorial*, 22 February 1938.

100. *Parl. Debates* (Lords), 5th ser., 1 March 1938, vol. 107, cols. 959–68.

101. Carr-Saunders to Sir Kingsley Wood, 21 December 1936; Wood to Carr-Saunders, 11 February 1937; S. P. Vivian to Blacker, 29 October 1937, PIC Papers X/9i.

102. *Eugenics Review* 17, no. 1 (April 1925): 8; *Times*, 9 January 1926.

103. Blacker, *Birth Control and the State*, pp. 60–61.

104. *Eugenics Review* 21, no. 3 (October 1929): 167.

105. Ibid. 21, no. 4 (January 1930): 251–55.

106. *News Chronicle*, 27 October 1937.

107. *New Generation* 13, no. 7 (July 1934): 75; 18, no. 1 (January 1939): 2.

108. Ibid. 12, no. 10 (October 1933): 113–14.

109. *Eugenics Review* 28, no. 1 (April 1936): 83–84.

110. *New Generation* 16, no. 5 (May 1937): 49–52; 18, no. 2 (February 1939): 13–15.

111. *Manchester Guardian*, 24 March 1937; *Eugenics Review*, 27, no. 1 (April 1935): 3–4.

112. *New Generation* 16, no. 8 (August 1937): 94.

113. *Eugenics Review* 28, no. 1 (April 1936): 83–84; *New Generation*, 12, no. 11 (November 1933): 131–32.

114. *Daily Telegraph*, 14, 15, 20 September 1937; *Birth Control News* 17, no. 6 (June 1939): 64.

115. Blacker to Newfield, 28 October 1935, Eugenics Society Papers, Eug./C.244.

116. *Daily Express*, 3 March 1937.

Chapter 11

1. C. P. Blacker, Memorandum, "Eugenic Problems Needing Research," 25 June 1937, Eugenics Society Papers, Eug./C.64.

2. See, for example, "Aims and Objects of the Eugenics Society," in *Eugenics Review* 26, no. 2 (July 1935): 135.

3. *Manchester Guardian*, 31 October 1930.

4. SPBCC, *Birth Control and Public Health*, preface.

5. Pell, *The Law of Births and Deaths*; Soloway, *Birth Control*, pp. 186–87.

6. *British Medical Journal*, pt. 2 (1920): 671; pt. 2 (1928): 310; pt. 2 (1928): 477–79; *Times*, 28 July 1928.

7. *British Medical Journal*, pt. 2 (1928): 547; Stevenson to Mallet, 21 May 1928, Eugenics Society Papers, Eug./I.2.

8. Moore to Mallet, April 1928, ibid., Eug./I.2.

9. Carr-Saunders to Blacker, 16 November 1930, ibid., Eug./C.56; Blacker to Eardley Holland, 23 November 1933, 22 August 1934, ibid., Eug./C.164.

10. *Eugenics Review* 12, no. 4 (January 1921): 297.

11. Ibid. 15, no. 4 (January 1923): 374.

12. Ibid. 18, no. 2 (July 1926): 131–34.

13. Huxley to Blacker, 5 September 1933; Blacker to Huxley, 11 September 1933, Eugenics Society Papers, Eug./C.185.

14. See, for example, *Daily Telegraph*, 8 September 1937.

15. *British Medical Journal*, pt. 1 (1938): 470–72.

16. *Eugenics Review* 34, no. 1 (April 1942): 4. Because of the outbreak of the war, the report was not published until 1942, and then in a limited edition which the *Eugenics Review* obtained.

17. Charles, *Twilight of Parenthood*, pp. 145–46, 161, 165, 168–69, 177, 180, 194–96.

18. See, for example, *Catholic News*, 18 March 1933; *Catholic Herald*, 5 May 1934; *Liverpool Daily Post*, 9 March 1936.

19. See Soloway, *Birth Control*, pp. 243–48, 254. In his 1930 encyclical, *Casti Connubi*, summarizing the Catholic church's mounting anxieties about the decline of sexual morality, Pope Pius IX condemned eugenics along with birth control, divorce, marital irregularities, and the denigration of love as depicted in films, theater, and the press.

20. See, for example, *New Generation*, December 1922, p. 6; July 1923, pp. 80–81; November 1925, p. 132.

21. Eugenics Society, Council Minutes 11 March 1931; Blacker to Newfield, 8 February 1934, 19 November 1935, Eugenics Society Papers, Eug./C.244.

22. *National Life* 2, no. 22 (December 1936): 269–71, 282–84; *Exeter Diocesan Gazette*, May 1933; *Birth Control News* 12, no. 3 (July 1933): 36; Fryer, *Birth Controllers*, pp. 65–66; Soloway, *Birth Control*, p. 251.

23. See the report of the Methodists Conference held in Liverpool 25 June 1939 in *Daily Telegraph*, and *Daily Herald*, 25 July 1939.

24. Carr-Saunders, *World Population*, p. 258.

25. Dawson of Penn, *Love-Marriage-Birth Control*, pp. 16–24.

26. *Parl. Debates* (Lords), 5th ser., December 1933, vol. 90, col. 680.

27. Ibid., 13 February 1934, cols. 804–14, 818–28; 20 March 1934, vol. 91, cols. 282–85.

28. *Birth Control News* 7, no. 8 (February 1934): 135.

29. *New Generation* 13, no. 2 (February 1934): 13–14; no. 4 (April 1934): 41–42; no. 2 (June 1934): 21.

30. Horder to Miss Holland, 1 March 1934, Eugenics Society Papers, Eug./D.16.

31. *Parl. Debates* (Lords), 5th ser., 13 February 1934, vol. 90, cols. 804–7.

32. Ibid., 21 June 1939, vol. 113, cols. 618–26; *Eugenics Review* 31, no. 2 (July 1939): 85–86; no. 3 (October 1939), p. 195.

33. *Eugenics Review* 28, no. 1 (April 1936): 58; no. 2 (July 1936): 127; no. 3 (October 1936): 222; no. 4 (January 1937): 292.

34. See, for example, NBCA, *Sixth Annual Report*; "Recommendations as to the Future Relations of the NBCA to the Eugenics Society," April 1937, Eugenics Society Papers, Eug./D.18.

35. *New Generation* 15, no. 11 (November 1936): 125; *Birmingham Gazette, Nottingham Journal*, 18 February 1938.

36. *British Medical Journal*, pt. 1 (1936): 135, 238, 390, 447–48; pt. 1 (1938): 484–85, 539–40, 591–92; *Lancet*, pt. 1 (1938): 235, 462.

37. *Birth Control News* 12, no. 7 (January 1934): 109.

38. Fuller to Blacker, 6 June 1936, Eugenics Society Papers, Eug./D.32.

39. *Eugenics Review* 26, no. 1 (April 1934): 4–5.

40. Ibid. 28, no. 3 (October 1936): 175–80; Carr-Saunders, *World Population*, p. 258.

41. *Eugenics Review* 28, no. 1 (April 1936): 69–70.

42. Ibid. 28, no. 4 (January 1937): 331–33; See also Frank White, *Birth Control and Its Opponents*.

43. Blacker, "Memorandum on Proposed Annual Conference of Representatives of Birth Control Clinics," Eugenics Society Papers, Eug./D.41; "Recommendations As to the Future Relations of the National Birth Control Association to the Eugenics Society," April 1937, Eug./D.18; Blacker to Dr. M. Jackson, 24 July 1939, Eug./C.173; *National Life*, 11 January 1937, pp. 296–97; *Eugenics Review* 29, no. 1 (April 1937): 7–8.

44. See *Parl. Debates* (Commons), 5th ser., 30 March 1938, vol. 333, cols. 2007–11; 16 December 1938, vol. 342, cols. 2420–38.

45. *Cavalcade*, 5 February 1938; *News Chronicle, Manchester News Chronicle*, 17 April 1939.

46. *Eugenics Review* 27, no. 1 (April 1935): 11–20.

47. Blacker to Carr-Saunders, 23 November 1933, 14 August 1935, Eugenics Society Papers, Eug./C.57; *Eugenics Review* 26, no. 4 (January 1935): 255–56.

48. Blacker to Carr-Saunders, 13 December 1934, 24 October 1935, Eugenics Society Papers, Eug./C.57.

49. Eugenics Society, Minutes of the Council, 2 April 1935; Blacker to Horder, 21, 25 March, 3, 17 April 1935, Eugenics Society Papers, Eug./C.170; Blacker to Newfield, 12 December 1935, Eug./C.244; Eugenics Society, *Annual Report of the Eugenics Society 1935–1936*.

50. See Eugenics Society, Minutes of the Council (1931–36), Eugenics Society Library; *Eugenics Review* 28, no. 4 (January 1937): 266, 331.

51. *Eugenics Review* 27, no. 4 (January 1936): 273. Lady Chambers to Blacker, 9 December 1937, Eugenics Society Papers, Eug./C.63.

52. Greta Jones, *Social Hygiene*, pp. 113–32.

53. *Eugenics Review* 30, no. 1 (April 1938): 4–5; Blacker, "Proposals As to the Formation of a Joint Committee to Deal with the Problems of Positive Eugenics," Eugenics Society Papers, Eug./D.163. Eugenics Society, Executive Committee Minutes, 5 January 1938, 1 November 1938; Minutes of the Council, 14 February 1938. The society gave the Population Policies Committee an initial grant of £300.

54. Lafitte continued to work with PEP after the war and in time became a professor of social administration at the University of Birmingham. For the relationship of the Eugenics Society with Lafitte and PEP see Eugenics Society Papers, Eug./C.199.

55. Blacker to Carr-Saunders, 29 September 1937, Eugenics Society Papers, Eug./C.57; Blacker to Horder, 19 January, 3 May 1938, Eug./C.172.

56. *Parl. Debates* (Commons), 5th ser., 29 November 1937, vol. 329, cols. 1759–60.

57. *Sunday Express*, 7 March 1937; *Morning Post*, 27 May 1937.

58. *Parl. Debates* (Lords), 5th ser., 21 June 1939, vol. 113, cols. 631–35.

59. *Western Daily Mail, Cardiff*, 26 May 1939.

60. See, for example, Ginsburg, *Parenthood and Poverty*, pp. 26–27, 33–34, 55–56.

61. *Yorkshire Telegraph and Star*, 8 March 1931; *Daily Mail*, 21 May 1931; *Morning Post*, 10 September 1935.

62. *Liverpool Post*, 3 August 1933.

63. See, for example, *Parl. Debates* (Commons), 5th ser., 10 February 1937, vol. 320, cols. 504–19.

64. *Western Daily Mail, Cardiff*, 26 May 1939.

65. *Morning Post*, 30 December 1936.

66. *Birth Control News* 17, no. 1 (November 1938): 4; *Daily Mirror*, 26 May 1939.

67. *Daily Herald*, 19 March 1937.

68. See, for example, *Parl. Debates* (Commons), 5th ser., 10 February 1937, vol. 320, cols. 522–26.

69. *Times*, 17 April 1937; *Daily Telegraph*, 1, 9 April 1937.

70. See Blacker and Glass, *Future of Our Population*, pp. 18–21; Blacker and Glass, *Population and Fertility*, pp. 100–101.

71. Charles, *Twilight of Parenthood*, pp. 189–90, 198–99.

72. Ibid., pp. 183–85.

73. Ibid., pp. 120, 126; Hogben, *Retreat from Reason*, pp. 43, 81–82.

74. See, for example, Darwin's evidence before the Royal Commission on Income Tax, 18 October 1919, Parl. Papers, Cmd. 285, p. 783; "Memorandum on the Evidence

Proposed to be Given Before the Royal Commission on the Income Tax," Eugenics Society Papers, Eug./D.106; *Eugenics Review* 12, no. 2 (July 1920): 93–97; no. 4 (January 1921): 280–82.

75. "Appeal for Eugenic Taxation," Eugenics Society Papers, Eug./D.106.

76. For Darwin's negotiations with M.P.s over taxation see letter, January 1927, ibid.; Eugenics Society, Minutes of the Council, 4 October 1927; *Eugenics Review* 20, no. 2 (July 1928): 76. 79. Blacker, *Birth Control and the State*, p. 63.

77. Eugenics Society, Minutes of the Council, 9 October 1929.

78. *New Generation* 9, no. 5 (May 1930): 52; 11, no. 5 (May 1932): 56.

79. *Eugenics Review* 24, no. 3 (October 1932): 260.

80. Blacker, "Memorandum on the Formation of An Institute of Family Relations" (1935): 5–9, Eugenics Society Papers, Eug./C.57.

81. On the issue of maternal mortality see Leathard, *The Fight for Family Planning*, pp. 37–38, 55, 62–64; Campbell, *Memorandum on Maternal Mortality*; Parl. Papers, Ministry of Health, *Final Report of Departmental Committee on Maternal Mortality and Morbidity*; Parl. Papers, Ministry of Health, *Report on an Investigation into Maternal Mortality*.

82. Blacker and Glass, *Future of Our Population*, pp. 20–22.

83. Blacker, "Memorandum on the Formation of an Institute of Family Relations," 1935, pp. 10–14, 23–24, Eugenics Society Papers, Eug./C.57.

Chapter 12

1. Booth, *Life and Labour of the People in London* 17:17–30; Rowntree, *Poverty: A Study of Town Life*, pp. 119–21, 134–35.

2. *Eugenics Review* 14, no. 1 (April 1922): 49–50.

3. See, for example, the *Evening Standard*, 10 January 1935; *Daily Mail*, 21 September 1935.

4. *Times*; *Glasgow Herald*, 11 February 1937.

5. *Daily Express*, 20 July 1934.

6. *Sunday Times*, 11 October 1936.

7. Glass, "The Fall in the Birth Rate."

8. *Times*, 11 February 1937.

9. *Evening Standard*, 10 January 1935.

10. *Eugenics Review* 29, no. 1 (April 1937): 45–47; *New Generation* 18, no. 12 (December 1939): 131.

11. For a notorious exception see Ludovici, *Lysistrata* ; Ludovici, *The Night-Hoers*; and Ludovici, *Man: An Indictment*.

12. *Sunday Chronicle*, 3 May 1935.

13. *Eugenics Review* 26, no. 3 (October 1934): 242–43.

14. See, for example, the *Manchester Evening Chronicle*, 18 March 1937.

15. *Reynolds Newspaper*, 18 April 1937; *Observer*, 6 March 1938; *Scotsman*, 7 March 1938.

16. *Manchester Evening News*, 18 March 1938.

17. Florence, *Birth Control on Trial*, pp. 136–39.

18. *Manchester Guardian*, 2 November 1937.

19. *Parl. Debates* (Commons), 5th ser., 29 November 1937, vol. 329, cols. 1787–91, 1810–11.

20. *Birth Control News* 16, no. 5 (December 1937): 1.

21. *Manchester Guardian*, 4 November 1937.

22. Charles, *Twilight of Parenthood*, pp. 198–200.

23. Ibid., p. 201. See also Charles, *The Practice of Birth Control*.

24. Florence, *Birth Control on Trial*, p. 119.

25. Charles, *Twilight of Parenthood*, p. 203.

26. Ibid., pp. 204, 213.

27. *Daily Herald*, 19 January 1937; *Evening Standard*, 4 March 1937; *Birth Control News* 15, no. 11 (April 1937): 134; Hubback to Blacker, 31 March 1936, Eugenics Society Papers, Eug./D.136; Eugenics Society, Minutes of the Council, 5 May 1936. On the interwar conflicts and divisions among feminists see Kent, "The Politics of Sexual Difference."

28. *The People*, 26 February 1939.

29. See "What Is Eugenics," pamphlet, ca. 1930, Eugenics Society Papers, Eug./C.170.

30. For the Family Endowment Society see MacNicol, *Family Allowances*, pp. 16–37.

31. Ibid., p. 7; Sidney Webb, *Decline in the Birth-Rate*, p. 16–17.

32. Whetham and Whetham, *The Family and the Nation*, pp. 190–94; *Sociological Papers* 3:74–80.

33. MacNicol, *Family Allowances*, pp. 87–88.

34. *Eugenics Review* 16, no. 3 (October 1924): 270–75.

35. Ibid., p. 270; MacNicol, *Family Allowances*, pp. 20–23.

36. Darwin to Havelock Ellis, 25 September 1920, Havelock Ellis Papers; *Eugenics Review* 12, no. 4 (January 1921): 282–84; 16, no. 4 (January 1924): 276–78.

37. *Eugenics Review* 16, no. 4 (January 1924): 276–78, 281–82.

38. MacNicol, *Family Allowances*, pp. 30–35. LSE provided an annual allowance of £30 a child to age thirteen followed by payments of £60 to the age of twenty-three if children were still in school.

39. Eugenics Society, *An Outline of a Practical Eugenic Policy*, p. 5.

40. See Family Endowment Society, *Memorandum on Family Allowances Presented to the Royal Commission*; MacNicol, *Family Allowances*, p. 35.

41. *Eugenics Review* 16, no. 1 (April 1924): 150–53.

42. MacNicol, *Family Allowances*, p. 35.

43. *Eugenics Review* 18, no. 2 (July 1926): 135–36.

44. Ibid. 16, no. 3 (October 1924): 283.

45. MacNicol, *Family Allowances*, p. 88; Rathbone, *The Disinherited Family*, p. 239.

46. Bennett, *Natural Selection*, p. 132–33.

47. Eugenics Society, Minutes of the Council, 9 October 1929.

48. Blacker to Fisher, 17 November 1931, 14 December 1933; Fisher to Blacker, 30 December 1931, Eugenics Society Papers, Eug./C.107, 108.

49. See Family Endowment Society, *Memorandum on Family Allowances Presented to the Royal Commission*; Family Endowment Society, *Memorandum on Family Allowances in the Teaching Profession*; Family Endowment Society, *The Case for Family*

Allowances among the Clergy; *Eugenics Review* 25, no. 1 (April 1933): 33–36.

50. *Eugenics Review* 23, no. 3 (October 1931): 201–2; 24, no. 2 (July 1932), p. 86.

51. Mallet, "The Reduction of the Fecundity of the Socially Inadequate," p. 364.

52. Chance to Blacker, 27 January 1932, and Blacker to Chance, 28 June 1934, Eugenics Society Papers, Eug./C.64; *Birth Control News* 7, no. 7 (January 1934): 111.

53. Michael Pease to Blacker, 1 January 1933, 5 August 1934, Eugenics Society Papers, Eug./C.269; MacNicol, *Family Allowances*, p. 83. See McDougall, "A Practicable Eugenic Suggestion."

54. For examples of the conflict see Blacker to W. T. J. Gun, 12 June 1932; Blacker to Fisher, 13, 20 June, 23 December 1932, 19 May, 14 December 1933; Fisher to Blacker, 20 December 1933; Blacker to Hubback, 18 December 1933, 1, 5 July 1934; Blacker to Darwin, 4 January 1934; "Minutes of the Family Allowance Sub-Committee," 25 July 1933, 9 January 1934, Eugenics Society Papers, Eug./D.65, C.107, 108, 177.

55. Blacker, *Eugenics and Family Allowances*; Penrose, "A National Population Policy Based on Eugenic Principles," 1934, Eugenics Society Papers, Eug./D.65.

56. Carr-Saunders, "Note on the Attitude to Family Allowances of the Eugenics Society," July 1934, ibid., Eug./C.57; Eugenics Society, "Minutes of the General Purposes Committee," 16 October, 6 November 1934, 15 January 1935.

57. Glass, *Struggle for Population*, pp. 87–89.

58. Blacker to Carr-Saunders, 2 December 1935, Eugenics Society Papers, Eug./C.57; *Eugenics Review* 27, no. 2 (July 1935): 91–93; *Birmingham Evening Star*, 13 July 1937.

59. *Birmingham Evening Star*, 13 July 1937.

60. *Sociological Review* 29, no. 3 (1937): 273–87.

61. *Eugenics Review* 27, no. 2 (July 1935): 93.

62. Eugenics Society, "Minutes of the General Purposes Committee," 4 August, 29 September 1936.

63. Lewis to Blacker, 25 July 1933, Eugenics Society Papers, Eug./C.206; Pease to Blacker, 8 December 1933, ibid., Eug./C.209.

64. Huxley to Blacker, 29 May 1933, ibid., Eug./C.209.

65. *Lancet*, pt. 1 (1933): 1265–66.

66. *Eugenics Review* 25, no. 2 (July 1933): 77–78; no. 3 (October 1933): 157–59, 179–81; *Lancet*, pt. 2 (1933): 297–98.

67. Blacker to A. H. W. James, 4, 10 October 1933, and James to Blacker, 7 October 1933, Eugenics Society Papers, Eug./C.191.

68. *Eugenics Review* 26, no. 3 (October 1934): 115; *Evening Standard*, 4 June 1940. Wilson, who had joined the Eugenics Society in 1932, was lost in aerial combat in 1940 at the age of fifty-five.

69. Blacker, *Eugenics in Retrospect*, p. 26. For examples see C. G. Campbell to Blacker, 29 January 1936; Blacker to Byron Bramwell, 7 February 1936, Eugenics Society Papers, Eug./C.37; and Blacker's correspondence with Norman A. Thompson, Eug./C.328.

70. Blacker, *Eugenics in Retrospect*, pp. 25–26.

71. *New Generation* 16, no. 2 (February 1937): 13–14; no. 12 (December 1937): 133–34. See also Soloway, *Birth Control*, pp. 162–65.

72. B. S. Bramwell to Blacker, 19 October 1934, Eugenics Society Papers,

Eug./C.36; Blacker to Carr-Saunders, 14 June 1934; Carr-Saunders to Blacker 15 June 1934, ibid., Eug./C.57.

73. Blacker to Huxley, 3 May 1935; Huxley to Blacker, 4 May 1935; Blacker, "Telephone Memorandum" of 7 May 1935, ibid., Eug./C.185.

74. Blacker to Duff, 22 July 1935, ibid., Eug./C.133; Duff to Horder, 8 October 1936, ibid., Eug./C.171. Duff's reports on Nazi eugenics are contained in Eug./C.132–33.

75. Blacker to Carr-Saunders, 8 February 1939, ibid., Eug./C.58; Glass, *Population Policies and Movements in Europe*, p. 305

76. Blacker to Newfield, 5 February 1934, 24 January 1938, Eugenics Society Papers, Eug./C.243, 245; Blacker to Duff, 23 December 1938, Eug./C.133.

77. Blacker to Penrose, 7 November 1938, and his "Note on Dr. Penrose's Memorandum," 16 November 1938, ibid., Eug./C.271.

78. *News Chronicle*, 2 April 1938; *Sunday Pictorial*, 3 April 1938.

79. *Daily Herald*, 18 January 1939; *Sunday Chronicle*, 22 January 1939; *Daily Mirror*, 18 January 1939.

80. *John Bull*, 10 December 1938; *Eugenics Review* 31, no. 3 (October 1939): 156.

81. *Eugenics Review* 31, no. 3 (October 1939): 157; Eugenics Society, *Aims and Objects*, p. 5.

82. Eugenics Society, *Aims and Objects*, p. 6.

83. Eugenics Society, Minutes of the Council, 3 July 1934; Blacker to Carr-Saunders, 14 February 1936, Eugenics Society Papers, Eug./C.57.

84. Blacker to Bramwell, 13 March 1935, Eugenics Society Papers, Eug./C.36.

85. *Birth Control News* 11, no. 12, (April 1933): 186–87; *Sunday Times*, 1 September 1935; Blacker to Bramwell, 13 March 1935, Eugenics Society Papers, Eug./C.36.

86. Eugenics Society, Minutes of the Executive Committee, 4 April, 4 July 1939.

87. Eugenics Society, Minutes of the Council, 10 October 1939; Minutes of the Emergency Committee, 7 November 1939; Blacker to Duff, 20 July 1944, Eugenics Society Papers, Eug./C.134. Duff served as the Eugenics Society's wartime representative on the council of the National Council for Maternity and Child Welfare.

88. Blacker to Duff, 4 October 1944, Eugenics Society Papers, Eug./C.134.

89. MacNicol, *Family Allowances*, pp. 89–91.

90. Ibid., pp. 92–94.

91. Eugenic Society, *Aims and Objects*, pp. 2–3.

92. Ibid., p. 2.

Chapter 13

1. Parl. Papers, *Current Trend of Population*.

2. Parl. Papers, *Social Insurance*, p. 154.

3. Ibid., pp. 8, 52–53; *Parl. Debates* (Commons), 5th ser., 16 July 1943, vol. 391, cols. 650–51. Churchill expressed his concerns in a March 1943 radio broadcast. See *The Listener*, 25 March 1943, pp. 363–65.

4. Harris, *William Beveridge*, p. 342.

5. Mitchell, *European Historical Statistics*, pp. 130, 134.

6. *Eugenics Review* 36, no. 1 (April 1944): 5–6.

7. Eugenics Society, "War Time Policy Comments," Eugenics Society Papers, Eug./D.248; Huxley to Horder, 29 September 1939, ibid., Eug./H.186.

8. *Eugenics Review* 31, no. 3 (October 1939): 151–52. See also 30, no. 3 (October 1938): 163.

9. Ibid. 31, no. 3 (October 1939): 153–54, 199–201.

10. Ibid. 32, no. 1 (April 1940): 7; no. 4 (January 1941): 114.

11. *Evening News*, 9 July 1941.

12. *Eugenics Review* 33, no. 2 (July 1940): 47–48, 55.

13. Ibid., no. 1 (April 1941): 28.

14. Eugenics Society, "War Time Policy Comments," Eugenics Society Papers, Eug./D.248.

15. The small membership dropped from 624 in 1939 to 495 at the end of the war. See Eugenics Society, Minutes of the Council, 16 November 1943; Eugenics Society Report 1944–1945.

16. Eugenics Society, Minutes of the Council, 10 October 1939; Reports, 1943–45.

17. Duff to Mrs. Collyer, 5 November 1940, Eugenics Society Papers, Eug./C.134.

18. Horder had written a foreword to Titmuss's *Poverty and Population*, the first of his many important works on social reform and administration.

19. See Titmuss and Titmuss, *Parents in Revolt*; Titmuss, "The End of Economic Parenthood," pp. 130–31. Blacker to Newfield, 30 June 1942, Eugenics Society Papers, Eug./C.333.

20. Duff to Mrs. Collyer, 15 September 1939; Titmuss to Duff, 18 September 1939, Eugenics Society Papers, Eug./C.134. See also Eugenics Society, Minutes of the Emergency Committee, 1939–1943.

21. Titmuss, *Birth, Poverty and Wealth*; Blacker to Newfield, 30 June 1942, Eugenics Society Papers, Eug./C.333. *Eugenics Review*, 34, no. 2 (July 1942): 52–53.

22. *Eugenics Review* 34, no. 4 (January 1943): 110.

23. Ibid. 32, no. 4 (January 1941): 112. Also no. 1 (April 1940): 7.

24. "Aims and Objects of the Eugenics Society: Moral and Scientific Basis" (1944), Eugenics Society Papers, Eug./C.134.

25. *Eugenics Review* 33, no. 4 (January 1942): 104–5.

26. Ibid. 32, no. 4 (January 1941): 113.

27. Ibid., no. 1 (April 1940): 6; no. 2 (July 1940): 70.

28. Ibid., no. 2 (July 1940): 43–46.

29. Titmuss, "The Social Environment and Eugenics," pp. 53–58.

30. *Eugenics Review* 33, no. 1 (April 1941): 4–6.

31. Ibid. 35, no. 3–4 (October–January 1943–44): 55–56.

32. "The Means of Family Planning," 28 July 1945, Eugenics Society Papers, Eug./C.199.

33. See, for example, Family Planning Association Report 1941–42 in *Eugenics Review* 34, no. 4 (January 1943): 129.

34. *British Medical Journal*, pt. 1 (1942): 81; Paterson, "Size of Family."

35. *Parl. Debates* (Lords), 5th ser., 8 June 1943, vol. 127, cols. 911–17; 16 July 1943, vol. 128, cols. 582–83.

36. *Eugenics Review* 36, no. 1 (April 1944): 40–41.

37. Ibid., pp. 9–16.

38. Mass Observation, *Britain and Her Birth-Rate*, pp. 92–96.

39. *Eugenics Review* 33, no. 2 (July 1941): 49–50; no. 4 (January 1942): 99–100; 34, no. 1 (April 1942): 7–12.

40. Parl. Papers, *Current Trend of Population*, pp. 2–12.

41. *Times*, 23, 29 June 1942.

42. *Eugenics Review* 34, no. 1 (April 1942): 7–8; no. 2 (July 1942): 47–48.

43. *British Medical Journal*, pt. 1 (1942): 394, 442–43.

44. See, for example, ibid., pp. 196–97, 272–73, 337, 423–24, 478; Blacker to Horder, Eugenics Society Papers, Eug./C.173.

45. *Eugenics Review* 34, no. 1 (April 1942): 9–12; 35, no. 1 (April 1943): 36–38.

46. Titmuss and Titmuss, *Parents in Revolt*, pp. 116–23.

47. *Parl. Debates* (Commons), 5th ser., 29 April, 6 May 1942, vol. 379, cols. 945–46, 1341–42.

48. Ibid., 23 April 1942, vol. 379, cols. 738–39; 9 July 1942, vol. 381, cols. 928–29.

49. Ibid., 3, 6 June 1943, vol. 390, cols. 371–72, 999–1000.

50. *Parl. Debates* (Lords), 5th ser., 8 June 1943, vol. 127, cols. 892–98.

51. Ibid., cols. 899–910, 917–22.

52. *Parl. Debates* (Commons), 5th ser., 16 July 1943, vol. 391, cols. 635–38.

53. Ibid., cols. 563–70.

54. Ibid., cols. 603–15.

55. Ibid., cols. 593–601.

56. Ibid., cols. 640–51, 922–29.

57. Parl. Papers, *Social Insurance*, pp. 8, 52–53, 154–57.

58. Titmuss to Blacker, 16 November 1941; Blacker to Titmuss, 19 November 1941, Eugenics Society Papers, Eug./C.133.

59. Beveridge, "Eugenic Aspects of Children's Allowances," pp. 117–23, 125.

60. Inge, *Diary of a Dean*, p. 14.

61. *Eugenics Review* 34, no. 4 (January 1943): 126–27.

62. Ibid. 36, no. 1 (April 1944): 17–18.

63. Ibid., pp. 21–22. Newfield to Blacker, 3 April 1943, Eugenics Society Papers, Eug./C.245.

64. Binney to Blacker, 21 July 1943, Eugenics Society Papers, Eug./C.199; *Eugenics Review* 36, no. 1 (April 1944): 18–20.

65. Minutes of the War Emergency Committee, 15 January 1940, Eugenics Society Papers, Eug./C.134.

66. Drysdale to Chance, 29 January 1942, Eugenics Society Papers, Eug./C.92.

67. For the varying reactions to Drysdale's letter see Eugenics Society Papers, Eug./C.92.

68. Blacker to Keynes, 20 January 1944; Keynes to Blacker, 25 January 1944, ibid., Eug./C.197. For the Malthusian League resolution see Miss O. M. Johnson to Blacker, 20 January 1944, ibid., or *British Medical Journal*, pt. 1 (1944): 169.

69. See, for example, *Eugenics Review* 32, no. 1 (April 1940): 3–4, 9; 33, no. 1 (April 1941): 6–7; no. 3 (October 1941): 69–72; Newfield to Hubback, 16 May 1940, Eugenics Society Papers, Eug./D.248.

70. *Eugenics Review* 34, no. 2 (July 1942): 51–52.

Chapter 14

1. Parl. Papers, *Report of the Royal Commission on Population*. See, in particular, Lewis-Fanning, *Report on an Enquiry into Family Limitation*, and Glass and Grebenik, *Trend and Pattern of Fertility*.

2. Eugenics Society, "Memorandum for the Royal Commission on Population: January 1945," Eugenics Society Papers, Eug./D.160, pp. 1–2.

3. Blacker, "Proposals As to the Formation of a Joint Committee to Deal With the Problems of Positive Eugenics," (1937) Eugenics Society Papers, Eug./D.163. Sir James Marchant to Horder, 6 June 1937, ibid., Eug./C.172. See also the *Times*, 19 March, 19 April 1937.

4. *Eugenics Review* 30, no. 1 (April 1938): 4–5.

5. See "Population Investigation Committee: Memorandum by War Emergency Committee," Eugenics Society Papers, Eug./C.161.

6. Minutes of War Emergency Committee, 14 April 1942; Carr-Saunders to Hubback, 30 July, Hubback to Carr-Saunders, 17 August 1942, Hubback to G. D. H. Cole, 24 July 1942, ibid., Eug./D.248.

7. Horder to Blacker, 15 December 1942, ibid., Eug./C.173; *Eugenics Review* 35, no. 1 (April 1943): 6–7; Glass to Carr-Saunders, 12 December 1944, 21 February 1945, PIC Papers VI/a.

8. PIC Papers VI/a; Memorandum to Sir John Anderson, 14 July 1943; Glass to Blacker, 30 July 1943; Carr-Saunders to Ernest Brown, 4 August 1943; Memorandum, 28 July 1943.

9. In addition to Carr-Saunders and the chairman, Lord Simon, who served in that capacity until 1946, some of the other Eugenics Society members or sympathizers who participated either directly or through their testimony were Professor A. W. Ellis, Eardley Holland, J. R. Hobhouse, Dr. A. S. Parkes, Godfrey Thomson, E. O. Lewis, Cyril Burt, J. A. Fraser Roberts, Eva Hubback, R. A. Fisher, R. R. Kuczynski, Grace Leybourne, Aubrey Lewis, and of course, Glass and Blacker.

10. See correspondence September–October 1944, PIC Papers VI/a; Blacker to Newfield, 18 December 1944, Eugenics Society Papers, Eug./C.245.

11. Cadbury to Blacker, 6, 8 September 1944, PIC Papers VI/a; L. Farrer-Brown, Nuffield Foundation, to Carr-Saunders 2 July 1945; Carr-Saunders to Blacker, 17 December 1945, ibid. VI/1a.

12. Blacker to Bramwell, 4 July 1945, Eugenics Society Papers, Eug./C.37; Blacker to Carr-Saunders, 17 April 1944, 4 July 1945, PIC Papers VI/1a.

13. Blacker to Carr-Saunders, 31 August 1944, Carr-Saunders Papers, 7/10; Blacker to Members of the Council, 20 October 1944, Eugenics Society Papers, Eug/D.160.

14. Eugenics Society, "Memorandum for the Royal Commission on Population," Eugenics Society Papers, Eug./D.160, p. 5.

15. Ibid., p. 6.

16. Ibid., pp. 8–12.

17. Ibid., pp. 3–4.

18. Carr-Saunders to Blacker, 16 June 1944, Eugenics Society Papers, Eug./D.160. See also Carr-Saunders's suggestions to Blacker in Carr-Saunders Papers, 7/10.

19. For a transcript of the Eugenics Society's testimony on 13 April 1945 see Eugenics Society Papers, Eug./D.160.

20. Blacker to Carr-Saunders, 31 July, 31 August 1944, Carr-Saunders to Blacker, 4 August 1944, Carr-Saunders Papers, 7/10. Carr-Saunders to Blacker, 16 June 1944, Eugenics Society Papers, Eug./D.160.

21. Glass and Grebenik, *Trend and Pattern of Fertility*.

22. Ibid., p. 110, table 40; pp. 112–13, table 42. For categories and social status see p. 21.

23. Glass to Carr-Saunders, 12 December 1944, PIC Papers VI/a.

24. For example, Hopkin, "The Measurement of Reproductivity"; Hajnal, "Births, Marriages and Reproductivity in England and Wales."

25. Mass Observation, *Britain and Her Birth-Rate*, pp. 7–13, 23.

26. Ibid., pp. 31–40.

27. Ibid., pp. 54–61.

28. Ibid., pp. 62–73.

29. *News Chronicle*, 21 February 1944.

30. Mass Observation, *Britain and Her Birth-Rate*, pp. 74–85.

31. Ibid., pp. 97–147.

32. Ibid., pp. 149–86.

33. Ibid., pp. 187–93.

34. Ibid., pp. 108–207.

35. Parl. Papers, *Report of the Royal Commission on Population*, pp. 158–59, 193–94; *Eugenics Review* 41, no. 3 (October 1949): 122–26.

36. For the passage of the Family Allowances Bill in 1945 see MacNicol, *Family Allowances*, chap. 7.

37. Mitchell, *European Historical Statistics*, p. 34

38. Blacker, *Eugenics: Galton and After*, pp. 142–44.

39. See, for example, *Parl. Debates* (Commons), 5th ser., 4 December 1940, vol. 367, cols. 602–7. Duff to Blacker, 4 November 1945; Blacker to Duff, 6 November 1945, Eugenics Society Papers, Eug./C.134.

40. "War Time Eugenic Measures in Germany," Eugenics Society Papers, Eug./D.248.

41. Blacker, *Eugenics: Galton and After*, p. 146.

42. The *Eugenics Review* ceased publishing in 1960. It was replaced by the *Journal of Biosocial Science*, which reflected more accurately the Eugenics Society's new orientation.

43. For the Gallup Poll see Eugenics Society Papers.

44. *Observer*, 20 October 1974.

45. See, for example, the *Times*, 14 June 1978, 10 March 1979.

46. Paul, "Eugenics and the Left," pp. 587–89.

47. Baker, "Memo to the Eugenics Society Council," 4 October 1961; Baker to Dr. Bertram, 26 December 1961, Eugenics Society Papers, Eug./C.13.

48. After his resignation as general secretary of the Eugenics Society, Blacker worked with Lord Simon on the 1955 PEP report, *World Population and Food Resources*, and was active with the International Planned Parenthood Federation.

49. Baker to Dr. Bertram, 26 December 1961, Eugenics Society Papers, Eug./C.13.

50. See for example, "Birth Dearth," in *Christian Century* 88 (1971): 1374.

51. *Times*, 19 July 1974, 14, 15 August 1975; *Sunday Times*, 31 January, 16 February 1977.

52. See, for example, the *Economist*, 27 May 1972, pp. 93–94; the *Times*, 17 October 1973, 19 July 1974, 6 February, 14, 15 August 1975; *Sunday Times*, 14 July 1974, 16 March 1975, 2 December 1976, 31 January, 16 July 1977. *Times Educational Supplement*, 9 February 1973, pp. 6–7, 18 April 1975, p. 4a; *Times Literary Supplement*, 7 September 1976, p. 11.

53. *Sunday Times*, 24 October 1984.

54. *New Society*, 2 July 1981, pp. 15–16.

55. *Listener*, 27 January 1977, p. 106.

56. *Geographic Magazine*, February 1979, p. 321; *Economist*, 3 February 1979, p. 48; 18 June 1983, p. 66.

57. *Economist*, 27 May 1972, pp. 93–94; *Times*, 31 October 1974.

58. *Sunday Times*, 16 March 1975; *Times Education Supplement*, 9 February 1973, p. 6; *Listener*, 27 January 1977, p. 106.

59. *Times Literary Supplement*, 30 April 1976; *Times Educational Supplement*, 29 November 1974, 25 March 1977; *Sunday Times*, 19 October 1981.

60. *Sunday Times*, 20, 27 October 1974.

61. Ibid.; *Times*, 21 October 1974.

62. *Times*, 21, 22 October 1974.

63. Wattenberg, *The Birth Dearth*, p. 81.

64. Paul, "Eugenics and the Left," p. 590.

Works Cited

The following bibliography consists of sources cited specifically in the preceding chapters. They represent only a portion of the extensive primary and secondary literature consulted for this book and available for the study of eugenics and birth control. Recent and more complete surveys of this literature can be found in the notes and "Essay on Sources" in Kevles, *In the Name of Eugenics* (pp. 303–405) and in the bibliography in Soloway, *Birth Control* (pp. 365–96).

Primary Sources

Manuscript Collections

Cardiff, Wales
The David Owen Centre, University College
  Family Planning Association Archives
    Birth Control Investigation Committee Papers
    National Birth Control Association Minutes and Correspondence
    National Birth Control Council Minutes and Correspondence

London
British Library
  William Boyd Carpenter Papers
  George Bernard Shaw Papers
  Marie Stopes Papers
British Library of Political and Economic Science
  William Beveridge Papers
  A. M. Carr-Saunders Papers
Contemporary Medical Archives Center, Wellcome Institute for the History of Medicine
  Eugenics Society Papers
Department of Population Studies, London School of Economics and Political Science
  Population Investigation Committee Papers
Eugenics Society Library
  Reports, Council Minute Books
  Press Cuttings 1907–1940, 14 vols.
National Maritime Museum (Greenwich)
  Arnold White Papers

Public Record Office
  Ministry of Health Papers
University College, The University of London
  Francis Galton Archives
  Karl Pearson Papers

New Haven, Connecticut
Stirling Library, Yale University
  Havelock Ellis Papers

Washington, D.C.
Library of Congress
  Margaret Sanger Papers

Government Documents and Official Publications

Parliamentary Debates (Great Britain)
Hansard Parliamentary Debates
  3d series, 1856–91
  4th series, 1892–1908
  5th series, 1909–80
  6th series, 1980–

Parliamentary Papers

Census of England and Wales, 1911: Fertility of Marriage. Part 1. Cd. 8678. London, 1917. Part 2. *Report*. Cd. 8491. London, 1923.
Census of England and Wales, 1931: General Report. London, 1950.
Census of England and Wales, 1931: Preliminary Report Including Tables of the Population. London, 1931.
Current Trend of Population in Great Britain. Cmd. 6358. London, 1942.
Final Report of the Health of Munition Workers Committee. Vol. 13. Cd. 9065. London, 1918.
Forty-fifth Annual Report of the Local Government Board: Supplement in Continuance of the Report of the Medical Officer of the Board for 1915–16. Containing a Report on Child Mortality at Ages 0–5. Cd. 8496. London, 1917–18.
Forty-second Annual Report of the Local Government Board 1912–1913: Supplement Containing a Second Report on Infant and Child Welfare. Cd. 6909. London, 1914.
Glass, D. V., and Grebenik, E. *The Trend and Pattern of Fertility in Great Britain: A Report on the Family Census of 1946*. Part 1. Papers of the Royal Commission on Population, vol. 6. London, 1954.
Lewis-Fanning, E. *Report on an Enquiry into Family Limitation and Its Influence on Human Fertility during the Past Fifty Years*. Papers of the Royal Commission on Population, vol. 1. London, 1949.
Memorandum by the Director-General, Army Medical Service, on the Physical Unfitness of Men Offering Themselves for Enlistment in the Army. Cd. 1501. London, 1903.
Ministry of Health, *Final Report of Departmental Committee on Maternal Mortality and Morbidity*. London, 1932.

Ministry of Health, *Report on an Investigation into Maternal Mortality.* Cmd. 5422. London, 1937.

Ministry of National Service 1917–1919, *Report upon the Physical Examination of Men of Military Age by National Service Medical Boards from November 1, 1917–October 31, 1918.* Cmd. 504. London, 1919.

Registrar-General 65th Annual Report. Cd. 2003. London, 1904.

Registrar-General 82d Annual Report. Cmd. 1017. London, 1920.

The Registrar-General's Statistical Review of England and Wales for the Year 1926. London, 1928.

The Registrar-General's Statistical Review of England and Wales for the Year 1927. London, 1929.

The Registrar-General's Statistical Review of England and Wales for the Year 1931. London, 1931.

Report of the Departmental Committee on Sterilisation (Joint Committee on Voluntary Sterilisation, June 1934). Cmd. 4485. London, 1934.

Report of the Inter-Departmental Committee on Physical Deterioration. Cd. 2175, 2210, 2186. London, 1904.

Report of the Mental Deficiency Committee, being a Joint Committee of the Board of Education and Board of Control. 3 vols. London, 1929.

Report of the Royal Commission on Divorce and Matrimonial Causes. Cd. 6478–82. London, 1912–13.

Report of the Royal Commission on Physical Training (Scotland). Cd. 1507, 1508. London, 1903.

Report of the Royal Commission on Population. Cmd. 7695. London, 1949.

Report of the Royal Commission on Population. Papers. 6 vols. London, 1950–54.

Report of the War Cabinet Committee on Women in Industry. Vol. 31. Cmd. 135. London, 1919.

Report of the Women's Employment Committee. Vol. 14. Cd. 9239. London, 1918.

Social Insurance and Allied Services. Cmd. 6404. London, 1942.

Journals, Periodicals, and Newspapers

Annals of Eugenics
Anti-Suffrage Review
Biometrika
The Birmingham Evening Star
The Birmingham Gazette
The Birmingham Post
Birth Control News
The Bournemouth Daily Echo
The Bristol Western Daily Press
The British Medical Journal
The Catholic Herald
The Catholic News
Cavalcade
The Chester Chronicle
Child Study

Christian Century
The Contemporary Review
The Daily Chronicle
The Daily Dispatch
The Daily Express
The Daily Herald
The Daily Mail
The Daily Mirror
The Daily News
The Daily Sketch
The Daily Telegraph
The Eastbourne Herald
The Economic Review
The Economist
The Edinburgh Review
The Englishwoman
The Eugenics Review
The Evening Standard
The Exeter Diocesan Gazette
The Fortnightly Review
Fraser's Magazine
Geographic Magazine
The Glasgow Herald
The Glasgow Sunday Mail
Guy's Hospital Gazette
Hibbert Journal
Hospital Social Service
John Bull
Journal of Biosocial Science
Journal of the Royal Statistical Society
The Lancet
The Listener
The Liverpool Daily Post
Macmillan's Magazine
The Malthusian
The Manchester City News
The Manchester Despatch
The Manchester Evening Chronicle
The Manchester Evening News
The Manchester Guardian
The Manchester News Chronicle
Medical Officer
The Medical Press and Circular
The Medical Times and Gazette
The Morning Post
The Nation

National Health
National Life
The National Review
Nature
New Generation
New Society
The New Statesman
The News Chronicle
News of the World
Nineteenth Century and After
The Northern Mail and Newcastle Chronicle
The Nottingham Journal
The Observer
The Pall Mall Gazette
The People
Public Opinion
Pulman's Weekly News, Somerset
The Quarterly Review
Reynold's Illustrated News
Reynolds Newspaper
The Ripon Gazette
The Scotsman
The Sheffield Daily Independent
The Sheffield Daily Telegraph
Social Studies of Science
The Sociological Review
The Spectator
Suffragette
The Sunday Chronicle
The Sunday Pictorial
Time and Tide
The Times
The Times Educational Supplement
The Times Literary Supplement
Votes for Women
The West Yorkshire Pioneer
The Western Daily Mail, Cardiff
The Western Daily Press, Bristol
The Western Morning News
The Westminster Review
The Yorkshire Telegraph and Star

Books, Pamphlets, and Reports

Aveling, Edward. *Darwinism and Small Families*. London, 1882.
Ayling, John. *Retreat from Parenthood*. London, 1930.

Barr, Sir James. *Aim and Scope of Eugenics*. Edinburgh, 1911.

Barrett, Lady Florence E. *Conception Control and Its Effects on the Individual and the Nation*. London, 1922.

Besant, Annie. *Law of Population: Its Consequences and Its Bearing upon Human Conduct and Morals*. London, 1881.

Beveridge, William. *Unemployment: A Problem of Industry*. London, 1909.

———. *Unemployment: A Problem of Industry*. Rev. ed. London, 1931.

Blacker, C. P. *Birth Control and the State: A Plea and a Forecast*. London, 1926.

———. *Eugenics and Family Allowances*. London, 1933.

———. *Eugenics: Galton and After*. London, 1952.

———. *Eugenics in Prospect and Retrospect*. London, 1945.

Blacker, C. P., and Glass, David V. *The Future of Our Population*. London, 1937.

———. *Population and Fertility*. London, 1938.

Blunt, Wilfred Scawen. *My Diaries: Being a Personal Narrative of Events 1888–1914*. New York, 1922.

Booth, Charles. *Life and Labour of the People in London*. 17 vols. London, 1902–4.

Bowley, Arthur L., and Hogg, Margaret H. *Has Poverty Diminished? A Sequel to "Livelihood and Poverty."* London, 1925.

Brown, J. B. *Young Men and Maidens: A Pastoral for the Times*. London, 1871.

Campbell, Janet. *Memorandum on Maternal Mortality*. London, 1924.

Cantlie, James. *Degeneration amongst Londoners*. Parkes Museum of Hygiene Lecture. London, 1885.

———. *Physical Efficiency: A Review of the Deleterious Effects of Town Life upon the Population of Britain, with Suggestions for Their Arrest*. London, 1906.

Carnegie United Kingdom Trust. *Report on the Physical Welfare of Mothers and Children: England and Wales*. 4 vols. London, 1917.

Carr-Saunders, A. M. *The Population Problem: A Study in Human Evolution*. Oxford, 1922.

———. *World Population: Past Growth and Present Trends*. London, 1936.

Cattell, Raymond. *The Fight for Our National Intelligence*. London, 1937.

Charles, Enid. *The Practice of Birth Control: An Analysis of 900 Women*. London, 1932.

———. *The Twilight of Parenthood: A Biological Study of the Decline of Population Growth*. London, 1934.

Clapperton, Jane H. *Scientific Meliorism*. London, 1885.

———. *A Vision of the Future Based on the Application of Ethical Principles*. London, 1904.

Crackanthorpe, Montague. *Population and Progress*. London, 1907.

Darwin, Charles. *The Descent of Man and Selection in Relation to Sex*. London, 1871.

———. *Organic Evolution: Outstanding Difficulties and Possible Explanations*. Cambridge, 1921.

———. *The Origin of Species by Means of Natural Selection or the Preservation of the Favoured Races in the Struggle for Life*. London, 1859.

———. *The Variation of Animals and Plants under Domestication*. New York, 1868.

Darwin, Leonard. *The Case for Eugenic Reform*. London, 1926.

————. *What Is Eugenics?* London, 1928.

Davies, Margaret L. *Maternity: Letters from Working Women.* London, 1915.

Dawson of Penn. *Love-Marriage-Birth Control.* London, 1922.

Drysdale, Charles Vickery. *The Empire and the Birth Rate: A Paper Read Before the Royal Colonial Institute, March 24, 1914.* London, 1914.

————. *Small or Large Families: Birth Control from the Moral, Racial, and Eugenic Standpoint.* New York, 1917.

Elderton, Ethel. *Report on the English Birth Rate. Part 1. England North of the Humber.* Eugenics Laboratory Memoirs 19 and 20. Cambridge, 1914.

Elderton, Ethel; Barrington, Amy; Jones, H. Gertrude; Laski, Harold; and Pearson, Karl. *On the Correlation of Fertility with Social Value: A Cooperative Study.* Eugenics Laboratory Memoir 18. London, 1913.

Ellis, Havelock. *Essays in War-Time: Further Studies in the Task of Social Hygiene.* Boston and New York, 1917.

————. *The Problem of Race Regeneration.* London, 1911.

————. *The Task of Social Hygiene.* London, 1912.

Eugenics Education Society. *Fourth Annual Report 1911–1912.* London, 1912.

————. *Problems in Eugenics: Papers Communicated to the First International Congress and Reports of Proceedings. Held at the University of London, July 24th to 30th, 1912.* 2 vols. London, 1912–13.

————. *Tenth Annual Report 1917–18.* London, 1918.

Eugenics Society. *The Aims and Objects of the Eugenics Society.* Rev. London, 1939.

————. *Annual Report of the Eugenics Society 1925–1926.* London, 1926.

————. *Annual Report of the Eugenics Society 1935–1936.* London, 1937.

————. *Annual Report of the Eugenics Society 1936–1937.* London, 1938.

————. *A Decade of Progress in Eugenics: Third International Congress of Eugenics, 1932.* Baltimore, 1934.

————. *An Outline of a Practical Eugenic Policy.* London, 1926.

Family Endowment Society. *The Case for Family Allowances among the Clergy.* London, 1933.

————. *Memorandum on Family Allowances in the Teaching Profession.* London, 1932.

————. *Memorandum on Family Allowances Presented to the Royal Commission on the Civil Service.* London, 1930.

Family Planning Association. *Report of the Family Planning Association 1939.* London, 1940.

Field, James A. *Essays on Population and Other Papers.* Chicago, 1931.

Florence, Lela S. *Birth Control on Trial.* London, 1930.

Galton, Francis. *English Men of Science: Their Nature and Nurture.* London, 1874.

————. *Essays in Eugenics.* London, 1909.

————. *Hereditary Genius: An Inquiry into Its Laws and Consequences.* New York, 1871.

————. *Inquiries into Human Faculty and Its Development.* London, 1883.

————. *Memories of My Life.* 3d ed. London, 1909.

————. *Natural Inheritance.* London, 1889.

————. *Tropical South Africa.* London, 1853.

General Medical Council. *Minutes of the General Medical Council, of Its Executive and Dental Committees, and of Its Three Branch Councils for the Year 1887*. Vol. 24. London, 1887.

Ginsburg, Louis. *Parenthood and Poverty: The Population Problem of Democracy*. Fabian Society Research Series No. 43. London, 1939.

Glass, David V. *Population Policies and Movements in Europe*. Oxford, 1940.

———. *The Struggle for Population*. Oxford, 1936.

Glyn, Elinor. *Romantic Adventure*. New York, 1937.

Greg, William Rathbone. *Enigmas of Life*. London, 1872.

Haycraft, John B. *Darwinism and Race Progress*. London, 1895.

Heron, David. *On the Relation of Fertility in Man to Social Status and on the Changes in This Relation That Have Taken Place during the Last Fifty Years*. Drapers Company Research Memoirs 1. London, 1906.

Hogben, Lancelot. *Dangerous Thoughts*. London, 1940.

———. *Retreat from Reason*. London, 1936.

Holyoake, Austin. *Large or Small Families? On Which Side Lies the Balance of Comfort?* London, 1870.

Houghton, Robert F. *National Ideals and Race Regeneration*. London, 1912.

Huxley, Thomas. *Evolution and Ethics and Other Essays*. New York, 1896.

Inge, William Ralph. *Diary of a Dean: St. Paul's 1911–1934*. London, 1949.

———. *Outspoken Essays*. 2d series. London, 1922.

In the High Court of Justice, Queen's Bench Division. June 18, 1877. The Queen v. Charles Bradlaugh and Annie Besant. 2d ed. London, 1888.

Jackson, Holbrook. *The Eighteen-Nineties*. London, 1913.

Jones, D. Caradog. *The Social Survey of Merseyside*. London, 1934.

Kidd, Benjamin. *Social Evolution*. 2d ed. London, 1894.

Knowlton, Charles. *The Fruits of Philosophy: An Essay on the Population Question*. London, 1877.

Kuczynski, Robert. *The Balance of Births and Deaths*. Vol. 1, *Western and Northern Europe*. New York, 1928.

———. *Population Movements*. Oxford, 1936.

Lambeth Conference. *Conference of Bishops of the Anglican Communion: Holden at Lambeth Palace, July 27 to August 5, 1908. Encyclical Letter from the Bishops, with the Resolutions and Reports*. London, 1908.

Leybourne, Grace, and White, K. *Education and the Birth Rate*. London, 1940.

Lidbetter, E. J. *Heredity and the Social Problem Group*. Vol. 1. London, 1933.

Ludovici, Anthony M. *Lysistrata or Woman's Future and Future Women*. London, 1924.

———. *Man: An Indictment*. London, 1931.

———. *The Night-Hoers or the Case against Birth-Control and an Alternative*. London, 1938.

McCleary, George F. *The Maternity and Child Welfare Movement*. London, 1935.

———. *The Menace of Depopulation*. London, 1937.

McKim, W. D. *Heredity and Human Progress*. London, 1900.

Malthus, Thomas R. *An Essay on the Principle of Population as It Affects the Future Improvement of Society*. London, 1798.

Marchant, James. *Birth Rate and Empire*. London, 1917.

————. *Cradles or Coffins? Our Greatest National Need.* London, 1916.

Mass Observation. *Britain and Her Birth-Rate: A Report Prepared by Mass-Observation for the Advertising Service Guild.* London, 1945.

Masterman, C. F. G. *The Condition of England.* London, 1909.

Masterman, C. F. G.; Pigou, A. C.; et al. *The Heart of the Empire: Discussions of Problems of Modern City Life in England, with an Essay on Imperialism.* London, 1901.

Meyer, F. B. *Religion and Race Regeneration.* London, 1912.

Morel, Benedict-Augustin. *Traité des dégénérescenses physiques intellectuelles et morales de l'espèce humaine.* Paris, 1857.

National Birth Control Association. *Sixth Annual Report 1935–1936.* London, 1937.

National Birth-Rate Commission. *Problems of Population and Parenthood: Being the Second Report of and the Chief Evidence Taken by the National Birth-Rate Commission, 1918–1920.* New York, 1920.

National Council of Public Morals. *The Declining Birth-Rate, Its Causes and Effects: Being the Report of and the Chief Evidence Taken by the National Birth-Rate Commission, Instituted, with Official Recognition, by the National Council of Public Morals—for the Promotion of Race Regeneration—Spiritual, Moral, and Physical.* Edited by James Marchant. London, 1916.

————. *The Ethics of Birth Control: Being the Report of the Special Committee Appointed by the National Council of Public Morals in Connection with the Investigations of the National Birth-Rate Commission.* London, 1925.

Newman, George. *Infant Mortality: A Social Problem.* London, 1906.

Newsholme, Arthur. *The Declining Birth-Rate: Its National and International Significance.* London, 1911.

————. *Health Problems in Organized Society: Studies in the Social Aspects of Public Health.* London, 1927.

Nordau, Max. *Degeneration.* London, 1892.

Owen, Harold. *Woman Adrift.* London, 1912.

Palmer, Mabel. *Life-Saving in Wartime: A Campaign Handbook (The Infant Welfare Propaganda Committee of the National League for Physical Education and Improvement).* London, 1916.

Pankhurst, Christabel. *The Great Scourge and How to End It.* London, 1913.

Pearson, Karl. *The Chances of Death and Other Studies in Evolution.* 2 vols. London, 1897.

————. *Darwinism, Medical Progress and Eugenics: The Cavendish Lecture, 1912. An Address to the Medical Profession.* London, 1912.

————. *The Ethic of Freethought and Other Addresses and Essays.* 2d ed. London, 1901.

————. *First Study of the Statistics of Pulmonary Tuberculosis.* London, 1910.

————. *The Groundwork of Eugenics.* Eugenics Laboratory Lecture Series 2. 2d ed. Cambridge, 1912.

————. *National Life from the Standpoint of Science.* London, 1901.

————. *National Life from the Standpoint of Science.* 2d ed. London, 1905.

————. *Nature and Nurture—The Problem of the Future: A Presidential Address at the Annual Meeting of the Social and Political Education League April 28, 1910.* London, 1910.

_____. *On the Handicapping of the First Born*. Eugenics Laboratory Lecture Series 10. Cambridge, 1914.

_____. *The Problem of Practical Eugenics*. Eugenics Laboratory Lecture Series 5. 2d ed. Cambridge, 1912.

Pell, Charles Edward. *The Law of Births and Deaths: Being a Study of the Variation in the Degree of Animal Fertility under the Influence of the Environment*. London, 1921.

Penrose, Lionel. *A Clinical and Genetic Study of 1280 Cases of Mental Defect*. London, 1938.

Petrie, William Flinders. *Janus in Modern Life*. New York, 1907.

Phillips, Marion, ed. *Women and the Labour Party*. London, 1918.

Problems of Population: Being the Report of the Proceedings of the Second General Assembly of the International Union for the Scientific Investigation of Population Problems. Edited by G. H. L. F. Pitt-Rivers. London, 1932.

Proceedings of the International Birth Control Conference, Zurich 1930. Edited by Ettie Sayer and Hannah Stone. London, 1932.

Queen's Hall Meeting on Constructive Birth Control: Speeches and Impressions. London, 1921.

Rathbone, Eleanor. *The Disinherited Family*. London, 1924.

Rentoul, Robert Reid. *Race Culture; Or, Race Suicide? (A Plea for the Unborn)*. London, 1906.

Report of the Anthropometric Committee of the British Association: Proceedings of the British Association for the Advancement of Science. London, 1883.

Report of the Proceedings of the National Conference on Infant Mortality, 1906. London, 1906.

Report of the Proceedings of the National Conference on Infant Mortality at St. George's Hotel. Liverpool, 1914.

Roberts, Robert. *The Classic Slum: Salford Life in the First Quarter of the Century*. Manchester, 1971.

Robertson, James Mackinnon. *Overpopulation: A Lecture Delivered for the Sunday Lecture Society, London, October 27, 1889, under the Title: "The Law of Population; Its Meaning and Menace."* London, 1890.

Robinson, W. J., ed. *Small or Large Families: Birth Control From the Moral, Racial, and Eugenic Standpoint*. New York, 1917.

Rowntree, B. Seebohm. *Poverty and Progress: A Second Social Survey of York*. London, 1941.

_____. *Poverty: A Study of Town Life*. London, 1901.

Saleeby, Caleb, W. *The Methods of Race Regeneration*. New York, 1911.

_____. *Parenthood and Race Culture: An Outline of Eugenics*. New York, 1910.

_____. *The Progress of Eugenics*. London, 1914.

_____. *Woman and Womanhood: A Search for Principles*. London, 1911.

_____. Shaw, George Bernard. *Preface to Three Plays by Brieux*. London, 1910.

Sidgwick, Mrs. Henry. *Health Statistics of Women Students of Cambridge and Oxford and of Their Sisters*. Cambridge, 1890.

_____. *University Education for Women: Presidential Address Delivered to the Education Society, Manchester University, on 21 November 1912*. Manchester, 1913.

Society for the Provision of Birth Control Clinics. *Birth Control and Public Health: A*

Report on Ten Years' Work of the Society for the Provision of Birth Control Clinics. London, 1932.

Sociological Society. *Sociological Papers.* 3 vols. London, 1905–1917.

Spencer, Herbert. *The Principles of Biology.* 2 vols. London, 1864, 1867.

————. *Social Statics: Or the Conditions Essential to Human Happiness Specified, and the First of Ten Developed.* London, 1851.

Stopes, Marie. *Contraception (Birth Control): Its Theory, History and Practice. A Manual for the Medical and Legal Professions.* London, 1923.

————. *A Letter to Working Mothers on How to Have Healthy Children and Avoid Weakening Pregnancies.* Leatherhead, 1919.

————. *Married Love.* London, 1918.

————. *Radiant Motherhood: A Book for Those Who Are Creating the Future.* London, 1920.

————. *Wise Parenthood: A Sequel to Married Love.* London, 1918.

Titmuss, Richard. *Birth, Poverty and Wealth. A Study of Infant Mortality.* London, 1943.

————. *Poverty and Population.* London, 1938.

Titmuss, Richard, and Titmuss, Kathleen. *Parents in Revolt: A Study of the Declining Birth-Rate in Acquisitive Societies.* London, 1942.

Webb, Beatrice. *Our Partnership.* London, 1948.

Webb, Sidney. *The Decline in the Birth-Rate.* London, 1907.

Webb, Sidney, and Webb, Beatrice. *English Poor Law History.* 3 vols. London, 1927–29.

————. *Industrial Democracy.* London, 1902.

Wells, H. G. *Mankind in the Making.* London, 1903.

Whetham, W. C. D. *Heredity and Society.* London, 1912.

Whetham, W. C. D., and Whetham, Catherine Durning. *The Family and the Nation: A Study in National Inheritance and Social Responsibility.* London, 1909.

White, Arnold. *Efficiency and Empire.* London, 1901.

————. *The Problems of a Great City.* London, 1887.

White, Frank W. *Birth Control and Its Opponents.* London, 1935.

————. *Posterity in the Light of Science, Philanthropy and Population.* London, 1929.

Winnington-Ingram, Arthur Foley. *A Charge Delivered to the Clergy and Church-wardens of London in St. Paul's Cathedral, October 19, 1905, at His Primary Visitation of the Diocese of London.* London, 1905.

Wright, Almroth E. *The Unexpurgated Case against Woman Suffrage.* London, 1913.

Articles and Essays

Allen, Grant. "Plain Words on the Woman Question." *Fortnightly Review* 46 (1889): 448–57.

Beveridge, William. "Eugenic Aspects of Children's Allowances." *Eugenics Review* 34, no. 4 (January 1943): 117–23, 125.

Blacker, C. P. "The Confluence of Psychiatry and Demography." *British Journal of Psychiatry* 123, no. 576 (1973):493–500.

————. "The Practice of Contraception." In *Proceedings of the International Birth*

Control Conference, Zurich 1930, edited by Ettie Sayer and Hanna Stone. London, 1932.

Bowley, A. L. "Births and Population in Great Britain." *Economic Journal* 34 (1924): 188–92.

———. "Economic Aspects of the Tendency of Population in Great Britain." In *Problems of Population: Being the Report of the Proceedings of the Second General Assembly of the International Union for the Scientific Investigation of Population Problems*, edited by G. H. L. F. Pitt-Rivers. London, 1932.

Cannan, Edward. "The Probability of a Cessation of the Growth of Population in England and Wales during the Next Century." *Economic Review* 5 (December 1895): 505–15.

Clouston, T. S. "The Psychological Dangers to Women in Modern Social Developments." In *The Position of Women: Actual and Ideal*. London, 1911.

Cookson, Montague. "The Morality of Married Life." *Fortnightly Review* 12 (October 1872): 397–412.

Darwin, Leonard. "Heredity and Environment: A Warning to Eugenists." *Eugenics Review* 8, no. 2 (July 1916): 93–122.

———. "The Society's Coming of Age: The Growth of the Eugenic Movement." *Eugenics Review* 21, no.1 (April 1929): 9–20.

Don, W. G., Deputy Surgeon-General, London Recruiting Staff. "Recruits and Recruiting." *The Journal of the United Services Institute* 33 (1889): 834–35.

Galton, Francis. "Hereditary Improvement." *Fraser's Magazine* 7 (January 1873): 116–30.

———. "Hereditary Talent and Character." *Macmillan's Magazine* 12 (June 1865): 157–66; (August 1865): 318–27.

———. "The Possible Improvement of the Human Breed under the Existing Conditions of Law and Sentiment." *Nature 64* (October 1901): 659–65.

———. "The Relative Supplies from Town and Country Families to the Population of Future Generations." *Journal of the Royal Statistical Society* 36 (1873): 19–26.

Glass, D. V. "The Fall in the Birth Rate." *Medical Press and Circular* (21 July 1937): 46–48.

Greenwood, Major; Brown, J. W.; and Wood, Frances. "The Fertility of the Middle Classes." *Eugenics Review* 12, no. 3 (October 1920): 158–211.

Hajnal, John. "Births, Marriages and Reproductivity in England and Wales, 1938–1947." In *Report of the Royal Commission on Population: Papers*. Vol. 2, *Reports and Selected Papers of the Statistics Committee*, pp.303–422. London, 1950.

Hamilton, C. J. "The Relation of Eugenics to Economics." *Eugenics Review* 3, no. 4 (January 1912): 295–305; 5, no. 2 (July 1913): 124–29.

Hill, Sir Leonard. "My Warning to England." *Evening News*, 5, 16 December 1936.

Himes, Norman, and Himes, Vera. "Birth Control for the British Working Classes: A Study of the First Thousand Cases to Visit an English Birth Control Clinic." *Hospital Social Service* 19 (1929): 578–617.

Hodson, Cora. "Contra-Selection in England." In International Eugenics Congress, *A Decade of Progress in Eugenics: Scientific Papers of the Third Interntional Congress of Eugenics, New York, August 21–23, 1932*. Baltimore, 1934.

Hopkin, Bryan. "The Measurement of Reproductivity." In *Report of the Royal Commission on Population*, pp. 241–59. Cmd. 7695. London, 1949.

Huxley, Julian. "Eugenics and Society." *Eugenics Review* 28, no. 1 (April 1936): 11–31.

Kuczynski, Robert. "The World's Future Population." In *Population. Lectures on the Harris Foundation*, pp. 298–302. Chicago, 1930.

Leybourne, Grace. "An Estimate of the Future Population of Great Britain." *Sociological Review* 26, no. 2 (1934): 130–38.

Linton, E. Lynn. "The Higher Education of Women." *Fortnightly Review* 40 (1886): 503–8.

MacArthur, Mary. "The Woman Trade Unionist's Point of View." In *Women and the Labour Party*, edited by Marion Phillips. London, 1918.

McDougall, William. "A Practicable Eugenic Suggestion." *Sociological Papers* 3 (1907).

Mallet, Bernard. "The Organisation of Registration and Its Bearing on Vital Statistics." *Journal of Royal Statistical Society* 80, no. 1 (January 1917): 1–24.

———. "The Reduction of the Fecundity of the Socially Inadequate." In *A Decade of Progress in Eugenics: Third International Congress of Eugenics, 1932.* Baltimore, 1934.

Masterman, C. F. G. "Realities at Home." In *The Heart of the Empire. Discussions of Problems of Modern City Life in England. With an Essay on Imperialism*, edited by C. F. G. Masterman. London, 1901.

Meath, Earl of. "Have We the Grit of Our Forefathers?" *Nineteenth Century* 64 (1908): 421–29.

Mumford, Alfred A. "Some Considerations on the Alleged Physical Deterioration of the British Race." *Fortnightly Review* 76 (1904): 324–38.

Newsholme, Arthur, and Stevenson, T. H. C. "The Decline of Human Fertility in the U.K. and Other Countries as Shown by Corrected Birth Rates." *Journal of the Royal Statistical Society* 69 (January 1906): 34–87.

Paterson, A. Spencer. "The Size of Family of the Business, Professional and Titled Classes." *Eugenics Review* 35, no. 3–4 (October–January, 1943–44): 57–70.

Pearson, Karl. "The Moral Basis of Socialism." In *Ethic of Free Thought and Other Addresses and Essays.* 2d ed., rev., pp. 301–29. London, 1901.

———. "On the Inheritance of the Mental and Moral Characters in Man, and Its Comparison with the Inheritance of the Physical Characters." The Huxley Lecture for 1903. *The Journal of the Anthropological Institute of Great Britain and Ireland* 33 (1903): 179–237.

———. "Reproductive Selection." In *The Chances of Death and Other Studies in Evolution*, 1:63–102. London,1897.

———. "Socialism and Natural Selection." In *The Chances of Death and Other Studies in Evolution*, 1:103–39. London, 1897.

———. "Socialism and Sex." In *The Ethic of Freethought and Addresses and Essays.* 2d ed., rev. Pp. 411–31. London, 1901.

———. "Socialism in Theory and Practice." In *The Ethic of Freethought and Other Addresses and Essays.* 2d ed., rev. Pp. 330–53. London, 1901.

———. "Variation in Man and Woman." In *Chances of Death and Other Studies in Evolution*, 1:256–377. London, 1897.

———. "The Woman's Question." In *The Ethic of Freethought and Other Addresses and Essays.* 2d ed., rev. Pp. 354–78. London, 1901.

Pearson, Karl, and Elderton, Ethel. "Further Evidence of Natural Selection in Man." *Biometrika* 10 (1915): 488–506.

Ruskin, John. "Of Queen's Gardens." In *Sesames and Lillies*. London, 1865.

Saleeby, Caleb. "The Nurture of the Race." In *Report of the Proceedings of the National Conference on Infant Mortality at St. George's Hotel*, pp. 140–46. Liverpool, 1914.

Shaw, George Bernard. "The Revolutionist's Handbook." In *Man and Superman: A Comedy and a Philosophy*. New York, 1947.

"Social Biology and Population Improvement." *Nature* 144 (16 September 1939): 521–22.

Stevenson, T. H. C. "The Fertility of Various Social Classes in England and Wales from the Middle of the Nineteenth Century to 1911." *The Journal of the Royal Statistical Society* 80 (May 1920): 401–44.

Titmuss, Richard. "The End of Economic Parenthood." *New Statesman and Nation*, 9 August 1941, pp. 130–31.

————. "The Social Environment and Eugenics." *Eugenics Review* 36, no. 2 (July 1944): 53–58.

Vines, J. H. "The Physique of Scottish Children." *The Westminster Review* 160 (1903): 319–22.

White, Arnold. "The Cult of Infirmity." *National Review* 34 (October 1899): 236–45.

Yule, G. Udny. "On the Changes in the Marriage and Birth-Rates in England and Wales during the Past Half Century, with an Inquiry as to Their Probable Causes." *The Journal of the Royal Statistical Society* 69 (March 1906): 88–132.

Secondary Sources

Books

Banks, J. A., and Banks, Olive. *Feminism and Family Planning in Victorian England*. Liverpool, 1964.

Bennett, J. H., ed. *Natural Selection, Heredity and Eugenics*. Oxford, 1983.

Braybon, Gail. *Women Workers in the First World War*. London, 1981.

Chase, Allan. *The Legacy of Malthus: The Social Costs of the New Scientific Racism*. New York, 1980.

Coale, Ansley J., and Watkins, Susan Cotts, eds. *The Decline of Fertility in Europe: The Revised Proceedings of a Conference on the Princeton European Fertility Project*. Princeton, 1986.

Cowan, Ruth S. *Sir Francis Galton and the Study of Heredity in the Nineteenth Century*. New York, 1984.

Dwork, Deborah. *War Is Good for Babies and Other Young Children: A History of the Infant and Child Welfare Movement in England 1898–1918*. London, 1987.

Farrall, Lyndsay. *The Origins and Growth of the English Eugenics Movement 1865–1925*. New York, 1985.

First, Ruth, and Scott, Ann. *Olive Schreiner*. New York, 1980.

Forrest, Derek W. *Francis Galton: The Life and Work of a Victorian Genius*. New York, 1974.

Freeden, Michael. *The New Liberalism: An Ideology of Social Reform*. Oxford, 1978.

Fryer, Peter. *The Birth Controllers*. London, 1965.

Garrard, John A. *The English and Immigration: A Comparative Study of the Jewish Influx, 1880–1910*. Oxford, 1971.

Gartner, Lloyd P. *The Jewish Immigrant in England, 1870–1914*. London, 1960.

Gilbert, Bentley B. *The Evolution of National Insurance in Great Britain: The Origins of the Welfare State*. London, 1966.

Hall, Ruth. *Passionate Crusader: The Life of Marie Stopes*. New York, 1977.

Haller, Mark. *Eugenics: Hereditarian Attitudes in American Thought*. New Brunswick, 1963.

Halsey, A. H., ed. *Trends in British Society since 1900: A Guide to the Changing Social Structure of Britain*. London, 1972.

Harris, José. *William Beveridge: A Biography*. Oxford, 1977.

Harrison, Brian. *Separate Spheres: The Opposition to Women's Suffrage in Britain, 1867–1928*. London, 1978.

Hubbard, Ruth, ed. *Women Look at Biology Looking at Women: A Collection of Feminist Critiques*. Boston, 1979.

Hynes, Samuel. *The Edwardian Turn of Mind*. Princeton, 1968.

Innes, J. W. *Class Fertility Trends in England and Wales, 1876–1934*. Princeton, 1938.

Jones, Gareth Stedman. *Outcast London: A Study in the Relationship between Classes in Victorian Society*. Oxford, 1971.

Jones, Greta. *Social Hygiene in Twentieth Century Britain*. London, 1986.

Kevles, Daniel J. *In the Name of Eugenics: Genetics and the Uses of Human Heredity*. New York, 1985.

Leathard, Audrey. *The Fight for Family Planning: The Development of Family Services in Britain, 1921–1974*. London, 1980.

Ledbetter, Rosanna. *A History of the Malthusian League, 1877–1927*. Columbus, 1976.

Lewis, Jane. *The Politics of Motherhood: Child and Maternal Welfare in England 1900–1939*. London, 1980.

McClaren, Angus. *Birth Control in Nineteenth Century England*. London, 1977.

MacKenzie, Donald. *Statistics in Britain, 1865–1930*. Edinburgh, 1981.

MacNicol, John. *Family Allowances: A Study in Social Policy Development*. London, 1980.

Mitchell, Brian R. *European Historical Statistics, 1750–1970*. London, 1975.

Mitchell, Brian, and Deane, Phyllis, eds. *Abstract of British Historical Statistics*. Cambridge, 1962.

Oldroyd, David, and Langham, Ian, eds. *The Wider Domain of Evolutionary Thought*. Dordrecht, 1983.

Pearson, E. S. *Karl Pearson: An Appreciation of Some Aspects of His Life and Work*. Cambridge, 1938.

Pearson, Karl. *The Life of Francis Galton*. 3 vols. London, 1914–30.

Pickens, Donald K. *Eugenics and the Progressives*. Nashville, 1968.

Provine, William B. *The Origin of Theoretical Population Genetics*. Chicago, 1971.

Read, Donald. *England 1868–1914*. London, 1979.

Saville, John. *Rural Depopulation in England and Wales*. London, 1957.

Searle, Geoffrey R. *Eugenics and Politics in Britain 1900–1914*. Leyden, 1976.
————. *The Quest for National Efficiency: A Study in British Politics and British Political Thought 1899–1914*. Berkeley and Los Angeles, 1971.
Semmel, Bernard. *Imperialism and Social Reform: English Social-Imperial Thought 1895–1914*. Cambridge, 1960.
————. *John Stuart Mill and the Pursuit of Virtue*. New Haven, 1984.
Skelley, Alan R. *The Victorian Army at Home: The Recruitment and Terms and Conditions of the British Regular, 1859–1899*. London, 1977.
Soloway, Richard A. *Birth Control and the Population Question in England, 1877–1930*. Chapel Hill, 1982.
————. *Prelates and People: Ecclesiastical Social Thought in England 1783–1852*. London, 1969.
Sutherland, Gillian. *Ability, Merit and Measurement: Mental Testing and English Education 1880–1940*. Oxford, 1984.
Teitelbaum, Michael S. *The British Fertility Decline: Demographic Transition in the Crucible of the Industrial Revolution*. Princeton, 1984.
Teitelbaum, Michael S., and Winter, Jay M. *The Fear of Population Decline*. Orlando, 1985.
Tranter, Neil L. *Population since the Industrial Revolution: The Case of England and Wales*. New York, 1973.
Wattenberg, Ben. *The Birth Dearth: What Happens When People in Free Countries Don't Have Enough Babies?* New York, 1987.
Webster, Charles, ed. *Biology, Medicine and Society 1840–1940*. Cambridge, 1981.
Werskey, Gary. *The Visible College*. London, 1978.
Winter, J. M. *The Great War and the British People*. Cambridge, 1986.
Wohl, Anthony S. *Endangered Lives: Public Health in Victorian Britain*. Cambridge, 1983.
Wrigley E. A., and Schofield, R. S. *The Population History of England, 1541–1871: A Reconstruction*. Cambridge, 1981.

Articles

Burstyn, Joan N. "Education and Sex: The Medical Case against Higher Education for Women in England, 1870–1900." *Proceedings of the American Philosophical Society* 117, no. 2 (April 1973): 79–89.
Conway, Jill. "Stereotypes of Femininity in a Theory of Sexual Evolution." *Victorian Studies* 14 (1970):47–62.
Cowan, Ruth S. "Francis Galton's Statistical Ideas: The Influence of Eugenics." *Isis* 63 (1972): 509–28.
————. "Nature and Nurture: The Interplay of Biology and Politics in the Work of Francis Galton." *Studies in the History of Biology* 1 (1977): 133–207.
D'Arcy, F. "The Malthusian League and the Resistance to Birth Control Propaganda in Late Victorian Britain." *Population Studies* 31, no. 3 (November 1977): 429–48.
Dyhouse, Carol. "Working Class Mothers and Infant Mortality in England, 1895–1914." *The Journal of Social History* 12 (1978): 248–67.
Farrall, Lyndsay A. "Controversy and Conflict in Science: A Case Study—The En-

glish Biometric School and Mendel's Laws." *Social Studies of Science* 5 (1975): 269–301.

_____. "The History of Eugenics: A Bibliographical Review." *Annals of Science* 36 (1979): 111–23.

Freeden, Michael. "Eugenics and Progressive Thought: A Study in Ideological Affinity." *The Historical Journal* 22 (1979): 645–71.

Froggart, P., and Nevin, N. C. "The 'Law of Ancestral Heredity' and the Mendelian-Ancestrian Controversy in England, 1889–1906." *Journal of Medical Genetics* 8 (1971): 1–36.

Gilbert, Bentley B. "Health and Politics: The British Physical Deterioration Report of 1904." *Bulletin of the History of Medicine* 39 (1965): 145–53.

_____. "Sir John Eldon Gorst and the Children of the Nation." *Bulletin of the History of Medicine* 28 (1954): 243–51.

Glass, David V. "A Note on the Under-registration of Births in Britain in the Nineteenth Century." *Population Studies* 5, no. 1 (1951): 70–80.

Harrison, Brian. "Women's Health and the Women's Movement in Britain 1840–1940." In *Biology, Medicine and Society 1840–1940*, edited by Charles Webster, pp. 15–71. Cambridge, 1981.

Hubbard, Ruth. "Have Only Men Evolved?" In *Women Look at Biology Looking at Women: A Collection of Feminist Critiques*, edited by Ruth Hubbard, pp. 7–35. Boston, 1979.

Jones, Greta. "Eugenics and Social Policy between the Wars." *The Historical Journal* 25 (1982): 717–28.

Kent, Susan. "The Politics of Sexual Difference: World War I and the Demise of British Feminism." *Journal of British Studies* 27, no. 3 (July 1988): 232–53.

Knodel, John, and van de Walle, Etienne. "Lessons from the Past." In *The Decline of Fertility in Europe: The Revised Proceedings of a Conference on the Princeton European Fertility Project*, edited by Ansley J. Coale and Susan Cott Watkins, pp. 390–419. Princeton, 1986.

MacKenzie, Donald. "Eugenics in Britain." *Social Studies of Science* 6 (1976): 499–532.

_____. "Karl Pearson and the Professional Middle Class." *Annals of Science* 36 (1979): 125–43.

_____. "Sociobiologists in Competition: The Biometrician-Mendelian Debate." In *Biology, Medicine and Society 1840–1940*, edited by Charles Webster, pp. 243–88. Cambridge, 1981.

Mosedale, S. Sleeth. "Science Corrupted: Victorian Biologists Consider 'The Woman Question.' " *Journal of the History of Biology* 9 (1978): 1–55.

Notestein, Frank W. "Economic Problems of Economic Change." In *Proceedings of the Eighth International Conference of Agricultural Economists*, pp. 13–31. London, 1953.

Paul, Diane. "Eugenics and the Left." *Journal of the History of Ideas* 45, no. 4 (1984): 567–90.

Richards, Evelleen. "Darwin and the Descent of Women." In *The Wider Domain of Evolutionary Thought*, edited by David Oldroyd and Ian Langham, pp. 57–111. Dordrecht, 1983.

Rollett, Constance, and Parker, Julia. "Population and Family." In *Trends in British Society since 1900: A Guide to the Changing Social Structure of Britain*, edited by A. H. Halsey, pp. 20–63. London, 1972.

Searle, Geoffrey R. "Eugenics and Class." In *Biology, Medicine and Society 1840–1940*, edited by Charles Webster, pp. 217–42. Cambridge, 1981.

––––––. "Eugenics and Politics in Britain in the 1930s." *Annals of Science* 36 (1979): 159–69.

Soloway, Richard A. "Counting the Degenerates: The Statistics of Race Deterioration in Edwardian England." *Journal of Contemporary History* 17 (1982): 137–64.

––––––. "Feminism, Fertility and Eugenics in Victorian and Edwardian England." In *Political Symbolism in Modern Europe*, edited by S. Drescher, D. Sabean, and A. Sharlin, pp. 121–45.

Spenceley, Geoff. "The Lace Associations: Philanthropic Movements to Preserve the Production of Hand-Made Lace in Late-Victorian and Edwardian England." *Victorian Studies* 16 (1973): 433–52.

Walkowitz, Judith. "Science, Feminism and Romance: The Men and Women's Club 1885–1889." *History Workshop* 21 (Spring 1986): 37–60.

Watkins, Susan Cotts. "Conclusions." In *The Decline of Fertility in Europe: The Revised Proceedings of a Conference on the Princeton European Fertility Project*, edited by Ansley J. Coale and Susan Cotts Watkins, pp. 420–49. Princeton, 1986.

Wise, M. J. "David V. Glass." *Biographical Memoirs of the Fellows of the Royal Society* 29 (November 1983): 201–25.

Dissertation

Szreter, S. "The Decline of Marital Fertility in England and Wales, ca. 1870–1914." Ph.D. diss., Cambridge University, 1984.

Index